THIRD EDITION

COGNITION

Margaret W. Matlin
State University of New York, Geneseo

THIRD EDITION

COGNITION

Margaret W. Matlin
State University of New York, Geneseo

Harcourt Brace Publishers

Fort Worth   Philadelphia   San Diego   New York   Orlando   Austin   San Antonio
Toronto   Montreal   London   Sydney   Tokyo

Publisher: Ted Buchholz
Acquisitions Editor: Christina N. Oldham
Senior Developmental Editor: Meera Dash
Project Editor: Margaret Allyson
Senior Production Manager: Tad Gaither
Art Director: Priscilla Mingus

Cover photograph by Michael Lupino

ISBN: 0-15-500571-5

Library of Congress Number: 92-075763

Printed in the United States of America

5 6 7 8 9 0 1 2 039 9 8 7 6 5 4

This book is dedicated to

Helen and Donald White
and
Clare and Harry Matlin

PREFACE

Our cognitive processes are truly impressive. We manage to recall the names of classmates from elementary school, details of events that occurred a decade ago, and even the meaning of foreign vocabulary words we haven't contemplated since high school. Young infants can distinguish subtle differences in speech sounds, and 6-year-olds know about 14,000 words, which they use to produce sentences that are both accurate and unique.

However, most cognitive psychology textbooks are written in such a dry, abstract, academic style that they fail to capture these inherently interesting capabilities. In the decade since the publication of my first edition of *Cognition*, I've received letters and comments from dozens of students and professors, telling me how much they enjoyed reading this textbook. Using their feedback, I have tried to revise the text so that the features readers most appreciate are even stronger than in the two previous editions.

FEATURES OF THE TEXTBOOK

I have now taught the Cognitive Psychology course approximately 20 times. In writing *Cognition*, I continually kept in mind students like those in my classes. Here are some of the ways in which I consider this book to be student-oriented:

1. The writing style is clear and interesting.
2. The text demonstrates that cognition is relevant to everyday, real-world experiences.
3. The book frequently examines how cognition can be applied to other disciplines, such as education, clinical psychology, law, geography, medicine, and consumer psychology.
4. Many easy-to-perform demonstrations illustrate important experiments in cognition and clarify central concepts.
5. Each new term is introduced in **boldface print** and is accompanied by a concise definition that appears in the same sentence.
6. An outline and a preview introduce the chapters, providing an appropriate framework for the new material.
7. Each major section in a chapter concludes with a summary, enabling students to review and consolidate material before moving to the next section, rather than waiting until the chapter's end for a single, lengthy summary.
8. Each chapter includes review questions and a list of new terms.
9. Each chapter concludes with a list of recommended readings and a brief description of each resource.
10. The first chapter introduces five major themes that are then traced throughout the book, providing students with a sense of continuity across many diverse topics.

ORGANIZATION

A textbook must be interesting and helpful. However, it must also reflect current developments in the discipline, and it must allow instructors to adapt its structure to their teaching plans. Instructors will therefore find the following features appealing:

1. *Cognition* offers a comprehensive overview of the field, including chapters on perception, memory, imagery, general knowledge, language, problem solving and creativity, reasoning, decision making, and the development of cognition.
2. Each chapter is a self-contained unit. For example, a new term such as *heuristics* is defined in every chapter in which it is used. This feature allows instructors considerable flexibility in the sequence of coverage. For example, some instructors may wish to cover the topic of imagery prior to the three chapters on memory.
3. Each section of a chapter is a discrete unit, particularly because every section is followed by a section summary. Instructors may choose to cover individual sections in a different order. For example, one instructor may decide to cover the section on schemas prior to the chapter on long-term memory. Another instructor might prefer to subdivide Chapter 12, on cognitive development, so that the first section of this chapter follows Chapter 5, the second section follows Chapter 7, and the third section follows Chapter 9.
4. Chapters 2 through 12 each include an in-depth section, which focuses on recent research on selected topics and provides details on research methods.
5. In all, the bibliography contains 1243 references, 796 of them from the last 10 years. As a consequence, the textbook provides a very current overview of the discipline.

HIGHLIGHTS OF THE THIRD EDITION

The discipline of cognitive psychology has made tremendous advances since the second edition of this textbook was published in 1989. Research in the areas of memory and language has been especially ambitious, and theoretical approaches to the discipline have been elaborated. Although every section of this textbook has been updated and rewritten, some of the more noteworthy changes are the following:

- Chapter 1 includes more material on neuroscience techniques, as well as a preview of the parallel distributed processing approach.

- Chapter 2 now examines David Marr's computational approach to pattern recognition, new material on the Stroop effect, and the topic of thought suppression.

- Chapter 3, on models of memory, contains updated material on the three theoretical approaches discussed in the second edition, as well as an examination of the parallel distributed processing approach to memory.

- Chapter 4 was created by reorganizing Chapters 2 and 3 from the previous edition; this new chapter focuses on sensory memory and short-term memory. The primary change in coverage is increased discussion of the working-memory view of short-term memory.

- Memory researchers have been especially active in the area of long-term memory (Chapter 5). New information is presented on encoding specificity, explicit versus implicit measures of memory, and ecological validity.

- In Chapter 6, the section on the characteristics of mental images has been reorganized. New material has been added on neuropsychological evidence for the similarity between imagery and perception, and new research on mental models is discussed.

- Chapter 7, on general knowledge, has been shortened and reorganized, with new material added on the tip-of-the-tongue phenomenon and metamemory.

- Research on language has been so productive that the third edition of *Cognition* requires two chapters to cover the material adequately. Chapter 8 examines language comprehension, with new material on theories of speech perception and metacomprehension.

- Two of the sections in Chapter 9 (Language Production) are entirely new. Researchers have produced new information about the writing process, certainly a cognitive activity familiar to both students and professors. Bilingualism is the second new topic. We now have abundant research on bilingualism. In addition, a substantial proportion of North Americans are now bilingual, and we need to appreciate their remarkable linguistic achievements.

- Chapter 10 has been shortened slightly, and new information has been added on the analogy approach to problem solving, as well as expert problem solving.

- Chapter 11 now combines the material on logical reasoning and decision making. The chapter contains new material on the belief-bias effect as well as overconfidence in decisions.

- Researchers in cognitive development (Chapter 12) have been especially active in recent years. The sections on memory in elderly people, metacognition in elderly people, and language development have undergone the most significant changes.

In preparing this new edition, I made every possible effort to include up-to-date research. I examined every relevant entry in *Psychological Abstracts* between 1988 and 1991. I also reviewed every relevant book cited in *Contemporary Psychology*. In addition, I wrote to more than 200 researchers, requesting reprints and preprints. The research on cognition is expanding at an ever-increasing rate, and I wanted this textbook to capture the excitement of the current research!

Professors should contact their Harcourt Brace & Company sales representative to obtain a copy of the Test Item File. This ancillary has been revised and expanded for the third edition of the textbook, with more emphasis on conceptual items and applications to real-world situations.

ACKNOWLEDGMENTS

I have many individuals to thank for their impressive efforts on this book. First, I would like to praise the people at Harcourt Brace & Company. Tina Oldham, my acquisitions editor, provided a framework for this revision; she also suggested areas that could be strengthened and new topics to be included. Meera Dash, my developmental editor, was invaluable in shaping the book. She arranged for a superb set of reviewers, helped make decisions about the structure of the book, and provided useful feedback on stylistic issues.

Margaret Allyson is an ideal project editor! Her intelligence, precision, organizational skills, and sense of humor transformed the production of this book into a pleasant and rewarding experience. I want to thank Linda Webster—once again—for her superb work in preparing the indexes for this textbook. Elizabeth Alvarez and J. R. Peacock also deserve my sincere thanks for their careful proofreading of the galley proofs and reference checking.

During my undergraduate and graduate training, many professors kindled my enthusiasm for the growing field of cognition. I would like to thank Gordon Bower, Albert Hastorf, Leonard Horowitz, and Eleanor Maccoby of Stanford University, and Edwin Martin, Arthur Melton, Richard Pew, and Robert Zajonc of the University of Michigan.

Many others have contributed in important ways to this book. Mary Gillan, Christine Lauer, Leslie Lauer, Heather Pival, and Sally Matlin helped locate references and prepare the bibliography. Also, Mary Lou Perry, Shirley Thompson, and Connie Ellis kept other aspects of my life running smoothly, allowing me more time to work on this writing project.

Others have helped in a variety of ways. Three members of Milne Library, SUNY Geneseo, deserve special thanks: Paula Henry ordered numerous books for me and informed me of interesting, relevant references. Judith Bushnell helped track down wayward references and conducted several computer searches for the In-Depth sections. Harriet Sleggs ordered dozens of books and articles through interlibrary loan.

In addition, a number of students contributed to the book and provided useful suggestions after reading the first two editions: Mary Jane Brennan, Miriam Dowd, Elizabeth Einemann, Michelle Fischer, Don Hudson, Jay Kleinman, Mary Kroll, Pamela Mead, Pamela Mino, Michelle Morante, Judith Rickey, Mary Riley, Margery Schemmel, Richard Slocum, John Tanchak, Heather Wallach, and Rachelle Yablin. Several Stanford University students provided insights about bilingualism: Laura Aizpuru, Sven Halstenburg, Rodrigo Liong, Jean Lu, Edwardo Martinez, Sally Matlin, Dorin Parasca, Laura Uribarri and other members of Casa Zapata. Other students provided references that were extremely useful: Ned Abbott, Patricia Kramer, Leslie Lauer, Sally Matlin, Christopher Piersante, Laura Segovia, and Nancy Tomassino. Thanks also to colleagues Ada Azodo, Hugh Foley, Ken Kallio, Lisbet Nielsen, Lori Van Wallendael, and Alan Welsh for making suggestions about references and improving the wording of passages in the text.

I would also like to express my appreciation to the reviewers. The reviewers who helped on the first edition included Richard Kasschau, University of Houston; Mark Ashcraft, Cleveland State University; Randolph Easton, Boston College; Barbara Goldman, University of Michigan—Dearborn; Harold Hawkins, University of Oregon; Joseph Hellige, University of Southern California; Richard High, Lehigh University; James Juola, University of Kansas; and R. A. Kinchla, Princeton University. The reviewers who gave assistance on the second edition included: Harriett Amster, University of Texas at Arlington; Francis T. Durso, University of Oklahoma; Susan E. Dutch, Westfield State College; Sallie Gordon, University of Utah; Richard Gottwald, University of Indiana at South Bend; Kenneth R. Graham, Muhlenberg College; Morton A. Heller, Winston-Salem State University; Michael W. O'Boyle, Iowa State University; David G. Payne, State University of New York at Binghamton; Louisa M. Slowiaczek, Loyola University of Chicago; Donald A. Smith, Northern Illinois University; Patricia Snyder, Albright College; and Richard K. Wagner, Florida State University. The excellent advice from these reviewers helped shape the first two editions and also guided me as I prepared this most recent version.

Reviewers for the third edition provided superb advice on the empirical and theoretical portions of this book, and they also gave useful guidance on the organizational and syntactic aspects of the manuscript. I would like to thank the following individuals for their careful, thoughtful work: John Flowers, University of Nebraska; Ira Fischler, University of Florida; Nancy Franklin, SUNY StonyBrook; Joanne Gallivan, University College of Cape Breton; Margaret Intons-Peterson, Indiana University; Christine Lofgren, University of California, Irvine; Bill McKeachie, University of Michigan; William Oliver, Florida State University; Andrea Richards, University of California, Los Angeles; Jonathan Schooler, University of Pittsburgh; and Jyotsna Vaid, Texas A & M University.

The final words of thanks belong to my family members. My husband, Arnie, and my daughters, Beth and Sally, deserve thanks for their enthusiasm, appreciation, help, and love. Their pride in my accomplishments makes it even more rewarding to be an author! Last, I would like to express my gratitude to four other important people in my life, my parents by birth and my parents by marriage: Helen and Donald White, and Clare and Harry Matlin.

Margaret W. Matlin

CONTENTS

CHAPTER 3

MODELS OF MEMORY 65

CHAPTER 4

SENSORY MEMORY AND SHORT-TERM MEMORY 101

CHAPTER 5

LONG-TERM MEMORY 131

CHAPTER 6

IMAGERY 172

CHAPTER 7

GENERAL KNOWLEDGE 212

CHAPTER 8

LANGUAGE COMPREHENSION: LISTENING AND READING 259

CHAPTER 9

LANGUAGE PRODUCTION: SPEAKING, WRITING, AND BILINGUALISM 302

CHAPTER 10

PROBLEM SOLVING AND CREATIVITY 330

CHAPTER 11

LOGICAL REASONING AND DECISION MAKING 377

CHAPTER 12

COGNITIVE DEVELOPMENT 436

THIRD EDITION

COGNITION

Margaret W. Matlin
State University of New York, Geneseo

C H A P T E R   1

INTRODUCTION

If you are like most students who have just begun to read this textbook, you would not yet feel qualified to offer a definition of the term *cognition*. Nevertheless, you have already engaged in a variety of cognitive processes in order to reach the middle of the first paragraph! For example, you used pattern recognition to interpret the assorted squiggles and lines that form the letters and words on this page. You consulted your memory to search for word meanings and to link together the ideas in this paragraph. Right now, as you contemplate your own thought processes, you are engaging in another component of cognition called *metacognition*. You may even have engaged in decision making if you tried to estimate how long it would take to read this first chapter.

Cognition, or mental activity, involves the acquisition, storage, retrieval, and use of knowledge. As you might imagine, cognition includes a wide range of mental processes if cognition is needed every time we acquire some information, place it in storage, retrieve it, or use that information. This textbook will explore a variety of mental processes, including perception, memory, imagery, language, problem solving, reasoning, and decision making.

A related term, **cognitive psychology,** has two meanings: Sometimes it is a synonym for the word *cognition*, and sometimes it refers to a particular approach to psychology. The **cognitive approach** is a theoretical orientation that proposes theories based on mental structures and processes (Craik, 1991). The cognitive approach is often contrasted with several other current psychological approaches: the behaviorist perspective, which emphasizes observable behaviors; the psychoanalytic perspective, which focuses on unconscious emotions; and the humanistic perspective, which emphasizes personal growth and interpersonal relationships.

Why should psychology students learn about cognition? One reason is that cognition is a major portion of the study of human psychology. What have you done in the last hour that did *not* require perception, memory, language, or some other higher mental process?

A second reason to study cognition is that the cognitive approach has widespread influence on other areas of psychology. For instance, social psychology has been deeply affected by cognitive psychology (e.g., Fiske & Taylor, 1991; Zebrowitz, 1990). The cognitive approach has also influenced educational psychology (e.g., Berger et al., 1987), developmental psychology (e.g., Simon, 1990), and consumer psychology (e.g., Bettman, 1986). Cognitive psychology has also had an impact on interdisciplinary areas. For example, a book by Lau and Sears (1986) examines political psychology from a cognitive perspective. In summary, an appreciation of cognitive psychology will help you understand many other areas of psychology.

The final reason for studying cognition is more personal. You own an impressive piece of equipment—your own mind—and you use this equipment every minute of the day. When you purchase a car, you typically receive a booklet that describes how it works. However, no one issued you an owner's manual for your mind when you were born. In a sense, this book is an owner's manual, describing what is known about how your mind works. In many cases, this book—like a car manual—also contains hints on how to improve performance.

The remainder of this introductory chapter consists of three parts. Following a brief history of cognitive psychology, we will outline its current status. The final part describes this textbook, including its content and major themes, as well as suggestions for using the book more effectively.

A BRIEF HISTORY OF THE COGNITIVE APPROACH
The Origins of Cognitive Psychology

Human thought processes have intrigued philosophers and other theorists for at least 2,000 years. For example, the Greek philosopher Aristotle proposed laws for learning and memory, and he emphasized the importance of mental imagery (Mayer, 1983). As Hearnshaw (1987) notes, cognitive psychology is both the oldest and the newest component in the history of psychology.

The Nineteenth Century. Theorists in the history of psychology often celebrate 1879 as the birth of scientific psychology. It was then that Wilhelm Wundt (pronounced "Voont") opened his laboratory in a small lecture room in Leipzig, Germany. Thus, psychology emerged as a new discipline that was separate from philosophy and physiology. Within several years, students flocked from around the world to study with Wundt, who eventually sponsored 186 PhD dissertations in psychology (Hearst, 1979).

Wundt proposed that psychology should study conscious experience, using introspection. **Introspection,** in this case, meant that trained observers attended carefully to their own sensations and reported them as objectively as possible (Gardner, 1985; Posner, 1986). These observers were encouraged to describe the sensations they felt, rather than the stimulus that produced the sensations. They were also instructed to report thoughts and images without attempting to give them meaning.

As Gardner (1985) stresses, Wundt's program was not simply stated once and then forgotten. Instead, Wundt worked continuously for 50 years to promote the introspective technique through journals and conferences. His work emphasized careful training of observers, the use of relevant controls, and the replication of experiments. These techniques have been incorporated in twentieth-century research on cognitive processes. For example, most of the research papers discussed in this book include several **replications,** or experiments in which a phenomenon is tested under different conditions.

In many ways, Wundt's careful, rigorous methods were similar to present-day cognitive research. Wundt specifically wrote, however, that higher mental processes such as thinking, language, and problem solving could not be appropriately investigated with the introspective technique.

Not all of Wundt's colleagues adopted the introspective technique, however. Hermann Ebbinghaus (1913), for example, devised his own methods for studying human memory. He constructed more than 2,000 nonsense syllables (for example, DAP) and tested his own ability to learn pairs of these stimuli. Ebbinghaus examined a variety of factors that might influence performance, such as the amount of time between list presentations. He specifically chose nonsense syllables rather than meaningful material so that the stimuli would not have previous associations with past experiences. Ebbinghaus's methods had a greater influence on cognitive psychology and on other areas of experimental psychology than did Wundt's introspection technique. For example, later researchers were more likely to conduct experiments testing how selected variables influenced memory than to ask observers to report the sensations produced by a stimulus. However, Gardner (1985) remarks that Ebbinghaus's methods encouraged decades of experimental psychologists to use meaningless material to study memory. Unfortunately, they avoided investigating the very different approach that humans adopt when they must recall meaningful material.

Meanwhile, at the end of the nineteenth century in the United States, American psychologists were more influenced by William James, who is often called the dean of American psychology. James was not much impressed with Wundt's introspection technique or Ebbinghaus's research with nonsense words. Instead, James preferred a more informal approach, emphasizing the kinds of psychological questions encountered in daily life. He is best known for his textbook, *Principles of Psychology*, published in 1890, which has been described as "probably the most significant psychological treatise ever written in America" (Evans, 1990, p. 11).

Principles of Psychology provides detailed descriptions about the stream of human experience and emphasizes that the human mind is active and inquiring. The book foreshadows numerous topics that currently fascinate cognitive psychologists, such as perception (Dember, 1990), attention (LaBerge, 1990), reasoning (Nickerson, 1990), and the tip-of-the-tongue phenomenon (Brown, 1990). Consider, for example, a portion of his description of the tip-of-the-tongue experience:

> Suppose we try to recall a forgotten name. The state of our consciousness is peculiar. There is a gap therein but no mere gap. It is a gap that is intensely active. A sort of wraith of the name is in it, beckoning us in a given direction, making us at moments tingle with the sense of our closeness and then letting us sink back without the longed-for term. (James, 1890, p. 251)

Perhaps James's most significant contributions to the field of cognitive psychology were his theories about memory. He proposed two different kinds of memory and distinguished between memory structure and memory processing, foreshadowing the important memory model proposed about 80 years later by Atkinson and Shiffrin (1968).

The Twentieth Century. In 1924, the American psychologist John B. Watson initiated a major new force in psychology known as behaviorism. **Behaviorism** is an approach that relies only on objective, observable reactions. The behaviorists believed that introspection was unscientific and that consciousness was far too vague to be investigated properly. In fact, their emphasis on observable behavior led them to reject any terms referring to mental events, such as *image, idea,* or *thought.* Many behaviorists classified thinking as simply subvocal speech. Presumably, appropriate equipment could detect the tiny movements made by the tongue (observable behaviors) during thinking. In other words, if you are thinking as you read this sentence, some early behaviorists would have said that you are really just talking to yourself, but so quietly that you cannot be heard. Behaviorists did not believe that vague, invisible constructs such as *thought* were necessary. Significantly, behaviorists were likely to avoid the human research participants favored by Wundt and Ebbinghaus, preferring instead the laboratory rat.

The study of mental activity was certainly hampered by behaviorists' refusal to study hidden processes. However, behaviorism still contributed significantly to the methods of current cognitive psychology (Simon, 1992a). Behaviorists stressed that concepts should be carefully and precisely defined. For example, *performance* might be defined as the number of trials that a rat required to complete a maze without error. Current cognitive psychology research also emphasizes precise definitions. For example, a cognitive researcher must use a precise definition for *memory.* In addition, behaviorism stressed experimental control. As a result, research psychologists primarily studied animals other than humans, because animals can be reared under far more carefully specified conditions than humans. Clearly, then, behaviorists rarely studied the kinds of human higher mental processes that interest contemporary cognitive psychologists.

Behaviorism thrived in the United States for several decades, but it had less influence on European psychology. An important new development in Europe at the turn of the century was Gestalt psychology. **Gestalt psychology** is an approach that emphasizes that humans have basic tendencies to organize what they see and that the whole is greater than the sum of its parts. Consider, for example, the first seven notes of the Alphabet Song ("AB-CD-EFG . . ."). The melody that results is more than simply seven tones strung together; it seems to have unity and organization. It has a Gestalt, or overall quality that transcends the individual elements (Gardner, 1985).

The Gestalt psychologists strongly objected to the introspective technique of analyzing experiences into separate components, because they stressed that the whole experience is inherently organized. The Gestalt psychologists constructed a number of laws that explain why certain components of a pattern seem to belong together. For example, the law of proximity or nearness states that items tend to be grouped together when they are physically close to each other.

Gestalt psychologists also emphasized the importance of insight in problem solving. Initially, the parts of a problem seem unrelated to each other, but with a sudden flash of insight, the parts fit together into a solution. Most of the early research in problem solving was conducted by Gestalt psychologists; their work represents an important contribution to cognitive psychology.

In the first part of this century, the behaviorists were dominant in the United States, and the Gestalt psychologists were influential on the Continent. Meanwhile, a British psychologist named Frederick C. Bartlett conducted his research on human memory. His important book, *Remembering: An Experimental and Social Study* (Bartlett, 1932), rejected the experimental methods of Ebbinghaus. Instead, Bartlett used meaningful material, such as lengthy stories, and he examined how people's mental set influenced their later recall of the material. He proposed that memory is a reconstructive process involving interpretations and transformations of the original material (Kendler, 1987).

Bartlett's work was largely ignored in the United States during the 1930s, because American psychologists were so devoted to the experimental methods of behaviorism. However, his work was later discovered by American psychologists, and it is quite similar to the schema-based approach to memory that we will explore in Chapters 5 and 7 (Mandler, 1985).

The Emergence of Contemporary Cognitive Psychology

We have briefly traced the historical roots of cognitive psychology, but when was this new approach actually "born"? Cognitive psychologists generally agree that the birth of cognitive psychology should be listed as 1956 (Eysenck, 1990; Gardner, 1985; Simon, 1981). During this prolific year, a large number of researchers published influential books and articles on attention, memory, language, concept formation, and problem solving. Some psychologists even specify a single *day* on which cognitive psychology was born. On September 11, 1956, many of the important researchers attended a symposium at the Massachusetts Institute of Technology. As George Miller recalled the event:

> I went away from the Symposium with a strong conviction, more intuitive than rational, that human experimental psychology, theoretical linguistics, and computer simulation of cognitive processes were all pieces of a larger whole, and that the future would see progressive elaboration and coordination of their shared concerns. (1979, p. 9)

Enthusiasm for the cognitive approach grew rapidly, so that by about 1960, the methodology, approach, and attitudes had changed substantially (Mandler, 1985). Another important turning point was the publication of Ulric Neisser's book *Cognitive Psychology* (Neisser, 1967). In fact, the increasing enthusiasm for the cognitive approach has sometimes been called the "cognitive revolution." Several factors contributed to the dramatic rise in popularity of cognitive psychology:

1. Psychologists were becoming increasingly disappointed with the behaviorist outlook that had dominated American psychology. Complex human behavior could not readily be explained using only the terms and concepts from

traditional behaviorist learning theory, such as stimuli, responses, and reinforcement. Because behaviorists limited themselves only to observable responses, many psychological activities could not be examined. For example, suppose we present an individual with a difficult problem (the stimulus). We wait 20 minutes until he or she produces the solution (the response). This exclusive focus on observable stimuli and responses tells us nothing about psychologically interesting processes, such as the thoughts and strategies involved in solving the problem (Eysenck & Keane, 1990).

2. Linguists, such as Noam Chomsky (1957), rejected the behaviorist approach to language acquisition and emphasized the mental processes we need for language. These linguists convinced many psychologists that the structure of language was too complex to be explained in behaviorist terms (Barsalou, 1992). Many linguists argued that humans have an inborn ability to master language, an idea that clearly contradicted the behaviorists' emphasis on learning in the acquisition of language.

3. Research in human memory began to blossom at the end of the 1950s. Researchers explored the possibility of different kinds of memory, examined the organization of memory, and proposed memory models. Behavioral terms could not be easily applied to memory phenomena.

4. Jean Piaget, a Swiss psychologist, had been constructing a new theory of developmental psychology that emphasized how children develop an appreciation of concepts, such as object permanence. Piaget's books began to be appreciated by American psychologists and educators toward the end of the 1950s.

5. One of the most important developments, the **information-processing approach,** evolved from computer science and communication science. Two important components of the information-processing approach are that (a) a mental process can be understood by comparing it with the operations of a computer and (b) a mental process can be interpreted as a flow of information through a series of stages.

Let us examine the information-processing approach in more detail. Consider, for example, the flow of information that occurs when you want to determine whether a particular bus goes to your desired destination in an unfamiliar city. First, data are received by the senses (the form of a large vehicle is registered on your retina), these data are compared with information stored in memory (the retinal image matches the information you have stored about buses), you seek additional information (you ask the driver about the destination), these data are compared with information stored in memory (the driver's reply matches the destination you have stored), and you make your decision (you plan to step into the bus). Notice, then, that the information-processing approach is concerned with both the flow of information within the organism and between the organism and the environment (Mandler, 1985).

Furthermore, the information-processing approach often attempts to understand a very sophisticated computer—the human brain (Evans, 1983). Computers are tools made by humans that capture a little of our cognitive flexibility (Sanford, 1985), and for that reason the computer is interesting. Furthermore, the information-processing approach argues that a number of simple mental operations can be grouped together to produce complex cognitive behavior, in the same way that complex tasks can be accomplished on the computer by stringing together a series of simple operations (Posner & McLeod, 1982).

For many years, the information-processing approach dominated cognitive psychology, and many people still favor this framework. However, in the last decade an increasing number of cognitive psychologists have abandoned the information-processing approach in favor of the parallel distributed processing approach, which we will discuss in the next section.

SECTION SUMMARY: A BRIEF HISTORY OF THE COGNITIVE APPROACH

1. Scientific psychology is often traced to Wilhelm Wundt, who developed the introspection technique.
2. Hermann Ebbinghaus studied human memory for nonsense syllables; his experimental methods were adopted by later researchers.
3. William James examined everyday psychological processes and stressed the active nature of the human mind.
4. Behaviorists were not interested in studying mental activity; however, behaviorist methodology had an important influence on current research in cognitive psychology.
5. Gestalt psychology emphasized organization in pattern perception and insight in problem solving.
6. Cognitive psychology began to emerge in the mid-1950s, encouraged by a disenchantment with behaviorism as well as a growth of interest in linguistics, human memory, Piagetian psychology, and the information-processing approach.
7. According to the information-processing approach, mental processes can be understood by comparison with a computer, and a mental process can be represented by information flowing through a series of stages.

THE CURRENT STATUS OF COGNITIVE PSYCHOLOGY

Clearly, cognitive psychology has had an enormous influence on the discipline of psychology. For example, almost all researchers recognize the importance of *mental representations*, a term that would have been forbidden by behaviorists several decades earlier (Gardner, 1985). The cognitive approach has also permeated most areas of psychology that had not previously emphasized thought processes. For example, Wyer and Srull (1986) emphasized that the cognitive approach "has had a revolutionary effect on social psychology" (p. 322). In fact, a survey of psychologists in U.S. colleges and universities reported that more than 75 percent claimed to be cognitive psychologists (Eysenck & Keane, 1990).

However, the discipline of cognitive psychology has its critics. Some claim that many subspecialties within cognitive psychology often do not communicate with one another. For example, a researcher in visual perception may have little contact with someone conducting research on understanding stories (Gardner, 1985).

One of the most common complaints in recent years concerns the issue of ecological validity. **Ecological validity** means that the results obtained in research should also apply to naturally occurring behavior in the real world (Cohen, 1989). Consider an experiment in which participants must memorize pairs of unrelated words, presented at 10-second intervals on a blank screen in a barren laboratory room. The results of this experiment might tell us something about the way memory operates. However, this task may have limited ecological validity, because real-life situations seldom involve this kind of controlled, context-free memorization. Furthermore, people may perform more competently in familiar environments than in laboratory settings (Rogoff, 1984).

Indeed, most cognitive psychologists prior to the 1980s did tend to conduct research in artificial laboratory environments, often using tasks that differed from daily cognitive activities. However, current researchers are much more likely to emphasize ecological validity. Psychologists interested in memory, for example, are currently studying real-life issues such as eyewitness testimony, absent-mindedness, and memory for conversations (Cohen, 1983, 1989). However, an important drawback to these real-life memory tasks is that they cannot be as rigorously controlled as in the laboratory. This issue of ecological validity will be discussed in more detail in Chapter 5. In general, most cognitive psychologists acknowledge that the discipline must advance by conducting *both* ecologically valid and laboratory-based research (Timberlake, 1984).

Several topics are critical in our discussion of contemporary cognitive psychology. First, we need to introduce the interdisciplinary area of cognitive science. Then we will look at two of the areas within cognitive science that have contributed most to cognitive psychology—neuroscience and artificial intelligence. Our final topic is the new approach to cognitive psychology called the parallel distributed processing approach.

Cognitive Science

Cognitive psychology is part of a broader field known as cognitive science. **Cognitive science** is a contemporary field of study that tries to answer questions about the nature of knowledge, its components, its development, and its use (Gardner,

1985). Cognitive science is interdisciplinary, including within its scope the fields of psychology, philosophy, linguistics, anthropology, artificial intelligence, and neuroscience (Gardner, 1985; Hunt, 1989). Some scholars also add sociology and economics to that interdisciplinary list (Gardner, 1985).

Theorists within the broad field of cognitive science agree that thinking involves the manipulation of internal representations of the external world (Hunt, 1989). Because cognitive scientists focus on these internal representations—also called *mental models*—you can see that this perspective clearly differs from the behaviorist approach. Cognitive scientists generally do not emphasize factors such as emotions or the differences between individuals (Gardner, 1985). They tend to value interdisciplinary studies. Unfortunately, the field has not yet reached the point where many fruitful interactions among the disciplines can be discussed (Keil, 1991; McTear, 1988). However, two areas in which researchers from other disciplines are especially likely to interact with psychologists are neuroscience and artificial intelligence. Let us turn our attention to these two topics.

Neuroscience

Cognitive **neuroscience** examines how the structure and function of the brain explain cognitive processes (Kosslyn & Koenig, 1992). In recent years, researchers have increased their efforts to build a bridge between cognitive psychology and neurosciences. LeDoux and Hirst (1986) discuss the need for these cooperative research efforts:

> The cognitive revolution is now in place. Cognition is *the* subject of contemporary psychology. This was achieved with little or no talk of neurons, action potentials, and neurotransmitters. Similarly, neuroscience has risen to an esteemed position among the biological sciences without much talk of cognitive processes. Do the fields need each other? Is there something to be gained by cross-disciplinary interchanges? Are interactions even possible? The answers are all yes because the problem of understanding the mind, unlike the would-be problem solvers, respects no disciplinary boundaries. (p. 2)

Naturally, neurological explanations for complex higher mental processes are often elusive. As Gardner (1985) writes, it is a cognitive challenge to build explanatory bridges between the level of the neuron and the level of the cognitive concept. Furthermore, the neuroscience approach is more likely to determine *where* a process takes place, rather than *how* that process works (Banks & Krajicek, 1991).

Let's examine some of the techniques used by neuroscientists that have provided particularly useful information for cognitive psychologists. We will begin with a method that examines a person who has experienced brain damage, and then we will consider three methods that study normal brains.

Brain Lesions. **Brain lesions** involve the destruction of tissue; these lesions are most often caused by strokes, tumors, or accidents. The study of lesions is one of the oldest techniques that neuroscientists have used to examine cognitive processes, with research first beginning in the 1860s. Some major advances were made following World War II, because many people with war-related injuries showed very specific language disorders. The laboratory researchers in New York, Oxford, Paris, Berlin, and Moscow began to share their findings with one another. They noticed similar cognitive disorders—even though the victims came from different cultures and spoke different languages (Gardner, 1985).

The study of brain lesions has greatly increased our understanding of the organization of the brain (Goodglass & Butters, 1988). Fortunately, the individuals with brain lesions can often compensate for their deficits within a short time. However, this compensation sometimes makes research findings less conclusive (Robinson & Petersen, 1986).

Regional Cerebral Blood-Flow Studies.

An active region of the brain requires more "metabolic fuel." Using the **regional cerebral blood-flow technique,** researchers can inject a small amount of a radioactive substance resembling glucose, which is the brain's major metabolic fuel. The neuroscientists can then record the cerebral blood flow to the active parts of the brain. Different cognitive tasks increase the regional cerebral blood flow in different areas of the brain. In Chapter 3, we will discuss how the regional cerebral blood-flow technique has been used to clarify the distinction between different types of memory. This technique is also called **positron emission tomography,** or **PET scan.**

Evoked Potential Technique.

When researchers use the **evoked potential technique,** they place electrodes on a person's scalp to record electrical signals generated from a large number of neurons located underneath the electrodes. This technique, like the regional cerebral blood-flow technique, cannot identify the response of a single neuron. However, it can identify electrical changes over very brief periods of time. The evoked potential technique responds in different ways to different task demands. Chapter 2 will discuss how this technique is used to study how people's attention patterns shift when they listen to an unexpected tone.

Single-Cell Recording Technique.

So far, we have examined three techniques that neuroscientists can use to study humans. In the **single-cell recording technique**—a technique that cannot safely be used on humans—researchers study characteristics of the nervous system in animals by inserting a tiny electrode next to (or even into) a single **neuron,** the basic cell in the nervous system. For example, a neuroscientist might insert an electrode into a neuron of a cat's visual cortex.

When Hubel and Wiesel (1965, 1979) used this technique, they found that some kinds of cells in the visual cortex responded vigorously only when lines were presented in a specific orientation. Other kinds of cells are even more specific in their "preferences"; the visual stimulus must have not only a specific orientation, but also a specific shape and direction of movement. More details on this technique can be found elsewhere (e.g., Hubel, 1982; Matlin & Foley, 1992). Clearly, this research has important implications for visual pattern recognition, because it provides a mechanism for recognizing certain patterns, such as letters of the alphabet. We will examine this research in Chapter 2.

A detailed investigation of the contribution of neuroscience research techniques to cognitive psychology is beyond the scope of this book. However, these techniques will be mentioned further in the chapters on perception and memory.

Artificial Intelligence

Artificial intelligence (AI) is the branch of computer science that attempts to write computer programs capable of the kind of higher mental processes traditionally associated only with humans (Gardner, 1985; Posner, 1986). Two topics that are often studied by researchers in artificial intelligence are language and problem solving; we will consider additional aspects of AI in Chapters 8 and 10.

The Machine Metaphor.
In recent years, many cognitive psychologists have adopted the computer as a machine metaphor for the human mind. As Cohen (1983) points out, the use of machine metaphors in psychology has a long history. As early as 430 B.C., philosophers compared the human mind to a machine (Marshall, 1977). Some of the metaphors for memory have included a wax tablet, a storehouse, and an extensively indexed library. The activity of the brain has been compared to a telephone exchange and to weaving on a loom. Thus, the computational (or computer) metaphor is the latest in a long list of mechanical and semimechanical metaphors.

According to the computational metaphor, the computer is a complex, multipurpose machine that processes information quickly and accurately. Researchers acknowledge obvious differences in physical structure between the computer and the human mind. However, they point out that both may operate according to similar general principles (Cohen, 1983; Eysenck, 1984; Miller, 1985). Like humans, computers have a variety of internal mechanisms. They have a central-processing mechanism with a limited capacity. This mechanism resembles limited attention in humans (as we'll discuss in the next chapter, we cannot pay attention to everything at once). Furthermore, computer systems distinguish between an active processor and a large-capacity information storage; cognitive psychologists often make a similar distinction in human memory between short-term and long-term memory. Also, both computers and humans can compare symbols and can make choices according to the results of the comparison. Researchers who favor the computational approach try to design the appropriate "software." With the right computer program, researchers hope to mimic the adaptability and the fluidity of human thought processes (McClelland et al., 1986).

AI researchers favor the analogy between the human mind and the computer because computer programs produce an account that must be detailed, precise, unambiguous, and logical. They can represent the functions of a computer with a flowchart that shows the sequence of stages in processing. The flowchart also illustrates the relationships between various internal functions. Suppose that the computer and the human show equivalent performance patterns on a particular task. Then the researcher can conclude that the program that directed the computer represents a good theory for describing the human's mental operations (Cohen, 1983; Eysenck, 1984).

A problem arises, however, in deciding what constitutes "equivalent performance." For example, a computer program may perform a series of mathematical calculations with an accuracy rate equal to that of a human. However, the computer is much faster; the two rates are not equivalent. Furthermore, human goals tend to be complex and fluid. People playing a game of chess may be concerned about how long the game lasts, about other social obligations, or about interpersonal interactions with their opponent. In contrast, the computer's goals are simple and rigid; the computer deals only with the outcome of the chess game (Eysenck, 1984; Neisser, 1963). In many respects, then, the performance patterns may not be equivalent.

Another issue that intrigues many AI researchers is whether a machine can think. Can a machine have conscious thoughts in the same sense that you and I have? This topic is beyond the scope of a cognition book, but if the question interests you, you can consult other resources such as a book by Dennett (1991) and articles by Searle (1990a, 1990b) and Churchland and Churchland (1990).

Computer Simulation. We need to draw a distinction between "pure AI" and computer simulation. **Pure AI** is an approach that seeks to accomplish a task as efficiently as possible. For example, the most successful computer programs for chess evaluate as many potential moves as possible in as little time as possible. A program that considers a larger number of moves is more likely to win the game. However, the strategies employed in these computer programs show little resemblance to the strategies humans use when they play chess. In contrast, **computer simulation** attempts to take human limitations into account. For example, most human chess players do not have the ability to evaluate several dozen potential moves at the same time. Therefore, a computer simulation should show similar limitations in its strategies.

Several areas in which computer-simulation research has been most active include basic visual processing, language processing, and problem solving. However, some tasks that humans accomplish quite easily seem to defy computer simulation. For example, any 10-year-old child can quickly locate a clock, read the pattern on the clock, and announce the time. However, this task cannot yet be simulated with a computer (Posner, 1986; Weisstein, 1973). Computers also cannot match humans' sophistication in learning languages, identifying objects in everyday scenes, or solving problems by drawing an analogy with other situations (Stillings et al., 1987).

Despite the limitations of computers, artificial intelligence has clearly had an important influence on research and theory in cognitive psychology; these contributions will be noted throughout the book. However, a more recent development called the parallel distributed processing approach has captured the imagination of many cognitive psychologists, thereby reducing the appeal of the classical AI approach. Let us now consider this new development.

The Parallel Distributed Processing Approach

In 1986, James McClelland, David Rumelhart, and their colleagues at the University of California, San Diego, published an enormously influential two-volume book called *Parallel Distributed Processing*. Palmer's (1987) review of these volumes captures the enthusiasm with which this new approach has been greeted, "These two volumes may turn out to be among the handful of most important books yet written for cognitive psychology" (p. 925).

The **parallel distributed processing approach** proposes that cognitive processes can be understood in terms of networks that link together neuron-like units. The parallel distributed processing approach is often refered to by its initials, the **PDP approach,** or by its alternate name, **connectionism.**

An undergraduate textbook in cognition cannot examine this elaborate theory or its application in detail. However, in this section we can outline its origins, its basic principles, and reactions to the PDP approach. The PDP approach will also be covered in some detail as a model of memory (Chapter 3), and it will be mentioned in several additional chapters.

The Origins of the PDP Approach. Some psychologists have traced the origins of the PDP approach back to William James's (1890) *Principles of Psychology* (e.g., Crovitz, 1990). We will begin with the more recent past, noting developments in both neuroscience and artificial intelligence—the two topics we have just discussed.

With the development of more sophisticated research techniques during the 1970s, neuroscientists were able to explore the structure of the **cerebral cortex,** the outer layer of the brain that is most responsible for cognitive processes. One important discovery was the numerous connections among neurons (e.g., Mountcastle, 1979). In fact, this pattern of interconnections resembled many elaborate networks.

In other words, many cognitive processes could not be localized in a particular pinpoint-sized portion of the brain; instead, the neural activity for a particular cognitive process seems to be distributed throughout a section of the brain. For example, we cannot pinpoint one small portion of your brain in which the name of your cognitive psychology professor is stored. Instead, that information is probably distributed throughout thousands of neurons in a region of your cerebral cortex. Those who favor the PDP approach decided that a model should be developed that resembled the important features of the brain, namely the numerous interconnections and the distributed nature of neural activity.

At the same time that theorists were learning about the features of the brain, they were becoming discouraged about the limits of the classical artificial intelligence approach favored by information-processing psychologists (e.g., Lupker, 1990). According to some classical AI models, processing was viewed as a series of discrete operations; one step must be completed before the system could go on to the next step in the flowchart (McClelland, 1988). This one-step-at-a-time approach may capture the leisurely series of operations you conduct when solving a long-division problem. However, it cannot explain how you can instantaneously perceive a visual scene (Churchland & Churchland, 1990; Martindale, 1991). When you look at a visual scene, the retina presents input to your cortex in the form of close to a million distinct signals—all at the same time.

In other words, many cognitive activities seem to involve **parallel processing,** with many signals handled at the same time, rather than **serial processing,** when only one item is handled at a given time. In short, processing appears to be both parallel and distributed, explaining the name *parallel distributed processing*.

The Basic Characteristics of the PDP Approach. The parallel distributed processing approach includes several important principles. Let us begin with the two principles we have just discussed and add other major points.

1. Many cognitive processes are based on parallel operations, not serial operations.
2. The neural activity underlying a particular cognitive action (for example, remembering a word) is typically distributed across a relatively broad area of the cortex, rather than being limited to a single, pinpoint-sized location.
3. If information is incomplete or faulty, you can still carry out most cognitive processes. For example, suppose a friend is describing Dr. Brown, noting that this individual is a short, very bright professor in the chemistry department, who is very politically active. You might say, "Oh, I think you mean Dr. Black in the physics department." Our memory and other cognitive processes are extremely flexible, tolerating cues that are partly inaccurate (Churchland & Churchland, 1990).
4. Some clues are more effective than others in helping us locate information in memory. For example, if you are trying to remind a friend about a movie you saw together, the name of the movie or the names of the major actors will certainly be more useful clues than the name of the cinematographer!

Chapter 3, on models of memory, will explore in more detail how the PDP approach accounts for the intricacy, flexibility, and accuracy of human memory. However, the most important characteristic of the PDP approach is that it is designed with the human brain as the basic model, rather than the serial computer (Palmer, 1987).

Reactions to the PDP Approach. Because the PDP approach is relatively new, we cannot assess its long-term impact. However, many cognitive scientists have greeted the PDP approach as a ground-breaking new framework (e.g., Bechtel & Abrahamsen, 1991; Palmer, 1987). They have even suggested that the PDP approach will produce a transformation of the field that is as dramatic as the "cognitive revolution," which replaced the earlier behaviorist approach.

Naturally, not all cognitive scientists share this enthusiasm (e.g., Fodor & Pylyshyn, 1988; Pinker & Mehler, 1988). However, numerous psychologists have embraced parallel distributed processing, developing models in areas as unrelated to each other as unconscious processes (Kihlstrom, 1987), slips of the tongue (Dell, 1986), and children's cognitive development (Bates & Elman, in press). With additional research, cognitive scientists should be able to determine whether the PDP approach can account for the broad range of skills represented by our cognitive processes.

SECTION SUMMARY: THE CURRENT STATUS OF COGNITIVE PSYCHOLOGY

1. Despite the widespread support for the cognitive approach to psychology, this approach has also been criticized.
2. One common complaint concerns the issue of ecological validity. However, ecologically valid research has increased in recent years.
3. Cognitive science includes the disciplines of psychology, philosophy, linguistics, anthropology, artificial intelligence, and neuroscience; cognitive scientists emphasize the importance of internal representations of the external world.
4. Neuroscientists search for brain-based explanations for cognitive processes, using techniques such as the study of brain lesions, regional cerebral blood-flow research, the evoked potential technique, and the single-cell recording technique.
5. Artificial intelligence approaches to cognition can involve designing computer programs to accomplish cognitive tasks as efficiently as possible (pure AI), or to accomplish these tasks while acknowledging human limitations (computer simulation).
6. An extremely influential new framework, called the parallel distributed processing approach, argues that cognitive scientists should abandon the serial computer as the basic model, instead proposing that the human brain provides the ideal model.
7. The PDP approach emphasizes that cognitive processes operate in parallel,

that neural activity is distributed across broad regions of the brain, that cognitive processes can be executed even when the information is incomplete or faulty, and that some clues are more effective than others in locating information in memory.

AN OVERVIEW OF THE BOOK

This textbook covers many different kinds of mental processes, beginning with perception and memory—two processes that are involved in virtually every other aspect of cognition. Later chapters discuss "higher order" cognition. As the name suggests, these higher order processes depend upon the more basic cognitive processes covered at the beginning of the book. The final chapter examines cognition across the life span. Let's preview Chapters 2 through 11.

A Preview of the Chapters

Perceptual processes **(Chapter 2)** involve the use of previous knowledge to interpret the stimuli that are registered by our senses. For example, pattern recognition allows you to recognize each of the letters on this page. Another perceptual process is attention. If you have ever tried to follow two conversations at the same time, you have probably noticed the limits of your attention!

Memory is the process of maintaining information over time. Memory is such an important part of cognition that it requires three chapters. **Chapter 3** examines four models of memory. One model emphasizes the difference between short-term and long-term memory, whereas the second model stresses that the accuracy of recall depends upon how deeply that information was processed. The third model focuses on the nature of the material stored in memory, and the fourth model is the parallel distributed processing approach, which we have just discussed.

Chapter 4, the second of the memory chapters, describes sensory and short-term memory. Have you ever heard a large clock chiming out the time when you were not really paying attention? Sensory memory makes the chimes still seem to ring inside your head for a couple of seconds after the physical stimulus has stopped. In the section on short-term memory, we will explore another phenomenon, which occurs when you forget someone's name that you heard just 30 seconds ago!

Chapter 5, the last memory chapter, focuses on long-term memory. We'll explore several factors, such as expertise and mood, that are related to people's ability to remember material for a long period of time. The section on autobiographical memory is concerned with our everyday memory experiences. For example, do you seem to have particularly vivid recall for the clothes you were wearing when an important event occurred? The final section of this chapter provides suggestions for memory improvement.

Chapter 6 examines imagery, which is the mental representation of things that are not physically present. An important controversy is whether mental images truly resemble perceptual images. For example, does your mental image of a clock resemble the visual image formed when you actually look at a clock? Another important topic concerns the mental representations we have for physical settings, such as the cognitive map you developed for your college campus.

Chapter 7 concerns general knowledge. One area of general knowledge is semantic memory, which includes factual knowledge about the world as well as knowledge about word meanings. General knowledge also includes schemas, which are generalized kinds of information about situations. For example, you have a schema for what happens during a child's birthday party. A final topic in this chapter is metacognition, which is your knowledge about your own cognitive processes. For instance, do you know whether you could remember the definition for *metacognition* if you were to be tested tomorrow morning?

Chapter 8 is the first of two chapters on language and it examines language comprehension. One component of language comprehension is understanding spoken language. A friend can mumble a sentence, and yet you can easily perceive the speech sounds and understand the meaning of that sentence. A second component of language comprehension is reading; you recognize words, figure out the meaning of unfamiliar words, and draw inferences that are not actually stated in a written passage.

Chapter 9, the second language chapter, investigates language production. When we speak, we need to select the content that we want to express, but we are also attuned to the social context of speech. For example, we make certain that the person with whom we are speaking has the appropriate background knowledge. Psychologists are just beginning to examine writing as a form of language production, but writing clearly involves different processes than speaking. The final topic is bilingualism; even though learning a single language is challenging, some people master two or more languages with fluency.

Chapter 10 considers problem solving. Suppose you want to solve a problem, such as how to cook some soup when the electricity has gone out. You'll need to represent the problem, perhaps in terms of a list, a mental image, or symbols. You can solve the problem by several strategies, such as dividing the problem into several smaller problems. Several factors that influence problem solving include expertise and whether the problem-solver has a mental set that blocks alternative approaches to the problem. Our final topic is creativity. Some research demonstrates, for example, that creativity can be squelched by telling people that they will be graded for their creative efforts.

Chapter 11 addresses logical reasoning and decision making. Reasoning involves drawing conclusions from several known facts. In many cases, a person's background knowledge interferes with accurate conclusions for reasoning problems. When we make decisions, we supply judgments about uncertain events. For example, people may cancel a trip to Europe after reading about a recent terrorist attack, even though statistics might show that chances of danger are small.

Chapter 12 examines cognitive processes in infants, children, and elderly adults. People in these three age groups are more competent than you might guess. For example, when the circumstances are right, 3-month-old infants can recall an event that occurred 5 weeks earlier. Young children are also quite accurate in

---

DEMONSTRATION 1.1

LOOKING AT UNUSUAL PARAGRAPHS.

How fast can you spot what is unusual about this paragraph? It looks so ordinary that you might think nothing was wrong with it at all, and, in fact, nothing is. But it is atypical. Why? Study its various parts, think about its curious wording, and you may hit upon a solution. But you must do it without aid; my plan is not to allow any scandalous misconduct in this psychological study. No doubt, if you work hard on this possibly frustrating task, its abnormality will soon dawn upon you. You cannot know until you try. But it is commonly a hard nut to crack. So, good luck!

I trust a solution is conspicuous now. Was it dramatic and fair, although odd? *Author's hint:* I cannot add my autograph to this communication and maintain its basic harmony.

---

recognizing whether they have seen something before. Finally, elderly people are very competent on many memory tasks, such as recognizing whether they have seen something before.

Themes in the Book

This book will stress certain themes and consistencies in cognitive processes. These themes can guide you, offering a framework for understanding many of the complexities of our mental abilities.

Theme 1 *The cognitive processes are active, rather than passive.* The behaviorists viewed humans as passive organisms; humans wait until a stimulus arrives from the environment, and then they respond. In contrast, the cognitive approach proposes that people are eager to acquire information. Furthermore, memory is a lively process, involving active synthesis, rather than passive storage. When you read, you actively draw inferences that were never directly stated. In summary, your mind is not a sponge that passively absorbs information leaking out from the environment. Instead, you continually search and synthesize.

Theme 2 *The cognitive processes are remarkably efficient and accurate.* The amount of material in your memory is awe-inspiring. Language development is similarly impressive because of the large number of new words and complex language structures that must be mastered. Naturally, humans make mistakes. However, these mistakes can often be traced to the use of a rational strategy. For instance, people frequently base their decisions on the ease with which examples spring to mind. This strategy often leads to a correct decision, but it can occasionally produce an error. Furthermore, many of the limitations in human information processing may actually be helpful. For instance, you may sometimes regret that you cannot remember information for more than a few seconds. However, if you retained all information forever, your memory would be hopelessly cluttered with facts that are no longer useful. Before you read further, try Demonstration 1.1, which is based on a demonstration by Hearst (1991).

Theme 3   *The cognitive processes handle positive information better than negative information.* We understand sentences better if they are worded in the affirmative, for example, "Mary is honest," rather than in the negative, "Mary is not dishonest." Reasoning tasks are also easier with positive than with negative information. Furthermore, we have trouble noticing when something is missing, as illustrated in Demonstration 1.1 (Hearst, 1991). Incidentally, if you are still puzzled, check the end of this chapter for the answer to the demonstration. We also tend to perform better on a variety of different tasks if the information is emotionally positive (that is, pleasant), rather than emotionally negative (unpleasant). In short, our cognitive processes are designed to handle *what is,* rather than *what is not* (Hearst, 1991).

Theme 4   *The cognitive processes are interrelated with one another; they do not operate in isolation.* This textbook devotes separate chapters to each topic. However, you should not conclude that each process can function by itself, without input from other processes. For example, decision making relies on perception, memory, general knowledge, and language. The higher mental processes depend on the careful integration of the more basic cognitive processes, so that tasks such as problem solving, logical reasoning, and decision making are impressively complex.

Theme 5   *Many cognitive processes rely on both bottom-up and top-down processing.* **Bottom-up processing** stresses the importance of information from the stimuli, whereas **top-down processing** stresses the influence of concepts, expectations, and memory upon the cognitive processes. Both factors work simultaneously to ensure that our cognitive processes are typically fast and accurate.

Consider pattern recognition. You recognize the professor for your cognitive psychology course partly because of the specific information from the stimulus— information about this person's face, height, shape, and so forth; bottom-up processing is important. At the same time, top-down processing operates because you have come to expect that the person standing in front of your classroom is that professor. Similarly, research by Brewer & Treyens (1981) shows that students who were asked to recall everything they saw in a college professor's office indeed recalled many of the stimuli they saw (bottom-up processing). However, they also "recalled" many objects—such as books—that could be expected but were not actually present (top-down processing).

How to Use the Book

This textbook includes several features that are designed to help you understand and remember the material. I would like to describe how you can use each of these features most effectively.

Notice that each chapter begins with an outline. When you start to read a new chapter, first examine the outline so that you can appreciate the general structure of a topic. For example, you can see that Chapter 2 contains two major sections, labeled *Pattern Recognition* and *Attention*.

Another feature in the next 11 chapters is a chapter preview, which is a short description of the material to be covered. This preview builds upon the framework provided in the outline and also defines some important new terms.

As you read the actual chapters, notice the numerous applications of cognitive psychology. The recent emphasis on ecological validity has produced many studies that describe our everyday cognitive activity. In addition, research in cognition has important applications in areas such as education, medicine, and clinical psychology. These examples provide concrete illustrations of psychological principles. As research on memory has demonstrated, people recall material better if it is concrete, rather than abstract, and if they try to determine whether it applies to themselves. Finally, a third kind of application in this book is the informal experiments or "demonstrations." Each demonstration requires little or no equipment, and you can perform most demonstrations by yourself. Students have reported that these demonstrations help make the material more memorable. Incidentally, more tips on improving memory will be discussed in Chapter 5.

Notice also that each new term appears in boldface type (for example, **cognition**) when it is first discussed. I have included the definition in the same sentence as the term, so you do not need to search an entire paragraph to determine the term's meaning. In some cases, a phonetic pronunciation is provided for a new word, with the accented syllable in italics. These pronunciation guides are not intended to insult your intelligence, but to aid your learning. Also, some of the same important terms appear in several different chapters. These terms will be defined each time they occur, so that the chapters can be read in any order.

Chapters 2 through 12 each contain an "In Depth" section, which examines recent research on a selected topic relevant to the chapter. These sections focus on experimental methodology and the outcome of the studies.

A unique feature of this textbook is a summary at the end of each major section in a chapter, rather than at the end of the entire chapter. For example, Chapter 2 includes two section summaries. This feature allows you to review the material more frequently and to master small manageable chunks before you move on to new material. When you reach the end of a section, test yourself to see whether you can remember the important points. Next read the section summary and notice which items you omitted or remembered incorrectly. Then test yourself again and recheck your accuracy. You may also find that you learn the material more efficiently if you read only one section—rather than an entire chapter—at a time.

A set of review questions and a list of new terms appear at the end of each chapter. Many review questions ask you to apply your knowledge to a practical problem. Other review questions encourage you to integrate information from several parts of a chapter. Notice that the new terms are listed in their order of appearance in the chapter. Check whether you can supply a definition and an example for each new term. You can locate the definition by checking the subject index at the end of the book.

The final feature of each chapter is a list of recommended readings. This list can supply you with resources if you want to write a paper on a particular topic or if an area is personally interesting. In general, I tried to locate books, chapters, and articles that provide more than an overview of the subject but are not overly technical.

One unusual aspect of cognition is that you are actually using cognition to learn about cognition! These suggestions may help you use your cognitive processes even more efficiently.

CHAPTER REVIEW QUESTIONS

1. What are cognition and cognitive psychology? Think about a career that you have selected and suggest several ways in which cognitive psychology may be relevant to that discipline.

2. Compare the following approaches to psychology with respect to their emphasis on higher mental processes: (a) Wundt's introspective technique, (b) William James's approach, (c) behaviorism, (d) Gestalt psychology, and (e) the cognitive approach.

3. The concept of ecological validity was introduced in this chapter. Compare the following approaches in terms of their concern about ecological validity: (a) Ebbinghaus's approach to memory, (b) James's approach to psychological processes, (c) Bartlett's approach to memory, (d) the cognitive psychology approach from several decades ago, and (e) the more recent cognitive psychology approach.

4. List several reasons for the increased interest in cognitive psychology and the decline of the behaviorist approach. Also, describe the area of cognitive science, noting the disciplines that contribute to this area.

5. What is artificial intelligence and how is the information-processing approach relevant to this topic? Think of a human cognitive process that might be interesting to people in artificial intelligence, and give examples of how the pure AI and the computer simulation investigations of this cognitive process might differ.

6. The section on neuroscience described several research techniques. Discuss these, contrasting each one with respect to these dimensions: (a) Can it be used with normal humans? (b) Can it be used with minimal harm and interference with normal processes? and (c) How precise is the information it yields?

7. How does the parallel distributed processing approach differ from the classical artificial intelligence approach? How is this new approach based on discoveries in neuroscience? What are its basic characteristics?

8. According to Theme 2, the cognitive processes are impressively efficient and accurate. However, we often tend to downplay our accuracy and emphasize our errors. Think about several occasions on which you have forgotten some-

thing, and contrast that number with the numerous occasions when you have accurately recalled material—for example, the names of people who attended your high school, the names of dozens of vegetables, the names of countries, and the names of popular songs and movies.

9. According to Theme 4, the cognitive processes are interrelated. Think about a problem you have solved recently, and point out how the solution to that problem depended upon perceptual processes, memory, language, and potentially some other cognitive processes.

10. Review each of the five themes of this book. Which of them seem consistent with your own experience, and which seem surprising?

NEW TERMS

cognition
cognitive psychology
cognitive approach
introspection
replications
behaviorism
Gestalt psychology
information-processing approach
ecological validity
cognitive science
neuroscience
brain lesions
regional cerebral blood-flow
    technique
positron emission tomography (PET
    scan)
evoked potential technique
single-cell recording technique

neuron
artificial intelligence (AI)
pure AI
computer simulation
parallel distributed processing
    approach
PDP approach
connectionism
cerebral cortex
parallel processing
serial processing
Theme 1
Theme 2
Theme 3
Theme 4
Theme 5
bottom-up processing
top-down processing

RECOMMENDED READINGS

Gardner, H. (1985). *The mind's new science: A history of the cognitive revolution.* New York: Basic Books. Howard Gardner's highly praised introduction to cognitive science provides a historical overview of the discipline. Cognitive psychology receives extra treatment, but excellent descriptions of the other disciplines within cognitive science are also included.

Kosslyn, S. M., & Koenig, O. (1992). *Wet mind: The new cognitive neuroscience.* New York: The Free Press. Stephen Kosslyn is a major researcher in the field of imagery, and this overview of neuroscience is one of the more readable accounts of this important field.

McClelland, J. L. (1988). Connectionist models and psychological evidence. *Journal of Memory and Language*, *27*, 107–123. The emerging parallel distributed processing approach is complex and challenging, but this article provides a brief overview, described in the words of one of the founders of the PDP approach.

Stillings, N. A., Feinstein, M. H., Garfield, J. L., Rissland, E. L., Rosenbaum, D. A., Weisler, S. E., & Baker-Ward, L. (1987). *Cognitive science: An introduction*. Cambridge, MA: MIT Press. This introductory textbook provides an excellent overview of cognitive science, including chapters on cognitive psychology, artificial intelligence, linguistics, neuroscience, and philosophy.

ANSWER TO DEMONSTRATION 1.1

The letter *e* is missing from this passage. Because of the frequency of this letter in English, a passage this long—without the letter *e*—is highly unusual.

PERCEPTUAL PROCESSES

Perception is a process that uses our previous knowledge to gather and interpret the stimuli that our senses register. Two aspects of perception that are most relevant for cognition are pattern recognition and attention.

Pattern recognition involves identifying a complex arrangement of sensory stimuli, such as a letter of the alphabet, a human face, or a complex scene. We will examine four theories of pattern recognition and then discuss how pattern recognition is influenced by both context and past experience.

If you have ever tried to study while a friend is talking, you can appreciate the limits of attention. Research demonstrates that performance usually suffers if attention must be divided between two or more tasks; however, practice may help. Also, when we selectively attend to one task, we recall very little about other irrelevant tasks. This chapter will discuss several theories of attention, including an in-depth section on feature-integration theory, as well as the biological basis of attention. Finally, we consider the topic of consciousness, including awareness about cognitive processes and thought suppression.

INTRODUCTION

You may be tempted to ignore perception because it seems so effortless. You turn your head, and your visual system immediately registers a wastebasket next to a pair of shoes. Your attention shifts to a sound in the hall, and you instantly recognize the footsteps of a friend. Admittedly, perception requires less effort than cognitive tasks such as problem solving or decision making. Still, no current computer can accomplish the impressive task of perceiving stimuli (Hoffman, 1986).

Perception involves using previous knowledge to gather and interpret the stimuli registered by the senses. For example, you used perception to interpret each of the letters on this page. Consider how you managed to perceive the letter n at the end of the word *perception*. You combined information registered by your eyes with your previous knowledge about the configuration of the letters of the alphabet as well as your previous knowledge about what to expect when your visual system has processed *perceptio-*. Notice that perception combines aspects of both the outside world (the stimuli) and your own inner world (your previous knowledge). Notice also that this process of pattern recognition is a good example of the fifth theme of this book: It combines bottom-up and top-down processing.

The topic of perception occupies an entire course in most colleges. We therefore cannot do justice to this discipline in just a single chapter; more details are available elsewhere (e.g., Coren et al, 1994; Goldstein, 1989; Matlin & Foley, 1992). Our discussion of perceptual processes will be limited to two topics that are particularly relevant to cognition: pattern recognition and attention. These processes are important because they prepare the "raw" sensory information so that it can be used in the more complex mental processes, which are discussed in later chapters

---

DEMONSTRATION 2.1

THE IMMEDIATE RECOGNITION OF PATTERNS.

Find a television set and turn it on; adjust the sound to "mute." Now change channels with your eyes closed. At each new channel, open your eyes and then immediately shut them. Notice how you can instantly identify and interpret the image on the TV screen, even though the image is one you did not expect and have never previously seen in that exact form. In less than a second and without major effort, you can identify colors, textures, contours, objects, and people. This demonstration was suggested by Irving Biederman (1990), who noted that people can usually interpret the meaning of a novel scene in 1/10 of a second. Notice also that you can recognize the rapidly presented images on MTV, even though they may be shown at a rate of 5 each second. Consistent with Theme 1, humans are impressively efficient in recognizing patterns.

---

of this book. Pattern recognition allows us to perceive a form in a stimulus, and attention is responsible for our more extensive processing of some information, while other information is neglected.

PATTERN RECOGNITION

To illustrate your own ability in recognizing patterns, try Demonstration 2.1. Within a fraction of a second, you can recognize meaningful patterns on the television set. **Pattern recognition** is the identification of a complex arrangement of sensory stimuli. When you recognize a pattern, your sensory processes transform and organize the raw information provided by your sensory receptors, and you compare the sensory stimuli with information in other memory storages. In some cases, pattern recognition involves applying a label to a particular arrangement of stimuli. For example, you recognize the letter Z, you recognize your Aunt Betty, and you recognize Beethoven's Fifth Symphony. In each case, you match a particular set of stimuli with a label stored in memory. In other cases, pattern recognition involves realizing that you have seen a particular pattern before. For example, you may notice a minor character in a movie. You recognize her face, even though you cannot attach a name or a label.

Our examination of pattern recognition begins with the major theories of pattern recognition. Then we will see how pattern recognition is facilitated by both the context in which the stimulus occurs and a person's previous experience with that stimulus.

Theories of Pattern Recognition

Many different theories of pattern recognition have been proposed, but we will look at only four of them. The first theory, template matching, is now generally

FIGURE 2.1	

Various Versions of the Letter Z.

acknowledged to be inadequate. Nonetheless, we will begin this section with an examination of the template-matching theory because it was the first modern theory; the three other theories represent more sophisticated developments. As you read about these theories, keep in mind that we do not need to choose just one theory. Humans are flexible creatures, and we may use different approaches on different pattern-recognition tasks.

Template-Matching Theory.   You look at a letter Z and you immediately recognize it. According to the **template-matching theory,** you compare a stimulus to a set of **templates**—specific patterns that you have stored in memory. After comparing the stimulus to a number of templates, you note the template that matches most closely. You've probably had the experience of trying to find a piece of a jigsaw puzzle that will complete part of the puzzle. The piece must fit precisely, or else it won't work. Similarly, the stimulus must fit the template precisely. Thus, the letter Q will not fit the template for the letter O because of the extra line on the bottom.

Some nonhuman pattern recognition systems are based on templates. For example, if you have a checking account, take out one of your checks and look at it. Notice the numbers at the bottom of the check, which are specially designed to be recognized by check-sorting computers. Each of the numbers has a constant, standardized shape. Furthermore, each of the numbers is distinctly different from the others. Humans sometimes write a number 4 that looks like a 9. The 4 on your check, however, looks very different from the 9, so the computer will not make errors in pattern recognition when the patterns are compared with the templates.

A template system may work well for computers that are provided with a standardized set of numbers. However, notice why templates are totally inadequate for explaining the complex process of pattern recognition in humans. One problem with the template-matching theory is that it is extremely inflexible. For example, if a letter differs from the appropriate template even slightly, the pattern would not be recognized. However, every day we succeed in recognizing letters that differ substantially from the classic version of a letter. Notice, for example, how all the Z's in Figure 2.1 differ from each other. The print types vary and the sizes vary.

Some Z's are fragmented, blurry, or rotated. Still, all of these patterns are recognizable Z's. Our pattern recognition procedure must therefore involve a more flexible system than matching a pattern against a specific template.

A second problem with the template system is that we would need an infinite number of templates in order to recognize all the possible variations found among letters and numbers—let alone faces and other shapes. How could all this information be stored?

Even if we could devise a modified template theory that was less bulky and more efficient than the one just described, we would have difficulty with patterns viewed from nonstandard angles. If you rotate Figure 2.1, or view it from a slant, the shape of the image on your retina changes drastically for each Z. Nonetheless, you still recognize the letters (Hoffman, 1986). In fact, Jolicoeur and Landau (1984) estimate that humans require as little as 15 milliseconds* of additional processing time to recognize a letter that has been rotated a complete 180°. A template theory would need to suggest a different template for each rotation of a figure, a clearly unwieldy proposal.

Finally, template models only work for isolated letters and other simple objects presented in their complete form (Pinker, 1984a). Look up from your textbook right now and notice the complex array of fragmented objects registered on your retina. Perhaps these include a lower edge of a lamp, a corner of a desk, and a part of a book. Nonetheless, you can sort out this jumble and recognize the shapes. How could the visual system include templates for lower edges of lamps and other fragments? Clearly, then, the template theory cannot handle the complexity of human visual processing.

Prototype Models. Prototype models are more flexible versions of template-matching theories. According to **prototype models,** we store **prototypes**—which are abstract, idealized patterns—in memory. When we see a stimulus, we compare it with a prototype. The match does not need to be exact; minor variations are allowed. If the match is close enough, we recognize the stimulus. If the match is inadequate, we compare the stimulus with other prototypes until we locate a match.

For example, think about the prototype you have developed for your best friend. This abstract, idealized pattern includes certain characteristic facial features, body build, and height. It does not include a specific set of clothing or a specific facial expression. After all, you have stored a prototype in memory, not a template. Thus you can recognize your friend even when the stimulus pattern and the prototype differ on certain features, such as hair length, the presence or absence of glasses, and clothing style.

A number of studies have demonstrated the usefulness of prototypes in perceiving geometric designs, letters of the alphabet, and cartoon-like drawings (Franks & Bransford, 1971; Posner et al., 1967; Rhodes et al., 1987). A study by Reed

---

* A millisecond is 1/1000 of a second.

DEMONSTRATION 2.2

FORMING PROTOTYPES OF FACES.

Examine the faces below, which belong to two different categories. Then cover up these two sets of faces.

Category 1

Category 2

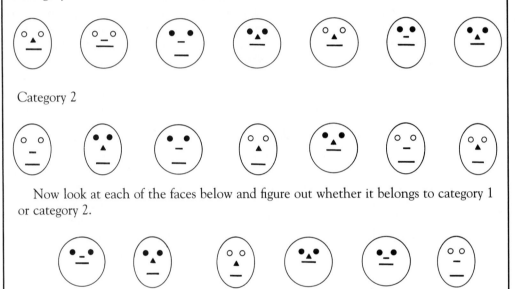

Now look at each of the faces below and figure out whether it belongs to category 1 or category 2.

(1972) demonstrates how prototype models can also be applied to the recognition of faces. Demonstration 2.2 is a modification of Reed's experiment. Participants in this experiment saw two categories of faces. As in Demonstration 2.2, no single feature reliably distinguished between the two categories of faces. For example, in Demonstration 2.2, the faces in Category 1 tend to have round heads, whereas the faces in Category 2 tend to have oval heads. However, there are exceptions in each category. Furthermore, the faces in Category 1 tend to have high mouths, whereas the faces in Category 2 tend to have low mouths—but again you can find exceptions. Other features, the shape of the nose and the shading of the eyes, are randomly distributed across the two categories.

After studying the faces for two minutes, Reed's participants were asked to classify 25 faces as belonging either to Category 1 or Category 2. The model that best predicted the participants' choices was a prototype model. In other words, the predominant strategy was to abstract a prototype representing each category. People then compared the novel patterns with each of the prototypes, emphasizing those features that best discriminated between the two categories. Thus, if you used a prototype approach in Demonstration 2.2, you first formed abstract prototypes for faces in Category 1 and Category 2. Then you compared each new picture with those two prototypes, paying particular attention to head shape and mouth position.

Prototype-matching theory is an appealing approach to the problem of pattern recognition. It describes how shapes can be easily recognized despite the variety of different representations of the same shape, the variety of orientations of the shape, and the fragmented view we often have of those shapes. However, the details of this approach have not yet been developed. For example, are there templates for prototypes (Spoehr & Lehmkuhle, 1982)? The next approach that we will consider, based on distinctive features, offers more neurological details—although this approach has other, different problems.

Incidentally, we will return to prototypes in Chapter 7, in which we will focus on the research of Eleanor Rosch and her colleagues. This chapter will consider how real-life categories—such as birds or tools or vehicles—are organized in terms of prototypes or best examples.

Distinctive-Features Models. The **distinctive-features models** state that we make discriminations among letters on the basis of a small number of characteristics. These characteristics that differentiate one letter from another are called **distinctive features.** According to the prototype models that were just discussed, people store an abstract, idealized version of each letter in their memory. In contrast, the distinctive-features models suggest that we store a list of feature components for each letter of the alphabet. For example, the letter G has a curved component and a horizontal line in the middle. When we see a new letter, we compare that letter with the lists of distinctive features that we have stored in memory.

Try Demonstration 2.3, which is based on a chart developed by Eleanor Gibson (1969). Distinctive-features models propose that these distinctive features remain constant, whether the letter is handwritten, printed, or typed. These models can explain how we perceive a wide variety of two-dimensional patterns, such as figures in a painting, designs on fabric, and illustrations in books. However, research testing distinctive-features models typically focuses on our ability to recognize letters and numbers.

Distinctive-features models are consistent with both psychological and physiological research. Research by Eleanor Gibson (1969) demonstrated that people require a relatively long time to decide whether some letters are different from one another when the letters share a large number of critical features. Note that the table in Demonstration 2.3 shows that the letters P and R are similar to each other on a large number of critical features; research participants made slow decisions about whether these two letters were different. In contrast, people decided relatively quickly whether other letter pairs—such as G and M—were different from

DEMONSTRATION 2.3

A DISTINCTIVE-FEATURES APPROACH (FROM GIBSON, 1969).

Eleanor Gibson proposed that letters differ from each other with respect to their distinctive features. She proposed the table that is reproduced below. Notice the top three kinds of features—straight, curve, and intersection. Notice that P and R share many features. However, Z and O have none of these kinds of features in common. Compare the following pairs of letters to determine the number of distinctive features they share: (1) E and F; (2) K and M; (3) Z and B; (4) N and M.

Features	A	E	F	H	I	L	T	K	M	N	V	W	X	Y	Z	B	C	D	G	J	O	P	R	Q	S	U
Straight																										
horizontal	+	+	+	+		+	+								+		+									
vertical		+	+	+	+	+	+	+	+	+				+		+		+				+	+			
diagonal /	+							+	+		+	+	+	+	+											
diagonal \	+							+	+	+	+	+	+	+								+	+			
Curve																										
closed																+		+			+	+	+	+		
open V																			+							+
open H																	+		+	+				+		
Intersection	+	+	+	+			+	+					+		+							+	+	+		
Redundancy																										
cyclic change		+						+			+				+								+			
symmetry	+	+		+	+		+	+	+		+	+	+	+		+	+	+			+					+
Discontinuity																										
vertical	+		+	+	+		+	+	+	+					+							+	+			
horizontal		+	+			+	+								+											

each other. Notice that G and M differ from each other in terms of many critical features. Garner's research (1979) confirmed that decision speed depends upon the number of shared distinctive features.

An important advantage of distinctive-features models is that they are compatible with some physiological evidence. As discussed in Chapter 1, the research team of Hubel and Wiesel inserted small wires, called microelectrodes, into a neuron in the visual cortex of anesthetized animals (Hubel, 1982; Hubel & Wiesel, 1965, 1979). Then they presented a simple visual stimulus, such as a vertical bar of light, directly in front of the animals' eyes. The researchers recorded the electrical response rate that the neuron produced to this stimulus, and then they presented a series of different stimuli. Figure 2.2 shows how one neuron might respond to bars with different orientations. Notice that this particular neuron responds most vigorously to a completely vertical bar; the response rate was much lower for lines with different orientations.

Furthermore, by moving the microelectrode to a new location just a hairbreadth away, Hubel and Wiesel located a different neuron that no longer responded so enthusiastically to a vertical bar. Instead, the preferred orientation was a bar rotated about 10°. Thus, a small patch of the visual cortex contained a variety of neurons, some especially responsive to vertical lines, some to horizontal lines, and some to specific diagonal lines. The visual system seems to contain specialized feature detectors "wired in," which facilitate the recognition of certain features of letters and simple patterns.

Let's compare the distinctive-features models with the other two approaches we have discussed. Probably the most important difference is that the distinctive-features approach proposes that pattern recognition involves detecting specific important parts of the stimulus. In contrast, the template model and prototype-matching theory emphasize the importance of the entire shape of the stimulus.

Klatzky (1980) proposes that prototype models and distinctive-features models may actually be compatible. For example, Klatzky notes that a prototype may consist of the features common to all or most instances of a pattern. To see how this explanation works, look back at Demonstration 2.2. Your prototype for the faces in Category 1 may have two features—round heads and high mouths. Your prototype for the faces in Category 2 may have two different features—oval heads and low mouths. The two prototypes may be similar with respect to other features, such as the absence of eyebrows and lack of hair. Thus, the prototype for Category 1 is both different from and similar to the prototype for Category 2 because both prototypes share only a moderate number of features. Similarly, the prototype for the letter O is both different from and similar to the prototype for the letter C. If prototypes are indeed based on distinctive features, future theorists may be able to integrate the two approaches.

We need to consider some basic problems with the distinctive-features approach. First, a theory of pattern recognition should not simply list the features in a simple shape; it must also describe the physical relationship among those features (Bruce, 1988). For example, in the letter T, the vertical line *supports* the horizontal line, whereas in the letter L, the vertical line rests at the side of the horizontal line.

In addition, Pinker (1984a) points out that the distinctive-features models were constructed to explain the relatively simple recognition of letters. However, natural

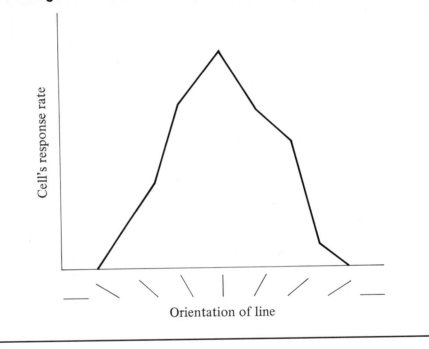

FIGURE 2.2

The Response Rate of a Hypothetical Cell in the Visual Cortex to Lines of Different Orientations. (Note that this cell responds most to vertical lines, less to diagonal lines, and least to horizontal lines.)

Cell's response rate

Orientation of line

shapes are much more complex. How can you recognize a horse? Do you analyze the stimulus into features, such as its mane, its hooves, and its head? This task is far more complicated than letter recognition. The final approach to pattern recognition specifically addresses how people recognize more complex kinds of stimuli found in everyday life.

The Computational Approach. The computational approach contains components of both the prototype approach and the distinctive-features approach, though its emphasis is different. The major aim of the **computational approach** is to develop computer-based theories that can accomplish some of the cognitive tasks that humans can achieve, such as the rapid, accurate recognition of three-dimensional objects (Biederman, 1987, 1990; Marr, 1982). The use of computers to simulate perceptual processes is known as **machine vision.**

Researchers who favor the computational approach typically do not examine the physiological aspects of pattern recognition. For example, one of the major contributors to this approach, David Marr (1982), wrote that an attempt to understand perception by investigating only the neurons is like trying to understand how birds fly by taking the physiological approach and studying their feathers. Similarly, he believed that a neuroscience approach could tell us *how* neurons operate, but not *why* they operate that way.

Until recently, the field of perception intrigued primarily psychologists, philosophers, and neuroscientists. However, in recent decades, computer scientists and researchers in artificial intelligence have also made important contributions (McArthur, 1982). These scientists are often less interested in figuring out exactly how perception occurs in humans than in understanding how perception is possible in any kind of organism or machine (Gardner, 1985; Yuille & Ullman, 1990).

Let us briefly consider Marr's description of the development of a three-dimensional (or 3-D) representation of a visual stimulus. Then we will examine how Irving Biederman has further developed the computational approach.

At the age of 32, David Marr discovered that he had leukemia. He decided to spend the last two years of his life writing a book titled *Vision* (Marr, 1982), which has had enormous influence on theories of pattern recognition. According to Marr, the first step in visual processing involves identifying an object's edges. Information about these edges is organized into an abstract representation that Marr called the **primal sketch.**

However, the goal of a visual system—whether in a computer or in a human— is to appreciate three-dimensional relationships, not simply an organized collection of edges. The primal sketch is first converted to a form that Marr called the $2^1/_2$- **D sketch,** which describes how the visible surfaces are oriented in relation to the viewer. The name $2^1/_2$-*D sketch* indicates that this intermediate representation is neither as primitive as a 2-D representation, nor as sophisticated as a 3-D representation. Finally, the $2^1/_2$ sketch is converted to a **3-D sketch,** which represents depth more accurately, including the complete third dimension, and shows the relationship of these shapes to each other. Whereas the $2^1/_2$-D sketch is represented from only one perspective—the viewer's—the 3-D sketch is more abstract, without any particular point of view.

David Marr and his colleagues suggested that 3-D representations of various shapes could be assigned to categories (e.g., Marr & Nishihara, 1978). Irving Biederman's recent work has explored the categorization of 3-D shapes more thoroughly in a theory called recognition-by-components (1987, 1990). The basic assumption of **recognition-by-components theory** is that a given view of an object can be represented as an arrangement of simple 3-D shapes, which he calls **geons,** a name that stands for *geometrical ions.* Geons resemble letters of the alphabet, because they can be combined to form something meaningful. Five of the proposed 24 geons are shown in Figure 2.3, together with various objects that can be constructed from the geons. Letters of the alphabet can be combined to form different meanings, depending upon the specific arrangements; *no* has a different meaning from *on.* Similarly, geons 3 and 5 from Figure 2.3 can be combined to form different meaningful objects; a cup is different from a pail. In general, an arrangement of

---

FIGURE 2.3

Examples of Geons (Left) and Representative Objects That Can Be Constructed from the Geons (Right). (From Biederman, 1990).

a.   b.

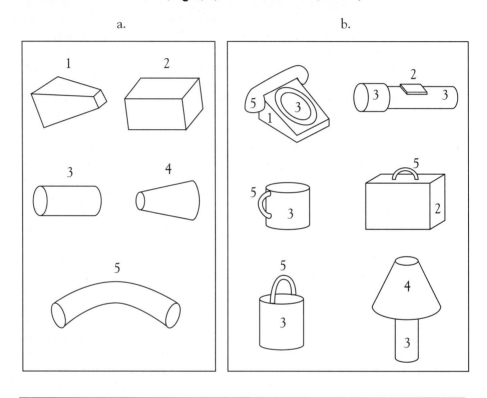

---

three geons is sufficient to permit the classification of any object. Notice, then, that Biederman's geon theory is essentially a feature theory for the recognition of objects (Oliver, 1992).

Although the recognition-by-components model has not yet been extensively tested, the early reports on normal humans and on people with specific visual deficits are compatible with the model (Banks & Krajicek, 1991). Additional work must be done to explain why we can identify not only isolated shapes, such as cups and pails, but also the complicated arrangements of numerous shapes, such as those we see when glancing quickly at a TV screen. The astonishing talents of the visual system, emphasized by Theme 2 of the book, can be partially described by the prototype, distinctive features, and computational approaches. However, even a combination of these three approaches cannot completely explain how you can glance at a scene and instantly recognize dozens of complex objects and their relationship with one another.

Top-Down Processing and Pattern Recognition

The theories of pattern recognition discussed so far have emphasized how people perceive isolated objects; we have not mentioned how knowledge and expectations might aid recognition. A perceiver tries to decipher a hastily written letter of the alphabet, without the benefit of the surrounding letters in the word. Another perceiver tries to identify an object that consists of a narrow, curved geon, attached to the side of a wider, cylindrical geon, without the reminder that the object resembles the coffee cup from breakfast.

Theme 5 emphasizes the difference between two kinds of processing. Let's review that distinction and see how these kinds of processes work together in a complementary fashion in pattern recognition. So far, our discussion of pattern recognition has emphasized **bottom-up processing** or **data-driven processing,** which stresses the importance of the stimulus in pattern recognition. Information about the stimulus arrives from the sensory receptors (from the bottom level in processing). The arrival of the information sets the pattern-recognition process into motion. The combination of simple, bottom-level features allows us to recognize more complex, whole patterns.

The other important process in pattern recognition is called **top-down processing** or **conceptually driven processing.** This approach stresses how a person's concepts and higher-level processes influence pattern recognition. According to this approach, our knowledge about how the world is organized helps in identifying patterns. We expect certain shapes to be found in certain locations, and we expect to encounter certain shapes because of past experiences. These expectations help us recognize patterns rapidly.

Cognitive psychologists propose that both bottom-up and top-down processing are necessary to explain the complexities of pattern recognition. As Palmer (1975a) notes, it is impossible to believe *only* in one or the other kind of processing; we cannot ask whether perceivers first interpret the whole or first interpret the parts. For example, a face is recognized because of two simultaneous processes: (a) when each shape—such as a pink oval representing the mouth—is placed in the context of a face, it becomes recognizable because of top-down processing and (b) bottom-up processing forces us to combine the component features into the perception of a face. Furthermore, top-down and bottom-up processing work smoothly together in seamless interaction to allow us to recognize patterns quickly and accurately (Hoffman, 1986).

Let's turn our attention to top-down processing. We will see how pattern recognition is facilitated by the context in which the stimulus appears and by past experience with the stimulus.

DEMONSTRATION 2.4

CONTEXT AND PATTERN RECOGNITION. CAN YOU READ THE FOLLOWING SENTENCE?

THE MAN RAN.

Context and Pattern Recognition. Before you read further, try Demonstration 2.4. As you can see, the same shape—an ambiguous letter—is sometimes perceived as an *H* and sometimes as an *A*. In this demonstration, you began to identify the whole word *THE*, and your tentative knowledge of that word helped to identify the second letter as an *H*. In other words, context facilitates pattern recognition.

Some of the research on context and pattern recognition focuses on identifying ambiguous objects. For example, Palmer (1975b) found that people were more likely to recognize an ambiguous figure when it was located in an appropriate context. Thus, in a kitchen scene, a loaf of bread was recognized more readily than a mailbox.

Most of the research on this topic examines how context enhances the recognition of letters of the alphabet. Psychologists who study reading realized that a theory of pattern recognition would be inadequate if it were based only on stimulus information. For example, suppose that we do identify each letter in terms of its distinctive features. In addition, suppose that each letter contains four distinctive features, a conservative guess. This would mean that a typical reader would need to make about 5,000 feature detections each minute, an outlandishly high estimate. Furthermore, do you have the impression that you really see and identify each letter in every sentence? You probably could read most sentences fairly well even if only half of the letters were present. F-r -x--pl-, -t's e-s- t- r--d t--s s--t-n--.

One of the most widely demonstrated phenomena in pattern recognition is the word superiority effect. According to the **word superiority effect,** we can identify a single letter more accurately and more rapidly when it appears in a word than when it appears in a string of unrelated letters. The word superiority effect was first reported more than a century ago (Cattell, 1886). During the current century, Reicher (1969) renewed psychologists' interest in the effect when he demonstrated that recognition accuracy was substantially higher when a letter appeared in a word, such as *work*, than in a nonword, such as *orwk*. Since then, dozens of studies have confirmed the importance of top-down processing in letter recognition (e.g., Chastain, 1981, 1986; Krueger, 1992; Pollatsek & Rayner, 1989; Taylor & Taylor, 1983; Wheeler, 1970).

One likely explanation for the word superiority effect involves an interaction between top-down and bottom-up processing (McClelland & Rumelhart, 1981;

Richman & Simon, 1989; Rumelhart & McClelland, 1982). This model is based on **parallel distributed processing,** the approach introduced in Chapter 1 that proposes that complex cognitive processes can be understood in terms of networks that link together related units. According to this connectionist model, when a person sees fragments of features in a word, these features activate letter units. These letter units then activate a word unit in the person's mental dictionary for that combination of letters. Once that word unit is activated, excitatory feedback helps in identifying individual letters. As a result, people can identify letters more quickly than if no word context provided excitatory feedback.

So far, we have seen that objects and letters can be more readily recognized when context is provided, demonstrating the importance of top-down processing. An additional way in which context can aid pattern recognition is that the context of a sentence can facilitate recognition of a word in a sentence. Many experiments have demonstrated that the context of a sentence, such as "Mary drank her orange _____," makes it easier to recognize a word, in this case, *juice*. In contrast, *juice* would take longer to recognize if it appeared alone or in an inappropriate context (Forster, 1981; Stanovich & West, 1981, 1983).

Let's discuss an interesting variant of these words-in-sentences studies. Rueckl and Oden (1986) demonstrated that both the features of the stimulus and the nature of the context influence word recognition; that is, bottom-up and top-down processing occur. These researchers used stimuli that were letters and letter-like characters. For example, one set of stimuli consisted of a perfectly formed letter *r*, a perfectly formed letter *n*, and three symbols that were intermediate between those two letters. Notice these stimuli arranged along the bottom of Figure 2.4. In each case, the letter pattern was embedded in the letter string "bea-s" so that there were five stimuli that ranged between "beans" and "bears."

The nature of the context was also varied by using the sentence frame, "The _____ raised (bears/beans) to supplement his income." The words chosen to fill the blank were carefully selected: "lion tamer," "zookeeper," "botanist," and "dairy farmer." You'll notice that a lion tamer and a zookeeper are more likely to raise bears, whereas the botanist and the dairy farmer are more likely to raise beans. Other similar ambiguous letters and sentence frames were also constructed, each using four different nouns or noun phrases.

On each trial, the participant saw one sentence for one second. Then the two test words were presented in upper-case letters (for example, *BEANS* and *BEARS*). People were told to select the word they had seen.

Figure 2.4 shows the results. As you can see, people were increasingly likely to choose the "bears" response when the segment on the right side of the letter was short, rather than long: The features of the stimulus are extremely important because pattern recognition operates in a bottom-up fashion. However, you'll also notice that people were consistently more likely to choose the "bears" response in the lion tamer and zookeeper sentences than in the botanist and dairy farmer sentences: The context is important because pattern recognition also operates in a top-down fashion.

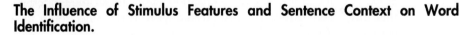

FIGURE 2.4

The Influence of Stimulus Features and Sentence Context on Word Identification.

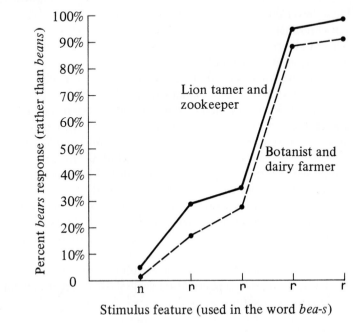

Think about how these context effects can influence the speed of reading. The previous letters in a word help you identify the remaining letters more quickly. Furthermore, the other words in a sentence help you identify the individual words more quickly. Without context to help you read quickly, you might still be reading the introduction to this chapter!

Past Experience and Pattern Recognition. We have seen that pattern recognition is facilitated by context. Pattern recognition is also facilitated when a person has had previous experience with an object. You can recognize a coffee cup more readily because you are familiar with this kind of object; people from another culture unaccustomed to coffee cups might have difficulty recognizing that distinctive shape if a blurry slide were quickly presented.

The importance of past experience has been demonstrated with studies using the priming technique. When the **priming technique** is used in research on pattern recognition, the researcher presents a stimulus, such as a word or a drawing of an object or face. Some time later, the researcher presents a different version of the stimulus, which contains less perceptual information (for example, just a few letters of a word or a very quickly presented image of an object). Priming is demonstrated if the research participants recognize this stimulus quickly, in comparison to a similar stimulus that had never been previously presented.

Consider, for example, a study on drawings of three-dimensional objects, such as those shown in Figure 2.5. As you can see, objects **a** and **b** are structurally possible in the real world. In contrast, **c** and **d** are known as "impossible figures"; they contain structural violations that prohibit their existence in three dimensions. Daniel Schacter and his colleagues (1991) presented figures like these to participants and asked them to decide whether the objects were possible or impossible. Later, the participants were tested to see if they could identify these objects and other, similar figures that had not been seen previously.

The results showed that previous exposure of the structurally possible figures did allow participants to identify them more quickly; priming was demonstrated. In contrast, there was no advantage to previous exposure of impossible figures. Tulving and Schacter (1990) speculate that the perceptual system has evolved so that priming works only for the stimuli that are ecologically valid, that is, likely to be encountered in everyday life. Consistent with Theme 2, our cognitive processes are remarkably efficient and accurate in helping us function in our everyday activities. Furthermore, previous exposure of the "possible figures" aided top-down processing, which facilitated pattern recognition.

SECTION SUMMARY: PATTERN RECOGNITION

1. Pattern recognition involves identifying a complex arrangement of sensory stimuli.
2. Four theories of pattern recognition have been proposed. Of these, the template-matching theory can be rejected because it cannot account for the complexity and speed of pattern recognition.
3. Prototype models propose that we compare each stimulus with a prototype. Experiments have demonstrated that people can form prototypes based on similar—but not identical—examples.
4. Distinctive-features models are supported by research showing that people require more time to make decisions about letters that share distinctive features.
5. The computational approach, which attempts to develop computer-based theories, is represented by Marr's theory of transforming primal sketches to $2^1/_2$-D sketches and finally 3-D sketches and by Biederman's recognition-by-components theory involving geons.
6. In bottom-up processing, pattern recognition begins with the arrival of the stimulus. Top-down processing emphasizes the role of context and expectations in identifying a pattern. Both processes are necessary to explain pattern recognition.

Representative Examples of Possible (a and b) and Impossible (c and d) Figures Used in the Pattern Recognition Studies of Schacter and His Colleagues (1991).

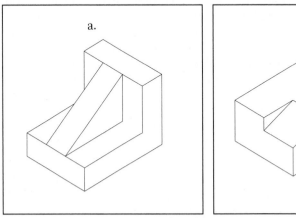

Possible Figures

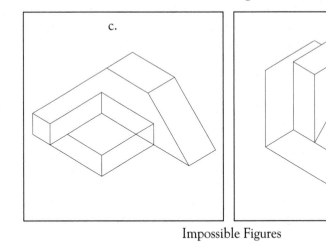

Impossible Figures

7. Research with figures, letters in words, and words in sentences has demonstrated that context facilitates pattern recognition.
8. Research using the priming technique demonstrates that previous exposure also enhances pattern recognition, at least when the stimuli are ones we could encounter in real life.

ATTENTION

Take a moment to pay attention to your attention processes. Close your eyes and try to notice every sound that is reaching your auditory system. Now continue to pay attention to those sounds and keep your eyes open, simultaneously expanding your attention to include visual stimuli. If you can manage this task, continue to include additional stimuli, specifically those that involve touch, smell, and taste. You'll discover that you cannot attend to everything at once.

In everyday speech, we use the word *attention* to include several different kinds of mental activity. Psychologists also use the word in many different contexts. Attention can refer to the kind of concentration on a mental task in which people try to exclude other interfering stimuli—for example, when taking an examination. It can refer to being prepared for further information—for example, when someone tells you to pay attention to an important announcement. It also refers to receiving several messages at once and ignoring all but one—for example, when you focus on one conversation at a noisy party. We will use a general definition of attention that applies to all these interpretations. **Attention** is a concentration of mental activity.

The topic of attention has varied in its popularity throughout the history of psychology. It intrigued the introspectionists in Europe, for example. In the United States, William James (1890) speculated about the number of ideas that could be attended to at one time—a speculation that still intrigues psychologists more than a century later. With the arrival of behaviorism, however, speculation about attention was considered inappropriate. Attention was regarded as such a hidden process that it was not a legitimate area for scientific study (Hirst, 1986). As recently as 1953, a major textbook on experimental psychology did not even mention attention (Eysenck, 1982; Osgood, 1953). However, in recent decades, attention has become a "hot topic." Attention has finally begun to receive the attention it deserves!

Attention is an important topic in its own right, and it is also important for other cognitive processes discussed in this book. For example, attention is an important factor in problem solving. As Chapter 10 describes, when people read a description of a problem, they inspect certain important sentences several times and disregard other sentences that seem trivial. Also, Chapter 11 explains how people make incorrect decisions when they pay attention to relatively unimportant information.

We will begin our discussion by considering two interrelated cognitive tasks, divided attention and selective attention. We will then examine explanations for attention, both theoretical and biological. Our final topic, consciousness, is closely related to attention.

Divided Attention

Imagine a busy executive, talking on her car phone as she drives to an important appointment. The telephone conversation captures her attention so completely that she misses the correct turnoff and wastes 15 minutes backtracking. The consequences of divided attention tasks can also be life-threatening. In Yugoslavia in 1976, two airplanes collided and all 176 passengers and crew members were killed. The air-traffic controller had been working without an assistant, and he was monitoring eleven aircraft simultaneously. In the preceding minutes, he had transmitted eight messages and received eleven (Barber, 1988). Humans are extremely competent, yet they cannot pay attention to everything at the same time.

In **divided attention** tasks, people must attend to several simultaneously active messages, responding to each as needed (Hawkins & Presson, 1986). In the laboratory, divided attention is typically studied by instructing participants to perform two tasks simultaneously. Unless the tasks have been well practiced, performance typically suffers. For example, consider a study by Neisser and Becklen (1975). A television screen was specially arranged to show two different kinds of games simultaneously, with the images overlapping completely. People were instructed to press a switch whenever a significant event occurred in either game. One game involved bouncing a ball, and the viewers pressed a switch whenever the ball was thrown from one player to another. The other game was a hand game you may have played when you were young. Viewers pressed a switch whenever one of the players managed to remove his hands quickly and slap the other player's hands.

People were easily able to follow one game at a time, even with the other game superimposed. However, their performance was extremely poor when they were instructed to follow both games simultaneously. For instance, the error rate for following two games was about eight times as high as the error rate for following a single game. According to Neisser and Becklen, there is a structured flow of information involved in the perception of events. If we are following one particular flow of information, it is extremely difficult to follow another, unrelated flow of information.

"Practice makes perfect," according to the popular saying. The research on practice and divided attention confirms the wisdom of that saying. For example, in two studies, college students were trained to read stories silently at the same time that they copied down irrelevant words dictated by the experimenter (Hirst et al., 1980; Spelke et al., 1976). At first, the students found it difficult to combine the two tasks; their reading speed decreased substantially, and their handwriting was illegible. However, after six weeks of training, they could read as quickly while taking dictation as when they were only reading. Their handwriting also improved.

Still, at this stage, they were not really attending to the dictated words; they were able to recall only 35 of the several thousand words they had written down. However, with more extensive training, they became so accomplished at this divided-attention task that they could even categorize the dictated word (for example by writing *fruit* when they heard the word *apple*) without any decline in their reading rate. As Hirst (1986) argues, practice seems to alter the limits of attentional capacity. Humans do not seem to have a built-in, fixed limit to the number of tasks they can perform simultaneously (Allport, 1989).

Selective Attention

Selective attention is closely related to divided attention. In divided attention, people are instructed to pay equal attention to several tasks. In **selective attention**, people are confronted with two or more simultaneous tasks and are required to focus their attention on one while disregarding the others (Hawkins & Presson, 1986). Selective-attention studies often show that people notice little about the irrelevant tasks. You have probably noticed that you can usually follow closely only one conversation at a noisy party; the content of the other conversations is generally not processed. You may have also experienced selective attention when picking up two stations on your radio. If you listen closely to one program, you notice only the superficial characteristics of the other.

At times, you might wish that attention were *not* so selective. Wouldn't it be wonderful to participate in one conversation, yet notice the details of all the other conversations going on around you? On the other hand, think how confusing this would be. Perhaps you would start talking about baseball—the topic of a neighboring conversation—when you had originally been talking about a friend's new job prospect. Furthermore, imagine the chaos you would experience if you simultaneously paid attention to all the information your senses register. You would notice hundreds of sights, sounds, smells, tastes, and touch sensations. It would be extremely difficult to focus your mental activity enough to respond appropriately to just a few of these sensations. Fortunately, selective attention can simplify our lives. As Theme 2 suggests, our cognitive apparatus is impressively well designed. Such features as selective attention, which may initially appear to be drawbacks, are really beneficial.

A classic study in selective attention was performed by Cherry (1953), who used the shadowing technique. In the **shadowing technique,** a person must listen to a series of words and repeat them after the speaker. Cherry asked people to wear earphones. They were told to shadow the message presented to one ear. Meanwhile, a second message was presented to the other ear, creating a situation known as **dichotic listening** (pronounced "die-*kot*-tick").

Cherry's results showed that people noticed very little about the second message. For example, Cherry sometimes changed the unattended, second message from English words to German words. People reported that they assumed that this unattended message was in English. In other words, their attention was so concentrated

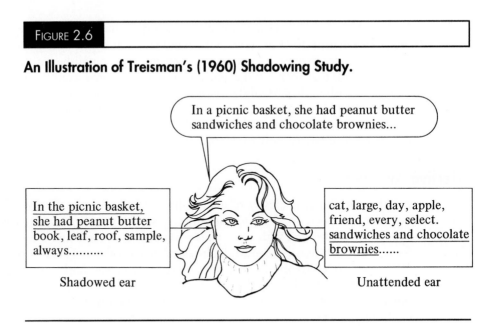

FIGURE 2.6

An Illustration of Treisman's (1960) Shadowing Study.

In a picnic basket, she had peanut butter sandwiches and chocolate brownies...

In the picnic basket, she had peanut butter book, leaf, roof, sample, always..........

Shadowed ear

cat, large, day, apple, friend, every, select. sandwiches and chocolate brownies......

Unattended ear

upon the attended message that they failed to notice the switch to a foreign language! People did notice, however, when the voice of the unattended message was switched from male to female. Thus, some characteristics of the unattended message can be detected.

If people can notice the gender of the speaker—or more likely, the pitch of the speaker's voice—what else do they notice? Moray (1959) found that people notice their own name if it is inserted in the unattended message. You have probably noticed this phenomenon. Even if you are paying close attention to one conversation at a party, you easily notice when your name is mentioned in a nearby conversation. Furthermore, in some cases people can follow meaning in the unattended ear. For example, Treisman (1960) presented two messages to the participants in her study. As Figure 2.6 illustrates, people were instructed to shadow one message and to leave the other message unattended. However, after a few words, the meaningful sentence in the to-be-shadowed ear was suddenly interrupted by a string of unrelated words. Simultaneously, that same sentence continued in the "unattended" ear. Treisman found that people sometimes followed the meaningful sentence and began to shadow the message in the ear that they were supposed to ignore. Thus, they might say, "In the picnic basket, she had peanut butter sandwiches and chocolate brownies." Interestingly, the participants in Treisman's study reported that they were unaware that the meaningful sentence had shifted to the unattended ear.

To what extent do people notice semantic aspects of the unattended message? This topic is controversial, because some studies suggest that people can notice the meaning of the unattended message, but other studies suggest they cannot (e.g.,

DEMONSTRATION 2.5

THE STROOP EFFECT.

For this project, you will need at least three colored markers, two sheets of paper, and a watch that can measure time in seconds. On the first sheet of paper, print in lower-case letters (in a column going from top to bottom) the following color names: red, blue, green, yellow, green, red, blue, yellow, blue, red, yellow, green, yellow, green, blue, red, red, green, yellow, blue. However, it is very important to print each word in an *inappropriate* color; for example, print the first word, *red,* in the color yellow.

On the second sheet of paper, make a column of 20 patches of color. Each patch should be equivalent in both size and color to the stimulus in the corresponding position on the first sheet of paper. (The task will be easier if you line up the two sheets of paper.)

Now take out a watch to measure your color-naming speed. First try sheet one; your task will be to say out loud the names of the ink colors on that sheet (ignoring the meaning of the words). Measure the amount of time it takes to go through that sheet five times. (Keep a tally of the number of repetitions.) Record that time.

Now repeat the task, measuring the amount of time it takes to say out loud the names of the ink colors on the second sheet. Again, go through that sheet five times, and record the total time. Did you take nearly twice as long on the task in which your attention was distracted by the meaning of the words?

Corteen & Wood, 1972; Hirst, 1986; Johnston & Dark, 1986; Wardlaw & Kroll, 1976). The answer probably depends upon task characteristics. For example, the meaning of the unattended message is more noticeable when that message is presented in the left ear (Dawson & Schell, 1982). Still, meaning is less noticeable than characteristics such as pitch (Allport, 1989).

In summary, when people's auditory attention is divided, they can notice some characteristics of the unattended message, such as the gender of the speaker and whether their own name is mentioned. On the other hand, they may be unaware of whether the unattended message is in English or in a foreign language. Finally, people can sometimes notice the meaning of the unattended message, but in some conditions, they do not.

So far, we have only examined selective attention on auditory tasks; people are instructed to shadow the message presented to one ear and ignore the message to the other ear. However, the selective attention task that has been most extensively researched demonstrates the difficulty of selective visual attention. Try Demonstration 2.5, which illustrates the famous Stroop effect. The **Stroop effect** refers to the observation that people take much longer to name the color of a stimulus when it is used in printing an incongruent word than when it appears as a solid color square. They have trouble saying "blue" when blue ink is used in printing the word *red.* Note that the Stroop effect demonstrates the effects of selective attention because people take longer to name a color when they are distracted by another feature of the stimulus, namely, the meaning of the words themselves.

The effect was first demonstrated by J. R. Stroop (1935), who found that people required an average of 110 seconds to name the ink color of 100 words that were incongruent color names (for example, blue ink used in writing the word *red*). In contrast, people required an average of only 63 seconds to name the ink color of 100 solid color squares. Since the original experiment, more than 400 additional studies have examined variations of the Stroop effect (MacLeod, 1991).

A recent review article by MacLeod (1991) examines a variety of explanations for the Stroop effect. MacLeod believes that the most promising account is provided by a parallel distributed processing approach (e.g., Cohen et al., 1990). According to this explanation, the Stroop task activates two pathways at the same time. One pathway is activated by the task of naming the ink color, and the other pathway is activated by the task of reading the word. Interference occurs when two competing pathways are active simultaneously, and task performance suffers.

Theories of Attention

Let us first consider some early theories of attention and then discuss Schneider and Shiffrin's theory of automatic versus controlled processing. The final portion of this section is an in-depth examination of Treisman's feature-integration theory.

Early Theories of Attention. The first theories of attention emphasized that people are extremely limited in the amount of information they can process at any given time. A common metaphor in these theories was the concept of a bottleneck. Just as the neck of a bottle restricts the flow from one region to another, **bottleneck theories** proposed a similar narrow passageway in human information processing. In other words, this bottleneck limits the quantity of information to which we can pay attention. Thus, when one message is currently flowing through a bottleneck, the other messages must be left behind. Many variations of this bottleneck theory were proposed (e.g., Broadbent, 1958; Deutsch & Deutsch, 1963; Triesman, 1964).

You'll recall from the section on theories of pattern recognition that the template theory was rejected because it was not flexible enough. Similarly, the bottleneck theories lost popularity because they underestimated the flexibility of human attention (Eysenck, 1982). No metaphor based on a simple machine or a simple structure can successfully account for the sophistication of human perceptual processes. The next two theories point out how the nature of the task, the amount of practice, and the stage in processing can all change the way people use attention.

Automatic Versus Controlled Processing. Walter Schneider and Richard Shiffrin have proposed two levels of processing relevant to attention. **Automatic processing** can be used on easy tasks involving highly familiar items. In contrast, **controlled processing** must be used on difficult tasks or tasks involving unfamiliar items. Furthermore, automatic processing is **parallel**; that is, you can handle two or more items at the same time. In contrast, controlled processing is **serial**; only one item can be handled at a time.

Automatic and controlled processing can be related to other topics discussed earlier in this chapter. We mentioned that people can use automatic processing on easy tasks with familiar items. Therefore, on a selective-attention task in which people use automatic processing, it should be relatively easy to pick up features of the unattended message. On a divided-attention task where both tasks require automatic processing, it should also be relatively easy to perform two tasks simultaneously. In addition, consider the relationship between practice and automatic processing. Tasks that have been extensively practiced will tend to involve automatic processing.

Now consider difficult tasks with unfamiliar items, which typically require controlled processing. On a selective-attention task in which people use controlled processing, very few features of the unattended message will be noticed. On a divided-attention task, it will be difficult to perform two tasks simultaneously. In addition, tasks that have *not* been extensively practiced will usually require controlled processing. To help you distinguish between these two terms, try thinking of examples of tasks that require either automatic or controlled processing.

The research by Schneider and Shiffrin examined the difference between automatic and controlled processing (Schneider & Shiffrin, 1977; Shiffrin & Schneider, 1977). Participants in these studies saw a rapid series of 20 pictures, or frames, on each trial. Each of four locations in a particular frame could be occupied by a number, a letter, or a set of dots. The numbers and letters could occupy one, two, or all four locations on a frame. Figure 2.7 shows a typical frame. Before seeing the 20 pictures, each participant was instructed to remember and look for either one or four targets. For example, a typical person might have been told to search the pictures for the four targets, B, P, Q, and Y. Notice, then, that both the size of the target set and the number of items in a frame were varied.

This study included two other important variables. The exposure time for each frame varied between 40 and 800 milliseconds. Finally, the difficulty of the task was varied. In the "consistent-mapping condition," the target-set items and the irrelevant items were from different categories. For example, a person might search for numbers, with the irrelevant items on a frame being letters. The "varied-mapping condition" was much more difficult. First of all, the target-set items and the irrelevant items were all from the same category. For example, a person might search for letters, with the irrelevant items also being letters. Furthermore, target-set items on one trial could become irrelevant items on the next trial. (For example, on Trial 1, you might search for an E, with irrelevant items being A, C, N, S, and so forth; on Trial 2, you might search for an S, with irrelevant items being E, A, C, N, and so forth.)

Let's consider the results of this study. The factors affecting accuracy were different for the two mapping conditions. In the easier, consistent-mapping condition, frame-exposure time was the only variable that influenced accuracy; people were

FIGURE 2.7

A Typical Frame in the Studies by Schneider and Shiffrin (1977).

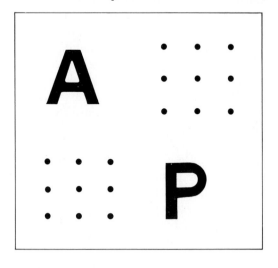

more accurate when they saw each frame for a long time. However, neither target-set size nor frame size influenced accuracy; that is, people were just as accurate when they were searching for four items as for one. People were also just as accurate when there were four letters or numbers on each frame as when there was only one letter or number. This consistent-mapping condition was so easy that people used *automatic processing*, even with a large number of target-set items and irrelevant items. People apparently conducted a parallel search, looking for all four targets in all four positions at the same time.

The varied-mapping condition produced different results. Exposure time influenced accuracy; as in the consistent-mapping condition, people were more accurate when the frames were exposed longer. However, the other two variables also influenced accuracy. People were more accurate when searching for one target than for four. They were also more accurate when there was only one letter or number on each frame than when there were four. In the varied-mapping condition, people were forced to use *controlled processing*, because the task could not be performed automatically. People in this condition apparently conducted a serial search, looking for each target—one at a time—through all items in a frame.

Schneider and Shiffrin's research inspired further research and theoretical debate (e.g., Cheng, 1985; Corballis, 1986; Fisher, 1984; Jonides et al., 1985; Ryan, 1983; Schneider & Shiffrin, 1985; Shiffrin & Schneider, 1984). For example, Fisher (1984) argued that there are clear limits to the amount of material that can be processed simultaneously. The maximum number of items that Schneider and

Shiffrin showed on each frame was only four. The limit for parallel search may not be much greater than four items. People probably cannot look at a frame of 10 items and search them all simultaneously and automatically.

◇ In Depth: *Feature-Integration Theory*

Anne Treisman, of the University of California at Berkeley, has further developed the distinction between the two kinds of perceptual processing. According to her **feature-integration theory,** we can sometimes process a scene automatically, with all parts of the scene processed at the same time; other scenes require focused attention, with each item in the scene processed one at a time (Treisman, 1988; Treisman & Gelade, 1980). Let's consider these two kinds of processing in more detail and then examine illusory conjunctions and other new developments.

Preattentive Processing and Focused Attention. The first stage of the theory, **preattentive processing,** involves the automatic registration of features, using parallel processing across the field. Preattentive processing, the relatively low-level kind of processing, is therefore roughly equivalent to Schneider and Shiffrin's automatic processing. This kind of processing is so effortless that we are not aware of it when it happens.

The second stage of Treisman's theory, **focused attention,** involves serial processing, in which objects are identified one at a time. Focused attention, the more demanding kind of processing, is required when the objects are more complex. Thus, focused attention is roughly equivalent to Schneider and Shiffrin's controlled search. Focused attention selects which features belong together—for example, which shape goes with which color.

Treisman and Gelade (1980) examined these two kinds of processing approaches by studying two different kinds of stimulus situations, one that used isolated features (and therefore involved preattentive processing) and one that used combinations of features (and therefore involved focused attention). Let's first consider the details of the research on preattentive processing. Treisman and Gelade proposed that if isolated features are processed automatically in preattentive processing, then people should be able to rapidly locate a target among its neighboring, irrelevant items. That target should seem to "pop out" of the display automatically, no matter how many items are in the display. In a series of studies, Treisman and Gelade discovered that if the target differed from the irrelevant items in the display with respect to a simple feature such as color or orientation, observers could detect the target just as fast when it was presented in an array of 30 items as when it was presented in an array of only 3 items (Treisman, 1986; Treisman & Gelade, 1980). Notice in section A of Demonstration 2.6 that the red X seems to "pop out," whether there are 2 or 29 irrelevant items. Preattentive processing can be accomplished in a parallel fashion and relatively automatically.

Now let's consider the details of the research on focused attention. Section B of Demonstration 2.6 requires searching for a target that is an object—that is, a

---

DEMONSTRATION 2.6

PREATTENTIVE PROCESSING VERSUS FOCUSED ATTENTION.

Locate two colored marking pens that have clear, bright colors, such as bright red and bright blue. Then follow the directions below for A and B.

A. On a plain sheet of white paper, make one red X, one blue X, and one red O, placing the figures in random order on the sheet. On a second sheet, make 1 blue X, 14 red O's, and 15 red X's, again placing the letters randomly. Ask a friend to locate the blue figure on each sheet and notice whether the two tasks take about the same time.

B. Keep the first sheet of paper from Part A. Take a third sheet, and place on it in random order 1 blue X, 9 red X's, 10 blue O's, and 10 red O's. Ask a friend to locate the blue X on each sheet and notice whether the second task takes substantially longer.

---

conjunction (or combination) of properties. When you search for a red X among red O's and blue X's, you must use focused attention because you are forced to focus attention on one item at a time, using serial processing. You are searching at the object level rather than the feature level. This task is more complex, and the time taken to find the target increases dramatically as a function of the number of distractors.

Theme 3 of this book states that our cognitive processes handle positive information better than negative information. Turn back to Demonstration 1.1 on page 19 to remind yourself about the difficulty of realizing that the solution was that the letter *e* was missing. The research of Treisman and her colleagues clearly provide additional support for that theme. For example, Treisman and Souther (1985) found that preattentive processing is typically used when a simple feature is *present* in a target; in contrast, focused processing is typically used when that same feature is *absent* from the target.

Figure 2.8 illustrates the displays that people examined in Treisman and Souther's study. In Figure 2.8a, participants searched for a circle with a line. Notice how this target seems to "pop out" from the display. In contrast, in Figure 2.8, people were told to search for a circle without a line. Notice how you must inspect this display more closely to determine that it indeed contains the target.

Figure 2.9 shows Treisman and Souther's results of the search times for targets without a line and for targets with a line. The data are reported for displays in which the target appeared and for displays in which the target was absent. You can see that when the target is a circle with a line, the number of items in the display has little effect on search times (either when the target appeared in the display or when it was absent). People who are searching for a feature that is present are using preattentive processing. In contrast, you can see that when the target is a circle without a line, the number of items in the display has a strong effect on search time (especially when the target is absent). When you are searching for a target with a missing feature—such as a circle with a missing line—you must use

---

FIGURE 2.8

The Stimuli Used in Treisman and Souther's (1985) Study.

A   B

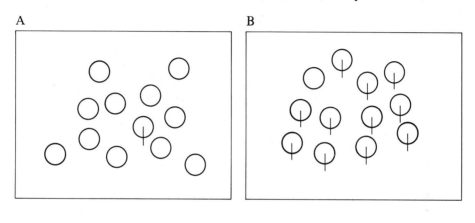

---

focused attention. This task is substantially more challenging than searching for a target that contains the specified feature (Treisman, 1991).

Illusory Conjunctions. Feature-integration theory argues that focused attention provides the "glue" to bind together the features of an object, such as its color and its shape. Treisman and her colleagues have demonstrated that when attention is either overloaded or distracted, illusory conjunctions can be produced. An **illusory conjunction** is an inappropriate combination of features, perhaps combining one object's shape with a nearby object's color.

For example, Treisman and Schmidt (1982) instructed people to look at displays that consisted of two black numbers on either side of a row of three larger, colored letters. The observers were specifically told to pay attention to the black numbers and to identify them, as well as anything they happened to notice about the colored letters.

Treisman and Schmidt (1982) found that the observers were highly accurate on the main task of reporting the black numbers; they were indeed paying attention to the numbers. The interesting observations came from the illusory conjunctions on the colored letters. On about one third of the trials, people reported an illusory conjunction. For example, a person who saw a red X and a green O might report having seen a red O. When these stimuli are deprived of focused attention, the features of an object can become "unglued" from each other and may be recombined randomly. This random recombination often produces illusory conjunctions.

Every minute of the day you fail to devote focused attention to a number of objects in your visual field. Why don't you experience illusory conjunctions more

FIGURE 2.9

The Results of Treisman and Souther's (1985) Study.

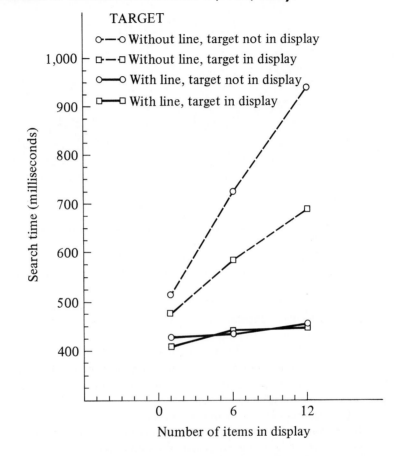

often? Treisman (1990) proposes that top-down processing—specifically our expectations and prior knowledge—helps to screen out inappropriate combinations. For example, in the vegetable section of your grocery store, a carrot might be registered in your peripheral vision while you are inspecting the green peppers. You are likely to keep the two principle features—the orange color and the slender, triangular shape—"glued" together appropriately. You are accustomed to orange carrots, so the illusory conjunction of a green carrot is unlikely. Top-down processing has such strong effects that the features remain combined, even with minimal attention.

We discussed the word superiority effect in the section on pattern recognition. Treisman and Souther (1986) demonstrated how the word superiority effect also operates in connection with illusory conjunctions. They briefly presented two nonsense words to observers, who were instructed to report what they saw. When nonsense words such as *dax* and *kay* had been presented, observers often reported seeing an English word such as *day*. When random-letter sequences are presented so quickly that the items do not receive focused attention, illusory conjunctions appear that are consistent with our expectations. Thus, top-down processing prevents us from seeing illusory conjunctions that are unlikely (such as green carrots) and encourages us to see illusory conjunctions that are highly likely (such as English words like *day*).

New Developments. The basic elements of feature-integration theory were proposed more than a decade ago. Since then, researchers have pointed out that the neurophysiological evidence on the mammalian visual system is consistent with the concept of separate storage systems for features like color and shape (Banks & Krajicek, 1991). Furthermore, most theories of vision now propose two subsystems, such as preattentive processing and focused attention (Enns & Rensink, 1991).

However, Treisman emphasizes that there is a continuum between preattentive processing and focused attention. Many tasks lie somewhere between those two extremes, rather than involving exclusively preattentive processing or exclusively focused attention (Treisman & Gormican, 1988). Furthermore, when participants have extensive practice in searching for conjunction targets that initially required focused attention, the targets can be located very rapidly (Treisman et al., 1992). For example, after 9,000 trials, participants were able to locate a target that was blue and X-shaped as quickly as they had located—prior to practice—a target that was simply blue. As we will see throughout Chapter 3, researchers often initially propose a theory that draws a clear-cut distinction between two or more psychological processes. With extensive research, however, theorists frequently conclude that reality is more complex. Rather than two clear-cut categories, we are more likely to find a continuum (as in Treisman's feature-integration theory) or blurry distinctions (as in the theories of memory in Chapter 3).

The Biological Basis of Attention

We noted at the beginning of this section on attention that the pioneering American psychologist William James had been interested in attention as a cognitive process. James described an early technique that appears to be an imaginative forerunner of the cerebral blood-flow techniques used in modern-day PET scans (James, 1890; Tulving, 1987). According to James, an Italian physician named Mosso placed a person horizontally on a delicately balanced table that could tip downward at either end when any imbalance occurred. Mosso asked the person to remain completely motionless and to engage in intellectual activity. Mosso reported that the table tipped downward at the head-end! Unfortunately, the technique is not sensitive enough to detect small-scale changes in blood flow, so I will not include a demonstration urging you to balance a friend on a table while he or she solves trigonometry problems.

In the past 10 to 15 years, a variety of sophisticated techniques have been developed. These techniques allow us a much more detailed understanding of the biological basis of attention than was available to psychologists who were developing theories in the 1960s and 1970s (Posner & Petersen, 1990). These studies have identified a network of areas throughout the brain that accomplish various attention tasks (Posner & Rothbart, 1991). For example, when attention is required to detect a target in a situation involving interference—such as a Stroop task—an area toward the front of the cerebral cortex is activated.

Michael Posner and his colleagues at the University of Oregon have provided an abundance of information about a region of the brain that is responsible for a different kind of attention. Imagine, for example, that you are searching the area around a bathroom sink for a lost contact lens. When you are attending to a location in space, the posterior attention network is activated. The **posterior attention network,** which is responsible for the kind of attention involving visual search, includes structures buried deep in the center of the brain as well as a part of the outer covering of the brain called the parietal cortex (Posner & Rothbart, 1991).

Figure 2.10 illustrates the specific portion of the cortex that is involved in visual-search attention. Notice that this region of the brain is distinctly different from the primary visual cortex, which is involved in recognizing letters in words, a perceptual process we discussed in the pattern-recognition half of this chapter.

How was the parietal cortex identified as a region of the brain involved in attention? Much of the research uses the **regional cerebral blood-flow technique,** the technique described in Chapter 1 that measures the blood flow within the cerebral cortex; changes in blood flow indicate neural activity. The parietal cortex shows increased blood flow when people pay attention to spatial locations (e.g., Corbetta et al., 1991; Posner et al., 1991).

Another important method in the research on the biological basis of attention involves clinical studies on people with **lesions,** or specific brain damage caused by strokes, accidents, or other traumas. People who have brain damage in the parietal region of the right hemisphere of the brain have trouble noticing a new visual stimulus that appears on the left side of their visual field. Those with damage in the left parietal region have trouble noticing a visual stimulus on the right side (Posner, 1991).

The German artist Anton Raderscheidt provides a particularly vivid example of the importance of the parietal cortex. The self-portraits he painted prior to suffering a stroke are full and complete. After suffering a stroke that damaged the right parietal cortex, his painting underwent a startling change. The first self-portrait painted after the stroke is reasonably complete on the right side of the

FIGURE 2.10

Regions of the Cerebral Cortex That Are Involved in Visual-Search Attention and Pattern Recognition (View of the Left Hemisphere, from the Side).

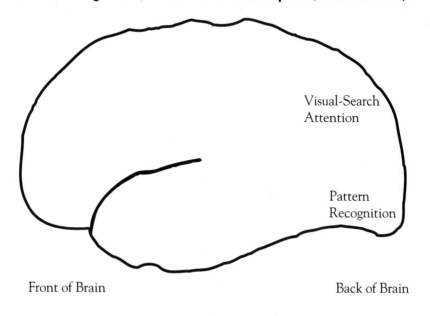

Visual-Search Attention

Pattern Recognition

Front of Brain   Back of Brain

paper, but the left side is completely blank! The artist seemed unable to attend to visual stimuli appearing in the left visual field. His later self-portraits showed greater development of the left side of the paper, but the detail was never as complete as on the right side (Wurtz et al., 1982).

Chapter 1 also described the **evoked potential technique,** which records electrical signals generated from a large number of neurons located underneath an electrode. This technique has been used to demonstrate direct neuron activity during attention. For example, a research group in Finland instructed people to listen to a series of tones. Most were tones of a particular pitch, but sometimes a higher pitched tone was included (e.g., Näätänen, 1982, 1985; Sams et al., 1985). In some conditions, the participants were instructed to press a response key whenever they heard this deviant tone. In these conditions, the electrical activity pattern showed a new component. However, this component was absent when participants were tested in other conditions, where they had been instructed to ignore the higher pitched tone. This research, therefore, identifies a clear-cut neurological correlate of attention.

In summary, research on the biological basis of attention has used cerebral blood-flow techniques as well as case studies of people with lesions to identify regions of the brain, such as the parietal cortex, that are responsible for attention. In addition, the evoked potential technique has established neuron activity that corresponds to attention processes. Future researchers will continue to combine the results of various neuroscience techniques to help us understand the biological explanations of attention.

Consciousness

Our final topic, consciousness, is controversial. One reason for the controversy is the variety of different definitions for the term (Farthing, 1992). For example, one book on consciousness lists seven different definitions (Wallace & Fisher, 1983). In this textbook, the word **consciousness** means awareness. Consciousness is closely related to attention, but the processes are not identical. After all, we are not aware or conscious of tasks we are performing with automatic processing or preattentive processing. For example, when you are driving, you may use automatic processing to put your foot on the brake in response to a red light. However, you may not be at all *conscious* that you performed this motor action.

As Chapter 1 noted, the behaviorists considered topics such as consciousness to be inappropriate for scientific study. By 1950, the study of consciousness had essentially vanished from the psychological scene (Hearnshaw, 1987). However, with the enthusiasm about cognitive psychology in the 1960s, consciousness edged back into psychology. In the last decade, consciousness has become a popular topic for books and review articles (Bowers & Meichenbaum, 1984; Farthing, 1992; Gardner, 1988; Kihlstrom, 1987; Mandler, 1985).

Two issues related to consciousness have been popular in recent years. The first topic concerns our ability to bring thoughts into consciousness; the second concerns our *inability* to let thoughts escape from consciousness.

Consciousness about Higher Mental Processes.
To what extent do we have access to our higher mental processes? For example, answer the following question: "What is your mother's maiden name?" Now answer this question: "How did you arrive at the answer to the first question?" As Miller (1962) points out, the answer appeared swiftly in your consciousness, but you probably cannot explain your thought processes. The name may have simply "popped" into memory.

Nisbett and Wilson (1977) argued that we often have little direct access to our thought processes. We may be fully conscious of the *products* of our thought processes (such as your mother's maiden name), but we are usually not conscious of the *process* that created the product. Most of Nisbett and Wilson's examples are from social psychology, but they also consider problem solving, an important topic in cognitive psychology. For example, they discuss the classic research by Maier (1931). In this study, two cords hung down from a ceiling, and participants in the study were told to tie the two ends of the cord together. (The cords were so far

---

DEMONSTRATION 2.7

THOUGHT SUPPRESSION.

This demonstration requires you to take a break from your reading and just relax for five minutes. Take a sheet of paper and a pen or pencil to record your thoughts as you simply let your mind wander. Your thoughts can include cognitive psychology, but they do not need to. Just jot down a brief note about each topic you think about as your mind wanders. One final instruction: During this exercise, *do not think about a white bear!*

---

apart that people could not hold one end and reach for the other end simultaneously.) The correct solution involved swinging one cord like a pendulum. When Maier casually swung a cord during the study, people typically reached the solution in less than a minute. However, when asked how they solved the problem, they typically provided answers that showed no consciousness of the process. A typical response was, "It just dawned on me."

Nisbett and Wilson's (1977) article stimulated discussion about the accuracy of introspections. Many researchers misinterpreted their claim: Nisbett and Wilson had said that we do not necessarily have access to our thought processes, but Bowers (1984) notes that several theorists mistakenly thought they had said it was *impossible* to have access to thought processes. As Chapter 7 discusses, we have limited access to some thought processes, but relatively complete access to other thought processes. In addition, researchers have specified how certain kinds of verbal reports can be most effectively gathered, so that they are accurate and do not interfere with normal cognitive processes (Ericsson & Simon, 1980, 1984).

Our thought processes are hidden, rather than overt. It is therefore challenging to design an experiment to measure these covert, private thoughts. Sometimes experiments yield different results, and sometimes different interpretations of these experiments yield different models. We saw, for example, that some psychologists prefer distinctive-features models of pattern recognition, whereas others prefer a computational approach. This controversy thrives because verbal reports about pattern recognition are not likely to be useful and because we cannot directly observe people recognizing patterns. Instead, we must examine the research that has been conducted and decide which explanations are most consistent with the data. In this chapter on perception and in the chapters that follow, we examine some processes for which we have rival explanations and some for which we have insufficient explanations. This uncertainty is an inevitable result in an area as complex, covert, and inaccessible as human cognition.

Thought Suppression. Before you read further, try Demonstration 2.7. Note whether you have difficulty carrying out the instructions.

The original source for the white bear study is literary, rather than scientific. Apparently, when the Russian novelist Dostoyevski was young, he tormented his young brother by telling him *not* to think of a white bear (Wegner et al., 1987). Similarly, if you have ever tried to avoid thinking about food when on a diet, you know the difficulty of trying to chase these undesired thoughts out of consciousness. Smokers trying to give up cigarettes and depressed people trying to cheer themselves can also verify that thought suppression is a difficult assignment. As Wegner and his colleagues (1987) point out, this process of **thought suppression** includes two components: (1) planning to eliminate a thought from consciousness and (2) carrying out that plan by suppressing all evidence of the thought, including the original plan.

To test the difficulty of Dostoyevski's task scientifically, Wegner and his coauthors instructed a group of students *not* to think about a white bear during a 5-minute period. Whenever they did think about a white bear, they rang a bell. They rang the bell an average of more than three times during the first minute in which they were supposed to be avoiding thoughts about the white bear, though they managed to limit their thoughts to about one instance per minute during the remainder of the 5-minute period. After this session, they were instructed to spend the next 5 minutes freely thinking about a white bear. This time, the white bears overpopulated consciousness, with close to five instances each minute. In contrast, another group of students who were instructed to think freely about a white bear—without a previous thought suppression session—thought about white bears an average of only three times each minute. In other words, initial suppression produces a rebound effect.

In his more recent work, Wegner (1992) has related the components of thought suppression to the concepts of controlled and automatic processing, which we introduced earlier in the chapter. Wegner proposes that when you try to suppress a thought, you engage in a controlled search for thoughts that are *not* the unwanted thought. For example, when you are on a diet, you consciously, systematically search for items other than food to think about—a friend, a movie, exercise. At the same time, you also engage in an automatic search for any signs of the unwanted thought; this process demands little attention and it occurs automatically. On a diet, this automatic search effortlessly produces thoughts about rich pastries and other caloric treats. When you stop trying to suppress a thought, you discard the controlled search for irrelevant items, but the automatic search continues. Consequently, you experience a rebound effect, with thoughts about the previously forbidden topic now overpopulating your consciousness!

In summary, we saw in the section on consciousness how our higher mental processes often fail to bring information to consciousness. This section on thought suppression suggests that we have difficulty eliminating some thoughts from consciousness; furthermore, the attempt to eliminate them may cause these thoughts to come back even stronger at a later time.

SECTION SUMMARY: ATTENTION

1. Attention is a concentration of mental activity.
2. Research on divided attention shows that performance may suffer when people must attend to several stimuli simultaneously. With extensive practice, performance on some divided-attention tasks can improve.
3. Selective-attention studies show that people using earphones on which they hear two different messages may notice little about the irrelevant message. They may notice the gender of the speaker and whether their own name is mentioned, but they may not notice whether the irrelevant message is in English; semantic aspects of the irrelevant message are occasionally processed. The Stroop effect is an example of a selective-attention task.
4. Early theories of attention emphasized a "bottleneck" that limits attention. A more recent theory, proposed by Schneider and Shiffrin, suggests that automatic processing is parallel, and it can be used on easy tasks with highly familiar items. Conversely, controlled processing is serial, and it must be used with difficult or unfamiliar tasks.
5. Treisman proposed a feature-integration theory containing two components: (1) preattentive processing, which can be used to search for isolated features and (2) focused attention, which must be used to search for combinations of features or for a feature that is missing. Illusory conjunctions may arise when attention is overloaded or distracted.
6. Biological research on attention has used cerebral blood-flow techniques as well as studies of people with lesions to locate regions of the brain (such as the parietal cortex) that are responsible for attention.
7. Consciousness, or awareness, is a topic that decreased in popularity during the behaviorist era, but it is once again popular. A controversy has arisen about the extent to which we are usually aware of our thought processes. Research on thought suppression illustrates the difficulty of eliminating some thoughts from consciousness.

CHAPTER REVIEW QUESTIONS

1. What is perception? Describe five different perceptual tasks that you have accomplished in the last five minutes.
2. Imagine that you are trying to read a sloppy number that appears in a friend's class notes. You conclude that it is an 8, rather than a 6 or a 3. Explain how you recognized that number, using template-matching theory, prototype models, and distinctive-features models.
3. Compare the first three theories of pattern recognition, mentioning (a) whether an entire letter or a part of a letter is stored in memory, (b) whether

the match must be exact or rough, and (c) the number of items that must be stored in memory to enable pattern recognition.

4. What is the goal of the computational approach to pattern recognition? Look up from your book and find a relatively simple portion of your visual field (for example, items on a desk surface). How would the three stages in David Marr's theory apply to this scene? Now identify two objects in that scene; how would Biederman's recognition-by-components theory describe how you recognize these objects?

5. Distinguish between bottom-up and top-down processing. Explain how top-down processing can aid the recognition of a variety of visual patterns by citing relevant studies. The chapter emphasized visual pattern recognition; provide examples of how top-down processing could help you recognize sounds, tastes, odors, and touch sensations.

6. What is divided attention? Give several examples of divided-attention tasks you have performed within the last 24 hours. What does the research show about the effects of practice on divided attention? Can you think of some examples of your own experience with practice and divided-attention performance?

7. What is selective attention? Give several examples of selective-attention tasks you have performed within the last 24 hours. Based on your knowledge of practice and *divided* attention, what predictions would you make about the effects of practice on noticing information about the irrelevant task in a selective-attention situation?

8. Imagine that you are trying to carry on a conversation with a friend at the same time you are reading an interesting article in a magazine. Describe how the bottleneck theories and automatic versus controlled processing would explain your performance. Now imagine that you are searching page 56 for the bold-faced phrase *posterior attention network*. What part of your brain is activated during this task?

9. What are the two basic stages of Treisman's feature-integration theory? How does this approach explain illusory conjunctions? Why don't we perceive illusory conjunctions more often?

10. Discuss Nisbett and Wilson's argument that we do not typically have access to our thought processes. Think of an example of each of the following tasks in which you can arrive at an answer without being conscious of the thought process: (a) speaking a sentence, (b) remembering information about a word's meaning, and (c) deciding the category to which an object belongs. Now try to think of cognitive processes where you seem to be more aware of the thought process. Finally, try to think of examples of occasions where thought suppression was difficult.

NEW TERMS

perception
pattern recognition
template-matching theory
templates
prototype models
prototypes
distinctive-features models
distinctive features
computational approach
machine vision
primal sketch
$2^1/_2$-D sketch
3-D sketch
recognition-by-components theory
geons
bottom-up processing
data-driven processing
top-down processing
conceptually driven processing
word superiority effect
parallel distributed processing
priming technique

attention
divided attention
selective attention
shadowing technique
dichotic listening
Stroop effect
bottleneck theories
automatic processing
controlled processing
parallel (processing)
serial (processing)
feature-integration theory
preattentive processing
focused attention
illusory conjunction
posterior attention network
PET scan
lesions
evoked potential technique
consciousness
thought suppression

RECOMMENDED READINGS

Coren, S., Ward, L. M., & Enns, J. (1994). *Sensation and perception* (4th ed.). Fort Worth, TX: Harcourt Brace Jovanovich. This textbook provides an overview of sensory processes and perception; the chapters on form and on learning and experience are most relevant to pattern perception.

Farthing, G. W. (1992). *The psychology of consciousness*. Englewood Cliffs, NJ: Prentice Hall. Farthing's book discusses various components of consciousness, including interesting topics such as introspection, the mind-body problem, daydreaming, and sleep.

Matlin, M. W., & Foley, H. J. (1992). *Sensation and perception* (3rd ed.). Boston: Allyn and Bacon. This textbook emphasizes a top-down approach to perception, exploring pattern recognition and other aspects of perceptual processes in some detail.

Osherson, D. N., Kosslyn, S. M., & Hollerbach, J. M. (Eds.). (1990). *An invitation to cognitive science* (Vol. 2). Cambridge, MA: MIT Press. Half of this volume focuses on visual cognition. Chapters 1 and 2 provide a sophisticated coverage of pattern perception.

Posner, M. I. (Ed.). (1989). *Foundations of cognitive science*. Cambridge, MA: MIT Press. The chapters of this handbook that are most relevant to perception include one on reading and one on visual attention.

MODELS OF MEMORY

Memory is a critical part of all cognitive processes, because it is involved whenever we maintain information over time. Chapter 3 is the first of three chapters about memory; it focuses on four important models of memory.

The Atkinson-Shiffrin model proposes that memory consists of three memory stores: sensory memory, short-term memory, and long-term memory. The model also includes control processes, such as the strategy of repeating information to maintain it in memory. Controversy surrounds the model's proposal that short-term memory and long-term memory constitute two different stores.

The levels-of-processing approach proposes that the way we process material influences how well we recall it. Deep processing (for example, in terms of a word's meaning) produces more permanent retention than shallow levels of processing (for example, in terms of a word's physical appearance). A kind of task that creates especially strong retention is a self-reference task, in which people are asked to judge whether a target word refers to themselves.

According to Tulving's model, episodic memory stores information about events, semantic memory stores organized knowledge about the world, and pro-cedural memory involves knowing how to do something. Tulving assembled the-oretical and research evidence for these distinctions, but skeptics have argued that the evidence is not convincing. In general, psychologists agree that procedural memory is different from the other two, but episodic memory and semantic memory may be similar.

A new, extremely influential approach to cognition is called parallel distributed processing (PDP), which proposes networks that link together neuron-like units. The PDP approach accounts for some important features of memory, such as the fact that when a person mentions a word or a name, we spontaneously recall numerous related items, and the fact that we can often retrieve correct information from a variety of clues, even when one of the clues is incorrect. This approach has won the enthusiasm of many supporters, but it is too new to draw conclusions about whether it can account for a wide variety of memory phenomena.

INTRODUCTION

Imagine that your memory were to fail right in the middle of the next sentence. You could not continue to read the sentence because you would be unable to recognize any letters or understand the meaning of any words. In fact, you wouldn't even be able to recall why the book was lying in front of you. You wouldn't remem-ber your name or your age, let alone the name of your cousin's girlfriend. Good friends would not look familiar. Furthermore, you wouldn't even be able to recall what you were thinking about just a minute ago.

Memory involves maintaining information over time. You can maintain this information for less than a second or as long as a lifetime. For example, you use memory to store the beginning of a word until you hear the end of the word. You also use memory to recall your own name, which you probably learned when you were about a year old.

Memory is so central to cognitive processes that it influences almost every aspect of every topic in this book. Pattern recognition and attention, two topics from Chapter 2, are clearly affected by our memory for shapes and attentional strategies. Memory occupies center stage in Chapters 4 and 5. In Chapter 6 we will discuss how images are stored in memory. Chapter 7 concentrates on memory for words, general knowledge, and concepts. In Chapters 8 and 9, memory is an important part of both language understanding and language production. As Theme 4 emphasizes, the cognitive processes are interrelated. Clearly, memory influences many other cognitive activities.

We will begin our examination of memory by introducing four influential models of memory. The first, proposed by Atkinson and Shiffrin, emphasizes the distinction between short-term memory and long-term memory. The second model stresses that memory is influenced by the way material is processed. The third model distinguishes among memory for events, memory for general information, and memory for procedures. Thus, these first three models focus on distinctions between kinds of memory, though the distinction may emphasize the length of storage, how the material is processed, or the nature of that material. In contrast, the fourth model—parallel distributed processing—proposes that memory should be viewed in terms of the interactions among basic neuron-like units.

Students often wonder why psychologists emphasize theories. Why can't they be happy simply conducting research? Cognitive psychologists, like other psychologists, frequently develop theoretical explanations. For example, you encountered several theories of pattern recognition and several theories of attention in Chapter 2. Memory is such a major topic in cognitive psychology that we need to set aside this entire chapter to address theoretical issues. One value of these theories is that they attempt to simplify and organize all the diverse phenomena we call "memory" (Fischler, 1992). Otherwise, we simply have a collection of memory phenomena, with no understanding about how they might be related to one another. Another value is that they guide further research, helping to identify unexplored areas.

We also need to stress that theories are not necessarily mutually exclusive. In the discussion of theories of pattern recognition in Chapter 2, we saw that the various theories could account for different tasks. Similarly, each of the four memory theories we examine in this chapter may help us understand different components of memory.

THE ATKINSON-SHIFFRIN MODEL

During the 1960s, psychologists became increasingly excited about information-processing approaches to memory. A number of different models of memory were proposed that outlined separate memory stores for different kinds of memory. These

FIGURE 3.1

Atkinson and Shiffrin's Model of Memory (Based on Atkinson & Shiffrin, 1968).

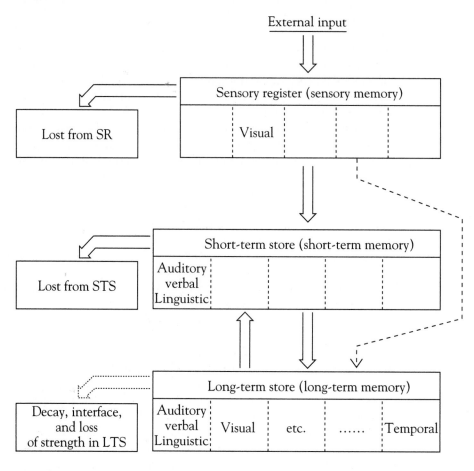

multistore models provided the first systematic account of the structures and processes that form the memory system (Eysenck & Keane, 1990).

The model that is most often referred to—and therefore sometimes called the "modal model"—was one proposed by Richard Atkinson and Richard Shiffrin (1968). Figure 3.1 shows this model, with arrows to indicate that information is transferred from one storage area to another. Let us examine the components of this influential model. Then we'll look at the experimental research and the case studies that neuroscientists have conducted. We will see that the model has some research support, but other results are not consistent with the model. We will conclude with an evaluation of the current status of this model.

Description of the Atkinson-Shiffrin Model

At the top of Figure 3.1, you can see how stimuli from the environment first enter sensory memory. **Sensory memory** is a large-capacity storage system that records information from each of the senses with reasonable accuracy. Although touch, smell, and taste can be represented in sensory memory, cognitive psychologists are especially likely to study **iconic memory** (visual sensory memory) and **echoic memory** (auditory sensory memory). In any case, information in sensory memory decays rapidly. Chapter 4 examines the research on sensory memory in much more detail.

Atkinson and Shiffrin's model proposes that material from sensory memory then passes on to short-term memory. **Short-term memory** (abbreviated **STM**) contains only the small amount of information that we are actively using. Atkinson and Shiffrin proposed that verbal information in STM is encoded acoustically, in terms of its sounds. Memories in STM are fragile—though not as fragile as those in sensory memory—and they can be lost from memory within about 30 seconds unless they are somehow repeated. Short-term memory is discussed in much more detail in the second part of Chapter 4.

According to the model, material finally passes from short-term memory to long-term memory. **Long-term memory** (abbreviated **LTM**) has a large capacity and contains memories that are decades old, in addition to memories that arrived several minutes ago. Atkinson and Shiffrin proposed that information in LTM is encoded semantically, in terms of its meaning. Memories in LTM are relatively permanent, and they are not likely to be lost. Chapter 5 examines the extensive research on long-term memory.

Suppose, for example, that a friend is reading a magazine article on food in China, and she relates to you an unusual fact:

In Eastern China, a featured item on the menu is deep-fried scorpion.

In terms of Atkinson and Shiffrin's model, the words in that sentence would first be registered in the auditory store of your sensory memory. That information could then be lost, or it could be transferred. In most cases involving transfer, the information would pass on to short-term memory, but that information could possibly be transferred from sensory memory to long-term memory, as the dotted line in Figure 3.1 suggests. Suppose, however, that the sentence about the deep-fried scorpion does arrive in short-term memory. One option is that this information may be lost from short-term memory. The other option is that it can pass on to long-term memory. If that information reaches long-term memory, it may be lost; however, the dotted line next to long-term memory suggests that loss from long-term memory is less likely than in the other two kinds of memory.

Notice that another arrow in Figure 3.1 indicates that information in long-term memory can pass back into short-term memory when we want to actively work with that information again. Suppose, for example, that an evening's conversation has drifted to the topic of deep-fried scorpions, and you wish to share your knowledge. You can retrieve this useful information from your relatively inactive long-term memory and bring it back to short-term memory.

So far, we have examined the model's **structural features,** which are the stable memory stores used during information processing. Atkinson and Shiffrin also proposed **control processes,** which are strategies that people use flexibly and voluntarily, depending upon the nature of the material and their own personal preferences. Chapter 7 examines these control processes in the section on meta-cognition. One important kind of control process is **rehearsal,** or the silent repetition of information that encourages it to recycle through short-term memory. For example, you may silently repeat information about deep-fried scorpions in order to recall it later. According to the model, information that is rehearsed frequently and kept for a long time in short-term memory is more likely to be transferred to long-term memory.

Control processes can operate in other ways in memory. For instance, people can decide whether they want to fill their short-term memory with material that needs to be remembered or to leave "work space" to think about something else. Furthermore, they can decide whether to use a particular memory strategy—such as a mental picture—to encode that sentence about deep-fried scorpions.

Research on the Atkinson-Shiffrin Model

The concept of sensory memory has created some controversy. In Chapter 4 we will see that current evidence suggests the possibility of at least two kinds of **iconic memory** (visual sensory memory) and two kinds of **echoic memory** (auditory sensory memory). Furthermore, some theorists have questioned whether the concept of iconic memory is even worth retaining. However, any controversy surrounding sensory memory has been greatly overshadowed by the controversy about another distinction in Atkinson and Shiffrin's model: the distinction between short-term memory and long-term memory. Numerous articles and books have debated this question (e.g., Baddeley, 1984, 1989; Melton, 1963; Squire, 1987; and Wickelgren, 1973). The consensus is that some research suggests that short-term memory really is different from long-term memory, but the evidence is not overwhelming. Wickelgren, for example, reviews a number of studies and concludes that several phenomena justify the distinction between short- and long-term memory. However, he concludes that the remainder of studies would be compatible with the view that humans really have only one kind of memory.

The issue, then, is whether we have enough evidence to support a model with two separate memory storages, a short-term memory that stores information for about 30 seconds or less and a long-term memory that stores material for long

| TABLE 3.1 | |

TWO LISTS SIMILAR TO THOSE USED BY KINTSCH AND BUSCHKE (1969).

LIST 1 (SEMANTICALLY SIMILAR PAIRS)	LIST 2 (ACOUSTICALLY SIMILAR PAIRS)
angry	tacks
pleased	so
forest	buy
sofa	owe
ocean	tied
woods	sew
carpet	their
sea	tax
happy	by
rug	there
mad	oh
couch	tide

periods of time. In general, psychologists prefer simple models, if these models can explain all of the data. However, suppose that we can demonstrate that certain factors have one kind of effect on material that is stored for short periods, and a different effect on material stored for longer periods. Then it is worthwhile to support a **duplex model,** or a model featuring two separate kinds of memory. Let us examine some representative research.

Kintsch and Buschke's Research. In one influential study, Kintsch and Buschke (1969) asked people to learn 16 English words in order. They proposed that the words from the beginning of the list would be in LTM when recall was requested because so much time had passed since they were presented. On the other hand, the most recent items should still be in STM. Their study focused upon one distinction that duplex theorists had proposed: material in STM is coded in terms of its acoustic or sound characteristics, whereas material in LTM is coded in terms of its semantic or meaning characteristics. The first study examined whether items at the beginning of the list—which were presumably in LTM— would be influenced by semantic factors. The second study examined whether items at the end of the list—which were presumably in STM—would be influenced by acoustic factors. Table 3.1 shows lists that are similar to the ones used in Kintsch and Buschke's research.

Notice that the first list contains pairs of synonyms, which are words that are similar to each other in *meaning*. This list resembles Kintsch and Buschke's semantically similar list. After the material had been presented, the experimenters supplied one word from the list, for example, *pleased*. The participants were requested to supply the next word in the list. The correct answer would be *forest*. However, suppose that a person confuses the word *pleased* with its synonym *happy*. Then this person might supply the word *rug* as the answer, because *rug* follows *happy*. Kintsch and Buschke measured the number of instances of this kind of semantic confusion that occurred for items in each part of the list. They found that items at the beginning of the list produced a greater number of semantic confusions than items at the end of the list. This result suggests that items at the beginning of the list, which should be in LTM, are coded in terms of their meaning.

The second list contains pairs of homonyms, which are words that are similar to each other in *sound*. This second list is comparable to Kintsch and Buschke's acoustically similar list. If a person confuses two words that sound the same, then he or she might see the word *so* and respond *their,* because *so* was confused with *sew,* which appeared before *their.* Kintsch and Buschke (1969) found that acoustic confusions were more likely at the end of the list than at the beginning of the list. This result suggests that items at the end of the list, which should be in STM, are coded in terms of their sound.

Evidence Against the Atkinson-Shiffrin Model.

In psychology, distinctions often seem crisp when they are first proposed. As more research and theory are produced, however, the distinctions seem to blur. For example, one crisp distinction used to be that short-term memory was acoustically coded, whereas long-term memory was semantically coded. We saw how this was demonstrated in the study by Kintsch and Buschke. However, more recent research has demonstrated that items in short-term memory can also be coded in terms of their meaning, a topic we will discuss in detail in Chapter 4. In addition, theorists pointed out that we often have a clear representation of the sound of an item in long-term memory; for example, the sound of a song may be encoded more clearly than its meaning. Thus, STM seems to be *primarily* acoustic, and LTM seems to be *primarily* semantic, but the distinction is fuzzy.

Experimental evidence also contradicts other features of the Atkinson-Shiffrin model. For example, the model proposes that information rehearsed for a long time in short-term memory is more likely to be transferred to long-term memory. However, earlier research by Tulving (1966) showed that in some situations the information people rehearsed frequently was not recalled any more accurately than unrehearsed information.

Neuroscience Research.

The neuroscience approach to memory has provided additional evidence for the Atkinson-Shiffrin model, especially through case studies of people with lesions. The most dramatic case was that of H.M., a man known only by his initials (Milner, 1966). In an attempt to cure H.M.'s serious epilepsy, neurosurgeons removed portions of his temporal lobes and his hippocampus. The operation successfully cured the epilepsy, but it left him with a severe kind of memory loss. H.M. can accurately recall events that occurred before his surgery and his short-term memory is also normal. However, he cannot learn or retain any new information. For example, anyone H.M. meets on a Monday would not look familiar on a Tuesday. Furthermore, he cannot recall more than 6 numbers in order, suggesting that his short-term memory is normal but he lacks the ability to transfer material from short-term memory to long-term memory (Squire, 1987).

The case of a second man, known as K.F., suggests roughly the opposite symptoms. K.F. had been in a motorcycle accident, which damaged a portion of the left side of his cerebral cortex. His long-term retention is normal, but his short-term memory is severely limited (Shallice & Warrington, 1970). For example, Philip Johnson-Laird (1988) reports on his own interactions with K.F. Johnson-Laird asked K.F. to repeat the sentence:

The dog bit the man and the man died.

K.F. repeated the sentence perfectly. Then Johnson-Laird asked him to repeat a second sentence:

The man the dog bit died.

This sentence was shorter but actually placed a greater burden on short-term memory; the subject, *the man* needs to be held in short-term memory—while processing the next three words—until reaching the main verb, *died.* K.F. was unable to repeat this second sentence.

The fact that H.M. has normal STM and abnormal LTM, whereas K.F. has abnormal STM and normal LTM, is often cited as strong evidence for the distinction between the two kinds of memory (e.g., Baddeley, 1990). However, the case of K.F. suggests a problem (Baddeley, 1990). The Atkinson-Shiffrin model proposes that information must pass through short-term memory before long-term learning can occur. If K.F. has abnormal short-term memory, how could his long-term memory be normal? It seems unlikely that all the material in his long-term memory came via the alternate route indicated in Figure 3.1, that is, directly from sensory memory.

The Current Status of the Atkinson-Shiffrin Model

The research on the distinction between short-term memory and long-term memory reveals mixed results. Some studies support the distinction, and many current models feature separate memories. Other research suggests that memory processes are similar—whether the information is stored in memory for several seconds or for many years. Many current cognitive theories still include a basic distinction between short-term memory and long-term memory (Estes, 1991). However, most models acknowledge that the Atkinson-Shiffrin model is too simple. For example, some proposals suggest that short-term memory is not a single storehouse with a limited capacity. Instead, it is probably a collection of temporary storehouses (Squire, 1987). We will examine this possibility in Chapter 4.

Despite the controversy over the distinction, however, most textbooks on memory or cognition discuss the research on short-term memory and long-term memory in different sections of the book. The rationale is that the studies in these two areas focus on different issues. For example, research on information stored in memory for brief periods frequently focuses on the limits of memory. In contrast, research on information stored in memory for longer periods usually examines topics such as autobiographical memory, encoding, and mnemonics. This book, too, considers short-term and long-term memory in two separate chapters. This division, however, reflects the nature of the tasks, rather than an enthusiastic endorsement of the Atkinson and Shiffrin model.

At about the time that many psychologists were growing dissatisfied with the duplex model proposed by Atkinson and Shiffrin, other researchers proposed a new theory. In this new levels-of-processing theory, other concepts were stressed, and the distinction between short-term memory and long-term memory was not emphasized.

SECTION SUMMARY: THE ATKINSON-SHIFFRIN MODEL

1. Memory involves maintaining information over time; memory is involved in almost every cognitive process.
2. The classic model of memory proposed by Atkinson and Shiffrin consists of three memory storage systems: sensory memory, short-term memory, and long-term memory.
3. The Atkinson-Shiffrin model also includes control processes, which are the strategies that people use voluntarily (for example, rehearsal).
4. The proposed distinction between short-term memory and long-term memory has inspired numerous studies. For example, some research shows that short-term memory is coded in terms of acoustics, whereas long-term memory is coded in terms of meaning. However, the experimental research on this issue and other proposed distinctions between STM and LTM does not provide clear-cut answers.
5. Similarly, the neuroscience case studies are not entirely consistent with the Atkinson-Shiffrin model.
6. Despite the mixed support, many contemporary cognitive theories distinguish between STM and LTM, though they are typically more complex than the Atkinson-Shiffrin model.

DEMONSTRATION 3.1

LEVELS OF PROCESSING.

Read each of the following questions and answer "yes" or "no" with respect to the word that follows.

1. Is the word in capital letters?   BOOK
2. Would the word fit the sentence:
    "I saw a _____ in a pond"?   duck
3. Does the word rhyme with BLUE?   safe
4. Would the word fit the sentence:
    "The girl walked down the _____"?   house
5. Does the word rhyme with FREIGHT?   WEIGHT
6. Is the word in small letters?   snow
7. Would the word fit the sentence:
    "The _____ was reading a book"?   STUDENT
8. Does the word rhyme with TYPE?   color
9. Is the word in capital letters?   flower
10. Would the word fit the sentence:
    "Last spring we saw a _____"?   robin
11. Does the word rhyme with SMALL?   HALL
12. Is the word in small letters?   TREE
13. Would the word fit the sentence:
    "My _____ is six feet tall"?   TEXTBOOK
14. Does the word rhyme with SAY?   day
15. Is the word in capital letters?   FOX

Now, without looking back over the words, try to remember as many of them as you can. Count the number correct for each of the three kinds of tasks: physical appearance, rhyming, and meaning.

THE LEVELS-OF-PROCESSING APPROACH

Before you read further, try Demonstration 3.1. Which kind of task produced the best recall? Was it the task in which you judged physical appearance, rhyming, or suitability in a sentence? This demonstration is based on a classic study by Craik and Tulving (1975) that explored levels of processing. Let's begin the discussion of this second model of memory by describing the levels-of-processing approach. Then we will look at the research, including an in-depth examination of an especially deep level of processing called the "self-reference effect." We'll end with an evaluation of the current status of this approach.

Description of the Levels-of-Processing Approach

The **levels-of-processing approach** proposes that deep, meaningful kinds of information processing lead to more permanent retention than shallow, sensory kinds of processing (Craik, 1979). For example, in Demonstration 3.1, you should have recalled more words when you judged a word's meaning (for example, whether the word would fit in a sentence), rather than its physical appearance (for example, whether it is in capital letters) or its sound (for example, whether it rhymes with a word). Because of its emphasis on whether the processing is deep or shallow, the theory is also called the **depth-of-processing approach.** In general, then, the more meaning a person extracts from a stimulus, the greater the depth of processing.

The levels-of-processing approach was proposed by Craik and Lockhart in 1972. Their paper has been one of the most influential in the area of human memory. In fact, Roediger (1980) pointed out that it had been quoted at least 700 times prior to 1980.

Let us examine the levels-of-processing theory in more detail. Craik and Lockhart (1972) proposed that people can analyze stimuli at a number of different levels. The shallow levels involve analysis in terms of physical or sensory characteristics, such as brightness or pitch. The deep levels involve analysis in terms of meaning. When you analyze for meaning, you may think of other, related associations, images, and past experiences related to the stimulus.

The by-product of all this analysis is a memory trace. If the stimulus is analyzed at a very shallow level (perhaps in terms of whether it had capital letters or whether it was printed in red), then that memory trace will be fragile and may be quickly forgotten. However, if the stimulus is analyzed at a very deep level (perhaps in terms of its semantic appropriateness in a sentence or in terms of the meaning category to which it belongs), then that memory trace will be durable: It will be remembered.

Craik and Lockhart also discussed rehearsal, the process of cycling information through memory, which we discussed in connection with the Atkinson-Shiffrin model. Craik and Lockhart proposed two kinds of rehearsal. **Maintenance rehearsal** merely repeats the kind of analysis that has already been carried out. In contrast, **elaborative rehearsal** involves a deeper, more meaningful analysis of the stimulus. Thus, if you see the word *book*, you could use maintenance rehearsal and simply repeat the sound of that word to yourself. On the other hand, you could use elaborative rehearsal by thinking of an image of a book or by relating the word *book* to another word on the list.

What will happen if you spend more time rehearsing? Craik and Lockhart (1972) predicted that the answer to this question depends on the kind of rehearsal you are using. If you are using shallow maintenance rehearsal, then increasing rehearsal time will not influence later recall. Simply repeating the word *book* five more times will not make it any more memorable. However, if you are using deep elaborative rehearsal, then an increase in rehearsal time *will* be helpful. During that time, you can dig out all kinds of extra images, associations, and memories to enrich the stimulus, and later recall will be more accurate.

Research on the Levels-of-Processing Approach

The major hypothesis emerging from Craik and Lockhart's (1972) paper was that deeper levels of processing should produce better recall. This hypothesis has been widely tested. For example, in an experiment similar to Demonstration 3.1, Craik and Tulving (1975) found that people were about three times as likely to recall a word if they had originally answered questions about its meaning than if they had originally answered questions about the word's physical appearance. Similarly, Parkin (1984) discovered that people who made semantic judgments about a word's category or its synonym performed much better on a surprise recall test than did people who made nonsemantic judgments (for example, about the number of vowels contained in a word or whether it had been printed only in capital letters).

Reviews of dozens of studies conclude that deep processing generally produces higher recall scores than shallow processing (Baddeley, 1990; Horton & Mills, 1984; Koriat & Melkman, 1987). Much of the research on this topic has focused on face recognition, the compatibility between encoding and retrieval, and the explanations for the effectiveness of deep processing. Let's examine these areas before the in-depth discussion of the self-reference effect, an especially popular research area in the last decade.

Depth of Processing and Face Recognition. Most of us can recall embarrassing incidents where we failed to recognize someone with whom we had interacted for many hours. For instance, a student in my cognitive psychology class named Michelle recalled how she had taken dancing lessons with another female student, totalling about three hours each week for two years. One day Michelle saw the other student in a shopping mall and did not recognize her. Michelle had apparently failed to use deep processing to encode her face; with different clothing, that face was now unrecognizable.

Research has shown that shallow processing of faces—like shallow processing of words—leads to poor recall. For instance, research participants recognize a greater number of photos of faces if they make judgments about whether a person is honest, rather than the gender of the person or the width of the person's nose (Sporer, 1991).

Bloom and Mudd (1991) have provided an appealing explanation. Their research demonstrated that people who had been instructed to judge whether a person was honest looked at the faces longer and made more eye movements compared to people who had been instructed to judge whether a person was male or female. These authors argue that deeper processing leads to encoding a greater number of features, and therefore superior recall. Alternately, when people make character judgments, they may encode the faces holistically, rather than in terms of isolated features (Wells & Hryciw, 1984). No matter which explanation is correct, you should emphasize deep processing the next time you want to remember somebody's face!

The Compatibility between Encoding and Retrieval.

Craik and Lockhart's (1972) original description of levels-of-processing theory emphasized **encoding,** or how items are placed into memory. It did not mention details about **retrieval,** or how items are recovered from memory. In a later paper, Craik and another colleague proposed that retrieval conditions should duplicate encoding conditions in order for deep processing to be highly effective (Moscovitch & Craik, 1976).

Let us consider a study that stresses the importance of the similarity between encoding and retrieval conditions. Suppose that you performed the various encoding tasks in Demonstration 3.1. Imagine, however, that you were then tested about rhyming patterns, rather than being tested for free recall. For example, a question might ask, "Was there a word on the list that rhymed with *toy?*" Bransford and his colleagues (1979) found that people performed better on this rhyming test if they had originally performed the rhyming encoding task, rather than the sentence encoding task. Thus, the presumably "shallow" acoustic task produced greater recall than the presumably "deep" semantic test. This research demonstrates that deep semantic processing may not be ideal unless the retrieval conditions are similar to the encoding conditions. We will return to discuss the importance of this compatibility when we consider encoding specificity in Chapter 5.

Explanations for the Effectiveness of Deep Processing.

Craik and Lockhart (1986) believe that deep levels of processing encourage recall because of two factors: distinctiveness and elaboration. **Distinctiveness** means that a stimulus is different from all other memory traces (Craik, 1979). For example, I can vividly recall a scene I witnessed during the 1970s. A friend had arranged for us to tour a nearby salt mine. Hundreds of feet below the earth's surface, we were traveling in a little cart through absolute darkness—until we suddenly came to a brightly lit area where five workers were nonchalantly sitting at a picnic area eating their lunch. That surreal image is so distinctly different from any scene I've experienced above ground that I'm unlikely to forget it! Researchers have supported the value of distinctiveness. For instance, people recall words with distinctive sequences of short and tall letters, such as *lymph, khaki,* and *afghan,* better than words with common orthographic sequences, such as *leaky, kennel,* and *airway* (Hunt & Elliot, 1980).

The second factor that operates with deep levels of processing is **elaboration,** which involves rich processing in terms of meaning (Anderson & Reder, 1979; Cohen et al., 1986). When you processed the word *duck* in Demonstration 3.1, for example, you might have thought about the fact that a duck is a bird, that it has feathers, that you have seen ducks on ponds, and many other possible associations. The semantic encoding encouraged rich processing. In contrast, if the instructions for that item had asked whether the word *duck* was in capital letters, you would simply answer yes or no; extensive elaboration would not be very likely.

Let's consider research on the importance of elaboration. Craik and Tulving (1975) asked participants to read sentences and decide whether the words that followed were appropriate to the sentences. Some of the sentence frames were simple, such as "She cooked the _____." Other sentence frames were elaborate, such as "The great bird swooped down and carried off the struggling _____." The word that followed these sentences was either appropriate (for example, *rabbit*) or inappropriate (for example, *book*). You'll notice that both kinds of sentences required deep or semantic processing. However, the more elaborate sentence frame produced far more accurate recall. Thus, more extensive elaboration leads to enhanced memory of stimuli.

Other research on elaboration emphasizes a practical point: In studying for a test, you will recall more if you elaborate on the material (Palmere et al., 1983). Palmere and his coauthors used a 32-paragraph essay on a fictitious African nation. Each paragraph contained only one major idea, and it consisted of four sentences—one main-idea sentence and three other sentences that provided examples for the main-idea sentence. In these studies, 8 of the 32 paragraphs remained intact; 8 had one sentence removed; 8 had two sentences removed; and 8 had all three example sentences removed. After participants had read the essay, they were tested for recall of the main ideas.

Figure 3.2 shows the results of three studies, each of which involved minor variations in presenting the paragraphs. The message is clear: more extensive elaboration—via a large number of examples—promotes greater recall of the main ideas. Try applying the results of this experiment in reading your textbooks or reviewing your class notes. First identify the main ideas, and then think up examples that illustrate the main ideas. In psychology courses such as cognitive psychology, it is reasonably easy to think up examples, particularly examples from your own experience. As the following in-depth section demonstrates, a particularly deep level of processing occurs when you process information in terms of your personal experience.

◇ In Depth: *The Self-Reference Effect*

We often deal with new information by relating it to ourselves. For example, students taking a course in abnormal psychology often suffer from "medical students' syndrome"—most psychological disorders seem to fit themselves! The professor describes how a depressed person feels pessimistic about the future, and suddenly dozens of students are wondering if their own pessimism means that they are clinically depressed.

FIGURE 3.2

The Number of Main Ideas Recalled, as a Function of Elaboration (Based on Palmere et al., 1983).

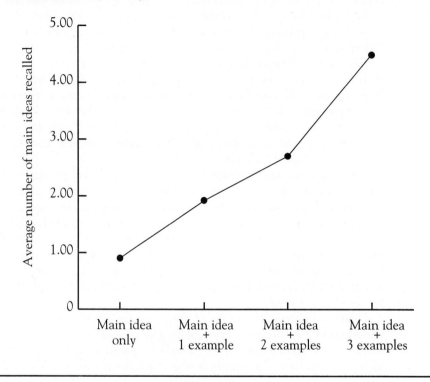

This personal framework for new information is an important topic in the levels-of-processing approach. Specifically, the **self-reference effect** points out that people recall more information when they try to relate that information to themselves. In the classic demonstration of the self-reference effect, Rogers, Kuiper, and Kirker (1977) asked participants to process lists of words according to the kinds of instructions usually studied in levels-of-processing research, that is, in terms of their physical characteristics, their acoustic (sound) characteristics, or their semantic (meaning) characteristics. However, other words were to be processed in terms of self-reference: People were asked to decide whether a particular word could be applied to themselves.

As Figure 3.3 illustrates, the self-reference task produced the best recall. Apparently, when we think about a word in connection with ourselves, we develop a particularly memorable coding for that word. For example, suppose that you are

---

FIGURE 3.3

Number of Words Recalled, as a Function of Level of Processing (Based on Rogers et al., 1977).

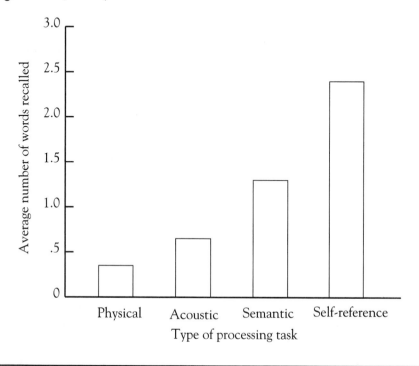

trying to decide whether the word *generous* applies to you yourself. You might remember how you loaned your notes to a friend who had missed class, and you shared a box of candy with the other people in the lounge—yes, *generous* does apply. The mental processes involved in the self-reference task seem to increase the chances that an item will be recalled.

The self-reference effect has been demonstrated repeatedly, for example with instructions to create mental imagery (Brown et al., 1986), with words related to creativity (Katz, 1987), and with paragraph-long prose passages (Reeder et al., 1987). The self-reference effect also works with children as young as 10 years of age (Halpin et al., 1984), as well as elderly adults (Rogers, 1983).

The research on the self-reference effect has also produced a strong demonstration of one of the themes of this book. As Theme 3 proposes, our cognitive system handles positive instances more effectively than negative instances. In the self-reference studies, people are more likely to recall a word that *does* apply to themselves than a word that does *not* (Bower & Gilligan, 1979; Ganellen & Carver, 1985; Mills, 1983). For example, the participants in Ganellen and Carver's study recalled 42 percent of the words that did apply to themselves, in contrast to 32 percent of words that did not apply.

Explanations for the Self-Reference Effect. Why should we recall information especially well when we apply it to ourselves? Belezza (1984) suggests that the self is treated as a rich and organized set of internal cues to which information can be associated. Klein and Kihlstrom (1986) focus especially on organization as an explanation for the self-reference effect. In particular, they suggested that when the task instructions asked people to judge whether a word was printed in small or capital letters, the participants inspected the words one at a time and were not inclined to organize those words together. When the task instructions asked whether a word fit the meaning of a sentence, people were also unlikely to organize the words together. However, when the instructions asked people to think about whether words applied to themselves, it might have been tempting to consider how some of these words were related to each other, because they were all applied to the same person.

In order to study the contribution of organization to the self-reference effect, Klein and Kihlstrom (1986) conducted a series of studies. In one study, for example, they included three conditions: (1) the "capital or small letters" (or structural) instructions; (2) instructions that asked whether the target word was a synonym of another word; and (3) the self-reference instructions ("Does this word describe you?"). As expected, people recalled only 5 percent in the structural condition, 13 percent in the semantic condition, and 27 percent in the self-reference condition. More important than this replication of the self-reference effect, however, is the pattern of organization shown in recall. When people in memory studies are told that they can recall words in any order they wish, they often show **clustering,** with related words appearing next to each other. People in Klein and Kihlstrom's study recalled an average of only one word in the structural condition, so clustering could not be measured. However, people showed substantially greater clustering in the self-reference task than on the other tasks.

In other studies, Klein and Kihlstrom (1986) carefully arranged the semantic and self-reference tasks so that the organization was equivalent for the two tasks. For example, in one study, the stimuli were words referring to professions, which could be well organized either semantically ("Does this job require a college education?") or according to self-reference ("Have you ever wanted to be a _____?"). With these special precautions, recall was virtually identical, 56 percent for the semantic task and 55 percent for the self-reference task. Thus, self-reference instructions may be effective because they encourage people to organize the trait words together into unified chunks.

Before you read further, try Demonstration 3.2, which focuses on a second potential explanation for the self-reference effect.

DEMONSTRATION 3.2

CONSTRUCTING SENTENCES.

Before you begin this demonstration, identify something that is enjoyable and interesting that you can do for a 5-minute break midway through this demonstration. Have that activity all set to go. Also, take out three sheets of paper.

On the first sheet of paper, write the numbers 1 through 20 on the left side. On the odd-numbered lines (1, 3, 5 . . .) write the last names of 10 current friends; on the even-numbered lines, copy the following last names: 2. Ziegler; 4. Dutton; 6. Gonzales; 8. McCrae; 10. Bunce; 12. Pletcher; 14. Wolter; 16. Henry; 18. Mann; 20. Burdett.

On the second sheet of paper, again write the numbers 1 through 20. Your task is to construct a sentence in which a name from the first sheet is linked with the corresponding word in the list below. For example, if the first name on your list were *Jones* and the first word on this list were *refrigerator*, you might construct a sentence like, *Jones created a large sandwich out of leftovers that filled the refrigerator*. Here is the list of words, in order:

1. snow	6. map	11. photograph	16. door
2. chair	7. bicycle	12. soup	17. cookie
3. library	8. candle	13. coat	18. book
4. leaf	9. football	14. bird	19. horse
5. apple	10. rug	15. car	20. shirt

As soon as you have finished writing these sentences, take a 5-minute break. Please try not to think about any of this material during your break. When you are finished, place these two sheets of paper where you cannot see them. Then turn to Demonstration 3.3, and look at the bottom line for further instructions (page 88).

Anthony Greenwald and Mahzarin Banaji (1989) reject the idea that the self is somehow unique in its ability to increase our memory ability. They propose, instead, that the self works like any other knowledge structure, but it is simply a very rich source of ideas. They propose that other rich sources of ideas, such as a friend's name, should also enhance recall. Their experiment resembled Demonstration 3.2; people produced names of friends and then constructed a sentence featuring each name, together with a concrete noun. People also constructed sentences using names supplied by the experimenter, just as you did.

The participants then completed a filler task in which they learned an assortment of trivial facts, and then they performed several recall tasks. Like you, they first provided free recall, listing the concrete nouns. For another task, called *cued recall*, they were given each of the 20 names and were asked to supply the noun that had been paired with each name.

FIGURE 3.4

Free Recall and Cued Recall for Nouns, as a Function of Whether the Nouns Had Been Paired with Names Generated by the Experimenter or by the Participant (From Greenwald & Banaji, 1989).

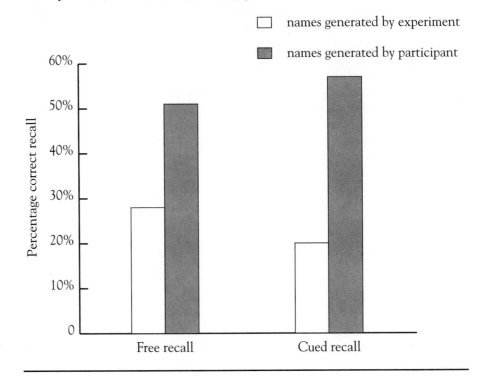

☐ names generated by experiment

▨ names generated by participant

Figure 3.4 shows the results of this study. As you can see, people recalled nearly twice as many of the nouns that had been paired with their friends' names, in comparison with nouns paired with strangers' names. Check how many of each group you recalled by counting the number of odd-numbered words you recalled from the list in Demonstration 3.2 and comparing it with the recall for even-numbered words. Figure 3.4 also shows that the contrast in recall was even greater for the cued recall task. Clearly, the self is not the only source of rich, memorable ideas. In addition, the name of each of our friends can serve as a nucleus around which new knowledge can be readily gathered.

Greenwald and Banaji's research illustrates an important point. The self-reference effect may operate in a fashion that is not particularly mysterious. Instead, it may work in a rather ordinary fashion, because the self is rich with associations and because, as we saw earlier, words related to the self tend to be organized into clusters.

Applications of the Self-Reference Effect. One important application of the self-reference effect is obvious: Whenever you want to remember material, try to relate it to your own experience—or to your friends. Reeder and his colleagues (1987) demonstrated that this technique works for prose passages, as well as isolated words.

The self-reference effect can also be applied to advertising. In one study, people made judgments about items that were pictured in advertisements (D'Ydewalle et al., 1985). A question about physical attributes might ask a person to judge a picture of a camera and answer the question, "Is there a red color in the picture?" A semantic question might ask, "Is it edible?" A self-reference question might ask, "Have you ever used this product?" The participants were later told to recall the brand names of the items. The self-reference instructions produced the best recall, followed by the semantic instructions. Performance was worst with the instructions on physical attributes.

As D'Ydewalle and his colleagues point out, advertisers make enormous efforts to construct a visually attractive ad. However, if they really want consumers to remember the brand name—presumably a major goal of an advertisement—they should invite consumers to process the picture at a deeper level, by considering how they themselves could use the product. Self-reference should encourage brand-name recall.

The Current Status of the Levels-of-Processing Approach

One major contribution of the levels-of-processing approach is that it emphasized the importance of the mental processes that occur when the material is being learned. Perhaps because of behaviorist influence, research in the 1950s and 1960s emphasized measurable variables, such as the number of times a stimulus had been exposed and the length of those exposures, rather than the hidden mental processes we use to learn the material. Another contribution is practical; we need to emphasize deep, meaningful processing if we want to improve retention.

However, the levels-of-processing approach also has drawbacks. The first problem is circularity: We have no independent assessment of depth (Nelson, 1977). Specifically, we say that if processing is deep, then retention will be better. Then we say that because the retention was better, the processing must have been deep. To avoid circularity, researchers need a measure of depth-of-processing *in advance* that can predict which conditions will produce the best retention.

A second problem is one we discussed earlier: Deep processing is not always better, because performance depends upon the way memory is tested. As discussed earlier, shallow processing—in terms of sound—is more effective than deep processing when memory is tested by asking whether any words on the list rhymed with *toy*.

In summary, then, the levels-of-processing approach played an important role in the history of cognitive psychology, and all current and future theories of memory need to acknowledge its contribution. However, the two major problems with the approach have prevented psychologists from developing that theory more completely.

SECTION SUMMARY: THE LEVELS-OF-PROCESSING APPROACH

1. The levels-of-processing approach suggests that deeper levels of processing produce more permanent retention than shallow levels of processing.
2. Levels of processing can explain face recognition; however, deep processing is only effective if retrieval conditions are similar to encoding conditions.
3. Distinctiveness and elaboration may be responsible for the effectiveness of deep levels of processing.
4. The self-reference task encourages especially deep levels of processing, resulting in enhanced memory. Self-reference instructions may encourage greater organization, and the self may serve as a rich source of associations.
5. The self-reference task can be applied to memory improvement and to advertisement.
6. Psychologists appreciate how the levels-of-processing approach emphasizes the mental processes that occur during learning; however, they criticize the circularity of the theory and the fact that "deeper is not always better."

TULVING'S MODEL:
EPISODIC, SEMANTIC, AND PROCEDURAL MEMORY

So far we have considered the Atkinson-Shiffrin model, which focuses on the length of time the material has been in memory, and the levels-of-processing approach, which focuses on how the material was processed during learning. A model proposed by Endel Tulving in 1972, in contrast, focuses on the *nature* of the material that is stored in memory. The original article was cited more than 500 times between 1972 and 1984 (McKoon et al., 1986). In more recent publications, Tulving has expanded his original model and discussed the distinctions in more detail (e.g., Tulving, 1983, 1984, 1986, 1987, 1989). Let us describe the model, look at the research, and evaluate it.

Description of Tulving's Model

Episodic memory stores information about when events happened and the relationship between those events. This information refers to your personal experience. Here are some examples of episodic memory:

1. The telephone rang a short while ago, followed by a thud when the snow fell off the roof.
2. I saw a student faint in class yesterday during a movie about neurosurgery.
3. I have a dental appointment at 3:30 tomorrow.

4. The first sentence I saw on this memory test was about a pauper. (Note that a list of items on a memory test is categorized as episodic memory.)

Semantic memory is the organized knowledge about the world. Semantic memory involves a fairly constant knowledge structure, in contrast to the changing events registered in episodic memory. It includes knowledge about words—as the name *semantic* implies—but it also includes many things we know that cannot readily be expressed in words. Incidentally, Tulving (1983) admits that the name *semantic memory* is too narrow; terms such as *generic memory* are more descriptive (Hintzman, 1978). However, people are now accustomed to the less accurate term, which this textbook will also use. Here are some examples of semantic memory:

1. I know that the meaning of the word *semantic* is closer to the meaning of the word *vocabulary* than it is to the word *disarmament*.
2. I remember that the chemical formula for water is H_2O.
3. I know what a French angelfish looks like.
4. I know that the shortest day of the year is in December.

More recently, Tulving has added a third category of memory to his model, called procedural memory (e.g., Squire, 1987; Tulving, 1987). Whereas episodic and semantic memory focus on factual information, **procedural memory** involves knowing how to do something, or learning connections between stimuli and responses. Some examples of procedural memory might include:

1. I know how to ride a bicycle.
2. I know how to tip the frying pan just right when making *injera*, an Ethiopian pancake.
3. I can start my car and put it into reverse.
4. I can dial the operator on the telephone.

Interestingly, procedural knowledge is often difficult to describe verbally. For example, you could read a book about how to ride a bicycle, yet that verbal information is unlikely to keep you from falling. Also, Demonstration 3.3 illustrates how your procedural knowledge can sometimes be more complete than comparable semantic knowledge.

In 1984, Endel Tulving received the Distinguished Scientific Contribution Award from the American Psychological Association. When receiving this award, he outlined why he supports a multiple-memory system (Tulving, 1985). Here are several reasons:

1. Profound generalizations cannot be made about all the different kinds of memory; a generalization about episodic memory may not apply to semantic memory.
2. Memory in humans has come about through a long evolutionary process, characterized by sudden twists, turns, and other irregularities. Human brain structures concerned with memory probably reflect these evolutionary quirks; they are likely to be complex (e.g., Sherry & Schacter, 1987).

DEMONSTRATION 3.3

COMPARING SEMANTIC AND PROCEDURAL KNOWLEDGE.

This demonstration requires you to be familiar with a standard keyboard, as found on a typewriter or a personal computer. (If you wouldn't know how to type your own name, then find a friend who can participate in this experiment.)

A. Without looking at a keyboard, describe which finger of which hand you would use to type each of the alphabet letters listed below; also describe whether the finger must reach up, reach down, or remain in place on the second row from the bottom on the typewriter.

a n y w h e r e y o u g o

B. Now sit down in front of a keyboard. Type the letters listed above.

If you are like most people, you will find that when you cannot look at a keyboard, your knowledge of the position of letters is minimal; your semantic knowledge about keyboard positions is weak. In contrast, you can rapidly type those letters without a single error; your procedural knowledge is superb.

Demonstration 3.2 (continued) Now recall on the third sheet of paper, in any order you like, the 20 words you learned for Demonstration 3.2.

---

3. The varieties of memory that seem so different cannot all involve the same underlying set of structures and processes. For example, consider the difference between (a) learning to adjust your motor movements when you wear eyeglasses that turn the world upside-down and (b) answering *yes* to the question "Is Abraham Lincoln dead?"

Initially, Tulving distinguished between only two kinds of memory, episodic and semantic (Tulving, 1983), so his description of the distinctions between these two is more complete. Demonstration 3.4 lists some of these distinctions from his list of 28 different contrasts. Try to decide whether the distinction between episodic and semantic memory seems like a useful one to you.

Research on Tulving's Model

Several kinds of research approaches have been used to explore the possible distinctions between different kinds of memory, though most examine the distinction between episodic and semantic memory. For example, Underwood and his colleagues (1978) tested 200 college students on 28 different measures of episodic

DEMONSTRATION 3.4

THE DISTINCTION BETWEEN EPISODIC AND SEMANTIC MEMORY.

Review the definitions of episodic and semantic memory, together with the examples provided. Now think of at least three of your own examples of each kind of memory. The chart below lists some of the dimensions on which Tulving (1983) suggests that episodic memory differs from semantic memory. Test each of your examples to see whether it is consistent with the characteristics listed in the chart. For example, do your examples of episodic memory seem to be derived from sensory experiences (for example, experiences you saw or heard), rather than comprehension (something you understood)?

CHARACTERISTIC	EPISODIC MEMORY	SEMANTIC MEMORY
1. Source of the information	Sensory experiences	Comprehension
2. Units of information	Episodes and events	Concepts, ideas, and facts
3. Organization	Time-related	Conceptual
4. Emotional content of the memory	More important	Less important
5. Likelihood of forgetting	Great	Small
6. Time required to remember the information	Relatively long time	Relatively short time
7. How tested in the laboratory	Recall of particular episodes	General knowledge
8. General usefulness	Less useful	More useful

memory and 5 different measures of semantic memory. The episodic memory tests included standard tasks such as free recall (which you tried in Demonstration 3.2) and serial learning (where people learn a list of words that must be recalled in the same order they originally appeared). The semantic memory tests mainly emphasized vocabulary.

In general, people's scores on the episodic memory tests were not closely correlated with their scores on the semantic memory tests. For example, a person who recalled a large number of words on a free recall test was not especially likely to have a superb vocabulary. If only one kind of memory were being assessed on these tasks, we would expect to find a high correlation among the tasks. The low correlations are consistent with a model in which episodic memory and semantic memory are separate.

Other research summarized by Shoben (1984) and Tulving (1983) also supports the distinction between episodic and semantic memory. For example, Shoben and his colleagues (1978) found that a variable related to semantic memory (sentence verification) influenced performance on a semantic memory task, whereas a variable related to episodic memory (sentence recognition) had no effect. In contrast, a variable related to episodic memory influenced performance on an episodic memory task, whereas a variable related to semantic memory had no effect.

However, other research does not support the episodic–semantic distinction. For example, Ratcliff and McKoon (1978) question the distinction that Tulving made about the organization of the two kinds of memory. If you look back at the third characteristic in Demonstration 3.4, you can see that Tulving proposed that episodic memory is time-related, whereas semantic memory is conceptual. Ratcliff and McKoon asked participants to study sentences such as "The pauper chopped wood and lugged water." This sentence would presumably enter episodic memory, which should emphasize relationships between words that appear close to each other in a sentence (because they would be close together in *time*). If episodic memory is indeed time-related, then the pair *pauper/wood* (a pair separated by one word) should be more closely related to each other than the pair *pauper/water* (a pair separated by four words). However, the results showed that these two pairs were related equally; the pauper was associated just as much with the water as with the wood. In contrast, the pair *wood/water* was not shown to be related. Even though these words appeared close together in time, their conceptual relationship is relatively weak. Tulving's theory claims that episodic memory is time-related, but Ratcliff and McKoon's study suggests that episodic memory emphasizes conceptual relationships.

Other distinctions from the table in Demonstration 3.4 have also been questioned by researchers. For example, in a test of the sixth characteristic, McKoon and Ratcliff (1986) demonstrated experimentally that episodic information can be recalled very quickly. And we can all think of examples where semantic information requires many minutes before it is recalled (Hirst, 1984; McKoon et al., 1986). If you've ever played Trivial Pursuit—a game that relies on retrieving off-beat, trivial information from semantic memory—you know how long retrieval from semantic memory can take!

Tulving argues that some of the strongest support for his theory comes from neuroscience research studies. Consider, for example, the studies measuring regional cerebral blood flow, a technique we discussed in Chapters 1 and 2. Tulving (1989) asked volunteers to perform a variety of semantic retrieval tasks in which they thought about general, impersonal knowledge. For instance, one professor recalled information about the history of astronomy. The cerebral blood-flow patterns showed greatest activity in the back part of the cerebral cortex. These same volunteers were also instructed to perform a variety of episodic retrieval tasks in which they thought about a particular personal experience. For example, this same professor recalled a Sunday afternoon excursion that had taken place a few days earlier. The cerebral blood-flow patterns showed greatest activity in the front part of the cerebral cortex.

Critics of Tulving's theory are not convinced by these neurological studies (e.g., Baddeley, 1984; McKoon et al., 1986). They argue that *any* two tasks—maybe even two semantic tasks—might differ in blood-flow patterns.

Tulving also believes that his theory is supported by observations of K.F., the man who had the motorcycle accident described on page 73 in connection with the distinction between short-term memory and long-term memory. Tulving (1989) argues that K.F. has impressive semantic memory but poor episodic memory. For example, he knows many things about the world, including knowledge about history, geography, politics, and music. He can also point out the location of his family's summer cottage in Ontario on a map of Canada, but he cannot retrieve from episodic memory any incident that occurred at the cabin.

Critics such as Eysenck and Keane (1990), however, argue that it isn't fair to compare amnesic individuals' semantic and episodic memory. After all, language and world information were typically acquired before the onset of amnesia. In contrast, the typical tests of episodic memory are based on information acquired after the onset of amnesia. A fair test would also assess newly learned semantic information and episodic information acquired long ago.

The Current Status of Tulving's Model

In general, reviews of the research on Tulving's model are skeptical about the distinction between episodic and semantic memory (e.g., Humphreys et al., 1989; Johnson & Hasher, 1987; Richardson-Klavehn & Bjork, 1988). Tulving himself even responded to a critical review of the literature by McKoon and her coauthors (1986) by saying that the evidence for this distinction is not strong. In fact, Tulving (1984, 1986) has revised his theory somewhat to suggest that episodic memory may be an important kind of semantic memory—in the way that apples are an important class within the category of fruit—rather than being an entirely separate system.

At present, researchers are much more likely to agree that procedural memory— the third category—represents a separate system (Baddeley, 1990). Knowing how to do something seems distinctly different from knowing or remembering information.

In discussing the Atkinson-Shiffrin model, we emphasized the convenience of distinguishing between short-term memory and long-term memory for the purpose of organizing the research—even if we are not convinced that the distinction actually occurs in human memory. Similarly, psychologists often distinguish between episodic, semantic, and procedural memory, even when they are not committed to a separate-memories model (e.g., Snodgrass, 1987). Accordingly, in this textbook Chapter 5 emphasizes episodic memory, and procedural memory is also mentioned. Chapter 7 explores semantic memory and the structure of our knowledge about the world.

SECTION SUMMARY: TULVING'S MODEL OF EPISODIC, SEMANTIC, AND PROCEDURAL MEMORY

1. Tulving proposed that episodic memory stores information about events, semantic memory stores organized knowledge about the world, and procedural memory involves knowing how to do something.
2. According to Tulving, episodic memory and semantic memory differ in terms of characteristics such as organization, likelihood of forgetting, and time required to remember the information.
3. Research on the distinction between kinds of memory has involved research on individual differences, experiments, measures of regional cerebral blood flow, and a case study of a brain-injured individual.
4. Researchers currently question the distinction between episodic memory and semantic memory, although they typically consider procedural memory to be different from the other two.

THE PARALLEL DISTRIBUTED PROCESSING APPROACH

Chapters 1 and 2 introduced the parallel distributed processing approach to cognition. In this chapter, we will explore in somewhat more detail how this approach explains the organization of memory. As you will note, this model differs from the other three because it does not focus on distinctions between different kinds of memory. Instead, the **parallel distributed processing approach** argues that cognitive processes can be understood in terms of networks that link together neuron-like units. The parallel distributed processing approach is often called either the **PDP approach** or **connectionism.** Because this approach is new and not yet fully developed or tested, we will limit our discussion to a description of the model and an assessment of its current status.

Description of the Parallel Distributed Processing Approach

Before you read further, try Demonstration 3.5, which illustrates some features of the PDP approach.

Human memory has a remarkable ability so familiar to us that we usually take it for granted: One thing reminds us of another (Johnson-Laird, 1988). Each of those clues in Task A of Demonstration 3.5 reminded you of several possible candidates. You probably thought of the correct answer after just a couple of clues, even though the description was not complete. Notice, however, that you did not conduct a complete search of all orange objects before beginning a second search

---

DEMONSTRATION 3.5

PARALLEL DISTRIBUTED PROCESSING.

For each of the two tasks below, read the set of clues and then guess as quickly as possible what thing is being described.

Task A

1. It is orange.
2. It grows below the ground.
3. It is a vegetable.
4. Rabbits characteristically like this item.

Task B

1. Its name starts with the letter *p*.
2. It inhabits barnyards.
3. It says "oink."
4. It is typically brown in color.

---

of all below-ground objects, then all vegetables, then all rabbit-endorsed items. In other words, your search for *carrot* was not serial, but parallel—consistent with the word *parallel* in parallel distributed processing.

Furthermore, notice that your memory can cope quite well, even if one of the clues is incorrect. In Task B, you searched for a barnyard-dwelling, oink-producing creature whose name starts with *p*. The word *pig* emerged, despite the misleading clue about the brown color. Similarly, if someone describes a classmate in your child development course who is a tall male from Saratoga Springs, you can identify the appropriate student, even if he is from Poughkeepsie.

Before we proceed further, note three characteristics of the memory searches you performed in Demonstration 3.5:

1. If a machine has one faulty part, it typically will not work, even if all other parts function well. If your car's battery is dead, the cooperative effort of all functioning parts still cannot make your car move forward. Human memory is much more flexible, active, and remarkable, consistent with Themes 1 and 2 of this book. Memory can still work well, even with some inappropriate input.

2. Memory storage is **content addressable;** that is, we can use attributes (such as an object's color) to locate material in memory.

3. Some clues are more effective than others in helping us locate material in

TABLE 3.2

ATTRIBUTES OF REPRESENTATIVE INDIVIDUALS WHOM A COLLEGE STUDENT MIGHT KNOW.

NAME	MAJOR	YEAR	POLITICAL ORIENTATION
1. Joe	Art	Junior	Liberal
2. Marti	Psychology	Sophomore	Liberal
3. Sam	Engineering	Senior	Conservative
4. Liz	Engineering	Sophomore	Conservative
5. Roberto	Psychology	Senior	Liberal

memory. For example, in Task B, most people would find the information about "oink" noises more useful than information about the number of legs the animal has.

James McClelland is one of the major developers of the PDP approach. McClelland (1981) described how our knowledge about a group of individuals might be stored by connections that link these people with their personal characteristics. His original example portrayed members of two gangs of small-time criminals, the Jets and the Sharks. We'll use a simpler and presumably more familiar example that features five college students. Table 3.2 lists these students, together with their college majors, year in school, and political orientation. Figure 3.5 shows how this information could be represented in network form. Notice that the figure represents only a fraction of the number of people a college student is likely to know and also just a fraction of the characteristics associated with each student. Try to imagine how large a piece of paper you would need to represent all the people you know, together with all the characteristics you consider relevant.

According to the PDP approach, each individual's characteristics are connected in a mutually excitatory network. If the connections among the characteristics are well established through extensive practice, then an appropriate clue allows you to locate the characteristics of a specified individual (McClelland, Rumelhart, & Hinton, 1986; Rumelhart et al., 1986).

Imagine that you want to locate the characteristics of Roberto, who is the only Roberto in the system. If you enter the system with the name *Roberto*, you can discover that he is a psychology major, a senior, and politically liberal. However,

FIGURE 3.5

A Sample of the Units and Connections that Represent the Individuals in Table 3.2.

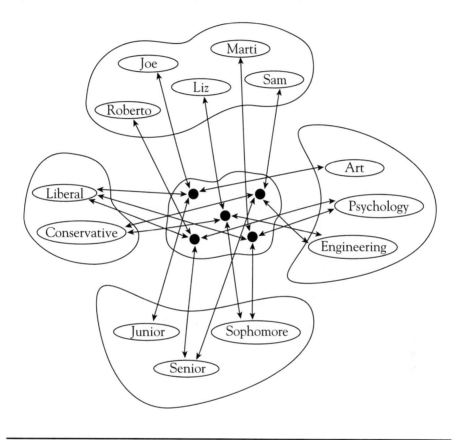

as we noted earlier, some clues are more effective than others. If we enter the system with the characteristic *psychology major,* our search produces ambiguity, because we locate two names—Marti and Roberto.

One advantage of the PDP model is that it allows us to explain how human memory can help us when some information is missing. Specifically, people can make a **spontaneous generalization,** which involves making inferences about general information that they never learned in the first place (McClelland, Rumelhart, & Hinton, 1986). For example, suppose that your memory stores the information in Figure 3.5 and similar information on other college students. Suppose, also, that someone were to ask you whether engineering students tend to be politically conservative. PDP theory suggests that the clue *engineering student* would activate information about all the engineering students you know, including information about their political orientation. You would reply that they do tend to be politically conservative, even though this factual statement is not directly stored in memory. (Our ability to make inferences will be discussed in more detail in Chapter 11.) Notice, then, that the structure of the PDP model makes some predictions about human cognitive processes, and these predictions can then be tested by researchers.

Spontaneous generalization involves making inferences about a category (for example, the category called "engineering student"). PDP models also allow us to fill in missing information about a particular person or an object; we make a **default assignment** based on information from similar people or objects. Suppose, for example, that you meet Christina, who happens to be an engineering student. Someone asks you about Christina's political preferences, and you have never discussed politics with her. This question will activate information about the political leanings of other engineers. Based on a default assignment, you will reply that she is probably conservative. Notice that both spontaneous generalization and default assignment can produce errors. For example, Christina may really be the president of your college's chapter of Democratic Socialists of America.

So far, our discussion of parallel distributed processing has been concrete and straightforward. In reality, the theory is extremely complex, sophisticated, and abstract (e.g., Eysenck & Keane, 1990; McClelland et al., 1986; Rumelhart et al., 1986; Schneider, 1987). Some of the other general characteristics of parallel distributed processing include the following:

1. A network contains basic neuron-like units, which are connected together so that a specific unit has many links to other units (hence the alternate name for the theory, *connectionism*).

2. A unit may affect other units by either exciting or inhibiting them.

3. Cognitive processes are based on parallel operations, rather than serial operations.

4. Knowledge is stored in the association of connections among the basic units. Notice that this view is very different from the common-sense idea that all the information you know about a particular person or object is stored in one specific location in the brain. In fact, the term *distributed processing* suggests that knowledge is distributed across many locations.

5. Every new event changes the strength of connections among relevant units. As a consequence, you are likely to respond differently the next time you experience a similar event. For example, while you have been reading about the PDP approach, you have been changing the strength of connections

between the name *PDP approach* and terms such as *content addressable* and *spontaneous generalization*. The next time you encounter the term *PDP approach*, all these related terms are likely to be activated.

6. Sometimes we have partial remembering for some information, rather than complete, perfect memory; the brain's capacity to provide partial memory is called **graceful degradation.** For example, in Chapter 7 we will discuss the **tip-of-the-tongue phenomenon,** which occurs when you know exactly which target you are seeking, and you may even know the target's first letter and number of syllables—but the word itself refuses to leap into memory.

The Current Status of the Parallel Distributed Processing Approach

The PDP approach represents the most important shift in theoretical orientations in psychology in recent decades (Schneider, 1987). Unfortunately, the approach is so new that researchers emphasize we cannot yet evaluate whether this approach can accommodate actual data (Schacter, 1990; Schneider, 1987). Some supporters are enthusiastic that the approach seems consistent with the neurological design of the brain (McNaughton & Morris, 1987); many are hopeful that PDP research may provide important links between psychology and neuroscience. However, other researchers are concerned that the PDP approach cannot account for certain memory phenomena. For example, Schacter (1990a) points out that current PDP models can explain situations where learning accumulates gradually across trials, but the models cannot yet provide a satisfactory account for our memory of a single episode. Also, the models have trouble explaining the rapid forgetting of extremely well-learned information that occurs when we learn additional information (McCloskey & Cohen, 1989; Ratcliff, 1990).

Each of the first three theoretical approaches—the Atkinson-Shiffrin model, the levels-of-processing approach, and Tulving's model—also generated tremendous enthusiasm when they were first proposed. However, the PDP approach is much broader, and it addresses perception, language, and decision making, as well as numerous aspects of memory. Still, we can speculate whether the enthusiasm that this approach initially generated will fade in the same way the excitement over the other three approaches has declined in recent decades—or whether the PDP approach will become the standard framework for analyzing human memory.

SECTION SUMMARY: THE PARALLEL DISTRIBUTED PROCESSING APPROACH

1. According to the PDP approach, the cognitive processes can be explained by networks linking together neuron-like units.
2. The PDP approach explains some important characteristics of memory:

(a) memory can function, even with inappropriate input; (b) we can use attributes to locate material in memory; (c) some clues are more effective than others in helping retrieve material from memory; (d) we can make spontaneous generalizations to construct general information about a category; (e) we can make default assignments to fill in missing information; and (f) we sometimes have partial memory for a target.

3. According to the PDP approach, memory consists of networks of interconnected units, which can either excite or inhibit each other; cognitive processes operate in a parallel fashion; knowledge is stored in the connections between units, and new events change the strengths of these connections.

4. The PDP approach has generated tremendous enthusiasm, though it may not be able to account for some memory characteristics; the approach is so new that it cannot yet be evaluated adequately.

REVIEW QUESTIONS

1. Two of the models discussed in this chapter emphasize the idea that there are different kinds of memory. Discuss the evidence for and against the short-term memory/long-term memory distinction and the episodic memory/semantic memory/procedural memory distinction.

2. What is rehearsal? How do the Atkinson-Shiffrin and levels-of-processing theories view its role in memory?

3. Some theorists stress the difference between structure and process. Compare the first three theories in terms of their relative emphasis on structure and process.

4. Suppose that a fourth-grade teacher asks his class to read a paragraph about mealtimes in the Bedouin culture. With respect to levels-of-processing theory, what kind of instructions should he use to encourage the greatest retention of material? What kind of instructions would be the least effective?

5. Discuss the self-reference effect, mentioning some of the research that has demonstrated this effect. What two explanations currently seem most likely?

6. At several points in the chapter, we discussed neuroscience research on the study of memory. If necessary, refer to Chapter 1 to describe these research techniques, and summarize the neuroscience findings about human memory.

7. Suppose that the Atkinson-Shiffrin theory and Tulving's theory were *both* correct. What six kinds of memory would we have? Give examples from your own experience of each of those six memory categories.

8. In the discussion of the PDP approach, we looked at an example of hypothetical college students. Select a topic with which you are familiar (e.g., popular singers, your own friends, American novelists, automobiles). Draw a diagram similar to Figure 3.5 to represent four or five examples of that

area; aside from the names of those examples, specify three other critical characteristics and draw in the connections among the items. For instance, if you select your own friends, draw a diagram showing five individuals and specifying three characteristics you consider important, besides their names.

9. Suppose that a friend is reading an introductory psychology textbook that mentions the PDP approach in passing. How would you describe the characteristics of this approach to your friend? Why is it called parallel distributed processing? What would you say about how this approach differs from traditional approaches?

10. Chapter 5 discusses memory improvement in some detail. However, this chapter offers a number of suggestions for enhancing memory. List as many of them as possible.

New Terms

memory
sensory memory
iconic memory
echoic memory
short-term memory (STM)
long-term memory (LTM)
structural features
control processes
rehearsal
duplex model
levels-of-processing approach
depth-of-processing approach
maintenance rehearsal
elaborative rehearsal
encoding
retrieval

distinctiveness
elaboration
self-reference effect
clustering
episodic memory
semantic memory
procedural memory
parallel distributed processing approach
PDP approach
connectionism
content addressable
spontaneous generalization
default assignment
graceful degradation
tip-of-the-tongue phenomenon

Recommended Readings

Baddeley, A. (1990). *Human memory: Theory and practice*. Boston: Allyn and Bacon. Baddeley is a key researcher in the area of human memory. His book discusses all four models of memory; however, it examines in greatest detail the Atkinson-Shiffrin model and the PDP approach.

Johnson-Laird, P. N. (1988). *The computer and the mind: An introduction to cognitive science*. Cambridge, MA: Harvard University Press. This book provides a clear overview of the PDP approach for those who are interested in more details about this important new approach.

Roediger, H. L., III, & Craik, F. I. M. (Eds.). (1989). *Varieties of memory and consciousness: Essays in honour of Endel Tulving.* Hillsdale, NJ: Erlbaum. Based on a conference that celebrated Tulving's 60th birthday, this book contains many chapters that discuss both Tulving's theory and the levels-of-processing approach.

Schacter, D. L. (1990). Memory. In M. I. Posner (Ed.), *Foundations of cognitive science* (pp. 683–725). Cambridge, MA: MIT Press. Schacter's chapter briefly outlines memory theory and research, placing the models of memory in a historical context.

Tulving, E. (1989). Remembering and knowing the past. *American Scientist, 77,* 361–367. This article, written for a lay audience, outlines the basic principles of Tulving's theory.

C H A P T E R 4

SENSORY MEMORY
AND SHORT-TERM MEMORY

PREVIEW

In this chapter we explore the two briefest kinds of memory: sensory memory and short-term memory. Both are limited in capacity and temporary in duration, in contrast to the long-term memory that we will examine in Chapter 5.

Sensory memory holds information in relatively unprocessed form. Visual sensory memory, also called iconic memory, holds material for a fraction of a second, thereby allowing time for that information to be processed after the stimulus has disappeared. Auditory sensory memory, also called echoic memory, holds material for 2 to 3 seconds after the stimulus has disappeared, so it is especially important when we process spoken language.

Short-term memory retains information for as long as 30 seconds. In contrast to sensory memory, information in short-term memory can be manipulated, for example, by comparing items and changing their order. Several decades ago, psychologists believed that short-term memory had a strict capacity, limited to between 5 and 9 items. We will see that the capacity of short-term memory is indeed limited, but many factors influence its limits. Furthermore, the information in short-term memory is often stored in terms of its sound, but it can also be stored in terms of its visual appearance and meaning. Finally, the most recent interpretation of short-term memory is called *working memory*. According to Baddeley's view, working memory consists of an auditory component, a visual-spatial component, and a central executive that coordinates information and plans strategies.

INTRODUCTION

In the last few minutes, dozens of items have entered your memory. The clear majority of those items were forgotten just moments later. This chapter focuses on these fleeting, fragile kinds of memory known as sensory memory and short-term memory. As we noted in Chapter 3, **sensory memory** is a large-capacity storage system that records information from each of the senses with reasonable accuracy. According to the Atkinson and Shiffrin (1968) model, material from sensory memory next passes to **short-term memory,** which contains only the small amount of material we are actively using. Much of the information in short-term memory is forgotten, and only a fraction passes on to long-term memory. Chapters 5, 6, and 7 will explore these more permanent memories. For now, let us examine memories that last substantially less than one minute.

SENSORY MEMORY

Sensory memory, also known as **sensory storage** or the **sensory register,** holds information in a relatively raw, unprocessed form for a short time after the physical stimulus is no longer available. Thus, sensory memory permits some trace of a stimulus to remain after the stimulus itself has disappeared. Try Demonstration 4.1

DEMONSTRATION 4.1

EXAMPLES OF SENSORY MEMORY.

Visual Sensory Memory.   Take a flashlight into a dark room and turn it on. Swing your wrist around in a circular motion, shining the flashlight onto a distant wall. If your motion is quick enough, you will see a complete circle. Your visual sensory memory stores the beginning of the circle while you examine the end of the circle.

Auditory Sensory Memory.   Take your hands and beat a quick rhythm on the desk. Can you still hear the echo after the beating is finished?

Tactile (Touch) Sensory Memory.   Take the palms of your hands and quickly rub them along a horizontal edge of your desk, moving your hands so that the heels touch first and the fingertips touch last. Can you still feel the sharp edge, even after your hand is off the desk?

---

so that you can appreciate several examples of sensory memory. Unfortunately, researchers have conducted only a few studies on sensory memory in the "minor" senses, such as touch, smell, and taste (e.g., Hill & Bliss, 1968). The vast majority of information concerns vision and hearing. Therefore, we will look only at visual sensory memory (iconic memory) and auditory sensory memory (echoic memory).

Why do we need sensory memory? Psychologists propose that sensory memory is necessary for two major reasons. First, the stimuli that bombard your senses are constantly and rapidly changing. For example, consider what happens when you read the sentence "Why do we need sensory memory?" aloud to a friend. The *wh* sound from the *why* is long gone by the time you speak the *y* sound of the word *memory*. However, a listener needs to retain this information about the pitch of your voice at the beginning of the sentence and compare it with similar information at the end of the sentence. The rising pitch in your voice allows the listener to decide that this sentence was a question. Listeners also need to retain an entire sentence so that they can determine which word in the sentence is stressed. Notice, for example, how the meaning of the sentence "I wouldn't buy tickets to hear him sing" changes, depending upon whether you stress the *I*, the *buy*, the *him*, or the *sing*.

A second reason why we need sensory memory is that we need to keep an accurate record of the sensory stimulation for a brief time while we select the most important stimuli for further processing. For example, think about the rich variety of stimuli that are now entertaining your senses. You can see the words on the page in front of you and other details of the surrounding area in which you are reading. Maybe you hear the squeak of your marker as it underlines an important point, and you may also hear faint music in the background. You can feel the pressure of your chair against your back and can also sense that your body is slightly tilted. You may be somewhat aware of the pain from yesterday's paper cut, and you may also notice that the room is exactly the temperature you find comfortable. Perhaps you can barely taste the toothpaste you used several hours ago or smell the distant aroma of cookies baking. You would be overwhelmed if you noticed all the information from all of your senses all of the time. Instead, your sensory memory keeps a record of the stimuli for a few moments, and the stimuli are quickly examined to determine which ones will receive further processing.

The second section of this chapter considers short-term memory, which differs from sensory memory in several respects:

1. Items remain in sensory memory for about 2 seconds or less, whereas they remain in short-term memory for as long as 30 seconds.
2. Information in sensory memory is relatively raw and unprocessed, whereas information in short-term memory can be manipulated (for example, by rehearsal, comparison, or changing the order of the items).
3. The information in sensory memory is a fairly accurate representation of the stimulus, whereas the information in short-term memory is more likely to be distorted and inaccurate.
4. Information is passively registered in sensory memory, whereas it is actively selected for entry into short-term memory (Estes, 1988).

Iconic Memory

Ulric Neisser, a major figure in the origins of cognitive psychology, proposed the name **iconic memory** to describe visual sensory memory. He wrote that iconic memory (pronounced "eye-*conn*-ick") involves the brief persistence of visual impressions that "makes them briefly available for processing even after the stimulus has terminated" (Neisser, 1967, p. 15). Whereas the term *iconic memory* refers to the memory process, the term **icon** refers to a particular visual impression, such as your impression of the letter A. You may have heard the words *icon* or *iconography* in an art class, referring to figures and the art of representing figures. Let's first look at Sperling's classic study on iconic memory and then consider more recent research.

Sperling's Research. George Sperling (1960) conducted one of the first demonstrations of iconic memory. His experiment cannot be illustrated without the use of special equipment. However, Demonstration 4.2 shows how experiments prior to Sperling's might have measured the size of iconic memory. You probably recalled only four or five letters in this demonstration. However, you may think you *saw* more than you were able to report. Perhaps you believe you saw about 10 items, rather than just 4 or 5. But does it seem that many of these 10 items faded during the time you took to report the earlier items?

DEMONSTRATION 4.2

THE WHOLE-REPORT TECHNIQUE.

WITH YOUR HAND, COVER THE CHART AT THE BOTTOM OF THIS DEM-
ONSTRATION AND DO NOT LOOK AT THE LETTERS UNTIL THE INSTRUC-
TIONS INDICATE TO DO SO! Find a room without outside light, and stand near the
light switch. As soon as you have finished reading these instructions, turn off the lights,
removing your hand from the chart. Quickly switch the light on and off, keeping it on
just a fraction of a second. Now try to recall as many of the letters as possible. OK, begin.

X	B	S	T
D	H	M	G
R	L	W	C

Sperling's objective was to measure the true size of iconic memory. To do this,
he needed to overcome the long amount of time that participants required to report
all the items in iconic memory. This problem plagued previous researchers, who
had used the method illustrated in Demonstration 4.2. This **whole-report technique** instructs people to report everything they saw. In contrast, Sperling's **partial-
report technique** instructs people to report only a specified portion of the display.
The same chart of letters is exposed very briefly. After the chart has disappeared,
participants hear a tone that indicates which portion of the display they must
report. Specifically, if they hear a high tone, they report the letters in the top row;
a middle tone indicates the middle row; and a low tone indicates the bottom row.

Imagine that you were a participant in Sperling's (1960) experiment. You would
see the display flashed briefly; then it disappears. Then suppose that you hear a low
tone, indicating that you should report as much as possible from the bottom line,
for example, *R L W C*. Notice that while you were looking at the letters, you had
no clue about which line in the display would be tested. Suppose that you manage
to recall three of those letters, *R L C*. If you recalled three letters from the bottom
row, we can assume that you could have also recalled three letters from the top
row if you had heard a high tone, or three letters from the middle row if you had
heard a middle tone. Thus, the number of items correct on any one line can be
multipled by three to obtain an estimate of the number of items the participant
actually saw in the entire display.

Sperling found that people recalled slightly more than three items from one line
when the partial-report technique was used. Therefore, he multiplied that figure
by three and estimated that people actually saw between 9 and 10 items out of the

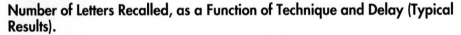

FIGURE 4.1

Number of Letters Recalled, as a Function of Technique and Delay (Typical Results).

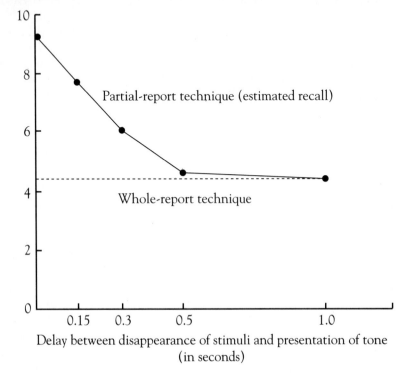

Delay between disappearance of stimuli and presentation of tone (in seconds)

12 possible items. However, suppose that the whole-report technique is used, rather than the partial-report technique. In this situation, the image of these 9 or 10 items fades so rapidly that a person can report only about 4 of them before the remaining items have disappeared from iconic memory.

Sperling also varied the length of the delay between the disappearance of the stimulus display and the sounding of the tone that indicated which line was to be recalled. If this partial-report tone sounded just as soon as the display disappeared, then people saw an estimated 9 to 10 items in the display—as we just discussed. However, if the partial-report tone was delayed as little as half a second, then people saw only an estimated 4.5 items. In other words, the iconic memory fades so rapidly that it is gone in half a second, and recall performance deteriorates to the same unspectacular level as in the whole-report technique. Figure 4.1 illustrates both the estimated recall with the partial-report technique and the recall using the whole-report technique.

Sperling's results produced enthusiastic responses from cognitive psychologists. These findings were quite compatible with an information-processing approach, such as the Atkinson-Shiffrin (1968) model. As Long (1980) describes, the information-processing approach emphasizes that perception is not an instantaneous result of stimulation. Instead, our visual experience is the product of a sequence of well-defined processes or stages, each requiring a measurable amount of time. Iconic storage permits a briefly presented stimulus to be prolonged, allowing for the next stage in information processing to begin.

The "Worth" of an Icon. Hundreds of other experiments followed Sperling's classic study, using a wide variety of research procedures (Long, 1980). They generally supported the concept of an icon that persisted 200 to 400 milliseconds— less than half a second—after disappearance of the stimulus (van der Heijden, 1981).

More recent research has concentrated on other characteristics of the icon. For example, consider a study by Geoffrey Loftus and his coauthors (1985) who wanted to measure the "worth" of an icon. That is, if observers are looking at pictures and they are *prevented* from using an icon, how much longer would each picture need to be exposed in order to compensate for the lack of an icon?

To answer this question, Loftus and his associates presented color slides of landscapes, for exposure durations that varied from 62 to 1,300 milliseconds. On some trials, a slide was immediately followed by a **mask,** a slide consisting of a jumble of black and gray lines on a white background. The immediate presentation of the mask prevented the persistence of an icon. On other trials, the mask was either delayed or absent. After 72 pictures had been presented, recognition was tested. These same 72 pictures were shown, together with 72 previously unseen pictures, and the participants were asked to respond whether each picture was old or new.

The participants' accuracy for each condition was calculated, and the accuracy rates provided some interesting information. For example, in one condition, pictures were presented for 270 milliseconds, and the mask was delayed, permitting the persistence of an icon. In this condition, participants correctly identified 69 percent of the pictures during the test phase. Let's now see how long a picture would have to be presented in the condition when icons could *not* be used, in order to achieve the same accuracy rate. Loftus and his colleagues calculated that pictures in the condition where they were immediately masked (therefore, using no icon) needed an exposure time of 370 milliseconds to achieve that same 69 percent accuracy rate. So, this research allows us to answer the question "How much is an icon worth?" Specifically, the icon is equal to about 100 milliseconds (which is 370 − 270 milliseconds) of additional exposure of a visual stimulus. Additional research by Loftus and his colleagues (1992) has replicated these data and also shown substantial individual differences in the rate at which an iconic image fades.

The Location of an Icon. Sperling's (1960) research initially produced enthusiasm, but in the last 20 years the concept of the icon has inspired both controversy and skepticism. One controversial issue, for example, is whether icons are stored in the visual receptors in the eye, rather than in some more central part of the brain. Specifically, Sakitt (1976) argued that the icon is stored in the rods, the light receptors that are sensitive to black-and-white stimuli but not to colored stimuli. Sakitt and her colleagues have continued to support this position (e.g., Long, 1980; Long & Beaton, 1982; Sakitt & Long, 1979). However, Banks and Barber (1977) demonstrated that iconic memory contains color information, and so cones must also be involved in iconic memory. Furthermore, Adelson (1978) found that, if anything, cones were more helpful than rods in iconic memory. Most psychologists believe, therefore, that icons must be stored at a higher level of visual processing than the receptors of the retina. Iconic memory appears to be a cognitive activity, rather than something limited to a portion of the eye.

Research by Di Lollo and his coworkers adds additional evidence against the receptor explanation and in favor of the cognitive explanation of iconic memory (Di Lollo, 1977, 1980; Di Lollo & Hogben, 1987). If the information is indeed stored in the retinal receptors, then a stimulus exposed for a longer time should probably increase the duration of iconic memory. No perceptual theory would suggest that iconic memory should *decrease* when the stimulus lasts longer. However, Di Lollo and his colleagues obtained a surprising and counterintuitive result. As stimulus duration is increased beyond about 10 milliseconds, the duration of iconic memory becomes progressively *shorter!* As Di Lollo (1992) explains, iconic memory is based on a period of information-processing activity. This period has a fixed duration, and the clock starts ticking at the very beginning of the stimulus presentation. In summary, Di Lollo's work suggests that the icon is stored in some more central part of the brain, rather than in the visual receptors of the eye.

The Usefulness of an Icon. In addition to the controversy about the physical location of the icon, another controversy has arisen about the usefulness of the icon. Haber (1983a, 1983b, 1985a) composed an "obituary" for the concept of the icon in a series of articles with gloomy titles such as "The icon is really dead." Haber's major argument is that the persistence of the visual stimulus does not play an important part in everyday perceptual activity. He claims that the concept of the icon might be useful if we frequently engaged in activities such as reading with only the brief flashes of light provided by lightning. Outside the laboratory, people spend most of their waking time viewing three-dimensional scenes featuring movement—not viewing briefly presented, two-dimensional letters. Haber also suggests that persistence of visual information would do more harm than good.

In general, psychologists rushed to resuscitate the icon after Haber pronounced it dead. For example, 32 authorities commented on Haber's (1983a) article in one journal, and Geoffrey Loftus (1985) notes that 30 of them found fault with Haber's argument. These authorities argued that the concept of the icon *is* useful. For example, motion pictures present brief flashes that need to be integrated in order to be perceived correctly; iconic memory aids this process. Furthermore, following the rise of computer technology, people spend considerable time looking at displays that resemble those used in laboratory experiments, and information about the icon can be useful in helping build more effective video display systems. In addition, the large-capacity storage provided in iconic memory is an extremely useful feature because, in combination with selective attention, it provides a mechanism for people to retain only a portion of all the stimuli reaching their senses. Finally, as Loftus (1983, 1985) points out, the techniques used to examine iconic memory may not be the most ecologically valid ones yet devised by cognitive psychologists. However, physicists study gravity via objects falling in near vacuums, rather than by observing leaves drifting gently from trees. Similarly, well-controlled laboratory conditions provide extremely useful information about human cognitive processes.

Directions for Further Research. It is difficult to predict the direction of future research on the icon. One possible issue is that iconic memory is not unitary; instead, two or more different kinds of brief visual memory may occur during the early stages of information processing (Coltheart, 1980; Cowan, 1988; Di Lollo & Dixon, 1988; Irwin & Yeomans, 1986). As we will note throughout this textbook, cognitive processes are seldom as simple as the earlier researchers proposed.

Another issue in future research may be to identify additional ways we use iconic memory in our daily lives. For example, iconic memory may help keep our visual world stable, despite constant eye movement (Banks & Krajicek, 1991; Irwin et al., 1990). Notice how, as you are reading this sentence, your eyes are jumping forward along the page. Iconic memory may help you preserve one image long enough so that it can be compared with an image registered after your eyes have moved ahead. From this comparison, you can conclude that the words have *not* changed position relative to each other and that your visual world has remained stable.

Echoic Memory

Neisser coined the phrase *echoic memory* to serve as the auditory equivalent of iconic memory. **Echoic memory** refers to auditory sensory memory, or the brief auditory impressions that persist after the sound itself has disappeared. A particular auditory impression is called an **echo,** because of its similarity to the echo that sometimes persists after a sound disappears. The name *echoic memory* seems particularly suitable at times. Have you ever noticed how you can "hear" a loud crash echoing inside your head after the sound has really stopped? You may also have noticed that when your professor has been lecturing, his or her words will "echo" in your head for a few moments after they have been spoken—fortunately just long enough for you to write them down.

FIGURE 4.2	

A Person Participating in an Echoic Memory Study.

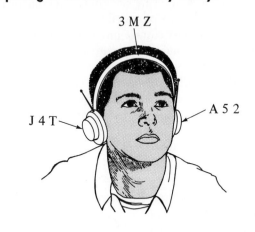

Darwin's Research. An important demonstration of echoic memory was a study modeled on Sperling's (1960) partial-report technique. You will recall that Sperling presented a visual display to participants and used an auditory signal to indicate which part of the display was to be reported. Darwin, Turvey, and Crowder (1972) neatly reversed Sperling's study by presenting an auditory display and using a visual signal to cue the partial report. These authors used special headphones to present three different auditory messages to the participants. Figure 4.2 illustrates how this was done. One group of items (J 4 T) was presented to a person's right ear. A second group of items (A 5 2) was presented to the left ear. A third group of items (3 M Z) was prepared by recording the list on both the right and left channels; this list was presented in such a way that it seemed to come from in between the right and the left ear—in other words, right in the middle. All three sequences were presented at the same time.

After hearing the sequences, people saw a visual cue on a screen, indicating which of the three sequences they should report. Specifically, a bar on the left meant that the participant should report the sequence from the left ear, a bar in the middle indicated the middle sequence, and a bar on the right indicated the sequence from the right ear.

Darwin and his coauthors found that the partial-report technique allowed people to report a larger estimated number of items than with the whole-report technique, in which people tried to report all nine items. These results are similar to the results for iconic memory. Thus, sensory memory stores items for a brief time—so brief that this memory is gone before people can list all the items in their sensory memory.

However, Darwin's study also pointed out some potential differences between the two kinds of sensory memory. Specifically, the maximum number of items correctly recalled in echoic memory was estimated to be about 5, which is considerably fewer than the 9 to 10 items in iconic memory. Darwin and his coauthors speculated that echoic memory was relatively small because people had difficulty separating the three different input channels. Another potential difference between echoic memory and iconic memory may be their duration. Darwin's study estimated that echoic memory could last as long as 2 seconds, in contrast to Sperling's estimate of a fraction of a second for iconic memory.

Later Research on Echoic Memory.

Robert Crowder (1982a) used a different technique to explore echoic memory. He presented two artificially produced vowel sounds, one after another. Sometimes, the vowels were highly similar to each other; for example, they might be two variants of the *a* sound in *cat*. Other times, the two vowels were identical. The two sounds were sometimes presented ½ second apart, and sometimes with longer gaps—ranging up to 5 seconds—between the two presentations. Participants were instructed to report for each trial whether the vowels were the same or different. Their responses were used to calculate an index of discrimination ability, that is, how accurately people reported whether the two sounds were different.

Figure 4.3 shows the results of Crowder's study. As you can see, performance is much more accurate when two vowels are presented less than a second apart. Performance seems to reach asymptote at about 3 seconds (that is, the curve remains essentially flat between 3 and 5 seconds). Crowder's study therefore identifies the upper limit of echoic memory to be about 3 seconds, slightly larger than the 2 seconds specified by Darwin and his coauthors (1972).

In discussing iconic memory, we noted that some theorists believe there is more than one kind of iconic memory. Similarly, theorists have proposed that there is more than one kind of echoic memory. For example, Cowan (1984, 1988) summarizes evidence for two kinds of auditory sensory memory. One kind, **short auditory storage,** is a simple store that involves no analysis of the stimulus and decays less than one second after the auditory stimulus has disappeared. **Long auditory storage,** in contrast, lasts several seconds; the material in this storage may be partly analyzed and transformed. Cowan suggests that a model of memory requires this longer kind of storage to account for a common phenomenon in auditory perception. Often, a single word spoken in a noisy environment cannot be deciphered until the listener has heard additional cues several seconds later in the sentence. Long auditory storage may retain this "mystery word," allowing later analysis.

Cowan makes an excellent point about the complexity of human cognitive processes. He notes that psychologists are taught to use parsimony as a guiding principle in constructing theories. That is, theories are supposed to be as simple as possible and still account for all the data. In the case of echoic memory, the rule of parsimony would suggest only a single kind of auditory memory storage. However, Cowan (1984) writes, "Nature may not equal this degree of parsimony" (p.

FIGURE 4.3

The Ability to Discriminate between Two Sounds (Based on Crowder, 1982a).

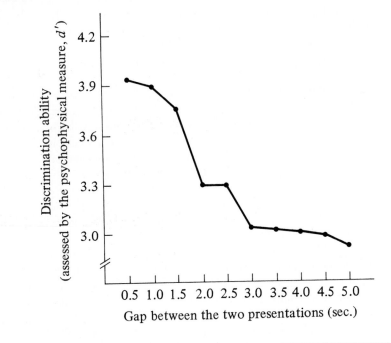

341). As we emphasize throughout this textbook, the truth about cognitive processes may be complex.

A final new development in echoic memory is that neuroscientists are beginning to study echoic memory. Näätänen and his colleagues in Finland use the evoked potential method described in Chapter 1 (Mäntysalo & Näätänen, 1987; Näätänen, 1986). In this research, a participant is told to concentrate on reading a book while a tone of a particular pitch is repeatedly presented. On some trials, however, a tone of a slightly different pitch is presented. By averaging together the values from the electroencephalograms, researchers have noticed that the new tone produces a shift in the wave pattern about 200 milliseconds after this tone has been presented. The neuronal representation decays about four seconds later, an interval that is roughly consistent with other estimates of the length of echoic memory. Researchers have tentatively located a site in the primary auditory cortex that seems to generate this change in the electroencephalogram. With additional research, we may be able to draw confident conclusions about the site within the brain where one component of echoic memory operates.

1. Sensory memory holds information in relatively unprocessed form; iconic memory and echoic memory have been studied most extensively.
2. Compared to short-term memory, sensory memory stores material for a shorter period of time; information is stored in a raw form that is fairly accurate, and registration is relatively passive.
3. Iconic memory has been repeatedly demonstrated. It lasts about 200 to 400 milliseconds and is roughly as helpful as about 100 milliseconds of additional stimulus viewing time.
4. Controversy has arisen over the location of iconic memory, the usefulness of the concept, and the ecological validity of the technique, although most researchers in this area support the concept. Iconic memory may involve several components.
5. Echoic memory has been demonstrated with a variety of techniques; it seems to last about 2 to 3 seconds.
6. Like iconic memory, echoic memory may not be unitary; a division between short auditory storage and long auditory storage has been proposed.
7. Neuroscientists have used the evoked potential method to examine the duration and the location of echoic memory in the auditory cortex.

SHORT-TERM MEMORY

You can probably recall a recent experience like this. You are standing in a telephone booth looking up a phone number. You find the number, repeat it to yourself, and close the phone book. You take out the coins, insert them, and raise your index finger to dial the number. Amazingly, you cannot remember it. The first digits were 586, and a 4 appeared somewhere, but you have no idea what the other numbers are!

This kind of forgetting occurs fairly often when you want to remember material for a short period of time. Perhaps 15 seconds pass while you close the phone book and insert the coins, yet some memories are so fragile that they evaporate before you can begin to use them. One characteristic of short-term memory specified in the Atkinson-Shiffrin (1968) model is that material is lost within 30 seconds unless it is somehow repeated.

Another characteristic of short-term memory described by Atkinson and Shiffrin is its clear-cut limits. You are certainly familiar with the strain you feel when you try to keep a list of items in short-term memory. Doesn't it seem that if one more item is added, one of the original items will need to be shoved out? These same limits are obvious when you try to learn how to do a new procedure that involves many rules or specifications (e.g., Carlson et al., 1989; Woltz, 1988). You

---

DEMONSTRATION 4.3

THE LIMITS OF SHORT-TERM MEMORY.

A. Try each of the following mental multiplication tasks. Be sure not to write down any of your calculations; do them entirely "in your head."
1. $7 \times 9 =$
2. $74 \times 9 =$
3. $74 \times 96 =$

B. Now read each of the following sentences, and construct a mental image of the action that is being described.
1. The repairperson departed.
2. The deliveryperson that the secretary met departed.
3. The salesperson that the doctor that the nurse despised met departed.

---

also become aware of these limits when you try mental arithmetic or read complicated sentences (Just & Carpenter, 1992; Waldrop, 1987). Demonstration 4.3 illustrates the limits of short-term memory for these two kinds of tasks. (Try each task in Sections A and B of Demonstration 4.3 before reading any further.) You probably had no difficulty with the first mathematics and reading tasks. The second tasks may have seemed more challenging, but manageable. The third tasks probably seemed beyond the limits of your short-term memory.

This part of the chapter explores the temporary storage of information, which is a feature of virtually all cognitive tasks (Schweickert, 1987). You may recall that Chapter 3 examined some of the research on short-term memory in connection with the Atkinson-Shiffrin model. In the current chapter, we will look at four topics: (1) the methodology in short-term memory research; (2) an in-depth coverage of the size of short-term memory; (3) the code in short-term memory; and (4) a new view of short-term memory, known as working memory.

The Methodology in Short-Term Memory Research

Demonstration 4.4 shows a modified version of the Brown/Peterson & Peterson technique, a method frequently used by researchers. John Brown (1958), a British psychologist, and Lloyd Peterson and Margaret Peterson (1959), two American psychologists, independently demonstrated that material held in memory for less than a minute could be forgotten. The technique therefore bears the names of both research groups.

DEMONSTRATION 4.4

A MODIFIED VERSION OF THE BROWN/PETERSON & PETERSON TECHNIQUE.

Take out five index cards. On one side of each card write a group of three words, one underneath another. On the opposite side write the three-digit number. Randomize the order of the cards and set them aside for a few minutes. Then show yourself the first card, with the side containing the words toward you, for about 2 seconds. Then immediately turn over the card and count backward by threes from the three-digit number. Go as fast as possible for 15–20 seconds. (If you can, convince a friend to time you.) Then write down as many of the three words as you can remember. Continue this process with the remaining four cards.

1. appeal
   temper   687
   burden
	4. flower
	   classic 573
	   predict

2. sober
   persuade   254
   content
	5. silken
	   idle 433
	   butcher

3. descend
   neglect   869
   elsewhere	

Peterson and Peterson, for example, asked people to study three letters. The participants then counted backward by threes for a short period and tried to recall the letters they had originally seen. On the first few trials, people recalled most of the letters. However, after several trials, the previous letters produced interference, and recall was poor. After a mere 5-second delay, people forgot approximately half of what they had seen. (See Figure 4.4.)

This dramatic demonstration of forgetting after a few seconds' delay had an important impact on memory research. Psychologists who had previously asked people to learn long lists of words—and recall them after lengthy delays—switched to investigating recall after just a few seconds' delay. The Brown/Peterson & Peterson technique was extremely popular during the 1960s and the early 1970s. As a consequence, psychologists conducted relatively little research on long-term memory during those years. Beginning in the late 1970s, researchers shifted their interest back to long-term memory, and this area of research is still more popular. Nonetheless, the early research using the Brown/Peterson & Peterson technique yielded important information about the fragility of memory for material stored just a few seconds.

FIGURE 4.4

Typical Results for Percentage Recalled with the Brown/Peterson & Peterson Technique.

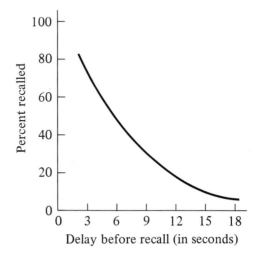

Two other techniques have been used in examining short-term memory. One way is to ask people to study a long list of items, perhaps 20 to 40 words long, and to recall as many of these words as possible. Then the researcher graphs the relationship between the position in which a word was presented (first, second, third, and so on) and the probability of recalling the word. Typically, the results resemble Figure 4.5. This relationship between a word's position and its recall is called a **serial position curve.** The curve usually shows accurate recall at the beginning and the end of the list and low recall in the middle (e.g., Greene & Samuel, 1986). Many researchers in short-term memory believe that the relatively accurate recall of words at the end of the list can be attributed to the fact that these items were still in short-term memory at the time of recall, although some researchers have proposed alternative interpretations (Baddeley & Hitch, 1993; Crowder, 1982b; R. L. Greene, 1986a, 1986b). Thus, one way of measuring the size of short-term memory is to count the number of accurately recalled items at the end of the list. Typically, the size of short-term memory is estimated to be two to seven items when the serial-position curve method is used.

More often, short-term memory size is measured in terms of **memory span,** or the number of items in a row that can be correctly recalled. Your ability to remember phone numbers is therefore a test of memory span. Several intelligence tests, such as the Wechsler Adult Intelligence Scale, include a test of memory span (Glanzer, 1982).

FIGURE 4.5

A Typical Serial Position Curve.

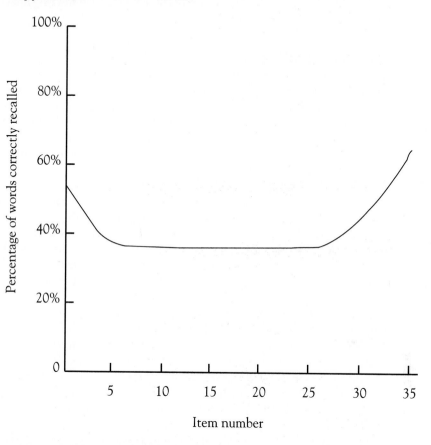

◇ *In Depth:* ***The Size of Short-Term Memory***

Suppose a friend told you his age: 19. You would have no trouble remembering that. Furthermore, you would have little trouble remembering a four-digit street address, such as 2614. However, a standard seven-digit phone number is more challenging—346-3421. If you add an area code to make the phone number 212-346-3421, you are unlikely to remember the entire number correctly. Clearly, short-term memory is limited (Anderson, 1991).

During the early excitement about short-term memory, researchers were convinced that we could specify with great precision the number of items that could be stored in short-term memory. However, more recent research suggests that pronunciation time is another important determinant of short-term memory. We also know that the storage capacity of short-term memory is not a simple issue; factors such as anxiety influence the number of items that can be held in temporary storage. Incidentally, the final section of this chapter—on working memory—raises additional questions about the size of short-term memory.

Miller's Magical Number. Researchers have been interested in the size of the memory span for more than a century. However, memory-span research gained particular importance in 1956 when George Miller wrote his famous article titled "The Magical Number Seven, Plus or Minus Two: Some Limits on Our Capacity for Processing Information." Miller proposed that people cannot keep many items in short-term memory at one time. Specifically, he suggested that people can remember about seven items (give or take two), or between five and nine items.

Miller used the term **chunk** to describe the basic unit in short-term memory. Thus, we can say that short-term memory holds about seven chunks. A chunk can be a single numeral or a single letter, because people can remember about seven numerals or letters if they are in random order. However, those numbers and letters can be organized into larger units. For example, perhaps your area code is 212 and all the phone numbers at your college begin with the same digits, 346. If 212 forms one chunk and 346 forms another chunk, then the phone number 212-346-3421 really contains only six chunks (that is, 1 + 1 + 4). It may be within your memory span.

Miller's (1956) article received major attention, and the concept of the magical number 7 ± 2 became a prominent fact known to most undergraduate psychology students. However, many people argued that Miller's term *chunk* was not a well-defined concept. For example, Simon (1974) complained that a major problem was that chunks were defined in a circular fashion. That is, a chunk is what there are seven of in short-term memory! In order for a chunk to be a more meaningful term, the chunk should be related to a different psychological task, independent of short-term memory performance.

The second task that Simon chose to examine was performance on long-term memory tasks. He reasoned that if the chunk is a real, legitimate concept, then the number of chunks in the stimulus list should be related to the amount of time that people take to commit a list to long-term memory. Simon then examined previous experiments that addressed this question. Indeed, the number of chunks in a stimulus showed a strong negative correlation with the amount of time required to learn that stimulus. He concluded that the chunk is a legitimate concept, because it is so closely related to learning time; and therefore, it is not simply an arbitrary term describing the seven units in memory.

Pronunciation Time. Other researchers have emphasized that pronunciation time may be even more important than the number of chunks formed by the items. For example, Schweickert and Boruff (1986) tested memory span for a variety of

---

DEMONSTRATION 4.5

PRONUNCIATION TIME AND MEMORY SPAN.

Read the following words. When you have finished, look away from the page and try to recall them.

    Chad, Burma, Greece, Cuba, Malta

Now try the task again with a different list of words. Again, read the words, look away, and recall them.

    Czechoslovakia, Somaliland, Nicaragua, Afghanistan, Venezuela

---

materials, such as consonants, numbers, nouns, shapes, color names, and nonsense words. With impressive consistency, people tended to recall the number of items that could be pronounced in about 1.5 seconds. These authors propose that the capacity of short-term memory is not determined by a fixed number of items or chunks in memory; instead, it is determined by the limited time for which the verbal trace of the items endures. In the case of nonsense syllables, a person might be able to pronounce only four items in 1.5 seconds; therefore, only four items will be recalled. In the case of numbers in the English language, a person can typically pronounce six items in 1.5 seconds, and so recall is somewhat greater. Incidentally, the importance of pronunciation time makes sense in light of the discussion in Chapter 3 of acoustic coding in short-term memory.

Researchers have also tested the pronunciation-time hypothesis for other kinds of items. Try Demonstration 4.5, which is a modification of a study by Baddeley and his colleagues (1975). These researchers found that people could accurately recall an average of 4.2 words from the list of countries with short names, but only 2.8 from the list of countries with long names.

However, the most systematic research has been conducted on the recall of numbers in a variety of languages. Naveh-Benjamin and Ayres (1986) tested memory spans for people who spoke English, Spanish, Hebrew, and Arabic. The English numbers between one and ten can be spoken rapidly; most of them are one-syllable words. Spanish and Hebrew have a somewhat greater average number of syllables for the numbers one to ten, and Arabic numbers are even longer. As you can see from Figure 4.6, the memory span is significantly greater for people speaking English than for people speaking the other three languages. Furthermore, the dotted line shows the pronunciation rate for each of the four languages. As you can see, greater memory spans result from languages that can be spoken rapidly. Clearly, pronunciation rate—as well as number of chunks—needs to be considered when discussing the capacity of short-term memory.

Anxiety and Memory Span. Numerous other factors influence the capacity of short-term memory. We'll look at just one factor, anxiety.

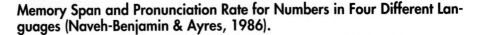

FIGURE 4.6

Memory Span and Pronunciation Rate for Numbers in Four Different Languages (Naveh-Benjamin & Ayres, 1986).

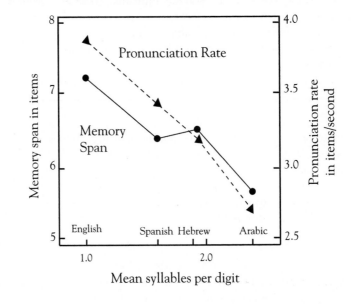

You probably will not be surprised to learn that highly anxious people have shorter memory spans than less anxious people. Darke (1988) administered a standardized measure, called the Test Anxiety Scale, to a large number of English-speaking college students. He then selected for further testing the students who scored in either the top 20 percent or the bottom 20 percent of the scale. Students in the high-anxiety group recalled an average of 8.8 numbers, whereas students in the low-anxiety group recalled an average of 10.4 numbers, a statistically significant difference. Naturally, factors other than anxiety (for example, intelligence) might be at least partly responsible for the difference in recall. Still, one reason that highly anxious people often perform poorly on examinations may be that anxiety can limit their memory span.

The Code in Short-Term Memory

Research on the capacity of short-term memory has received the best publicity. However, psychologists have been equally intrigued by the way material is coded. You may recall our discussion of acoustic coding in STM in the Atkinson-Shiffrin model (Chapter 3). Let's consider the issue in greater detail.

Suppose that you have just called the post office to find the zip code for a friend in Menlo Park, California. The clerk tells you "94025." How do you keep *94025* in your short-term memory until you can write it down? Do you store it in terms of the way it sounds, the way it looks, or some aspect of its meaning? In other words, how are items coded in your short-term memory?

You might be likely to answer that you seemed to code *94025* in terms of its sound. Can you almost "hear" yourself repeating *94025* over and over to yourself? In fact, you would probably code in terms of sound, even if you initially looked at a visual version of the zip code, located on a page of a directory. As you will see, the evidence strongly favors an acoustic code—that is, storage in terms of the sound of an item. However, as Postman (1975) and Crowder (1982b) warn us, the acoustic code is certainly not the only code used in short-term memory. An item can also be coded in terms of a **visual code,** involving the physical appearance of the item, or in terms of a **semantic code,** involving the item's meaning.

Acoustic Coding in Short-Term Memory. Numerous experiments have demonstrated the importance of acoustic coding in short-term memory (e.g., Conrad, 1964). The study by Kintsch and Buschke (1969), discussed in connection with the Atkinson-Shiffrin model, also supports acoustic coding. We will look at another representative study, performed by Wickelgren (1965). On each trial, Wickelgren presented a tape recording of an eight-item list, consisting of four letters and four digits in random order. Thus, a typical item might be *4NF9G27P.* As soon as the tape was finished, people tried to recall the list. Wickelgren was particularly interested in the kinds of substitutions people made. For example, if they did not correctly recall the *P* at the end of the list, what did they recall in its place? He found that people tended to substitute an item that was acoustically similar. For example, instead of the last *P,* they might substitute a *B, C, D, E, G, T,* or *V,* all letters with the "ee" sound. Furthermore, if they substituted a number for *P,* it would most likely be the similar-sounding number *3.*

Some recent research by Brandimonte and her colleagues (1992) shows that suppressing the acoustic coding in short-term memory can have an important effect on long-term memory. Let's compare the performance for two groups of participants in one of their studies. In one condition, which we'll call the control group, people saw six pictures of objects, such as the ones labeled "original picture" in Figure 4.7. The series was repeated until they knew the pictures in order. On the second task, they were asked to create a mental image of each picture in the series, and to subtract a specified part from each image. They were told to name the resulting image. For example, if they had created a mental image of the piece of candy in Figure 4.7 and they subtracted the specified part, they should end up describing the resulting image as a fish. Similarly, the pipe minus the specified part should be described as a bowl. The participants in this control condition succeeded in naming an average of 2.7 items correctly, out of a maximum of 6.0 items.

In a different condition, which involved verbal suppression, students performed the same tasks—with one exception: While they were learning the original list of

FIGURE 4.7

Two of the Stimuli Used in the Study by Brandimonte et al. (1992).

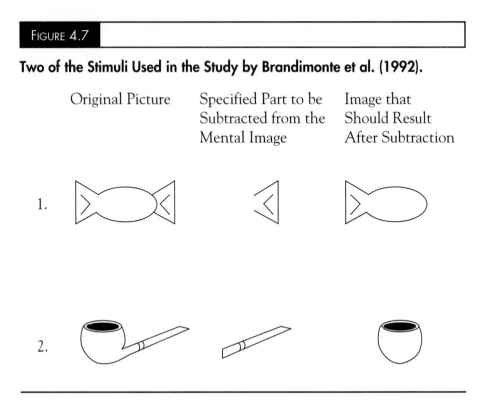

| Original Picture | Specified Part to be Subtracted from the Mental Image | Image that Should Result After Subtraction |

pictures, they were instructed to repeat an irrelevant sound (*la-la-la* . . .). Notice that this repetition would block the acoustic representation of each picture. You can't say *candy* or *pipe* to yourself if you are chanting *la-la-la* out loud! How well did these people do on the task of naming the image that was created by subtracting the specified part? As it turned out, they performed significantly better than people in the control condition, naming an average of 3.8 items correctly. Because acoustic coding was difficult, they were probably more likely to use visual coding. In the picture subtraction task, they found it relatively simple to subtract a part from a visual image. In contrast, the people in the control condition were more likely to use acoustical encoding. Therefore, they had difficulty subtracting a part from a stimulus that had been coded as a word, such as *candy* or *pipe*.

This research illustrates that we can encourage people to avoid acoustic encoding in short-term memory, and an alternate encoding may actually enhance later performance. Let's now consider these alternate encodings, specifically, visual and semantic codes.

Visual Coding in Short-Term Memory. As the research by Brandimonte and her coauthors showed, items can also be coded in short-term memory in terms of their visual characteristics. We will also discuss visual images in memory in Chapter 6.

One of the most convincing illustrations of visual coding in short-term memory was a study by Posner and Keele (1967). In their experiment, people saw pairs of letters such as A-A, A-a, A-B, and A-b. Sometimes the two letters were presented at the same time, but other times there was a brief delay between the two letters. In each case, people were requested to answer whether the letters had identical names or not. Posner and Keele were particularly interested to see whether people took longer to respond *yes* to A-a pairs than to A-A pairs. After all, if items are stored merely in terms of their *sounds*, then the response to A-a should be as fast as the response to A-A. However, if items are stored in terms of the way they look, then A-a pairs should take longer because the visual symbols must be translated into the appropriate names. A-A pairs, in contrast, would require no translation.

Posner and Keele found that when the delay between the two letters was less than 1.5 seconds, A-a pairs did indeed take longer than A-A pairs. However, when the delay was longer than 1.5 seconds, A-a pairs and A-A pairs took the same amount of time. Apparently, we initially code the pair A-a in terms of the physical appearance of the letters, but after 1.5 seconds the letters are coded in terms of the identical letter name, "Ay." Thus, a visual code can be stored in short-term memory for very brief periods. However, this visual code seems to be quite fragile, because it is soon replaced by an auditory code.

Semantic Coding in Short-Term Memory. We also have substantial evidence that items in short-term memory can be coded in terms of their meaning. For example, consider a study by Wickens and his colleagues (1976). Their technique is based on a concept from memory called proactive inhibition. **Proactive inhibition (PI)** means that people have trouble learning new material because previously learned material keeps interfering with new learning. Suppose you had previously learned the items *XCJ*, *HBR*, and *TSV* in a Brown/Peterson & Peterson test of short-term memory. You will then have trouble remembering a fourth item, *KRN*, because the three previous items keep interfering. However, if the experimenter shifts the category of the fourth item from letters to, say, numbers, your memory will improve. You will experience a **release from proactive inhibition;** performance on the new, different item (say, *529*) will be almost as high as it had been on the first item, *XCJ*.

Many experiments have demonstrated release from PI when the category of items is shifted, as from letters to numbers. However, Wickens and his coauthors (1976) demonstrated that release from PI could also be obtained when the semantic class of items is shifted. They gave people three trials on the Brown/Peterson & Peterson test, with each trial consisting of three names of fruits, similar to those in Table 4.1. Thus, on Trial 1 a person might see *banana*, *peach*, and *apple*, followed by the three-digit number 259. After counting backward by threes from this number for 18 seconds, they tried to recall the three words.

TABLE 4.1

THE SETUP FOR EXPERIMENTS ON RELEASE FROM PI.

CONDITION	TRIAL 1	TRIAL 2	TRIAL 3	TRIAL 4
Fruits (control)	banana peach apple	plum apricot lime	melon lemon grape	orange cherry pineapple
Vegetables	banana peach apple	plum apricot lime	melon lemon grape	onion radish potato
Flowers	banana peach apple	plum apricot lime	melon lemon grape	daises violet tulip
Meats	banana peach apple	plum apricot lime	melon lemon grape	salami bacon hamburger
Professions	banana peach apple	plum apricot lime	melon lemon grape	doctor teacher lawyer

Everyone received the same three trials concerning fruits, but five different kinds of material were presented on the fourth trial: fruits, vegetables, flowers, meats, and professions. We would expect the buildup of PI to be the greatest for the people who had to remember fruits on the fourth trial; their performance should be poor. After all, their memories should be full of other fruits that would be interfering with the new fruits. However, if meaning is important in short-term memory, performance in the other four conditions should depend upon the semantic similarity between these items and fruit. For example, people who received vegetables on the fourth trial should do rather poorly, since fruits and vegetables are similar—they are both edible and grow in the ground. People who received flowers and meats should do somewhat better, because flowers and meats share only one attribute with fruits. However, people who received professions should do the best of all, because professions are not edible and do not grow in the ground.

Figure 4.8 is an example of the kind of results every researcher hopes to find. Note that the results are exactly as predicted. In summary, meaning is important in short-term memory because old words interfere with the recall of new words

FIGURE 4.8

Release from PI, as a Function of Semantic Similarity (Based on Wickens et al., 1976).

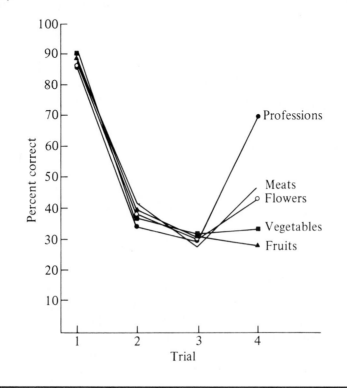

that are similar in meaning. Furthermore, the degree of semantic similarity is related to the amount of interference.

In this section, we have explored the various ways in which information is stored in short-term memory. An auditory code is most common. However, in certain situations, people can use either visual or semantic codes.

Working Memory: A New View of Short-Term Memory

Earlier, we noted that many current researchers and theorists are proposing that neither iconic memory nor echoic memory is unitary. They argue, instead, that iconic memory and echoic memory each have at least two components. Therefore, you should not be surprised to learn that psychologists have also proposed several components for short-term memory. As Schneider (1993) emphasizes, multiple memory systems have evolved that are specialized for different tasks.

Alan Baddeley (1986, 1992) has developed the most complete description of a multicomponent interpretation of short-term memory, which he calls working memory. According to Baddeley, **working memory** is a three-part system that temporarily holds and manipulates information as we perform cognitive tasks. Notice that Baddeley's working memory is not simply a passive storehouse with a number of shelves to hold chunks of information. His emphasis on the manipulation of information means that working memory is more like a workbench where material is constantly being handled, combined, and transformed.

Before we examine the three components, let's see why Baddeley felt compelled to conclude that working memory is not unitary. In a classic study, Baddeley and Hitch (1974) presented a string of random numbers and instructed people to rehearse them while performing a reasoning task. The sequence of numbers varied in length from zero to eight items. Thus, the longer list approached the upper limit of short-term memory, according to the 7 ± 2 proposal. The reasoning task required participants to judge whether certain statements about letter order were correct or incorrect. For example, when the two letters BA appeared, participants should respond to the statement "A follows B" by pressing a "yes" button. If BA was accompanied by the statement "B follows A," participants should press the "no" button.

Imagine yourself performing this task. Wouldn't you think you would take longer and make more errors if you had to keep rehearsing eight numerals, instead of only one? In fact, Baddeley and Hitch discovered that people required less than a second longer when instructed to rehearse eight numerals, in contrast to a task that required no rehearsal. Even more impressive, the error rate remained at about 5 percent, no matter how many numerals the participants rehearsed! These data clearly contradicted the view that temporary storage has only about seven slots. Instead, short-term memory or working memory seems to have several components, which can operate partially independently of each other. Baddeley proposed three components for working memory: a phonological loop, a visuospatial sketch pad, and a central executive (Baddeley, 1986, 1988, 1992; Baddeley & Hitch, 1974).

Phonological Loop. According to Baddeley's model, the **phonological loop** stores a limited number of sounds, and the memory trace decays within 2 seconds unless the material is rehearsed. Notice that this description is consistent with the information on pronunciation time discussed in the In-Depth section. Because the material in the phonological loop is coded acoustically, items that sound the same are also confused with one another and are more readily forgotten.

Recent research by Martin (1993) provides neuropsychological evidence for a separate phonological loop. Martin tested a woman known as E. A. who demonstrated normal sentence comprehension. However, she showed a very specific deficit for remembering phonological information. For example, she could not retain words presented in Spanish. Apparently, the phonological loop is not critical for language comprehension.

Visuospatial Sketch Pad. According to Baddeley's model, the second component of working memory is the **visuospatial sketch pad,** which stores visual and spatial information—much like how you use a pad of paper to work out a problem in geometry. Chapter 6 examines the kinds of mental manipulations we perform on visual images, such as rotating and comparing them. In the study by Brandimonte and his colleagues (1992), the people who were instructed to repeat *la-la-la* were presumably forced to use the visuospatial sketch pad because their phonological loop was busy repeating the syllable.

Like the phonological loop, the capacity of the visuospatial sketch pad is limited (Frick, 1988, 1990). If you try to solve a geometry problem on a scratch pad that's too small, you will make some errors. Similarly, when too many items are supplied to the sketch pad, you cannot represent them accurately enough to be successfully recovered. Keep in mind, however, that the limits of the phonological loop and the visuospatial sketch pad are independent. As Baddeley and Hitch (1974) discovered, you can rehearse numbers in the phonological loop while making decisions about the spatial arrangement of letters on the visuospatial sketch pad.

Central Executive. According to Baddeley's model, the **central executive** integrates information from the phonological loop and the visuospatial sketch pad, as well as from long-term memory; the central executive also plays a major role in attention and in planning and controlling behavior (Baddeley, 1988, 1992; Morris, 1987; Morris & Jones, 1990). Baddeley (1992) admits that the central executive is more difficult to study using research techniques, in comparison to the other two systems. However, it plays a critical role in the overall functions of working memory. As Baddeley (1986) points out, if we concentrate on, say, the phonological loop, the situation would resemble a critical analysis of *Hamlet* that focuses on a minor character Polonius and completely ignores the prince of Denmark!

Baddeley proposes that the central executive works like a supervisor or scheduler. The executive decides which issues deserve attention and which should be ignored. The executive also selects strategies, figuring out how to tackle a problem. We will examine this issue of strategy selection more completely in Chapter 7, in connection with metacognition. Finally, like any competent supervisor, the central executive gathers information from a variety of sources. To continue this metaphor, the central executive in working memory synthesizes the information from the two assistants, the phonological loop and the visuospatial sketch pad, and also from the large library known as long-term memory. In the next chapter, we will examine the characteristics of this remarkable storehouse. In contrast to the restricted capacity of sensory memory and short-term memory, long-term memory has no limits.

SECTION SUMMARY: SHORT-TERM MEMORY

1. As the Brown/Peterson & Peterson technique shows, a large proportion of material is forgotten in short-term memory after just a few seconds' delay.

2. The size of short-term memory is small; according to Miller's classic article, it is limited to 7 ± 2 chunks, but others argue that it is more closely related to pronunciation time; that is, with longer words, less material is remembered. In addition, short-term memory is influenced by factors such as an individual's anxiety level.

3. Information in short-term memory is usually stored in terms of an auditory code; however, in some circumstances, semantic and visual cues can also be used.

4. According to Baddeley's model of short-term memory, working memory consists of a phonological loop and a visuospatial sketch pad—each of which has independent capacity limits—and a central executive that integrates information, plans, and controls behavior.

CHAPTER REVIEW QUESTIONS

1. Think of an example of echoic memory and of short-term memory (one stored in terms of an auditory code). Try to recall the list of distinctions between sensory memory and short-term memory from the beginning of the chapter and point out how those two examples illustrate these distinctions.

2. We discussed sensory memory for sights and sounds. Sperling's (1960) method of examining iconic memory was modified to test echoic memory. Describe these studies. How could the method be adapted to test sensory memory for touch?

3. Explain why sensory memory is necessary in vision and hearing. How is sensory memory related to the information about attention discussed in Chapter 2? Why is sensory memory necessary for pattern recognition (also discussed in Chapter 2)?

4. When the concept of iconic memory was first proposed, it was greeted enthusiastically. More recently, this concept has inspired controversy. Discuss recent developments and arguments in this area.

5. According to a quote by Cowan in this chapter, echoic memory may not be as simple as we once thought. Review Cowan's proposal about two kinds of echoic memory and point out how one of these may share some characteristics with short-term memory.

6. Describe Miller's classic notion about the magical number 7. Why are chunks relevant to this notion, and what more recent evidence suggests that this number may not be as firm as we once thought?

7. Which component of Baddeley's model is relevant for the research on pronunciation time? Describe this research and point out what the research suggests about the limits of this component of working memory.

8. The section on anxiety and short-term memory described a study about individual differences in anxiety level. Speculate how each of these findings might be integrated into Baddeley's concept of working memory.

9. What kinds of codes can be used for items stored in short-term memory? Review the research that has been conducted in this area.

10. Why did Baddeley reject the classic conception of a single storehouse for short-term memory? What did he suggest instead? Can you think of examples from your own experience where you make simultaneous use of Baddeley's two proposed storehouses?

11. Recent theories of sensory memory have proposed dividing both iconic memory and echoic memory into two or more components. However, no one has suggested a concept similar to a central executive for sensory memory. Can you think why the concept of a central executive is not necessary for sensory memory?

NEW TERMS

sensory memory	long auditory storage
short-term memory	serial position curve
sensory storage	memory span
sensory register	chunk
iconic memory	visual code
icon	semantic code
whole-report technique	proactive inhibition (PI)
partial-report technique	release from proactive inhibition
mask	working memory
echoic memory	phonological loop
echo	visuospatial sketch pad
short auditory storage	central executive

RECOMMENDED READINGS

Baddeley, A. (1986). *Working memory*. Oxford, England: Clarendon Press. This book provides a comprehensive discussion of Baddeley's model of working memory, including background history, relevant research, and speculations.

Baddeley, A. (1990). *Human memory: Theory and practice*. Boston: Allyn and Bacon. Baddeley's textbook provides a good description of sensory memory and places the discussion of working memory within the general topic of short-term memory; Chapters 2 through 5 are especially relevant.

Just, M. A., & Carpenter, P. A. (1992). A capacity theory of comprehension: Individual differences in working memory. *Psychological Review, 99*, 122–149. This review article outlines why working memory is important in language comprehension; it therefore provides a good bridge between the current material on short-term memory and the material you will read in Chapter 8.

C H A P T E R   5

LONG-TERM MEMORY

PREVIEW

A number of factors can dramatically influence the accuracy of long-term memory. For example, if you have ever returned to a once-familiar location and experienced a flood of long-lost memories, you know the importance of context. Memory accuracy can also be influenced by the way memory is assessed, as the In-Depth section on explicit versus implicit memory illustrates. Mood also affects recall; for example, memory is better when the material being learned is consistent with a person's current mood. Finally, people who have expert knowledge in an area recall more than novices.

One important topic in the research on autobiographical memory is flashbulb memories, which bring forth a vivid memory about an emotionally arousing event. Because memory is influenced by our general knowledge about objects and events (schemas), we sometimes mistakenly "recall" events that never really happened. We may also have difficulty deciding whether we truly performed an action we intended to do, or we may forget to perform an action in the future. The research on eyewitness testimony has implications for the courtroom, and the debate about ecological validity considers whether research on real-world topics such as eyewitness testimony is more useful than laboratory research.

In the third section of this chapter, we consider three mnemonic devices: visual imagery; the method of loci (in which items are linked with locations); and organization. We also examine four more general strategies: external memory aids; practice; a multimodal approach (which emphasizes the complexity of factors that influence memory); and metamemory, which is your knowledge about your memory.

INTRODUCTION

Chapter 4 emphasized the fragility of sensory and short-term memory. All too often, information that we want to retain will disappear from memory—after less than a minute. In contrast, this chapter demonstrates that material retained in long-term memory can be amazingly resistant to forgetting.

Think about the information stored in your own long-term memory. For example, can you recall the details about how you learned you had been accepted into the college you now attend? If you received a letter of acceptance, for instance, can you remember where you were standing when you opened the letter, what you were wearing, and whom you told first? Or perhaps you recognize a magazine advertisement, even though you originally saw that ad several years earlier. Indeed, Standing (1973) found that people who had seen 10,000 pictures later recognized most of them. From one set of pictures, he estimated that if people were shown 1,000,000 pictures, they would retain 731,400 of them 2 days later.

Twentieth-century residents of industrialized countries need to have enormous memory capacities (Cohen, 1989). We continuously meet new people, travel to unfamiliar places, and master new skills. During almost every waking moment, we are bombarded with written and spoken information. Think about the number of items you need to learn and remember in an average day, and contrast your memory requirements with those of a resident of a rural community in the 1600s. People rarely met an unfamiliar person. They carried out similar activites each day and rarely traveled beyond their own community. Isn't it amazing that you can store thousands of times more material in your own memory, using virtually the same cognitive equipment? You may forget some information, as any test-taker can verify. However, consistent with Theme 2, long-term memory is remarkably efficient (Cohen, 1989).

We must also admire the length of time for which memories can be stored. At some point while you are reading this chapter, try Demonstration 5.1, which illustrates the durability of some memories. This demonstration is based on the research of Bahrick (1984), who tested retention of Spanish learned in high school or college. The interval between acquisition and retrieval ranged from 0 to 50 years. The participants recall was far from perfect. However, even 50 years later, people remembered about 40 percent of the vocabulary, idioms, and grammar they had originally learned. Bahrich proposed the name **permastore** to refer to this relatively permanent, very long-term form of memory.

Only a handful of studies have attempted to explore long-term memories that endure for half a century. Most of the research discussed in the present chapter examines retention intervals of a few minutes or several hours. We will begin by considering some factors that influence accuracy. The second section discusses autobiographical memory for the events in one's own life. The last section of the chapter suggests strategies for memory improvement.

DETERMINANTS OF ACCURACY

We have noted that long-term memory is typically robust. Individuals can remember a large number of vocabulary words from a foreign language, even though a half-century has passed since they learned that *abajo* means *down*. As you might expect, accuracy is influenced by a number of factors; we will examine four of these factors in this section.

Although these four factors may at first glance seem unrelated, each focuses on the importance of context. This textbook first emphasized contextual issues in Chapter 2, when we saw how context facilitates pattern recognition. Furthermore, in Chapter 3, the discussion of the levels of processing approach examined how memory depends upon context. We saw that recall is good when the context at the time of retrieval matches the context at the time of encoding. For example, people performed well on a retrieval task that emphasized the sound of a word if the encoding task had required judgments about whether two words sounded similar. In contrast, recall is poor when retrieval context does not match encoding context. For example, people performed poorly on a retrieval task emphasizing a word's sound if the encoding task had required judgments about word meaning.

DEMONSTRATION 5.1

VERY LONG-TERM MEMORY.

For this demonstration, you will need to locate at least one person who studied either Spanish or French but has not used the language in the last year. Ask the volunteer how many years have passed since studying the foreign language. Then hand him or her the appropriate list of vocabulary words (either in Spanish or French), with the instructions to take as long as necessary to supply the English translation. (The answers are at the end of the chapter.)

Spanish

1. ferrocarril _____
2. gato _____
3. hermana _____
4. cama _____
5. cabeza _____
6. manzana _____
7. corazón _____
8. zapato _____
9. silla _____
10. cocina _____

11. camino _____
12. diablo _____
13. naranja _____
14. pájaro _____
15. abuelo _____
16. brazo _____
17. falda _____
18. desayuno _____
19. ventana _____
20. luna _____

French

1. chemin de fer _____
2. chat _____
3. sœur _____
4. lit _____
5. tête _____
6. pomme _____
7. cœur _____
8. chaussure _____
9. chaise _____
10. cuisine _____

11. rue _____
12. satan _____
13. orange _____
14. oiseau _____
15. grand-père _____
16. bras _____
17. jupe _____
18. petit déjeuner _____
19. fenêtre _____
20. lune _____

You may wish to locate several individuals, so that you can determine whether recall decreases for longer retention intervals. (To provide a larger sample, your instructor may choose to gather the data from the entire class.) Incidentally, Bahrick (1984) found that recall for Spanish-English vocabulary declined rapidly in the initial years when people were no longer actively studying Spanish, but the decrease then leveled off after about three years.

In the current section on determinants of accuracy, context emerges once again as an important factor. We will begin by directly addressing the issue of context, elaborating on encoding specificity. Then the In-Depth section explores how memory can be measured either explicitly or implicitly. Explicit measures emphasize top-down processing; when retrieval is assessed by an explicit measure, performance is better when encoding also emphasized top-down processing. In contrast, implicit measures emphasize bottom-up processing; when retrieval is assessed by an implicit measure, performance is better when encoding also emphasized bottom-up processing.

The research on mood also underscores the importance of context. For example, people recall material more accurately if its emotional tone matches their mood. Furthermore, people often remember material better if their mood during encoding matches their mood during recall.

The final determinant of accuracy—expertise—is related to context in a different fashion. As we will demonstrate, a person's expertise is limited to a specific context. For example, someone who is an expert in chess may not be astonishingly talented in other domains.

The importance of context emphasizes the complexities of human long-term memory. We cannot consider an isolated learner, someone who is oblivious to the richness of contextual cues in the outside world. Instead, humans are situated within a broader framework, and they take their surroundings into account (e.g., Lave, 1988). Let us begin our discussion of determinants of accuracy by exploring this context in more detail.

The Effects of Context: Encoding Specificity

Does this scenario sound familiar? You are in the bedroom and realize that you need something from the kitchen. Once you arrive in the kitchen, however, you have no idea why you made the trip. Without the context in which you encoded the item you wanted, you cannot retrieve this memory. You return to the bedroom, which is rich with contextual cues, and you immediately remember what you wanted. Similarly, an isolated question on an exam may look completely unfamiliar, although you would have remembered the answer in the correct context.

These examples illustrate the **encoding specificity principle,** which states that recall is better if the retrieval context is like the encoding context (Begg & White, 1985; Tulving, 1983). In contrast, forgetting occurs when the two contexts do not match. Let's consider more information about the importance of context in long-term memory.

Research on Encoding Specificity.
In a representative study, Geiselman and Glenny (1977) presented words visually to the participants in their experiment. The participants were asked to imagine each of the words as being spoken by a familiar person; some were instructed to imagine a female voice, and others were

FIGURE 5.1

Percentage of Participants Who Correctly Recognized a Word, as a Function of Encoding Condition and Retrieval Condition (Based on Geiselman and Glenny, 1977).

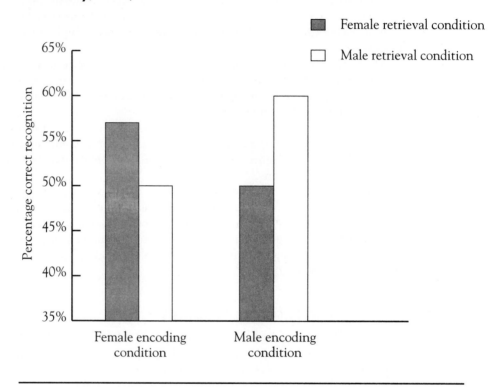

instructed to imagine a male voice. Later, recognition was tested by having a male or a female speaker say each word; the participants were instructed to indicate whether each word was old or new. For some people, the gender of the speaker matched the gender of the imagined voice; others had a mismatch between the encoding context and the retrieval context. As Figure 5.1 illustrates, recognition was substantially more likely when the contexts matched. This study also illustrates that "context" is not limited to physical locations; context can include other cues present during encoding and recall, such as a speaker's voice or your own mood.

Everyone reading this book can readily think of real-life examples of the importance of context. Psychologists have also explained why context effects help us to function even more effectively in our daily lives. After all, we don't want to remember numerous details that were important in a previous context but are no longer relevant (Bjork & Bjork, 1988). For instance, you don't want your memory to be cluttered with details about your third-grade classroom or the class-trip you took in high school.

However, we have a problem: context effects are sometimes difficult to demonstrate reliably in the laboratory (Bjork & Richardson-Klavehn, 1987; Smith, 1988). An inspection of the 29 laboratory research studies on this topic found that 27 showed at least some evidence of context effects (Smith, 1988). However, psychologists have difficulty explaining why context effects may be important in one experiment (e.g., Smith et al., 1978), and yet context has absolutely no influence in a highly similar replication experiment (e.g., Bjork & Richardson-Klavehn, 1987).

One explanation for some of the inconsistencies is called the outshining hypothesis. This explanation is based on a principle from astronomy (Smith, 1988). Imagine that you are looking up in the sky on a moonless night, and you can just barely see a particular star. You would have more difficulty seeing this star when the moon is full, and the star would be completely outshone by the sun in the daytime. Similarly, the **outshining hypothesis** proposes that context can trigger memory when better memory cues are absent; however, context can be completely outshone when other, better cues are present. In general, when the material to be recalled has been well learned, then the memory cues from that material should be strong enough to outshine the relatively weak context cues. When the material has *not* been well learned, context cues can help trigger memory (Smith, 1988). In short, context should be especially important when you have not yet mastered the material.

Other Illustrations of Context Effects. Let's consider two variations of the context-effects research that have practical implications. First, several psychologists have shown that the context in which human faces are observed can influence the ability to remember the faces (Davies, 1988). You can certainly remember occasions in which you have failed to recognize a classmate whom you see in a new setting.

The second variation is relevant to Chapter 6 on imagery. We can enhance memory by trying to *imagine* the context in which we originally encoded information (Smith, 1988). Have you ever tried to create a mental image of a page from a textbook to help reconstruct the answer to a question on a test? Smith (1988) suggests an additional factor—in addition to the outshining hypothesis—to explain some of the inconsistencies in the research on context effects. Specifically, in the conditions where researchers do not reinstate the actual context cues, the participants may spontaneously reinstate their own imaginary versions. Sometimes you don't need to return to the bedroom to remember why you had departed for the kitchen; a mental image of the bedroom may trigger your memory.

In summary, then, memory is sometimes enhanced when the retrieval context resembles the encoding context, though the context effect may be outshone when stronger memory cues are present. Furthermore, the effects of context can be demonstrated for visual material such as human faces—as well as verbal material—and also when context is created through mental imagery.

◇ In Depth: **Explicit Versus Implicit Measures of Memory**

Imagine this scene. A young woman is walking aimlessly down the street, and she is eventually picked up by the police. She seems to be suffering from an extreme form of amnesia, because she has lost all memory of who she is. Unfortunately, she is carrying no identification. Then the police have a breakthrough idea; they ask her to begin dialing phone numbers. As it turns out, she dials her mother's number—though she is not aware whose number she is dialing.

Daniel Schacter tells this story to illustrate the difference between explicit and implicit measures of memory—a difference that can be demonstrated for people with normal memory as well as for those who have amnesia (Adler, 1991). Let us clarify the basic concepts of this distinction and then look at some research.

Definitions and Examples. Demonstration 5.2 provides two examples of explicit memory measures and two examples of implicit memory measures. Try these examples before you read further.

An **explicit memory measure** requires the participants to remember information. Almost all of the research we have discussed in Chapters 3, 4, and 5 have used explicit memory tests. The most common explicit memory measure is **recall,** in which the participant must reproduce items that had been learned earlier. Another explicit memory measure is **recognition,** in which the participant must identify which items on a list had appeared on a previous list.

In contrast, an **implicit memory measure** requires the participant to perform a task—to *do* something. In Schacter's anecdote about the woman with amnesia, dialing a phone number was a test of implicit memory. Implicit memory shows the effects of previous experience that creep out in our ongoing behavior, when we are not making a conscious effort to recall the past (Roediger, 1991).

Researchers have devised numerous measures of implicit memory; you tried two of these in Demonstration 5.2. If the words in the original list were stored in your memory, you would complete those words (for example, *vessel* and *village*) faster than words that had not been on the list (for example, *letter* and *plastic*). Furthermore, you would be likely to supply those words on a **repetition priming task,** in which a recent exposure to an item affects the way you process it. In contrast, words that were not primed—because they did not appear on the list—would be less likely to be supplied as answers to those questions. (Thus, the words *kitchen, reindeer,* and *bookstore* would be relatively likely to be supplied as answers to the three questions, in contrast to unprimed words.)

One of the critical distinctions between explicit and implicit memory measures is that explicit memory tasks require conscious recollection of previous experiences

DEMONSTRATION 5.2

EXPLICIT AND IMPLICIT MEMORY MEASURES.

Take out a piece of scratch paper. Then read the following list of words:

picture   commerce   motion   village   vessel   window   number   reindeer
custom   amount   fellow   advice   dozen   flower   kitchen   bookstore

Now cover up that list. Take a break for a few minutes and then try the following tasks:

A. Explicit Memory Measures
   1. Recall: On the piece of scratch paper, write down as many of those words as you can recall.

   2. Recognition: From the list below, circle the words that appeared on the original list:

   woodpile   fellow   leaflet   fitness   number   butter   motion   table
   people   dozen   napkin   picture   kitchen   bookstore   cradle   advice

B. Implicit Memory Measures
   1. Word completion: From the word fragments below, provide an appropriate, complete word.

   v s e _   l t e _   v l a e _   p a t c _   m t o _   m n a _   n t b o _
   c m e c _   a v c _   t b e _   f o e _   c r o _   h m w r   b o s o e _

   2. Repetition priming: Perform the following tasks:
      • Name three rooms in a typical house.
      • Name three items associated with Christmas.
      • Name three different kinds of stores.

(Graf & Schacter, 1985; Hirst, 1989). For example, you needed to make a conscious effort to remember the words on the original list in order to decide whether the word *fellow* had appeared there. In contrast, implicit memory tasks do not require conscious recollection of previous experiences. To complete the word *village* from the fragments, you did not need to recall having seen it on the original list. In fact, you probably could have completed that word rapidly, even if you did not remember the word during the two explicit memory tasks.

You may recall that consciousness was discussed in Chapter 2 in connection with perceptual attention. In that chapter, we examined Nisbett and Wilson's

(1977) argument that we often have little direct awareness of our thought processes. Lockhart (1989) points out that implicit memory may be the norm—especially if we include infants and nonhuman species, and explicit memory may be limited to some of the activities of the most highly evolved species.

Clearly, implicit memory is one of the "hot topics" in current research on memory (Mitchell, 1991). Psychologists are excited about paradoxes, and paradoxes are common when we compare performance on explicit and implicit memory tasks. In some studies, amnesic patients perform disastrously on explicit memory tasks, but they score well on implicit memory tasks. In other studies involving people with normal memories, experimental variables have potent effects on one kind of test, but no effects (or even the opposite effect) on the other kind of test (Schacter et al., 1989). Let's now consider the experimental research on explicit and implicit memory.

Research on Amnesic Patients. Some of the pioneering work on implicit memory in amnesics was conducted by Elizabeth Warrington and Lawrence Weiskrantz (1970). They examined four amnesics, one whose temporal lobe had been surgically removed and three with Korsakoff's syndrome, a disorder associated with severe alcoholism, which involves brain damage and amnesia. These researchers presented some English words and then gave the amnesics recall and recognition tasks. Compared to normal control group participants, the amnesics performed much poorer on both of these explicit memory tasks.

So far, then, the results are not surprising. However, both groups also completed two implicit memory tasks. These were presented as word guessing games, though they actually assessed recall for words shown earlier. In one, the previously presented English words were shown in a mutilated form that was difficult to read. Participants were told to guess which word was represented. In the second implicit memory task, people saw the first few letters, and they were instructed to produce the first word that came to mind. Amazingly, the implicit memory performance of the amnesics and the control group participants were virtually identical. Both groups correctly identified about 45 percent of the mutilated words, and both groups correctly completed about 65 percent of the word stems. These results have been replicated many times since the original research, as noted in reviews of the literature (e.g., MacLeod & Bassili, 1989; Roediger, 1990).

The research by Warrington and Weiskrantz (1970) is a good example of a concept called *dissociation*. A **dissociation** occurs when a variable has large effects on one kind of test, but little or no effects on another kind of test; a dissociation also occurs when a variable has one kind of effect if measured by Test A, and the opposite effect if measured by Test B (Roediger et al., 1989). Thus, the term dissociation is similar to the concept of a statistical interaction, which you may already know from a course in statistics. In Warrington and Weiskrantz's data, the dissociation was evident because the variable of memory status (amnesic versus control) had a major effect when measured by explicit memory tests and no effect when measured by implicit memory tests.

These results and similar findings on amnesics might have been dismissed as simply an interesting quirk, limited to a small number of people with a memory deficit. However, researchers then discovered similar dissociations in data collected on normal adults.

Research with Normal Adults. A variety of studies have demonstrated dissociations in adults who have no identified brain damage. For example, normal people may score higher on an explicit test when they have processed stimuli semantically rather than perceptually. On an implicit test, however, they may score higher when the material is processed perceptually rather than semantically. (e.g., Jacoby, 1983).

Let's look in more detail at an excellent example of dissociation, using normal college students. Mary Susan Weldon and Henry Roediger (1987) decided to examine a well-known phenomenon called the picture superiority effect. Research on the **picture superiority effect** shows that pictures are usually remembered better than words. In typical research, participants study either pictures that have obvious names (for example, a picture of an elephant) or names of concrete objects (for example, the word *elephant*). Later, they are asked to recall names of the items seen previously. They typically recall a significantly larger number of pictures than names.

Previous research had tested the picture superiority effect only with explicit memory measures, specifically, recall and recognition. What would happen if memory were assessed using implicit memory measures—in addition to explicit measures?

Weldon and Roediger (1987) showed students slides that contained either a simple black-on-white line drawing or the typed name of a concrete object. Later, the students either supplied recall (an explicit measure) or completed a word fragment, such as e_ep_n_ for the word *elephant* (an implicit measure). They were allowed 5 minutes for the recall task, and they were allowed to recall the words in any order they wished. For the word-fragment task, they were allowed 20 seconds for each item. They also completed word fragments for other, similar items that had not appeared on the slides, to provide a comparison with nonstudied items.

Figure 5.2 shows how recall depends upon the original method of processing. As you can see, the explicit memory measure showed the usual picture superiority effect; participants recalled more of the items originally seen as pictures, rather than words. Notice, however, that the results are dramatically reversed for the implicit memory measure. On this word-fragment task, they performed much better on the items originally seen as words, rather than pictures. In fact, their performance on the items originally seen as pictures was not much better than their performance on some nonstudied items. In other words, Figure 5.2 clearly illustrates

FIGURE 5.2

Performance on a Recall Test and a Word-Completion Task, as a Function of Method of Presentation (Picture or Name) (Based on Weldon & Roediger, 1987).

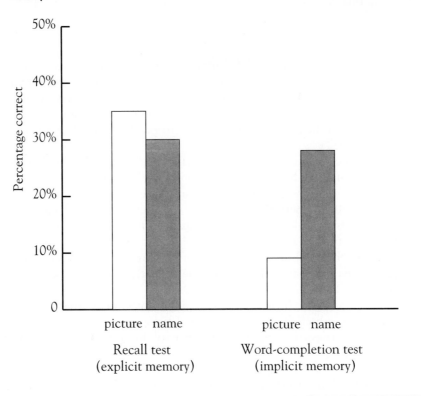

a dissociation, with different results for explicit memory measures than for implicit memory measures.

Roediger and his colleagues explain how these results resemble the encoding specificity principle examined in the previous section (Roediger, 1990; Roediger et al., 1989). That is, test performance is better when the retrieval context is like the encoding context. These authors argue that when people saw a picture of an elephant, their encoding emphasized top-down processing, with the meaning of the elephant receiving special prominence. They argue that explicit memory tests—such as free-recall tests—emphasize top-down processing. Therefore, performance is good because the two contexts match. Similarly, when people saw the word *elephant,* they encoded the word in terms of its letters (emphasizing bottom-up processing). Implicit memory tests—such as word-completion tests—emphasize

---

DEMONSTRATION 5.3

LISTS OF ITEMS.

Take out a piece of paper and make three columns of numbers from 1 to 10. For the first set of numbers, list 10 colors in any order you wish. For the next set, list 10 desserts. Finally, list 10 professors from whom you have taken courses.

Now arrange each of the three lists in alphabetical order on a separate piece of paper, and set the original lists aside. Rank each item with respect to the other members of the list. For example, give your favorite color a rank of 1 and your least favorite color a rank of 10. Finally, transfer each of those ranks back to the original list. At this point, each of the 10 items on each of the three lists should now have a rank next to it.

---

bottom-up processing. Once again, performance is good because the two contexts match. In contrast, the encoding specificity principle states that retrieval is poor when the retrieval context does not match the encoding context, and the data in Figure 5.2 certainly confirm this part of the principle.

Current Status of Implicit Memory. The excitement about implicit memory seems to be growing even stronger in the 1990s, as memory researchers explore these new ways of assessing memory. However, the explanations for the numerous examples of dissociation—and for other discoveries about implicit memory—are not yet focused. Some psychologists favor explanations emphasizing context and the encoding specificity principle. Others propose that the results can best be explained in terms of multiple memory systems, such as Tulving's theory that we examined in Chapter 3 (e.g., Schacter, 1990; Tulving & Schacter, 1990).

Other researchers are attempting to relate the new information about implicit memory to other areas, such as social psychology and developmental psychology (Roediger, 1990). Some have also speculated about the implications for education (Roediger, 1990). For example, educators may want to use implicit memory tests, rather than explicit memory tests, to assess some forms of learning. Furthermore, researchers should examine how advertisers and the media affect our implicit memory and influence our actions when we buy products, vote for candidates, and make other decisions (Oliver, 1992). The material on implicit memory has important implications for all psychology because it illustrates that we may know more than what we reveal in actual recall.

Mood

Try Demonstration 5.3 before you read further. This demonstration illustrates one way in which mood or emotion can influence memory. Later in this discussion, we will see the importance of context once again: Memory is influenced by whether the emotional tone of the material matches your current mood. Furthermore, memory can be influenced by the match between your mood during encoding and your mood during retrieval.

Memory for Words Differing in Emotion. For nearly a century, psychologists have been interested in the way that emotional tone can influence memory. In a typical study, people learn lists of words that are pleasant, neutral, or unpleasant. Then their recall is tested after a delay of several minutes to several months. In a review of the literature, we found that pleasant items are often recalled better than either negative or neutral items, particularly if the delay is long (Matlin & Stang, 1978). For example, in the 52 studies we located involving long-term memory, pleasant items were recalled significantly more accurately than unpleasant items in 39 of the studies. We proposed that this selective recall of pleasant items is part of a more general Pollyanna Principle. The **Pollyanna Principle** states that pleasant items are usually processed more efficiently and more accurately than less pleasant items. The principle holds true for a wide variety of phenomena in perception, language, and decision making.

Demonstration 5.3 illustrates another aspect of the Pollyanna Principle: We remember pleasant items *before* less pleasant items. Inspect your responses for Demonstration 5.3. Did you list the colors you like (those with ranks of 1, 2, and 3) prior to the colors you detest (those with ranks of 8, 9, and 10)? Are your favorite desserts first on the list? My colleagues and I found that when people made lists of fruits, vegetables, and professors, the pleasant items "tumbled out" of memory prior to neutral or unpleasant items (Matlin et al., 1979). For example, the correlation* between pleasantness and order in the list was +.87 for colors and +.69 for desserts; both relationships are highly significant. Matlin and Stang (1978) proposed that pleasant items seem to be stored more accessibly in memory. As a result, they can be recalled quickly and accurately. The Pollyanna Principle is consistent with Theme 3 of this book: Positive information is processed more efficiently than negative information.

Mood Congruence. A second category of studies about mood and memory is called **mood congruence,** which means that memory is better when the material to be learned is congruent with a person's current mood. Thus, a person who is in a pleasant mood should learn pleasant material better than unpleasant material, whereas a person in an unpleasant mood should learn unpleasant material better (Bower, 1987).

As Blaney (1986) points out, there are two major ways to examine mood congruence. One way is to study people who differ from each other in general mood. In these studies of individual differences, depressed people tend to recall more

---

* A correlation is a statistical measure of the strength of the relationship between two variables, where .00 represents no relationship and +1.00 represents a strong positive relationship.

negative material, whereas people who are not depressed tend to recall more positive material (Blaney, 1986). These findings are important for clinical psychologists. If depressed people tend to forget the positive experiences that have happened to them, recalling only the negative experiences, the depression could increase still further.

A second way to examine mood congruence is to manipulate people's moods, for example by asking them to think about particularly happy or unhappy events from their past. Blaney reviewed 29 articles in which mood was experimentally induced; in all, 25 of these articles demonstrated mood congruence, 3 showed no significant differences, and 1 showed mood-*in*congruent bias in recall. Thus, mood has an important effect on memory for different kinds of material (Mayer, 1986).

Mood-State Dependence. According to **mood-state dependence,** your recall when you are in a particular mood depends partly on your mood when you originally learned the material. In this research, the emotional nature of the material doesn't matter. Instead, the important variable is whether the mood during encoding matches the mood during recall. Notice, then, that mood-state dependence is one example of the encoding specificity principle, a concept we discussed at the beginning of the chapter.

The research on mood-state dependence is inconsistent (e.g., Blaney, 1986; Bower, 1987; Bower & Mayer, 1989), and mood-state dependence doesn't seem to be as reliable as mood congruence. Consider this study that *failed* to demonstrate mood-state dependence. Bower and Mayer (1985) hypnotized participants in their study. Then the participants were asked to recall either a happy or a sad event from their lives, thereby inducing either a happy or a sad mood. During this first mood state, the participants heard a list of English words. A second mood state (either happy or sad) was then induced, and participants heard a second list. After a break, a third mood state (again, either happy or sad) was induced, and the participants were instructed to recall the words from each of the lists.

If mood-state dependence were to operate successfully in this study, we would expect recall to be better when the mood during recall matched the mood during encoding. For example, a person who is happy during recall should remember more from the list encoded during a happy mood (rather than a sad mood). However, people in this study recalled 57 percent of material in the conditions where encoding matched recall mood and 56 percent in conditions where the moods did not match.

Fortunately, a new statistical technique allows us to draw conclusions where research results are inconsistent. The **meta-analysis technique** provides a statistical method for synthesizing numerous studies on a single topic. A meta-analysis can combine numerous previous studies into one enormous superstudy that can provide a general picture of the research. The increasing popularity of this technique can help us resolve some of the controversies in cognitive psychology.

Claudia Ucros (1989) conducted a meta-analysis on the research on mood-state dependence. She found a moderately strong relationship between matching mood states and amount of material recalled. Furthermore, a number of variables influenced the strength of that relationship. For example, mood-state dependence was especially likely to operate if the stimulus material was real-life events, rather than material such as sentences constructed by the researchers. Also, adults were more likely than children to show the effect. In ideal circumstances, the effects of mood-state dependence can be strong, but, like encoding specificity, it will not always operate.

Expertise

So far, we have examined how three important factors influence the amount of material people recall. We have seen that memory performance is enhanced when the retrieval context resembles the encoding context. Furthermore, the advantage of matching contexts applies not only in the general issue of encoding specificity, but also in the more specific domains of methods of testing (that is, explicit versus implicit memory tests) and mood.

Expertise is a fourth factor that dramatically influences long-term memory. Once again, context plays an important role, though the nature of its role is different.

Consider a typical study of expertise, the case of an expert restaurant waiter studied by Ericsson (1985). This waiter, known by the initials J. C., was able to memorize up to 20 complete dinner orders in a typical restaurant setting. In a laboratory setting, Ericsson re-created the restaurant task by pairing a picture of a face with a dinner order, which could contain one of eight meat entrees, one of five meat temperatures (rare to well-done), one of five salad dressings, and one of three side dishes. In other words, there were 600 possible dinner orders! On this laboratory task, J. C. required dramatically less time to study the orders than did the college students who also participated in the study. Furthermore, J. C. made virtually no errors in recalling the orders for tables of three, five, and eight customers. A critical difference, too, was the difference in memory strategy between J. C. and the college students. They tended to store the orders as a list and to recall the orders in the same order in which they had been presented. In contrast, J. C. recalled all information from one category together, usually using a memory strategy. For example, he recalled all salad dressings together, encoding them in terms of the first letters of their names (for example, Bleu cheese, Oil-and-vinegar, Oil-and-vinegar, Thousand Island became BOOT).

J. C.'s expertise produced outstanding recall in one specific context; he could remember a remarkable number of restaurant orders. However, expertise in one area seldom indicates outstanding general memory skills (Ericsson & Smith, 1991). For example, chess masters are outstanding in their memory for chess positions, but they do not differ from control subjects in their basic cognitive and perceptual abilities.

Let us consider a study that demonstrates how expertise is context-specific. Bellezza and Buck (1988) examined two areas of expertise: plays of college football and knowledge of clothing. On the first day of the study, a test of knowledge for the two areas was administered. On the second day, people learned material related to the two areas. One group of participants learned paired associates (for example, a football term such as *scrimmage* paired together with an unrelated noun such as *lemonade*). A second group of participants read a passage describing either a nonstandard football game or nonstandard clothing at a wedding (for example, "As the attendants got ready, they wrapped themselves in cheesecloth and wore epaulets on each shoulder"). The third day of the experiment, participants recalled the material they had learned on the previous day. For both the paired-associate task and the passage recall, people who had scored high on the knowledge test tended to recall more information—but only in their area of expertise.

This study shows, then, that an "expert" on football may recall information about a football game, but this same expert does not perform any better than average when the tasks concern clothing. Similarly, a clothing "expert" performs very well on tasks related to clothing, but not on tasks related to football. In other words, expertise is context-specific.

Why is expertise so helpful in remembering material? Experts have several advantages over nonexperts (Bellezza & Buck, 1988; Cohen, 1989; Ericsson, 1988; Ericsson & Polson, 1988; Ericsson & Smith, 1991a; Intons-Peterson & Smyth, 1987):

1. Experts possess a well-organized, carefully learned knowledge structure.
2. Experts have more vivid visual images for the items they must recall. (If you know more about clothing than football, you can visualize an epaulet better than a scrimmage.)
3. Experts are more likely to reorganize the material they must recall, forming meaningful chunks that group related material together. (Those of us with no experience in remembering restaurant orders would be unlikely to regroup the customers' orders so that salad dressings were separate from side dishes.)
4. Experts rehearse in a different fashion. (For example, actors rehearse their lines by focusing on words that are likely to trigger recall.)
5. Experts are better at reconstructing missing portions of information from material that is partially remembered.

The information on expertise has a practical application for eyewitness testimony, a topic we will examine more thoroughly in the next section. Specifically, people are more accurate in identifying members of their own race than members of another race, a phenomenon called **own-race bias** (Brigham & Malpass, 1985). In a review of the literature, for example, both black and white individuals were substantially more accurate in recognizing faces of people of their own race (Bothwell et al., 1989). The results of the effect are somewhat decreased when people have greater contact with members of the other race. Thus, we would expect that a white college student with many black friends would develop expertise in recognizing the facial features of black individuals.

SECTION SUMMARY: DETERMINANTS OF ACCURACY

1. Long-term memory can store an impressive amount of material for an impressive length of time.
2. The encoding specificity principle states that recall is better if the retrieval context resembles the encoding context; although the encoding specificity principle often operates, it may not be substantial when better cues than context are present.
3. Explicit memory measures require participants to remember information, whereas implicit memory measures require them to perform a task. Amnesics perform worse than people with intact memories on explicit memory tasks, but similarly on implicit memory tasks. Also, in research with normal college students, pictures are remembered better than words on explicit memory tasks, but the reverse is true for implicit memory tasks. The data can be interpreted in an encoding-specificity context.
4. In general, people recall pleasant material more accurately than less pleasant material. People also recall material more accurately when that material is consistent with their mood (mood congruence). Although there are many exceptions, people also tend to remember material better if their mood during encoding matches their mood during recall (mood-state dependence).
5. Expertise has an important effect on long-term memory; the advantage is explained by factors such as a well-organized knowledge structure and differences in study patterns, rehearsal, and reconstruction. However, expertise is context-specific.

AUTOBIOGRAPHICAL MEMORY

Autobiographical memory is memory for events from one's own life (Neisser, 1989). In general, the research on autobiographical or **everyday memory** involves recall for naturally occurring events that happen outside the laboratory. A glance through some of the recent studies in this area suggests the wide variety of topics within autobiographical memory: memories of the first year in college (Pillemer et al., 1988); estimating the dates of personal events, academic lectures, and recent political events (Brown, 1990; Rubin & Baddeley, 1989; Thompson et al., 1988); recognizing faces at a 25th high-school reunion (Bruck et al., 1991); and women students' recall of their first menstrual period (Pillemer et al., 1987).

In this section on autobiographical memory, we'll first examine especially vivid memories and then see how autobiographical memories can become schematized when they are not especially vivid. We'll then see what kind of errors occur when

DEMONSTRATION 5.4

FLASHBULB MEMORY.

Ask several acquaintances whether they can identify any memories of a very surprising, emotional event. Tell them, for example, that many people can recall in vivid detail the circumstances in which they learned about the death of President Kennedy or, more recently, the fall of the Berlin Wall, or an important world crisis. Other vivid memories focus on more personally important events. Ask these people to tell you about the memory, particularly noting any small details that they recall.

we are trying to remember to do something. The following section focuses on eyewitness testimony, a topic that has obvious applications in the courtroom. Our final topic concerns the debate about ecological validity and the value of research on autobiographical memory.

Flashbulb Memories

Try Demonstration 5.4 on flashbulb memory before you read further. **Flashbulb memory** is the memory for the situation in which we first learned of a very surprising and emotionally arousing event (Brown & Kulik, 1977).

My clearest flashbulb memory, like many of my generation, is of learning that President John Kennedy had been shot. I was a sophomore at Stanford University, just ready for a midday class in German. I had entered the classroom from the right, and I was just about to sit down at a long table on the right-hand side of the classroom. The sun was streaming in from the left. There was only one other person seated in the classroom, a blond fellow named Dewey. He turned around and said, "Did you hear that President Kennedy has been shot?" I also recall my reaction and the reactions of others as they entered the class. Kennedy was shot about 30 years ago, yet trivial details of that news are stunningly clear to many today. You can probably think of personal events in your own life that triggered flashbulb memories—the death of a relative, a piece of important good news, or an amazing surprise.

The Classic Research. Brown and Kulik point out that these flashbulb memories are clearly not as accurate as a photograph in which a true flashbulb has been fired. For example, I don't remember what books I was carrying or what Dewey was wearing. Nonetheless, they do include details that would be missing from a neutral memory of comparable age.

To examine flashbulb memories, Brown and Kulik questioned people to see whether various national events triggered these memories. Six kinds of information were most likely to be listed in these flashbulb memories: the place, the ongoing event that was interrupted by the news, the person who gave them the news, their own feelings, the emotions in others, and the aftermath. Check the responses to Demonstration 5.4 to see if these items were included in the recall.

Brown and Kulik concluded that the two main determinants of flashbulb memory were a high level of surprise and a high level of emotional arousal or perceived importance. These authors also proposed that these surprising, arousing events were more likely to be rehearsed, either silently or in conversation. Consequently, the memory of these events is more elaborated than that of more ordinary daily events.

These vivid memories may capture highly positive as well as tragic events. For example, an Indian friend of mine recalls in detail the circumstances in which Mohandas Gandhi, the nonviolent political leader, spoke to a crowd of people in Gauhati, India. My friend was only 5 years old, yet he vividly recalls Gandhi, wearing a white outfit and accompanied by two women. He can recall that his aunt, who was with him, was wearing a white sari with a gold and red border, and he can distinctly remember how the heat of the day had made him very thirsty. Rubin and Kozin (1984) studied similar vivid memories for events in people's lives. These vivid memories had to meet the criteria of being clear and detailed, and almost lifelike, in order to be included in the study. However, they were not required to be caused by surprising or consequential events. The participants in this study were asked to describe the three clearest memories from their past.

What kind of events did people supply? Of these memories, 18 percent concerned injuries or accidents to the participants or their friends. Other frequent categories included sports, love relationships, animals, and events from the first week of college. Interestingly, however, only 3 percent of the events were judged to have any national importance. In general, people reported that their vivid memories were consequential and surprising, and they also reported rehearsing the memories frequently. Rubin and Kozin conclude that almost all autobiographical memories have flashbulb-like clarity immediately after they occur. However, flashbulb memories and vivid memories—which may really be equivalent—maintain this clarity for a longer time than "garden-variety" memories, because they are rehearsed more often.

More Recent Research.   In the last decade, the research on flashbulb memories has addressed whether these memories are somehow special, or whether they simply represent the more impressive end of normal memory. Christianson (1989) questioned Swedish citizens about their memories of the assassination of Swedish prime minister Olof Palme, who was shot in Stockholm in 1986. Christianson found that one year later, people did recall more circumstantial information about the assassination than about a personal event from the same time period. However, many of the specific details had begun to slip away by 1987. Only about half of the people could accurately recall what they were doing when they learned about the assassination, and only 25 percent remembered what clothes they were wearing.

DEMONSTRATION 5.5

THE SCHEMATIZATION OF MEMORY.

Describe what you ate for lunch exactly one week ago. Also note where you sat and with whom you ate. What time did you eat lunch? What did you carry with you to lunch? What foods did you finish, and what did you leave on your plate?

As McCloskey and his colleagues (1988) conclude, "flashbulb memories are neither uniformly accurate nor immune to forgetting" (p. 177). The ordinary mechanisms, which serve us well in our everyday life, are powerful enough to produce even more accurate (though not perfect) recall when we experience a surprising event of great importance.

Schemas and Autobiographical Memory

Try Demonstration 5.5 on memory schemas before you read further. A **schema** is our general knowledge about an object or an event that has been acquired from past experience (Cohen, 1989). Schemas are abstracted from a large number of specific examples of events in our lives, and these schemas summarize the important characteristics contained in the events. For example, you have probably developed a schema for "eating lunch." You tend to sit in a particular area with a constant group of people. Conversation topics may also be reasonably standardized.

As Barclay (1986) writes, you notice common features through repeated exposure to similar kinds of activities. Thus, for autobiographical material, schemas lead to the organized storage in memory of everyday information about yourself. Typically, memory capacity limitations prevent us from remembering precise details about our daily life (Did that green salad contain carrot shreds?). However, schemas allow us to process large amounts of material because we can summarize the regularities in our lives. After some time, any single event is not distinguishable from other, similar events. Therefore, when you were asked to recall the details of last week's lunch, you probably reconstructed a plausible, "generic" memory based on many similar events.

The concept of schemas also suggests that we may mistakenly "recall" events that never really happened, as long as they are conceptually similar to the schemas we have developed. Furthermore, the generic aspects of events may become blended as time passes, particularly because you continue to experience similar events. Inaccuracy should also increase as time passes. Neisser (1988) calls this kind of inaccuracy **repisodic memory** (note the pun with *episodic memory*), meaning the recall of a supposed event that is really the blending of details over repeated and related episodes. The schematization of memory is an example of Theme 1 of the book: The cognitive processes actively reshape and categorize our memories. It also illustrates part of Theme 2 of this book: Errors in cognitive processing can often be traced to logical strategies, such as mistakenly recalling an event similar to one that had actually happened.

Craig Barclay and his colleagues have provided research evidence for the importance of schemas in memory (Barclay, 1986; Barclay & Wellman, 1986). Three students kept records of memorable daily events for a period of 4 months. Then, 2½ years later, they were asked to read an item and decide whether it was exactly what they had originally written or an item that was unfamiliar. The students correctly recognized about 85 percent of the original items, a testimony to their accuracy. However, they also said that they recognized about 50 percent of the items that were actually schematic versions, rather than the true originals. For example, a student originally wrote:

> I went shopping downtown looking for an anniversary present for my parents but couldn't find a thing. I get so frustrated when I can't find what I want.

About half the time, this same student might say, "Yes, I recognize it" to a version that read:

> I went shopping downtown. I must have gone to 10 stores before giving up and going home. I get so frustrated when I can't find what I want.

This research illustrates that our general schemas for events in memory are likely to provoke "false alarms" reasonably often. That is, we are likely to think we recognize something that is really not familiar. However, we are persuaded because it matches quite nicely our more generalized schema. Perhaps one reason that our flashbulb memories seem so vivid is that each of these memories is unique and unrepeated, in sharp contrast to the more pedestrian, generic quality of the more abundant memory schemas. Incidentally, Chapter 7 will examine schemas in more detail.

Memory for Action

Something like this has certainly happened to you: You borrowed a book from a friend, and you distinctly remember returning it to him or her. However, the next day, you find the book is still on your desk. Apparently, you simply *imagined* returning the book. This process of trying to discriminate between memories of real and imagined events is called **reality monitoring** (Johnson, 1988). Reality monitoring involves memory about actions that may have been performed in the past; this section will also discuss remembering to do actions in the future.

Reality Monitoring. It should be easy to distinguish between real actions (giving the book to a friend) and imagined actions (thinking that you gave the book to a friend). However, making this decision is often difficult. For example, Anderson (1984) found that people had trouble remembering whether they had really

---

DEMONSTRATION 5.6

REMEMBERING TO DO THINGS.

Take 10 index cards and hand them out to 10 acquaintances. Instruct five of them to return the cards to you tomorrow at approximately the same time of the day. (You may want to specify that they can return the cards by slipping them under your door, noting the time at which they do so.) Instruct the other five to return the cards seven days from now, at approximately the same time. In each case, make note of the number who successfully return the cards on time. You may also wish to ask them to share their memory strategies.

---

traced a pen along a specified outline, or whether they had simply imagined themselves doing it. According to Johnson and Raye (1981), we decide that we really did perform an action if our memory is rich with perceptual details and if it requires little cognitive effort to reconstruct that memory. In contrast, we decide that we merely imagined performing the action if the memory lacks perceptual details and if reconstruction requires great cognitive effort.

Consider this example. You are trying to recall whether you took an antibiotic that was prescribed for an illness. You examine your memory and realize that you can readily "see" the pill in your hand and "feel" the glass of water at your lips. The memory is rich with perceptual detail, and that memory came readily to mind—without any of the cognitive effort that would have been required in constructing an imagined experience. As a consequence, you conclude that you really did take the pill.

Prospective Memory. Some time today, try Demonstration 5.6, which involves remembering to do things, or **prospective memory.** In this textbook's three chapters on memory, the major focus is on retrospective memory, or recalling information that has been previously learned. Rather than focusing on the past, prospective memory investigates how we remember to perform actions in the future (Harris, 1984). Some typical prospective memory tasks might include remembering to mail a letter, to take the cookies out of the oven, to let the dog out before you leave the house, and to bring your tennis racquet to gym class. In many cases, the primary challenge is to *remember* to perform an action in the future. However, sometimes the primary challenge is to remember the content of that action. You are certainly familiar with the feeling that you are supposed to do something, but you cannot remember *what* it was (Koriat et al., 1990).

One intriguing component of prospective memory is absentmindedness (e.g., Reason, 1984; Reason & Mycielska, 1982). Most people do not publicly reveal their slips, so if you feel that you are the only person who gets into bed with your shoes on or writes a check and then puts the checkbook back without tearing out the check, you'll want to read Reason's work on the subject.

Reason (1984) notes that several common characteristics encourage absent-minded behavior. These slips are more likely in highly familiar surroundings when you are performing tasks automatically. Slips are also more likely if you are pre-occupied, distracted, or feeling time pressure. In most cases, absentmindedness is simply irritating. However, sometimes these slips can produce an airplane collision, such as the disastrous Tenerife accident of 1977, or the nuclear accident at Three Mile Island in 1979.

Most of the research on prospective memory involves laboratory research that is designed to be naturalistic. In a representative study, students received eight postcards to mail back to the experimenter, one a week for 8 weeks (Meacham, 1982; Meacham & Singer, 1977). Some students were instructed to mail them once a week on a specified different day of each week, whereas others were instructed to mail them every Wednesday. Furthermore, some students were told that they would receive up to $5.00 payment for conscientiously mailing the cards; others received no payment. Meacham and Singer found that people in the "every Wednesday" condition were no more likely to mail the cards than those in the random-day condition. However, greed was an effective motivator. The average participant in the paid condition returned only 1.4 cards late, in contrast to 2.1 late cards in the unpaid condition.

In this section we have examined memory for your own actions—whether you have done something in the past and whether you will remember to do something in the future. Now let us turn to memory for other people's actions, in the form of eyewitness testimony.

Eyewitness Testimony

In 1979, a Catholic priest awaited trial for several armed robberies in Delaware. Seven witnesses had identified him as the "gentleman bandit," referring to the robber's polite manners and elegant clothes. During the trial, many witnesses identified the priest as the one who had committed the robberies. Suddenly, however, the trial was halted; another man had confessed to the robberies (Loftus & Ketcham, 1991).

Reports like this one have led psychologists to question the reliability of eye-witness testimony. However, in close to 80,000 cases each year in the United States, the only critical evidence against a person who has been arrested is eye-witness identification (Goldstein et al., 1989). By one estimate, more than 2,000 people are wrongfully convicted each year in the United States on the basis of a faulty eyewitness testimony (Loftus & Ketcham, 1991).

Throughout our discussion of memory, we have emphasized that human memory is reasonably accurate, but it is not flawless. Eyewitness testimonies, like other memories, are generally accurate, but these reports can also be flawed. Similar to other kinds of memory, eyewitness testimony can be influenced by pre-existing schemas (List, 1986). The problem is that when an eyewitness testimony is inaccurate, the wrong person may go to jail or—in the worst case—be executed by mistake (Loftus & Ketcham, 1991). Let us consider how inaccuracies can arise when people identify faces and when they are given misleading information after the event that they had witnessed.

Identifying Faces. Think about the factors that might influence how accurate you would be in identifying faces in an eyewitness situation. Fortunately, we have extensive information on this topic. For example, Shapiro and Penrod (1986) located 128 research studies about facial recognition, which involved 960 experimental conditions and a total of 16,950 participants. With the data from these studies, they conducted a meta-analysis, the statistical analysis we discussed earlier. This meta-analysis confirmed the own-race bias that we mentioned in connection with expertise; people indeed remember faces better when those faces are of their own race. Let us discuss other factors that influence identification accuracy, based on Shapiro and Penrod's analysis as well as other research.

In general, as you might expect, identification accuracy is better when people devote greater time and attention to looking at the face (Ellis, 1984; Shapiro & Penrod, 1986). Furthermore, people are less accurate when something distracts attention away from the face. For example, if a robber is holding a gun, eyewitnesses are likely to focus on the gun rather than the details of the robber's face (Cutler et al., 1987; Ellis, 1984; Loftus, 1979).

The length of the retention interval also influences facial recognition (Shapiro & Penrod, 1986; Shepherd et al., 1982). Still, as Ellis (1984) concludes, "delay intervals even as long as weeks or months do not automatically reduce recognition accuracy" (p. 25). However, if pictures of other faces, such as misleading composite faces, are shown during the delay interval, accuracy is substantially reduced (Davies & Jenkins, 1985; Jenkins & Davies, 1985). Obviously, all of these factors that influence the accuracy of facial identification have important practical implications in the courtroom.

Misleading Post-Event Information. Errors in eyewitness testimony can arise not only from misleading pictures of faces, but also from misleading information that is supplied after the original event. In the classic experiment in this area, for example, Loftus and her coauthors (1978) showed participants in the study a series of slides. In this sequence, a sports car stopped at an intersection, and then it turned and hit a pedestrian. Half of the participants saw a slide with a yield sign at the intersection; the other half saw a stop sign. Twenty minutes to 1 week after the slides had been shown, the participants answered questions about the details of the accident. A critical question contained information that was either consistent or inconsistent with a detail in the original slide series, or else did not mention the detail. For example, some people who had seen the yield sign were asked, "Did another car pass the red Datsun while it was stopped at the yield sign?" (consistent).

FIGURE 5.3

The Effect of Type of Information and Delay on Proportion of Correct Answers (Loftus et al., 1978).

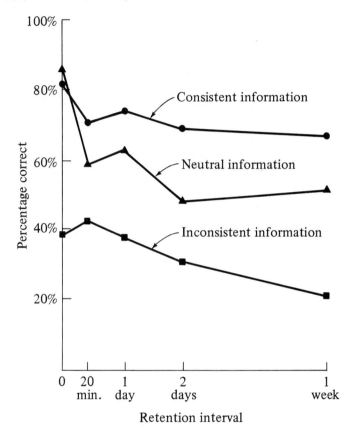

Other people were asked, "Did another car pass the red Datsun while it was stopped at the stop sign?" (inconsistent). For still other people, the sign was not mentioned (neutral). Then participants were shown two slides, one with a stop sign and one with a yield sign, and they were asked to select which slide they had seen. As Figure 5.3 shows, people who saw the inconsistent information were much less accurate than people in the other two conditions. Their selections were based on the information in the questionnaire, rather than the original slide. Several studies have replicated the detrimental effects of misleading post-event information (e.g., Shaughnessy & Mand, 1982).

In other studies, researchers introduce misleading information so that the participants in the research create new, incorrect memories. Nevertheless, the participants are as confident about the accuracy of these new memories as they are about their genuine memories (Loftus et al., 1989; Loftus & Hoffman, 1989). However, the descriptions of these two kinds of memories are actually somewhat different. Schooler and his coauthors (1986) asked the participants in their study to describe in detail what they had seen in a previous series of slides. Those who had actually seen a stop sign were likely to emphasize perceptual details of the scene; these details were rarely mentioned by those who had been told misleading information about the stop sign. Notice that these findings are consistent with Johnson and Raye's (1981) explanation of memory monitoring. If an event really happened, the scene is more likely to have rich perceptual detail than if we had merely imagined the event. Jurors in a court case who are trying to decide whether an eyewitness really saw an event should base their decision on the level of perceptual detail, rather than the level of the eyewitness's confidence about the memory.

Ecological Validity and Autobiographical Memory Research

In Chapter 1 we introduced the concept of **ecological validity,** which means that the results obtained in research should also hold true in "real life." More than any other area of cognition, the research on long-term memory has embraced the concept of ecological validity. This section on autobiographical memory has examined such real-world phenomena as flashbulb memories, schematic memories for everyday events, absentmindedness in our daily lives, and eyewitness testimonies in the courtroom. Clearly, this emphasis on real-life applications is a dramatic departure from the controlled laboratory settings used for memory research during the 1960s and 1970s (Morris, 1988). Now that you have read about some of the research in real-world settings, you are in a better position to appreciate the debate about ecological validity.

In 1989, an article by Banaji and Crowder appeared in a prominent journal. The title of the article, "The Bankruptcy of Everyday Memory," made the authors' position quite clear. Banaji and Crowder claimed that the research methods used to explore everyday memory were unsophisticated. They also argued that the kind of well-controlled memory research conducted in the laboratory could indeed have important implications for our daily memory tasks.

Many researchers rushed to the aid of the everyday memory studies. For example, Ceci and Bronfenbrenner (1991) pointed out that the laboratory and the real-world setting often yield different results. Their research showed how young children used a much different system to remember to check a clock when they were in a real kitchen than when they were in a lab setting. Other researchers complained that Banaji and Crowder had not examined some of the better developed examples of everyday memory (Conway, 1991).

Probably the wisest conclusion about this controversy is that *both* the laboratory and the real-world approaches can advance our understanding of human memory. In the words of Endel Tulving (1991), whose memory research has spanned several decades:

> There is no law that says that good facts or ideas can come out of one type of approach only if some other approach is suppressed. As in other fields of science, there is room for many different kinds of facts and ideas about memory and for many approaches. (p. 42)

SECTION SUMMARY: AUTOBIOGRAPHICAL MEMORY

1. Flashbulb memories and other vivid memories are rich with information, but specific details seem to fade as time passes.
2. Memory schemas encourage us to mistakenly recall events that never really occurred, as long as these events are similar to a schema.
3. According to the work on reality monitoring, we decide whether we really did perform an action on the basis of perceptual details and cognitive effort.
4. The research on prospective memory includes absentmindedness and factors that influence accuracy.
5. Factors that influence eyewitness testimony for faces include time and attention in looking at the face, the own-race bias, length of retention interval, and misleading information.
6. When misleading information is introduced after an event that a witness has seen, he or she may recall that incorrect information, rather than the original event; although people may be confident about these incorrect memories, the memories lack perceptual detail.
7. The controversy over the value of research in everyday memory is best resolved by emphasizing that both laboratory research and research in the real world can help us understand human memory.

MEMORY IMPROVEMENT

Our discussion of memory has already emphasized a particularly important suggestion for improving memory performance. As you know from the discussion of levels of processing in Chapter 3, recall is superior if information is processed at a deep level. Therefore, whenever you need to learn some information, concentrate on its meaning and try to develop rich, elaborate encodings. Whenever possible, try to relate the material to your own experiences because the self-reference effect demonstrates that this kind of encoding is particularly helpful.

In this section, we will consider seven additional methods for improving memory. The first three methods emphasize mnemonics (pronounced ni-*mon*-icks, with a silent *m*). **Mnemonics** is the use of a strategy to help memory; these include visual

DEMONSTRATION 5.7

INSTRUCTIONS AND MEMORY.

Learn the following list of pairs by repeating the members of each pair several times. For example, if the pair is CAT–WINDOW, say over and over to yourself, "CAT–WINDOW, CAT–WINDOW, CAT–WINDOW." Just repeat the words, and do not use any other study method. Allow yourself one minute for this list.

CUSTARD–LUMBER   IVY–MOTHER
JAIL–CLOWN   LIZARD–PAPER
ENVELOPE–SLIPPER   SCISSORS–BEAR
SHEEPSKIN–CANDLE   CANDY–MOUNTAIN
FRECKLES–APPLE   BOOK–PAINT
HAMMER–STAR   TREE–OCEAN

Now, cover up the pairs above. Try to recall as many responses as possible.

ENVELOPE   _____   JAIL   _____
FRECKLES   _____   IVY   _____
TREE   _____   SHEEPSKIN   _____
CANDY   _____   BOOK   _____
SCISSORS   _____   LIZARD   _____
CUSTARD   _____   HAMMER   _____

Learn the following list of pairs by visualizing a mental picture in which the two objects in each pair are in some kind of vivid interaction. For example, if the pair is CAT–WINDOW, you might make up a picture of a cat jumping through a closed window, with the glass shattering all about. Just make up a picture and do not use any other study method. Allow yourself one minute for this list.

SOAP–MERMAID   MIRROR–RABBIT
FOOTBALL–LAKE   HOUSE–DIAMOND
PENCIL–LETTUCE   LAMB–MOON
CAR–HONEY   BREAD–GLASS
CANDLE–DANCER   LIPS–MONKEY
DANDELION–FLEA   DOLLAR–ELEPHANT

Now, cover up the pairs above. Try to recall as many responses as possible.

CANDLE   _____   DOLLAR   _____
DANDELION   _____   CAR   _____
BREAD   _____   LIPS   _____
MIRROR   _____   PENCIL   _____
LAMB   _____   SOAP   _____
FOOTBALL   _____   HOUSE   _____

Now, count the number of correct responses on each list. Did you recall a greater number of words with the imagery instructions? Incidentally, you may have found it very difficult to *avoid* using imagery on the first list, because you are reading a section about memory improvement. In that case, your recall scores were probably similar for the two lists. You may wish to test a friend, instead.

imagery, the method of loci, and organization. Memory can also be enhanced via four more general methods, which include external memory aids, practice, the multimodal approach, and—perhaps most important—metamemory. Notice that each of these methods makes use of familiar concepts; we remember more effectively if we pay attention, use deep levels of processing and distinctive cues, and emphasize effective retrieval strategies (Fischler, 1992).

Mnemonics Using Imagery

Imagery refers to the mental representations of objects or actions that are not physically present. Chapter 6 examines the nature of these mental images; however, we are currently interested in how imagery can enhance memory.

Try Demonstration 5.7 before you read further. Which set of instructions produced the highest recall, the repetition or the imagery instructions?

This demonstration is a simplified version of a study by Bower and Winzenz (1970). They used concrete nouns in their study and tested participants in four different conditions: (1) repetition, in which people repeated the pairs silently to themselves; (2) sentence reading, in which people read sentences devised by the experimenters, and each pair was included in one sentence; (3) sentence generation, in which people made up a sentence about each pair and said it aloud; and (4) imagery, in which people tried to construct a mental picture of the two words in vivid interaction with each other.

After learning several lists of words, the participants saw the first word of each pair and were asked to supply the second word. The results were quite remarkable. Out of a possible 15 items, people in the repetition condition recalled only 5.2. In contrast, people in the imagery condition recalled 12.7 words—more than twice as many! Research shows that visual imagery is a powerful strategy for enhancing memory (Bellezza, 1986; McDaniel & Pressley, 1987).

Perhaps you have read an article in a popular magazine that suggested you should create an unusual or bizarre image. In fact, the research on imagery shows that bizarre images do not consistently work more effectively than ordinary images in enhancing memory (Einstein & McDaniel, 1987; Einstein et al., 1989).

However, the research consistently shows that imagery is most effective when the items that must be recalled are shown interacting with each other (Begg, 1982). For example, if you want to remember the pair *elephant* and *dollar bill*, try to visualize an elephant holding the bill in its trunk, rather than these two items separated from each other.

The **keyword method** is a mnemonic device that uses mental imagery to help people remember unfamiliar vocabulary items (Desrochers & Begg, 1987). Imagine that you are learning Spanish, and you want to remember that the unfamiliar Spanish word *rodilla* means *knee* in English. From the word *rodilla* you could derive a similar-sounding English keyword, *rodeo*. Then imagine a cowboy at a rodeo with his knees conspicuously protruding, as in Figure 5.4.

FIGURE 5.4	

The Keyword Representation for the Pair of Words *rodilla-knee.*

Research on the keyword method confirms that it can help students who are trying to learn new English vocabulary words or foreign-language vocabulary (Desrochers & Begg, 1987; McDaniel et al., 1987). For example, Kasper and Glass (1988) found that college students recalled significantly more Spanish vocabulary if they used the keyword method than if they simply rehearsed the material by repeating it over and over. The keyword method has also been used to help individuals with Alzheimer's disease learn people's names (Hill et al., 1987).

Method of Loci

The **method of loci** instructs people to associate items to be learned with a series of physical locations. It combines imagery with other memory aids. The method of loci (pronounced *low*-sigh) is one of the oldest mnemonic devices (Snowman, 1987). The basic rules for using this method involve (1) visualizing a series of places, in a specific sequence, that you know well; (2) making up an image to represent each item you want to remember; and (3) associating the items, one by one, with the corresponding location in memory. A clear strength of the method of loci is that it takes advantage of the encoding specificity principle discussed earlier in the chapter; the material is encoded together with memory cues that are so familiar that they are virtually guaranteed to be available at the time of recall (Oliver, 1992).

Gordon Bower (1970) describes how we might use the method of loci for a familiar sequence of loci associated with a home, such as the driveway, the garage, the front door, the coat closet, and the kitchen sink. If you need to remember a grocery shopping list (for example, hot dogs, cat food, tomatoes, bananas, and orange juice), you could make up a vivid image for each item. Then imagine each item in its appropriate place. You could imagine giant *hot dogs* rolling down the *driveway*, a monstrous *cat eating food* in the *garage*, ripe *tomatoes* splattering all over the *front door*, and a quart of *orange juice* gurgling down the *kitchen sink*. When you enter the supermarket, you can mentally walk the route from the driveway to the kitchen sink, recalling the items in order.

The method sounds unlikely, but does it work? In a representative experiment by Groninger (1971), participants in one condition were told to think of 25 locations that could be placed in order. Then they mentally pictured items on a 25-word list, using the method of loci. Participants in the control condition simply learned the 25 words in order, using any method they wanted. Everyone was instructed not to rehearse the material any further. Then everyone returned for testing 1 week and 5 weeks later, and those people who said they had rehearsed the material were eliminated from the study. Figure 5.5 shows the results of the study. As you can see, the method of loci was particularly effective—relative to the control group—when recall was measured 5 weeks after learning.

Organization

Organization is the attempt to bring order and pattern to the material we learn. In **chunking,** for example, we combine several small units into larger units. For instance, try Demonstration 5.8, which is a modification of a study by Bower and Springston (1970). These researchers found much better recall when a string of letters was grouped according to meaningful, familiar units, rather than in arbitrary groups of three. In Demonstration 5.8, you probably recalled a greater number of items on the second list, which was organized according to familiar chunks, than on either the list where the letters were grouped in arbitrary units or the ungrouped list.

Another effective way to organize material is to construct a hierarchy. A **hierarchy** is a system in which items are arranged in a series of classes, from the most general classes to the most specific. For example, Figure 5.6 presents part of a hierarchy for animals.

Bower, Clark, Lesgold, and Winzenz (1969) asked people to learn words that belonged to four hierarchies similar to the one in Figure 5.6. Some people learned the words in an organized fashion, and the words were presented in the format of the upside-down trees you see in Figure 5.6. Other people saw the same words,

FIGURE 5.5

Percentage of Words Recalled in the Correct Order, as a Function of Condition and Delay (Based on Groninger, 1971).

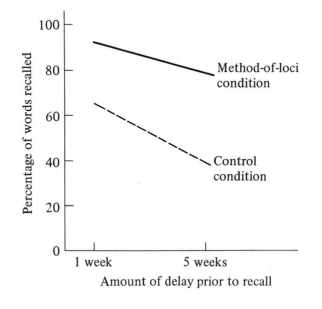

but the words were randomly scattered throughout the different positions in each tree. Thus, there was no pattern for the words. The group who had learned the organized structure performed much better. For instance, on the first trial, the group who learned the organized structure recalled an average of 73 words, in comparison to only 21 for the group who learned the random structure. Other studies (e.g., Wittrock, 1974) have shown that hierarchical organization is useful even for recalling words chosen at random from a dictionary. Structure and organization clearly enhance recall (Hirst, 1988).

A hierarchy is a form of outline. An outline is valuable because it provides organization and structure for concepts that you learn in a particular discipline. Naturally, the material is usually not as simple as a list of individual words, but the ideas can still be arranged into a series of classes. For example, this chapter is divided into three general areas: determinants of accuracy, autobiographical memory, and memory improvement. See if you can construct a hierarchy similar to Figure 5.6 that includes more specific topics for this chapter. Then check back with the outline at the beginning of the chapter to see whether you omitted anything. If you study the outline of each chapter, you will have an organized structure that can help your recall on an examination.

CHUNKING.

Read this list of letters and then cover them up. Try to recall them as accurately as possible.

    YMC   AJF   KFB   INB   CLS   DTV

Now read this list of letters and then cover them up. Try to recall them as accurately as possible.

    AMA   PHD   TWA   VCR   XKE   SDI

Finally, read this list of letters and then cover them up. Try to recall them as accurately as possible.

    NZKLEQBNPIJWUYHRTM

Another popular mnemonic that makes use of organization is the **first-letter technique,** which involves taking the first letter of each word you want to remember and composing a word or a sentence from these letters (Herrmann, 1991). Maybe you learned the colors of the rainbow by using the mediator ROY G. BIV to recall Red, Orange, Yellow, Green, Blue, Indigo, and Violet. As you may have learned, the notes that fall on the lines in a musical selection can be remembered by taking the first letters of the sentence, "Every Good Boy Does Fine," and the notes that fall between the lines spell FACE.

Students frequently use first-letter mnemonics (Gruneberg, 1978). In one group of medical students, for example, more than half used this technique at least occasionally in preparing for anatomy examinations. The pharmaceutical company Merck, Sharp & Dome (1980) prepared a medical mnemonics handbook for physicians. A typical example is to be used in the treatment of trauma from sports injuries: PRICE (Position, Rest, Ice, Compression, Elevation). However, the effectiveness of the first-letter technique has not been convincingly demonstrated. Morris (1978) reports that the first-letter technique helps recall if the order of the items is important. On the other hand, it is less useful when you need to remember unrelated items. Carlson, Zimmer, and Glover (1981) also found that first-letter techniques did not aid memory, though they admit that they may not have allowed the participants enough study time to benefit fully from the mnemonics. In summary, the first-letter technique is a popular one, and one that many of us *believe* must work; however, it may not really deserve its popularity.

So far, we have seen how organization can enhance memory through the use of chunking, a hierarchy, or a first-letter mnemonic. A fourth organizational method, called the **narrative technique,** instructs people to make up stories to link a series of words together. In one study, Bower and Clark (1969) told one group of people

FIGURE 5.6

An Example of a Hierarchy.

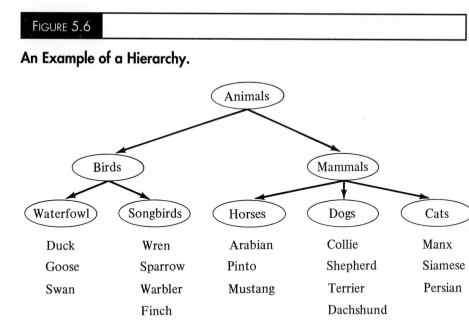

Waterfowl	Songbirds	Horses	Dogs	Cats
Duck	Wren	Arabian	Collie	Manx
Goose	Sparrow	Pinto	Shepherd	Siamese
Swan	Warbler	Mustang	Terrier	Persian
	Finch		Dachshund	

to make up narrative stories that incorporated a set of English words. Different people—the control group—spent the same amount of time learning these words, but they were simply told to study and learn each list. After 12 lists had been presented, the participants were instructed to recall the words on all 12 lists. Figure 5.7 shows the impressive results. As you can see, the two groups show no overlap whatsoever. Clearly, the narrative technique is an effective way to enhance memory. However, we should stress that techniques such as this are effective only if a narrative can be generated easily and reliably during both learning and recall (Bellezza, 1987). A narrative will not be helpful if it hangs together so loosely that you cannot remember the story!

External Memory Aids

So far, we have examined three mnemonic strategies that offer specific instructions on transforming material so that it becomes more memorable. You can construct mental images, try the method of loci to link items with physical locations, or use one of several organizational techniques. Let us now turn to four more general approaches to memory improvement.

One general strategy is to use an **external memory aid,** which is defined as any device, external to the person, that facilitates memory in some way (Intons-Peterson & Newsome, 1992). Taking notes on a lecture is one obvious external memory aid; research confirms that students usually recall more material if they have taken

FIGURE 5.7

Recall as a Function of Learning Condition: Narrative Versus Control (From Bower & Clark, 1969).

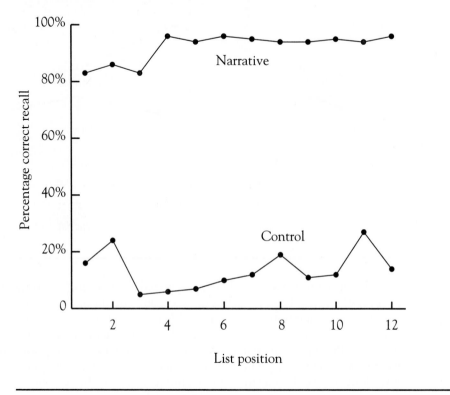

notes (Intons-Peterson & Newsome, 1992; Kiewra, 1985). Other external memory aids include a shopping list, a bookmark, asking someone else to remind you to do something, a whistling teapot—reminding you to take the pot off the stove—and dozens of commercial memory aids (Intons-Peterson & Fournier, 1986; Intons-Peterson, 1993). A typical commercial memory aid is a credit card case that sounds an alarm if you forget to get your credit card back from the clerk (Herrmann & Petro, 1990). In each case, the external memory aid eases the burden of remembering too much information. Naturally, these aids are helpful only if they can be easily used and if they successfully remind us about what we are supposed to remember. If you switch your ring to another finger to remind you to turn off your stove before leaving the apartment, you may find yourself pondering, "Now what was this reminder supposed to remind me to do?"

Practice

Another general memory-improvement strategy sounds almost too obvious to mention: The more you practice, the more you remember. However, even college students forget the rule that "practice makes perfect." Every semester, students in some of my classes will come to my office to discuss how they can improve their performance on exams. One of my first questions is, "How long did you spend studying?" An amazing number will say something like, "Well, I read every chapter and I looked over my notes." Most of us cannot master material with only one exposure to a textbook and a cursory inspection of lecture notes. Instead, the task requires reading the material two or three times, each time practicing the retrieval of information. (For example, what are the memory techniques we have discussed so far?)

The **total time hypothesis** states that the amount you learn depends on the total time you devote to learning (Baddeley, 1990). Keep in mind, however, that an hour spent actively learning the material, using deep levels of processing, may be more valuable than two hours in which your eyes simply drift across the pages. Also keep in mind a second point, the **distribution of practice effect;** in general, you learn more if you spread your learning trials over time, rather than learning the material all at once (Baddeley, 1990). Research on real-life material, such as high school math and Spanish vocabulary, confirms the distribution of practice effect (Bahrick & Hall, 1991; Bahrick & Phelps, 1987).

The Multimodal Approach

In the last 15 years, psychologists have become increasingly critical of the mnemonics approach to memory improvement. These researchers complain that the traditional approach to memory improvement has been too simplistic; it implies that a single solution can be found to help all people with their memory difficulties (e.g., Herrmann, 1991; Herrmann & Searleman, 1990; Poon, 1980; Wilson, 1984, 1987).

The most readable summary of the new approaches to memory improvement is a book by Douglas Herrmann (1991) called *Super Memory*. Elaborating on the work of Wilson and of Poon, as well as on his own research, Herrmann's **multimodal approach** emphasizes that there is no simple, improve-your-memory-overnight answer to memory problems. He stresses that people who seriously want to improve their memories must adopt a complete approach to memory improvement. This complete approach involves attention to your physical and mental condition (for example, by getting sufficient sleep and maintaining an optimum level of daily activity). It also involves concern about memory attitude (for example, by keeping a memory diary in order to provide an accurate impression of typical memory behavior) and concern about social context (for example, by making conversation in order to "buy time" while you gather information to help you remember some critical fact).

Herrmann also makes numerous suggestions about mental manipulations, such as rehearsing an item, focusing attention on details that should be registered, and encouraging deep levels of processing by paying attention to semantic and emotional aspects of the material to be remembered. Finally, Herrmann emphasizes that people who want to improve their memories should develop a repertoire of several memory manipulations. Again, there is no single, perfect mnemonic device. For example, Herrmann gives several pages of recommendations on how to acquire and remember people's names. One of these recommendations for learning a new name involves the following steps:

1. Say the name aloud.
2. Ask the person a question, using his or her name.
3. Say the name at least once in conversation.
4. End the conversation by thinking of a rhyme for the name, deciding whom the person looks like, or—if possible—jotting down the name unobtrusively.

Herrmann and others argue that this more comprehensive multimodal approach to memory improvement is essential because the more traditional methods may have limited usefulness. For example, people who have learned how to use a mnemonic device may indeed show short-term improvement in memory. However, people later fail to apply these methods to new tasks, and they stop using them (Herrmann et al., 1987). Memory improvement should involve more comprehensive approaches that attend to the numerous factors affecting memory. In addition, memory improvement must involve the development of a flexible repertoire of techniques to aid each specific kind of memory task.

Metamemory

So far, you have learned that you can improve your memory by using imagery, the method of loci, organization, external memory aids, practice, and the multimodal approach to memory. However, all of these techniques are limited in their effectiveness if you fail to use your metamemory. **Metamemory** is your knowledge and awareness about your own memory. The topic of metamemory will be examined much more thoroughly in the chapter on general knowledge (Chapter 7).

To learn most effectively, you need to know what kind of strategies work best for you, how long you can study before your attention wanders, the time of day during which you learn the most, and so forth. In addition to knowing your memory's strengths and weaknesses, you also need to know how to regulate your memory and related processes (McKeachie et al., 1985). You need to know how to plan your study activities, how to regulate your attention, and how to monitor whether you are understanding the material you are reading. You need to know that you should spend more time on a difficult part of the chapter—such as the discussion of explicit versus implicit measures of memory (Matlin, 1993).

In fact, metamemory is probably the most important component of memory improvement. Consistent with Theme 2 of this book, we humans possess remarkably proficient cognitive processes. When we exercise our metamemory appropriately, we can develop study strategies that make the best possible use of these remarkable processes.

SECTION SUMMARY: MEMORY IMPROVEMENT

1. Three specific methods of memory improvement include visual imagery (constructing interacting mental images and the keyword method), the method of loci, and organization (chunking, a hierarchy, the first-letter technique, and the narrative technique).
2. Four more general strategies of memory improvement include external memory aids, practice (the total time hypothesis and the distribution of practice effect), the multimodal approach, and metamemory.

CHAPTER REVIEW QUESTIONS

1. What is encoding specificity? How is the outshining hypothesis relevant to the research on encoding specificity? How is encoding specificity related to the topic of mood-state dependence?
2. Give several examples of explicit and implicit memory tasks you have performed in the past few days. How is the concept of dissociation relevant in the research on explicit and implicit memory that has been conducted on both amnesic patients and normal adults?
3. According to one saying, "The more you know, the easier it is to learn." What evidence do we have for this statement in the material discussed in this chapter? How can educators take advantage of this saying?
4. Define the term *autobiographical memory* and mention several topics that have been studied in this area. How does research in this area differ from more traditional laboratory research, and what is the debate concerning ecological validity?
5. Describe how schemas could lead to a distortion in the recall of a flashbulb memory. How might misleading post-event information also influence this recall?
6. The topics of mood and emotion were examined in the sections on the determinants of accuracy and flashbulb memories. What does this research show? Think of examples from your own experience related to these two topics.
7. Describe an example of an occasion where you had difficulty on a reality monitoring task. According to Johnson and Raye, how do people decide

whether or not an event really happened? The section on memory for action also discussed prospective memory. Describe several prospective memory tasks you currently face. How could external memory aids help you remember to do these things?

8. Discuss as many of the mnemonic techniques from this chapter as you can remember. Describe how you can use each one to remember some information from this chapter for your next cognitive psychology examination.

9. Some theorists have argued that mnemonic techniques are effective primarily because they encourage deeper encoding of the material. Review the techniques and show how most of them emphasize deep, rather than shallow, levels of processing.

10. Why are some current memory researchers critical of the traditional mnemonics approach to memory improvement? Why do the multimodal approach and the metamemory approach emphasize a more comprehensive, complex approach to memory improvement?

NEW TERMS

permastore
encoding specificity principle
outshining hypothesis
explicit memory measure
recall
recognition
implicit memory measure
repetition priming task
dissociation
picture superiority effect
Pollyanna Principle
mood congruence
mood-state dependence
meta-analysis technique
own-race bias
autobiographical memory
everyday memory
flashbulb memory
schema

repisodic memory
reality monitoring
prospective memory
ecological validity
mnemonics
imagery
keyword method
method of loci
organization
chunking
hierarchy
first-letter technique
narrative technique
external memory aid
total time hypothesis
distribution of practice effect
multimodal approach
metamemory

RECOMMENDED READINGS

Cohen, G. (1989). *Memory in the real world*. London: Lawrence Erlbaum. Cohen's book is a clear, interesting, and well-written overview of the research on autobiographical memory.

Davies, G. M., & Thomson, D. M. (Eds.). (1988). *Memory in context: Context in memory*. Chichester, England: John Wiley & Sons. Encoding specificity is thoroughly covered in this book, which also includes information on face recognition, mood and memory, and eyewitness testimony.

Ericsson, K. A., & Smith, J. (Eds.). (1991b). *Toward a general theory of expertise: Prospects and limits*. New York: Cambridge University Press. This edited volume explores expert knowledge in areas as diverse as chess, music, and sports.

Herrmann, D. J. (1991). *Super memory*. Emmaus, PA: Rodale Press. Herrmann's book describes the multimodal approach to memory improvement. An especially useful part of the book is a list of a wide variety of memory techniques.

Lewandowsky, S., Dunn, J. C., & Kirsner, K. (Eds.). (1989). *Implicit memory: Theoretical issues*. Hillsdale, NJ: Lawrence Erlbaum. This is an excellent book on the distinction between explicit and implicit memory, covering both theory and research.

Loftus, E. F., & Ketcham, K. (1991). *Witness for the defense*. New York: St. Martin's Press. Elizabeth Loftus is probably the best known researcher on eyewitness testimony. This book, written for a popular audience, discusses not only research in this area, but also her personal experiences in providing expert testimony in the courtroom.

ANSWERS TO DEMONSTRATION 5.1.

1. railroad	6. apple	11. street	16. arm
2. cat	7. heart	12. devil	17. skirt
3. sister	8. shoe	13. orange	18. breakfast
4. bed	9. chair	14. bird	19. window
5. head	10. kitchen	15. grandfather	20. moon

IMAGERY

INTRODUCTION

THE CHARACTERISTICS OF MENTAL IMAGES

    IMAGERY AND ROTATION

    IMAGERY AND SIZE

    IMAGERY AND SHAPE

    IMAGERY AND PART-WHOLE RELATIONSHIPS

    IMAGERY AND AMBIGUOUS FIGURES

    IMAGERY AND INTERFERENCE

    OTHER VISION-LIKE PROCESSES

    NEUROPSYCHOLOGICAL EVIDENCE FOR THE SIMILARITY BETWEEN IMAGERY

        AND PERCEPTION

    THE IMAGERY CONTROVERSY

COGNITIVE MAPS

    COGNITIVE MAPS AND DISTANCE

    COGNITIVE MAPS AND SHAPE

    COGNITIVE MAPS AND RELATIVE POSITIONS

    IN DEPTH: USING VERBAL DESCRIPTIONS TO CREATE MENTAL MODELS

The last three chapters have emphasized memory for verbal material. Now we shift our focus to more pictorial material as we investigate mental imagery, specifically, the characteristics of mental images and cognitive maps.

Psychologists have devised some clever research techniques to identify the characteristics of mental images. In many ways, mental images and the perception of real objects are similar; for example, our mental images of elephants are larger than our mental images of rabbits. This section also examines a controversy about how we store mental images in memory—are images stored in a picture-like code or a more abstract description?

A cognitive map is an internal representation of your spatial environment. For example, you have a cognitive map of the town or city in which your college is located. Our cognitive maps show certain systematic distortions. For example, you are likely to remember city streets as intersecting at right angles, even when the angles are not so regular. As a final topic in this chapter, we will consider how people can create mental models of their environment on the basis of verbal descriptions.

INTRODUCTION

Which is larger, a tennis ball or the rounded portion of a lightbulb? Which is darker green, a frozen pea or a pine tree? Which is higher off the ground, the tip of a racehorse's tail or its rear knee? When people try to answer these questions, many report that their "mind's eye" seems to see the tennis ball, the pine tree, or the horse (Kosslyn, 1990). This chapter examines **imagery,** which is the mental representation of things that are not physically present.

Although imagery and perception share some important characteristics, the two systems also differ. For example, a perceptual stimulus stimulates the sensory receptors, such as the rods and cones of the eye; these receptors are not activated during imagery. Furthermore, imagery only occurs in specific circumstances (Kosslyn, 1988). An image of a racehorse comes to mind only when you begin to perform the comparison. Also, the range of individual differences among normal individuals is more striking in the case of visual imagery than in the case of perception. When asked to describe a girl carrying an umbrella, a "high-imager" will provide a description that is rich in visual detail, even including specifics about the color of her boots and the shape of the umbrella handle (Reisberg et al., 1986). In contrast, a "low-imager" may report a vague description that lacks richness and detail.

How often do we use imagery? Inspired by the research on everyday cognition in areas such as memory, Stephen Kosslyn and his colleagues (1990) asked students to keep a diary listing the instances of mental imagery that occurred in their daily lives. The students reported that about two-thirds of their images were visual;

images involving hearing, touch, taste, and smell were much less common. Psychologists' research preferences show a similar lopsidedness. Although they occasionally study topics such as auditory or smell imagery (e.g., Intons-Peterson & McDaniel, 1991; Reisberg, 1992), most of the research examines visual imagery.

Imagery has received more than 2,500 years of attention in Western thought (Yuille, 1985). Even the first psychologists considered imagery to be an important part of the discipline (Gardner, 1985). For example, Wundt and his followers carefully analyzed the self-reports provided in the introspections that trained subjects provided about imagery. However, American behaviorists, such as John Watson, were strongly opposed to research on any process as unobservable as mental imagery. As a consequence, research and theories about imagery declined sharply during the 40-year period in which behaviorism was dominant (Kent, 1990; Yuille, 1983). Frederick Bartlett maintained an interest in imagery in Great Britain, and Jean Piaget explored developmental aspects of imagery in continental Europe (Yuille, 1985). Nonetheless, these psychologists were unable to inspire enthusiasm about imagery in the United States. As behaviorism declined in popularity, however, cognitive psychologists rediscovered imagery and have made it one of the most controversial areas in contemporary cognitive psychology.

This chapter explores two aspects of mental images. The first section examines the nature of mental images, with an emphasis on the way these mental images are stored. The second section focuses on cognitive maps, or the representation of geographic information.

THE CHARACTERISTICS OF MENTAL IMAGES

As you might expect, research on mental imagery is difficult to conduct, especially because mental images are not directly observable and because they fade quickly (Finke, 1989). However, psychologists have recently begun to apply some of the research techniques developed for studying visual perception, so the investigation of imagery has made impressive advances in recent decades (Finke & Shepard, 1986). Try Demonstration 6.1, which illustrates one important research technique.

One of the major controversies in this field concerns the extent to which imagery processes resemble perceptual experiences. Many theorists, such as Finke (1989) and Kosslyn (1990), argue that information is stored in analog codes. An **analog code** is a representation that closely resembles the physical object. (Notice that the word *analog* suggests the word *analogy*, such as the analogy between the real object and the mental picture.) Suppose that you are looking at a picture of a star above a picture of a cross, and then the star is moved closer to the cross. An analog representation of that movement will have to represent the same set of intermediate states that your visual system registers during the actual physical movement (Rumelhart & Norman, 1988).

In contrast, other theorists such as Pylyshyn (1978, 1984) argue that we store images in terms of a propositional code. A **propositional code** is an abstract, language-like representation; storage is neither visual nor spatial, and it does not

DEMONSTRATION 6.1

MENTAL ROTATION (FROM SHEPARD & METZLER, 1971).

Which of these pairs of objects are the same, and which are different?

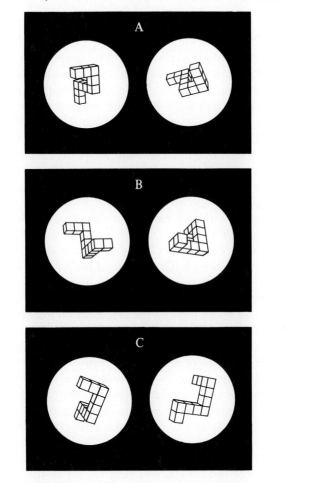

resemble the original stimulus. Thus, if you close your eyes and try to visualize your best friend's face, that face will be captured by a set of abstract propositions specifying each facial feature.

The controversy about analog versus propositional coding has not been resolved, although most researchers seem to favor the analog approach. Like most controversies in psychology, both positions are probably at least partially correct. However, it will be useful as you read the following pages to decide which studies support the analog-code hypothesis and which support the propositional hypothesis. At the end of this section, we will return to the discussion of the way in which information is stored. First, however, we must examine the research on the characteristics of mental images, which has important implications for the nature of the storage code.

Imagery and Rotation

A major stumbling block to the study of imagery is that cognitive processes are generally unobservable. However, some other cognitive processes can be studied more readily than imagery. For example, we can examine memory for verbal material by asking people to write down the words they have learned. Their recall provides some hints about memory processes. Now think how you might study mental images. Compared with verbal memory, this mental process is elusive and inaccessible. It's tempting to suggest that we should simply ask people to introspect about their mental images and use these reports as a basis for a description of mental imagery. However, as Pinker (1985) writes, these introspective reports can be unreliable and biased because we may not have conscious access to the processes involved in imagery. (You'll recall that the consciousness section of Chapter 2 discussed this issue.)

It's interesting to contemplate how much less productive the research on mental imagery might have been if Roger Shepard hadn't had an unusual half-dream on November 16, 1968. He was just emerging from sleep on that morning when he visualized a three-dimensional structure majestically turning in space (Shepard, 1978). This vivid image inspired the first study on imagery that used careful controls and measurement procedures—the first study that made those inaccessible mental images more accessible. It provided objective, quantitative data that could satisfy some of the more permissive behaviorists (Cooper & Shepard, 1984).

You tried the experiment in Demonstration 6.1, which is based on this study by Shepard and his coauthor, Jacqueline Metzler (1971). Notice that in the top pair of designs, the left-hand figure can be changed into the right-hand figure by keeping the figure flat on the page and rotating it clockwise. Suddenly, the two figures match up, and you reply "same." The middle pair, however, requires a rotation in a third dimension. You may, for example, take the two-block "arm" that is jutting out toward you and push it over to the left and away from you. Suddenly, again, the figures match up, and you reply "same." In the case of the bottom figure, every attempt to rotate the figure produces a mismatch, and you conclude "different."

Shepard and Metzler asked eight long-suffering people to judge 1,600 pairs of line drawings like these. The participants pulled a lever with their right hand if they judged the figures to be the same, and they pulled another lever with their left hand if they judged the figures to be different. In each case, the experimenters measured the amount of time required for a decision.

Does it take longer to rotate pairs in depth, as in the middle pair, than to rotate

Reaction Time for Deciding That Pairs of Figures Are the Same, as a Function of the Angle of Rotation and the Nature of Rotation (Shepard & Metzler, 1971). [Note: The centers of the circles indicate the means, and the bars on either side provide an index of the variability of those means.]

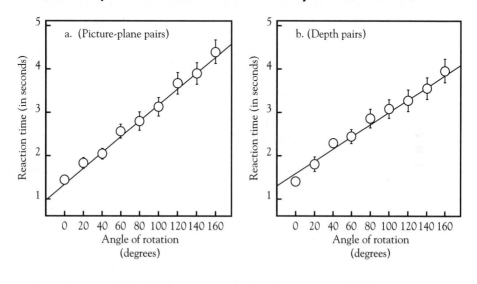

them in the picture plane, as in the top pair? Figure 6.1 shows the results for the two kinds of pairs. First, notice that the two graphs are very similar. Secondly, notice that in each graph, decision time was strongly influenced by the amount of rotation required to match a figure up with its mate. Rotating a figure 160° requires much more time than rotating it a mere 20°. As you can see, the relationship between rotation and reaction time is strictly linear in both figures.

The Shepard and Metzler study is an excellent demonstration that illustrates how the operations we perform on objects in our mind are similar to the operations we would perform on actual physical objects. If you were holding two figures in your hands, trying to decide whether they were the same, you would find that rotating a figure in depth would be no more difficult than rotating it while holding it flat. However, you would take longer rotating a figure 160° than rotating it 20°.

The study on geometric figures has been replicated with other stimuli, such as letters of the alphabet (e.g., Cooper & Shepard, 1973; Jordan & Huntsman, 1990; Just & Carpenter, 1985). We also know that people rotate familiar figures more quickly than unfamiliar figures, and they rotate clear pictures more rapidly than blurry pictures (Duncan & Bourg, 1983; Jolicoeur et al., 1987). Furthermore, with

---

DEMONSTRATION 6.2

IMAGERY AND SIZE.

A. Imagine an elephant standing next to a rabbit. Now answer this question: *Does a rabbit have a beak?*

B. Imagine a fly standing next to a rabbit. Now answer this question: *Does a rabbit have an eyebrow?*

In which picture was the rabbit the largest, A or B? Which picture seemed to have more detail in the area you were examining for the beak or the eyebrow, A or B?

---

practice, we can rotate figures more rapidly. In a representative study, Jolicoeur (1985) found that after 50 trials, the average participant reduced the rotation time from 1.3 seconds to 1.0 seconds.

In general, the research on rotating figures and letters provides some of the strongest support for the analog coding approach. We seem to treat mental images the same way we treat physical objects when we rotate them through space.

Imagery and Size

The first systematic research on imagery demonstrated that people treat mental images the same way they treat physical objects when they rotate them in space. Researchers immediately began to examine other attributes of mental images, such as their size and shape. Try Demonstration 6.2 before you read further.

Kosslyn's Research.   Questions like those in Demonstration 6.2 were part of a carefully planned series of experiments conducted by a major researcher in imagery, Stephen Kosslyn. Kosslyn (1975) wanted to discover whether people would make faster judgments about large images than about small images. You can anticipate a major problem with this research area: How can we control the size of someone's mental image? Kosslyn figured that a mental image of an elephant next to a rabbit would force people to imagine a relatively small rabbit. In contrast, a mental image of a fly next to a rabbit would produce a relatively large rabbit.

When you see *real-life* pictures of animals, you can see all the details quite clearly on a large picture. On the other hand, details are squeezed in so close together on a small picture that it is difficult to make judgments about them. If this same rule for real-life pictures also holds true for pictures in our heads, then people should make judgments more quickly with a large mental image (as in a rabbit next to a fly) than with a small mental image (as in a rabbit next to an elephant). In the experiment, people made judgments about objects, for example, whether a rabbit had legs. Kosslyn's results support his prediction; judgments were 0.21 seconds faster with a large mental image than with a small mental image. This difference was very substantial, given the small amount of time required to make these judgments.

Kosslyn was concerned, however, that critics might argue that the results could be due to some aspect of elephants and flies other than their relative size. For example, people might find elephants so fascinating that the rabbit part of the elephant-rabbit mental image is relatively undeveloped. In a second experiment, therefore, Kosslyn (1975) asked participants to imagine various animals next to either a monstrous fly (one that was as big as an elephant) or next to a minuscule elephant (one that was as small as a fly). The results showed that judgments were 0.29 seconds faster with a large mental image (that is, when the animal is next to the minuscule elephant) than with a small mental image (that is, when the animal is next to the monstrous fly). In other words, these two experiments demonstrate that characteristics are easier to "see" when the mental image is large, and the effect cannot be explained by another factor, the relative interest of the competing figure.

Kosslyn anticipated yet another argument that his critics might make. Perhaps people take longer to create a small mental image than to create a large mental image. Perhaps, then, these small mental images are relatively incomplete at the time of the test, when people are asked to make judgments about the images, and consequently those judgments take longer. In a final experiment Kosslyn (1975) asked people to imagine an animal and to make the mental image of the animal into a "picture" of specified dimensions. When an image was clearly in mind, the participants gave a signal. The results of this study showed that it took much longer to create *large* mental images. Kosslyn therefore answered another potential criticism of his study, and at the same time provided further support for the analogy between physical objects and mental images. After all, it takes longer to fill in all the detail on a large painting than on a small painting. Similarly, it takes longer to "paint" a large mental image than a small one.

In other research on the relationship between size and response time, Kosslyn and his colleagues (1978) demonstrated that people took a long time to scan the distance between two faroff points on a mental map that they had created. In contrast, they scanned the distance between two nearby points quite rapidly.

Experimenter Expectancy. Kosslyn's research had eliminated several alternative explanations that critics might suggest to explain his data. However, Intons-Peterson (1983) has argued that these results could perhaps be produced by experimenter expectancy. In **experimenter expectancy,** the experimenters' biases influence the outcomes of the experiment. For example, experimenters who conduct research in mental imagery know that longer distances should require longer search times. Experimenters could somehow transmit these expectations to the participants in the study. These participants might (either consciously or unconsciously) adjust their search speeds according to the expectations.

FIGURE 6.2

Relationships between Distance and Reaction Time, as Predicted by Exper-imenter-Expectancy Explanation and as Actually Demonstrated by Partic-ipants in the Experiment (Based on Jolicoeur & Kosslyn, 1985a).

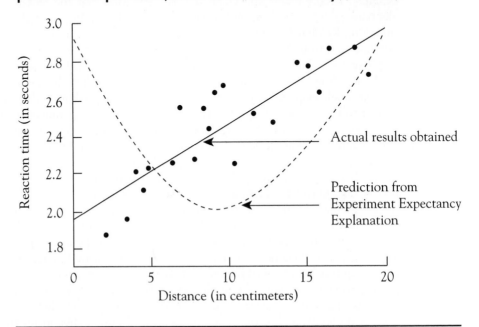

To answer this criticism, Jolicoeur and Kosslyn (1985a, 1985b) repeated Kosslyn and his coauthors' (1978) mental map experiment. However, the two people who conducted the experiment were not familiar with the research on mental imagery, and they were given elaborate and convincing (but incorrect) explanations about why their results *should* show a U-shaped relationship between distance and scanning time. (The explanation involved Gestalt organizational principles, discussed in Chapter 1.) Participants in the experiment studied a map in order to create a mental image of various locations on the map, such as a large tree and a hut. Then the experimenter named a location on the map and instructed the participant to "focus" on this location. The experimenter then named a second location and asked the participant to imagine a small black speck moving in a straight line from the original location toward the second location. The participants were told to press a button when the speck "arrived" at the destination.

Did the results show the typical relationship between distance and time, with longer distances requiring more time, or did they show the U-shaped results that the experimenters had been led to expect the participants to supply? Figure 6.2 illustrates the U-shaped results that the experimenters should have obtained if experimenter expectancy had been operating. It also shows that the results actually obtained in the experiment demonstrated the by-now typical linear relationship, in which it takes longer to scan a large mental distance. Experimenter expectancy cannot account for the obtained results.

Moyer's Research. Robert Moyer has provided additional information about how the relative size of mental images corresponds to the relative size of physical objects. Moyer (1973) used a principle from **psychophysics,** the area of psychology that measures people's reactions to perceptual stimuli. In psychophysics, we know that when people are asked to judge which of two lines is longer, they take longer to make a decision if the lines are almost equal. If the lines are clearly different from one another, the decision is much faster.

Moyer searched for evidence of an **internal psychophysics,** one that operates on images stored inside the head, rather than images on paper. He proposed that people should take longer to decide which was larger, a moth or a flea, than to decide which was larger, a moose or a roach. This prediction, remember, was based on the longer decision times for physical objects when the two choices are similar in size.

Participants in Moyer's (1973) experiment saw many different pairs of names for animals, with the animals ranging in size from a flea to a whale. Moyer measured how long it took people to decide which member of the pair was larger. Then people assigned a number to each animal name, estimating that animal's size. The results showed evidence of an internal psychophysics. There was a **symbolic distance effect;** that is, the smaller the difference in size between the two animals, the longer was the decision time (Moyer & Dumais, 1978). Thus it took longer to decide whether an ant (whose size was ranked 1) was larger than a bee (size ranking of 2) than it took to compare an ant with an elk (size rankings of 1 and 7). Moyer argued that people convert the animal names into mental images that preserve the sizes of the animals. Decisions regarding relative size take a long time if two objects are similar, whether the objects are in our minds or physically in front of us.

Intons-Peterson's Research. So far, we have only considered visual images, asking questions about the sizes of imagined animals and the distances on imagined maps. Margaret Intons-Peterson (one of the creators of the Brown/Peterson & Peterson technique for assessing short-term memory) provides some interesting information about *auditory* distance.

Imagine a cat purring, and create a mental image of its pitch. Now with that auditory image firmly in mind, move the pitch upward to the pitch of a telephone ringing. Intons-Peterson and her colleagues (1992) asked students to perform a similar task in which two imagined sounds were separated by a large distance. She found that people required a long time to "travel" that mental distance. As you can see from Figure 6.3, however, people were able to "travel" a small mental distance much more quickly. For example, a typical participant might require less

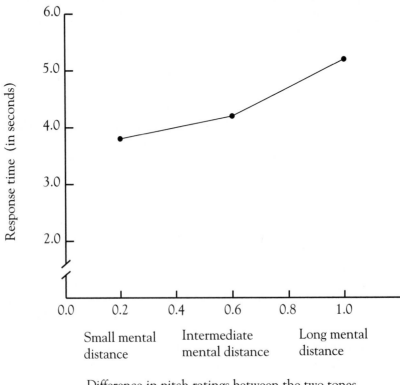

| FIGURE 6.3 | |

Amount of Time Taken to "Travel" a Mental Distance between Two Tones, as a Function of the Separation between These Two Tones (Based on Intons-Peterson et al., 1992).

Difference in pitch ratings between the two tones

than 4 seconds to move the pitch upward from "purring cat" to "ticking clock." Just as Kosslyn and his colleagues (1978) showed that long distances require more time on a *visual* mental map, Intons-Peterson showed that long distances require more time on an *auditory* mental map.

In addition, Intons-Peterson and her coworkers were able to demonstrate a symbolic distance effect with auditory images. You'll recall from Moyer's research on visual images that people take a long time to decide whether a bee is larger than an ant. In contrast, they could rapidly decide whether an elk is larger than an ant. Basically, then, when two objects are similar in size, it will take a long time to decide which is larger. In a second experiment, Intons-Peterson and her associates (1992) found that people take a long time to decide whether the pitch of a

---

DEMONSTRATION 6.3

IMAGERY AND ANGLES.

For each pair below, imagine two standard, nondigital clocks. Each clock should represent one of the specified times. Compare these two mental clocks and decide which clock has the smaller angle between the hour hand and the minute hand. Notice which two tasks seem to take longer.

1. 3:20 and 7:25
2. 4:10 and 9:23
3. 2:45 and 1:05
4. 3:15 and 5:30

---

purring cat is lower than the pitch of a ticking clock. However, they could rapidly decide whether the pitch of a purring cat is lower than the pitch of a ringing telephone.

Students in my cognitive psychology classes often have difficulty sorting out the research on size and mental imagery. Remember from Kosslyn's research and Intons-Peterson's first study that it takes longer to travel a large mental distance, whether that distance is visual or auditory. In contrast, Moyer's research and Intons-Peterson's second study illustrated the symbolic distance effect; when two stimuli are similar, it takes longer to decide which one is bigger (in the case of visual imagery) or which one is lower in pitch (in the case of auditory imagery). The symbolic distance effect always involves a comparison, such as two visual images or else two auditory images.

Imagery and Shape

Try Demonstration 6.3, which is similar to a study by Allan Paivio, one of the pioneers in research on imagery. In solving each problem in this demonstration, you probably seemed to consult two pictures that you created in your head. The task seemed to require imagery, rather than verbal reasoning.

Paivio (1978a) worked with a very basic kind of shape, the angle formed by the two hands on a mental clock. He decided to work with these particular shapes because these angles could be measured more precisely and consistently than the shape of imagined animals or other objects. Paivio asked people to make decisions, such as the ones described in Demonstration 6.3, and then he measured each decision time.

Paivio's results showed that decision time was related to the size of the difference between the angles. If the hands in the two clocks that were being compared create angles that are almost equal (for example, 3:20 and 7:25), the decision about which angle was smaller required a relatively long time. In contrast, the decision was easy

FIGURE 6.4

Decisions about Angles.

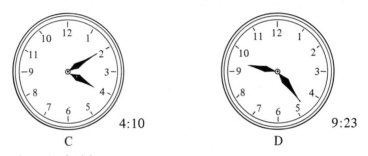

A difficult decision:
Which angle between the hands is smaller, clock A or clock B?

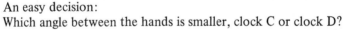

An easy decision:
Which angle between the hands is smaller, clock C or clock D?

---

and rapid when the two angles were quite different (for example, 4:10 and 9:23). Figure 6.4 shows a difficult decision and an easy one.

This finding provides more evidence for an "internal psychophysics," like the study by Moyer (1973) that we discussed in the Imagery and Size section. With real objects, people take longer to make a decision if two objects are similar than if there is a clear-cut difference. In the same way, people should take longer when the mental objects are similar to each other. Paivio therefore tested pairs of times corresponding to several angle size differences. For example, some pairs had a 30° difference between the angles, and some had a 150° difference.

Paivio also examined individual differences, a topic we should discuss before we look at his results. Some people are quite good at mental imagery tasks: Just mention the time 9:23 to them, and a mental picture of a clock reading 9:23 pops immediately into their heads. Other people have to struggle to make up an image. Slowly they picture the small hand set at the 9, then they try to keep the small hand glued there while they create a large hand pointing to the lower right-hand

FIGURE 6.5

The Influence of Angle Difference on Reaction Time, for High-Imagery and Low-Imagery People (From Paivio, 1978b).

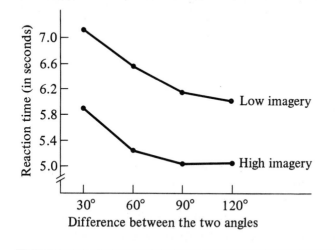

corner. Paivio gave the participants in his study several standardized tests for mental-imagery ability (e.g., predicting what a colored block would look like if subdivided into smaller blocks). Based on these test results, people were categorized as having either high-imagery or low-imagery.

Let us see how angle difference and imagery ability influenced reaction time, that is, the amount of time required to decide which angle is smaller. As Figure 6.5 shows, the study provided additional evidence for internal psychophysics. Notice how the reaction times are much longer when the two shapes are similar (that is, the angle difference is small). Notice, also, that high-imagery people have consistently shorter reaction times than the low-imagery people.

Paivio argues that this study offers strong support for the proposal that people use analog codes—rather than propositional codes—in problems like the mental clock task. First of all, the participants' reaction times were closely related to the angle differences, corresponding to the true, physical differences on "real" clocks. Secondly, the reaction times were related to imagery ability. Additional data showed that reaction times were not related to verbal ability; we would expect these two factors to be related if images were stored in a language-like propositional code.

Other research on imagery and shape provides additional support for analog codes. For example, Shepard and Chipman (1970) asked people to construct mental images of the shapes of various states—such as Colorado and West Virginia—and to make judgments about the shape similarity for various pairs of mental images. Their judgments were highly similar to the judgments they made when

---

DEMONSTRATION 6.4

IMAGERY AND PART-WHOLE RELATIONSHIPS.

Cover these instructions before asking a friend to look at this figure. Then cover up the figure and ask your friend whether it contained a parallelogram.

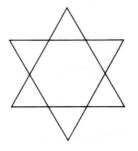

---

judging actual sketches of the states' shapes. Once again, people's judgments about the shape of mental images are similar to their judgments about the shape of physical stimuli.

Let's review the conclusions thus far about the characteristics of mental images:

1. When people rotate a mental image, a large rotation takes them longer, just as they take longer when rotating a physical stimulus by a large degree.
2. People make size judgments in a similar fashion for mental images and physical stimuli; this conclusion holds true for both visual and auditory images.
3. People make decisions about shape in a similar fashion for mental images and physical stimuli; this conclusion holds true for both simple shapes (angles formed by hands on a clock) and complex shapes (geographic regions).

Now let's consider some additional research on imagery.

Imagery and Part-Whole Relationships

Try Demonstration 6.4 and note whether your friend reported seeing a parallelogram. For most people, this is a difficult question. Reed (1974) was interested in people's ability to decide whether a pattern was a portion of a pattern they had seen earlier. He therefore presented a series of pattern pairs, first a pattern like the Star of David in Demonstration 6.4, and then, after a brief delay, a second pattern (for example, a parallelogram). In half of the cases the second pattern was truly part of the first one; in the other half of the cases it was not (for example, a rectangle).

If people store mental images in their heads that correspond to the physical objects that they have seen, they should be able to produce the mental image and

Figure 6.6

An Example of an Ambiguous Figure from Chambers and Reisberg's (1985) Study.

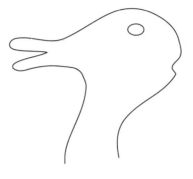

adjust the parallelogram into place in their mental image. However, the participants in Reed's study were correct only 14 percent of the time on this particular
example. Overall, they were correct only 55 percent of the time, hardly better than
chance. This lack of accuracy, Reed argued, suggests that people could not have
been storing mental pictures. Instead, he proposed that people store pictures as
descriptions, in propositional codes. Your friend may have stored the description
in Demonstration 6.4 as "two triangles, one pointing up and the other pointing
down, placed on top of each other." When asked whether the figure contained a
parallelogram, your friend may have searched through that verbal description and
found only triangles, not parallelograms.

Notice that Reed's research is not consistent with the analog code argument.
At least in some circumstances, people may not store information about a picture
in terms of a picture-like representation. Instead, they may use language-like
descriptions, consistent with the propositional-code argument.

Imagery and Ambiguous Figures

One controversial question is whether visual imagery resembles perception in the
way we process ambiguous stimuli. For example, you can interpret the ambiguous
stimulus in Figure 6.6 in two ways: a rabbit facing to the right or a duck facing to
the left. Chambers and Reisberg (1985) showed this figure to participants for 5
seconds, asked them to create a clear mental image of the figure, and then removed
it. Participants were then asked to give a second, different interpretation of the
figure. None of the 15 people were able to do so, even though several of them
were high-imagery individuals. However, when they were asked to draw the figure
from memory and then reinterpret it, all 15 reported a second interpretation.

DEMONSTRATION 6.5

REINTERPRETING AMBIGUOUS STIMULI.

Imagine the capital letter **H.** Now imagine the capital letter **X** directly on top of the **H,** so that the four corners of each letter match up exactly. From this mental image, what new shapes and objects do you see in your "mind's eye"?

Chambers and Reisberg's (1985) research on ambiguous figures suggests that a language-like propositional code can dominate over an analog code. In this study, apparently, the initial interpretation of the figure is strong (Finke, 1989). Top-down processes—similar to those we explored in Chapter 2—can interfere with alternate interpretations. These results parallel those of Reed (1974) in which two triangles could not be reinterpreted to contain a parallelogram. Both of these studies required participants to manipulate a mental image of an abstract sketch that had just been presented, rather than asking them to create their own images of elephants, clocks, or West Virginia. Tasks using abstract shapes may encourage a propositional code, rather than an analog code. Similarly, when I was working on a jigsaw puzzle recently, I found myself searching for missing pieces to which I had attached labels, for instance, "angel with outstretched wings." In cases such as these, storage may be predominantly propositional.

In some circumstances, however, mental images can be as susceptible to reinterpretation as visual stimuli are. For example, Finke and his colleagues (1989) asked people to combine two mental images, as in Demonstration 6.5. The participants in this study were indeed able to come up with new interpretations for these ambiguous stimuli. In addition to a combined **X** and **H** figure, they reported some new geometric shapes (for example, right triangles), some new letters (for example, M), and some objects (for example, a bow tie). Furthermore, Peterson and her colleagues (1992) showed that people could indeed produce reinterpretations of the duck-rabbit ambiguous figure if they were encouraged to pay attention to specified parts of the image. In summary, visual images can be reinterpreted when the stimuli and instructions are ideal; coding can apparently involve analogs in some circumstances.

Imagery and Interference

Try to get a mental image of a good friend's face at the same time as your eyes wander over this page. You will probably find it a difficult task, because you are trying to look at the words on the page and to look (with your "mind's eye") at your friend. You cannot look two places at once, and so you experience interference. Research has demonstrated that visual perception can interfere with visual imagery, and visual imagery can also interfere with visual perception.

Visual Tasks Interfering with Visual Imagery. Brooks (1968) demonstrated that visual perception can interfere with a task that requires visual imagery. Participants in this study saw a block letter, such as the *L* in Figure 6.7. Then, from memory, people were instructed to make a decision about each corner in the figure. Specifically, they were told to answer "yes" if a corner was located at the extreme part of the figure (either the extreme top or the extreme bottom). If a corner was not located at an extreme part (i.e., if it was in the middle), they should answer "no." Starting at the asterisk in Figure 6.7(a), for example, and moving clockwise around the figure, notice that the responses should be "yes, yes, no, no, yes, yes."

Brooks asked participants to give their answers by responding in one of three different ways: (1) vocal (saying "yes" or "no" out loud); (2) tapping (using the left hand to answer "yes" and the right hand to answer "no"); and (3) pointing (looking at a complex spatial arrangement of pairs of Y's and N's—such as in Figure 6.7(b)—pointing to either the Y or the N).

Brooks reasoned that the pointing task would require a great deal of visual perception in order to scan the display of Y's and N's. In contrast, visual perception in the vocal or tapping conditions would be minimal. Therefore, to the extent that a person's mental image of that letter is visual, people would find it difficult to provide responses requiring visual perception. Brooks' results showed that people

---

FIGURE 6.7

An Example of a Block Diagram and an Answer Sheet for the Pointing Condition, Similar to Those Used by Brooks (1968). (a) A block letter: Subjects classified each corner as to whether it was at an extreme part of the figure or not. (b) An answer sheet for the pointing condition: Subjects pointed to Y or N to indicate the answer (correct answers are underlined).

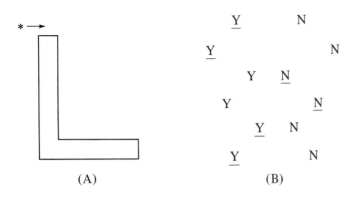

(A)   (B)

took about twice as long on the pointing task as on the other tasks; visual perception interfered with the visual image.

However, you might be suspicious about these results. How do we know that the pointing task is not simply a more difficult one, without considering interference? Fortunately, Brooks included another condition, in which people were asked to remember sentences and make judgments about the words in the sentence. This task was largely verbal or vocal, rather than spatial. The participants in this condition responded quickly for tapping and pointing, but they experienced interference when the vocal response was required, and their reaction times were much longer. Thus, visual perception interferes with a visual image, and a verbal task interferes with a verbal image. This experiment thus provides evidence that we store a memory of a picture (such as a picture of the letter L) in terms of what it looks like in its arrangement in space rather than in terms of a string of verbal descriptions of its shape.

Visual Imagery Interfering with Visual Tasks. If stimuli we really see can interfere with things we see in our mental images, will the reverse also be true? That is, can a mental image interfere when we are trying to see a physical stimulus? Segal and Fusella (1970) asked participants to make a visual image (for example, a volcano or a tree) or an auditory image (for example, the sound of an oboe or a typewriter). As soon as each person had formed the requested image, the experimenters presented either a sound on the harmonica (auditory signal), a small blue arrow (visual signal), or nothing. People performed much less accurately in detecting the physical stimulus when the image and the signal were in the same sensory mode. In other words, it was easier to see the arrow when they were imagining the sound of a typewriter than when they were imaging the shape of a tree. On the other hand, it was easier to hear the harmonica when they were imagining the shape of a tree than when they were imagining the sound of a typewriter. Once again, visual images seem to involve visual activity. In addition, auditory images seem to involve auditory activity.

Additional research by Segal and her coauthors has confirmed that images interfere with perception (Segal, 1971; Segal & Gordon, 1969). These researchers have found that people have trouble detecting external stimuli when they are actively creating mental images. However, Farah and Smith (1983) were not able to replicate this research. It is surprising that the interference and imagery research has not been more extensive, because in everyday life, we often experience conflicts between imagery and perception.

Other Vision-like Processes

Other research has explored additional similarities between imagery and visual processes. For example, one characteristic of the visual system is that acuity (or the ability to see small details) is better for objects that are registered in the center of the retina and worse for objects registered in the periphery. Finke and Kosslyn (1980) presented two dots about a centimeter apart; they asked participants in their study to indicate how far into their peripheral vision the dots could be moved before the acuity was so poor that the dots blurred together. Other participants performed the same task by *imagining* the dots moving out into the periphery. The perception and imagery instructions produced highly similar results, particularly for people with vivid imagery.

Another visual phenomenon discovered by perception researchers is called the **oblique effect,** which means that acuity is better for narrow stripes if they are oriented either horizontally or vertically than if they are oriented diagonally. Kosslyn (1983) reproduced the oblique effect using imagery instructions. This study demonstrates once again the similarity between perception and imagery. However, the study also has additional significance. Critics have proposed that the experimental results in imagery experiments might be traceable to demand characteristics. Earlier we discussed experimenter expectancy, a process by which the experimenter's expectations might be transmitted to participants in an experiment. **Demand characteristics** include all the cues that might convey the experimenter's hypothesis to the participant. Experimenter expectancy is one source of these cues, but there are numerous other demand characteristics, as well. For example, in many cases, participants may be able to guess the results that the experimenter wants. For instance, they may guess that an auditory image is supposed to interfere with an auditory perception. However, the oblique effect is virtually unknown to people without a background in the field of perception. It seems highly unlikely that the participants in Kosslyn's study could have guessed the results.

Other imagery phenomena resembling vision that have been demonstrated with visual imagery include stabilized images. Kosslyn (1983) showed that when people imagine a pattern at a particular location for a long period, it is more difficult to imagine a new pattern at that same location; this phenomenon is directly parallel to visual experience. Furthermore, another visual phenomenon involves complementary colors as afterimages: After viewing green, we see faint red. Complementary color afterimages can also be produced by imagery as well as by physical stimuli (Finke & Schmidt, 1978).

Additional research has explored more complex vision-like perceptions. For example, imagery can help people form a strong visual figure that is distinct from superimposed, distracting stimuli (Cave & Kosslyn, 1989). Visual illusions have also been demonstrated with imagery (Wallace, 1984). In short, imagery operates like perception for a wide variety of visual phenomena.

Neuropsychological Evidence for the Similarity between Imagery and Perception

We have examined many studies that demonstrate how people seem to treat mental images the same way they treat visual stimuli; imagery and perception appear to involve similar psychological processes. But how similar are imagery and perception at the physiological level? As Finke (1989) notes, mental imagery does not involve the rods and cones in the retina, or the parts of the visual system between the retina and the cortex. This makes sense; no visual stimuli are available to stimulate the retinal receptors, for example.

However, physiological structures at more advanced levels of visual processing do seem to be activated when we construct mental images (Simon, 1992b). Martha Farah (1988) recently received the Troland award in experimental psychology from the National Academy of Sciences for her research on vision. She has gathered some compelling evidence that the visual processing areas of the cerebral cortex are implicated in visual mental imagery.

The research summarized in Farah's review uses many of the techniques discussed in the section on neuroscience in Chapter 1. For example, researchers have studied individuals with lesions (damage) in the visual cortex. Many of these people cannot use mental imagery, even though their other cognitive abilities are normal.

A variety of studies have used the regional cerebral blood-flow method to assess which areas of the brain show increased blood flow when people engage in tasks that require visual imagery. Again, the visual cortex, located at the back of the brain, is most active (Farah, 1988; Kosslyn & Koenig, 1992). In a representative study, for example, Goldenberg and his colleagues (1988) found that this region showed increased blood flow when people were asked to make judgments that required visual imagery in order to make a decision (for example, "The green of pine trees is darker than that of grass. Correct or incorrect?"). In contrast, this region did not show increased blood flow for judgments involving minimal visual imagery (for example, "Columbus named the natives of America Indians because he believed he was in India. Correct or incorrect?"). Furthermore, using the evoked potential technique, Farah and her colleagues (1988) found that imagery influenced the evoked potentials that occurred when people viewed real visual stimuli.

The neuropsychological evidence is particularly compelling because it avoids the problem of demand characteristics that we discussed earlier. As Farah (1988) points out, people are not likely to know which parts of their brains are typically active during vision. Furthermore, they are not likely to be able to voluntarily change their electrical activity in their brains or force more blood to flow into the visual cortex! As Farah concludes:

> Across a variety of tasks, it has been found that imagery engages the visual cortex, whereas other tasks, many of which are highly similar save for the absence of visual imagery, do not. (p. 312)

The Imagery Controversy

Howard Gardner (1985) writes in his chronicle of the history of cognitive science, "Probably no research in recent cognitive studies has generated so much controversy as work on imagery" (p. 330). Let's first examine the analog position, and then we will consider the propositional view. It is important to know that these two positions differ in their emphasis on the similarity between mental images and physical stimuli. However, the two positions are not *completely* different from each other, and they may apply to different kinds of tasks.

The Analog Position. In examining the characteristics of mental images, we discovered many ways in which our reactions to mental images are the same as our reactions to real objects. (You may wish to review those similarities quickly.) Indeed, the majority of the research supports this position.

Kosslyn and others support a structural theory of imagery, which proposes that "similar mechanisms in the visual system are activated when objects or events are imagined as when the same objects or events are actually perceived" (Finke, 1989, p. 41). Kosslyn has developed a theory of imagery that has been implemented by a computer-simulation model (Kosslyn, 1981, 1987; Kosslyn & Koenig, 1992). This theory is complex, and it will only be briefly summarized in this textbook. According to this theory, images have two important components. The first is the **surface representation,** which is a quasi-pictorial representation. This representation depicts an object, and it is responsible for the experience we report of having a picturelike mental image. The surface representation is produced in the visual cortex, somewhat similar to the way a visual image is produced when we see a real, physical object. The second component of Kosslyn's theory is the **deep representation.** This is the information that is stored in long-term memory and is used to generate the surface representation. Two different kinds of deep representations can generate surface representations: (1) literal information, which consists of encodings of how something looked, and (2) propositional information, which describes an object or a scene in verbal terms.

How does Kosslyn's theory account for the generation of an image? According to Kosslyn, image generation occurs when a surface image is formed on the basis of information stored in long-term memory (that is, the deep representation). This image generation is accomplished by four processing components:

1. The *picture* process converts information encoded in a literal encoding into a surface image. The image can come in different sizes and locations, depending on the "instructions" given to the picture process.
2. The *find* process searches the surface image for a particular part. (For example, suppose someone is describing a person to you and then says, "He has red hair." You must find the neutral-colored hair in your surface image and correct the hair color.)
3. The *put* process performs several functions that are necessary to create a portion of an image at the correct location, for example by adjusting the size of one part of the image.
4. The *image* process coordinates the other three components and determines other characteristics such as whether the image will be detailed or relatively simple.

Kosslyn proposes additional processes that allow a person to scan to a correct location (for example, to look at the rear end of the mental image of a frog when asked, "Does a frog have a tail?"), to change the size of the mental image, and to rotate the figure.

The Propositional Position.

Pylyshyn (1978, 1984) has been the strongest opponent of the "pictures-in-the head" hypothesis. He agrees that people *do* experience mental images; it would be foolish to argue otherwise. However, Pylyshyn says that these images are epiphenomenal, which means that the images are simply "tacked on" later, after an item has been recovered from (propositional) storage. He proposes that information is actually stored in terms of propositions, or abstract concepts that describe relationships between items. People remove a proposition from storage and use that propositional information to construct a mental image. Pylyshyn argues that it would be awkward—and perhaps even unworkable—to store information in terms of mental images, because a huge storage space would be required to store all the images people claim they have.

Pylyshyn also emphasizes the differences between perceptual experiences and mental images. For example, a real photograph can be reexamined and reinterpreted. However, Reed's (1974) research showed that a mental image cannot be reinterpreted in order to locate a hidden part that was not originally noticed. Also, Chambers and Reisberg's (1985) study underscored how a mental image of some ambiguous stimuli cannot be readily reinterpreted, even though people can easily reinterpret a visual stimulus.

Furthermore, Pylyshyn points out that operations are possible for perceiving real objects that are impossible for mental images. Pylyshyn (1984) suggests an informal experiment to demonstrate this last point:

> Form a clear, stable image of a favorite familiar scene. Can you now imagine it as a photographic negative, out of focus, in mirror-image inversion, upside down? (pp. 227–228).

Indeed, you will probably find it difficult to make these transformations, because mental images do not always mimic perceptual experiences.

We cannot completely resolve the imagery controversy at this time. Imagery is such a hidden process that research is especially difficult. At present, we can probably conclude that with most stimuli and most tasks, storage seems to involve an analog code. For some kinds of stimuli and several specific tasks, however, a propositional code may be used. In many respects—though certainly not all—mental images resemble the perceptions of real objects.

SECTION SUMMARY: THE CHARACTERISTICS OF MENTAL IMAGES

1. An important controversy in imagery is whether information is stored in

analog or propositional codes; research on the characteristics of mental images has attempted to address this issue.

2. The amount of time it takes to rotate a mental image depends on the degree of rotation required, just as when rotating a real, physical object.

3. People take longer to make judgments about the characteristics of small mental images than of large mental images. Also, it takes longer to travel a large mental distance. Finally, when two mental images are similar, comparisons take longer than when the images are different.

4. When judging shapes, people take longer to make decisions about two similar angles formed by hands on a clock; when judging the shape of states, people make decisions about mental images that resemble their decisions about physical stimuli.

5. People have difficulty identifying that a part belongs to a whole if they have not included the part in their original verbal description of the whole.

6. Some ambiguous figures (for example, representational sketches) are difficult to reinterpret in a mental image; other figures (for example, superimposed letters) can be readily reinterpreted.

7. Visual tasks interfere with visual imagery, and verbal tasks interfere with verbal imagery. Furthermore, visual imagery may interfere with visual tasks, and auditory imagery may interfere with auditory tasks.

8. Other vision-like properties of mental images include acuity for objects registered in the retina's periphery, the oblique effect, the stabilized-image phenomenon, the formation of a visual figure, and visual illusions.

9. According to neuropsychological research, visual imagery involves the visual processing areas of the cerebral cortex.

10. The analog position has been developed into a theory by Kosslyn that includes both surface and deep representations. The propositional position, as expressed by Pylyshyn, argues that images are simply "tacked on" to the propositional code. At present, most (but not all) research supports the analog position.

COGNITIVE MAPS

You have probably had an experience like this. You just arrived in a new environment, perhaps for your first year of college. You ask for directions, let's say, to the library. You hear the reply, "OK, it's simple. You go up the hill, staying to the right of the Blake Building. Then you take a left, and Newton will be on your right. The library will be over on your left." You struggle to recall some landmarks from the orientation tour. Was Newton next to the college union, or was it over near the administration building? Valiantly, you try to incorporate this new information into your discouragingly hazy mental map.

So far, this chapter has examined the general characteristics of mental images and how they are stored in memory. Now we consider a related topic, cognitive maps. **Cognitive maps** are the internal representations of the way our spatial environment is arranged (Ormrod et al., 1988). Research on cognitive maps has examined environmental spaces that range in size from classrooms, to neighborhoods, to cities, countries, and larger geographic regions (Weatherford, 1985). Typically, these studies emphasize real-world settings and ecological validity.

In general, researchers have not discussed the way in which cognitive maps are encoded, that is, whether the code is analog or propositional. However, most researchers who have raised this issue conclude that cognitive maps must be both analog and propositional in nature (e.g., Gärling et al., 1985; McNamara et al., 1989; Russell & Ward, 1982). Your mental map for a particular city may therefore include both a picture-like image of the relationship among several streets and buildings, as well as propositions, such as "The Ethiopian restaurant is in northwest Toronto." Information on your mental map may include landmark knowledge and procedural knowledge (for example, "To get to the Ethiopian restaurant, go north from the hotel parking lot and turn left on Bloor"). Your mental map may also include survey knowledge, which is the relationship among locations that can be directly acquired by learning a map or by repeatedly exploring an environment (Schwartz & Kulhavy, 1988; Thorndyke & Goldin, 1983).

In this section on cognitive maps, we will consider how cognitive maps represent distance, shape, and orientation. Finally, the In-Depth section will examine how we can construct mental models of our environment, based on a verbal description.

Theme 2 of this book states that cognitive processes are generally accurate. This generalization also applies to cognitive maps, because our mental representations of the environment usually reflect reality with reasonable accuracy, whether these cognitive maps depict college campuses or larger geographic regions. However, the second part of Theme 2 states that when people do make errors in their cognitive processes, those mistakes can often be traced to a rational strategy. We saw an example of this principle in Chapter 5 on the schematic nature of memory: People tend to believe that certain events occurred in their lives, as long as these events are conceptually similar to the schemas they have already developed. Similarly, the mistakes people make in their cognitive maps "make sense." These mistakes are systematic distortions of reality. They reflect a tendency to base our judgments on variables that are typically relevant, and to judge our environment as being more regular and orderly than it really is. We will see that people tend to show systematic distortions in distance, shape, and orientation.

Cognitive Maps and Distance

How far is it from your college library to the classroom in which your cognitive psychology course is taught? How many miles separate the city in which you were born from the city where your home is currently located? When people make distance estimates like these, their estimates are often distorted by factors such as the number of intervening cities, road-route distance, and semantic categories.

Number of Intervening Cities. In one of the first systematic studies about distance in cognitive maps, Thorndyke (1981) constructed a map of a hypothetical region with cities distributed throughout the map at 100, 200, 300, and 400 miles from each other. Between any two cities on the map, there were 0, 1, 2, or 3 other cities along the route, and Thorndyke was interested in the relationship between the number of intervening cities and distance estimation. Participants in the experiment alternated between study trials and recall trials until they had accurately reconstructed the map on two consecutive trials. Finally, they received a sheet listing the 64 possible city pairs, and were instructed to estimate the distance between each pair of cities.

The number of intervening cities had a clear-cut influence on their estimates. For example, when the cities were really 300 miles apart on the map, people estimated that they were 280 miles apart when there were no intervening cities, but they were estimated to be 350 miles apart with three intervening cities. Notice that this error is a sensible one, however. In general, if two cities are randomly distributed through a region, any two cities *are* indeed farther apart when there are three other cities between them; two cities with no other intervening cities are likely to be closer together.

Road-Route Distance. People consider two cities to be physically closer together (as measured by a straight line) if the road connecting them is a straight line, rather than an indirect route. McNamara and his colleagues (1984) used a clever way of obtaining distance estimates. Their basic concern was that psychologists should use tasks that miminize demand characteristics in order to assess the properties of mental representations more accurately (McNamara, 1986). Mental images are especially hidden and covert, and we want to make these processes overt and measurable. The methods we use to make these processes overt should not require too much effort, or else the overt responses will not accurately reflect the covert processes. For example, suppose the researchers select distance estimates as the overt response. These estimates may be difficult to make, because they rely on memory and judgment. Unfortunately, they may not accurately reflect the "map in the head."

How else can researchers assess this "map in the head"? McNamara and his coauthors used a priming task, a method we also examined in Chapter 5. In many studies on language, people are asked to judge whether they recognize a word as having appeared in some material they read earlier. They tend to recognize the target word faster if it was immediately preceded in the recognition test by a word from the same earlier sentence as the target, in contrast to a word from a different sentence. This tendency for a nearby word to facilitate recognition of a target word is called a **priming effect**. McNamara and his colleagues used the priming effect to investigate, indirectly, people's mental maps. Recognition of a target city's name should be faster if that city is preceded by the name of a city perceived to be nearby

---

FIGURE 6.8

Map Similar to One Used by McNamara et al. (1984).

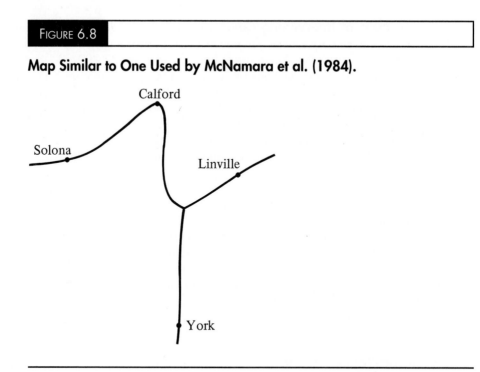

---

on the map. In contrast, the name of a faraway city should not facilitate recognition.

McNamara and his coauthors (1984) presented a hypothetical map of a region, containing 16 city names arranged along roadways. Figure 6.8 is similar to a small portion of the map. Notice that the city of Calford is equally far "as the crow flies" from the cities of Solona and Linville. However, traveling along the road, Calford is closer to Solona. The critical question is whether Calford is primed more by the name *Solona* than by the name *Linville*.

The experiment began with a series of study-test trials until participants could place the cities accurately on a blank map. This procedure ensured that they had indeed developed a mental map. A recognition test followed: City names were presented one at a time, and the participants were instructed to decide whether the city name was on the map they had just learned.

The results showed that people did respond relatively quickly when the target city was preceded by a city name that was connected to it by a direct road route. In contrast, people responded relatively slowly when the preceding city name was not directly connected with the target city. For example, a typical participant would recognize *Calford* much more quickly when preceded by the name *Solona* than when preceded by the name *Linville*. The priming effect demonstrates that road-route distance matters more than distance measured "as the crow flies" on people's cognitive maps. However, the emphasis on road-route distance is another distortion that makes good sense. In real life, we humans cannot travel along the route that crows fly; we travel along roads. It is therefore perfectly rational to think of distance in terms of road-route distance, rather than crow-flight distance.

Semantic Categories. The Computing and Media Center on my college campus seems closer to the College Union than it is to a clothing store. The clothing store is actually closer, but my distance estimate is distorted because the Computing and Media Center and the Union are clustered together in my semantic memory. The clothing store does not belong to this cluster, even though no physical boundary divides campus buildings from off-campus locations.

Research by Stephen Hirtle and his colleagues illustrates how semantic factors influence distance estimates for landmarks located within a town. For example, Hirtle and Mascolo (1986) constructed a hypothetical map of a town that included some landmarks associated with town government (for example, court house, police station, town hall) and some landmarks associated with recreation (for example, park, golf course, beach). After learning the locations on the map, the map was removed and people estimated the distance between pairs of landmarks. The results showed that people tended to shift each landmark closer to other landmarks that belonged to the same cluster. For example, the court house might

---

MENTAL MAPS AND CURVES.

Look at the portion of the map below, which shows a river and two nearby streets. Study this map for about 5 seconds. Then close the book and try to sketch the map as accurately as possible. The results will be discussed in the next section.

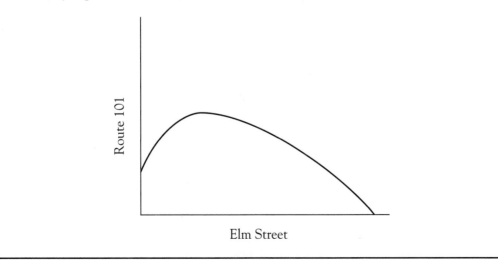

be remembered as being close to the police station and the town hall. The shifts occurred for members of the same semantic cluster, but not for members of different semantic clusters; the court house did not move closer to the park.

The same influence of semantic categories occurred when Hirtle and Jonides (1985) asked University of Michigan students to estimate distances between pairs of landmarks in Ann Arbor. The students showed a clustering bias; members of the same cluster were judged to be closer to each other than members of different clusters—even when the actual distances were the same.

Thus, both laboratory research (Hirtle & Mascolo, 1986) and research using ecologically valid stimuli (Hirtle & Jonides, 1985) confirm an additional distortion in distance estimates: When two places seem semantically close, we believe they are geographically close. Once again, however, this error makes sense; in general, our experience with real-life experiences tells us that landmarks with similar functions are likely to be close to each other. Be sure you have tried Demonstration 6.6 on page 199 before you read further.

Cognitive Maps and Shape

Our cognitive maps represent not only distances, but shapes. These shapes are evident in map features such as the angles formed by intersecting streets and the curves illustrating the bends in rivers. Once again, the research shows a systematic distortion; people tend to construct cognitive maps in which the shapes are more regular than they are in reality.

Angles. Consider the research by Moar and Bower (1983), who studied people's cognitive maps of Cambridge, England. All of the participants in the study had lived in Cambridge for at least 5 years. Moar and Bower wanted to determine people's estimates for the angles formed by the intersection of two streets. They were particularly interested in the angle estimates for sets of three streets that formed large triangles within the city of Cambridge. The participants showed a clear tendency to "regularize" the angles so that they were more like 90° angles. For example, three streets formed a triangle that contained real angles of 67°, 63°, and 50°. However, these same angles were estimated to be 84°, 78°, and 88°. In all, seven of the nine angles were significantly biased in the direction of a 90° angle. Furthermore, you know that the angles within a triangle should sum to 180°. Notice, however, that the angles in people's cognitive-triangle maps do not necessarily sum to 180°. (In this particular example, for instance, the angles sum to 250°.)

What explains this systematic distortion? Moar and Bower (1983) suggest that we employ a **heuristic,** or simple rule-of-thumb. In general, as a rule-of-thumb, when two roads meet, they form a 90° angle. It is easier to represent angles in a mental map as being closer to 90° than they really are. Similarly, as you recall from the discussion of schematization of memory, it is easier to store a schematic version of an event, rather than a precise version of the event that accurately represents all the little details.

Curves. The New York State Thruway runs in an east-west direction across the state, though it curves somewhat in certain areas. To me, the upward curve south of Rochester seems symmetrical, equally arched on each side of the city. However, when I checked the map, the curve is much steeper on the eastern side.

Research confirms that people tend to use a **symmetry heuristic;** figures are remembered as being more symmetrical and regular than they truly are. For example, Tversky and Schiano (1989) showed students maplike diagrams in which an irregularly shaped curve was said to be a river, bordered by two streets. These diagrams resembled the figure in Demonstration 6.6. The participants studied each figure for 5 seconds and then drew it from memory.

The results showed that for 7 of the 8 figures, people drew the figure as being more symmetrical than it had been in the original sketch. Now check your own figure from Demonstration 6.6 and see whether the symmetry heuristic also operated in your drawing.

Cognitive Maps and Relative Positions

Which city is farther west, San Diego, California, or Reno, Nevada? If you are like most people—and the participants in a study by Stevens and Coupe (1978)—the question seems ludicrously easy. Of course San Diego is farther west, because California is west of Nevada. However, if you consult a map, you'll discover that Reno is in fact west of San Diego. Which city is farther north, Detroit or its "twin city" across the river, Windsor, in Ontario, Canada? Again, the answer seems obvious; any Canadian city must be north of a U.S. city!

Barbara Tversky (1981) argues that cognitive maps often reveal two additional kinds of heuristics. We use these heuristics when we try to capture the orientation of features on our mental maps. Geographic regions are typically irregular in shape, and landmarks are typically irregularly scattered through space. We tend to represent features as being more regular than they really are—just as we represent the angles of intersecting streets as being close to 90° and we represent curves as being symmetrical. The two heuristics that operate for the relative positions of features are called the rotation heuristic and the aligment heuristic.

The Rotation Heuristic. According to the **rotation heuristic,** figures that are slightly tilted will be remembered as being either more vertical or more horizontal than they really are. For example, Figure 6.9 shows that the coastline of California is slanted at a significant angle. The rotation heuristic makes the orientation more vertical by rotating the coastline. If your cognitive map suffers from the distorting effects of the rotation heuristic, you will conclude (erroneously) that San Diego is

---

FIGURE 6.9

According to the Rotation Heuristic, We Tend to Rotate the Coastline of California Into a More Nearly Vertical Orientation and Incorrectly Conclude That San Diego Is Farther West Than Reno.

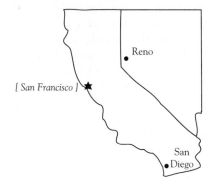

---

west of Reno. Similarly the rotation heuristic leads you to the wrong decision about Detroit and Windsor; Windsor, in Canada, is actually *south* of Detroit.

Let us look at some research on the rotation heuristic. Tversky (1981) studied people's mental maps for the geographic region of the San Francisco Bay area. This region slants substantially, as Figure 6.9 shows. However, 69 percent of the students at a Bay area college in this region showed evidence of the rotation heuristic. In their mental maps, the coastline was rotated in a more north-south direction than is true on a geographically correct map. Keep in mind, though, that some students—in fact, 31 percent of them—were not influenced by this heuristic.

The Alignment Heuristic. According to the **alignment heuristic,** figures will be remembered as being more lined up than they really are. To test the alignment heuristic, Tversky (1981) presented pairs of cities to students, who were asked to select which member of each pair was north (or east). For example, one of those pairs was Rome-Philadelphia. As Figure 6.10 shows, Rome is actually north of Philadelphia. However, because of the alignment heuristic, people tend to line up the United States and Europe so that they are in the same latitude. Because we know that Rome is in southern Europe and Philadelphia is at the north end of the United States, we conclude—incorrectly—that Philadelphia is north of Rome.

Tversky's results indicated that the students showed a consistent tendency to use the alignment heuristic. For example, 78 percent judged Philadelphia to be north of Rome, and 12 percent judged that they were the same latitude. Only 10 percent correctly answered that Rome is north of Philadelphia. On all eight pairs tested, an average of 66 percent supplied the incorrect answer.

FIGURE 6.10

According to the Alignment Heuristic, We Tend to Line Up Europe and the United States and Incorrectly Conclude That Philadelphia Is North of Rome.

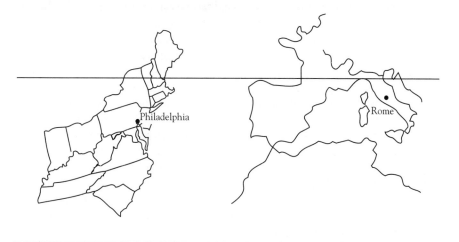

The rotation heuristic and the alignment heuristic may initially sound similar. However, the rotation heuristic involves rotating a single coastline, country, building, or other figure in a clockwise or counterclockwise fashion so that its border is oriented in a nearly vertical or horizontal direction. In contrast, the alignment heuristic involves lining up a number of separate countries, buildings, or other figures in a straight row. Both heuristics are similar, however, because they encourage us to construct cognitive maps that are orderly.

The heuristics we have examined in this chapter make sense. For example, our cities tend to have right angles, pictures are generally hung on walls in a vertical orientation, rather than at a slant, and houses are typically lined up evenly along the streets. However, when we rely too strongly on these heuristics, we miss the important details that make each stimulus unique. When our top-down cognitive processes are too active, we fail to pay sufficient attention to bottom-up information. In fact, the angle at the intersection is really 70°, that coastline does not run exactly north-south, and those continents are not really arranged in a horizontal line.

We have been stressing the similarity among the various heuristics. However, Tversky (1991a) points out some noticeable differences. For example, the symmetry heuristic, which would be used for representing curves, is equally strong in perception and in memory. In contrast, the rotation and alignment heuristics are small in perception; with the actual maps in front of us, we show little distortion. However, the distortions produced by these two heuristics are much stronger in memory than in perception.

◇ In Depth: **Using Verbal Descriptions to Create Mental Models**

In everyday life, we often hear or read descriptions of a particular environment. A friend calls to give you directions to her house. You have never traveled there before, yet you find yourself creating a cognitive map to represent the route. Similarly, a neighbor describes the setting in which his car was hit by a truck, or you read a mystery novel explaining where the dead body was found in relation to the broken vase and the butler's fingerprints. Again, you create cognitive maps. These cognitive maps allow us to simulate spatial aspects of our external environment (Rumelhart & Norman, 1988).

One of the themes of this textbook is that cognitive processes are active. When we hear a description, we do not simply store these isolated statements in a passive fashion. Instead, we actively create a mental model that represents the relevant features of a scene. In fact, people who had been asked to draw maps of environments that they had read about were just as accurate in their re-creation as people who learned this same information by studying a map (Taylor & Tversky, 1992).

In this In-Depth section, we will examine how people create these mental models, based on verbal description. Let us begin by considering the initial research. Then we will examine the spatial framework model, as well as other information about the characteristics of mental models.

Franklin and Tversky's Research.   Before you read further, try Demonstration 6.7, which is based on a story used in a series of studies conducted by Nancy Franklin and Barbara Tversky (1990). Franklin and Tversky presented descriptions of 10 different scenes, depicting a hotel lobby, an opera theater, a barn, and so forth. Each description mentioned five objects located in a plausible position in relation to the observer (either above, below, in front, in back, and to either the left or the right side). Only five objects were mentioned, so that the memory load would not be overwhelming. After reading each description, the participants were instructed to imagine that they were rotating to face a different object. They were then asked to specify which object was located in each of several directions (for example, "above your head"). In all cases, the researchers measured how long the participant took to respond to the question.

Franklin and Tversky were especially interested in discovering whether response time depended upon the location of the object that was being tested. Can we make all those decisions equally quickly? In contrast, did your experience with Demonstration 6.7 suggest that some decisions are easier than others?

As you can see from Figure 6.11, people could rapidly answer which objects were above and below; reaction times were short. They required a somewhat longer amount of time to decide which objects were ahead or behind, and decisions about which objects were to the right and to the left required the longest amount of time. Figure 6.11 also allows us to contrast pairs of items. You can see that "above" and "below" decisions took equally long. Also, "right" and "left" decisions took

DEMONSTRATION 6.7

CREATING A MENTAL MODEL.

Take a piece of paper and cover the portion labeled "Further Instructions." Read the story. When you have finished reading it, cover up the story and follow the Further Instructions.

The Story

You are at the Jefferson Plaza Hotel, where you have just taken the escalator from the first to the second floor. You will be meeting someone for dinner in a few minutes. You now stand next to the top of the escalator, where you have a view of the first floor as well as the second floor. You first look directly to your left, where you see a shimmering indoor fountain about 10 yards beyond a carpeted walkway. Though you cannot see beyond the low, stone wall that surrounds it, you suppose that its bottom is littered with nickels and pennies that hotel guests have tossed in. The view down onto the first floor allows you to see that directly below you is a darkened, candle-lit tavern. It looks very plush, and every table you see seems to be filled with well-dressed patrons. Looking directly behind you, you see through the window of the hotel's barbershop. You can see an older gentleman, whose chest is covered by a white sheet, being shaved by a much younger man. You next look straight ahead of you, where you see a quaint little giftshop just on the other side of the escalator. You're a sucker for little ceramic statues, and you squint your eyes to try to read the hours of operation posted on the store's entrance. Hanging from the high ceiling directly above you, you see a giant banner welcoming the Elks convention to the hotel. It is made from white lettering sewn onto a blue background, and it looks to you to be about 25 feet long. (Based on Tversky, 1991b, p. 133)

Further Instructions

Now imagine that you have turned to face the barber shop. Cover up the story above and answer the following questions:

1. What is above your head?
2. What is below your feet?
3. What is ahead of you?
4. What is behind you?
5. What is to your right?

FIGURE 6.11

Response Times for Questions about Various Directions in Relation to the Upright Observer (Based on Franklin & Tversky, 1990).

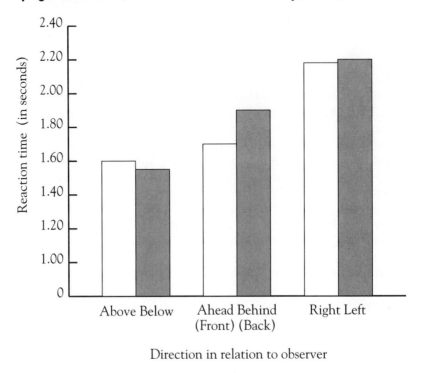

Direction in relation to observer

---

equally long. However, people judged much more quickly what was "ahead" as opposed to "behind."

Franklin and Tversky (1990) replicated these results in two additional studies; again, the vertical dimension was systematically favored. They also asked participants to describe how they thought they had performed the task. All participants reported that they had constructed images of the environment as they were reading. Most also reported that they had constructed imagery that represented the observer's point of view. (Did you use imagery in Demonstration 6.7, and did you adopt the observer's viewpoint?)

The Spatial Framework Model. Franklin and Tversky (1990) compare three potential models that could explain how people might explore their imagined environments. They reject the equiavailability model and the mental transformation model, and they favor the spatial framework model.

According to the equiavailability model, people can make decisions equally rapidly about all directions, because all locations are equally available to the observer. Clearly, the data in Figure 6.11 do not support the equiavailability model.

According to the mental transformation model, readers are immersed in an imagined environment. To inspect the locations of the specified objects, you must mentally turn your body or your head. The response times should depend upon the amount of mental movement needed to inspect each location. You should respond most quickly to objects in front of you, because these objects require no mental movement. You should take somewhat longer to identify objects to your right, left, above, and below; however, these four response times should be similar because all are 90° away from the front. In contrast, objects behind you should have the longest response times, because you would need to mentally rotate your head 180° to locate these objects in your mind's eye. The mental transformation model is consistent with the research by Shepard and Metzler (1971) examined at the beginning of the chapter, which showed that decision time depended on the number of degrees that a figure needed to be rotated. Notice, however, that the data in Figure 6.11 do not match these predictions.

Apparently, then, we respond differently when we imagine ourselves in a described environment, surrounded by objects. Our judgments about these mental models are not based simply on perceptions. (In contrast, you'll recall that we emphasized throughout the first section of this chapter that mental images *mirrored* perceptions.) Instead, the **spatial framework model** emphasizes that our conceptions of space differ from our perceptions of space, and certain spatial directions are especially prominent in our thinking (Franklin & Tversky, 1990; Tversky, 1991b).

Specifically, the spatial framework model states that when we are in a typical upright position, the vertical or above/below dimension is especially prominent. This dimension has special significance for two reasons. First, the vertical dimension is correlated with gravity, an advantage that neither of the two other dimensions share. Gravity has an important asymmetric effect on the world we perceive; objects fall downward, not upward. It is reasonable to think that, because of its association with gravity, the above/below dimension should be particularly important and thus particularly accessible. Second, the vertical dimension on an upright human's body is physically asymmetric. That is, the top (head) and bottom (feet) are easy to tell apart, and so we do not confuse them with each other. These two factors combine to help us make judgments on the above/below dimension very rapidly, as Figure 6.11 shows.

The next most prominent dimension is the front/back dimension. This dimension is not correlated with gravity in upright observers. However, we can view and interact with objects in front of us more readily than with objects in back of us, introducing an additional asymmetry. Also, the human's front half is not symmetric with the back half, again making it easy to distinguish between front and back. These two characteristics lead to judgment times for the front/back dimension that are fast, although not as fast as for the above/below dimension.

The least prominent dimension is right/left. This dimension is not correlated with gravity, and we can perceive objects equally well whether they are on the right or the left. Furthermore, except for minor preferences most of us have in manipulating objects with our right or left hand, this dimension does not have the degree of asymmetry we find for front versus back. And finally, a human's right half is roughly symmetrical with the left half. You can probably remember occasions when you confused your right and left hands, or when you told someone to turn left rather than right. Additional processing time may be required to ensure that you do not make this error, so right/left decisions take longer.

In summary, then, the spatial framework characterizes the vertical dimension for the upright observer as most prominent, the front/back dimension as next most prominent, and the right/left dimension as least prominent. The pattern of response times in Figure 6.11 supports this characterization.

Further Research on Mental Models. In additional studies, Franklin and Tversky (1990) used scenarios that described observers looking at scenes while reclining. As you might expect, people took longer to make all judgments, because we do not typically interact with the world from a reclining position! Now the front/back decisions were the fastest. This makes sense if we consider the important asymmetries that exist for reclining observers. Because you can lie on your back, front, and sides, *none* of your body dimensions is consistently associated with gravity. The most important asymmetries that remain are the perceptual and functional asymmetries of front/back. So now this front/back dimension becomes most prominent; accordingly, people answer questions most quickly about the front/back dimension.

So far, all the research we have discussed used scenarios written in the second person. (Notice the number of *you* sentences in Demonstration 6.7, for example.) Perhaps people can construct mental models from verbal descriptions when the text suggests that the reader is observing a scene. However, do people construct these models when the text involves the third person? If a mystery novel describes what Detective Brown sees upon arriving at the scene of the crime, do we readers jump into the scene and adopt Detective Brown's perspective—or do we remain outside the scene, like a viewer watching a movie? Bryant, Tversky, and Franklin (1992) found that readers prefer to adopt the perspective of an involved person.

Furthermore, Franklin and her colleagues (1992) presented narratives describing objects from the perspective of two different observers in the same environment. Interestingly, participants in these studies did not take the viewpoints of the two observers in turn. Instead, they adopted a neutral perspective that incorporated information from both observers.

All the research on mental models is an excellent testimony for the active nature of human cognitive processes. We take in information and go beyond the information we have been given, constructing a model to represent our knowledge. As we will see in the next chapter, this tendency to go beyond the given information is an important general characteristic of our cognitive processes.

Section Summary: Cognitive Maps

1. Cognitive maps usually reflect reality with reasonable accuracy, but systematic errors reflect the tendency to base our judgments on variables that are typically relevant and to judge our environment as being more regular than it really is.
2. Estimates of distance on cognitive maps can be distorted by the number of intervening cities, road-route distance (rather than distance "as the crow flies"), and the semantic categories representing the landmarks on the cognitive maps.
3. Shapes on cognitive maps can be distorted so that angles of intersecting streets are closer to 90° and curves are more nearly symmetrical.
4. The relative positions of features on cognitive maps can be distorted so that slightly tilted figures will be remembered as being more vertical or more horizontal than they really are (rotation heuristic), and a series of figures will be remembered as being more lined up than it really is (alignment heuristic).
5. We often create mental models of environments on the basis of a verbal description. In these mental models, the vertical dimension has special prominence (when we are in the normal upright position), followed by the front/back dimension, and then the right/left dimension; these data are explained by the spatial framework model.

Chapter Review Questions

1. Summarize the two theories of the characteristics of mental images: the analog code and the propositional viewpoint. Describe the findings about mental rotations, size, shape, part-whole relationships, and any other topics you recall. In each case, note which theory the results support.
2. Almost all of this chapter dealt with visual imagery, because little information is available about imagery in the other senses. How might you design a study on taste imagery that would be conceptually similar to one of the studies mentioned in this chapter? See whether you can also design studies to examine smell, hearing, and touch, basing these studies on the experiments discussed in this chapter.
3. Which areas of research provided the strongest support for the propositional storage of information about objects? I mentioned my own experience with

using a propositional code for a jigsaw-puzzle piece; can you think of an occasion where you seemed to use a propositional code for an unfamiliar stimulus?

4. How do the studies on imagery and interference support the viewpoint that visual activity is involved in visual imagery, and auditory activity is involved in auditory imagery?

5. What are experimenter expectancy and demand characteristics? Describe one study for each of these concepts that suggests that the results of imagery experiments are unlikely to be traced to these factors alone.

6. What kind of neuropsychological evidence do we have that suggests visual imagery resembles visual perception? How is visual imagery different from visual perception?

7. Cognitive maps sometimes correspond to reality, but sometimes they do not. Discuss the factors that seem to produce systematic distortions when people estimate distances on mental maps.

8. What are the heuristics that cause systematic distortions in the shapes and relative positions represented on cognitive maps? How are these related to two concepts discussed in other chapters, top-down processing (Chapter 2) and schemas (Chapter 5).

9. According to Franklin and Tversky, the three dimensions in our mental models are *not* created equal. Which dimension has special prominence for an upright observer, and which has the least prominence? How does the spatial framework model explain these differences?

10. The material we discussed in the first portion of this chapter emphasized that mental imagery resembles perception. However, the material on cognitive maps pointed out that these cognitive maps may be influenced by our conceptions as well as our perceptions. Discuss these points, including some information about mental models.

NEW TERMS

imagery
analog code
propositional code
experimenter expectancy
psychophysics
internal psychophysics
symbolic distance effect
oblique effect
demand characteristics

surface representation
deep representation
cognitive maps
priming effect
heuristic
symmetry heuristic
rotation heuristic
alignment heuristic
spatial framework model

RECOMMENDED READINGS

Finke, R. A. (1989). *Principles of mental imagery*. Cambridge, MA: MIT Press. Finke, a well-known researcher in imagery, has written a clear, well-organized overview of the characteristics of mental images.

Kosslyn, S. M., & Koenig, O. (1992). *Wet mind: The new cognitive neuroscience*. New York: The Free Press. Only a portion of this book focuses on visual cognition and imagery. However, the discussion of the biological underpinnings of imagery and other cognitive processes will be useful to those interested in neuroscience.

Reisberg, D. (Ed.). (1992). *Auditory imagery*. Hillsdale, NJ: Erlbaum. This collection of 10 chapters on auditory images offers a helpful supplement to the material in this chapter, which primarily emphasizes visual images.

Tversky, B. (1991b). Spatial mental models. *The Psychology of Learning and Motivation, 27*, 109–145. Tversky's chapter provides a solid overview of the research covered in the In-Depth section on mental models.

GENERAL KNOWLEDGE

PREVIEW

The three major topics covered in this chapter are semantic memory, schemas, and metacognition.

Semantic memory involves our organized knowledge about the world. We will look at four different theories that attempt to explain how all this information could be stored and used in memory.

A schema is a generalized kind of knowledge about situations and events. One kind of schema is a script, which describes an expected sequence of events. For example, most people have a well-defined "restaurant script," which specifies all the events that are likely to occur when you dine in a restaurant. Schemas influence our memories during four processes: when we select the material we want to remember, when we store the meaning of a verbal passage, when we interpret material, and when we form a single, integrated representation in memory. Although schemas can cause inaccuracies during these stages, we are often more accurate than schema theory proposes.

Metacognition involves knowledge and awareness about our own cognitive processes. For example, you are often aware of the characteristics of a word on the tip of your tongue (for instance, the first letter of the target word), even if you cannot recover that word. In the In-Depth section on metamemory, we will see that college students can predict what they will remember from some memory tasks. However, they often spend too much time studying material they already know, and insufficient time on difficult material they have not yet mastered.

INTRODUCTION

If you are a typical adult, you know the meaning of at least 20,000 to 40,000 words (Baddeley, 1990). You also know a tremendous amount of information about each of those words; you know that a cat has fur, that an apple is red, and that a car is a better example of a vehicle than an elevator.

Furthermore, when you hear a sentence, you know much more than the simple combination of words would suggest (Eysenck & Keane, 1990). Consider the following sentence:

> When Lisa was on her way back from the store with the balloon, she fell and the balloon floated away.

Think about all the facts you take for granted and all the reasonable inferences you make. For instance, Lisa is probably a child, not a 40-year-old. Also, she bought the balloon in the store; the balloon was attached to a string; the balloon was inflated with a light gas; when she fell, she let go of the string; she may have scraped her knee; it may have bled. A sentence that initially seemed simple is immediately enriched by an astonishing amount of information about objects and events in our world. (Incidentally, Chapter 8 will explore the way we make inferences during reading.)

In addition, you have some knowledge about *what* you know. You may know that you know the capital of Utah, but you know you cannot recall the names of your senators. You know you can remember your French vocabulary well enough for tomorrow's quiz, but you know you cannot recall the definition of the alignment heuristic.

So far, we have focused on the retention and retrieval processes involved in remembering isolated episodic information (Chapters 4 and 5), as well as the encoding processes for visual and spatial information (Chapter 6). In the present chapter, we shift our attention to semantic information and general knowledge.

This chapter offers testimony to our impressive cognitive abilities; we have an enormous amount of information at our disposal (Shoben, 1988). This chapter also confirms the active nature of our cognitive processes. In Chapter 6, we saw that people can use the information in a verbal description to actively construct a mental model of an environment. In the current chapter, we will see that when people are given one bit of information, they can go beyond the given information to actively retrieve other stored information about word relationships and other likely inferences. Let us explore how people go beyond the given information in semantic memory, schemas, and metacognition.

THE STRUCTURE OF SEMANTIC MEMORY

As we discussed in earlier chapters, **semantic memory** is organized knowledge about the world. We contrasted semantic memory with episodic memory, which contains information about time-dated events. As we emphasized, the distinction between semantic and episodic memory is not clear-cut. However, the phrase "It happened to me" is always implied in episodic memory, which emphasizes when, where, or how this event occurred (Chang, 1986). In contrast, semantic memory involves knowledge without reference to how that information was acquired. An example of semantic memory would be, "The solar system has nine planets." An example of episodic memory would be, "This morning I was told that the solar system has nine planets" (Chang, 1986). As you may also recall, psychologists use the term *semantic memory* in a broad sense. It includes encyclopedic knowledge (for example, "Martin Luther King was born in Atlanta, Georgia") as well as lexical or language knowledge (for example, "The word *snow* is related to the word *rain*"). Let us consider several possible models of how semantic memory is organized. These include the feature comparison model, network models, the exemplar approach, and the prototype approach.

The Feature Comparison Model

One logical way to organize semantic memory would be in terms of lists of features. According to the **feature comparison model,** concepts are stored in memory

---

FIGURE 7.1

The Feature Comparison Model of Semantic Memory (From Smith, 1978. Courtesy of Lawrence Erlbaum Associates, Inc.).

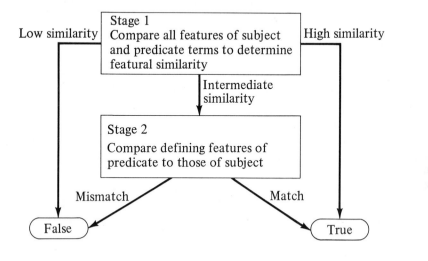

---

according to a list of features or attributes (Smith, Shoben, & Rips, 1974). A two-stage decision process is necessary to make judgments about these concepts. We will first look at the structure these authors propose for semantic memory and then examine the decision process.

Consider the concept *cat* for a moment. We could make up a list of features that are often relevant to cats:

has fur
dislikes water
has four legs
meows
has a tail
chases mice

The decision process described by Smith and his coauthors becomes relevant when people must answer a question such as "Is a cat an animal?" In the first stage of the decision process, people compare all the features of the subject of the sentence, *cat*, and the predicate, *animal*. Figure 7.1 shows an outline of the model.

Three decisions are possible at Stage 1. First of all, the subject term and the predicate term may show low similarity, and so the person quickly replies "false" to the question. For example, the question "Is a robin a pencil?" has such little similarity between the two terms that you would immediately answer "false." In a

---

DEMONSTRATION 7.1

THE SENTENCE VERIFICATION TECHNIQUE.

For each of the items below, answer *as quickly as possible* either true or false.

1. A poodle is a dog.
2. A squirrel is an animal.
3. A flower is a rock.
4. A carrot is a vegetable.
5. A mango is a fruit.
6. A petunia is a tree.
7. A robin is a bird.
8. A rutabaga is a vegetable.

---

second situation, the subject and the predicate terms may show high similarity, leading to a quick "true" answer. "Is a cat an animal?" leads to an immediate "true." Note, however, that a Stage 2 comparison is required if there is intermediate similarity between the subject and the predicate; these decisions take longer.

Smith and his coauthors propose that the features used in the feature comparison model are either defining features or characteristic features. **Defining features** are those features that are necessary to the meaning of the item. For example, the defining features of a robin include that it is living and has feathers and a red breast. **Characteristic features** are those features that are merely descriptive but are not essential. For example, the characteristic features of a robin include that it flies, perches in trees, is not domesticated, and is small in size.

The feature comparison model has been tested by researchers using the sentence verification technique. In the **sentence verification technique,** people see simple sentences, and they must consult their stored semantic knowledge to determine whether the sentences are true or false (Kounios et al., 1987). Demonstration 7.1 shows the kinds of items presented in the sentence verification technique. In general, people are highly accurate on this task, so researchers do not need to compare the error rate across experimental conditions. Instead, they measure response latencies. Two experimental conditions might produce response latencies that differ by one-tenth of a second. You might initially think this sounds like a trivial difference. However, if this difference is consistently found for most participants, it is worth exploring. A stable difference may reveal something important about the structure of semantic memory.

One common finding in research using the sentence verification technique is the typicality effect. In the **typicality effect,** people reach decisions faster when an item is a typical member of a category, rather than an unusual member. For example, in Demonstration 7.1, you probably decided quickly that a carrot is a vegetable, but you paused before deciding that a rutabaga is a vegetable. In a typical study,

Katz (1981) presented high-typicality sentences such as "A globe is round" and low-typicality sentences such as "A barrel is round." Reaction times were about 0.3 seconds faster for typical items than for atypical items.

The feature comparison model can explain these results. For example, a carrot is a typical member of its category, so the features of carrots and vegetables are highly similar. People quickly answer the question "Is a carrot a vegetable?" because they only require Stage 1 processing in the model. However, the rutabaga is an example of an atypical vegetable. People require much longer to answer the question "Is a rutabaga a vegetable?" because the decision requires Stage 2 processing as well as Stage 1 processing.

Unfortunately, the feature comparison model has difficulty explaining other semantic memory findings that have been obtained with the sentence verification technique. For example, a second common finding with this technique (beyond the typicality effect) is the category size effect. According to the **category size effect,** people reach decisions faster when an item is a member of a small category, rather than a large category. For example, in Demonstration 7.1, you probably decided quickly that a poodle is a dog, whereas you took longer to decide that a squirrel is an animal. After all, *dog* has fewer category members than *animal* does. However, the feature comparison model would predict the opposite, because small categories have a larger number of defining features (for example, the category *dog* has a greater number of defining features than the category *animal*). Therefore, comparing the features should take *longer* during Stage 2.

Another major problem with the feature comparison model is that nonexperts may not be guided by defining features (Malt, 1990). Furthermore, the model does not provide any objective way to distinguish between defining and characteristic attributes (Eysenck & Keane, 1990). Also, we seem to know that robins are birds without resorting to a formal comparison of features (Cohen, 1983). Finally, the feature comparison model does not explain how the members of categories are related to one another, which is a distinct advantage of the network models we discuss next.

Network Models

Think for a moment about the large number of associations you have to the word *apple*. How can we find an effective way to represent the different aspects of meaning for *apple* that are stored in memory? A number of theorists favor network models. Originally, a network was an arrangement of threads in a net-like structure, with many connections among these threads. Similarly, a **network model** of semantic memory proposes a net-like organization of concepts in memory, with many interconnections. The meaning of a particular concept, such as *apple*, depends on the concepts to which it is connected.

We will consider the network model developed by Collins and Loftus (1975) and then examine Anderson's (1983a, 1990) ACT* theory. A third network theory, the parallel distributed processing approach, was discussed in Chapter 3. Turn

FIGURE 7.2

An Example of a Network Structure for the Concept *Apple*.

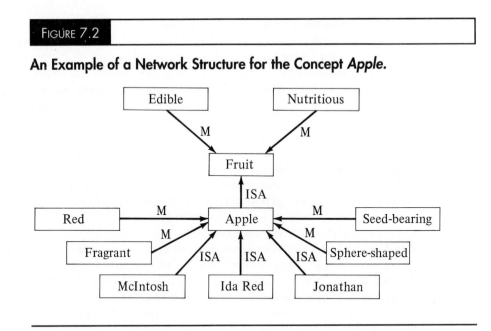

back to Figure 3.5 (page 95) to refresh your memory of a representative network. In brief, the **parallel distributed processing (PDP) approach** argues that cognitive processes can be understood in terms of networks that link together neuron-like units. The PDP approach does not distinguish between episodic and semantic memory (Johnson & Hasher, 1987), so that episodic facts are intertwined with semantic information.

The Collins and Loftus Network Model. Collins and Loftus (1975) developed a theory based on earlier models (e.g., Collins & Quillian, 1969) in which meaning is represented by hypothetical networks. The **Collins and Loftus network model** proposes that semantic memory is organized in terms of net-like structures, with many interconnections; when we retrieve information, activation spreads to related concepts.

In this model, each concept can be represented as a **node,** or location in a network. Links or associations connect a particular node with other concept nodes. Figure 7.2 shows a small portion of the network that might surround the concept *apple.* Keep in mind that each of the other concepts in this figure has its own individual network structures. Imagine networks surrounding each concept in Figure 7.2 and then add a few more concepts to your mental picture. You can appreciate the richness and complexity of semantic memory!

The semantic network theory proposes different kinds of links between concepts. Two kinds of links shown in Figure 7.2 are a superordinate link and a modifier link. A **superordinate link,** represented by the label ISA to represent the words *is a*, shows that one concept is a member of a larger class. For example, the concept *McIntosh* has a superordinate link to the concept *apple*. A **modifier link,** represented by the label M, shows the properties of a concept. For example, the property *red* is connected to *apple* via a modifier link.

We have examined the structure of semantic networks. How do they work? When the name of a concept is mentioned, the node representing that concept is activated. The activation expands or spreads from that node to other nodes with which it is connected, a process called **spread of activation.** The activation spreads first to all the nodes linked to the original node and then spreads to more remote nodes. As activation spreads, it grows weaker at the more remote nodes. When a node has been activated, an activation tag is left behind along with information about the nature of the activation.

Let's consider how the Collins-Loftus model would explain what happens in a sentence verification task. Suppose you hear the sentence "A McIntosh is a fruit." This model proposes that the nodes *McIntosh* and *fruit* will be activated. The activation at each of these nodes will spread, and the node *apple* will receive some of this spreading activation from each of two sources. An **intersection** occurs when spreading activation from two different sources arrives at the same node. Thus *apple* represents an intersection. When a search of memory produces an intersection, we then evaluate the information in the activation tags. "A McIntosh is a fruit" therefore deserves a "yes" answer on the basis of information in the activation tags.

However, consider what happens when an intersection cannot be found. Consider the sentence "An apple is a mammal." In this case, activation would spread from both *apple* and *mammal*, but no intersection would be found. You can't get there from here, so that sentence deserves a "no" answer.

As Collins and Loftus (1975) also proposed, links that are frequently used have greater strengths. As a result, these links allow faster travel times between the nodes. For example, the link between carrot and vegetable is stronger than the link between rutabaga and vegetable. Therefore, the typicality effect is easy to explain. We make decisions quickly when a word is a typical member of a category because a strong link connects the word with the category name.

The concept of spreading activation is an appealing one, although it has its critics (McKoon & Ratcliff, 1992; Ratcliff & McKoon, 1988). In general, however, the Collins and Loftus model has been superseded by more complex theories that attempt to explain broader aspects of general knowledge. These theories include the PDP approach, which we examined in Chapter 3, and Anderson's ACT* theory.

Anderson's ACT* Theory. One of the most influential theorists in contemporary cognitive psychology is John Anderson of Carnegie Mellon University. Anderson constructed a series of network models (Anderson, 1976, 1983a, 1985, 1990). The most current version is called **ACT*** (to be read "Act-star"); ACT stands for the Adaptive Control of Thought, and the asterisk indicates that this version is a modification of the original ACT model. ACT* attempts to account for all of cognition, including memory, language, learning, reasoning, decision making, and so forth. Anderson believes that the mind is unitary and that all the higher cognitive processes are different products of the same underlying system. (In contrast, other theorists propose that the language system, for example, is governed by different principles than memory or decision making.) The ACT* model emphasizes the concept of control, which is the feature that provides direction to thought and supervises the transition between thoughts.

Obviously, a theory that attempts to explain all of cognition is extremely complex. We will therefore consider an overview of ACT* as described in Anderson's (1983a) book *The Architecture of Cognition* and then discuss his more specific view of semantic memory. Anderson makes a basic distinction between declarative and procedural knowledge. **Declarative knowledge** is knowledge about facts and things (in other words, the essence of this current chapter). In contrast, **procedural knowledge** is knowledge about how to perform actions. Another important feature of Anderson's theory is **working memory,** which is the active part of the declarative memory system—it is the portion that is currently "working." You'll recall our discussion of the characteristics of working memory from Chapter 4.

Black (1984) presents a simplified example. Suppose you are trying to set the time on a new digital watch, using the instruction booklet. First, you activate the goal of wanting to set the watch; that goal is therefore in working memory. The goal of setting the watch would then activate a procedure such as "If the goal is to set a watch, then look at the instruction booklet." Looking at the instruction booklet activates the procedures of processing the verbal material and the pictures in the booklet. After comprehending the material, the contents of the booklet are stored in the declarative network. The declarative network contains an interconnected set of propositions (for example, "the watch has three buttons"), visual images (for example, the locations of the buttons), and information about the order of events (for example, "set the date first, then hours, then minutes, then the seconds").

Let us now focus on declarative knowledge, which is responsible for semantic memory. According to Anderson (1976, 1983a, 1985), the meaning of a sentence can be represented by a propositional network, or pattern of interconnected propositions. We discussed propositions in Chapter 6. Anderson's definition of a proposition, however, is somewhat more precise: A **proposition** is the smallest unit of knowledge that can be judged either true or false. For instance, the phrase *white cat* does not qualify as a proposition because we cannot find out whether it is true or false unless we know something more about the white cat. However, each of the following three statements is a proposition:

1. Susan gave a cat to Maria.
2. The cat was white.
3. Maria is the president of the club.

FIGURE 7.3

A Propositional Network Representing the Sentence "Susan gave a white cat to Maria, who is the president of the club."

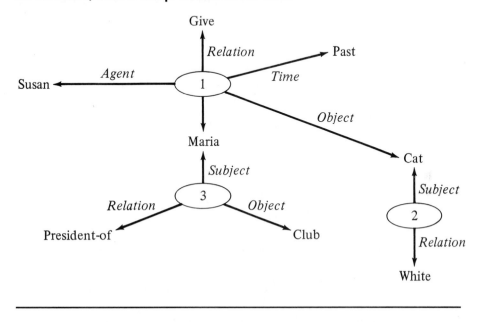

These three propositions can appear by themselves, but they can also be combined into a sentence, such as the following:

Susan gave a white cat to Maria, who is the president of the club.

Figure 7.3 shows how this sentence could be represented by a propositional network. As you can see, each of the three propositions in the sentence is represented by a node, and the links are represented by arrows. Notice, too, that the propositional network represents the important relations in the three propositions, but not the exact wording. Propositions are abstract; they do not represent a specific set of words. (Later in the chapter, we will look at research that demonstrates how we tend to remember the gist or general message of language, rather than the specific wording of sentences.)

Furthermore, Anderson suggests that each of the concepts in a proposition can be represented by a network as well. Figure 7.4 illustrates just a small part of the representation of the word *cat* in memory. Try to imagine what the propositional network in Figure 7.3 would look like if each of the concepts in that network were to be replaced by an expanded network representing the richness of meanings you

A Partial Representation of CAT in Memory.

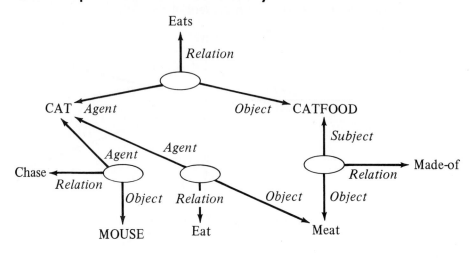

have acquired. Obviously, these networks need to be complicated in order to accurately represent the dozens of associations we have for each item in semantic memory.

Anderson's model of semantic memory makes some additional proposals. For example, similar to the Collins-Loftus model, the links vary in strength, and they become stronger as they are used more often. Also, the model assumes that at any given moment, as many as 10 nodes are represented in working memory. Furthermore, the model proposes that activation can spread. However, Anderson argues that there is a limited capacity to the spread of activation. Thus, if many links are activated simultaneously, each link receives relatively little activation (Anderson, 1983b).

Anderson's model has been highly praised for its skill in integrating cognitive processes and for its scholarship (e.g., Black, 1984; Lehnert, 1984). However, others have been critical about some of its general attributes. Johnson-Laird and his coauthors (1984), for example, complain that network models only provide connections between words; they do not make connections to the representations of those words in the real world. It seems likely that semantic theories in the future will attempt to be even more comprehensive and make those final connections to real-world objects.

Let us review the two major categories of semantic memory models we have examined so far. The feature comparison model suggests that concepts are stored in memory according to a list of attributes. We decide whether a cat is an animal by comparing the features of *cat* with the features of *animal*. In contrast, the three network models emphasize the interconnections among concepts in memory. These three theories included an early model by Collins and Loftus (1975) that introduced the concept of spreading activation, the parallel distributed processing approach, discussed in Chapter 3, and Anderson's (1983a) ACT* theory, which describes how sentences—as well as words—can be represented by networks. The two theories we will now consider differ somewhat from the feature comparison model and the network models because they are more concerned with answering questions about categories. For instance, if we see a strange creature in a zoo, how do we decide whether it is a bird or a mammal? As one group of theorists noted:

> People clearly are quite proficient at dividing the world into categories. . . . People can learn to distinguish between cows and horses, between saddle horses and draft horses, between Belgians and Percherons. (Holland et al., 1987, p. 179)

The two theories that emphasize the relationship among items in categories are the exemplar approach and the prototype approach.

The Exemplar Approach

The **exemplar approach** argues that we first learn some specific examples of a concept and then classify a new stimulus by deciding how closely it resembles those specific examples. For example, suppose that you have just read four case studies, each describing a depressed individual. You then decide to read a fifth case study and find that this individual also fits into the category "depressed person" because this description closely resembles one previously described.

According to the exemplar approach, people do not perform any kind of abstraction process (Hintzman, 1986; Medin, 1989; Medin & Schaffer, 1978; Shoben, 1988). That is, while reading those four case studies, you did not figure out what general characteristics the individuals tended to have in common because, as the exemplar model suggests, if you were to summarize information, you would have discarded useful data; as a consequence, your predictions would be less accurate.

Consider Barsalou's (1992) description about the category of *bachelor*. This category might be represented by memories of many specific bachelors you have known. You do not abstract a general statement, such as *unmarried adult human male*. Instead, you represent the concept *bachelor* with a loose collection of memories for exemplars (John, Pete, Guillermo, Steve, and so on). When you meet a new person, you decide whether he is a bachelor by comparing his attributes with the attributes of people in a number of different categories. If this new person matches Pete's attributes, for example, you conclude that he is a bachelor.

Barsalou points out some possible problems with the exemplar approach. For example, this theory suggests that people store an immense amount of specific exemplar information; human memory may not be capable of storing this much detail. A more serious problem is that we clearly *do* make abstractions about categories, based on the exemplars. Let us now turn to prototype theory, which emphasizes our tendency to derive these abstract properties.

The Prototype Approach

According to a theory proposed by Eleanor Rosch (1973), categories are organized according to **prototypes,** which are items that best represent examples of a category. According to this **prototype approach,** people decide whether an item belongs to a category by comparing that item with a prototype. If the item is similar to the prototype, the item is included in the category. However, if the item is sufficiently different, it is placed in another category where it more closely resembles that category's prototype. You'll notice how this approach resembles the prototype view of pattern perception, whereas the exemplar approach is similar to the template view.

As Rumelhart and Norman (1988) point out, the prototype of a category does not really need to exist. For example, if I were to ask you to describe a prototypical animal, you might tell me about a four-legged creature with fur, a tail, and a size somewhere between a large dog and a cow—something exactly like no creature on earth. Thus, a prototype is an idealized example.

Rosch also points out that members of a category differ in their **prototypicality,** or degree to which they are prototypical. A robin and a sparrow are very prototypical birds, whereas ostriches and penguins are nonprototypes. Think of a prototype, or most typical member, for a particular group on your campus, such as a fraternity, sorority, or other club. Also think of a nonprototype ("You mean he's a Theta Kappa? He doesn't seem at all like one!"). Now think of a prototype for a professor, a fruit, and a murder weapon, and then think of a nonprototype for each category. For example, a tomato is a nonprototypical fruit, and an icicle is a nonprototypical murder weapon.

The prototype approach has had an important impact on cognitive psychology, and it has also influenced other disciplines within psychology (Rosch, 1988). For example, Mayer and Bower (1986) discovered that people use prototypes to organize personality concepts, such as "extrovert." Clinical psychologists also use prototypes for various psychological disorders, such as "aggressive-impulsive child" (Horowitz et al., 1981). Furthermore, emotions such as anger may be organized according to prototypes (Russell, 1990).

Eleanor Rosch and her coauthors, as well as other researchers, have conducted numerous studies on the characteristics of prototypes. They have demonstrated that all members of categories are *not* created equal (Malt & Smith, 1984). Instead, a category tends to have a **graded structure,** beginning with the most representative or prototypical members and continuing on through the category's nonprototypical members (Barsalou, 1985, 1987; Neisser, 1987). Let us examine several important characteristics of prototypes. Then we will discuss another important component of Rosch's prototype theory, levels of categorization.

Characteristics of Prototypes. Prototypes differ from the nonprototypical members of categories in several respects. As you will see, prototypes have a special, privileged status (Smith, 1989).

1. *Prototypes are supplied as examples of a category.* Several studies have shown that people judge some items to be "better" examples of a concept than some other items. In one study, for example, Mervis, Catlin, and Rosch (1976) looked at some category norms that had already been collected. The norms had been constructed by asking people to provide examples of eight different categories, such as birds, fruit, sports, and weapons. Other people supplied prototype ratings for each of these examples. A statistical analysis showed that the items that were rated most prototypical were the same items that people supplied most often in the category norms. For instance, for the category *bird*, people would consider *robin* to be very prototypical, and *robin* is very frequently listed as an example of this category *bird*. In contrast, people would rate *penguin* as low on the prototype scale, and *penguin* is only rarely listed as an example of the category *bird*. Thus, if someone asks you to name a member of a category, you will probably name a prototype.

Earlier, we discussed the typicality effect; people reach decisions faster when an item is a typical member of a category. Thus, prototypes are supplied more often as examples, and they are also judged more rapidly.

2. *Prototypes serve as reference points.* Before reading further, turn the page and try Demonstration 7.2, which illustrates how prototypes serve as reference points. This demonstration is based on two studies by Rosch (1975a). In the first study, similar to part A in the demonstration, people saw pairs of numbers, colors, or lines. For the numbers, one member of each pair was a prototype—that is, a multiple of 10 that should be relevant in our decimal number system (for example, 10, 50, or 100). The other member of the pair was a number of about the same size, but not a multiple of 10 (for example, 11, 48, or 103). For the colors, one member of each pair was a prototype color (red, yellow, green, and blue), and the other member was a nonprototype color (for example, purplish red). For the lines, one member was a line in a "standard" position (exactly horizontal, exactly vertical, and 45° diagonal) and the other member was a line in a position rotated 10° from the standard position. In each case, then, Rosch wanted to determine which pair member served as a reference point, that is, the stimulus with which the other member was compared.

Her results showed quite clearly that the prototypes tended to serve as the reference points. For example, people were more likely to say "11 is essentially 10," rather than "10 is essentially 11." Check your answers in Demonstration 7.2. Did the prototypes, which are multiples of 10, occur second in the sentence, as if they were standards to which all other numbers are compared?

Rosch's second study used a different method, which was more physical than linguistic. As in part B in Demonstration 7.2, people placed pairs of items (for example, two numbers) on a blank surface. When the prototype served as the

---

DEMONSTRATION 7.2

PROTOTYPES AS REFERENCE POINTS.

A. Pairs of items are listed below, together with a sentence containing two blanks. Choose one item to fill the first blank, and place the other item in the second blank. Take your time, try the items both ways, and choose the way in which the "sentence" seems to make the most sense.

1. (10, 11)   _____ is essentially _____.
2. (103, 100)   _____ is sort of _____.
3. (48, 50)   _____ is roughly _____.
4. (1000, 1004)   _____ is basically _____.

B. Take out four sheets of blank paper. Take the first number of each of the pairs listed below, and place it near the left-hand margin of a sheet of paper. Then draw a line to represent how far away the second number is from the first, as in the illustration below. Judge each pair in isolation from the other pairs. The same number appears more than once, but you do not need to be consistent in your judgments. Work as quickly as you can. Here is an example:

```
100        107
 •—————————•
```

1. (14, 10)
2. (10, 13)
3. (10, 14)
4. (13, 10)

---

reference point, the other item was placed relatively close to it. However, when the nonprototype served as the reference point, the other item was placed relatively far away. Now check your own responses on this task by measuring the distance between each of the pairs of items. Is the distance between 10 and 13 shorter than the distance between 13 and 10, as Rosch would predict?

Notice what Rosch's results are saying: The distance from 10 to 13 is less than the distance from 13 to 10. This contradicts everything your third-grade teacher taught you about arithmetic. The human mind does not treat these distances as equal, however. Instead, prototype numbers serve as reference points or landmarks, and other numbers are compared with these landmarks.

3. *Prototypes are judged more quickly after priming.* We discussed priming in Chapter 6 in connection with cognitive maps; people recognize a city name more quickly if it was preceded by the name of a nearby city. More generally, the **priming effect** means that people respond faster to an item if it was preceded by a similar item.

The research shows that priming helps prototypes more than it helps nonprototypes. Imagine, for example, that you are participating in a study on priming. Your task is to judge pairs of similar colors and to respond whether they are the same or not. On some occasions, the name of the color is shown to you before you must judge the pair of colors; these are the primed trials. On other occasions, no color name is supplied to you as a "warning"; these are the unprimed trials. Rosch (1975b) tried this priming setup for both prototype colors (for example, a good, bright red) and nonprototype colors (for example, a muddy red).

Rosch's results showed that priming was very helpful for prototypical colors; people responded more quickly after primed trials than after nonprimed trials. However, priming actually inhibited the judgments for nonprototypical colors, even after two weeks of practice. In other words, if you see the word *red*, you expect to see true, fire-engine red colors. If you see, instead, dark, muddy red colors, the priming offers no advantage. Instead, you pause as you work to reconcile your image of a bright, vivid color with the muddy colors you actually see before you.

4. *Prototypes can substitute for a category name in a sentence.* Try Demonstration 7.3, which illustrates a typical study on substituting other words for category names (Rosch, 1977). As you'll probably discover, prototypes can substitute quite well for the category name. However, a sentence is bizarre when a nonprototype is substituted. Check over your responses from this demonstration. It seems peculiar to have 20 penguins sitting on telephone wires. Sentences 3, 6, 9, 12, and 15 involve nonprototypes and probably seemed more bizarre than those involving prototypes.

5. *Prototypes share common attributes in a family resemblance category.* Before we examine this issue, let's introduce a new term, *family resemblance*. **Family resemblance** means that no single attribute is shared by all examples of a concept; however, each example has at least one attribute in common with some other example of the concept. As the philosopher Wittgenstein (1953) pointed out, some concepts are difficult to describe in terms of specific defining features. For example, consider the concept of *games*. Think about the games you know. What single attribute do they all have in common? How is Monopoly similar to volleyball? You might respond that both involve competition, but then what about the children's game, "Ring around the Rosie"? Some games involve skill, but others depend upon luck. Notice how each game shares some attributes with some other game, yet no one attribute is shared by all games. In fact, the members of the concept *games* have a family resemblance to one another.

Rosch and Mervis (1975) examined the role of prototypes in family resemblances. Specifically, they proposed that the items that people judge to be most

---

DEMONSTRATION 7.3

SUBSTITUTING PROTOTYPES AND NONPROTOTYPES IN SENTENCES.

Examine each of the sentences below and rate them as to how normal or how bizarre each one seems to you. Use this scale:

1	2	3	4	5	6	7
Normal					Bizarre	

Rating

_____   1. Twenty birds sat on a telephone wire outside my window.
_____   2. Twenty sparrows sat on a telephone wire outside my window.
_____   3. Twenty penguins sat on a telephone wire outside my window.
_____   4. One of my favorite desserts is fruit pie.
_____   5. One of my favorite desserts is apple pie.
_____   6. One of my favorite desserts is olive pie.
_____   7. How can I go to the fair without a vehicle?
_____   8. How can I go to the fair without a truck?
_____   9. How can I go to the fair without an elevator?
_____ 10. The robbers had many weapons.
_____ 11. The robbers had many guns.
_____ 12. The robbers had many bricks.
_____ 13. We like to watch sports on television.
_____ 14. We like to watch baseball on television.
_____ 15. We like to watch sunbathing on television.

---

prototypical will have the greatest number of attributes in common with other members of the category. In one study, for example, they used members of categories that had previously been rated for their prototypicality; we will call these ratings **prototype ratings.** Table 7.1 shows three of the categories. For vehicles, notice that *car* was rated as the most prototypical member, whereas *elevator* was rated as least prototypical. Check over these lists to see whether they agree with your ideas of which items are the best and worst examples of each category. Rosch and Mervis asked a new group of people to list the attributes possessed by each item. For the word *dog*, for instance, they were told to list attributes like having four legs, barking, having fur, and so on.

Two judges then gathered together all the items and all the attributes for each category. From this information they calculated a number that showed the extent to which an item's attributes were also shared by other members of the same category. For example, *car* would probably share its attributes with many other members of the vehicle category. Like many other items on that list, it has wheels, moves horizontally, uses fuel, and encloses the passenger. An *elevator*, on the other

TABLE 7.1

PROTOTYPE RATINGS FOR WORDS IN THREE CATEGORIES (FROM ROSCH AND MERVIS, 1975).

| | CATEGORY | | |
ITEM	VEHICLE	VEGETABLE	CLOTHING
1	Car	Peas	Pants
2	Truck	Carrots	Shirt
3	Bus	String beans	Dress
4	Motorcycle	Spinach	Skirt
5	Train	Broccoli	Jacket
6	Trolley car	Asparagus	Coat
7	Bicycle	Corn	Sweater
8	Airplane	Cauliflower	Underwear
9	Boat	Brussels sprouts	Socks
10	Tractor	Lettuce	Pajamas
11	Cart	Beets	Bathing suit
12	Wheelchair	Tomato	Shoes
13	Tank	Lima beans	Vest
14	Raft	Eggplant	Tie
15	Sled	Onion	Mittens
16	Horse	Potato	Hat
17	Blimp	Yam	Apron
18	Skates	Mushroom	Purse
19	Wheelbarrow	Pumpkin	Wristwatch
20	Elevator	Rice	Necklace

hand, shares its attributes with few other members: it operates by pulleys, moves vertically, and is usually enclosed within a building.

Rosch and Mervis therefore had two measures for each category member: its prototypicality rating and its rating of the number of common attributes. By statistical calculations, they showed that the two measures were closely related. In other words, if an item had been rated as highly prototypical (*car*), it was also likely to be rated as having many attributes in common with other members of the category. However, if an item had been rated as low on the prototype scale (for instance, *elevator*), it was likely to have few attributes in common.

This relationship makes sense. Think about a prototypical example of the concept *game*, for instance. To me, Monopoly is prototypical, and it shares many attributes with many other games. "Ring around the Rosie," however, is not prototypical, and it shares few other attributes with games like Ping-Pong, Scrabble, and chess. See whether this relationship holds true for the following concepts: attractive person, profession, and adventure movie. In each case, it is probably difficult to find one attribute that applies to all members of the category. However, you can list several attributes that apply to several members. Furthermore, as Rosch and Mervis demonstrated, the most prototypical member of each category has the greatest number of attributes in common with the other members.

Two studies have been critical of the concept of family resemblance; they claim that people may prefer simpler strategies than sorting in terms of family resemblance. For example, in one study, Medin and his colleagues (1987) designed bug-like cartoon creatures in family-resemblance categories. People showed a systematic tendency to sort in terms of a single attribute (for example, round head versus angular head), rather than in terms of family resemblance. Similarly, Ward and Scott (1987) found that people sorted human cartoon faces in terms of a single attribute, rather than family resemblance. It's not yet clear whether these results are damaging for the concept of family resemblance and for prototype theory. Defenders of prototype theory may criticize these studies, for example, because they use artificial stimuli (cartoon figures with arbitrary combinations of attributes) rather than the objects found in true, natural categories. However, the concept of family resemblance may not be applicable to as many situations as was originally thought.

Levels of Categorization. We have just examined five characteristics of prototypes that differentiate them from nonprototypes. The second major portion of Eleanor Rosch's theory looks at the way that our semantic categories are structured in terms of different levels.

Consider these examples. You can call the wooden structure upon which you are sitting by several different names: furniture, chair, or deskchair. You can refer to your pet as a dog, a spaniel, or a cocker spaniel. You can tighten the mirror on your car with a tool, a screwdriver, or a Phillips screwdriver. In other words, an object can belong to many different, related categories.

Some category levels are called **superordinate-level categories,** which means higher level or more general. Furniture, animal, and tool are all examples of superordinate category levels. **Basic-level categories** are more specific, but not as specific as you can go. Chair, cat, and screwdriver are examples of basic-level categories. Finally, **subordinate-level categories** mean lower level or more specific categories. Deskchair, Siamese, and Phillips screwdriver are examples of subordinate categories. However, basic level categories have special status, as you will learn in this section.

It may be useful to review these terms by thinking of examples of basic-level and subordinate categories for some superordinate terms you use often, such as musical instrument, vehicle, and clothing. Also, be certain that you know the difference between the terms *prototype* and *basic-level category*. A prototype is a best example of a category, whether the category level is superordinate, basic-level, or subordinate. Let us look at several important characteristics of basic-level categories.

1. *Members of basic-level categories have attributes in common.* As Rosch and her colleagues (1976) proposed, groups of objects that belong together share correlated features that are obviously different from the features of other objects. To test this idea, they set up nine categories, using each of the three proposed levels. For example, one category used *tool* as a superordinate-level category, *screwdriver* as a basic-level category, and *Phillips screwdriver* as a subordinate-level category.

People were instructed to list all the attributes they could think of that were true for all members of the specified category. For example, for *screwdriver*, someone might list "metal protrusion," "ridged handle," and "about 4–10 inches long."

Rosch and her colleagues then tallied up the attributes that people frequently listed for each item on the list. They found that people listed very few of the same attributes for superordinate-level items. This makes sense—how many attributes can you supply that would hold true for all tools, for example? However, they listed a large number of attributes for basic-level items. For example, all screwdrivers share a large number of characteristics, many more than are shared by all tools. People did not supply many more attributes for subordinate-level items than for basic-level items, however. Again, this makes sense. For the item *Phillips screwdriver*, we cannot add many attributes to the list we constructed for *screwdriver*.

Tversky and Hemenway (1984) provide more evidence for the generalization that members of basic-level categories have many attributes in common. These researchers asked participants to list attributes for items at the three category levels: superordinate, basic, and subordinate. The attributes were divided into two kinds: parts (for example, *stem* for an apple) and nonparts (for example, *round* for an apple).

Figure 7.5 shows the results. As you can see, both kinds of attributes show the same pattern. Tversky and Hemenway conclude from several studies that people associate few, if any, attributes with superordinate-level categories. However, they associate a much larger number of attributes with basic-level categories. Thus, the basic level of reference appears to have a special, privileged status, in contrast with the superordinate level.

2. *Members of basic-level categories have shapes in common.* Another study by Rosch and her colleagues (1976) examined the extent to which members of a category have the same shape. Pictures of objects were made the same size, and their outlines were lined up in order to measure the extent of the overlap in their shapes. The overlap was greatest for members of basic-level categories. For example, the overlap in shape would not be extensive for members of the superordinate category *furniture*. A lamp and a chair have very different outlines. However, members of the basic-level category *chair* would have similar shapes; think of a desk

FIGURE 7.5

Average Number of Parts and Nonparts Attributes Listed by Participants, as a Function of Level of Categorization (Tversky & Hemenway, 1984).

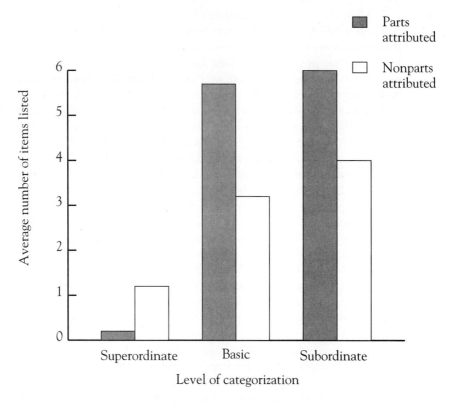

chair and a kitchen chair. There was a little bit more overlap for subordinate-level categories than for basic-level categories. For example, "deskchairs" overlapped more than "chairs" did. In summary, then, shapes overlap to an increasingly greater extent as we move from superordinate to basic-level to subordinate categories. However, the most impressive improvement in the overlap is between the superordinate and the basic-level categories.

3. *Basic-level names are used to identify objects.* Try naming some of the objects that you can see from where you are sitting. You are likely to use basic-level names for these objects. You will mention *pen*, for example, rather than the superordinate *writing instrument* or the subordinate *Bic fine-point pen*. Rosch and her colleagues (1976) asked people to look at pictures and identify the objects; they found that people preferred to use basic-level names. Apparently, the basic-level name gives

enough information without being overly detailed. Other researchers demonstrated that this effect was not simply produced by a preference for shorter words (Murphy & Smith, 1982). Furthermore, people use basic-level names to refer to events as well as objects (Morris & Murphy, 1990). Once again, the basic level has special status.

4. *Basic-level names produce the priming effect.* As we saw earlier, members of the same basic-level category share the same general shape. For example, members of the category *chair* look roughly the same. We would expect, therefore, that when people hear the word *chair*, they would form a mental image that would resemble most chairs.

The reason that the mental image is relevant is that Rosch and her colleagues (1976) wanted to see whether priming with basic-level names would be helpful. In one variation of the priming technique, the experimenter gives the name of the object, and the participants decide whether two pictures that follow are the same or different. For example, you might hear the word *carrot* and see a picture of two identical carrots. Presumably, priming works because the presentation of the word allows you to make a mental image of this word, which helps when you make the later decision.

At any rate, the results showed that priming with basic-level names *was* helpful—it did help to see a basic-level term like *carrot* before judging the carrots. However, priming with superordinate names (such as *vegetable*) was *not* helpful. Apparently, when you hear the word *vegetable*, you do not develop a mental image that is specific enough to prepare you for judging carrots. When you want to warn people that something is happening, warn them with a basic-level term—shout "Fire!" not "Danger!"

5. *Experts use subordinate categories differently.* So far, we have seen that members of basic-level categories have attributes and shapes in common. Also, they are used to identify objects, and basic-level names produce the priming effect. Tanaka and Taylor (1991) note that basic-level categories may have special status for those of us who are not experts in an area. However, for an expert, the subordinate-level categories may also have "privileged" status. For example, those of you who are experts on birds may be able to list a large number of attributes for *Baltimore orioles* (subordinate level) that you would not list for *orioles* (basic level).

Tanaka and Taylor located 12 dog experts and 12 bird experts, all with at least 10 years of experience in their field. These experts were asked to list features of either dogs or birds at the superordinate level, the basic level, and the subordinate level. On the average, these experts listed 10 new characteristics for the basic level that were not mentioned at the superordinate level and 10 new characteristics for the subordinate level were not mentioned at the basic level. In contrast, the comparable figures for novices were 11 new characteristics for the basic level and 6 for the subordinate level. In other words, experts show substantially more differentiation at the subordinate level than novices do. Similar findings have been reported for musicians making judgments about musical instruments (Palmer et al., 1989). It seems, then, that basic-level categories do not have special status for experts, because subordinate-level categories are equally privileged.

Conclusions about the Prototype Approach. One advantage of the prototype approach is that it can account for our ability to form concepts for groups that are loosely structured. For example, we can create a concept for stimuli that merely share a family resemblance to one another, such as *games*. As Barsalou (1992) points out, prototype models work especially well for categories whose exemplars have no single characteristic in common.

Furthermore, the prototype approach explains how we can reduce all the information about a wide variety of stimuli into a single, idealized abstraction. We do not need to retain an enormous amount of information about an enormous number of exemplars. However, in many cases, we do store specific information about exemplars. An ideal prototype model would therefore need to include a mechanism for storing this specific information, as well as abstract prototypes (Barsalou, 1990, 1992).

An ideal prototype model must also acknowledge that concepts can be unstable. We saw in the previous section that conceptual structure can change as people acquire expertise; the subordinate-level categories can become fine-tuned. Furthermore, our notions about the ideal prototype can shift as the context changes. For example, under normal circumstances, Americans regard a robin to be a more prototypical bird than a swan. However, when instructed to take the viewpoint of the average Chinese citizen, Americans believe that a swan is a more prototypical bird (Barsalou, 1989). To account for the complexity of the concepts we store in semantic memory, an ideal theory must explain how concepts are often stable. However, this theory must also explain how concepts can be altered by factors such as expertise and context.

SECTION SUMMARY: THE STRUCTURE OF SEMANTIC MEMORY

1. The information on general knowledge in this chapter illustrates that human cognitive abilities are both impressive and active.
2. The feature comparison model proposes that concepts are stored in terms of a list of features. Some decisions about semantic memory can be made rapidly while others require two stages.
3. Three network models include one proposed by Collins and Loftus (with interconnecting concepts and spreading activation), the PDP approach (whose neuron-like components were discussed in Chapter 3), and Anderson's ACT* approach (in which both sentences and concepts can be represented by a network structure).

4. The exemplar approach argues that we classify new stimuli in terms of their resemblance to specific examplars.

5. According to Rosch's prototype theory, people compare new stimuli with an idealized prototype in order to categorize them. Prototypes are frequently supplied when people compile a list of category examples, they serve as reference points, they are judged more quickly after priming, they can substitute for a category name, and they share common attributes in a family resemblance category.

6. Rosch's theory also proposes that basic-level categories have attributes and shapes in common; basic-level names are used to identify objects and to produce the priming effect; however, experts also make good use of subordinate categories.

SCHEMAS

So far, this chapter on general knowledge has focused on words, concepts, and, occasionally, sentences. However, human cognitive processes also involve knowledge units that are much larger. Our knowledge includes information about familiar situations, events, and the relationships about these situations and events. These generalized kinds of knowledge about situations and events are called **schemas.** You may recall that we discussed the concept of schemas in Chapter 5 in connection with autobiographical memory. In that chapter, we saw how people can develop schemas for certain repeated events in their lives, such as shopping for a gift. A schema represents "generic" information that includes not only events from one's life but also general knowledge about procedures, sequences of events, and social situations (Thorndyke, 1984).

Schema theories propose that people encode this generic information in memory and use it to understand and remember new examples of the schema. To be more specific, schemas guide our recognition and understanding of new examples by providing expectations about what should occur (Thorndyke, 1984). Schemas therefore exploit top-down processing, one of the principles of cognitive processes emphasized in Theme 5. Furthermore, schemas allow us to predict what will happen in a new situation (Norman, 1982). In most situations, these predictions will be correct; schemas are **heuristics,** or rules-of-thumb that are generally accurate.

Sometimes schemas can lead us astray, and we make errors. However, these errors usually make sense. Consistent with Theme 2, our cognitive processes are generally accurate and the mistakes are typically rational. Eysenck (1984) proposes an example: Suppose that you need to find the bathroom in an unfamiliar house. You would use your schema-based knowledge to eliminate the living room as a likely place to find it. This strategy would be correct about 99 percent of the time. However, this strategy can produce an error, because in about 1 percent of homes (including my own during graduate school), the bathroom is directly adjacent to the living room.

AN APPLICATION OF A SCRIPT.

Read the following paragraph from an article by Abelson (1981, p. 715):

John was feeling very hungry as he entered the restaurant. He settled himself at a table and noticed that the waiter was nearby. Suddenly, however, he realized that he'd forgotten his reading glasses.

Now, explain how Sentence 3 is related to Sentence 2.

Schema theories are popular when psychologists try to explain how people remember complex events (Alba & Hasher, 1983; Shoben, 1988). However, the concept of the schema has even earlier origins in psychology. Piaget's work in the 1920s investigated schemas in infants, and Bartlett's research in the 1920s tested memory for schemas in adults.

In this section on schemas, we will first examine one kind of schema called a script. The remainder of the section will explore how schemas operate in memory during the processes of selection, abstraction, interpretation, and integration.

Scripts

A **script** is a simple, well-structured sequence of events, involved in most of our daily processing (Mandler, 1984; Rumelhart & Norman, 1988). Although the terms *schema* and *script* are often used interchangeably, *script* is actually a narrower term, referring to events that happen across a period of time.

Consider the simple story in Demonstration 7.4. This task seems ridiculously easy. Of course John would need his glasses to read the menu that the waiter would bring to him. However, no menu was explicitly mentioned. Nonetheless, the first mention of entering the restaurant activates the expectation of certain predictable events. In fact, something that could be called a "restaurant script" was called forth, involving a standard sequence of events that a customer might expect in a restaurant (Abelson, 1981).

We can also have scripts for visiting a dentist's office, for how a board meeting should be run, and even for events that do not have the outcome we expected (Foti & Lord, 1987; Read & Cesa, 1991). Let's first consider some of the research on scripts and then examine an artificial intelligence approach used in developing scripts.

Research on Scripts.   In the previous section, we noted that experts differ from novices in the richness of their subordinate-level categories. You will not be surprised to learn that experts also differ from novices in their understanding of scripts.

For example, Pryor and Merluzzi (1985) examined two common social scripts, "getting a date" and "going on a first date." College students who were "experts"— because they had been on many dates—were able to place the events in their proper script sequence much more quickly than less socially experienced students.

A second study examines the difference between scripts and categories. This chapter has explored both scripts and categories, which are important components of the structure of knowledge. The two terms differ, however, in that scripts represent sequences of events, whereas categories represent clusters of objects. Barsalou and Sewell (1985) have demonstrated that scripts and categories also differ in the way they are recovered from memory. As part of their experiment, Barsalou and Sewell asked participants to recall items from the script "How to write a letter" and from the category *tools*. On some occasions, they were instructed to recall the items in any order they wished. On other occasions, they were told to recall the items in a specified order, from most typical representative to least typical representative. Barsalou and Sewell measured the number of items recalled in each 5-second period. In the script condition, people recalled roughly a constant number of items for each 5-second period of recall, whereas in the category condition, people started with a burst of examples and rapidly decreased their output toward the end of recall. We saw in the section on natural categories that typical examples are recalled quickly and at the beginning of the list of items. However, the structure of scripts is different. Perhaps because they are often constrained by the sequence of events, the components of a script are recalled at an even, steady pace.

Can people see the similarity between two kinds of scripts that have similar kinds of motives and outcomes? Seifert and her colleagues (1986) examined thematically similar episodes. For example, one episode occurred in an academic setting. It concerned Dr. Popoff, who knew that his graduate student Mike was unhappy with the research facilities. When Dr. Popoff discovered that Mike had been accepted at a rival university, he quickly offered Mike abundant research equipment, but by then Mike had already decided to transfer. A second episode occurred in a romance setting. Phil and his secretary were in love, but Phil kept postponing asking her to marry him. Meanwhile, the secretary fell in love with an accountant. When Phil found out, he proposed to her, but by then she and the accountant were already making honeymoon plans. Notice that these two passages show high thematic similarity.

Seifert and her colleagues used the priming technique described earlier in this book. They wanted to discover whether people would recognize a test sentence more quickly if that sentence were preceded by a priming sentence from the thematically similar story. (You may recall that psychologists interpret faster reaction times after a priming stimulus to be an indication that the participant regards the priming stimulus and the test stimulus to be conceptually related.)

The results of the study showed that the response time for a test sentence was facilitated by the priming sentence *only* if the participants had been urged to pay attention to repeated themes in the stories they were reading. Otherwise, people did not seem to make the connection between the two stories. If you plan to inspire a friend to behave in a more noble fashion, and you decide to tell Aesop's fables or other exemplary tales, you would be wise to point out that the fable might be connected with current behavior! People do not spontaneously detect abstract similarities in scripts.

Artificial Intelligence Approaches to Scripts. The first systematic effort to use an artificial intelligence approach to scripts was a computer program called Search of Associative Memory, or **SAM.** Roger Schank and his coauthors developed SAM so that it could process printed stories on a limited number of topics, recognize that a given script applies, and make predictions about which events are most likely to occur—in much greater detail than contained in the original story (Schank, 1982; Schank & Abelson, 1977; Schank and the Yale AI Project, 1975).

For example, suppose that the original study contained this sparse outline of a restaurant script:

John went to a restaurant. The hostess seated John. The hostess gave John a menu. John ordered lobster. He was served quickly. He left a large tip. He left the restaurant.

SAM was able to provide a paraphrase that included predictions about other intervening events:

John decided he was going to a restaurant. He went to one. He asked the hostess for a table. She told him he could go to it. He went to it. She went to it. He sat down in a chair. He got a menu from her. He read it. A waiter saw John at the table. The waiter went to it. John ordered lobster. A chef cooked it. The waiter got it from the chef. The waiter served it quickly to John. He ate it. He asked the waiter for a check. John got it from the waiter. John remembered the waiter had served him quickly. John left the waiter a large tip. John paid the check. He left the restaurant. (Schank and the Yale AI Project, 1975)

Now SAM is not a stimulating writer—you wouldn't hire SAM to write restaurant reviews for *Gourmet* magazine. Still, the program includes abundant information beyond the contents of the original, brief story. Scripts are the source of these additional elaborations and predictions.

The original SAM program has been modified. For example, one more recent variant includes a memory organization packet or **MOP,** which includes generalized groups of events called "scenes" (Schank, 1982; Seifert et al., 1986). The **MOP** specifies how the scenes are organized; for example, entering a restaurant comes before ordering. The scenes, however, are relatively abstract, and the same scene can be used in different MOPs. For example, an ordering scene could be used in both a restaurant and an ordering from a catalog MOP. This MOP program is therefore designed to be more flexible, because the scenes can be recombined in many fashions. This flexibility is also necessary because the model needs to account for people's adaptability when they have initially used an inappropriate script (McKoon et al., 1989).

In the remainder of this section, we will investigate how schemas operate in four phases of memory. According to Alba and Hasher (1983), schemas may operate at four different phases:

1. during the selection of material to be remembered;
2. during abstraction (when meaning is stored, but not the specifics of the message);
3. during interpretation (when relevant prior knowledge aids comprehension);
4. during integration (when a single memory representation is formed).

Schemas and Memory Selection

Try Demonstration 7.5 when you have the opportunity. This demonstration is based on a study by Brewer and Treyens (1981). These authors asked participants in their study to wait, one at a time, in the room pictured in the demonstration. Each time, the experimenter explained that this was his office, and he needed to check the laboratory to see if the previous participant had completed the experiment. After 35 seconds, the experimenter asked the participant to move to a nearby room. Here, each person was given a surprise test: Recall everything in the room in which he or she had waited.

The results showed that people were highly likely to recall objects consistent with the "office schema"—nearly everyone remembered the desk, the chair next to the desk, and the wall. However, few recalled the wine bottle and the coffee pot, and only one remembered the picnic basket. These items were not consistent with the office schema. (In addition, some remembered items that were *not* in the room; nine remembered books, though none had been in sight. This supplying of schema-consistent items represents an interesting reconstruction error.)

As Alba and Hasher (1983) point out, schema theories propose three conditions that determine whether a piece of information will be selected for encoding:

1. A person must have a relevant schema, such as an "office schema."
2. The schema must be activated. For example, the participants in Brewer and Treyen's study must realize that they are in an office.
3. The incoming information must be important with respect to the schema. For example, the chair and the desk are important components of the "office schema."

Schema theory predicts that the storage process is highly selective, producing inaccuracies in memory. Alba and Hasher feel, however, that schema theory is overly pessimistic; memory is highly accurate in many cases, even when stimuli are not consistent with a schema. It seems safe to take the position proposed in Theme 2 of this book: Memory is generally very accurate, but many errors in memory can be traced to rational mistakes. In this case, people adopt the heuristic, "When overwhelmed with stimuli, encode mainly the stimuli consistent with the schema."

DEMONSTRATION 7.5

SCHEMAS AND MEMORY (BASED ON BREWER & TREYENS, 1981).

After reading these instructions, cover them and the rest of the text in this demonstration so that only the picture shows. Present the picture to a friend, with the instructions, "Look at this picture of a psychologist's office for a brief time." Half a minute later, close the book and ask your friend to list everything that was in the room.

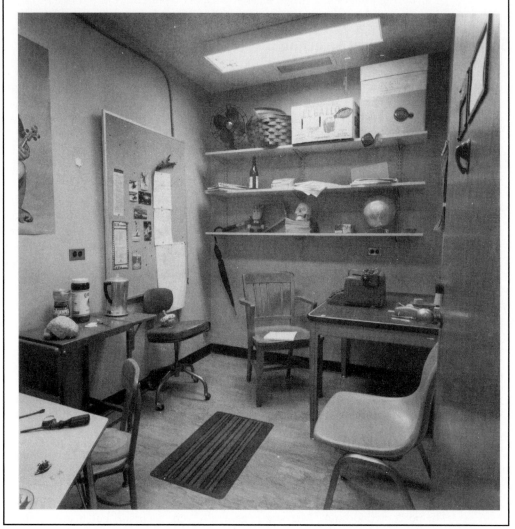

DEMONSTRATION 7.6

CONSTRUCTIVE MEMORY (BASED ON JENKINS, 1974).

Part 1

Read each sentence, count to five, answer the question, and go on to the next sentence.

SENTENCE	QUESTION
The girl broke the window on the porch.	Broke what?
The tree in the front yard shaded the man who was smoking his pipe.	Where?
The cat, running from the barking dog, jumped on the table.	From what?
The tree was tall.	Was what?
The cat running from the dog jumped on the table.	Where?
The girl who lives next door broke the window on the porch.	Lives where?
The scared cat was running from the barking dog.	What was?
The girl lives next door.	Who does?
The tree shaded the man who was smoking his pipe.	What did?
The scared cat jumped on the table.	What did?
The girl who lives next door broke the large window.	Broke what?
The man was smoking his pipe.	Who was?
The large window was on the porch.	Where?
The tall tree was in the front yard.	What was?
The cat jumped on the table.	Where?
The tall tree in the front yard shaded the man.	Did what?
The dog was barking.	Was what?
The window was large.	What was?

Part 2

Cover the preceding sentences. Now read each of the following sentences and decide whether it is a sentence from the list in Part 1.

1. The girl who lives next door broke the window.   (old _____, new _____)
2. The tree was in the front yard.   (old _____, new _____)
3. The scared cat, running from the barking dog, jumped on the table.   (old _____, new _____)
4. The window was on the porch.   (old _____, new _____)
5. The tree in the front yard shaded the man.   (old _____, new _____)
6. The cat was running from the dog.   (old _____, new _____)
7. The tall tree shaded the man who was smoking his pipe.   (old _____, new _____)

(continued on page 242)

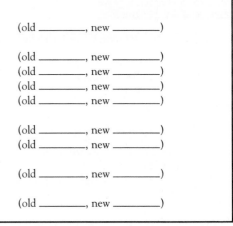

8. The scared cat was running from the dog.   (old _____, new _____)
9. The girl who lives next door broke the large window
   on the porch.   (old _____, new _____)
10. The tall tree shaded the girl who broke the window.   (old _____, new _____)
11. The cat was running from the barking dog.   (old _____, new _____)
12. The girl broke the large window.   (old _____, new _____)
13. The scared cat ran from the barking dog that jumped
    on the table.   (old _____, new _____)
14. The girl broke the large window on the porch.   (old _____, new _____)
15. The scared cat which broke the window on the porch
    climbed the tree.   (old _____, new _____)
16. The tall tree in the front yard shaded the man who
    was smoking his pipe.   (old _____, new _____)

Schemas and Memory Abstraction

Abstraction is a memory process that stores the meaning of a message without storing the exact words and grammatical structures. You can recall much of the information about the prototype approach, for example, without recalling a single sentence in its exact original form.

In a classic study, Sachs (1967) asked people to listen to a story that contained a critical sentence, and she interrupted the story shortly after they had heard that critical sentence. At this point, she asked the participants to judge whether they had seen a particular sentence. In some cases, she showed them a sentence that was identical to the critical sentence. In other cases, this new sentence was similar in meaning to the critical sentence, but different either in its arrangement of words or its **syntax** (grammatical form). In still other cases, this new sentence was different in meaning from the original sentence.

Sachs found that people did not pay much attention to word arrangement or syntax. They frequently thought they had seen a sentence that actually had very different word order from the original. People's **verbatim,** or word-for-word, memory is far from spectacular a few minutes after a passage has been presented. However, performance was quite accurate for sentences with the meaning changes. People cannot be tricked into thinking, for example, that they had seen a sentence with a meaning very different from the original. We store the meaning of prose even if we forget the exact wording.

Now try Demonstration 7.6—if you haven't already done so. This is a simpler version of a study by Bransford and Franks (1971). How many sentences in the second half had you seen before? The answer is at the end of this section.

Bransford and Franks asked the participants in their study to listen to sentences that belonged to several different stories. Then they were given a recognition test that included new sentences, many of which were combinations of the earlier sentences. Nonetheless, people were convinced that they had seen them before. They were particularly certain that they had heard complex sentences, such as "The tall tree in the front yard shaded the man who was smoking his pipe." In contrast, they were quite confident that they had not seen simple sentences, such as "The cat was scared." Furthermore, they did not think that they had seen sentences that violated the meaning of the earlier sentences—for example "The scared cat which broke the window on the porch climbed the tree."

Bransford and Franks proposed a constructive model of memory for prose material. According to the **constructive model of memory,** people integrate information from individual sentences in order to construct larger ideas. People therefore think that they have already seen those complex sentences because they had combined the various facts in memory. Once sentences are fused in memory, we cannot untangle them into their original components and recall those components verbatim.

These results surprised many people. The experiment has been successfully repeated in a variety of experimental situations (Flagg et al., 1975). However, many psychologists criticized the Bransford and Franks (1971) results. Some suggested, for example, that people really did not understand the task instructions; perhaps they thought they were merely to choose the sentences that had the same *meaning* as the original. The alternative interpretation was dismissed by Flagg and his colleagues, however, because their research showed that people really *did* understand the instructions.

How well can people remember meaning? The studies of Sachs (1967) and Bransford and Franks (1971) have shown that people remember the general meaning of the material they hear, even though they forget the specific form of the sentences (as Sachs showed) or the specific sentences they have seen (as Bransford and Franks showed). In the laboratory, people are at a disadvantage because the nature of human memory does not allow them to recall the precise words. However, in real life this disadvantage is seldom important. Typically, we do not need to recall the original sentences exactly. Instead, we can synthesize many isolated bits of information into a well-organized whole and recall the meaning of a passage.

Notice that the constructive nature of memory emphasizes the active nature of our cognitive processes, consistent with Theme 1 of this book. Sentences do not passively enter memory, where each is stored separately. Instead, we try to make sense out of sentences that seem to be related to each other. We combine the sentences into a coherent story, fitting the pieces together.

Constructive memory also illustrates Theme 2. Although memory is generally accurate, the errors in information processing can often be traced to generally useful strategies. In real life, a useful heuristic is to fuse sentences together. However, this heuristic can lead us astray if it is applied inappropriately. Check to see whether you applied the constructive model of memory inappropriately in Demonstration 7.6. In fact, every one of those sentences in the test was new. Before you read the next section, try Demonstration 7.7.

DEMONSTRATION 7.7

CONTEXT AND RECALL.

Read the following paragraph. Then close your book and recall as much of it as you can.

The procedure is actually quite simple. First you arrange things into different groups depending on their makeup. Of course, one pile may be sufficient depending on how much there is to do. If you have to go somewhere else due to lack of facilities, that is the next step; otherwise you are pretty well set. It is important not to overdo any particular endeavor. That is, it is better to do too few things at once than too many. In the short run this may not seem important, but complications from doing too many can easily arise. A mistake can be expensive as well. The manipulation of the appropriate mechanisms should be self-explanatory, and we need not dwell on it here. At first the whole procedure will seem complicated. Soon, however, it will become just another facet of life. It is difficult to foresee any end to the necessity for this task in the immediate future, but then one never can tell.

Schemas and Interpretations in Memory

In many cases, people add their own information to the material they encounter, and they remember this information as having been present in the original material. Thus, recall can contain **inferences** or logical conclusions that were never part of the original stimulus material.

Research in this area began with the studies of Frederick Bartlett (1932), a memory researcher who used natural language material. As we've mentioned before, his theories and techniques foreshadowed the approaches of contemporary cognitive psychologists. Unlike Ebbinghaus, who favored the use of nonsense words, Bartlett believed that the most interesting aspect of memory was the complex interaction between the material presented by the experimenter and the prior knowledge of the participants in the experiment. Furthermore, Bartlett argued that as time passes after hearing the original story, the recalled story borrows more heavily from previous knowledge and less from the information in the original story (Dooling & Christiaansen, 1977).

Bransford, Barclay, and Franks (1972) provided further evidence about the fusing of previous knowledge and information in stimulus material. These authors studied how people constructed mental models, based on verbal descriptions—a topic we considered in Chapter 6. They gave some people a sentence such as:

1. *Three turtles rested beside a floating log, and a fish swam beneath them.*

Others heard a sentence such as:

2. *Three turtles rested on a floating log, and a fish swam beneath them.*

Notice that the only difference between these two sentences is the word *beside* or *on*.

Later, everyone received a recognition test containing sentences such as:

3. *Three turtles rested (beside/on) a floating log, and a fish swam beneath it.*

Let us discuss this recognition sentence before examining the results. Sentence 3 contains *it* rather than *them* and can be derived from Sentence 2. Our knowledge of spatial relations tells us that if the turtles are on the log and a fish is beneath them, then the fish must also be beneath the log. That recognition sentence is therefore a reasonable inference. Notice, however, that the recognition sentence is not necessarily an inference from Sentence 1; it is ambiguous whether the fish are swimming beneath the log.

The results of the study showed that people who had seen Sentence 2 often reported that they recognized Sentence 3. However, people who had seen Sentence 1 were much less likely to say that they recognized Sentence 3. Bransford and his coauthors (1972) explain that people who saw Sentence 2 construct an idea by fusing that sentence with what they know about the world. As a result, they believe that they have seen a sentence that was never presented, even though it is a reasonable inference.

In the studies we have discussed so far, background knowledge misleads people, and they recall inferences that were not actually stated. Once more, a strategy that is typically helpful can lead us astray. In everyday life, background knowledge is often very helpful. How was your recall for Demonstration 7.7, which was adapted from a study by Bransford and Johnson (1972)? How would your recall have been if you had been told that it was a paragraph about doing laundry? Reread that paragraph, within the context of doing laundry. Once you know that it is about laundry, all your background knowledge about the washing process helps you fit the puzzling parts together into a meaningful paragraph. Bransford and Johnson found that people who knew the topic of the paragraph before reading it recalled 73 percent more material than people who did not know the topic. This kind of background knowledge improves performance because the background knowledge is consistent with the information in the paragraph.

Our background knowledge can also help us recall stories. Bower (1976) argues that simple stories have definite, regular structures. People become familiar with the basic structure of stories from their prior experience with stories in their culture. They use this structure in sorting out any new stories they hear. Once again, when background information is consistent with the stimulus materials, this background information is clearly helpful.

This material on schemas and memory interpretations can be applied to advertising. Suppose that an ad says, "Four out of five doctors recommend the ingredients in Gonif's brand medication." You might reasonably infer, therefore, that four out of five doctors would also recommend Gonif's medication itself, even though the ad never said so.

Research by Harris and his colleagues (1989) shows that people who read advertisements may jump to conclusions, remembering inferences that were never actually stated. In their research, college students read stories that contained several advertising slogans. Some slogans made a direct claim (for example, *Tylenol cures colds*), whereas others merely implied the same claim (for example, *Tylenol fights colds*). On a multiple-choice task that followed, people who had seen the implied-claim version often selected the direct-claim version instead. You can see why these results suggest that consumers should be careful. If an advertiser implies that a particular product has outstanding properties, make certain that you do not jump to inappropriate conclusions; you are likely to remember those inferences, rather than the actual stated information.

After reading about the experimental evidence for humans' tendencies to draw inappropriate inferences, you might conclude that people inevitably draw conclusions based on inferences from their daily experience. Alba and Hasher (1983) note, however, that inference-making is not an *obligatory* process. Several researchers have found that inference-making occurs only in limited situations; people often recall material accurately, just as it was originally presented. Further research must address the issue of when memory is schematic and when it is accurate. In many cases, then, schemas can indeed influence inferences in memory. However, consistent with Theme 2, memory can often be highly accurate.

Schemas and Integration in Memory

Another process in memory formation is integration. Schema theories argue that a single, integrated representation is created in memory from the information that was selected in the first phase, abstracted in the second phase, and interpreted (with the aid of background knowledge) in the third phase. In fact, some researchers argue that schemas exert a more powerful effect during the integration and retrieval phases than during the earlier phases of memory (e.g., Bloom, 1988; Kardash et al., 1988).

For example, a number of studies show that background knowledge does not influence recall if that recall is tested immediately after the material is learned. However, after a longer delay, the material has been integrated with existing schemas; recall is now altered. For instance, Harris and his colleagues (1989) asked college students in Kansas to read a story that was consistent with either American or traditional Mexican culture. A representative story about planning a date in the Mexican culture included a sentence about the young man's older sister accompanying the couple as a chaperone; the American version had no chaperone. When story recall was tested 30 minutes after reading the material, the students showed no tendency for the Mexican-script stories to shift in the direction consistent with American schemas. After a 2-day delay, however, a significant number of story details had shifted.

As Harris and his colleagues (1988) points out, schemas about our culture can influence our initial understanding of a story about another culture. However, an important additional source of cultural distortion occurs during delayed recall. We do not remember the details, so we reconstruct information that is consistent with our own cultural schemas.

Although people often integrate material in memory, Alba and Hasher (1983) once again cite experimental evidence that fails to demonstrate integration. In many cases, people store within memory several separate, unintegrated units of the original stimulus complex. Memory integration does occur, but it is not inevitable.

In summary, schemas can influence memory, from the initial selection of material, through abstraction and interpretation, and including the final process of integration. However, we must stress the following points:

1. We often *do* select material that is inconsistent with our schemas.
2. We can recall the exact surface material as it was originally presented—otherwise, chorus directors would have resigned long ago.
3. We often fail to apply our background knowledge when we need to interpret new material.
4. We may keep the elements in memory isolated from each other rather than integrated together.

Thus, schemas clearly influence memory, but the influence is far from complete.

SECTION SUMMARY: SCHEMAS

1. Research on scripts shows that experts can arrange events in an appropriate order more quickly than novices; also, people show different time patterns in recalling material from scripts and categories; furthermore, people may not detect abstract similarities between two scripts unless the similarities are pointed out.
2. Computer programs have been devised to elaborate on a sparse outline of a script; any computer program must reflect the flexibility with which humans use scripts.
3. Schemas operate in the selection of memories; for example, people recall items consistent with an office schema.
4. Schemas encourage memory abstraction, so that the details of the original message are lost, but the general meaning is retained.
5. Schemas influence the interpretations in memory; people may recall inferences that never appeared in the original material. However, background information often helps us interpret unclear information. Unfortunately, people often recall incorrect inferences from advertisements.
6. Schemas encourage an integrated representation in memory; research shows that people may misremember material so that it is more consistent with their schemas, including their cultural schemas.

7. Schemas can have important influences on memory, but this influence is not inevitable.

METACOGNITION

We have discussed several kinds of knowledge in this chapter, including knowledge about words, concepts, situations, and events. Our last topic is somewhat different. **Metacognition** is your knowledge of and awareness about cognitive processes. Thus, we shift from knowledge about the outside world to knowledge about the processes inside your head.

Think about the variety of metacognitive knowledge you possess. For example, if I were to ask you the name of the researcher who is associated with the prototype approach to semantic memory, you could tell me whether or not the researcher's name is on the tip of your tongue. You also know what kinds of factors influence your own cognitive processes (for example, time of day, motivation, type of material, and social circumstances). Furthermore, you can also assess whether you are adequately prepared for the next exam you will take.

Metacognition is an intriguing process because we use our cognitive processes to contemplate our cognitive processes. Metacognition is important because our knowledge about our cognitive processes can guide us in arranging circumstances and selecting strategies to improve future cognitive performances.

In this chapter, we will examine the tip-of-the-tongue phenomenon and metamemory, two very important kinds of metacognition. In Chapter 8, we will look at metacomprehension, which focuses on your knowledge about whether you have understood a passage you have just read. In Chapter 10, we will discuss whether people can accurately predict how close they are to solving a cognitive problem. Finally, Chapter 12 considers the development of metacognition.

The Tip-of-the-Tongue Phenomenon

Try Demonstration 7.8 to see whether any of the definitions encourage you into a tip-of-the-tongue experience. The **tip-of-the-tongue phenomenon** refers to the sensation we have when we are confident that we know the word for which we are searching, yet we cannot recall it. Brown and McNeill's (1966) study is the classic one on this topic. Let's examine this phenomenon and then see how it is related to metacognition.

Brown and McNeill's description of a man "seized" by a tip-of-the-tongue state might capture the torment you may feel when you fail to snatch a word from the tip of your tongue:

The signs of it were unmistakable; he would appear to be in mild torment, something like the brink of a sneeze, and if he found the word his relief was considerable. (p. 326)

DEMONSTRATION 7.8

THE TIP-OF-THE-TONGUE PHENOMENON.

Look at each of the definitions below. For each definition, supply the appropriate word if you know it. Indicate "Don't know" for those that you are certain you don't know. Mark TOT next to those for which you are reasonably certain you know the word, though you can't recall it now. For these words, supply at least one word that sounds similar to the target word. The answers appear later in the chapter.

1. An absolute ruler, a tyrant.
2. A stone having a cavity lined with crystals.
3. A great circle of the earth passing through the geographic poles and any given point on the earth's surface.
4. Worthy of respect or reverence by reason of age and dignity.
5. Shedding leaves each year, as opposed to evergreen.
6. A person appointed to act as a substitute for another.
7. Five offspring born at a single birth.
8. A special quality of leadership that captures the popular imagination and inspires unswerving allegiance.
9. The red coloring matter of the red blood corpuscles.
10. Flying reptiles that were extinct at the end of the Mesozoic Era.
11. A spring from which hot water, steam, or mud gushes out at intervals, found in Yellowstone National Park.
12. The second stomach of a bird, which has thick, muscular walls.

The similarity between "the brink of a sneeze" and the irritation of the tip-of-the-tongue experience is amazing! Don't you wish you had a substance similar to pepper that could coax the missing word out of memory?

At any rate, Brown and McNeill produced the tip-of-the-tongue state by giving people the definition for an uncommon English word, such as *cloaca, ambergris,* and *nepotism.* Sometimes people supplied the appropriate word immediately, and other times they were confident that they did not know the word. However, in some cases, the definition produced a tip-of-the-tongue state. In these cases, the experimenter asked people to provide words that resembled the target word in terms of sound, but not meaning. For example, when the target word was *sampan,* people provided these similar-sounding words: *Saipan, Siam, Cheyenne, sarong, sanching,* and *symphoon.*

Brown and McNeill's results showed that the similar-sounding words were indeed very similar to the target words. The similar-sounding words matched the target's first letter 49 percent of the time, and they matched the target's number of syllables 48 percent of the time.

Brown and McNeill (1966) proposed that our long-term memory for words and definitions is like a dictionary. However, our mental dictionaries are much more flexible than the alphabetized version you have on your bookshelf. We can recover words from memory by either their meaning or their sound, and we need not examine the entries in alphabetical order.

Alan Brown (1991) has reviewed 25 years of research on the tip-of-the-tongue experience. He concludes that people report that the experience occurs about once a week in their daily lives, although elderly people report it somewhat more often than younger adults. People successfully retrieve the word they are seeking about half the time, often within the first two minutes of the tip-of-the-tongue experience.

In general, the research also shows that people are correct in guessing the first letter of the target word between 50 percent and 70 percent of the time. People are also highly accurate in guessing the appropriate number of syllables (between 47 percent and 83 percent correct guesses). However, these figures are less impressive once you realize that people could be quite accurate by simply guessing. The higher accuracy rates are usually obtained with proper names, which are typically limited to one- and two-syllable words.

Now check your own accuracy for Demonstration 7.8, and notice whether your similar-sounding words resemble the targets in terms of first letter and number of syllables. The target words were:

1. despot	5. deciduous	9. hemoglobin
2. geode	6. surrogate	10. pterodactyl
3. meridian	7. quintuplets	11. geyser
4. venerable	8. charisma	12. gizzard

Incidentally, the tip-of-the-tongue phenomenon is consistent with the concept of graceful degradation, discussed in connection with the parallel distributed processing approach (p. 97). That is, we often remember some partial information, even if we cannot recover the exact target we are searching for in memory.

Think about the reason why the tip-of-the-tongue phenomenon is one kind of metacognition. People know enough about their memory to report, "This word is on the tip of my tongue." Their knowledge is indeed fairly accurate, because they are likely to be able to identify the first letter and the number of syllables in the target word. They are also likely to provide similar-sounding words that really do resemble the target word. Finally, in about half the cases, they successfully retrieve the word for which they were searching, an indication that they were indeed in hot pursuit of the target word.

◇ In Depth: *Metamemory*

Have you ever been in this position? You thought you knew the material for a midterm, and, in fact, you expected to receive a fairly high grade. However, when the midterms were handed back, you received a C. If this sounds familiar, you have been the victim of a metamemory failure. **Metamemory** refers to people's knowledge and awareness of their memory. Let's first examine the accuracy of metamemory and then consider how metamemory is related to memory performance. Then we will ask whether people are aware of the factors that can affect memory. The final issue to discuss is whether people are effective in using metamemory to regulate their study strategies.

Chapter 5 foreshadowed the importance of metamemory. In the section on memory improvement, we introduced a number of memory strategies. However, these strategies have limited value unless you use your metamemory to decide what you already know and what needs more review. Metamemory will also help you identify which memory strategies work best for you and which ones are inefficient. This In-Depth section therefore suggests some practical tips for memory improvement and performance on examinations. As you read this material, try to identify where your metamemory may need some improvement.

The Accuracy of Metamemory. Under ideal conditions, metamemory can be outstanding. Consider, for instance, a study by Eugene Lovelace (1984). Lovelace presented pairs of unrelated English words (e.g., DISEASE-RAILROAD). The participants were told that they would be tested for paired-associate learning, that is, they would later see the first word in the pair and be asked to supply the second word. There were four learning conditions: S1 people saw each pair for 8 seconds on a single study trial; S2 people saw each pair for 4 seconds on each of two successive study trials; S4 people saw each pair for 2 seconds on each of four successive study trials; and people in the T2 condition saw each pair for 4 seconds on each of two successive study trials with a test trial in between. After the final exposure of each pair, the participants rated each pair for the likelihood of their answering the item correctly on a later test. Finally, they were tested for recall.

Figure 7.6 shows the results. The most striking finding is that people can predict which items they will recall. When they give a rating of 5 to an item, they do in fact recall it about 90 percent of the time when they are tested later; when they give a rating of 1, they recall it less than half of the time. Notice, too, that the relationship between confidence rating and proportion correct holds true for all four conditions. These findings can be applied to your classroom performance. If you know that you will be tested on a specific list of items—such as foreign-language vocabulary or definitions for psychology terms—you are likely to be reasonably accurate in estimating whether you know the material.

Metamemory is less accurate when the task is not so clear-cut. In most college courses, you seldom know exactly what material will be on the test. Furthermore, you need to master concepts, not pairs of words, and it seems to be more difficult to assess whether you will remember conceptual material.

A study by Ruth Maki and Sharon Berry (1984) has important implications for your performance in psychology courses. They examined college students' abilities to predict how well they would perform on a test covering material they had read

FIGURE 7.6

Probability of Recalling an Item, as a Function of Experimental Condition and Rated Likelihood of Answering the Question (Lovelace, 1984).

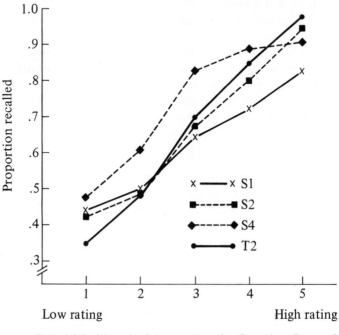

Rated Likelihood of Answering the Question Correctly
on a Later Test

in a psychology textbook. Students read sections from an introductory textbook and then estimated how well they thought they would perform on a multiple-choice question on that section. The next day, they were tested on their performance, and half of the students were given feedback about whether they had answered each question correctly. On the third day, they read further sections, and on the fourth day, they received their final test.

Surprisingly, feedback about test performance did not influence the accuracy with which students predicted their performance on the test. Figure 7.7, therefore, does not include this variable. However, the figure does include another variable, the student's ability, which was assessed in terms of whether the student scored in the top half or the bottom half of the group on the first of the two tests. Notice that the students who were above average did indeed predict with some accuracy that they would do well on the items they answered correctly, in contrast to the

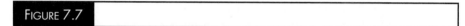

FIGURE 7.7

Average Ratings of Performance on Future Multiple-Choice Questions, as a Function of the Ability Level of the Student and Whether the Item Was Later Answered Correctly or Incorrectly.

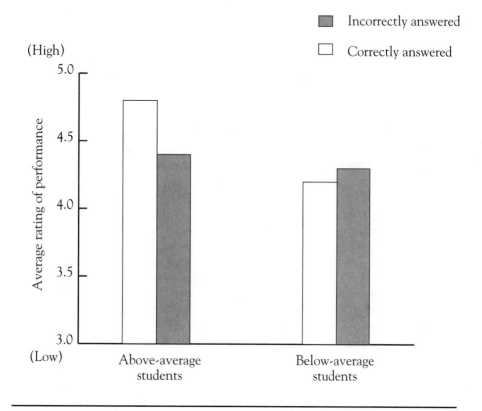

items they answered incorrectly. However, the students who were below average did not accurately predict their performance. In fact, they were slightly more confident about the items they had actually answered *incorrectly!* This observation brings us to our next topic.

The Relationship Between Metamemory and Memory Performance.

We saw that good students are better than poor students in accurately assessing what they know. In a related study, Leal (1987) gave introductory psychology students a questionnaire to test their knowledge about metamemory. Typical questions assessed whether students knew that relearning is easier than learning material for the first time, and that material at the beginning and end of a list is learned better than material in the middle. The results showed that some of the individual metamemory questions were significantly correlated with performance on classroom examinations. For instance, students who reported that they organize material in a meaningful manner and test themselves prior to an exam were likely to do well on classroom exams. However, the total score on the metamemory questionnaire was not correlated with exam performance. Apparently, some components of metamemory are not really related to exam scores.

As you may know from other courses, an ideal study for examining cause-and-effect relationships in psychology should involve an experiment, rather than correlational methods. Unfortunately, the relationship between metamemory and memory performance has not yet been investigated using the experimental method. Here is an important question, ready to be tested experimentally: If we were to teach metacognitive skills to college students, would they score higher than students in a control group, who had not been instructed in metacognitive techniques?

Awareness of Factors Affecting Memory.

Think about someone you know with a high grade point average. Can this person's high grades be traced more to high ability or to hard work? According to Devolder and Pressley (1989), North American students give more credit to innate ability than to hard work. However, students need to be aware that effort and strategic factors can be just as important as ability, or sometimes even more important.

Are students aware that some memory strategies are more effective than others? Here again, students are not sufficiently aware of the importance of strategic factors. Suzuki-Slakter (1988) instructed one group of students to memorize material by simply repeating it—a strategy that you know is relatively ineffective. These students seriously overestimated their performance. Another group was told to make up stories and images about the items—a strategy you know to be effective. These students *underestimated* their performance.

Other studies have found that people are not aware that the keyword method (which was illustrated in Figure 5.4) is much more effective than mere repetition (Pressley et al., 1984, 1988). However, when people practiced both methods and saw their superior performance with the keyword method, they were much more likely to use this method in the future. This research highlights an important point: Try using various study strategies, then test yourself. You'll be much more likely to revise your strategies if you can demonstrate that they improve your performance.

Regulating Study Strategies.

You may have developed your metamemory to the point that you know exactly which study strategies work best in which circumstances. However, your exam performance may still be less than ideal if you have not effectively regulated your study strategies. Specifically, you need to adjust your time allotment so that you spend much more time on the items you have not yet mastered than on those that you know you'll remember.

Thomas Nelson and R. Jacob Leonesio (1988) examined how students distribute their study time when they are allowed to study at their own pace. They found that students did allocate more study time for the items they believed would be difficult to master. The correlations here averaged about +.30 (where .00 would indicate no relationship and +1.00 would be a perfect correlation). Now, if students were ideal study-machines, they would spend very little time studying items they already know. Instead, they would concentrate their study time on the items that seem more difficult. The correlation would be much closer to +1.00.

Unfortunately, however, students are less than ideal in regulating their study strategies. They spend longer than necessary studying items they already know and not enough time studying the ones they have not yet mastered. Let's translate these findings to apply to the way you might study this current chapter for an examination tomorrow—assuming that you are a typical student. You may decide that you know the material on the tip-of-the-tongue phenomenon fairly well, but you are not confident about the theories of semantic memory. You might indeed spend somewhat longer studying semantic memory. However, you would be likely to distribute your study time too evenly across the chapter, reviewing what you already know. (Can't you see yourself pausing to reminisce about your experiences with the tip-of-the-tongue effect, meanwhile breezing too quickly over the finer points of the network models of semantic memory?) Try to figure out some system that ensures more attention to difficult items.

Throughout this section on metamemory, we have discussed how attention to your metamemory can improve performance. You need to know memory strategies, such as those outlined in Chapter 5. However, you also need to know how to use them effectively by selecting the strategies that work well for you and help you distribute your study time effectively.

SECTION SUMMARY: METACOGNITION

1. Two important components of metacognition are the tip-of-the-tongue phenomenon and metamemory.
2. Research on the tip-of-the-tongue phenomenon shows that when people cannot remember the word for which they are searching, they still can identify its important attributes.
3. People's metamemories are quite accurate when the task is clear-cut; when the material involves concepts and you do not know what will be tested, metamemory accuracy is not as impressive.
4. Good students are somewhat better than poor students in estimating their test performance; also, some components of metamemory are correlated with memory performance.
5. Students are not sufficiently aware that effort is related to test scores or that some memory strategies are more effective than others.

6. Students spend somewhat more time studying difficult material, rather than easy material, but ideally they should spend even more time on the difficult items.

CHAPTER REVIEW QUESTIONS

1. Suppose that a true-false question on an examination reads, "A script is a kind of schema." Describe how you would process that question in terms of the feature comparison model and the two network models discussed in this chapter.
2. The concept of priming was introduced in Chapter 6. Review the research on priming from that chapter, and summarize the information on priming from the current chapter. How is top-down processing related to priming?
3. Think of a prototype for the category *household pet*, such as a dog, and contrast it with a nonprototypical pet, a skunk. Compare these two animals with respect to (a) whether they would be supplied as examples, (b) the extent to which they would be used as a reference point in trying to describe another household pet, (c) how quickly they would be judged after priming, and (d) whether they can substitute for a category name in a sentence.
4. Consider the basic-level category *dime*, in contrast to the superordinate *money*, and the subordinate *1986 dime*. Discuss how members of this basic-level category (a) share attributes in common and (b) have shapes in common. Discuss also how the basic-level name would be used to identify objects.
5. Name three scripts with which you are very familiar. How would these scripts be considered heuristics, rather than exact predictors of what will happen the next time you find yourself in one of the situations described in the script?
6. The exemplar approach to semantic memory differs from the prototype approach because those who favor exemplars believe that we can retain specific information about specific examples. How does this distinction also apply to the material on schemas in memory, with respect to recalling specific information?
7. Human cognitive processes seem to prefer prototypes, basic-level categories, and schemas. Discuss this general statement, providing experimental support from this chapter.
8. Think of a schema that could influence your recall of a scene or an event. Explain how that schema might influence memory during selection, abstraction, interpretation, and integration.
9. In general, how accurate is our metacognition? Provide examples from the tip-of-the-tongue phenomenon and various metamemory tasks.

10. Think of a high-school student or a student who is just beginning college. Imagine that this person is asking you for advice on how to study. What information can you provide from the discussion of metamemory? Give as many hints as possible.

NEW TERMS

semantic memory
feature comparison model
defining features
characteristic features
sentence verification technique
typicality effect
category size effect
network model
parallel distributed processing (PDP)
    approach
Collins and Loftus network model
node
superordinate link
modifier link
spread of activation
intersection
ACT*
declarative knowledge
procedural knowledge
working memory
proposition
exemplar approach

prototypes
prototype approach
prototypicality
graded structure
priming effect
family resemblance
prototype ratings
superordinate-level categories
basic-level categories
subordinate-level categories
schemas
heuristics
script
SAM
MOP
syntax
verbatim
constructive model of memory
inferences
metacognition
tip-of-the-tongue phenomenon
metamemory

RECOMMENDED READINGS

Barsalou, L. W. (1992). *Cognitive psychology: An overview for cognitive scientists.* Hillsdale, NJ: Erlbaum. Lawrence Barsalou is a prominent researcher in the area of semantic memory. His chapters on categorization and knowledge in memory would be useful for students who want an advanced-level, theoretical treatment of these topics.

Brown, A. S. (1991). A review of the tip-of-the-tongue experience. *Psychological Bulletin, 109,* 204–223. Brown's article provides a recent review of the topic, including questions for which we do not yet have answers.

Nelson, T. O. (Ed.). (1992). *Metacognition: Core readings*. Boston, MA: Allyn & Bacon. Here is an excellent collection of theoretical and empirical articles about metacognition.

Shoben, E. J. (1988). The representation of knowledge. In M. F. McTear (Ed.), *Understanding cognitive science* (pp. 102–119). Chichester, England: Ellis Horwood. Shoben's chapter provides a cohesive discussion of theories of semantic memory.

Vosniadou, S., & Ortony, A. (Eds.). (1989). *Similarity and analogical reasoning*. New York: Cambridge University Press. The first part of the book contains some excellent articles on the structure of concepts.

LANGUAGE COMPREHENSION: LISTENING AND READING

PREVIEW

Chapters 8 and 9 examine the psychological aspects of language. Specifically, Chapter 8 emphasizes language comprehension in the form of listening and reading. Chapter 9 will emphasize speaking, writing, and bilingualism.

A necessary first stage in comprehending language is speech perception, which involves translating sounds into speech units. When we perceive speech, we fill in missing sounds and determine the boundaries between words, often with the aid of context. As listeners, we process language in terms of groups of words called constituents. We also listen to surface structure and determine the underlying, deep structure of a sentence. Sentences are harder to understand if they contain negatives, the passive voice, or ambiguities.

Reading involves perceptual processes such as eye movement and letter recognition, as well as word recognition. Context is important when we need to understand the meaning of an unfamiliar word. When we read, we frequently draw inferences that were not actually stated in the written passage. Unfortunately, people are not exceptionally accurate in their metacomprehension; for example, college students cannot accurately predict how well they will do on a reading comprehension test. Finally, research on artificial intelligence emphasizes the competence of humans in language comprehension skills.

INTRODUCTION

Imagine what would happen if language suddenly became illegal. You wouldn't be allowed to speak, to read, to write, or to use words in memory or thought. Think about the disastrous consequences for your daily life. You couldn't discuss which movie to see next Friday. You couldn't attend any lectures or read any books. In fact, you wouldn't attend school at all, because basic information about registration could not be communicated. Furthermore, you wouldn't *need* to attend school, because all the professions requiring verbal communication—are there any that do not?—would be banned. Even people who lead relatively solitary lives would experience a transformation, because they would be deprived of language from television, radio, books, and newspapers (J. Greene, 1986). We have difficulty imagining even the most primitive society without language.

In Chapters 8 and 9, we will examine **psycholinguistics,** or the psychological aspects of language. Psycholinguistics examines how people learn and use language to communicate ideas (Taylor & Taylor, 1990). Language provides the best example of one theme of this textbook, the interrelatedness of the cognitive processes; virtually every topic discussed so far makes some contribution to language. For example, perception is involved when we hear speech or read words. Echoic memory and short-term memory help us store the stimuli long enough to process and interpret them. Long-term memory provides continuity between the material we processed long ago and the material we now encounter. Clearly, memory is an essential component of language (Garman, 1990). Furthermore, language is influenced by semantic memory, schemas, and the tip-of-the-tongue phenomenon.

This list of cognitive processes that contribute to language should foreshadow why the mastery of language is such a complex accomplishment. Even though it is complicated, we still use language with little difficulty (Singer, 1990). People are remarkably efficient and accurate in understanding and producing language, consistent with Theme 2 of this textbook. The chapters on language should also convince you that humans are active information processors (Theme 1). Rather than passively listening to language, we actively consult our previous knowledge, use various strategies, form expectations, and draw conclusions. When we speak, we must ascertain what our listeners already know and what other facts must be conveyed. Language is not only our most remarkable cognitive achievement, but it is also the most social of our cognitive processes.

The first of our two chapters on language focuses on language comprehension, a topic that can be subdivided into listening and reading. The second chapter will explore language production, which involves speaking and writing; the topic of bilingualism will also be explored in that chapter.

The first parts of Chapters 8 and 9 deal with auditory language, whereas the second parts of each chapter deal with visual language. The spoken and written forms of language clearly share important similarities. To comprehend either form of language, we must retrieve the meaning of each word, analyze relationships between words, and extract meaning (Singer, 1990). Indeed, people who are good readers are also effective listeners (Townsend et al., 1987). However, the processes differ in important respects (Brown, 1986; Danks & End, 1987; Liberman, 1992):

1. Humans have spoken language over the past 1 million to 3 million years, but writing systems have been created only during the last 6,000 years.
2. All language communities have a fully developed spoken language, but reading and writing are less common.
3. Children learn to speak early in their lives, with relatively little coaching; they must be taught to read and write, often with great difficulty.
4. A reader can reread a difficult passage; a listener cannot "re-listen."

With these comparisons in mind, let us explore the auditory and visual components of language comprehension.

UNDERSTANDING SPOKEN LANGUAGE

The process of understanding language, often called **language comprehension,** involves using permanently stored knowledge to interpret new input. We listen to a set of sounds and manage to make sense of them, using our extensive knowledge of sounds, words, language rules, and the world. We can also go beyond the information given, managing to interpret metaphors (for example, *The camel is the taxi of the desert.*) and schemas (Glucksberg, 1989).

The following topics will be discussed in this section of the chapter: speech perception, constituent structure, transformational grammar, and factors affecting comprehension. These topics focus on three different levels of analysis. Speech perception emphasizes the sounds of language, and constituent structure focuses on understanding phrases. Transformational grammar and comprehension factors focus on the sentence level.

Speech Perception

When we understand spoken language, we must first analyze the sounds of speech. In **speech perception,** the listener's auditory system translates sound vibrations into a string of sounds that the listener perceives to be speech.

Speech perception is extremely complex, and more details on the process may be pursued in other books (e.g., Coren et al., 1994; Matlin & Foley, 1992; Handel, 1989). To most of us, however, speech perception does not seem complex, because we usually pay no attention to it. Instead, we usually attend to what the speaker is saying. We notice greetings, warnings, questions, and statements, but we do not notice the vehicle that is used to deliver this information (Darwin, 1976).

The next time you listen to a radio announcer, pay no attention to the meaning of his or her words, but notice the sounds instead. (You can attend to sound more readily if you tune in on a program in a language you do not understand.) Think about the string of sounds—vowels for which the vocal tract remains open (for example, the sounds *a* and *e*), stop consonants for which the vocal track closes completely and then quickly opens up (for example, the sounds *p* and *k*), and other sounds, such as *f* and *r*, in which the vocal tract performs other contortions. You'll hear occasional brief quiet periods in this string of sounds, but most of the words are simply run together in one continuous series.

Let us consider several facts about speech perception:

1. Information about sounds is transmitted in parallel.
2. Context allows listeners to fill in missing sounds.
3. Visual cues from the speaker's mouth help us interpret ambiguous sounds.
4. Listeners can impose boundaries between words.

After examining these aspects of speech perception, we will consider theories of speech perception.

Parallel Transmission. When we read the letters in a sentence, the letters follow one another, like beads on a string. However, the story is different for **phonemes** (pronounced "*foe*-neem"), which are the basic units of spoken language (for example, the sounds *a*, *k*, and *th*). The sound of a phoneme does not follow neatly after the preceding phoneme (Jusczyk, 1986; Luce & Pisoni, 1987). Instead of transmitting the phonemes one at a time, some of the sounds are transmitted

FIGURE 8.1	

Parallel Transmission, Showing How More Than One Phoneme Is Transmitted at a Time.

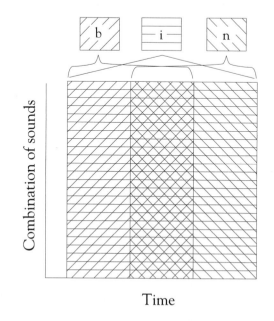

at about the same time. The term **parallel transmission** refers to this tendency for the phonemes to overlap somewhat as they are spoken.

For example, suppose that a speaker is saying the English word *bin*, as Figure 8.1 illustrates. The first consonant, *b*, carries its sound through the first two-thirds of the word, so that it influences the sound of the *i*. Because the vowel *i* spreads its transmission throughout the entire word, it influences the sounds of both the *b* and the *n*. The last consonant, *n*, actually begins its sound during the middle of the word, and thus it influences the sound of the *i*. Therefore, each phoneme's sound is modified by the surrounding phonemes.

Because of parallel transmission, speech sounds flow together. This means that a small segment of speech cannot carry all the information about one phoneme, because that information is spread across several segments. Furthermore, a phoneme's sound can change, depending on which phonemes precede and follow it. Phonemes often do not have a single, constant pronunciation. For example, a *d* might sound different in a *di* combination than it sounds in a *du* combination.

From our discussion so far, you might conclude that there is no stability in the sound of a phoneme. However, Cole and Scott (1974) have argued that, in spite of the variation provided from the surrounding sounds, all consonant phonemes have some invariant features. An **invariant feature** in speech perception is a sound cue that accompanies a particular phoneme, no matter what vowels surround it. For example, Cole and Scott argue that the phoneme s always has a hissing sound. Furthermore, a ʒ always differs from an s because its pitch is lower. Sometimes the invariant features are specific enough so that a person can identify the consonant. In other cases, the invariant features allow the listener to narrow down the possibilities to two or three phonemes.

Context and Speech Perception.

People are active listeners, consistent with Theme 1. Instead of passively receiving speech sounds, they can use context as a cue to help them figure out a sound or a word.

Warren and his colleagues have demonstrated in several experiments that people tend to show **phonemic restoration:** They can fill in sounds that are missing, using context as a cue. For example, Warren (1970) played a recording of a sentence: *The state governors met with their respective legi*latures convening in the capital city.* The first s in the word *legislatures* was replaced with an ordinary cough lasting 0.12 seconds. Of the 20 people who heard the recording, 19 reported that there were no sounds missing from the recording! (The one remaining person reported the wrong sound as missing.)

We are accustomed to having occasional phonemes masked by extraneous noises, and we are quite good at reconstructing the missing sounds. Think about the number of times extraneous noises have interfered with your professors' lectures. People knock books off desks, cough, turn pages, and whisper. Still, you can figure out the appropriate words.

Warren and Warren (1970) showed that people are skilled at using the meaning of a sentence to select the correct word from several options. They played four sentences for their subjects:

> It was found that the *eel was on the axle.
> It was found that the *eel was on the shoe.
> It was found that the *eel was on the orange.
> It was found that the *eel was on the table.

The four sentences were identical with one exception: A different word was spliced onto the end of each sentence. As before, a cough was inserted in the location shown by the asterisk. The "word" *eel was heard as *wheel* in the first sentence, *heel* in the second sentence, *peel* in the third, and *meal* in the fourth. In this study, then, people could not use surrounding sounds to reconstruct the word, yet they were able to reconstruct the word on the basis of a context cue that occurred four words later!

Notice that phonemic restoration is a kind of illusion (Warren, 1984). People think they hear a phoneme, even though the correct sound vibrations never reached their ears. Phonemic restoration is a well-documented phenomenon, and it has been demonstrated in numerous studies, (e.g., Samuel, 1981, 1987; Samuel

DEMONSTRATION 8.1

CONTEXT AND MISPRONUNCIATIONS.

Practice reading these sentences until you can read them smoothly. Then read them to a friend. Ask your friend to report which word in each sentence was mispronounced and to identify which sound in the word was incorrect.

1. In all the gunfusion, the mystery man escaped from the mansion.
2. When I was working pizily in the library, the fire alarm rang out.
3. The messemger ran up to the professor and handed her a proclamation.
4. It has been zuggested that students be required to preregister.
5. The president reacted vavorably to all of the committee's suggestions.

& Ressler, 1986). Other research has demonstrated that people are highly accurate in reconstructing a word that is missed during speech perception, particularly when that word is highly predictable from context (Cooper et al., 1985; Salasoo & Pisoni, 1985).

Our ability to perceive a word on the basis of context also allows us to handle sloppy pronunciations. Try Demonstration 8.1, which is a modification of a study by Cole (1973). In Cole's study, people often did not notice mispronunciations when they occurred in the context of a sentence (for example, the *gunfusion* sentence). However, they accurately distinguished syllables such as *gun* and *con* when the isolated syllables were presented.

Because we are so tolerant of mispronunciations in sentences, we often fail to notice startling mispronunciations that children make. Think back about a song that you sang when you were a child in which you included totally inappropriate words. One of my students recalled singing a Christmas carol in which the shepherds "washed their socks by night," rather than "watched their flocks by night." Another student recalled singing a Christmas carol with these words, "O come all ye hateful: Joy, Phil, and their trumpet." Many songs that children learn are never explained to them, and so they make up versions that make sense. However, these versions sound close enough to the standard that adults will not detect the errors. A classroom may have 25 second-graders, all reciting their own variants of the "Pledge of Allegiance"!

We have seen in this section that context has an important influence on the speech we hear. You may recall a similar discussion about the effects of context in Chapter 2 when we examined the influence of context on visual pattern perception. In the context of a kitchen scene, we see a loaf of bread, rather than a mailbox. In the context of an axle, we hear the word *wheel*, rather than *peel*. Although other explanations have been offered (e.g., Kintsch, 1988), one likely explanation for the influence of context on perception is top-down processing. Whether we are

---

DEMONSTRATION 8.2

VISUAL CUES AND SPEECH PERCEPTION (BASED ON SMYTH ET AL., 1987).

The next time you are in a room with both a television and a radio, try this exercise. Switch the TV set to the news or some other program where someone is talking straight to the camera; keep the volume low. Now turn on your radio and tune it between two stations, so that it produces a hissing noise. Turn the radio's volume up until you have difficulty understanding what the person on television is saying; the radio's "white noise" should nearly mask the speaker's voice. Face the TV screen and close your eyes; try to understand the spoken words. Now open your eyes. Do you find that speech perception is now much easier?

---

looking or listening, we use our knowledge and expectations to help the recognition process. Understanding language is not merely a passive process where words flow into our ears, providing data for bottom-up processing. Instead, we actively use the information we know to create expectations about what we might hear. Consistent with Theme 5 of this textbook, top-down processing influences our cognitive activities.

Visual Cues as an Aid to Speech Perception.   Try Demonstration 8.2 when you have the opportunity. Smyth and her colleagues (1987) point out how this simple exercise illustrates the contribution of visual cues to speech perception. Information from the speaker's lips and face helps resolve ambiguities from the speech signal, much as contextual cues help us choose between *wheel* and *peel* (Dodd & Campbell, 1986). Similarly, you can hear conversation better when speaking directly to a person than when speaking over the telephone (Massaro, 1989). Even with a superb telephone connection, we miss the lip cues that would tell us whether the speaker was discussing *Harry* or *Mary*.

However, adults with normal hearing often do not learn to notice or take advantage of these visual cues. In fact, we are likely to appreciate visual cues only in unusual circumstances. For example, you may notice a poorly dubbed movie, in which the actors' lips move independently of the sounds presumably coming from those lips (Massaro, 1987).

Word Boundaries.   Have you ever heard a conversation in an unfamiliar language? The words seem to run together in a continuous stream, with no boundaries separating them. You may think that the boundaries between words seem much more distinct in English, almost as clear-cut as the white spaces that identify the boundaries of written English. In most cases, however, the actual acoustic stimulus of spoken language shows no clear-cut pauses to mark the boundaries. An actual physical event, such as a pause, marks a word boundary less than 40 percent of the time (Cole & Jakimik, 1980; Flores d'Arcais, 1988).

Consider this visual analog of the problem confronting our auditory system (Jusczyk, 1986) as you read the following line:

THEREDONATEAKETTLEOFTENCHIPS.

Without the white spaces (the visual equivalent of pauses in speech), you probably found the task difficult. Did you read the line as, "There, Don ate a kettle of ten chips," "There, donate a kettle of ten chips," or "The red on a tea kettle often chips"?

Children have to learn where the boundaries between words are located, and they make frequent mistakes. Dr. Eleanor Maccoby told her child psychology class at Stanford University about a child who thought that toast was called "jamonit." It seems that his mother handed him a piece of toast every morning and asked, "Would you like some jam on it?" Not only had the child acquired the wrong label for toast, but he had also failed to identify two boundaries. Children's mispronunciations in songs, which we discussed in the previous section, frequently involve boundary errors.

Children are not alone in boundary errors, however. Safire (1979) comments about a grandmother who made an interesting misinterpretation of "the girl with kaleidoscope eyes" from the Beatles' song "Lucy in the Sky with Diamonds." Because of her greater familiarity with illness than with psychedelic experiences, she thought that the line was "the girl with colitis goes by." We use our knowledge to interpret ambiguous phonemes and impose boundaries between words. Most of the time, this knowledge leads us to the correct conclusions, but sometimes it leads to humorous misinterpretations.

Theories of Speech Perception.

The theories that explain speech perception generally fall into two categories. Some believe that speech requires a special mechanism to explain our impressive skill in this area. Others admire humans' skill in speech perception, but argue that the same general mechanism that handles other cognitive processes also handles speech perception.

The **special mechanism approach,** also known as the **motor theory of speech perception,** argues that humans have a specialized device that allows them to decode speech stimuli by connecting the stimuli they hear with the way these sounds are produced by the speaker. In other words, speech perception is closely linked with speech production. The major proponents of this approach, Alvin Liberman and Ignatius Mattingly, argue that this unique ability to perceive speech resembles the special sound localization abilities found in barn owls and bats (Liberman & Mattingly, 1989; Mattingly & Liberman, 1988).

More specifically, Liberman and Mattingly argue that humans possess a **phonetic module,** a special-purpose neural mechanism that facilitates speech perception. This phonetic module enables listeners to segment the blurred stream of auditory information that reaches their ears, so that they can perceive distinct phonemes and words. One argument in favor of the phonetic module was thought to be categorical perception. Computers can be used to generate a range of sounds that form a gradual continuum between two phonemes, for example, between the sounds of *b* and *p*. Even though these stimuli form a smooth continuum, people who hear this series of sounds typically show **categorical perception,** hearing one clear-cut phoneme or the other. Intriguingly, people do not report hearing a sound partway between a *b* and a *p*.

In contrast, the **general mechanism approach** argues that we can explain speech perception without any special phonetic module. People who favor this approach propose that humans process speech sounds and nonspeech sounds using the same neural mechanisms. Speech perception is therefore a learned ability—indeed, a very impressive learned ability—rather than an innate ability all humans are born with.

At present, the evidence seems to favor the general mechanism approach, with the strongest evidence from the following sets of studies:

1. The same categorical perception has been demonstrated with an impressive variety of nonhuman animals, including chinchillas, Japanese quail, and macaque monkeys (Kuhl, 1989; Miller, 1990; Moody et al., 1990). Because these nonhuman species do not have human language abilities, they should not have a special phonetic module.
2. Humans exhibit categorical perception for complex *nonspeech* sounds. Thus, categorical perception is a general characteristic, not limited to humans and not limited to speech (Jusczyk, 1986).
3. People's judgments about phonemes are influenced by visual cues. For example, suppose people hear the auditory stimulus *ba* and see lip movements appropriate to a sound somewhere between *ba* and *da*. According to Massaro, they are extremely unlikely to report hearing the clear-cut sound *ba*—even though that was the sound reaching their ears (Massaro, 1987; Massaro & Cohen, 1990). Thus, speech perception is flexible.

In summary, our ability to perceive speech sounds is impressive. However, this ability can probably be explained by our general perceptual skill, rather than any special innate speech mechanism. We learn to distinguish speech sounds, the same as we learn other cognitive accomplishments.

Constituent Structure

So far, we have considered only isolated speech sounds and (in Chapter 7) isolated words and concepts. However, if you want to understand a sentence, you also need to master **syntax,** which is grammatical form or sentence structure. Syntax involves the way in which words are arranged in a sentence. For example, if your professor tells the class, "Our next examination will be on Wednesday," you must be able to decode the grammatical structure of that sentence. As if you were solving a jigsaw puzzle, you combine the meanings of those words so that the sentence makes

DEMONSTRATION 8.3

CONSTITUENT STRUCTURE.

Arrange the words in each of these sentences into natural groups. Do this by writing down the words that go together and circling that group. You may arrange the sentences into as many groups as you like, but you must use all the words.

1. Parents were assisting the advanced teenage pupils.
2. The young woman carried the heavy painting.
3. Waiters who remember well serve orders correctly.

Check to see whether your answers agree with the groupings proposed for these sentences in the discussion of constituent structure.

sense. Obviously, the process must happen quickly, because you need to understand this sentence before the professor begins to describe the material to be covered on the examination. Before we discuss this component of comprehension, try Demonstration 8.3.

The Nature of Constituents.   One widely accepted view of language comprehension involves constituents (e.g., Singer, 1990). A **constituent** is a phrase or basic unit in a sentence, usually containing more than one word but less than an entire sentence. According to Clark and Clark (1977), "As a rough guide, a constituent is a group of words that can be replaced by a single word without a change in function and without doing violence to the rest of the sentence" (p. 48).

For example, suppose that we have the sentence:

The young woman carried the heavy painting.

We can break this sentence down into two **immediate constituents,** the largest and highest level parts: *the young woman* and *carried the heavy painting.* Each of those constituents can be further subdivided until we have the **ultimate constituents,** or the individual words. Figure 8.2 shows how this sentence can be repeatedly subdivided into its constituents by using **rewrite rules.**

Notice how Clark and Clark's replacement rule can be applied. For example, *the young woman* can be replaced by *Susan, Hepzibah,* or *she* without altering the structure of the rest of the sentence. Similarly, the constituent *young woman* can be replaced by a single word such as *teenager* or *student.* However, we cannot create a constituent out of *woman carried the,* because there is no single word having the same function that we can substitute.

Why should listeners bother with constituents? Why shouldn't we simply process the words one at a time? As it turns out, we often need information from the

FIGURE 8.2

An Example of Constituents.

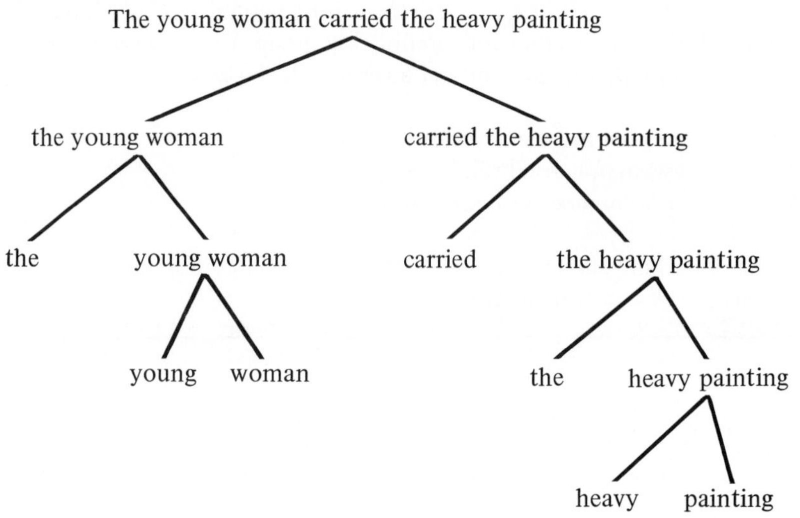

The young woman carried the heavy painting

the young woman   carried the heavy painting

the   young woman   carried   the heavy painting

young   woman   the   heavy painting

heavy   painting

entire constituent unit in order to give us cues about the meaning of the words. For example, consider the word *painting* in the sentence we analyzed. *Painting* could be a verb or it could be a noun. However, from the context in which *painting* appears—the constituent *the heavy painting*—we know that the noun version is appropriate. Other words are even more ambiguous. The word *block*, for example, has many meanings in isolation, and the other words in the constituent help to identify the appropriate meaning. Thus, context is helpful in figuring out the meaning of words, just as it is helpful in identifying the individual phonemes in a word.

Constituents and Understanding. Understanding a sentence involves several important processes:

1. Hearing the speech sounds;
2. Storing a representation of the speech sounds in short-term memory;
3. Locating the meanings of the words in semantic memory;
4. Organizing the representations of the speech sounds into constituents;
5. Determining the meaning of the constituents;
6. Combining the constituents to figure out the meaning of the whole sentence; and
7. Forgetting the exact wording of the constituents, retaining only the gist.

Do not think of these seven processes as occurring one at a time, in a neat, orderly sequence. If you are listening to a lecture, for example, you may be hearing, storing, locating, organizing, determining, combining, and forgetting—all at the same time. Thus, you may be forgetting Sentence 1 while you are performing steps 3, 4, 5, and 6 on Sentence 2 and hearing and storing Sentence 3. Also, notice that the last step of this sequence involves forgetting the exact wording and retaining only the gist, a process that was discussed in detail in Chapter 7.

The Psychological Reality of Constituent Structure. What evidence do we have for constituent structure? How do we know that people dissect the sentences they hear into these constituent parts? Let us consider an example of a study that demonstrates this process (Martin, 1970). An abbreviated version of this study was shown in Demonstration 8.3. Look at the answers you gave for that exercise.

Martin asked college students to draw circles around the words in a sentence that seemed to go together. As in Demonstration 8.3, they were told to make as many groups as they wished. Martin tabulated the results in terms of the number of times each word was included in the same circle as other words. He found a very strong tendency for certain words to be placed together. For example, the auxiliary verb almost always appeared with the main verb, as in the phrase *were assisting*. The adjective next to the object was almost always in the same circle as the object, as in the phrase *teenage pupils*. Check to see whether you showed this same pattern. Similarly, in Sentence 2, did you place *young* and *woman* together, and *heavy* and *painting* together? In Sentence 3, was *who remember well* included in the same circle?

Other studies have used verbatim (word-for-word) memory to investigate the psychological reality of constituent structure. These studies demonstrate that people remember words better if they are from the constituent that is currently being processed. Jarvella (1971) presented two kinds of passages, such as:

1. The confidence of Kofach was not unfounded.
   To stack the meeting for McDonald,
   the union had even brought in outsiders.
2. Kofach had been persuaded by the international
   to stack the meeting for McDonald.
   The union had even brought in outsiders.

Notice that the actual words in the second and third lines are identical in Passage 1 and Passage 2. However, in Passage 1, *to stack the meeting for McDonald* belongs with the third line. In contrast, in Passage 2, this same phrase belongs with the first line.

Jarvella interrupted people just after they had finished reading the third line and asked them to recall what they had read. As you would expect, recall in both conditions was excellent for the very most recent material, such as the line *the union had even brought in outsiders*. The interesting finding was that recall of the second line, *to stack the meeting for McDonald*, was excellent for people who saw Passage 1. That second line was part of a constituent that they were currently processing. In contrast, recall of the second line was poor for people who saw Passage 2. For them, that line was part of a constituent that they had already completed. Consequently, they did not need to remember it verbatim. In another study, Jarvella demonstrated that people remembered the general meaning of these previous constituents (e.g., the second line of Passage 2), even though their verbatim recall was poor.

Language comprehension clearly depends on memory processes. This theme has been further developed by theorists who propose that part of short-term memory is set aside as a buffer that contains verbatim information about constituents from earlier in the text (Kintsch & van Dijk, 1978; Miller & Kintsch, 1980; Singer, 1990). New information is presented in a new cycle, and it enters short-term memory; this new information is interpreted with the aid of the old information in the buffer. Information is then transferred to long-term memory, and a new cycle begins. Fletcher (1981) tested this hypothesis by presenting material from *Reader's Digest* articles; the memory status of portions of this material had been established by pretesting. Participants were then shown a probe word, which was selected from one of four locations in the cycle, as based on the theories of Kintsch and his colleagues:

1. words from earlier cycles, not held in memory buffer;
2. words from the next-to-last cycle, not held in memory buffer;
3. words from the next-to-last cycle, held in memory buffer; and
4. words from most recent cycle.

The participants in the study pressed buttons to indicate whether or not each specified probe word had occurred in the passage. Fletcher's results showed that words from Category 2 were recalled no better than the words from Category 1. However, words from Category 3 were recalled much more accurately. In summary, words that are currently held in the memory buffer have a greater likelihood of being recalled.

Strategies for Identifying Constituents.

We have been discussing how constituents are stored in memory. Let us now consider how listeners divide sentences up into their constituents. Kimball (1973) proposed that listeners have developed a variety of strategies. One strategy, for example, concerns function words. **Function words** are words, such as prepositions and conjunctions, that are very important for the structure of a grammatical sentence. Kimball suggested that whenever listeners find a function word, they begin a new constituent. For example, in the sentence

Mary said that the boy went to the store.

listeners would begin new constituents when they hear the words *that* and *to*.

Kimball also proposed that listeners develop a second strategy to accompany the first strategy. As soon as a function word indicates the beginning of a constituent, the listeners search for content words. **Content words** are words, such as nouns and verbs, that refer to persons, objects, and actions. For example, a function word such as *in* alerts the listener to search for a noun. The listener knows that a noun must come, no matter how many other words intervene. Imagine yourself listening to a sentence:

In the deep, dark, long-forgotten . . .

You know that the noun must come eventually!

Clark and Clark (1977) point out other strategies, including the use of affixes. Affixes are word parts, such as *-er*, *-y*, and *-ly*, that indicate the part of speech of a word. Thus, *-er* words are typically nouns, *-y* words are typically adjectives, and *-ly* words are typically adverbs. (However, there are exceptions, such as the adjective *clever*.) Listeners use these word parts to identify parts of speech.

These strategies are not foolproof. They do not always guarantee a solution, and they may lead us astray. However, they *usually* allow us to understand a sentence correctly. Thus, these language comprehension strategies can be called heuristics. As we have discussed in earlier chapters, **heuristics** are rules of thumb that are useful in solving problems. We will also see in later chapters that heuristics can help us solve problems and make decisions.

Transformational Grammar

People usually think of a sentence as an orderly sequence of words, typically lined up in a row on a piece of paper. Noam Chomsky (1957, 1965) caused great excitement among psychologists by proposing that there is more to a sentence than meets the eye. His work on the psychology of language was mentioned in your textbook's Introduction as one of the forces that led to the decreased popularity of behaviorism. The behaviorists emphasized the observable aspects of language behavior. In contrast, Chomsky argued that human language abilities could only be explained in terms of a complex system of rules and principles represented in the minds of speakers. He is clearly one of the most influential theorists in modern linguistics (Tartter, 1986; Wasow, 1989).

Specifically, Chomsky devised a model of **transformational grammar** to convert underlying, deep structure into the surface structure of a sentence. **Surface structure** is represented by the words that are actually spoken or written. In contrast, the **deep structure** is the underlying, more abstract meaning of the sentence. Let us examine these two kinds of structures in more detail.

Chomsky pointed out that two sentences may have very different surface structures but very similar deep structures. Consider the following two sentences:

Sara threw the ball.
The ball was thrown by Sara.

Notice how different the surface structures are: None of the words occupies the same position in the two sentences, and three of the words in the second sentence do not appear in the first sentence. However, "deep down," speakers of English feel that the sentences have identical core meanings.

Chomsky also pointed out that two sentences may have very similar surface structures but very different deep structures, as in these two sentences:

John is easy to please.
John is eager to please.

These sentences differ by only a single word, yet their meanings are quite different.

Two sentences can have identical surface structures but very different deep structures; these are called **ambiguous sentences.** Here is a sampling:

The shooting of the hunters was terrible.
They are cooking apples.
The lamb is too hot to eat.

Notice that rewrite rules can be used to generate two different kinds of constituent structures. (In fact, try making two diagrams like the one in Figure 8.2 to represent *They are cooking apples.*) We will discuss ambiguity in more detail later in this section.

Chomsky proposed that people understand sentences by transforming the surface structure into a basic, deep structure or **kernel** form. They use transformational rules to convert surface structure to deep structure during understanding. They also use transformational rules to convert deep structure to surface structure during speech production or writing.

Chomsky's ideas about transformational grammar inspired dozens of studies during the 1960s and 1970s. For example, Mehler (1963) found that people recalled kernel sentences, such as *The biologist has made the discovery*, much more accurately than sentences that involved several transformations, such as *Hasn't the discovery been made by the biologist?* (a negative-passive-question variant of the kernel).

Not all of the evidence for Chomsky's theory was favorable, however. For example, the sentence *The cookies were smelled by John* should theoretically take less time to process than the sentence *The cookies were smelled* because the second sentence requires an additional transformation to drop the *by John*. However, Slobin's (1966) research demonstrated that the second sentence actually took *less* time to verify.

In general, psychologists support Chomsky's notion of the distinction between surface and deep structure. However, they are less enthusiastic about the notion of a close correspondence between the number of transformations and psychological complexity (Prideaux, 1985; Tartter, 1986). Furthermore, Chomsky's more recent theories place less emphasis on transformations than on the grammatical information contained in the individual words of a sentence (Chomsky, 1973,

1981; Wasow, 1989). For example, the word *greet* not only conveys information about the word's meaning, but it also specifies the requirement that *greet* must be followed by a noun, as in the sentence, *Joe greeted his opponent* (Ratner & Gleason, 1993a).

Factors Affecting Comprehension

The research on transformational grammar sparked an interest in the factors that can influence our understanding of sentences. As this section will demonstrate, we have more difficulty understanding sentences (1) if they contain negatives, such as *not*; (2) if they are in the passive rather than the active voice; and (3) if they are ambiguous.

Negatives. Several years ago, the first sentence in a newspaper article read,

> ALBANY—The Assembly yesterday overwhelmingly approved a state Equal Rights Amendment free of revisions intended to restrict its influence on a woman's right to an abortion.

This sentence requires several readings to understand exactly what the Assembly decided, because it contains so many implied negatives. If a sentence contains a negative word, such as *no* or *not*, or an implied negative, the sentence almost always requires more processing time than a similar affirmative sentence (Taylor & Taylor, 1990).

In a classic study, Clark and Chase (1972) asked people to verify statements, such as:

> Star is above plus.   *
> ‡

The participants responded more quickly if the sentences were affirmative than if they contained the negative form *isn't* (for example, *Plus isn't above star*), and they also made fewer errors.

If we have difficulty understanding a sentence with one negative, how about a sentence with two or three negatives? For example, is this sentence true?

> Few people strongly deny that the world is not flat. (Sherman, 1976, p. 145)

With three negatives, the sentence is almost incomprehensible! As you might expect, understanding decreases as the number of negatives increases. Sherman (1976) found that people understood every one of the affirmative sentences, but they understood only 59 percent of the sentences with four negatives. In other words, performance in this condition was only slightly better than guessing (which would produce 50 percent correct responses).

This discussion of negatives should remind you of Theme 3: Our cognitive processes handle positive information better than negative information. Quite simply, we can deal more easily with something that exists than something that does not exist.

The Passive Voice. As discussed earlier, Chomsky (1957, 1965) pointed out that the active and passive forms of a sentence may differ in surface structure but have similar deep structures. However, the active form is more basic whereas the passive form requires additional words. Furthermore, in modern English we use the active form seven times as often as the passive (Svartik, 1966). Some passive forms sound awkward, and some verbs do not even have any sensible passive forms (Anisfeld & Klenbort, 1973). What passive forms could you possibly concoct for the verbs *sleep, resemble, be,* and *cost?*

The active form is also easier to understand. For example, Hornby (1974) asked people to judge whether a picture correctly represented a sentence. People responded faster if the sentences were active, such as *The girl is petting the cat,* than if the sentences were passive, such as *The cat is being petted by the girl.*

The passive voice used to be very popular in scientific writing. As a result, scientific writing often sounded extremely pompous. Fortunately for those of us who want to understand scientific writing, current style manuals now recommend the active voice (for example, the *Publication Manual of the American Psychological Association,* 1983).

Ambiguity. We discussed ambiguous sentences in connection with Chomsky's transformational grammar. Let us discuss the different kinds of ambiguity and the effect of ambiguity on understanding.

There are three kinds of ambiguity. The first kind is **lexical ambiguity,** in which a word has two different meanings. Consider the following sentence:

Time flies like an arrow,
but fruit flies like a banana.

The sentence is startling because the word *flies* is ambiguous, but the first part of the sentence led us to anticipate only one interpretation. Many puns and riddles are based on lexical ambiguity.

A second type of ambiguity involves **surface structure ambiguity,** in which words can be grouped together in more than one way. Suppose that a friend said, "The only ones who volunteered are a few incompetent people like John and you." Notice that the sentence is ambiguous because the last part can be grouped as either (incompetent people like John) (and you) or (incompetent people like John and you).

A third type of ambiguity involves **deep structure ambiguity,** in which the essential logical relations between phrases can be interpreted in two ways. For example, suppose you saw a newspaper heading that read:

Senator found drunk on Capitol steps.

As discussed earlier, an ambiguous sentence occurs when a single surface structure has two different deep structures.

Several studies have demonstrated that ambiguous sentences are more difficult to understand. Foss (1970), for example, asked people to listen to ambiguous and unambiguous sentences. At the same time, they also performed an additional task, which involved pressing a button every time they heard the sound *b* in a sentence. People took longer to press the button if they were listening to an ambiguous sentence. Foss reasoned that ambiguous sentences are more difficult to understand, so listeners have less processing capacity available to use in other tasks.

Theorists disagree about how listeners process ambiguous material (Holmes et al., 1987). Theorists who favor a parallel distributed processing approach argue that when people encounter a potential ambiguity, the activation builds up for all meanings of the ambiguous item; however, the degree of activation depends on the frequency of the meanings and the context (Simpson, 1984; Simpson & Burgess, 1985). Thus, in the sentence *Pat took the money to the bank,* the "financial institution" interpretation of *bank* would receive the most activation because it is the most common interpretation and because the context of *money* suggests this meaning. But, presumably, other meanings of *bank* (as in *riverbank, blood bank,* and *banking an airplane*) also receive some minimal activation.

In contrast, other theorists argue that context constrains the meaning activation at the very beginning, limiting meaning-access to only a single interpretation that is appropriate to the sentence context (Glucksberg et al., 1986). Subjectively speaking, this explanation may *seem* more appealing. I don't think I consider all the multiple meanings of the word *bank* in an ambiguous sentence. However, you'll recall from Chapter 2 that we may have limited awareness of some cognitive processes. In the case of ambiguity, our introspective understanding may not match the covert processes that actually occur.

SECTION SUMMARY: UNDERSTANDING SPOKEN LANGUAGE

1. In speech perception, information about the sounds in a syllable is sent in parallel, rather than one phoneme at a time.
2. When a sound is missing from speech, listeners demonstrate phonemic restoration, using context to help them perceive the missing sound. Context also helps determine the boundaries between words.
3. According to current research, speech perception does not require a special phonetic module; instead, the general mechanism approach is favored.
4. Listeners use the information in constituent units to determine meaning. Part of short-term memory is set aside for previous constituents. Listeners develop heuristics for partitioning a sentence into its constituents.

5. Chomsky's theory of transformational grammar proposed that transformational rules are used to transform deep structure into surface structure.
6. Sentences are more difficult to understand if they contain negatives, if they are in the passive voice, and if they are ambiguous.

READING

In just a few decades, the topic of reading has changed its status enormously among psychologists. As recently as the 1960s, psychologists knew embarrassingly little about reading. In fact, one of the major books on reading during that era was a reprint of a book originally published in 1908 (Huey, 1968). The introduction to the 1968 edition pointed out that no new information had been gathered on many aspects of reading during the previous 60 years! Today, reading is one of the most important topics in cognitive psychology (Johnson, 1991). When I revised the material on reading for this edition of your textbook, for example, I gathered information from 22 relevant books and several dozen articles published in the last decade. Students who want more information about this complex topic might be especially interested in the books by Crowder and Wagner (1992), Just and Carpenter (1987), and Rayner and Pollatsek (1989).

Our discussion of reading is not confined just to Chapter 8, because we have already discussed components of reading, such as letter recognition (Chapter 2), memory for written material (Chapters 4, 5, and 7), and the construction of mental models from written text (Chapter 6). In Chapter 9 we will examine how people read problems, and in Chapter 12 we'll mention children's knowledge about the reading process. As emphasized throughout the book, the cognitive processes are interrelated. Reading is an important cognitive activity that uses virtually every process discussed in this textbook, demonstrating how the cognitive processes are interrelated (Theme 4).

This section begins with a discussion of the more perceptual aspects of reading and then considers how we manage to read isolated words. As we progress to increasingly larger units, we will discuss reading comprehension and inferences in reading. The next topic—even further from the perceptual level—is metacomprehension. Finally, our discussion of artificial intelligence and reading points out how difficult it is for machines to accomplish even some of the simpler reading tasks we take for granted.

Perceptual Processes

For a moment, become aware of the way your eyes are moving as you read this page. Notice that your eyes make a series of little jumps as they move across the page. **Saccadic movement** refers to these very rapid movements of the eyes from one spot to the next. Your eyes must make these movements in order to bring the center of the retina—where vision is sharpest—into position over the words you want to read. **Fixations** occur during the period between these saccadic movements; during a fixation, the visual system acquires the useful information for reading (Blanchard, 1987).

Researchers have developed a number of methods for assessing perceptual processes in reading. One very useful method is the **gaze-contingent paradigm,** which involves tracking readers' eyes as they read material displayed on a cathode-ray tube and changing the text display as the readers progress through a passage. With this method, researchers can selectively replace letters in certain regions of the display. For example, they can replace all letters more than 10 letters to the right of the letter that the observer is viewing; a string of irrelevant letters can be substituted (e.g., rmot lfe ...). The researchers note whether this text alteration changed any measures of reading. If the measures do change, then they conclude that the letters in the altered region would normally be included in the **perceptual span**—the region seen during the pause between saccadic movements (Underwood & McConkie, 1985). The gaze-contingent paradigm has been used to demonstrate that the perceptual span normally includes letters lying about four positions to the left of the letter you are directly looking at, and the letters about eight positions to the right of that central letter. Thus, the perceptual span is definitely lopsided, probably because we are looking for reading cues in the text that lies to the right.

Other research has demonstrated that saccadic eye movements have several predictable patterns. For example, when the eye jumps forward in a saccadic eye movement, it rarely moves to a blank space between sentences or between words (McConkie, 1983; McConkie & Zóla, 1984). The eye usually jumps past the word *the,* and it also skips a word that is highly predictable in a sentence (Balota et al., 1985; O'Regan, 1979). However, the size of the saccadic movement is small if the next word in the sentence is misspelled or if it is a long word (McConkie & Zóla, 1984; O'Regan, 1980). Again, these strategies make sense, because a large saccadic movement would be unwise if the material is puzzling or long.

Our saccadic movements are also sensitive to thematic aspects of the material we are reading. For example, if we read a story with a surprise ending, we make a larger number of saccadic movements as we reread the puzzling passage (Blanchard & Iran-Nejad, 1987).

Good readers differ from poor readers with respect to the kind of saccadic movements their eyes make. Figure 8.3 shows how two readers might differ in their eye movements. The good reader makes larger jumps and is also less likely to move backward to earlier material in the sentence. Furthermore, although this cannot be seen in the diagram, the good reader pauses for a short time before making the next saccadic movement. A typical good reader might pause for ⅕ second each time, whereas a poor reader might pause for ½ second. Thus, good and poor readers differ with respect to the size of the eye movements, as well as the number of backward eye movements and the duration of the fixation pause.

You may wish to review the section in Chapter 2 on pattern recognition, which provides information on how we recognize letters when we read. That section

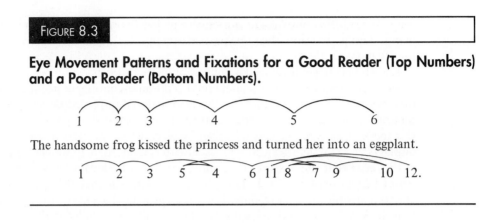

FIGURE 8.3

Eye Movement Patterns and Fixations for a Good Reader (Top Numbers) and a Poor Reader (Bottom Numbers).

The handsome frog kissed the princess and turned her into an eggplant.

considered theories of pattern recognition and discussed how context aids the recognition of letters and other patterns.

Theories of Word Recognition

You just read the word *Recognition* in the title of this section. Somehow, you were able to look at that pattern of letters and recognize that word. How did you accomplish this? Three different hypotheses have been developed to explain how readers recognize printed words when they read to themselves. One hypothesis, which we will call the **direct-access hypothesis,** states that the reader can recognize a word directly from the printed letters. That is, you look at the word *recognition* and the visual pattern is sufficient to let you locate information about the meaning of the word in semantic memory.

Another hypothesis, which we will call the **indirect-access hypothesis,** states that "there is an *obligatory* translation from ink marks on the page to some form of speech code in order to gain access to a store of word meanings during reading" (Besner et al., 1981, p. 415). Notice that the process is indirect because of the necessary intermediate step of converting the visual stimulus into a sound stimulus.

Think about whether you seem to use this intermediate step when you read. When you read, do you have a speech-like representation of the words? You probably read silently, but does it seem that you have an auditory image of what you are reading? Perhaps you are concluding that you sometimes have direct access and sometimes require the intermediate step involving the sound of a word.

The third hypothesis, called the **dual-encoding hypothesis,** states that semantic memory can be reached either directly, through the visual route, or indirectly, through the sound route. Thus, visual symbols can be encoded in two ways.

The direct-access hypothesis and the indirect-access hypothesis are parallel to the whole-word and the phonics methods of teaching reading (Doctor & Coltheart, 1980). As you may know, some educators favor the **whole-word approach,** which argues that readers do not stop to identify the individual letters in a word; instead, they can recognize the whole word. Educators who endorse this approach empha-size that the correspondence between the written and spoken codes in English is notoriously complex (Seidenberg & McClelland, 1989); they therefore argue against the phonics approach.

However, other educators favor the **phonics approach,** which states that readers recognize words by sounding out the individual letters in the word. If your grade school teachers told you to "sound out the word" when you stumbled on a new word, they championed the phonics approach. The phonics approach stresses that sound is a necessary intermediate step in reading. The argument between the whole-word supporters and the phonics supporters is just as feverish among edu-cators as is the argument between direct-access supporters and indirect-access supporters among psychologists (Wilkinson, 1992). Let us consider the evidence for the three competing hypotheses.

The Direct-Access Hypothesis.

One kind of evidence for the hypothesis that words can be recognized directly—without a translation into sound—comes from homonyms. As you may recall, homonyms are words that are spelled differently but sound the same. When you see the two homonyms *their* and *there*, you know that they have different meanings. If each of those visual stimuli were translated into sound, as the indirect-access hypothesis claims, then we would be left with two identical sounds. It would be difficult to explain how those two identical sounds could then lead to the two different meanings.

More support for the direct-access hypothesis comes from a study by Bradshaw and Nettleton (1974). They presented pairs of words that were similar in spelling but not in sound, such as *mown–down, horse–worse,* and *quart–part.* When subjects pronounced the first member of the pair out loud, it took them somewhat longer to pronounce the second member—interference arose because the two words were not pronounced similarly. However, this effect did not occur in silent reading. When people read the first word silently, there was no delay in pronouncing the second word. This suggests that silent reading does not lead to a silent pronunci-ation of the word, because there was no evidence for any interference.

Perhaps the strongest evidence for the direct-access hypothesis comes from clin-ical observations of **deep dyslexia,** a severe reading disorder in which people are unable to translate printed words into sounds. For example, these people are unable to pronounce simple nonsense words, such as *dap, ish,* and *lar.* They also are unable to judge which visually presented words rhyme with each other. Clearly, these people cannot use the intermediate step of translating words into sound. Never-theless, they are able to look at a printed word and identify its meaning (Besner et al., 1981; Coltheart, et al., 1980). Thus, it is possible to read without an oblig-atory translation into a speech code.

The Indirect-Access Hypothesis.

Several studies indicate that visual stimuli may be translated into sound during reading. Hardyck and Petrinovitch (1970), for example, noted that people often sound out words when the material is difficult. (Incidentally, did you sound out the name *Petrinovitch* when you read it?) When people were prevented from making any lip movements, they had trouble reading difficult material. This indicates that people are translating the visual stimulus into sound.

Word sounds are also important when children begin to read. Wagner and Torgesen (1987) summarize numerous studies demonstrating that children with high phonological awareness have superior reading skills. That is, the children who are able to identify sound patterns in a word also receive higher scores on reading achievement tests.

A study by Doctor and Coltheart (1980) also supports the indirect-access hypothesis. Children saw sentences such as, "He ran threw the street," and were asked to decide whether these sentences were meaningful or not. Doctor and Coltheart found that the children were likely to judge sentences as meaningful if they *sounded* meaningful. For example, "He ran threw the street" would be pronounced just the same as the meaningful sentence, "He ran through the street." Therefore, they judged that sentence as meaningful. In contrast, they did not judge sentences as meaningful if they remained meaningless when they were pronounced, for example, "He ran sew the street."

Other evidence for the indirect-access hypothesis comes from Van Orden (1987), who found that readers made frequent errors when they were instructed to categorize homonyms. In a typical task, readers were instructed to decide whether a particular stimulus (for example, *rose*) belonged to a previously specified category (for example, *flower*). The interesting question is how readers would respond to homonyms (for example, *rows*, rather than *rose*). Van Orden found that the participants in his study often agreed that a *rows* is indeed a *flower*, suggesting that the printed word was translated into a sound representation.

The Dual-Encoding Hypothesis. Some results favor a direct access to word recognition, whereas others favor an intermediate step involving a word's sound. The dual-encoding hypothesis, which argues that both routes are possible, is currently most popular (Van Orden et al., 1990). The flexibility of this hypothesis is certainly one of its strengths. It argues that the characteristics of the reader and the characteristics of the reading material determine whether access is direct or indirect.

For example, Baron and Strawson (1976) identified both direct- and indirect-access readers in their study. One set of readers read words more quickly if the words conformed to the standard spelling-sound correspondence rules (for example, *sweet*) than if they violated the rules (for example, *sword*). Furthermore, in an independent test, these people relied heavily on spelling-sound correspondence rules. These are the people who choose indirect access and encode the visual stimulus into sound before recognition. The other set of readers did not show much difference in reading speed between regular and irregular words. Also, they did not

---

DEMONSTRATION 8.4

FIGURING OUT THE MEANING OF A WORD FROM CONTEXT (BASED ON STERNBERG & POWELL, 1983).

Read the paragraph below. Then define, as precisely as possible, the two words that are italicized.

Two ill-dressed people—the one a tired woman of middle years and the other a tense young man—sat around a fire where the common meal was almost ready. The mother, Tanith, peered at her son through the *oam* of the bubbling stew. It had been a long time since his last *ceilidh* and Tobar had changed greatly; where once he had seemed all legs and clumsy joints, he now was well-formed and in control of his hard, young body. As they ate, Tobar told of his past year, re-creating for Tanith how he had wandered long and far in his quest to gain the skills he would need to be permitted to rejoin the company. Then all too soon, their brief *ceilidh* over, Tobar walked over to touch his mother's arm and quickly left.

---

rely heavily on the spelling-sound correspondence rules. These are the direct-access readers.

In addition, Mason (1978) found that "mature readers"—for example, college students—were more likely to use the direct-access method. This makes sense. When children first learn to read, they rely on sound (as the study by Doctor and Coltheart, 1980, showed). As they mature, they often skip that intermediate step.

Other factors may also determine whether people select the direct- or the indirect-access method. For example, you will recall that Hardyck and Petrinovitch (1970) found that people sounded out words when the words were difficult. Try to notice whether you are more likely to sound out unfamiliar words than ones you know well.

Furthermore, we sometimes choose the indirect-access method when we are under stress. When you are reading the questions on an essay examination, you might find yourself **subvocalizing,** sounding out the words silently. However, if you are by yourself in a quiet room, you will probably not subvocalize when you are reading the Sunday comics. As Besner and his colleagues (1981) conclude, word sounds may be important if the text is difficult and if it requires elaborate processing of grammatical structure. In these cases, comprehension may involve storing of phonological information in short-term memory for several seconds.

At present, the dual-encoding hypothesis seems like a wise compromise. However, the conclusions may change within the next decade as some researchers begin to argue more strongly for the indirect-access hypothesis (e.g., Perfetti & Bell, 1991; Van Orden et al., 1990). The conclusions may also be influenced by some of the new research techniques in neuroscience. For example, cerebral blood-flow studies may be able to show us whether the auditory areas of the brain are activated during word recognition (e.g., Petersen et al., 1988; Posner et al., 1988).

Discovering the Meaning of an Unfamiliar Word

Try Demonstration 8.4, which is an example of the passages used by Sternberg and Powell (1983) in their work on verbal comprehension. Let us examine their theory of how people use context to discover the meanings of unfamiliar words.

Sternberg and Powell point out that when we read, we often come upon a word whose meaning is unfamiliar. We then typically attempt to use the context in which the word occurs to figure out its meaning. Sternberg and Powell propose that context can provide several kinds of information cues about meaning, including the following:

1. Temporal cues indicate how often X (the unknown word) occurs or how long it lasts.
2. Spatial cues identify X's location.
3. Value cues suggest the emotion that X arouses.
4. Functional descriptive cues describe the possible actions X can perform.
5. Stative descriptive cues concern the physical properties of X (that is, its physical state).

For example, consider the sentence:

At dawn, the *blen* arose on the horizon and shone brightly.

This sentence contains several contextual cues that make it easy to infer the meaning of *blen*. The phrase *at dawn* provides a temporal cue, about the time at which the arising of the *blen* occurred. *Arose* is a functional descriptive cue, describing an action that a *blen* could perform. (Notice how this cue limits the possible candidates for *blen* to those things that move or appear to move.) *On the horizon* provides a spatial cue. *Shone* is an additional functional descriptive cue, further limiting the possible candidates for *blen*. Finally, *brightly* provides a stative descriptive cue, describing a property of the shining of the *blen*, that is, its brightness. With all these different cues, an experienced reader can easily understand that the nonsense word *blen* is a synonym for the familiar word *sun*.

Naturally, we do not always use contextual cues in decoding a word's meaning, and when we do use them, they do not always work. For example, we are more likely to use contextual cues if an unknown word appears in a variety of different contexts. A variety of contexts increases the likelihood that a wide range of cues will be supplied about the word. In this case the reader is more likely to obtain a full picture of the scope of the word's meaning. In contrast, merely repeating an unknown word in the same context is *not* particularly helpful.

To test their theory about the importance of contextual cues, Sternberg and Powell (1983) asked high-school students to read passages like the one in Demonstration 8.4. Then the students provided a definition for each of the italicized words in the passage (for example, *oam* and *ceilidh* in Demonstration 8.4). Three

---

DEMONSTRATION 8.5

READING SENTENCES.

Read each of the following sentences, which were used in research by MacDonald and her colleagues (1992, pp. 93–95). They will be discussed in the following section.

1. The soldiers warned about the dangers before the midnight raid.
2. A yellow frisby dropped from the roof onto the narrow driveway.
3. The evil genie served the golden figs in the ancient temple.
4. The frightened kid pushed through the crowd to the front row.

---

trained raters judged the quality of these definitions, and then a "definition goodness" score was calculated for each of the words. Powell herself then examined each of the passages and counted the number of occurrences of each kind of contextual cue. The results showed a strong correlation between the two measures: Words that appeared in a rich context of different cues were more accurately defined by the students who had read the passages.

As you might expect, the students in Sternberg and Powell's study differed in their ability to use contextual cues and to provide accurate definitions. The students who were particularly good at this task were also found to have higher scores on tests of vocabulary, reading comprehension, and general intelligence.

Furthermore, Daneman and Green (1986) found that the ability to use contextual cues is related to working-memory span. College students tried to guess the meaning of unusual words on the basis of sentence context, and these definitions were rated for accuracy on a scale from 0 to 4. Their memory span for words in a sentence was also tested. Figure 8.4 shows that people with relatively large memory spans provide better definitions. In addition, people who have small memory spans probably devote so much of their attention to reading that they have less attention "left over" to remember the important contextual cues. (Incidentally, in the passage in Demonstration 8.4, *oam* means steam and a *ceilidh* is a visit.)

Reading and Working Memory

Let us now consider a second role for working memory; people with large memory capacities are not only better in decoding words, but they also excel in decoding sentences. Try Demonstration 8.5, if you haven't already done so. As you probably realized, each of these sentences contained a temporary ambiguity. For example, after reading the initial words of the sentence, *The soldiers warned about the dangers* . . . , you may have considered two meanings. Perhaps the soldiers were the ones who did the warning, or perhaps someone else warned them. MacDonald, Just, and Carpenter (1992) propose a model in which both of these interpretations of *warned*

FIGURE 8.4

The Relationship between Memory Span and Accuracy of Definition for an Unfamiliar Word.

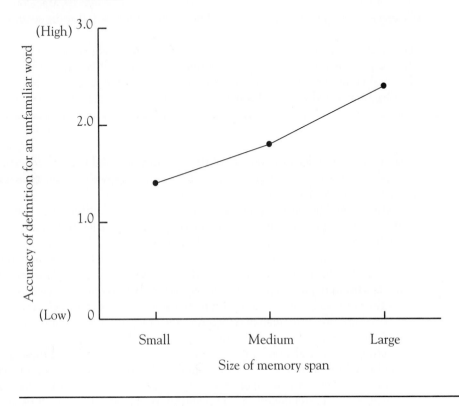

are initially activated. However, readers who have large working-memory capacities maintain both potential representations until they have read several words further in the sentence. In contrast, readers who have smaller working-memory capacities keep only the more likely representation. In the previous example, readers with limited working-memory capacities immediately reject the possibility that someone else warned the soldiers; they only maintain the most obvious meaning, that the soldiers did the warning.

In other articles, Marcel Just and his colleagues describe how working-memory capacity constrains our reading comprehension (Just & Carpenter, 1992; King & Just, 1991). People who can maintain many items in memory while they unravel a sentence are more accurate and more rapid in understanding complicated sentences, such as *The reporter that the senator attacked admitted the error*. This research on reading and working memory is a good illustration of Theme 4. The cognitive processes do not operate in isolation, and reading skill depends heavily upon memory capacity.

Reading Comprehension

We began this section on reading with an introduction to perceptual aspects of reading, particularly eye movements. Then we moved on to consider how people recognize individual words and how they interpret sentences. Now we need to consider larger conceptual units in reading, beyond the level of the sentence. Frederick Bartlett (1932) was concerned with these larger units when he conducted research on memory for stories more than half a century ago. However, for the next few decades psychologists and linguists concentrated primarily on words and sentences. For example, a prominent review article on psycholinguistics written in 1974 claimed that the basic problem in psycholinguistics was this: What happens when we understand *sentences?* (Johnson-Laird, 1974; Kintsch, 1984). In recent years, however, researchers have enthusiastically tackled larger issues, including the understanding of schemas, scripts, and stories.

In the previous section, we considered the importance of context in understanding words. In this section, we will see that context is also important when we move beyond the level of the word. As Sharkey and Sharkey (1987a, 1987b) observe, it is more difficult to define context on this grander scale, but context is still important. For example, consider how much easier it is to read an article in the sports section of the newspaper once you realize that you can fit it into the context of a particular script about an "ambitious athlete carrying on in a competition regardless of a severe injury." At all levels of reading comprehension, there is an interaction between the processing of the physical stimuli (bottom-up processing) and the context provided by expectations and previous knowledge (top-down processing), as Theme 5 suggests. Two important components of reading comprehension are the specific background knowledge of the reader and forming a well-organized representation of the text.

Specific Background Knowledge. Quite simply, the more you know about a topic, the easier it is to learn even more. Consider a study by Spilich and his colleagues (1979). These researchers used a passage written about baseball, a topic about which people have widely different amounts of knowledge. The participants in this study were divided into high- and low-knowledge groups on the basis of a 45-item test of baseball knowledge. The baseball text was then presented to them, and they wrote down as much as they could recall from the passage. The high-knowledge people recalled an average of 48 statements, whereas the low-knowledge people recalled only 31.

The two groups also showed qualitative differences in recall. The baseball fans recalled more statements about actions that were important to the outcome of the game, and they were also likely to recall the events in the correct order. In contrast, people with less knowledge about baseball were more likely to recall details that were peripheral to the game. For example, they often mentioned information about the weather and what the crowd was thinking. Their lack of knowledge made it more difficult for them to recognize how various actions were relevant to the game. Background information therefore provides a meaningful context for the acquisition of new information. This information provides a conceptual structure or schema that contains the implications of facts and bits of information that seem unrelated when read by a person with little background knowledge (Just & Carpenter, 1984). As we have seen throughout this textbook, expectations and top-down processing are more predominant for experts than for novices.

Forming a Coherent Representation of the Text.   Reading comprehension is enormously more complicated than simply fitting words and phrases together. In addition, readers must gather information together, making the message both cohesive and stable. Readers assume that writers intend their messages to "hang together." As a result, they interpret unclear sections as clearly as they can, and they seek relevance and connections even when the material is not well structured (Foss & Speer, 1991).

Furthermore, we often construct mental models of the material we are reading. In Chapter 6, we saw that people construct mental models based on a written description of an environment. Similarly, readers construct internal representations that include descriptions of the cast of characters in a story. This descriptive information may include the characters' occupations, relationships, personal traits, goals, plans, and actions (Bower, 1989; Bower & Morrow, 1990).

Competent readers manage to construct coherent representations of the material they have read. Consider research in which high-school students were instructed to read short passages of text (Meyer et al., 1980). One passage, for example, consisted of two paragraphs about oil spills from supertankers. After reading a passage, the students were asked to write down all they could remember from the passage. The researchers then categorized the responses in terms of whether the students had organized their recall in the same fashion used in the original article. The results showed that about three-quarters of students who had received high scores on a reading comprehension test used the same structure, in contrast to less than one-quarter of the students who had received low scores. Thus, reading comprehension tends to be associated with understanding the organization of a text passage.

When people read a story, they show a characteristic pattern as they attempt to understand what is happening (Haberlandt et al., 1980; Mandler & Johnson, 1977). At the beginning, the reader identifies the main character, encodes the problem facing this character, and determines where the episode is located. Thus, the processing load is large at the beginning of an episode. At the end of a story, the reader rehearses specific details and chunks the information for memory storage;

again, the processing load is large. In contrast, the middle of a story is less challenging.

When people try to form a coherent representation of the text they are reading, they often make inferences that go beyond the information supplied by the writer. Let's consider this topic in more detail.

◇ In Depth: **Inferences in Reading**

We discussed inferences in Chapter 7 in connection with the influence of schemas on memory. People combine their information about the world with the information presented in a passage, and they draw a reasonable conclusion based on that combination. Consistent with Theme 1, people are active information processors. We also saw that the inference can become part of memory; for example, people mistakenly believe that the experimenter had presented the inference during the study. In some cases, then, inferences can produce errors. However, drawing inferences is generally a useful heuristic. Consistent with Theme 2, this strategy usually enables us to draw correct conclusions and to make necessary links between the sentences in a passage.

Let us begin this section by considering how our knowledge about scripts can encourage inferences. Then we will consider various factors that encourage us to make inferences. Finally, we'll discuss higher levels of inference.

Scripts and Inferences.   In Chapter 7, we discussed the term **script,** which is a simple, well-structured sequence of events, such as going to a restaurant. A written passage that triggers a familiar script is especially likely to inspire an inference about some other part of the script that might be relevant. For example, Noel Sharkey presented brief passages that should activate a specific script (Sharkey, 1986; Sharkey & Mitchell, 1985). Here is a typical passage:

> The children's birthday party was going quite well.
> They all sat round the table prepared to sing.

Presumably, these two sentences are sufficient to activate the "children's birthday party" script. The sentences were then removed, and one of three words appeared: (1) a word related to the script (for example, *candles*), (2) a word unrelated to the script (for example, *rabbits*), or (3) a nonsense word (for example, *asintar*). Participants were instructed to judge as quickly as possible whether the item was an English word or not. People made judgments significantly faster when the word was related to the birthday party script. For instance, they decided that *candles* was an English word much more rapidly than they decided about *rabbits*.

Karl Haberlandt and Geoffrey Bingham (1984) also examined the importance of scripts in reading. They constructed pairs of sentences that were parts of established scripts, such as the "lighting a fire" script. Half of the sentences were presented in a forward direction, such as: *He got some logs. He lit the wood.* Half were presented in a backward direction, such as: *He blew on the flame. He lit the wood.* Participants in the study were asked to read all sentences carefully and judge as quickly as possible whether the two sentences in a pair were related to each other. The results showed that people made twice as many errors on backward pairs as on forward pairs. Furthermore, their decision latencies were significantly longer on the backward pairs. Apparently, events must be presented in the correct chronological order to activate the appropriate script.

Factors that Encourage Inferences.

Readers do not always draw inferences when they process a written passage (McKoon & Ratcliff, 1992b). In general, readers are rather cautious. Reading is complicated enough without doing even more work to fill in the gaps (Rayner & Pollatsek, 1989). However, we are especially likely to draw an inference if a passage does not seem to fit the current context. For example, suppose you saw these sentences:

> The hamburger chain owner was afraid his love for french fries would ruin his marriage. He decided to join a health club in order to save his marriage.

If you are like most people, you needed to create an explanation for these puzzling bits of information, probably inferring that the owner was overweight and his wife disliked obesity (Eysenck & Keane, 1990; Thorndyke, 1976).

As you might expect, people who have been instructed to read a passage carefully are especially likely to draw inferences during reading (Van Oostendorp, 1991). When reading slowly and carefully, we have the time to search for connections that we might otherwise miss.

Another factor that determines whether or not we draw an inference is the kind of inference required by the passage. Let's consider in some detail a study by Colleen Seifert, Scott Robertson, and John Black (1985) that explores this issue. They examined four kinds of inferences that people could draw when reading a story. Specifically, people can make inferences about the goal, the plan, the action, or the state of characters in a story. Let us identify each of these components in a sample story:

The King's Heir

Provo is a picturesque kingdom in France.
Corman was heir to the throne of Provo.

GOAL: He wanted to be king.
        He was so tired of waiting.

PLAN: He decided to poison the king.
        He thought arsenic would work well.
        Corman went to the storeroom.

STATE: There was arsenic in the storeroom.
              He hid the poison in his coat.
              The king was looking out the window.
              His cup was on the table near the door.

ACTION: Corman put poison in the king's drink.
              The king felt ill after drinking.
              Corman called for the physician.
              Corman told the king he should take care of himself.
              The king fell to the floor.
              Corman knew he would soon be king. (p. 420)

Notice that each of the four critical sentences that appear directly after the words GOAL, PLAN, STATE, and ACTION would be a logical inference from the preceding information in the passage. For example, if we know that Corman was heir to a kingdom, we can logically surmise that his goal would be to become king.

Participants in the study read the narrative with two of the four critical sentences left out. For example, part of one version might move directly from the sentence *Corman was heir to the throne of Provo* to the sentence *He was so tired of waiting*. Would people draw the proper inference that Corman wanted to become king? Seifert and her colleagues (1985) measured inference-drawing by giving a recognition test 20 minutes after participants had read the passages. The recognition test contained some sentences that had actually appeared in the story, some sentences that were inferences (with all four kinds of inferences represented), and some that were unrelated. In each case, participants rated the sentence on a 7-point scale, where 1 indicated that an item had definitely not been seen and 7 indicated that it definitely had been seen.

Figure 8.5 shows the recognition ratings when the critical sentences were either present or absent. Notice that people are almost as likely to "recognize" a sentence when it was absent as when it was present if that sentence represents an inference about a goal, a plan, or an action. The inference was incorporated into memory nearly as firmly as a sentence that had actually been presented! In contrast, people were unsure about whether they had seen an inference about a state, if it had not really been presented. People are not as likely to draw inferences about states.

As Seifert and her colleagues (1985) conclude, readers can make an enormous number of inferences from a text. However, they probably don't have the processing capacity to make all these inferences at once. Instead, they need to be selective. In the kind of story narrative Seifert and her coauthors studied, the readers chose to make inferences about goals, plans, and actions. Seifert (1990) suggests that these event-based inferences are especially helpful because readers predict what will come next in a text, they explain why events occur, and they also bridge gaps in the sequence of events. Inferences about states may be helpful in descriptive passages where the physical appearance of an object or the layout of a scene is central to a passage. However, inferences about states are not very useful when the story emphasizes actions and events.

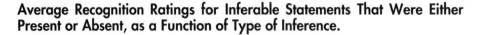

FIGURE 8.5

Average Recognition Ratings for Inferable Statements That Were Either Present or Absent, as a Function of Type of Inference.

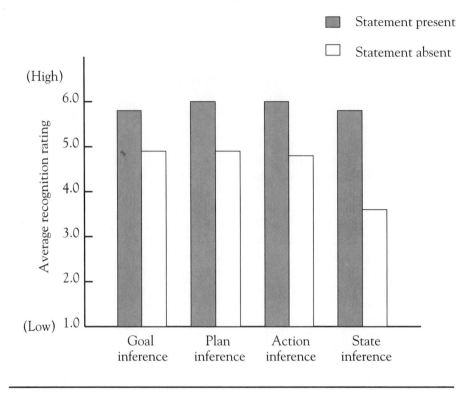

This section has focused on factors that affect inferences, and we discussed in some detail that some inferences are more probable than others. In focusing on these details, however, let's not lose sight of the power of those inferences. As Figure 8.5 showed, we are almost as likely to remember reading these inferences as to remember statements that actually occurred in the text. Our inferences blend with the text, forming a cohesive story. We retain the gist or general meaning of a passage, forgetting that we actually constructed some of the elements of that story.

Higher Level Inferences. Researchers are beginning to explore higher levels of inference, including very abstract themes. Colleen Seifert (1990), for example, presents a passage describing a man who was being considered for a Supreme Court appointment some years ago:

Ginsberg has been accused of using marijuana during his teaching years, threatening his appointment to the Supreme Court. A lawyer who is said to have been a close friend of Ginsberg during his days at Harvard refused to comment. (p. 115)

In order to make sense of this passage, we need to make inferences based on a wide variety of "facts" from our general knowledge storehouse.

Another higher level inference involves our own preference for the way we want a story to turn out. Perhaps you've turned the pages of a fast-paced spy novel and mentally shouted to your favorite character, "Watch out!" In fact, Allbritton and Gerrig (1991) found that readers did generate what they called *participatory responses* when they became involved in a story. These mental preferences for the story's outcome can be so strong that they can actually interfere with readers' ability to judge how the story actually turned out, making us pause as we try to decide whether that unhappy ending really did occur. In fact, you may find yourself so hopeful about a happy ending you've constructed that you read the final sentences over several times, trying to convince yourself that the hero or heroine didn't die!

In summary, we are likely to draw inferences that are consistent with a script. Inferences are especially likely if a passage does not fit the current context, if we read slowly, and if the inference involves a goal, a plan, or an action. In addition, we draw higher level, more abstract inferences about people's intentions, as well as inferences based on our own preferences.

Metacomprehension

Did you understand the material on inferences in reading? How much longer can you read today before you feel you can't absorb any more? Are you aware you've started a new section under the topic of reading? As you think about these issues, you are engaging in metacomprehension. **Metacomprehension** refers to our thoughts about reading comprehension; it is one kind of metacognition. (If your metacomprehension is excellent, you are now saying to yourself something like, "OK, this topic is going to be related to the material in Chapter 7, on the tip-of-the-tongue phenomenon and metamemory.") How accurate is the typical college student's metacomprehension, and how can metacomprehension be improved?

Metacomprehension Accuracy. In general, college students are not very accurate in their metacomprehension skills. For example, they may *think* that they understood something they read because they are familiar with its general topic, but they have not retained specific information (Glenberg et al., 1987).

Let us consider a representative study on metacomprehension. Pressley and Ghatala (1988) tested introductory psychology students to assess their metacomprehension as well as their performance on two other metacognitive tasks. Metacomprehension was tested using the reading comprehension tests from the Scholastic Aptitude Test (SAT). If you took the SAT, you'll recall that items on this portion of the SAT typically contain between one and three paragraphs, in

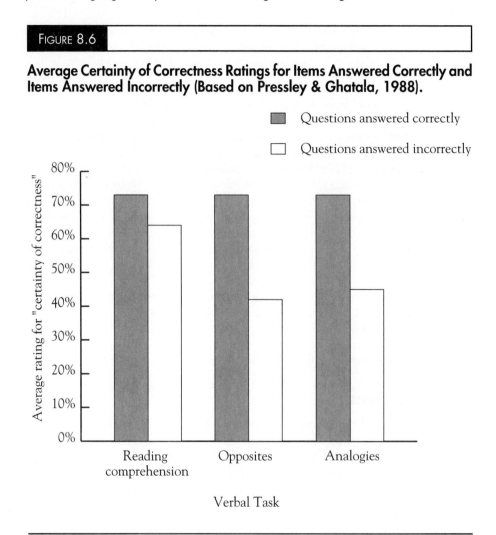

FIGURE 8.6

Average Certainty of Correctness Ratings for Items Answered Correctly and Items Answered Incorrectly (Based on Pressley & Ghatala, 1988).

essay form, followed by several multiple-choice questions. After the students in Pressley and Ghatala's study had answered the multiple-choice questions, they then rated how certain they were that they had answered the questions correctly. If they were absolutely certain that their answer had been correct, they were told to answer 100 percent. If they were just guessing, they were told to report 20 percent (representing guessing at the chance level among five possible answers on the test). This certainty rating served as the measure of metacomprehension.

Figure 8.6 shows the students' average certainty ratings for the items they had actually answered correctly and for those answered incorrectly. When they had actually answered the reading comprehension questions correctly, they supplied an average certainty rating of 73 percent. In other words, they were fairly confident about these items, which is appropriate. However, notice the average certainty rating for the items that they answered *incorrectly*. Here, they supplied an average certainty rating of about 64 percent. Unfortunately, this is about the same level of confidence they showed for the items they answered correctly! Furthermore, these data suggest that students are highly overconfident in many cases; they believe they know what they have just finished reading, even when they answer the questions incorrectly.

For comparison's sake, let's see how those same students performed on two other metacognition tests, based on other verbal portions of the SAT. If you took the SAT, you may remember that one verbal task asks you to select a word that is the opposite of a listed word. (For example, "Which word is the opposite of *irreparable? amiable, mendable, grateful, confusing,* or *divisible.*") Notice that the students were much more confident about the items they had answered correctly (73 percent) than the items they had answered incorrectly (42 percent). The third verbal task involved the analogies test (for example, "*intruder* is to *privacy* as *animal* is to *forest, ripple* is to *calm . . .*"). Once more the contrast is clear; they were much more certain about items they had answered correctly (72 percent) than about items they had answered incorrectly (46 percent). In short, students are reasonably accurate in assessing their performance on two vocabulary tests, but they are not very accurate in assessing their reading comprehension.

Improving Metacomprehension. Ideally, students should be accurate in assessing whether they understand what they have read; their subjective assessments should match their performance on an objective test. One effective way to improve metacomprehension is to take a pretest, which can supply feedback about comprehension before taking the actual examination (Glenberg et al., 1987).

Metacomprehension involves accurately assessing whether or not you understand a written passage. It also involves regulating your reading, so that you know how to read more effectively. For example, Kaufman and her colleagues (1985) found that good and poor readers differed in their awareness that certain reading strategies were useful. Good readers were more likely to report that they found it helpful to try to make connections among the ideas they had read and to try to create visual images based on descriptions in the text.

Psychologists and educators are beginning to examine some of the metacomprehension strategies that can enhance reading comprehension. Demonstration 8.6 will help you consider your own metacomprehension skills and think about some strategies for self-management, based on suggestions offered by Baker (1989), Bereiter and Bird (1985), Garner (1987), and Nist and Mealey (1991).

Artificial Intelligence and Reading

As discussed earlier in this textbook, **artificial intelligence (AI)** is the area of computer science that attempts to construct computers that can execute human-like cognitive processes. As Judith Greene (1986) writes, the goal of AI is to

DEMONSTRATION 8.6

ASSESSING METACOMPREHENSION SKILLS.

Answer each of the following questions about your own metacomprehension. If you answer "no" to any question, devise a plan for improving metacomprehension that you can apply as you read the next assigned chapter in this textbook.

1. In general, are you accurate in predicting your performance on exam questions related to reading?
2. After reading a chapter in this textbook, do you test your comprehension by quizzing yourself on the list of new terms and on the review questions?
3. After you have read a short section (roughly a page in length), do you make yourself summarize what you have just read—using your own words?
4. Do you reread a portion when it isn't making sense or when you realize you haven't been paying attention?
5. Do you try to draw connections between the ideas in the textbook?
6. When you read a term you do not know, do you try to determine its meaning by looking up its meaning in a dictionary or the index of this textbook?
7. When you review material prior to a test, do you spend more time on the material you consider difficult than on the material you consider easy?

develop computer programs that will make a computer behave "as if" it were intelligent. When developing AI models of language, the basic rationale of the approach we will discuss is that computers are dumb. They start off with no knowledge whatsoever about **natural language,** that is, ordinary human language with all its sloppiness, ambiguities, and complexities. The researcher has to write into the program all the information that is necessary to make the computer behave as if it comprehends sentences typed on its keyboard. The program must be in the form of detailed instructions, and the computer must be given specific programming operations for analyzing all input.

Researchers in artificial intelligence claim three benefits from developing computer programs capable of language comprehension:

1. The operations have to be stated very precisely in the form of objective instructions that a computer program can carry out. This requirement forces researchers to be very specific about the components of their theory of language comprehension.
2. The process of deciding what information should be provided to the computer database may reveal insights about what processes must be involved in human language comprehension.
3. Researchers' theories of language can be tested by running the program to see whether it responds correctly to the typed sentences (J. Greene, 1986).

How can researchers tell whether a computer really "understands" a fragment of language? Perhaps the sentences it generates may simply reflect the information that the programmer put into the program. Typically, researchers demand that the output must be in a different format from the input. For example, if the input is a story, the output must be a summary that captures the important points. The output cannot simply match the input.

Chapter 1 pointed out the distinction between artificial intelligence (specifically "pure AI") and computer simulation. **Pure AI** seeks to accomplish a task as efficiently as possible, whereas **computer simulation** tries to take human limitations into account. Thus, a computer simulation model of sentence comprehension should reflect the difficulty humans have in understanding ambiguous sentences, and it should also have problems interpreting long, complex sentences (Singer, 1990).

Researchers have been intrigued with computer simulation of language comprehension since the discipline of artificial intelligence began about 40 years ago. In the 1950s, for example, some researchers tried to program a computer to translate English into Russian. This may seem like a fairly easy task until you consider the problems presented by ambiguities and idioms. Legend has it that an early researcher programmed his computer to translate "the spirit is willing but the flesh is weak," initially into Russian and then back into English. The retranslated English read: "The vodka is good but the meat is rotten" (Tartter, 1986). Clearly, any accurate translation would involve extensive familiarity with both language and world knowledge, more comparable to an encyclopedia than a dictionary.

Let us consider one example of a program designed to perform reading tasks. One specific script-based program has been given the unattractive name of **FRUMP,** standing for Fast Reading Understanding and Memory Program (De Jong, 1982). The goal of FRUMP is to summarize newspaper stories, written in ordinary language. When it was developed, FRUMP could interpret about 10 percent of UPI (United Press International) news wires (Kintsch, 1984). It works by applying world knowledge, based on 48 different scripts. Presumably, if a greater number of scripts were provided, it could summarize an even larger number of stories. The program is designed to make a guess about which scripts are relevant to a story, and then to search the text to see if the guess is confirmed. Only those sentences relevant to the script will be processed. FRUMP makes a good summary of only the main points; everything else is disregarded.

As Kintsch (1984) notes, there is only one time when FRUMP uses a bottom-up approach—at the beginning when it is searching the words to decide what script to use. The rest of the process is top-down, because it is based on script information.

Consider, for example, the "vehicle accident" script, which is activated when the text contains information about some kind of vehicle striking some physical object in some location. The script contains information to report number of people killed, number of people injured, and the cause of the accident. On the basis of the "vehicle accident" script, FRUMP reported on a news article, "A vehicle accident occurred in Colorado. A plane hit the ground. 1 person died." FRUMP did manage to capture the facts of this story, though it missed the major reason that the item was newsworthy: Yes, one person was killed, but 21 survived!

FRUMP also occasionally misinterprets figures of speech. For example, it processed the headline "Pope's Death Shakes the Western Hemisphere" and interpreted it as, "There was an earthquake in the Western Hemisphere. The Pope Died." FRUMP had been programmed to interpret the word *shake* as belonging to the "earthquake" script!

We can be impressed that FRUMP manages to process a reasonable number of newspaper stories, but its errors tend to highlight the extensive capabilities of human readers. The work on computer simulation points out our tremendous flexibility and our astonishing storehouse of world knowledge, consistent with Theme 2 of this textbook. We humans can manage to read a handwritten address scrawled on an envelope, yet no machine has yet been designed to accomplish this relatively simple task with great accuracy (Kosslyn & Koenig, 1992). Furthermore, we humans can effortlessly recognize words at the rate of about 200 words per minute. We can discover the meaning of an unfamiliar word and also understand an intricate sentence. We manage to draw inferences that are not stated in the text we are reading, and we can also assess (though not with tremendous accuracy) whether we have understood the material we have just read. Now let us turn to an even more remarkable human ability, language production.

SECTION SUMMARY: READING

1. The eyes make saccadic movements during reading; the perceptual span during fixation includes roughly four letters to the left of center and eight letters to the right.
2. In contrast to poor readers, good readers make larger saccadic movements, pause for a shorter amount of time, and move backward less often.
3. Of the three hypotheses of word recognition, the current favorite is the dual-encoding hypothesis, which states that semantic memory can be reached either directly through the visual route or indirectly through the sound route.
4. Readers use a variety of contextual cues to determine the meaning of an unfamiliar word; people who score high on tests of vocabulary, reading comprehension, intelligence, and short-term memory are particularly skilled at figuring out a word's meaning from context.
5. Specific background knowledge in an area facilitates reading.
6. Skilled readers summarize a passage using the same organizational framework as the text itself. In reading a story, the processing load is greatest at the beginning and the end of the story.
7. Research on inferences shows that people draw inferences that are consistent

with a script. Also, inferences are most likely if a passage does not fit the context, if people read slowly, and if the inference involves a goal, a plan, or an action. Finally, people also draw higher level inferences.

8. Research on metacomprehension shows that college students are not highly accurate in predicting whether they have understood a written passage.

9. Computer simulation programs, such as one called FRUMP designed to read newspaper stories, point out human competence in a wide variety of reading tasks.

CHAPTER REVIEW QUESTIONS

1. What is parallel transmission, and why does it present a problem when psychologists try to explain speech perception?

2. What kind of arguments support the general mechanism approach to speech perception? Why is this approach consistent with the view that cognitive processes are interrelated?

3. Construct a simple sentence and divide it into constituents. Explain how these constituents are important in language comprehension. Next, construct a different sentence, one that has the same deep structure as your original sentence, but different surface structure. Now think of a pun that has a single surface structure but two different deep structures.

4. Context is an important concept throughout this chapter. Discuss the importance of context in speech perception, the processing of ambiguous words, discovering the meaning of an unfamiliar word, and background knowledge in reading.

5. Compare your language comprehension while listening with your language comprehension while reading. Which processes are similar and which are different?

6. You are reading a sentence right now. Describe the processes involved as you (a) move your eyes, (b) perceive the letters, and (c) recognize the words.

7. Review the three theories of word recognition. Describe the situations in which the direct-access hypothesis is most likely to apply and those in which the indirect-access hypothesis is most likely.

8. Describe several ways in which people make inferences during reading comprehension. Use examples from your own experience to illustrate these methods. How do these inferences illustrate the theme that concerns the active nature of cognitive processes?

9. What kind of metacomprehension tasks are relevant when you are reading this textbook? List as many tasks as possible. Why do you suppose that metacomprehension for reading long passages of text would be less accurate than metamemory for vocabulary words (Chapter 7)?

10. Discuss the variety of other cognitive skills involved in understanding spoken language and reading. Then, moving in the opposite direction, list the variety of other cognitive skills that depend upon understanding spoken language and reading.

NEW TERMS

psycholinguistics
language comprehension
speech perception
phonemes
parallel transmission
invariant feature
phonemic restoration
special mechanism approach
motor theory of speech perception
phonetic module
categorical perception
general mechanism approach
syntax
constituent
immediate constituents
ultimate constituents
rewrite rules
function words
content words
heuristics
transformational grammar
surface structure

deep structure
ambiguous sentences
kernel
lexical ambiguity
deep structure ambiguity
saccadic movement
gaze-contingent paradigm
perceptual span
direct-access hypothesis
indirect-access hypothesis
dual-encoding hypothesis
whole-word approach
phonics approach
deep dyslexia
subvocalizing
script
metacomprehension
artificial intelligence (AI)
natural language
Pure AI
computer simulation
FRUMP

RECOMMENDED READINGS

Crowder, R. G., & Wagner, R. K. (1992). *The psychology of reading: An introduction* (2nd ed.). New York: Oxford University Press. This is an excellent summary of the psychological components of reading, including the topics covered in Chapter 8 as well as reading development, spelling, and dyslexia.

Garner, R. (1987). *Metacognition and reading comprehension.* Norwood, NJ: Ablex. Garner's very readable book examines metacomprehension, and it would be especially useful for anyone who is interested in the educational aspects of reading.

Gleason, J. B., & Ratner, N. B. (Eds.). (1993a). *Psycholinguistics*. Fort Worth, TX: Harcourt Brace Jovanovich. This upper-level textbook includes 11 chapters, many written by well-known psycholinguists. Chapters in *Psycholinguistics* that are especially relevant to this chapter cover speech perception, sentence processing, discourse processes, and reading.

Seifert, C. M. (1990). Content-based inferences in text. *The Psychology of Learning and Motivation, 25*, 103–122. This chapter provides a concise and helpful overview of inferences in reading, the subject of our In-Depth section in this chapter.

Singer, M. (1990). *Psychology of language: An introduction to sentence and discourse processes*. Hillsdale, NJ: Erlbaum. This is one of the more clearly written textbooks on psycholinguistics. It is especially strong in the topics covered in this chapter, with an emphasis on language comprehension, inferences, and understanding stories.

LANGUAGE PRODUCTION: SPEAKING, WRITING, AND BILINGUALISM

Whereas Chapter 8 examined language comprehension (listening and reading), Chapter 9 focuses on language production, specifically speaking, writing, and bilingualism.

Speaking requires impressive planning; for example, we need to plan how to arrange the words in an orderly sequence. Although most of our spoken language is error free, we sometimes make speech errors such as slips of the tongue. Two other features of spoken language include the gestures that often accompany our speech and the social context of speech (for example, making sure that your conversational partner shares the same background information).

Although writing occupies a large portion of college students' course work, psychologists have only recently begun to study the writing process. Writing shares some characteristics with speaking, but other characteristics—such as the complexity of the language—are different. Writing consists of three tasks that often overlap in time: planning, sentence generation, and revision.

Bilinguals seem to have a number of advantages over monolinguals. For example, they are more aware of language structure, and they perform better on tests of cognitive flexibility and nonverbal intelligence. In general, people who acquire a second language during childhood show a greater mastery of that language than those who learn the language as adults.

INTRODUCTION

Every time a person comprehends language, someone else needs to produce language. If psychologists distributed their research equitably, we would therefore know just as much about language production as we know about language comprehension; in effect, Chapter 9 would be the same length as Chapter 8.

However, one psychologist estimates that only 5 percent of published papers in psycholinguistics focus on language production (Dell, 1985). These results are somewhat surprising, given that language production is overt—and therefore much more measurable than the covert processes involved in language comprehension (Foss, 1988). However, research on language comprehension is actually easier to conduct, because researchers find it easier to control what a person hears or reads than to control what a person wishes to say or write (Fromkin, 1993; Stemberger, 1991). Fortunately, however, psychologists are becoming increasingly interested in language production (Foss, 1988). They have also begun a systematic investigation of the way people produce written language; writing was not even mentioned in the previous edition of this textbook.

Let us begin by examining spoken language, and then we'll consider written language. Our final topic, bilingualism, involves all the impressive skills of both language comprehension and language production and thus will serve as the final section on language in these two chapters.

SPEAKING

The Dutch psycholinguist Willem Levelt begins his book *Speaking: From Intention to Articulation* with the following paragraph:

> Talking is one of our dearest occupations. We spend hours a day conversing, telling stories, teaching, quarreling, . . . and, of course, speaking to ourselves. Speaking is, moreover, one of our most complex cognitive, linguistic, and motor skills. Articulation flows automatically, at a rate of about fifteen speech sounds per second, while we are attending only to the ideas we want to get across to our interlocutors. (Levelt, 1989, p. i)

In this section of the chapter, we will examine how people select the content of their conversations. We will then see how our speech errors show systematic patterns and how our gestures accompany spoken language in a systematic fashion. Our final topic is the social context of speech; we need to keep in mind that language serves a social function and is therefore sensitive to social regulations. Throughout this entire section, notice that the cognitive processes are impressively active—consistent with Theme 1—as they simultaneously juggle meaning, the mechanics of speech, and the subtle nature of social interactions.

Selecting the Content of Speech

Speech production requires a series of stages. We begin by working out the gist or the overall meaning of what we intend to say. Then we devise the general structure of the sentence without selecting the exact words. During the third stage, we choose both the words and their forms (for example, not just the word *eat* but the form *am eating*). In the fourth and final stage, we convert these intentions into overt speech by articulating the phonemes (Garrett, 1984).

In the last chapter, we emphasized that several stages of speech comprehension may take place simultaneously. Similarly, those four stages of speech production also overlap in time. We often pronounce several phonemes in a sentence before we have completely worked out the general structure for the last part of that sentence. In general, research with reaction-time data suggests that we tend to select the exact subject of a sentence when we begin a sentence; at this point, however, the verb is only partially selected (Lindsley, 1975).

Typically, we plan ahead for more than one sentence when we are speaking (Holmes, 1984). When we are talking for an extended period (for example, telling someone about summer plans), we alternate between hesitant phases and fluent phases. We speak haltingly and slowly as we plan what we will say. During the fluent phase, we are rewarded for our earlier planning, and the words flow more easily (Beattie, 1983; Levelt, 1989).

A major problem arises when we utter a statement. We may have a general thought that we want to express, or we may have a mental image that needs to be

---

DEMONSTRATION 9.1

DESCRIBING YOUR HOME.

Think about your home or some other residence that you know well. On a piece of paper, briefly describe the layout of that residence.

---

conveyed verbally. These rather shapeless ideas need to be translated into a statement that has a disciplined, linear shape, with words following another in time. This problem of arranging words in an ordered, linear sequence is called **the linearization problem** (Bock, 1987; Foss, 1988). Try noticing how linearization ordinarily occurs quite effortlessly; consistent with Theme 2, we accomplish this challenging task quite readily. Occasionally, however, you may find yourself struggling, trying to say everything at the very beginning.

One important issue in selecting the words we wish to say is whether we choose the active or the passive voice. Another issue is the content of speech, which has been studied in people's descriptions of their homes. Try Demonstration 9.1 now, before you read further.

Selecting the Active or the Passive Voice. In Chapter 8, we noted that the active voice is much easier to understand than the passive voice. We also know that people are more likely to produce the active voice. In Taylor and Taylor's (1990) tabulation of spoken language samples, the simple active form (for example, *He read the book*) occurred 81 percent of the time, in contrast to 14 percent for the simple passive form (for example, *The book was read by him*).

However, our selection of the active versus the passive voice can also be influenced by the sentence heard immediately beforehand. Participants in a study by Bock (1986) heard isolated sentences, with the instructions that they would be asked to recognize them later. In fact, the true purpose of each sentence was to act as a prime for a picture-description task that followed immediately after. For example, a participant might read either the active priming sentence *A brick struck the car's windshield* or the passive priming sentence *The car's windshield was struck by a brick*. Then the participant saw a target picture, which might show a bolt of lightning striking a church. Bock asked the participant to describe the picture, and she noted whether the sentence produced was active or passive.

When human agents were involved in the picture's activity, people almost always used the active voice. It is far more natural to say, "The boy punched the man" than to say, "The man was punched by the boy." The priming condition (active vs. passive) had no influence on people's choices, as shown in Figure 9.1. However, when there was a nonhuman agent (as in the example of lightning striking the church) people were more likely to use the active voice in the sentence they produced if the prime had been active. If the prime had been passive, people

FIGURE 9.1

The Influence of the Prime in Word Choice in Describing a Picture.

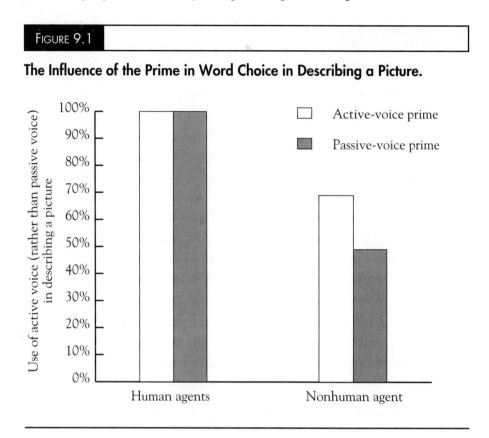

used the passive voice relatively often. People therefore show an inclination to produce a sentence that mimics the form of a preceding sentence.

Constructing Descriptions.   Psychologists have also studied the general way in which people plan their speech, for example, when they are asked to describe something. Linde and Labov (1975) asked New York City residents to describe the layout of their apartments. The respondents were quite uniform in their descriptions—they began at the outside entrance, and proceeded to name each room. They also included instructions about how to reach each room. A typical description was:

> You walked in the front door.
> There was a narrow hallway.
> To the left, the first door you came to was a tiny bedroom.
> Then there was a kitchen,
> and then a bathroom,
> and then the main room was in the back, living room, I guess
> (p. 927)

Linde and Labov found that the "guided tour" description was most common. In contrast, people seldom described the layout in terms of a map of the apartment. Only 3 percent of the people in their study presented an overview of the apartment's floor plan. Now look at the description you wrote in Demonstration 9.1 and notice whether you described a visitor's route through the home or a maplike description.

Speech Errors

The speech that most people produce is generally very well formed (Bock, 1987; Deese, 1984), consistent with Theme 2. However, the speech we use in everyday conversation differs from perfect English in several respects. People often pause in the middle of sentences. They may start a new sentence before finishing the previous one. They sometimes use extra words, such as *oh, well,* and *um.*

Mackay and Osgood (1959) found that professors are just as guilty of speech errors as everyone else. They recorded the speech of 13 professors who attended a conference at the University of Illinois. The following excerpt is representative of the kind of errors they found—with pauses represented by ellipses (. . .):

> As far as I know, no one yet has done the in a way obvious now and interesting problem of . . . doing a in a sense a structural frequency study of the alternative . . . syntactical . . . in a given language, say, like English, the alternative . . . possible structures, and how what their hierarchical . . . probability of occurrence structure is. Now, it seems to me you w-w-will need that kind of data as base line. . . . (p. 25)

Furthermore, when former U.S. President George Bush was asked by reporters about his accomplishments, he replied:

> I see no media mention of it, but we entered in—you asked what time it is and I'm telling you how to build a watch here—but we had Boris Yeltsin here the other day. And I think of my times campaigning in Iowa, years ago, and how there was a—Iowa has kind of, I single out Iowa, it's kind of an international state in a sense and has a great interest in all these things—and we had Yeltsin standing here in the Rose Garden, and we entered into a deal to eliminate the biggest and most threatening ballistic missiles . . . and it was almost, "Ho-hum, what have you done for me recently?" ("Overheard," 1992)

Thus, even high-status speakers do not always produce flawless English.

Researchers have been particularly interested in the kind of speech errors called slips-of-the-tongue. **Slips-of-the-tongue** are errors in which sounds or entire words are rearranged between two or more different words. Dell (1986) proposes three kinds of errors:

1. Sound errors occur when sounds in nearby words are exchanged, for example, *Snow flurries* → *flow snurries.*
2. Morpheme errors occur when morphemes (or smallest meaningful units in

FIGURE 9.2	

An Example of Dell's Model of Sound Processing in Sentence Production (Simplified).

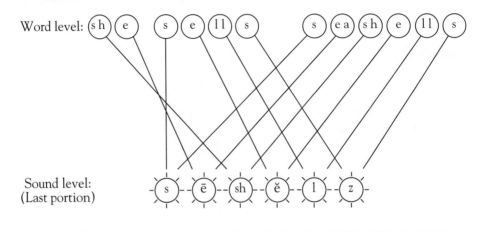

language, such as -ly or in-) are exchanged in nearby words, for example, *Self-destruct instruction* → *self-instruct destruction.*

3. Word errors occur when words are exchanged, for example, *Writing a letter to my mother* → *writing a mother to my letter.*

Each of these three kinds of errors can take several forms, in addition to the exchange errors in the previous examples. For example, there are anticipation errors (*Reading list* → *leading list*), perseveration errors (*Waking rabbits* → *waking wabbits*), and deletions (*Same state* → *same sate*).

In almost all cases, the errors occur across items from the same category. For instance, in sound errors, initial consonants interact with initial consonants (as in the *flow snurries* example). In morpheme errors, prefixes substitute for prefixes (as

DEMONSTRATION 9.2

SLIPS-OF-THE-TONGUE

Keep a record of all the slips-of-the-tongue that you either hear or make yourself in the next week. Classify each slip as a sound error, morpheme error, or word error. Furthermore, decide whether the error is an exchange, an anticipation, a perseveration, an addition, or some other form. Also note whether the error occurs across items from the same category. Finally, see if you can determine why the error occurred, using an analysis similar to Dell's.

in the *self-instruct* example). In word errors, members of the same grammatical category are interchanged (as in the *mother to my letter* example).

Dell (1986) has proposed an elaborate and comprehensive theory for speech errors that is similar to the parallel distributed processing approach and involves the concept of spreading activation. Let us consider a brief overview of what might happen to encourage a sound error. Dell proposes that when a speaker is constructing a sentence, he or she constructs a representation at the word level. This representation must be fairly well constructed before representation can be constructed at the sound level. When a person wants to speak, the words required for a sentence will activate the sound elements to which they are linked. For example, Figure 9.2 shows how the activation might work for the sounds in the last word of the tongue-twister *She sells seashells*.

Usually, we utter the sounds that are most highly activated, and usually these highly activated sounds are the appropriate ones. However, each sound can be activated by several different words. Notice, for example, that the *sh* sound in the sound level representation of seashells (that is, *seshelz*) is highly "charged" because it receives activation from the first word in the sentence, *she*, as well as the *sh* in *seashells*. As Dell says, errors are a natural result from the theory's assumptions. Incorrect items can sometimes have activation levels that are just as high as (or higher than) the correct items. By mistake, these incorrect items may be selected. A speaker is highly likely to say, *She sells sheashells*, particularly because the rhythm of the sentence encourages a further resemblance between the *she* and the *sea* in *seashells*.

Try Demonstration 9.2 to determine what kinds of slips-of-the-tongue are typically found in your daily experience. Incidentally, Ferber (1991) suggests that listeners often fail to detect slips-of-the-tongue, thereby committing what we could call "slips-of-the-ear." As you know from the material on context and phonemic restoration from Chapter 8, context effects and top-down processing (Theme 5) are often so strong that we fail to notice speech errors.

Gestures

So far, we have been discussing the production of speech sounds. David McNeill (1985) argues that another important component of language production is gestures. **Gestures** can be defined as the movements of the arms and hands that accompany speech. McNeill suggests, in fact, that speech and gestures are closely connected, both generated by the same psychological processes. Gestures develop together with speech as children learn to communicate, and gestures disappear when people develop speech disorders as adults.

McNeill found that people show remarkable uniformity in their use of gestures. For example, people who had just watched a television cartoon were asked to describe the sequence of events. Even though they were tested separately, the participants showed similar hand motions as they pointed upward to describe the cartoon character climbing up a drainspout, and they swung an elevated hand to

---

DEMONSTRATION 9.3

GESTURES ACCOMPANYING SPEECH.

The next time a friend mentions having seen an action movie, and you have a few minutes, ask this person to describe the movie. Notice whether gestures are used to indicate action in the movie. Are gestures also used for emphasis? How else are gestures used in this description?

---

indicate chasing someone with a stick. Gestures add to spoken language, providing richness and an extra dimension. In fact, Cassell and McNeill (1991) argue that a gesture is like a second eye, providing a new dimension similar to the binocular vision we achieve with two eyes.

Gestures can convey actions, and they can also signal that the speech they accompany is important. For example, I notice that when I'm lecturing to a class and I say, "I really want to emphasize that . . . ," my hands rise up, with palms facing the students, and my hands move up and down rhythmically with those words.

Now that you are sensitized to the linguistic importance of gestures, try noticing how seldom we speak without gestures. Furthermore, read Demonstration 9.3 and try it at the next appropriate occasion.

The Social Context of Speech

When we speak, we need to attend to the content of speech. We need to produce error-free speech, accompanied by appropriate gestures. In addition to these challenging assignments, we also need to be attuned to the social context of speech.

As Herbert Clark (1985) argues, language is really a social instrument. We direct our words to other people, and our goal is not merely to express our thoughts aloud but to affect the people with whom we are talking. Clark proposes that conversation is like a complicated dance. Speakers cannot simply utter words aloud and expect to be understood. Instead, speakers must consider their conversation partners, make numerous assumptions about those partners, and design their utterances appropriately.

This complicated dance involves precise coordination. Two people going simultaneously through a doorway need to coordinate their motor actions. Similarly, two speakers need to coordinate turn-taking, they need to coordinate their understanding of ambiguous terms, and they need to understand each other's intentions. When Helen tells Sam, *The Bakers are on their way,* both participants in the conversation need to understand that this is an indirect invitation for Sam to start dinner, rather than to call the police for protection (Clark, 1985). Conversation involves an implicit contract in which the speaker must ensure that the listener has the proper contextual background for the message (Harris et al., 1980).

The knowledge of these social rules that underlie language is called **pragmatics** (Carroll, 1986). Included in the topic of pragmatics are common ground, the given-new strategy, knowledge about conversational format, and an understanding of directives.

Common Ground.

Suppose that a young man named Andy asks Lisa, "How was your weekend?" and Lisa answers, "It was like being in Conshohocken again." Andy will understand this reply only if they share a similar understanding about the characteristics or events that took place in Conshohocken. In fact, we would expect Lisa to make this remark only if she were certain that she and Andy shared appropriate common ground (Gerrig & Littman, 1990).

Common ground means that the conversationalists share the similar background knowledge, schemas, and experiences that are necessary for mutual understanding. To guarantee conversational coherence, the speakers must collaborate to make certain that they share common ground. Clark and Wilkes-Gibbs (1986) examined how this collaboration process operates when people work together to arrange complex figures. Demonstration 9.4 is a modification of their study.

The participants in the study played this game for six trials. (Each trial consisted of arranging all 12 figures in order.) On the first trial, the director required an average of nearly four turns to describe a figure and make certain that the matcher understood the reference. However, as Figure 9.3 shows, the director and the matcher soon developed a mutual shorthand. Just as two dancers become more skilled at coordinating their movements as they practice together, conversational partners become more skilled in communicating efficiently.

The Given-New Strategy.

Another way in which speakers coordinate their conversations is called the given-new strategy (Clark, 1985; Haviland & Clark, 1974). According to the **given-new strategy,** a speaker's sentence contains some "given" information, with which the listener is already familiar, and some new information. This enables the listener to integrate the new information into memory along with the old memory. For example, consider the sentence:

The story Dr. Jones told was excellent.

The given information is that Dr. Jones told a story, whereas the new information was that the story was excellent.

Notice how the given information can be conveyed quite subtly. Thus, *Jim, too, snores at night* refers to the given information that someone else snores as well. *Julia's diamonds are real, though* (with the name *Julia* emphasized) implies that someone else's diamonds are not. Finally, *When did Tim stop drinking?* implies that Tim had been drinking previously. For the speaker to convey the new information successfully, however, the given information must match the information already

---

DEMONSTRATION 9.4

COLLABORATING TO ESTABLISH COMMON GROUND.

For this demonstration, you need to make two photocopies of these figures. Then locate two volunteers and a watch that can measure time in seconds. Cut the figures apart, keeping each sheet's figures in a separate pile and making certain the dot is at the top of each figure. Appoint one person to be the "director"; this person should arrange the figures in random order in two rows of six figures each. This person's task is to describe the first figure in enough detail so that the "matcher" is able to identify that figure and place it in position 1 in front of him or her. (Neither person should be able to see the other's figures.) The goal is for the matcher to place all 12 figures in the same order as the director's figures. They may use any kind of verbal descriptions they choose, but no gestures or imitation of body position. Record how long it takes them to reach their goal, and then make sure that the figures do match up. Ask them to try the game two more times, with the same person serving as director. Record the times again, and note whether the time decreases on the second and third trials; are they increasingly efficient in establishing common ground? Do they tend to develop a standard vocabulary (for example, "the ice skater") to refer to a given figure?

---

in the listener's memory. Thus, a speaker would be more successful with this sequence:

We carried the books downstairs. The books were heavy.

than with this sequence:

We carried the school supplies downstairs. The books were heavy.

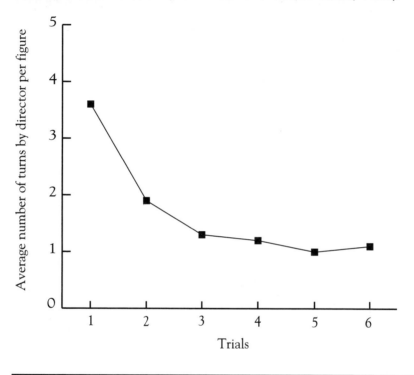

FIGURE 9.3

Average Number of Turns that Directors Required for Each Figure, as a Function of Trial Number (From Clark and Wilkes-Gibbs, 1986).

In the first case, the sentence *The books were heavy* is easy to interpret because it matches information that the previous sentence established in memory. In the second case, an extra step is required, as the listener must reason that the school supplies included books. Ordinarily, we converse as if speakers and listeners have unspoken contracts to obey the given-new rule; that is, the speaker must provide the appropriate framework within which the new information can be understood.

Conversational Format. We also have social rules about the format of our conversations. One rule is that the speakers should alternate (Goodwin, 1981; McLaughlin, 1984). Speakers do not talk at the same time, and they do not typically leave long pauses in the middle of the conversation. Think about this rule of alternation and how it applies in different situations. In a telephone conversation, for example, alternation is required in the beginning interchanges. The answerer must speak first, but this speech segment must be brief. The answerer may say "Hello," or "Dr. Jones speaking," or "Yeah," but longer segments will not be tolerated. When I call my accountant, for example, the receptionist who answers the phone manages to condense "Kasdin, Saiger, Rossman, Elder & Gould" into something that lasts 1 second and sounds like "Kasgrsmeldrgld." The person who called must then provide identification and expect a brief acknowledgment from the answerer before proceeding with the message.

Similarly, we begin our conversations with people we meet with an alternation pattern:

JOE: Hi, Maria, how are you?
MARIA: Hi. Fine. How about you?

Proper etiquette also specifies that the closing of conversations must be highly structured (Ervin-Tripp, 1993). Pay attention to this structure the next time you overhear a telephone conversation. The speakers may require numerous alternations to "wind down" a conversation. Certainly, a polite adult cannot end a conversation by flinging a simple "good-bye" into a random pause in the interchange. A typical ending might be this:

A. Well, I'm really glad you called, Jean.
B. I'm glad I found you home.
A. You're right, I haven't been home much. Let's get together, OK?
B. OK. And say hello to Jim.
A. Yes, and say hi to your family.
B. See you.
A. 'Bye now.

Typically, the leave-taking portion of the conversation involves either specific or vague plans for contact in the future (Clark, 1985).

Directives. Ervin-Tripp (1976, 1993) has studied the social aspects of a particular kind of sentence called a directive. A **directive** is a sentence that requests someone to do something. Ervin-Tripp gathered large samples of speech in natural settings and found six different kinds of directives used in American English. Each kind of directive seemed to be used in certain, well-defined circumstances. For example, one kind of directive was used to express need. It was used either by a higher-ranking person in a work setting, as when a physician says to a nurse, "I'll need an ear curette in room 3," or in families, as when a child says to a parent, "I need a drink, Daddy." Another kind of directive is very abbreviated, because the necessary action is obvious. Thus, a customer may say to a waitress, "Tea, with lemon."

In general, the most polite directives require more words (Brown & Levinson, 1987). For example, "Could you possibly by any chance lend me your car for just a few minutes?" would be considered more polite than, "Could you lend me your car?"

Sometimes, directives are asked in the form of indirect questions. However, the speaker does not really need information, but services. For example, a teacher might ask a class, "What are you laughing at?" The teacher is not really concerned about the source of the laughter; it is a request for silence. Finally, some directives take the form of hints. You probably know someone who says, "I wonder if there is any butter in the refrigerator," instead of the more *direct* directive, "Would you get me some butter, please." Both of these directives can easily be misinterpreted, either intentionally or unintentionally.

Notice that many requests are in the form of questions that provide listeners with options. The options allow them either to comply with the request or to give some good reason why they cannot comply. These questions whose syntax does not match their intended purpose are called **indirect speech acts** (Green, 1989). Gibbs (1986) investigated the hypothesis that speakers will state their requests in a format that anticipates potential obstacles to compliance. Participants in this study read scenarios of everyday situations, such as going to a restaurant and ordering something that might no longer be available. They were asked to imagine themselves in this scenario and write down one sentence that they might say.

The results showed that people were most likely to frame their requests in terms of a possible obstacle that might create a problem. In the restaurant scenario, for example, 68 percent of the sentences began, "Do you have . . . "; requests such as "I'd like . . . " were much less common. Try noticing how you word your own requests. Do you tend to address a potential obstacle? For example, I recall an occasion when I wanted to call a professor at a large university. Aware that I would speak to one of many secretaries, who might not know about this professor's habits, I asked almost automatically, "Do you know what Dr. New's schedule will be for the day?"

Also, consider how we may occasionally phrase a request in an extremely indirect fashion. Valian (1985) provides an example of how we communicate more than we say. On seeing her neighbor in the elevator, she asked, "Has your designer made any progress on the soundproofing?" After a blank moment, the neighbor smiles and answers, "Oh, has our music been bothering you again?" The question about the designer let the neighbor know that the noise had still been bothersome and reminded him of an earlier promise.

SECTION SUMMARY: SPEAKING

1. Although studies on language production are much less common than studies on language comprehension, psychologists are becoming increasingly interested in language production.
2. Four stages in speech production include working out the gist, the general structure, the word choice, and phoneme articulation.
3. People typically select the active voice, except when the preceding sentence

involves the passive voice and no human agents; routes are typically used when describing a home.

4. According to Dell, slips-of-the-tongue occur because a speech sound other than the intended one is highly activated.

5. Gestures and speech are interconnected, providing additional richness and emphasis.

6. The pragmatic rules of speech include common ground, the given-new strategy, appropriate conversational format, and the skillful use of directives.

WRITING

Writing is a cognitive task that is both difficult and time consuming. It is also an important component of many people's occupations. For example, technical and professional people reported that in a typical working day they spent an average of about 30 percent of their time writing (Faigley & Miller, 1982; Kellogg, 1989a). However, research on the cognitive processes in writing is relatively new—with the first article appearing in the 1970s—and relatively limited (Hayes, 1989). We noted earlier in this chapter that research on *understanding* speech is more common than research on the act of speaking. The contrast is even more dramatic when we compare written language; research on reading is overwhelmingly more common than research on writing.

Comparing Speaking and Writing

Naturally, speaking and writing share many similar cognitive components. However, Ellis and Beattie (1986) point out some differing characteristics. Compared to speaking, writing is more likely to:

1. Occur in isolation from other people;
2. Involve delayed social feedback (if any);
3. Require extensive revising and editing;
4. Involve syntactically and lexically complex language; and
5. Be recorded in a potentially permanent form.

In one study comparing speaking and writing, Chafe and Danielewicz (1987) examined professors and graduate students. These researchers collected both formal and informal samples of speech (in lectures and in casual conversation) and writing (in professional articles and in personal letters). The comparison revealed that written language showed significantly more varied vocabulary than spoken language, whether formal or informal. In contrast, spoken language was much more likely than written language to include **hedges,** which are phrases—such as *sort of* and *kind of*—that limit the generality of the statement. Spoken language was also much more likely to show involvement with the audience and reference to oneself.

Cognitive Tasks Involved in Writing

Several psychologists have described the cognitive tasks that comprise writing. These include planning, sentence generating, and revising. However, like the similar stages we discussed in both understanding and producing spoken language, these tasks often overlap (Hayes, 1989a; Hayes & Flower, 1986; Kellogg, 1987). For example, you may be planning your overall writing strategy while generating parts of several sentences. All components of the task are complex, and they strain the limits of attention (Kellogg, 1989). As Flower and Hayes (1980) described the process:

> Writing is the act of dealing with an excessive number of simultaneous demands or constraints. Viewed this way, a writer in the act is a thinker on a full-time cognitive overload. (p. 33)

Still, consistent with Theme 2, we manage to coordinate these tasks quite skillfully as we produce written language.

Planning.   A writing plan includes at least three kinds of elements: (1) goals to express content knowledge about the topic; (2) goals unrelated to content, such as the form of the essay or persuasive techniques; and (3) goals to use certain words and phrases that sound appropriate. Research by Hayes (1989a) shows that the amount of planning and the quality of planning are highly correlated with the quality of the written text.

Perhaps you had a high-school teacher who insisted that you outline a paper before you began to write. Research by Kellogg (1988, 1990) strongly supports this strategy. College students who were instructed to prepare a written outline later wrote significantly better essays than students in a control group. Kellogg suggests that an outline may help to alleviate attention overload. In addition, an outline may help students overcome the linearization problem, which occurs in writing as well as in speaking. You've probably had the experience of beginning to write a paper only to find that each of several interrelated ideas needs to be placed first! An outline helps sort these ideas into an orderly, linear sequence.

Some researchers have begun to explore how the planning process is influenced by using a computer. Hayes (1989a) cites research by Haas showing that writers were less likely to preplan writing when they used a computer than when they used pen and paper. They also planned less at a conceptual level when they used a computer.

Sentence Generation.   Before you read further, try Demonstration 9.5, which requires you to generate some sentences. During sentence generation, the writer must translate the general ideas developed during planning, thus creating the actual sentences of the text. Even the most detailed outline must be greatly expanded during this process.

GENERATING SENTENCES.

For this exercise, you should be alone in a room, with no one else present to inhibit your spontaneity. Take a piece of paper on which you will write two sentences. For this writing task, however, say out loud the thoughts you are considering while you write each sentence. The results will be discussed later in this section.

1. Write one sentence to answer the question, "What is the most important characteristic that a good student should have?"
2. Write one sentence to answer the question, "What do you consider to be your strongest personality characteristic—the one that you most admire in yourself?"

One important characteristic of sentence generation is that the final essay is typically at least eight times longer than even the most elaborate outline. Another important characteristic is that hesitant phases tend to alternate with fluent phases, just as we discussed for spoken language. For example, one research project asked college graduates to think aloud as they described their writing process. When asked to describe her job, one woman generated the following passage (the dashes indicate pauses of 2 seconds or more):

> The best thing about it is—what? Something about using my mind—it allows me the opportunity to—uh—I want to write something about my ideas—to put ideas into action—or—to develop my ideas into—what?—into a meaningful form? Oh, bleh!—say it allows me—to use—Na—allows me—scratch that. The best thing about it is it allows me to use—my mind and ideas in a productive way. (adapted from Hayes, 1989a, p. 213)

Now think back on your own pattern when you were writing the sentences in Demonstration 9.5. Did you show a similar pattern of pauses alternating with fluent writing?

Revision.   In order to revise what you have written, you need to reconsider the goals of the text, to predict how well the text accomplishes these goals, and to propose improved ways to accomplish those goals (Hayes, 1989a). College students show tremendous individual differences in this area. Hayes (1989a) studied college students who were writing research papers for a class. Some students revised their original papers dramatically, often completely abandoning earlier drafts to begin a new version. Others showed little or no global revision, making changes only at the word or sentence level.

In another study, Hayes and his colleagues (1987) compared the revision capabilities of seven expert writers and seven first-year college students. Everyone was given the same poorly written two-page letter and was asked to revise it for an audience of young college students. The first-year students were likely to approach the text one sentence at a time, fixing relatively minor problems with spelling and grammar, but ignoring problems of organization, focus, and transition between ideas. The students were also more likely to judge some defective sentences as being appropriate. For example, several students found no fault with the sentence, "In sports like fencing for a long time many of our varsity team members had no previous experience anyway." Finally, the students were less likely than the expert writers to diagnose the source of a problem with a sentence. For example, a student might say, "This sentence just doesn't sound right," whereas an expert might say, "The subject and the verb don't agree here."

In other situations, however, expertise can be a drawback. Specifically, if you know too much, you may not recognize that the text could be unclear to readers with little background knowledge. Hayes (1989a) found that students who had acquired background knowledge on a topic were *less* likely to identify problem passages in an unclear essay on that topic. Ideally, writers should be sensitive to grammatical and organizational problems when they are revising a writing sample. However, they must also be able to adopt the viewpoint of a naive reader, who may not have enough background knowledge to understand a difficult technical paper.

SECTION SUMMARY: WRITING

1. In contrast to speaking, writing is an isolated task with less social feedback; it involves extensive revision and complex language and is also more permanent than speech.
2. The quality of writing is related to the amount and the quality of planning; outlining also enhances writing quality.
3. When people generate sentences during writing, the final essay is much longer than the outline; writers' fluent phases alternate with hesitant phases.
4. Expert writers are more likely than beginning college students to revise the organization, focus, and transitions in a paper; they are also more likely to notice defective sentences and to diagnose their specific problem; however, people who have background knowledge in an area may not be sensitive to the difficulties the text would present for naive readers.

BILINGUALISM

In these two chapters on language, we have considered four astonishingly complicated cognitive tasks: speech comprehension, reading, speaking, and writing. These tasks require the simultaneous coordination of cognitive skills, social knowledge, and physical gestures. We can marvel that human beings can manage all these tasks in one language—and then we remind ourselves that many people master two or more languages.

Only a fraction of North Americans consider themselves bilinguals, yet Snow (1993) points out that most of the people in the world are at least somewhat bilingual. Some people live in officially bilingual regions, such as Quebec, Belgium, and Switzerland. Some become bilingual because their home language is not the language used for school and business (for example, Zulu speakers in South Africa who must learn English). Immigrants frequently need to master the language of their new country. Figure 9.4 shows a message sent to Boston residents, reminding us that people who learn a second language often need to learn new written characters, as well as words and syntax. People also become bilinguals because colonization has imposed another language upon them, because they have studied language in school, or because they grew up in homes where two languages were used routinely.

A **bilingual** speaker is a person who uses two languages that differ in speech sounds, vocabulary, and syntax. Technically, we should use the term **multilingual** to refer to someone who uses more than two languages, but psycholinguists often use the term *bilingual* to include *multilinguals* as well (Taylor & Taylor, 1990). The bilingual's native language is referred to as the **first language** or **L1,** and the non-native language is the **second language** or **L2.**

A pioneer in research on bilingualism, Wallace Lambert, received the 1990 Distinguished Scientific Award for the Applications of Psychology, given by the American Psychological Association. Lambert introduced an important distinction between additive and subtractive bilingualism. In **additive bilingualism,** an individual acquires proficiency in a second language with no loss in his or her first language; both languages are associated with respect and prestige. For example, English speakers in Quebec usually learn French if they run a business. In **subtractive bilingualism,** the new language replaces the first language. Unfortunately, most linguistic minority groups in the United States and Canada are pressured to develop high-level skills in English at the expense of their first language, producing subtractive bilingualism (Lambert, 1990).

The North American educational system values additive bilingualism; we want our nonminority, middle-class children to acquire French or German. However, that same educational system seldom sees the value of keeping a child fluent in a first language such as Spanish, Vietnamese, or Arabic; subtractive bilingualism often predominates for immigrant children.

As you can imagine, the topic of bilingualism has important political and social psychological implications, especially when educators and politicians make statements about various ethnic groups. These same social psychological forces are important when an individual wants to become bilingual. One of the most important predictors in acquiring a second language is a person's attitude toward the people who speak that language. In fact, researchers have tried to predict the ability of English Canadian high-school students in learning French (Gardner & Lambert,

---

A Notice Sent to Boston Residents by a Telephone Company. The Languages on the Notice Include English, Portuguese, Spanish, Vietnamese, French, Chinese, and Cambodian.

What You Should Know About Automatic Dialing Services.

This is an important notice. Please have it translated.

Este é um aviso importante. Queira mandá-lo traduzir.

Este es un aviso importante. Sírvase mandarlo traducir.

ĐÂY LÀ MỘT BẢN THÔNG CÁO QUAN TRỌNG
XIN VUI LÒNG CHO DỊCH LẠI THÔNG CÁO ẤY

Ceci est important. Veuillez faire traduire.

本通知很重要。请将之译成中文。

នេះគឺជាដំណឹងល្អ សូមមេត្តាបកប្រែជូនផង

1959; Lambert, 1992). The students' *attitude* toward French Canadians was just as important as their cognitive, language-learning *aptitude*. Not surprisingly, the relationship between attitudes and language proficiency also works in the reverse direction; elementary school English Canadians who learn French develop more positive attitudes toward French Canadians than do children in a control group (Lambert, 1987).

The topic of bilingualism is so interesting and complex that some colleges offer an entire course in the subject. We will limit our discussion here to three cognitive issues: (1) the advantages and disadvantages of bilingualism, (2) code switching, and (3) an in-depth consideration of the relationship between age of acquisition and proficiency in the second language.

Advantages and Disadvantages of Bilingualism

The early theorists suggested that bilingualism is harmful. For example, Jespersen (1922) said, "The brain effort required to master the two languages instead of one certainly diminishes the child's power of learning other things which might and ought to be learnt" (p. 148). According to that view, an individual's cognitive capacity is limited, and thought is less efficient because the brain stores two linguistic systems (Lambert, 1990). The early research on bilingualism seemed to support that conclusion. However, this research was seriously flawed; lower-class bilinguals were compared with middle-class monolinguals, with all of the achievement and IQ testing conducted in the monolingual child's language (Reynolds, 1991a).

You can imagine, then, the impact caused by the first well-controlled study comparing monolinguals with bilinguals: Bilinguals were found to be more advanced in school, they scored better on tests of first language skills, and they showed greater mental flexibility (Peal & Lambert, 1962). The original research was conducted in Montreal, and the results have been confirmed by carefully conducted research in Singapore, Switzerland, South Africa, Israel, and New York (Lambert, 1990).

In addition to gaining fluency in a second language, bilinguals seem to have a number of advantages over monolinguals.

1. Bilinguals actually acquire more expertise in their native (first) language. For example, English-speaking Canadian children whose classes are taught in French gain greater understanding of English language structure (Diaz, 1985; Lambert et al., 1991).

2. Bilinguals are more aware that the names assigned to concepts are arbitrary (Bialystok, 1987, 1988; Hakuta, 1986). For example, monolingual children cannot imagine that a cow could just as easily have been assigned the name, *dog*.

3. Bilingual children are more sensitive to some pragmatic aspects of language. For example, English-speaking children whose classes are taught in French are more aware that when you speak to a blindfolded child, you need to supply additional information (Genesee et al., 1975).

4. Bilingual children are more likely to show cognitive flexibility on tests of creativity, such as thinking of a wide variety of different uses for a paper clip (Scott, 1973).

5. Bilinguals also perform better on tests of nonverbal intelligence that require reorganization of visual patterns, and on concept formation tasks that require mental flexibility (Peal & Lambert, 1962).

Are there any *disadvantages* to being bilingual? People who use two languages extensively may subtly alter their pronunciation of some speech sounds in both languages (Caramazza et al., 1973). Bilinguals are also slightly slower in making some kinds of decisions about language, though these are unlikely to hamper communication. For example, an English-French bilingual may be momentarily uncertain whether a passage is written in English or in French (Taylor & Taylor, 1990). Bilinguals may also take somewhat longer to decide whether a string of letters (either a nonsense word or an English word) is actually an English word (Ransdell & Fischler, 1987). As Insup Taylor—a multilingual who speaks Korean, Japanese, and English—concludes in her psycholinguistics textbook, "Bilinguals may experience a slight disadvantage in language-processing speed over monolinguals, but this disadvantage is far outweighed by the advantages of being able to function in two languages (Taylor & Taylor, 1990, p. 340).

Code Switching

Code switching refers to a bilingual's tendency to switch from one language to another when speaking to other bilinguals. To quote the title of an article on code switching, "Sometimes I'll start a sentence in English y termino en español" (Poplack, 1980). A bilingual is especially likely to switch to another language for a phrase that is overlearned or better expressed in that language (Taylor & Taylor, 1990).

Intriguingly, people may prefer to switch codes to their second language when they need to talk about something embarrassing. In one study, Cantonese-English bilinguals in Hong Kong were asked to discuss an embarrassing topic (for example, a personally embarrassing episode they experienced recently). They talked longer on these embarrassing subjects in English than in Cantonese, their first language. Obviously, code switching involves social factors as well as linguistic factors (Bond & Lai, 1986; Romaine, 1989).

◇ In Depth: *Second-Language Proficiency as a Function of Age of Acquisition*

A number of years ago, I recall meeting a family who had moved to the United States from Iceland and had been in their new country only one week. Both highly intelligent and highly educated parents had studied English in school for at least 10 years, yet they clearly struggled to understand and produce conversational speech. In contrast, their 4-year-old son had already picked up a good deal of English with no formal training. When the time came to leave, the parents haltingly said their goodbyes, and the 4-year-old—in unaccented English—shouted enthusiastically, "See you later, alligator!"

This anecdote raises the question about the relationship between the age at which you begin to learn a second language and your eventual proficiency in that language. We will focus on a study by Johnson and Newport (1989) after considering some background research. Finally, we will consider possible explanations for these results.

Background Research.   You probably will not be surprised to learn that people who acquire a second language during early childhood are more likely to master the **phonology,** or speech sounds, of this second language than those who acquire a second language during adulthood (Snow, 1993; Taylor & Taylor, 1990). A representative study examined immigrants to Great Britain from 20 different language backgrounds that included such diverse languages as Armenian, Cantonese, and Spanish (Tahta et al., 1981). Each individual read a short passage in English, and this reading was graded by three English-speaking judges. The results showed a clear-cut relationship between age at which the individual began to learn English and the rated degree of foreign accent. Those who had learned English before 7 years of age were judged to have no foreign accent, whereas those who had learned English after age 14 typically spoke with a stronger accent.

Other language skills are also influenced by the **age-at-arrival effect;** that is, people are more likely to be proficient at a second language if they immigrated to the second country at an early age. For example, Mägiste (1986) found that German children who moved to Sweden at age 8 required only four years to name objects just as quickly in Swedish as in German. In contrast, German children who moved to Sweden at age 14 required six years to reach the same degree of proficiency in naming objects. Similarly, age at arrival is correlated with an individual's skill in understanding English sentences that are accompanied by a noisy background.

Related research comes from information about congenitally deaf individuals for whom American Sign Language is the first language. Deaf children whose parents are also deaf are exposed to sign language from birth, but children of hearing parents learn sign language at a later age, once they reach school. Newport studied only individuals who had at least 40 years' experience with sign language (Newport, 1990; Newport & Supalla, 1993). Thus, the researchers could be confident that their research participants had achieved asymptotic performance (that is, ultimate expertise in sign language). The results were clear. People who were exposed to sign language at birth received higher scores than those who had learned sign language between the ages of 4 and 6, who in turn received higher scores than those who had learned it after the age of 11. Furthermore, the advantage of early acquisition held true for both comprehension and production.

In summary, this research has shown an age-at-arrival effect for the mastery of speech sounds and skill at naming objects. Furthermore, age of acquisition is correlated with sign-language proficiency. The research of Jacqueline Johnson and Elisa Newport (1989) then examined how age at arrival seems to be related to proficiency in some grammatical forms in English.

Johnson and Newport's Research. Johnson and Newport decided to study Chinese and Korean speakers who had learned English as a second language. These two Asian languages were selected because they are less similar to English than European languages, such as Spanish and French. Thus, speakers of both Asian languages would be expected to have difficulty mastering English syntax. All speakers were selected from the students and faculty at the University of Illinois, so they currently shared a similar English-speaking environment.

Each research participant was tested extensively for mastery of English grammar. In each case, the participant judged whether or not a spoken sentence was grammatically correct. A total of 12 different grammatical rules were tested. Here are some representative rule types and examples of ungrammatical sentences:

1. Past tense: Yesterday the hunter shoots a deer.
2. Pronouns: Susan is making some cookies for we.
3. Prepositions: The man climbed the ladder up carefully.

FIGURE 9.5

The Relationship Between Age at Arrival in the United States and Total Score on the Test of English Grammar (From Johnson & Newport, 1989).

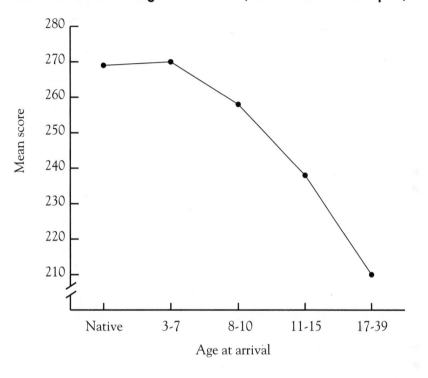

4. Wh- questions: When Sam will fix his car?
5. Word order: Martha a question asked the policeman.

Figure 9.5 shows the relationship between age of arrival in the United States and total score on this test of English grammar. As you can see, people who arrived in the United States between 3 and 7 years of age received scores identical to the scores received by native speakers of English. Beyond the age of 7, however, age of arrival had a major impact on test scores. Overall, the data showed a strong negative correlation between age at arrival and grammatical proficiency. The correlation coefficient (r) was −.77, which was highly significant. (An r of .00 would indicate no relationship, whereas an r of −1.00 would be a perfect negative correlation.)

At this point, you may wonder whether those who acquired English at an early age had simply spent more years in the United States and therefore had more years of practice speaking English, thus producing higher scores. However, the correlation coefficient between years in the United States and test scores was not significant ($r = .16$). Thus, this alternate explanation cannot account for the major part of the relationship between age of arrival and mastery of these grammatical forms.

Explanations for the Results. Why do people seem to have a special advantage when they learn a foreign language during childhood? Some years ago, Lenneberg (1967) suggested that humans have a critical period for language acquisition. According to the **critical period hypothesis,** learners are best able to achieve a particular skill during a limited period, early in their maturational development (Hurford, 1991). Johnson and Newport (1989) support the general notion of a critical period for the acquisition of some forms of language. As they say, "Human beings appear to have a special capacity for acquiring language in childhood, regardless of whether the language is their first or second." (p. 95)

To some extent, children may learn a second language more effectively than adults because of neurological explanations. An older person's brain may be less plastic and less able to accomplish the reorganization required in learning a new language. However, other factors may also facilitate language acquisition in younger people. For example, young children may be less inhibited about trying out a sentence that might be incorrect (Harley, 1986; Johnson & Newport, 1989).

Johnson and Newport also comment in more detail about the nature of the proposed critical period for second-language acquisition. First, Lenneberg (1967) had proposed that normal language learning was possible prior to puberty, but performance dropped suddenly at the onset of puberty. However, as you can see from Figure 9.5, the decline seems to be gradual, beginning well before puberty. Secondly, people *can* learn a second language during adulthood. Their scores suggest considerable proficiency, even if they do not typically achieve the same fluency that a native speaker might have. However, individual differences are extensive for people who learn a second language as adults; some achieve a competence that almost rivals a native speaker's command of English, whereas others find difficulty with the many different components of our challenging English language.

Keep in mind, too, that we should not generalize these results inappropriately. Adults whose first language is closer to English may learn to speak English quite well.

As a final exercise in helping you understand bilingualism, try Demonstration 9.6 at your next opportunity. Quite clearly, bilinguals and multilinguals provide the best demonstration of how Theme 2 applies to language, because they manage to master accurate and rapid communication in two or more languages.

SECTION SUMMARY: BILINGUALISM

1. In additive bilingualism, both languages are associated with prestige; in subtractive bilingualism, the first language is considered less prestigious, and

---

DEMONSTRATION 9.6

EXPLORING BILINGUALISM.

If you are fortunate enough to be a bilingual or a multilingual, you can answer these questions yourself. If you are not, perhaps you know someone well enough that you would feel comfortable asking him or her the following questions:

1. How old were you when you were first exposed to your second language?
2. Under what circumstances did you acquire this second language? For example, did you have formal lessons in this language?
3. When you began to learn this second language, did you find yourself becoming any less fluent in your native language? If so, can you provide any examples?
4. Do you think you have any special insights about the nature of language that a monolingual may not have?
5. When you are with another person who is bilingual in the same languages you speak, do you find yourself switching back and forth between the two languages? Can you think of any particular situations in which you might be especially likely to switch from one language to the other?
6. If you had to talk about something embarrassing that happened to you, in which language would you choose to discuss it? Are there any topics or kinds of conversation for which you prefer one language, rather than the other?
7. Does the North American culture (including peer groups) discourage bilinguals from using their first language?

---

proficiency in this language may be lost as the second language is acquired. Attitudes are an important determinant of bilingual skills.

2. Well-controlled research shows that bilinguals have an advantage over monolinguals in their understanding of first-language structure, the arbitrary nature of concept names, and pragmatic aspects of language; bilinguals also receive higher scores on tests of cognitive flexibility and nonverbal intelligence. However, bilinguals may alter the pronunciation of speech sounds and they may take longer to make some language-processing decisions.
3. Bilinguals may engage in code switching, and they may prefer to discuss embarrassing topics in their second language.
4. People who acquire a second language at an early age are better at phonology and naming objects, compared to those who learn a second language during adulthood; early language acquisition is also advantageous for those who learn American Sign Language.
5. According to Johnson and Newport, Chinese and Koreans who learn English at an early age also show greater mastery of some forms of English grammar.

CHAPTER REVIEW QUESTIONS

1. In general, what are the important cognitive tasks involved in language production (Chapter 9) that are not required in language comprehension (Chapter 8)?
2. What information do we have about the way people plan their sentences? What effect can a previous sentence have on the specific word choices planned for the next sentence?
3. What is the linearization problem? Why would it be more relevant in language production—either speaking or writing—than it would be when you create a mental image (Chapter 6)?
4. Think of a speech error you recently heard or made yourself. What kind of error is this, according to Dell's classification, and how would Dell's theory explain this particular error?
5. How are gestures important in the production of language, and what do they contribute to spoken language?
6. Analyze the next conversation you overhear from the viewpoint of the social context of speech. Pay particular attention to (a) the establishment of common ground, (b) the given-new strategy, (c) conversational format, and (d) directives.
7. What are the differences between writing and speaking? How do both of these cognitive tasks illustrate how the different phases of language production overlap?
8. Based on the material in this chapter, what hints could you adopt to produce a better paper the next time you are given a formal writing assignment?
9. What are additive and subtractive bilingualism? What advantages do bilinguals have over monolinguals, and what are their potential disadvantages?
10. In what areas do bilinguals seem to have an advantage if they acquire their second language during childhood, rather than adulthood? How does the critical period hypothesis relate to these findings? Why should you be cautious about overgeneralizing these results?

NEW TERMS

the linearization problem
slips-of-the-tongue
gestures
pragmatics
common ground
given-new strategy
directive
indirect speech acts
hedges
bilingual

multilingual
first language (L1)
second language (L2)
additive bilingualism
subtractive bilingualism
code switching
phonology
age-at-arrival effect
critical period hypothesis

RECOMMENDED READINGS

Gleason, J. B., & Ratner, N. B. (1993). *Psycholinguistics*. Fort Worth, TX: Harcourt Brace Jovanovich. Two well-written chapters in this book—one on conversational discourse and one on bilingualism—are especially strong, current discussions of the research.

Hayes, J. R. (1989a). Writing research: The analysis of a very complex task. In D. Klahr & K. Kotovsky (Eds), *Complex information processing: The impact of Herbert A. Simon* (pp. 209–234). Hillsdale, NJ: Erlbaum. At present, this chapter offers the best summary of the research on cognitive aspects of writing.

Reynolds, A. G. (Ed.). (1991b). *Bilingualism, multiculturalism, and second language learning: The McGill Conference in Honour of Wallace E. Lambert*. Hillsdale, NJ: Erlbaum. In this volume, a number of researchers who have been associated with Wallace Lambert summarize the research on linguistic and social consequences of bilingualism.

Taylor, I., & Taylor, M. M. (1990). *Psycholinguistics: Learning and using language*. Englewood Cliffs, NJ: Prentice Hall. This undergraduate textbook contains relevant material on social aspects of conversation and bilingualism.

CHAPTER 10

PROBLEM SOLVING AND CREATIVITY

PREVIEW

We use problem solving when we want to reach a particular goal, but that goal cannot be easily reached. This chapter considers four aspects of problem solving: (1) understanding the problem, (2) problem-solving approaches, (3) factors that influence problem solving, and (4) creativity.

When you understand a problem, you construct an internal representation of the problem. You can use many alternate methods to represent the problem, such as lists, graphs, and visual images.

Some problem-solving approaches involve algorithms, which are methods that will always produce a solution. Heuristics, in contrast, do not always produce a solution, though they require less time. Two heuristics are the means-ends heuristic and the analogy approach; in the In-Depth section on the analogy approach, we'll explore why this heuristic is not used more effectively.

Several factors influence the way people approach and solve problems. For instance, the recent research on expertise has identified seven advantages that experts have over novices. Mental set and functional fixedness are barriers to problem solving that involve cognitive rigidity. Furthermore, the approach you take to solving a problem also depends upon whether the problem is well defined and whether it requires insight.

Creativity can be defined as finding a solution that is both unusual and useful. We will consider two methods designed to enhance creativity. Also, we'll examine how creativity can be influenced by taking a break (incubation) and by social factors, such as having your work evaluated.

INTRODUCTION

You solve dozens of problems every day. Think about all the problems you solved yesterday, for example. Perhaps you wanted to leave a note for a professor, but you had no pen or pencil. An essay exam may have asked you to compare two theories that seemed entirely unrelated. Perhaps you had planned to make an interesting main course for dinner but arrived home to find bare cupboards. In spite of the fact that you spent most of the day solving problems, you may have sat down to relax late at night—and solved more problems. Perhaps you played a card game or read a mystery novel or solved a crossword puzzle.

Problem solving is inescapable in everyday life. In fact, most jobs require some kind of problem solving—whether we consider managers, auto mechanics, doctors, teachers, counselors, or some other occupation (Lesgold, 1988; Sinnott, 1989).

You use **problem solving** when you want to reach a certain goal, but that goal is not readily available. You face a problem whenever a gap exists between where you are now and where you want to be—and you do not know how to cross that gap (Hayes, 1989b; Mayer, 1985).

A problem consists of three features: (1) the original state, (2) the goal state, and (3) the rules. For example, suppose you want to go shopping in a nearby town. The **original state** describes the situation at the beginning of the problem. In this case, it might be, "I am in my room, five miles from that town, with no car and no public transportation." The **goal state** is reached when the problem is solved. Here, it would be, "I want to be in a town five miles away." The **rules** describe the restrictions that must be followed in proceding from the original state to the goal state. The rules in this hypothetical problem might include the following: "I can't borrow a car from a stranger" and "I can't drive a stick-shift car." Think about a problem you have recently solved and determine the original state, goal state, and rules, so that you are familiar with these terms.

One aspect of problem solving that has received relatively little attention is problem *finding* (Brown & Walter, 1990). One example of problem finding was reported by leaders of a British company, who discovered that they were requesting unnecessary paperwork from their employees. The company leaders had previously been unaware that any problem existed. One year after finding the problem, 26 million cards and sheets of paper were eliminated—and presumably employees felt less overwhelmed (Bransford et al., 1987). However, the solution would never have occurred if the problem hadn't first been discovered.

Children seem to seek out problems spontaneously, though adults typically do not (Thomas, 1989). Some educators argue that our formal education discourages us from learning to find problems and ask questions (Brown & Walter, 1990). One writer observed:

> Recently a teacher was overheard to announce: "When I want your questions, I'll give them to you." Much of school practice consists of giving definite, almost concrete answers. Perhaps boredom sets in as answers are given to questions that were never asked. (Gowin, 1981, p. 127)

Because so little information on problem finding is available, this chapter will emphasize problem solving. Throughout this chapter, we will emphasize the active nature of cognitive processes in problem solving, consistent with Theme 1. When people solve problems, they seldom take a random, trial-and-error approach, blindly trying different options until one option finally provides a solution. Instead, they plan their attacks, typically breaking a problem into its component steps and devising a plan for solving each component. In addition to plans, problem solvers also use strategies. We will emphasize that people frequently use certain kinds of strategies that are likely to produce a solution relatively quickly. As this textbook stresses, humans are not passive beings that absorb information from the environment. Instead, we plan our approach to problems, choosing strategies that are likely to provide useful solutions.

Our first topic in this chapter is understanding the problem. Then we will consider a variety of problem-solving approaches, as well as factors that influence problem solving. Our final topic is a particularly puzzling area of problem solving: creativity.

UNDERSTANDING THE PROBLEM

Some years ago, the companies in a New York City skyscraper faced a major problem. The people in the building were continually complaining that the elevators moved too slowly. Numerous consultants were brought in, but the complaints only increased. When people threatened to move out, plans were drawn up to add an extremely expensive new set of elevators. Before reconstruction began, however, someone decided to add mirrors in the lobbies near the elevators. The complaints stopped. Apparently, the original problem-solvers had not properly understood the problem. In fact, the real problem wasn't the speed of the elevators, but the boredom of waiting for them to arrive (Thomas, 1989).

What do we mean when we say that we understand a problem? According to Greeno (1977), **understanding** involves constructing an internal representation. For example, if you understand a sentence, you create some internal representation or pattern in your head so that concepts are related to each other in the same way that they are related to each other in the original sentence. To create this pattern in your head you must use background knowledge, such as the meaning of the various words in the sentence.

Greeno believes that understanding has three requirements: coherence, correspondence, and relationship to background knowledge. Let us look at each of these components in more detail.

A coherent representation is a pattern that is connected, so that all the parts make sense. For example, consider Greeno's sentence, "Tree trunks are straws for thirsty leaves and branches" (p. 44). That sentence remains at the level of complete nonsense unless you see that it is based on the similarity of tree trunks and straws in moving liquid. Once you see the analogy, the fragments of the sentence become united. Similarly, look back at Demonstration 7.7. When you originally read that paragraph, it had no coherent representation in your head because many fragments were unrelated. However, once you had been told that the paragraph was about washing clothes, everything made sense. You had a coherent representation.

Greeno also proposes that understanding requires a close correspondence between the internal representation and the material that is being understood. Sometimes the internal representation is incomplete, and sometimes it is inaccurate. Important relations among the parts may be left out or mismatched. Think about an occasion when you noticed that an internal representation and the material to be understood did not correspond. I recall my mother giving her friend a recipe for yogurt, which included the sentence, "Then you put the yogurt in a warm blanket." The friend looked quite pained and asked, "But isn't it awfully messy to wash the blanket out?" The friend's internal representation unfortunately omitted the fact that the yogurt was in a container.

DEMONSTRATION 10.1

THE FIVE-HANDED-MONSTER PROBLEM (FROM SIMON & HAYES, 1976, P. 168).

Read over this problem and underline the parts of the sentences you consider most important.

1. Three five-handed extraterrestrial monsters were holding three crystal globes.
2. Because of the quantum-mechanical peculiarities of their neighborhood, both monsters and globes come in exactly three sizes with no others permitted: small, medium, and large.
3. The medium-sized monster was holding the small globe; the small monster was holding the large globe; and the large monster was holding the medium-sized globe.
4. Since this situation offended their keenly developed sense of symmetry, they proceeded to transfer globes from one monster to another so that each monster would have a globe proportionate to his own size.
5. Monster etiquette complicated the solution of the problem since it requires: that only one globe may be transferred at a time; that if a monster is holding two globes, only the larger of the two may be transferred; and that a globe may not be transferred to a monster who is holding a larger globe.
6. By what sequence of transfers could the monsters have solved this problem?

Greeno's third criterion for good understanding is that the material to be understood must be related to the understander's background knowledge. This point has probably occurred to you if you have ever found yourself enrolled in an advanced-level course without the proper prerequisite courses or if you have ever looked at a professional article in an area unfamiliar to you. Vocabulary and concepts must be familiar for material to be understood. Greeno summarizes his previous research on this topic, which involved people solving probability problems. Those who were told the meanings of basic concepts in probability were better at solving word problems than those who were only taught the formulas.

The first step in understanding a problem is deciding what information is crucial and which is irrelevant. The second step is deciding how to represent the problem.

Paying Attention to Important Information

To understand a problem, you must pay attention to the crucial information, ignoring irrelevant information. Notice, then, that one complex cognitive task—problem solving—relies on another cognitive activity—attention. This is another example of the inter-relatedness of our cognitive processes (Theme 4). Read over the problem in Demonstration 10.1 and decide which parts are most important.

DEMONSTRATION 10.2

USING SYMBOLS IN PROBLEM SOLVING.

Solve the following problem: Mary is ten years younger than twice Susan's age. Five years from now, Mary will be eight years older than Susan's age at that time. How old are Mary and Susan? (The answer is found in the discussion in the text.)

Simon and Hayes (1976) asked 20 people to solve this problem, thinking aloud as they worked. The authors recorded what the participants said and also recorded the number of times each sentence was reread before the participants made their first move. Sentence 3 was reread a total of 23 times; this sentence describes the present situation. Sentence 4 was reread only nine times; this sentence describes the goal state. Sentence 5 was reread 32 times; this sentence describes the rules. All other sentences combined were reread only five times.

What kinds of sentences did people pay attention to? Simon and Hayes argue that they will reread a sentence if (1) they believe the information in the sentence is relevant to the task and (2) they have not stored the information in memory. For instance, Sentences 1 and 2 contain information that is either irrelevant (for example, that the monsters each have five hands) or repeated later (for example, the sizes of the monsters and the globes). The last part of Sentence 4 is relevant to the task, but the information in that sentence—that each monster must hold a globe of a corresponding size—can easily be stored in memory. Consequently it does not deserve rereading.

Sentences 3 and 5, in contrast, are both relevant and complicated. These are the sentences that are difficult to store in memory. As a result, people must return to these sentences and reread them before they begin the problem. Furthermore, Simon and Hayes (1976) noticed that people also reread these sentences *after* they had begun to make moves. They seldom reread the other sentences once they had begun the problem.

Were your judgments about the importance of the sentences in Demonstration 10.1 similar to the rereading patterns that Simon and Hayes found? Did you tend to ignore parts of certain sentences? One person in the Simon and Hayes study read the phrase, "Because of the quantum-mechanical pecularities of their neighborhood . . . " and commented, "Forget that garbage!" (Hayes, 1978, p. 198). You may have had the same response.

In Chapter 8 we discussed computer programs designed to process natural English, such as articles in newspapers. Kintsch and Greeno (1985) have designed a program that solves arithmetic word problems, such as "Joe has eight marbles. He has five more marbles than Tom. How many marbles does Tom have?" Obviously, the arithmetic operation in this question is no challenge to a computer. However, humans can easily pay attention to some words and ignore others. A major challenge in designing a computer program is specifying how the system determines which words deserve attention.

Attention is also important in problem understanding because competing thoughts can produce divided attention. Bransford and Stein (1984) presented algebra word problems to a group of college students. You remember these problems—a typical one might ask about a train traveling in one direction and a bird flying in another direction. The students were asked to note their thoughts and feelings as they inspected the problem. For a substantial number of students, their initial reactions to the problem included thoughts, such as "Oh no, this is a mathematical word problem—I hate those things" and "Boy, am I going to look stupid!" These negative thoughts occurred frequently throughout the 5 minutes allotted to the task. Clearly, they drained attention from the central task of problem solving. Real-world problem solving frequently occurs in divided-attention tasks. Hunt and Lansman (1986) point out, for example, that the task of driving a car through an unfamiliar city in rush-hour traffic is a divided-attention issue. You must solve the problem of reaching your goal while watching other cars, pedestrians, and traffic lights.

Consider, too, the number of problems we face in everyday life in which the major challenge is discovering what information is important and what is irrelevant. Your statistics professor, for example, may include a problem on a test that has many details about the experimental design that are really not important for the solution of the problem. There may even be extra statistical information that you will not need in finding the answer. The challenge in the problem may really be to decide what information merits attention. Also, consider how this idea of discovering essential information can be applied to some riddles. Halpern (1989) poses this one:

> Suppose you are a bus driver. On the first stop you pick up 6 men and 2 women. At the second stop 2 men leave and 1 woman boards the bus. At the third stop 1 man leaves and 2 women enter the bus. At the fourth stop 3 men get on and 3 women get off. At the fifth stop, 2 men get off, 3 men get on, 1 woman gets off and 2 women get on. What is the bus driver's name? (p. 392)

A major problem in understanding a problem is focusing on the appropriate part of the problem (Mayer, 1989). If you paid attention to the bus driver problem, you could solve it without rereading it. However, if you didn't pay attention, you can locate the answer in the first sentence.

Methods of Representing the Problem

As soon as the problem solver has decided which information is essential and which can be disregarded, the next step is to find a good way to represent the problem. Simon and Hayes (1976) argue that people regard problems like the one in Demonstration 10.1 as a "cover story" for the "real problem." Thus they must discover the abstract puzzle underneath all the details, and then they must find a good way to represent this abstract puzzle. Think about your reaction to Demonstration 10.1, for example. Did you really think it was a problem about five-handed monsters? Instead, you probably saw it as a puzzle in which certain objects were to be exchanged according to certain rules.

If people regard problems as being abstract, then a difficulty arises. After all, an abstract problem is difficult to keep in memory while you perform operations. Therefore, people typically invent some method of representing the abstract problem in a concrete way—a particular concrete way that shows only the essential information.

Symbols. Sometimes the most effective way to represent an abstract problem is by using symbols, as students learn to do in high-school algebra. Try Demonstration 10.2, for example. The usual way of solving this problem is to let a symbol such as m represent Mary's age and a symbol such as s represent Susan's age. We can then "translate" each sentence into a formula. The first sentence becomes:

$$m = 2s - 10$$

The second sentence becomes:

$$m + 5 = s + 5 + 8$$

Now we can substitute for m in the second equation:

$$2s - 10 + 5 = s + 5 + 8$$

Therefore we find that:

$$s = 18$$

Substituting for s in the first equation, we find that:

$$m = 26$$

Finally, we have to translate the symbols back into words; Susan is 18 and Mary is 26.

Of course, as you learned in algebra, the major problem is learning to translate words into symbols. Schoenfield (1982) describes how calculus students were asked to rephrase simple algebra problem statements so that they were more understandable. About 10 percent of the rephrasings included information that directly contradicted the input, and 20 percent contained information that was so confused that it was unintelligible. If you misunderstand a problem, you will not translate it accurately into symbols. (And, incidentally, a proper understanding of a problem does not guarantee an appropriate translation into symbols!)

It seems likely that many errors occur in translating words into symbols, because people either have difficulty with the linguistic interpretation of the words or because they fail to remember all the critical material. In previous chapters, we have seen that people remember material that is consistent with their prior schemas. This same schema-consistent processing occurs when people try to solve problems (Mayer, 1989).

One common problem in translating sentences into symbols is that the problem solver often simplifies the sentence, thereby misrepresenting the information. Mayer (1982, 1985) asked college students to read a series of eight algebra story problems, and then recall them later. The problems contained some relational propositions such as "the rate in still water is 12 miles per hour more than the rate of the current" and simpler propositions such as "the cost of the candy is $1.70 per pound." The participants recalled only 71 percent of the relational propositions correctly, in contrast to 91 percent of the simpler propositions. Further analysis showed that the errors on the relational propositions frequently involved changing those statements into simpler forms, such as "the rate in still water is 12 miles per hour."

A further problem arises in the translation process because people bring their previous misconceptions with them when they begin to solve a problem. For example, several researchers have asked students without any background in physics to solve physics problems (Donley & Ashcraft, 1992; Green et al., 1985). Many of them hold misconceptions about the way objects move. Unfortunately, these misconceptions interfere with the proper translation of words into symbols.

Lists. In many problems, however, translating words into symbols will not get us very far. For example, the monster problem in Demonstration 10.1 cannot be

---

TABLE 10.1

REPRESENTING THE MONSTER PROBLEM IN A LIST.

	MONSTER SIZE	GLOBE SIZE
Step 1	Small Medium Large	Medium Large Small
Step 2	Small Medium Large	Medium — Large, Small
Step 3	Small Medium Large	— Medium Large, Small

TABLE 10.2

REPRESENTING THE MONSTER PROBLEM IN A MATRIX.

| | MONSTER SIZE | | |
	SMALL	MEDIUM	LARGE
Step 1	Medium	Large	Small
Step 2	Medium	—	Large, Small
Step 3	—	Medium	Large, Small

handled by the symbols used in an algebra problem. We could approach the problem by making a list, as in Table 10.1. However, notice how quickly the list becomes bulky. It is hard to keep track of which monster has which ball, so in this instance a list is not very helpful. Now try Demonstration 10.3 before you read further.

Matrices. Simon and Hayes (1976b) found that more than 50 percent of participants spontaneously constructed some kind of matrix to represent the monster

DEMONSTRATION 10.3

THE COIN PROBLEM (BASED ON KEREN, 1984).

Three coins are supposed to be distributed between two children according to the following procedure. A regular deck of 52 cards (containing 26 red-faced and 26 black-faced cards) is well shuffled, and a card is randomly picked up. If the card is black, Chris gets a coin; if it's red, Pat gets a coin. After returning the card, the deck is again well shuffled and the second coin is distributed according to the same rule (black card, the coin goes to Chris; red card, the coin goes to Pat). Again the card is returned, the deck is well shuffled, and the third coin is distributed according to the same rule. Specify all the possibilities in which the three coins might be distributed between the two children. Now choose which of the following is most likely to occur:

a. One child will get 3 coins—the other none.
b. One child will get 2 coins—the other one.
c. Possibilities (a) and (b) are equally likely.

The answer is discussed in Figure 10.1.

FIGURE 10.1	

A Hierarchical Tree Diagram Used to Solve Demonstration 10.3.

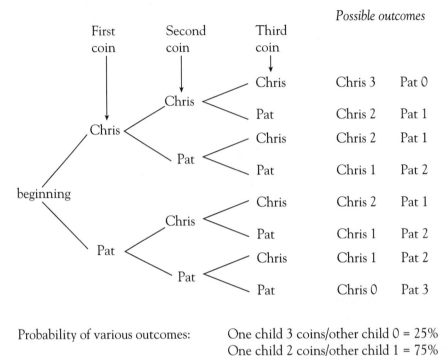

Possible outcomes

First coin	Second coin	Third coin		
		Chris	Chris 3	Pat 0
	Chris	Pat	Chris 2	Pat 1
Chris		Chris	Chris 2	Pat 1
	Pat	Pat	Chris 1	Pat 2
beginning		Chris	Chris 2	Pat 1
	Chris	Pat	Chris 1	Pat 2
Pat		Chris	Chris 1	Pat 2
	Pat	Pat	Chris 0	Pat 3

Probability of various outcomes: One child 3 coins/other child 0 = 25%
One child 2 coins/other child 1 = 75%

Therefore, the correct answer to Demonstration 10.3 is b.

problem. A **matrix** is a chart that shows the possible combinations. In the case of the monster problem, the matrix shows which monster has which globe at different times, as in Table 10.2. A matrix is an excellent way to keep track of objects, particularly when the problem is a complex one and the relevant information is categorical (Halpern, 1989).

Hierarchical Tree Diagram. Demonstration 10.3 showed a problem that can be represented in several different ways. One way, for example, is to list the four possible outcomes: Chris 3, Pat 0; Chris 0, Pat 3; Chris 2, Pat 1; and Chris 1, Pat 2. However, a list format is deceptive because it encourages the problem solver to assume that all the options on the list are equally probable. When Keren (1984) presented this problem to college students, only 40 percent who used the list format eventually produced the correct answer.

A more satisfactory alternative for representing the problem is a **hierarchical tree diagram,** a figure that uses a treelike structure to specify every possible outcome and is especially effective in assessing the mathematical probability of various outcomes (Halpern, 1989). Notice that in Figure 10.1 the hierarchical tree diagram shows how the 2 coin/1 coin distribution can occur in six ways. In contrast, the 0 coin/3 coin distribution can occur in only two ways. Keren found that 80 percent of students who used a hierarchical tree diagram eventually produced the correct answer. In other words, the hierarchical tree diagram was twice as successful as the simple list in producing the correct response.

Graphs. For some problems, however, symbols, lists, matrices, and hierarchical tree diagrams are not useful. Consider, for example, the Buddhist monk problem in Demonstration 10.4. An effective way to approach this problem is by making a graph. As Figure 10.2 shows, we can use one line to show the monk going up the mountain on the first day. We use another line to show the monk coming down the mountain several days later. The point at which the lines cross tell us the spot that the monk will pass at the same time on each of the two days. I have drawn the lines so that they cross at a point 1,200 feet up the mountain at 1:00 P.M. However, even if you vary the monk's rate (for example, so that he goes up slowly and comes down quickly), the two paths must always cross at some point.

Visual Images. Other people prefer to solve the Buddhist monk problem visually. One young woman who chose a visual approach to this problem reported the following:

DEMONSTRATION 10.4

THE BUDDHIST MONK PROBLEM.

Exactly at sunrise one morning, a Buddhist monk set out to climb a tall mountain. The narrow path was not more than a foot or two wide, and it wound around the mountain to a beautiful, glittering temple at the mountain peak.

The monk climbed the path at varying rates of speed. He stopped many times along the way to rest and to eat the fruit he carried with him. He reached the temple just before sunset. At the temple, he fasted and meditated for several days. Then he began his journey back along the same path, starting at sunrise and walking, as before, at variable speeds with many stops along the way. However, his average speed going down the hill was greater than his average climbing speed.

Prove that there must be a spot along the path that the monk will pass on both trips at exactly the same time of day. (The answer is found in Figure 10.2.)

FIGURE 10.2

A Graphic Representation of the Buddhist Monk Problem.

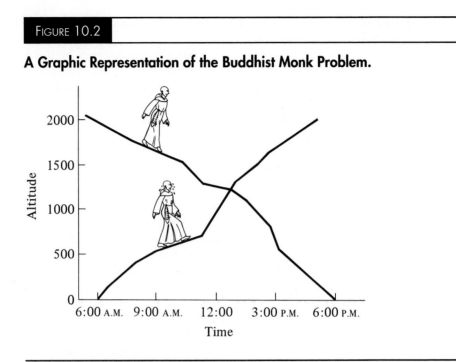

I tried this and that, until I got fed up with the whole thing, but the image of that monk in his saffron robe walking up the hill kept persisting in my mind. Then a moment came when, superimposed on this image, I saw another, more transparent one, of the monk walking *down* the hill, and I realized in a flash that the two figures *must* meet at some point some time—regardless at what speed they walk and how often each of them stops. Then I reasoned out what I already knew: whether the monk descends two days or three days later comes to the same; so I was quite justified in letting him descend on the same day, in duplicate so to speak. (Koestler, 1964, p. 184)

As Koestler points out, a visual image has the advantage of being *irrational*. After all, how could the monk meet himself coming down the mountain? Thus, the visual image can let us escape from the boundaries of traditional representations. At the same time, however, the visual image is somewhat concrete; it serves as a symbol for a theory that has not yet been thoroughly developed. This may partially explain why visual representations are particularly useful in solving novel problems (Kaufmann, 1985).

We need to point out that problem-solvers do not exclusively use just verbal representations or just imagery to solve a puzzle. For example, the image of the monks is certainly associated with some words (Gellatly, 1986a). Also, some imagery representations may be more effective than others. For example, Adeyemo (1990) asked college students to construct a novel coat rack, given only a specified

---

REPRESENTATIONS OF PROBLEMS.

Read the information and answer the question at the bottom of the demonstration. (The answer is at the end of the chapter.)

Five people are in a hospital. Each one has only one disease, and each has a different disease. Each one occupies a separate room; room numbers are 101–105.

1. The person with asthma is in Room 101.
2. Ms. Jones has heart disease.
3. Ms. Green is in Room 105.
4. Ms. Smith has tuberculosis.
5. The woman with mononucleosis is in Room 104.
6. Ms. Thomas is in Room 101.
7. Ms. Smith is in Room 102.
8. One of the patients, other than Ms. Anderson, has gall bladder disease.

What disease does Ms. Anderson have and in what room is she?

---

set of equipment. Students who created an image of an imaginary structure were much more successful in solving the problem than were students who created an image of a familiar coat rack.

Which Method is Best? We have seen that problems can be represented by symbols, lists, matrices, hierarchical tree diagrams, graphs, and visual images. Naturally, some problems cannot be represented by some of the methods. For example, the Buddhist monk problem will not fit into a matrix. However, as we saw in the case of Keren's coin study, some problems can be represented in several possible ways. Now that you have been exposed to six different representational formats, try Demonstration 10.5.

Which method works best for this particular problem? Schwartz (1971) examined this question in an article, "Modes of Representation and Problem Solving: Well Evolved is Half Solved." He gave people problems that involved "whodunit" types of solutions, such as the hospital-room problem. The participants were encouraged to show all their work, so that Schwartz could observe how they represented the problem.

Schwartz found that the representation method was related to whether the participants solved the problem. When people used a matrix to represent this kind of problem, 74 percent reached the solution. Other representations produced a solution between 40 percent and 55 percent of the time. People who did not use any particular representation method were successful only 25 percent of the time. For this kind of problem (though clearly not for all problems), the matrix representation was clearly the most effective.

We should point out, however, that Schwartz's study shows only that the representation method is related to the frequency of solution. We may be tempted to conclude that this method *caused* a higher frequency of solution, so that problem solvers could improve their accuracy by shifting to matrix representations. However, another interpretation for the data is that people who choose matrix representations are good problem solvers, and people who choose other representations are poor problem solvers. Telling these other people about matrix representation may not aid them substantially. At present, however, we can conclude that people who spontaneously use matrix representations are effective in solving this kind of problem.

SECTION SUMMARY: UNDERSTANDING THE PROBLEM

1. An important part of problem solving is problem finding; formal education places little emphasis on this part of the task.
2. Understanding the problem requires constructing an internal representation of the problem, which should have coherence, correspondence, and relationship to background knowledge.
3. People pay attention to the parts of the problem that seem relevant to the task and that are not stored in memory.
4. Methods for representing problems include symbols, lists, matrices, hierarchical tree diagrams, graphs, and visual images. For certain problems, some methods are more likely than others to produce a correct solution.

PROBLEM-SOLVING APPROACHES

Once you have represented the problem, you can use many different strategies to attack it. Some strategies are very time consuming. An **algorithm** is a method that will always produce a solution to the problem, sooner or later. One example of an algorithm is the method called **systematic random search,** in which you try out all possible answers using a specified system. For example, a high-school student faced with the algebra problem in Demonstration 10.2 could begin with $m = 0$ and $s = 0$ and try all possible values for m and s until the solution is reached. With such an inefficient algorithm, however, the exam would probably be over by the time the solution was obtained.

Newell and Simon (1972) observe that the time taken to search for an answer to a problem is roughly proportional to the total size of the problem space. The **problem space** is all the possible solutions to the problem that have occurred to the problem solver. Thus, the problem may have other solutions, but if the problem solver is not aware of these solutions, they are not included in the problem space.

Notice how the problem space can vary. The problem space for the anagram YBO is very small, whereas the problem space for the anagram LSSTNEUIAMYOUL is enormous.

Algorithms are often inefficient and unsophisticated. Other, more sophisticated methods cut down the part of the space that must be explored to find a solution. The problem solver thus begins with a large space at first. However, she or he applies relevant information about the problem in order to reduce the size of the problem space, leaving a relatively small space to examine. For example, to solve that lengthy anagram, you might pick out initial combinations of letters that are pronounceable, thereby narrowing the problem space (Greeno & Simon, 1988). Perhaps you would reject combinations such as LS, LT, and LN, but consider LE, LU, and hopefully SI. This strategy would probably lead you to a solution much faster than a systematic random search of all the more than 87 billion possible arrangements of the 14 letters in SIMULTANEOUSLY.

The strategy of looking only for pronounceable letter combinations is an example of a heuristic. As you know from other chapters, a heuristic is a rule of thumb. In problem solving, a **heuristic** is a rule of thumb involving a selective search, looking at only the portions of the problem space that are most likely to produce a solution.

We noted that algorithms such as a systematic random search will always produce a solution, although you may age a few years in the process. Heuristics, in contrast, do not guarantee a solution. For example, suppose you were given the anagram IPMHYLOD. If you used a heuristic of rejecting unlikely initial combinations such as LY, you would fail to find the correct solution, LYMPHOID. When making a decision, you'll need to weigh the benefits of an algorithm's speed against the costs of possibly missing the correct solution (Anderson, 1991; Du Boulay, 1989).

Psychologists have conducted more research on problem solvers' heuristics than on their algorithms. One reason is that algorithms do not exist for most everyday problems (for example, how to get to a nearby town). Furthermore, people are more likely to use heuristics. Two of the most widely used heuristics are means-ends analysis and the analogy.

The Means-Ends Heuristic

When you use the means-ends heuristic, you divide the problem into a number of **subproblems,** or smaller problems. You then solve each subproblem by detecting the difference between the original state and the goal state and then reducing the difference between these two states. The name **means-ends analysis** is appropriate, because it involves figuring out the "ends" you want and then figuring out the "means" you will use to reach those ends. As Sweller and Levine (1982) note, means-ends analysis concentrates the problem solver's attention on the difference between the current problem state and the goal state.

Every day we all solve problems by using means-ends analysis. Suppose, for example, that you are in the library at 9:37 in the morning and have just realized that you must miss an 11:00 class in industrial psychology because you must register for next semester's courses during that period. You know that the lecture will be important, and there will be an examination during the next class session that includes material from the class you must miss. Because of the exam, you realize that no one will lend you the notes long enough to copy them—not even your good friend Susan, who takes meticulous notes and would ordinarily be most cooperative. The original state, unfortunately, has you in the registration line at 11:00 while Susan takes notes that you may never see. The goal state would have you holding a copy of those fine notes. The problem has three subproblems: (1) discover a way for Susan to take notes for you, as well as herself; (2) discover a way to notify Susan; and (3) discover how to obtain those notes. You may solve the three subproblems separately. For example, you may realize that Rodney Wong in your 10:00 class passes by your industrial psych classroom and can see Susan—you have solved the second subproblem. Then it occurs to you that you can ask a librarian for a piece of carbon paper and some sheets of paper and ask Rodney to bring them to Susan; she can make a carbon copy as she takes notes for herself. The third subproblem is the easiest; Susan can bring the copy of the notes to the cafeteria, where you always eat lunch together.

When you use means-ends analysis to solve a problem, you can proceed in either the forward direction, from the initial state to the goal state, or backward from the goal state to the initial state. Thus, you may solve the third subproblem prior to the first subproblem. Try noticing the kinds of problems you might solve using means-ends analysis, perhaps writing a term paper for a history course, solving a problem in a statistics class, or figuring out the solution to numerous everyday dilemmas. Let us now examine some of the research showing how people use means-ends analysis in solving problems, as well as computer simulation investigations of this heuristic.

Research on the Means-Ends Heuristic.

Research demonstrates that people do organize problems in terms of subproblems. Greeno (1974) used the Hobbits-and-Orcs problem in Demonstration 10.6. His study showed that people pause at points in the problem and plan their strategy for the next few moves. They do not move ahead at a steady pace through a long series of individual moves. Specifically, people took a long time before the first move and before two other critical moves. At each of these points, they were tackling a subproblem and needed to organize a group of moves.

In some cases, means-ends analysis might not be the best approach. Sometimes the solution to a problem depends on temporarily *increasing* the difference between the original state and the goal state. For example, how did you solve the Hobbits-and-Orcs problem in Demonstration 10.6? Maybe you concentrated on reducing the difference between the original state (all creatures on the right side) and the

DEMONSTRATION 10.6

THE HOBBITS-AND-ORCS PROBLEM.

Try solving this problem. (The answer is at the end of the chapter.)

Three Hobbits and three Orcs arrive at a river bank, and they all wish to cross onto the other side. Fortunately, there is a boat, but unfortunately, the boat can only hold two creatures at one time. Also, there is another problem. Orcs are vicious creatures, and whenever there are more Orcs than Hobbits on one side of the river, the Orcs will immediately attack the Hobbits and eat them up. Consequently, you should be certain that you never leave more Orcs than Hobbits on any river bank. How should the problem be solved? (It must be added that the Orcs, though vicious, can be trusted to bring the boat back!)

goal state (all creatures on the left side) and you therefore only moved them from right to left. If you did, you would have ignored some steps that were crucial for the solution of the problem: moving creatures *backward* across the river to the right side of the river.

A study by Thomas (1974) emphasizes people's reluctance to move away from the goal state—even if the answer ultimately depends on this temporary detour. One group of participants in this study worked through the Hobbits-and-Orcs problems in the normal order; they served as the control group. In contrast, a part-whole group began by solving the *last* part of the problem, starting at one of the points that required moving away from the goal. Then the part-whole group solved the entire problem, from beginning to end.

Figure 10.3 shows the results. As you can see, people in the part-whole group gained an initial advantage from their experience on the last part of the problem:

FIGURE 10.3

Average Number of Moves in Each of the Two Parts of the Hobbits-and-Orcs Problem, as a Function of the Group. (Note: Small Number of Moves Represents Good Performance.)

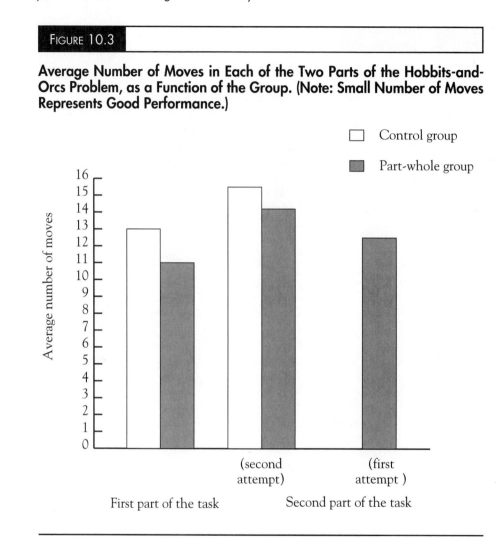

They performed significantly better than the control group on the first part of the task. However, the difference between the two groups was not statistically significant for the second part of the problem: Both groups performed relatively poorly because they were reluctant to make the necessary detour. Notice, in contrast, that the part-whole group actually performed worse the second time around on the last part of the problem. When they tried it the first time, the detour was less apparent than it was the second time, with the background of progress through the first part of the problem (Gilhooly, 1982).

In real life, as in Hobbits-and-Orcs problems, we sometimes find that the best way to move forward is to move backward temporarily. Think of an occasion when you were working on one of the later subproblems in a problem and discovered that a solution to an earlier subproblem was inadequate. For example, when you are writing a paper based on library research, you might discover that the resources you gathered during an earlier stage were not sufficient. Now you need to move backward to that earlier subproblem and revisit the library. You'll probably resent this task, especially because it seems to increase the difference between the original state and the goal state. In short, to solve a problem with means-ends analysis, we must sometimes violate a strict difference-reduction strategy.

Computer Simulation. Newell and Simon (1972) have examined means-ends analysis with a computer simulation approach. As discussed earlier in the book, in **computer simulation** a researcher writes a computer program that will perform a task the same way that a human would. For example, a researcher might try to write a computer program for the Hobbits-and-Orcs problem. The program should make some false starts, just as the human would. The program should be no better at solving the problem than a human would be, and it also should be no worse. The researcher tests the program by having it solve a problem and noting whether the steps it takes match the steps that humans would take in solving the problem. In studying problem solving, computer simulation offers the same advantage mentioned in connection with computer simulation of language processes: It forces the theorist to be clear and unambiguous about the components of the theory (Gilhooly, 1982; Greeno & Simon, 1988).

Sometimes the computer program's performance does not match the performance of human problem solvers. This failure indicates to the researchers that their theory needs to be revised. If the researchers have created a program that does mimic human behavior, however, this success does *not* automatically imply that humans actually solve problems in this fashion. It is possible, for example, that another task could be devised for which the computer program and the human problem solver would perform differently. In psychology, we cannot "prove" that a theory is correct; we can only demonstrate that it is compatible or consistent with behavior. Thus, if a program does predict how humans will solve a problem, a theory can be tentatively accepted. If it does not predict problem solutions, a theory can be rejected.

What is the advantage of computer simulation? Why is it preferable to a theory stated in standard English? Many cognitive psychologists favor computer simulation because it allows them to express their theories in precise computer language. In contrast, standard English is much less explicit.

Newell and Simon developed a computer program called **General Problem Solver** or **GPS,** which is a program whose basic strategy is means-ends analysis. The goal of the GPS is not simply to solve problems in the most efficient way, but to mimic the processes that normal humans use when they tackle these problems (Gardner, 1985). GPS has three different methods:

1. The transform method, which involves matching the original state to the goal state and finding the difference between them and then reducing the

difference by producing a new and different state. As a final step, this new state is transformed into the goal state.

2. The apply-operator method, which involves determining whether the operator (an action that changes the problem from one state to another) can be applied to the original state. If so, apply the operator; if not, change it to a new state before applying the operator.

3. The reduce method, which involves searching for an operator that would help reduce the difference and then applying it to the original state to produce a new state.

Notice that these three methods are different ways of changing the original state into the goal state. The transform method involves creating a new, transition state; the apply-operator method involves finding a state to which the operator can be applied; and the reduce method involves a search for the right operator for the situation.

The General Problem Solver program developed by Newell and Simon was the first to simulate a variety of human symbolic behavior (Gardner, 1985). GPS therefore has had an important impact on the history of cognitive psychology. It was used to solve transport problems like that of the Hobbits and Orcs, and it was successful in simulating human performance on this kind of problem.

In addition, the GPS was used in studying a number of general problems, such as the grammatical analysis of sentences, proofs in logic, and trigonometry problems. The GPS was eventually discarded by Newell and Simon because its generality was not as great as they had wished (Gardner, 1985). However, GPS is important because it helped us understand better how humans solve problems using means-ends analysis (Greeno & Simon, 1988).

◇ In Depth: **The Analogy Approach**

Every day you use analogies to solve problems. To solve a problem on a mathematics problem set, you refer to previous problems in your textbook. To pronounce an unfamiliar English word, you think about other words with similar spellings. Analogies also figure prominently in creative breakthroughs in art and science. For example, some of Einstein's theories developed out of analogies (Keane, 1988).

In an **analogy,** we use a solution to an earlier problem to help with a new one. Analogies pervade human thinking. Whenever we try to solve a new problem by referring to a known, familiar problem, we are using an analogy (Halpern et al., 1990). Educators are clearly aware of the power of analogies. In a survey conducted by Halpern (1987), virtually every college-level course in critical thinking or creative thinking emphasized course instruction on using analogies.

Researchers have enthusiastically examined how problem solvers use analogies. In fact, a book on analogical problem solving argues that analogies constitute a prototypical research topic in cognitive psychology (Keane, 1988). Let's now examine a portion of this research, beginning with an overview of some important background studies and then focusing on some recent research by Laura Novick.

Background Research. The challenge for people who use the analogy strategy is to determine the *real* problem, that is, the abstract puzzle underneath all the details. In the section on understanding problems, we emphasized that the problem solver must peel away the unimportant layers in order to reach the core of the problem. For example, when you attacked Demonstration 10.6, you realized that you did not need to know anything about Hobbits and Orcs—except for characteristics that were relevant for getting them across the stream. The story could just as well have concerned residents of different planets. These sets of problems with the same underlying structures and solutions—but with different specific details and contexts—are called **problem isomorphs.**

If people appreciate the concept of problem isomorphs, then they should be able to classify various kinds of algebra word problems. In one study, Hinsley, Hayes, and Simon (1977) wanted to see whether people could classify various kinds of algebra word problems. They asked high-school and college students who had taken courses in algebra to sort problems selected from a high-school algebra textbook. They were given 76 problems and were simply told to sort the cards into piles by problem type. The phrase "problem type" was not defined, nor was the number of piles. People did categorize the word problems into clusters. Furthermore, they showed strong agreement about what the categories were.

In their research, Hinsley and his co-workers devised 18 different clusters of algebra problems. The following three examples are typical:

1. *River current.* A river steamer goes 36 miles downstream in the same amount of time that it travels 14 miles upstream. In still water, the steamer would travel at a rate that is 12 miles an hour faster than the rate of the current. What is the rate of the current?
2. *Work.* Mr. Jones takes 3 minutes less than Mr. Smith to assemble a machine when each works alone. One day, Mr. Jones spent 6 minutes assembling a machine and then left; Mr. Smith finished the machine in 4 more minutes. How long would it take Mr. Jones, working alone, to assemble a machine?
3. *Number.* In a certain number, the digit in the units place is 1 more than 3 times the digit in the tens place. If you switch the numbers around, you get a number that is 8 times the sum of the digits. What is that number?

Hinsley and his co-workers found that people could categorize a problem very early during its presentation. As they write,

For example, after hearing the three words, "A river steamer . . ." from a river current problem, one subject said, "It's going to be one of those river things with upstream, downstream, and still water. You are going to compare times upstream and down-stream . . . " (p. 97)

People may be able to categorize problem types. However, researchers typically find that people often ignore these analogies when they actually need to solve a problem. For example, Reed (1977) found that people often showed little transfer between the Hobbits-and-Orcs problem you saw in Demonstration 10.6 and a similar but more difficult problem traditionally known as the "jealous-husbands problem." Holyoak and Koh (1987) have confirmed that people are often reluctant to see the analogy between a problem they have solved and a new problem isomorph.

Reed and his coauthors (1985) are also pessimistic about students' ability to use analogy information appropriately. In a series of experiments, these authors demonstrated that students in a college algebra course had difficulty transferring their knowledge between similar problems for distance, mixture, and work-rate word problems. In particular, they tended to make errors when substituting a new numerical value for the appropriate numerical value in the original problem. The authors suggest that students would make fewer errors if they were to construct tables listing the values of the important variables in both the original and the new problem.

This research shows that the analogy strategy should be useful. However, problem solvers too often fail to detect the analogy, and they may also make errors in interpreting it. VanLehn (1989) concludes in his summary of this research that people seldom notice a potential analogy, and when they do notice the analogy, it is likely to be based on superficial features, rather than true, structural similarities.

Novick's Research. Let's now consider research by Laura Novick (1988), which explores why people have difficulty transferring their knowledge from one problem to a second, analogical problem. As she points out, experimenters and people who read about the research on analogical problem solving find this research puzzling. It seems so obvious that a person who has been given a problem to solve should search back to find other, similar problems solved just minutes earlier! The difficulty, according to Novick, is that problem solvers—especially novice problem solvers—focus on salient **surface features,** which are the specific objects and terms used in the question. For example, recall that the person in the research by Hinsley and his coauthors (1977) classified a problem as a river current problem after hearing only three words, "A river steamer . . . " Unfortunately, these problem solvers may fail to emphasize the **structural features,** the underlying core that must be understood in order to solve the problem correctly.

Let's use some standard terminology for analogical problem solving. Imagine that you are currently trying to solve a problem; this current problem is called the **target problem.** To solve the target problem, you should look for a similar problem you solved in the past, called a **source problem.**

Novick wanted to see how the expertise of the problem solvers influenced the way they selected a source problem. In particular, she proposed that novice problem

---

DEMONSTRATION 10.7

A TYPICAL PROBLEM FROM NOVICK'S (1988, P. 513) RESEARCH.

Mr. and Mrs. Renshaw were planning how to arrange vegetable plants in their new garden. They agreed on the total number of plants to buy, but not on how many of each kind to get. Mr. Renshaw wanted to have a few kinds of vegetables and ten of each kind. Mrs. Renshaw wanted more kinds of vegetables, so she suggested having only four of each kind. Mr. Renshaw didn't like that because if some of the plants died, there wouldn't be very many of each kind. So they agreed to have five of each vegetable. But then their daughter pointed out that there was room in the garden for two more plants, although then there wouldn't be the same number of each kind of vegetable. To remedy this, she suggested buying six of each vegetable. Everyone was satisfied with this plan. Given this information, what is the fewest number of vegetable plants the Renshaws could have in their garden? The answer to this problem appears at the end of the chapter.

---

solvers would select a source problem that resembled the surface features of the target problem. In contrast, expert problem solvers would be more likely to select a source problem that resembled the structural features of the target problem.

Novick tested college undergraduates and categorized them into expertise categories (experts, high novices, and low novices) on the basis of their scores on the mathematics section of the Scholastic Aptitude Test (SAT). She argued that the SAT is a valid way to categorize students in her research because the problems on that test are similar to the problems she presented to the students. Demonstration 10.7 shows a typical problem from Novick's research.

Imagine that you are a participant in Novick's study. In the beginning, you are given three problems to solve, including the one in Demonstration 10.7; these serve as the source problems. Each problem is also accompanied by an explanation of the solution. For example, you might see the explanation for this problem that is shown at the end of this chapter, on page 374. After these three problems, Novick hands you the target problem, and you are instructed to solve it. This target problem resembles the *surface* features of the first source problem. However, it resembles the *structural* features of the second source problem, because it requires you to figure out the lowest common multiple (for example, $10 \times 4 \times 5$ in Demonstration 10.7). The only similarity that the target problem shares with the third source problem is that both require some arithmetic calculations.

Novick examined college students' calculations for the target problem in this study to determine whether their solution relied on the earlier problem that had been similar in surface features or the one that had been similar in structural features. As you can see in Figure 10.4, the experts were slightly more likely to emphasize structural similarity, whereas both categories of novices were much more likely to emphasize surface similarity.

FIGURE 10.4

Kind of Source Problem Selected for Solving the Target Problem, as a Function of Level of Expertise of Problem Solver (Based on Novick, 1988).

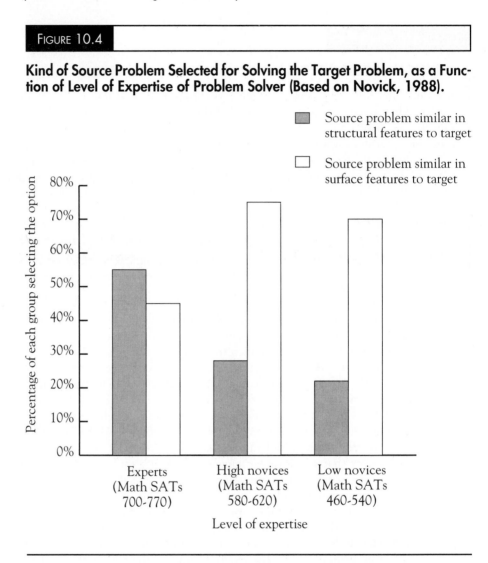

Thus, Novick's research shows us that experts are often able to unpeel the layers of math problems and notice that at the core, two problems share structural similarities. To solve the target problem, the expert uses the strategies that were successful in solving that structurally similar source problem. In contrast, people with less expertise miss the appropriate analogy, relying instead on similarities that are unimportant.

In a later article, Laura Novick and Keith Holyoak (1991) pointed out that successful problem solving by analogy requires four different processes:

1. Retrieval, or locating the appropriate source problem;

2. Mapping, or constructing orderly correspondences between the parts of the source problem and the parts of the target problem;
3. Adaptation, or determining how to use the same procedures for the target problem that were successful for the source problem; and
4. Learning, or figuring out an abstract schema for the entire class of problems that the source problem and the target represent.

The research on using analogies to solve problems suggests that analogies are extremely useful—when they are used appropriately. Unfortunately, however, the appropriate use of analogies requires four intellectually challenging hurdles. As a consequence, novice problem solvers may not be successful in exploiting these analogies.

SECTION SUMMARY: PROBLEM-SOLVING APPROACHES

1. With algorithms, such as the systematic random search, the problem solver eventually reaches a solution, but this method is very time consuming; in contrast, heuristics examine only part of the problem space, but they do not guarantee a solution.
2. One heuristic is the means-ends heuristic, which involves dividing the problem into subproblems; people are reluctant to move away from the goal state in solving a subproblem. The General Problem Solver is a computer program designed to use means-ends analysis.
3. Another heuristic is the analogy approach; people are aware of problem isomorphs, but they seldom spontaneously draw analogies to previous problems.
4. According to Novick's research, novices typically focus on salient surface features, whereas experts frequently emphasize the structural features that the target problem and the source problem share.

FACTORS THAT INFLUENCE PROBLEM SOLVING

How will you approach the next problem you face, and how successfully will you solve it? We cannot answer that question unless we know some information about you—the problem solver—and about the problem you are about to attack. For example, we would want to know about your level of expertise and whether you have a certain mental set. Relevant characteristics of the problem include the functional fixedness of any objects to be used in solving the problem, whether the problem is well-defined or ill-defined, and whether the problem requires insight.

Expertise

As we saw in Novick's research, experts and novices differ in the way they use the analogy approach. How else do experts differ from novices in the way they solve problems? Experts aren't simply "smarter" than other people. For instance, Ceci and Liker (1986, 1988) found that people who were experts at betting for horse races did not have higher IQs than nonexperts. Furthermore, experts excel primarily in their own domains of expertise (Glaser & Chi, 1988). You wouldn't expect a racetrack expert to excel at the problem of creating a Northern Italian meal from unfamiliar ingredients!

Let's trace how experts differ from novices during many phases of problem solving. We'll begin with some of the basic, early steps, then remind you about how experts differ from novices in intermediate phases, such as appreciating structural similarities, and finally consider more general issues, such as metacognition.

Memory. Experts differ from novices with respect to their memory for information related to their area (Chi et al., 1982; Glaser & Chi, 1988). For example, expert chess players have much better memory than novices for various chess positions. De Groot (1966) briefly showed chess positions to novices and experts and then requested recall. The experts were far superior in recalling the positions, even though they were no better at remembering random arrangements of the chess pieces. In other words, their memory is better only if the chess arrangement fits into a particular schema. Similarly, people who are experts at the game Othello are also superior at recalling meaningful game patterns, but not random positions (Wolff et al., 1984). Because memory for relevant information is an important part of problem solving (Anderson, 1987), the experts have a clear advantage over the novices in game performance.

Knowledge Base. Novices and experts also differ substantially in their knowledge base, or schemas (Hunt, 1989). Chi (1981) found in their study of physics problem solving that the novices simply lacked important knowledge about the principles of physics. As we discussed in previous chapters, you need the appropriate schemas in order to understand a topic properly.

Representation. Furthermore, novices and experts represent the problems differently. Larkin (1983, 1985) found that the novices in her study were likely to use naive problem representations, involving objects in the real world such as blocks, pulleys, and toboggans. The experts were able to construct physical representations about abstract ideas such as force and momentum. Other researchers have found similar results (e.g., de Jong & Ferguson-Hessler, 1986; Ferguson-Hessler & de Jong, 1987). Experts are also more likely to use appropriate mental images or diagrams, which are likely to facilitate problem solving (Clement, 1991; Larkin & Simon, 1987).

Appreciating Structural Similarity. As we emphasized in the In-Depth section, experts are more likely than novices to appreciate the structural similarity between mathematics problems; they are less likely to be distracted by surface similarities. The same findings have been reported for experts and novices solving physics problems (Glaser & Chi, 1988; Hardiman et al., 1989).

Elaborating on Initial States. Experts are more thorough than novices in thinking about the initial states of a problem. For example, Voss and his coauthors studied three groups of people with differing levels of expertise about the Soviet Union (Voss et al., 1983; Voss & Post, 1988). The experts on this task were political scientists whose area was Soviet affairs. The two novice groups included one group of chemistry professors and one group of students. These researchers examined the protocols, or spoken records collected during problem solving. The Soviet experts frequently began by identifying possible constraints in the problem, such as the amount of usable land and Soviet ideology. In all, 24 percent of the protocols of the Soviet experts elaborated on the initial state of the problem, in contrast to only 1 percent of the protocols of each novice group.

Speed and Efficiency. As you might expect, experts are much faster than novices, and they solve problems with little error. Their operations become more automatic, and a particular stimulus situation also quickly triggers a response (Glaser & Chi, 1988). Experts also seem to have a more coherent, efficient plan for problem solving (Hershey et al., 1990).

On some tasks, experts may solve problems faster because they use parallel processing, rather than serial processing. As the discussion on attention in Chapter 2 noted, parallel processing handles two or more items at the same time. In contrast, serial processing handles only one item at a time. Novick and Coté (1992) examined experts who reported that they could solve anagrams quickly, and novices, who said their anagram-solving skills were "awful." The experts solved this anagrams so quickly that they must have been considering several alternate solutions at the same time. To experts, the solution to anagrams such as DNSUO, RCWDO, and IASYD seemed to "pop out" in less than 2 seconds. In contrast, the novices were probably using serial processing. (Incidentally, are you a novice or an expert anagram solver?)

Metacognitive Skills. Experts are better at monitoring their problem solving; you may recall that Chapter 7 discussed that self-monitoring is a component of metacognition. Experts seem to be better at judging the difficulty of a problem. They are also more aware when they are making an error, and they are more skilled at allocating their time appropriately when solving problems (Glaser & Chi, 1988). In short, experts are more skilled at numerous phases of problem solving and are even more skilled at knowing how well they are doing in solving the problem at hand.

DEMONSTRATION 10.8

MENTAL SET.

Try these two examples to see the effects of mental set.

A.   Luchins' (1942) Water-Jar Problem
Imagine that you have three jars, A, B, and C. In each of seven problems the capacity of the three jars is listed. You must use these jars in order to obtain the amount of liquid specified in the "Goal" column. You may obtain the goal amount by adding or subtracting the quantities listed in A, B, and C. (The answers can be found in the discussion of the experiment.)

PROBLEM	A	B	C	GOAL
1	24	130	3	100
2	9	44	7	21
3	21	58	4	29
4	12	160	25	98
5	19	75	5	46
6	23	49	3	20
7	18	48	4	22

B.   A Number Puzzle
You are no doubt familiar with the kind of number puzzles in which you try to figure out the pattern for the order of numbers. Why are these numbers arranged in this order?

8,   5,   4,   9,   1,   7,   6,   3,   2,   0

The answer appears at the end of the chapter.

Mental Set

Try the two parts of Demonstration 10.8, which illustrate mental set. When problem solvers have a **mental set,** they keep trying the same solution they have used in previous problems, even though the problem could be approached via other, easier ways. Mental sets involve a kind of mindless rigidity that blocks effective problem solving (Langer, 1989). Although problem solving demands both top-down and bottom-up processing (Theme 5), overactive top-down processing produces a counterproductive mental set. The classic experiment on mental set is the Luchins (1942) water-jar problem, illustrated in the first part of Demonstration 10.8.

The best way to solve Problem 1 is to fill up jar B and remove one jarful with jar A and two jarsful with jar C. Because Problems 1–5 can all be solved in this fashion, they create a set for the problem solver. Most people will keep using this method when they reach Problems 6 and 7. However, this past learning will actually be a disadvantage, because there are easier, more direct ways of solving these later problems. Problem 6 can be solved by subtracting C from A, and Problem 7 can be solved by adding C to A. Luchins found that almost all of the participants to whom he gave such complex problems as 1–5 persisted in the same complex kind of solution on later problems. On the other hand, control-group participants, who began right away with problems such as 6 and 7, almost always solved the problem in the easier fashion.

A mental set often works against us in our everyday experiences, too. Consider, for example, the problem of getting to a particular location in a nearby city. Perhaps you devised a long, elaborate route involving many turns—a route that you have used for years—only to find out that someone else had discovered a simpler, more direct route on the first try.

So far, we have considered two characteristics of the *problem solver*—expertise and mental set—that influence how a problem is solved. Now we will examine three characteristics of a *problem*—other than the nature of the problem itself—that influence problem solving: functional fixedness, whether the problem is well defined or ill defined, and whether or not the problem requires insight. We need to emphasize as well that some problems are simply more difficult than others (e.g., Kotovsky & Kushmerick, 1991; Kotovsky & Simon, 1990). For example, Kotovsky and his coauthors (1985) examined a problem called the Tower of Hanoi, which resembles the monster-and-globe problem you tried in Demonstration 10.1. They found that different problem isomorphs varied greatly in their difficulty, with one isomorph requiring 16 times as long to solve as other versions; memory load was a strong determinant of problem difficulty. Let us now turn to three other important determinants of problem solving.

Functional Fixedness

Functional fixedness means that the functions or uses we assign to objects tend to remain fixed or stable. To overcome functional fixedness, we need to think flexibly about other ways that objects can be used. My sister, for example, described a creative solution to a problem she faced on a business trip. She had purchased a take-out dinner from a wonderful Indian restaurant. Back in her hotel, she discovered that the bag contained no plastic spoons or forks, and the hotel dining room had closed several hours earlier. What to do? She searched the hotel room, discovered an attractive new shoehorn in the "complimentary packet," washed it thoroughly, and enjoyed her chicken biriyani. To overcome functional fixedness, she had to realize that an object designed for one particular function (putting on shoes) can also serve another function (conveying food to the mouth).

The history of technology offers numerous examples of overcoming functional fixedness. For instance, the steam engine was used for a century to pump water out of mines before an inventor realized that it could be used as a source of locomotive power (Gellatly, 1986a).

Notice, incidentally, that *functional fixedness* describes a characteristic of objects in a problem-solving task, whereas *mental set* describes a characteristic of problem solvers. However, both characteristics block effective problem solving. Also, research has demonstrated that the two concepts are related. For example, Mc-Kelvie (1984) administered the Luchins water-jar problem to college students, and then four weeks later he administered a functional fixedness task to the same students. The people who were most susceptible to mental set also had the most difficulty in overcoming functional fixedness.

The classic study in functional fixedness is called Duncker's candle problem (Duncker, 1945). Imagine that you have been led to a room that contains a table. On the table are three objects, a candle, a box of matches, and a box of thumbtacks. Your task is to find a way to attach the candle to the wall of the room so that it burns properly, using no other objects than those on the table. Most people approach this problem by trying to tack the candle to the wall or by using melted wax to try to glue it up; both tactics fail miserably! The solution involves overcoming functional fixedness by tacking the empty matchbox to the wall to serve as a candle holder.

Functional fixedness and mental sets are two more examples of the part of Theme 2 that states that mistakes in cognitive processing can often be traced to a strategy that is basically very rational. In general, objects in our world have fixed functions. For example, we use a hammer to pound in a nail and a wrench to tighten a bolt. The strategy of using one tool for one task and another tool for another task is generally very wise; after all, each was specifically designed for its own task. Functional fixedness occurs, however, when we apply that strategy too rigidly and fail to realize, for instance, that if all other tools are missing, a wrench could be used to pound in the nail. Similarly, it is generally a wise strategy to use the knowledge you learned in solving earlier problems to solve the present problem. If an old idea works well, keep using it! However, in the case of mental sets, we apply the strategy gained from past experience too rigidly and fail to notice more efficient solutions.

Well-Defined and Ill-Defined Problems

Most of the problems we have considered so far could be called well defined. A **well-defined problem** is one in which the original state, the goal state, and the rules are all clearly specified. In addition, we have some systematic way to help us decide whether a solution is correct (Kahney, 1986; Reitman, 1964). In an anagram, for example, we know when we have reached a correct decision.

However, most of our daily problems are ill defined. An **ill-defined problem** is one in which the original state, the goal state, or the rules are unclear. Furthermore, we have no systematic way of telling whether a solution to an ill-defined problem is correct (Reitman, 1964). Some representative ill-defined problems include saving money for college tuition, de-escalating the nuclear arms race, and improving the environment (Halpern, 1989).

Simon (1973) describes another ill-defined problem: an architect designing a house. Notice, incidentally, that an architect could take a well-defined approach to the problem by selecting a standard house design and duplicating it. If she intends to create an original design, however, the problem is certainly ill defined. She could consider all kinds of structures, such as a geodesic dome, an A-frame, arches, and so on. She would also have to consider many varieties of material, such as wood, metal, concrete, camel's hides, marble, granite, rubber, ice (as Simon notes, don't object to ice—it's been done). Furthermore, there would be many different ways of proceeding. She might start with floor plans, or with the design for the front of the building, or with a list of needs stipulated by the client. Very few aspects of this problem are clearly defined. Furthermore, the architect would have no way of knowing whether or not she has reached a correct solution, though she certainly would know whether she had solved an anagram correctly.

We discussed algorithms and heuristics that could be used to solve well-defined problems. One of these heuristics can also be used for ill-defined problems; you can divide a problem into several subproblems. Another strategy is to add more structure to the situation. One difficulty with an ill-defined problem is that the task has so few constraints or limitations. To reach a solution, we must somehow restrict the possibilities. For example, when faced with the ill-defined problem of writing a paper for your course in cognitive psychology, you might restrict the possibilities by considering only those topics that relate to education.

Other strategies for solving ill-defined problems include starting to work on the problem even if you do not yet understand it completely and stopping when you have a solution, although it may not be the best possible solution. Because an ill-defined problem has no single, ideal solution, we can adopt a different criterion for success than with a well-defined problem.

Insight and Non-Insight Problems

Try Demonstration 10.9, which illustrates two typical insight problems. When we experience **insight,** the solution to a problem suddenly enters our minds and we immediately realize that the solution is correct (Baron, 1988).

The concept of insight was very important to Gestalt psychologists. As Chapter 1 described, Gestalt psychologists emphasized the importance of organizational tendencies. They argued that the parts of a problem may initially seem unrelated to one another, but a sudden flash of insight could make the parts fit together into a solution. If you solved the problems successfully in Demonstration 10.9, you are familiar with this feeling of sudden success.

DEMONSTRATION 10.9

TWO INSIGHT PROBLEMS.

A. The Nine-Dot Problem
Connect these nine dots with four connected straight lines. Do not lift your pencil from the paper when you draw the four lines.

• • •

• • •

• • •

B. The Triangle Problem
With six matches, construct four equilateral triangles. One complete match must make up one side of each triangle.

The answers to these two problems appear at the end of the chapter.

Behaviorist psychologists rejected the concept of insight because insight's emphasis on a sudden cognitive reorganization was not compatible with their emphasis on observable behavior. However, with the rise of the cognitive approach, psychologists once again use the term freely.

Janet Metcalfe argues that people working on insight problems experience a sudden leap in their confidence about being close to a correct solution. In contrast, our confidence builds gradually for problems that do not require insight, such as standard high-school algebra problems (Metcalfe & Wiebe, 1987). In fact, Metcalfe and Wiebe argue that the sudden rise in confidence can be used to distinguish insight from non-insight problems.

Let us examine Metcalfe's (1986) paper on solution patterns for insight problems. Metcalfe posed the following problem to students:

A stranger approached a museum curator and offered him an ancient bronze coin. The coin had an authentic appearance and was marked with the date 544 B.C. The curator had happily made acquisitions from suspicious sources before, but this time he promptly called the police and had the stranger arrested. Why? (p. 624)

As students worked on this problem, they supplied ratings every 10 seconds on a "feeling-of-warmth" scale. A rating of 0 indicated that they were completely "cold" about the problem, with no glimmer of a solution. A score of 10 meant that they were certain they had a solution.

As you can see from Figure 10.5, the warmth ratings showed only gradual increases until they soared dramatically with the discovery of the correct solution.

FIGURE 10.5

"Warmth Ratings" for Answers That Were Correct, as a Function of Time of Rating Prior to Answering (Based on Metcalfe, 1986).

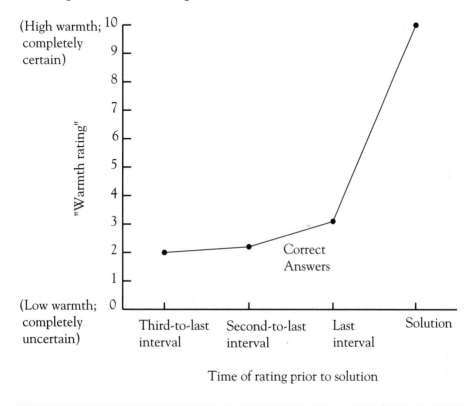

If you figured out the answer to the coin question, did you experience this same sudden burst of certainty? (Incidentally, the answer to this problem is that someone who had actually lived in 544 B.C. could not possibly have used the designation B.C. to indicate the birth of Christ half a millennium later.)

SECTION SUMMARY: FACTORS THAT INFLUENCE PROBLEM SOLVING

1. Experts differ from novices with respect to their memory for task-related material, their knowledge base, method of problem representation, appreciation of structural similarity, greater elaboration on initial states, speed and efficiency, and metacognitive self-monitoring.

2. Problem solving is also influenced by an individual's mental set, which inhibits effective solutions.

3. Three characteristics of a problem—other than the nature of the problem itself—are functional fixedness, whether the problem is well defined or ill defined, and whether or not the problem requires insight.

4. Functional fixedness means that the way in which we use objects tends to remain stable; both functional fixedness and mental sets can be traced to very rational cognitive strategies.

5. Ill-defined problems, in contrast to well-defined problems, lack clearly specified original states, goal states, rules, and criteria for deciding whether a solution is correct; they are therefore likely to be approached via different strategies than those used for well-defined problems.

6. Insight problems, in contrast to non-insight problems, are solved when the answer appears suddenly; "feelings-of-warmth" ratings rise abruptly, just prior to solution.

CREATIVITY

Perhaps you breathed a sigh of relief as you finished the sections on problem solving and prepared to read a section on creativity. Problem solving sounds so routine, whereas creativity sounds inspired. People who solve problems sit around working out their means-ends analyses, whereas people who think creatively have light bulbs flashing above their heads.

Truthfully, however, creativity is an area of problem solving. Creativity, like the areas of problem solving we have already considered, requires moving from an original state to a goal state. However, creativity is more controversial because we have no single standardized definition of creativity and no single widely accepted way to measure it. We will discuss definitions and measurement techniques and then examine several factors that may influence creativity.

Definitions

An entire chapter could be written on the variety of definitions for creativity. However, most theorists agree that novelty is a necessary component of creativity (e.g., Baron, 1988; Eysenck, 1990; Gilhooly, 1988; Mumford & Gustafson, 1988). However, novelty is not enough. The answer we seek must also allow us to reach our goal; it must be practical and useful. Suppose I asked you to construct a creative answer to the question, "How can you roast a pig?" The nineteenth-century essayist Charles Lamb observed that one way to roast a pig would be to put it into a house and then burn the house down. This answer meets the criterion of novelty, though it does not fulfil the usefulness requirement. To most theorists, then, **creativity** involves finding a solution that is both unusual and useful.

You will notice that the definition of creativity did not specify intelligence. Certainly the two concepts are related, though they are not identical (Baron, 1988;

Haensly & Reynolds, 1989; Sternberg, 1990). If we look at a broad sample of people, intelligence is somewhat correlated with creativity. As Hayes (1989c) suggests, one explanation for this general correlation is that a person must be at least moderately intelligent to attain an occupation that encourages creative projects. However, if you examine professionals in a given occupation (who therefore met the minimum criterion for intelligence), the more creative people and the less creative people are likely to have similar IQs. Intelligence is necessary—but not sufficient—to produce creativity.

Measuring Creativity

If theorists disagree about the definition of creativity, how can they possibly agree about how to measure it? As you might imagine, they do not agree at all. Furthermore, no current test of creativity consistently predicts which people will be more creative in real-life situations. Numerous tests are available, however; Mansfield and Busse (1981) discuss 20 different measures, for example.

Let us consider three different approaches to creativity: Guilford's (1967) Divergent Production Tests, Mednick and Mednick's (1967) Remote Associates Test, and Amabile's (1983) more recent consensual assessment technique.

Divergent Production. Guilford's (1967) test emerges from his idea that people have at least 120 different, independent kinds of mental abilities. Some of these abilities involve memory, some involve evaluating or judging, and some (in fact, 24) involve divergent production. In **divergent production,** people make a number of varied responses to each test item. Demonstration 10.10 shows some of the 24 ways in which Guilford measured divergent production.

Guilford discusses some of the support for **Divergent Production Tests.** In one study, for example, public relations and advertising employees were judged by their superiors to be either "creative" or "less creative." All employees then took the Divergent Production Tests. On five of the eight tests, the creative employees did significantly better than less creative employees. On the other hand, Guilford comments, "Correlations between DP (Divergent Production) test scores and criteria of creativity during the years through high school have not been spectacular, to say the least" (p. 163). Others criticize the concept of divergent production, noting that *number* of unusual ideas bears little relationship to creativity (Nickerson et al., 1985) and that different measures of divergent production are not as highly correlated with each other as they should be (Brown, 1989).

Remote Associates Test. The Remote Associates Test (RAT) was devised by Mednick and Mednick (1967) to measure their concept of creativity. Try Demonstration 10.11 to see several examples of the kind of problems on the RAT. These authors interpreted creativity to mean the ability to see relationships among

---

DEMONSTRATION 10.10

DIVERGENT PRODUCTION TESTS.

Try the following items, which are similar to Guilford's (1967) Divergent Production Tests.

1. Here is a simple, familiar form: a circle. How many pictures of real objects can you make using a circle, in a one-minute period?

2. Many words begin with an L and end with an N. List as many words as possible, in a one-minute period, that have the form L_____N. (They can have any number of letters in between the L and the N.)

3. Suppose that people reached their final height at the age of 2, and so normal adult height was less than a meter. In a one-minute period, list as many consequences as possible that would result from this change.

4. Here is a list of names. They can be classified in many ways. For example, one classification would be in terms of the number of syllables; SALLY, MAYA, and HAROLD have two syllables, whereas BETH, GAIL, and JOHN have one syllable. Classify them in as many ways as possible, in a one-minute period.

BETH   HAROLD   GAIL   JOHN   MAYA   SALLY

5. Here are four shapes. Combine them to make each of the following objects: a face, a lamp, a piece of playground equipment, a tree. Each shape may be used once, many times, or not at all in forming each object, and it may be expanded or shrunk to any size.

---

ideas that are remote from one another. Creative people can take far-flung ideas and combine them into new associations that meet certain criteria.

As Demonstration 10.11 shows, the **Remote Associates Test** is a test of creativity; the items consist of three words that must be linked together with a single word.

DEMONSTRATION 10.11

REMOTE ASSOCIATES.

For each set of three words, try to think of a fourth word that is related to all three words. For example, the words ROUGH, COLD, and BEER suggest the word DRAFT, because of the phrases, ROUGH DRAFT, COLD DRAFT, and DRAFT BEER. (The answers are at the end of the chapter.)

1. CHARMING	STUDENT	VALIANT
2. FOOD	CATCHER	HOT
3. HEARTED	FEET	BITTER
4. DARK	SHOT	SUN
5. CANADIAN	GOLF	SANDWICH
6. TUG	GRAVY	SHOW
7. ATTORNEY	SELF	SPENDING
8. MAGIC	PITCH	POWER
9. ARM	COAL	PEACH
10. TYPE	GHOST	STORY

Mednick and Mednick (1967) cite several studies demonstrating a relationship between RAT scores and creative performance. For example, scientists in a chemical firm who have high RAT scores also have high job classifications. Also, psychology graduate students who have high RAT scores tend to be rated as highly creative by their research advisors. Furthermore, technicians with IBM who have high RAT scores are more likely to make award-winning suggestions for improvement of the company.

A study by Andrews (1975) points out that creativity, as assessed by tests such as the RAT, may be related to real-life creativity only if all the circumstances are ideal. He located 115 scientists who had directed research projects. The scientists took the RAT, and they also answered questions about the laboratory environment in which they worked. Independent judgments were obtained on the quality of their scientific output. Andrews found no relationship between RAT measures and scientific output. However, he conducted another analysis and found that there *was* a relationship if the environmental factors were examined as well. Some of the scientists worked in a situation in which they had opportunities for innovation, made decisions about the research, felt professionally secure, and worked independently. For these scientists, high RAT scorers had greater scientific output than low RAT scorers. For the people who worked in less pleasant situations, there was no significant correlation. Andrews' results therefore suggest that in ideal work settings, scores on the RAT may be related to real-life measures of creativity.

However, not all the research offers optimism for the RAT. Reviews of the research on the RAT conclude that people who score high on the RAT sometimes show superior creative achievement, but sometimes they do not (Baron, 1988;

Brown, 1989; Nickerson et al., 1985). Unfortunately, the reasons for the inconsistent results are not clear.

Consensual Assessment Technique.

Teresa Amabile has developed a third alternative to the measurement of creativity. She points out that we can look at creativity as a property of *products*, rather than of people. According to the **consensual assessment technique,** a product should be considered creative if observers who are familiar with the area agree that it is indeed creative (Amabile, 1983, 1990). Her research indicates that observers who are familiar with an area tend to agree with one another in their creativity assessments. For example, trained artists rated young girls' artwork in one study (Amabile, 1982), and they agreed with one another about assessments of which artwork was creative and which was not. Their ratings also tended to agree with the ratings of art teachers and the ratings of novices.

Amabile's technique has some clear advantages. For example, it's hard to argue with the logic of a definition of creativity that can be paraphrased, "If experts think this work is creative, then it is." In addition, the straightforward measurement technique makes it easier to conduct research on the factors that influence creativity. We will look at some of this research in the final section.

Factors Influencing Creativity

Psychologists may disagree about how to define and measure creativity. However, they would agree in supporting efforts to enhance creativity. Let's consider two popular techniques designed to enhance creativity and then consider two additional factors that can affect creativity.

Brainstorming.

One of the most common approaches to encouraging creativity is Osborn's (1957) brainstorming principle. **Brainstorming** is a process conducted in a group setting in which there are four basic guidelines:

1. Evaluation of ideas must be withheld until later; thus criticism is ruled out.
2. The wilder the idea, the better. It is easier to tame an idea later than to think one up.
3. The greater the number of ideas, the better.
4. People can combine two or more ideas proposed by others.

Osborn maintains that the spirit of a brainstorming session is important. People should encourage themselves as well as encourage one another. Complete friendliness and a relaxed frame of mind are especially important.

The brainstorming technique has had good publicity in the popular press. Recently, however, psychologists have become increasingly skeptical about the value of this technique (e.g., Gilhooly, 1988; Weisberg, 1986). Weisberg's review of the literature, for example, questions both the assumptions underlying brainstorming and its practical usefulness. Weisberg does not agree with the assumption that creativity depends on the number of diverse ideas produced. Perhaps more important, research suggests that people can often be more creative working alone than working in groups. Furthermore, brainstorming groups may produce a greater *number* of ideas than groups urged to think critically, but their ideas are often lower in quality. Brainstorming may indeed be effective in some circumstances, but it does not seem to guarantee creative production of ideas.

Synectics. Another approach to encouraging creativity is called synectics (Gordon, 1961). **Synectics** encourages the use of analogies in creative thinking. The method includes the following kinds of analogies:

1. The personal analogy encourages you to place yourself directly in the situation. For example, if you want to make a particular machine work more efficiently, imagine that you are that machine.
2. The direct analogy encourages you to find something else that solves the problem you are examining. Very often it is helpful to look at solutions provided by human or animal biology. Alexander Graham Bell did this when he considered how the relatively huge bones of the human ear could be moved by a relatively delicate membrane, and he invented the telephone, in which a piece of steel is moved by a membrane. More recently, biologist Michael Zasloff was searching for a new approach to the study of infectious diseases. He pondered why frogs, which live in scummy, bacteria-filled ponds, don't have trouble with infections. His study led him to the discovery of naturally occurring substances in frog skin that can kill a range of microbes ("Ribbiting Evidence," 1987).
3. The symbolic analogy uses objective, impersonal, or poetic images to describe a problem. Gordon describes a synectics group that designed a new, smaller automobile jack by first thinking of the Indian rope trick (the one you may have seen in cartoons, in which a turbaned Indian makes a soft rope rigid enough to climb on).

Gordon describes how the synectics method has been used in industry, business, and education. For example, participants in a synectics session on the problem of science and public policy tried imaging themselves as nocturnal animals and as little fish being swallowed by big fish on the Florida Keys. The answer finally emerged when they formed an analogy between the government and the garment industry. They concluded that the government—like successful garment designers—should seek nontraditional solutions to problems.

Does the synectics method work? As Gilhooly (1988) points out, the method has been widely used by industries and other organizations. However, we do not yet have substantial research to document whether it truly enhances creativity.

Incubation and Creativity. Have you ever worked on a creative project and come to an impasse—then found that the solution lept into your mind after taking

FIGURE 10.6

The Influence of Evaluation Expectation and Working Condition on Creativity (Based on Amabile, 1983).

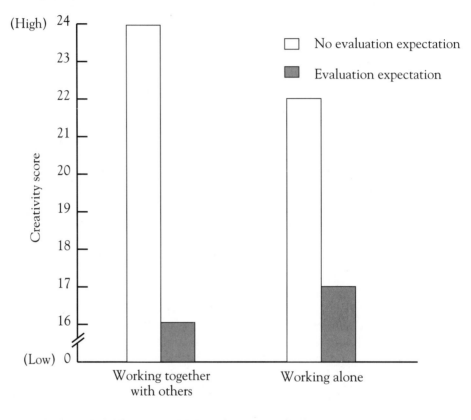

a break? Many artists, scientists, and other creative people testify that incubation helps them solve problems creatively. **Incubation** means that you are more likely to solve a difficult problem if a delay is placed between a period of intense work on the problem and a second work session (Yaniv & Meyer, 1987).

Incubation sounds plausible. However, incubation is seldom demonstrated in well-controlled research (Baron, 1988; Gilhooly, 1988), even though the anecdotal evidence is abundant. Perhaps more ecologically valid research should be conducted with creative individuals solving real-life artistic, scientific, and conceptual problems.

Assuming that incubation occasionally does work, what would be some likely mechanisms? Some theorists propose that unconscious processes are at work during that incubation period. Another possibility is that inappropriate mental sets may decay during that delay period (Gilhooly, 1988). Furthermore, this incubation period may allow time for the spread of activation between related concepts, especially for tasks that require verbal creativity (Yaniv & Meyer, 1987).

Social Factors Influencing Creativity.

You may have noticed that our discussion of factors influencing creativity has been rather tentative so far. We have described two methods that are supposed to enhance creativity, yet research support for their efficacy is slim. We also lack strong evidence for the value of incubation. Fortunately, the research on social factors is much more impressive.

For example, we know that creativity is reduced when people know that others will be evaluating their work (Amabile, 1983, 1990). In a representative experiment, college students were told to compose a poem. Half were told that the experimenter was simply interested in their handwriting, not the content of the poem, and therefore they did not expect to be evaluated on their poems. The other half were told that the experimenter was interested in the poem's content, and they would receive a copy of the judges' evaluations of their poems. Therefore these people expected to be evaluated. Half of the people in each of these groups worked alone, and half worked with others who were also composing poems.

Each of the poems was judged according to the consensual assessment technique, using judges who were poets. Figure 10.6 shows the results. As you can see, people produced poems that were much less creative when they expected to be evaluated. Creativity was inhibited by evaluation expectation, whether people worked in isolation or with others. However, people were equally creative in the "working together" and "working alone" conditions.

Amabile (1983) presents other convincing evidence that evaluation expectation can undermine creativity. For instance, the effect holds true for both adults and children, and for both artistic creativity and verbal creativity (Amabile, 1983, 1990; Hennessey & Amabile, 1984, 1988). When you expect your work to be evaluated, the product may not be less appealing or less technically appropriate, but it is likely to be less creative.

Research has also documented how other social factors can influence creativity. Amabile (1990) outlines how creativity is reduced under these conditions:

1. When someone is watching you while you are working;
2. When you are offered a reward for being creative;
3. When you must compete for prizes; and
4. When someone restricts your choices about how you can express your creativity.

Undergraduate students in psychology often think that all the interesting research questions may have been answered. In the area of creativity, we certainly have not answered all the questions. Furthermore, if we take seriously the challenge of problem finding that was raised at the beginning of the chapter, we probably have not yet identified many of the interesting questions.

SECTION SUMMARY: CREATIVITY

1. Numerous definitions have been proposed for creativity; one common definition is that creativity involves finding a solution that is both unusual and useful.
2. Creativity can be measured by Guilford's Divergent Production Test and Mednick and Mednick's Remote Associates Test; results on the validity of these tests are mixed. A newer method is Amabile's consensual assessment technique, in which a product is considered to be creative if experts in the area agree that it is creative.
3. Although brainstorming and the synectics approach are widely used, not much research exists as evidence of their effectiveness; similarly, well-controlled research seldom supports the concept of incubation.
4. The social conditions that can influence creativity include the anticipation of evaluation, being watched while working, being offered a reward, competition, and restricted choice.

CHAPTER REVIEW QUESTIONS

1. Identify a well-defined problem that you are currently facing as a student. Describe the original state, the goal state, and the rules. Repeat this process for an ill-defined problem that you are likely to encounter in your future profession. Specify which parts of the problem are ill defined.
2. Try to recall a problem that you found difficult to understand, either from an academic area or from everyday life. Which of Greeno's three requirements for understanding (coherence, correspondence, and relationship to background knowledge) were not met in this problem?
3. This chapter examined six different methods of representing a problem. Return to the description of these methods and point out how each method could be used to solve a problem you have faced either in college classes or in your personal life during recent weeks.
4. How do algorithms differ from heuristics in problem solving? When you solve problems, what situations suggest which of the two approaches? Describe a situation in which the means-ends heuristic was more useful than an algorithm.
5. What are the barriers that prevent our successful use of the analogy approach to problem solving? Think of an area in which you have expertise (an academic subject, a hobby, or work-related knowledge) and point out how Novick's research could apply to your appreciation of the structural similarities shared by problem isomorphs.
6. Think of an area in which you consider yourself an expert. Recall the section on expertise and point out the seven cognitive areas in which you are likely to have an advantage over a novice.

7. How are mental set and functional fixedness related to each other, and how do they limit problem solving? Why would incubation—when it works—help in overcoming these two barriers to effective problem solving?

8. The topic of metacognition was mentioned twice in this chapter. Discuss these two topics, and point out how metacognitive measures can help us determine which problems require insight and which do not.

9. Describe how Amabile defines creativity and discuss how the various social factors can influence creativity. From this information, describe a situation that is most likely to *enhance* creativity.

10. Imagine that you are a supervisor of 10 employees in a small company. Describe how you might use brainstorming and synectics to reach a creative solution to a company problem. Also, list appropriate cautions about these techniques. Finally, outline how you could do research to test the effectiveness of these two techniques, using Amabile's method of measuring creativity.

NEW TERMS

problem solving
original state
goal state
rules
understanding
matrix
hierarchical tree diagram
algorithm
systematic random search
problem space
heuristic
subproblems
means-ends analysis
computer simulation
General Problem Solver (GPS)
analogy
problem isomorphs

surface features
structural features
target problem
source problem
mental set
functional fixedness
well-defined problem
ill-defined problem
insight
creativity
divergent production
Divergent Production Tests
Remote Associates Test
consensual assessment technique
brainstorming
synectics
incubation

RECOMMENDED READINGS

Adams, J. L. (1986). *The care and feeding of ideas: A guide to encouraging creativity.* Reading, MA: Addison-Wesley. Adams is an engineer with expertise in enhancing creativity in scientists. This book offers a wealth of interesting suggestions, though readers should be encouraged to keep in mind that research has not been conducted about the usefulness of most of the described techniques.

Chi, M. T. H., Glaser, R., & Farr, M. J. (Eds.). (1988). *The nature of expertise.* Hillsdale, NJ: Erlbaum. This book includes chapters by many well-known figures in cognitive psychology; the overview chapter is especially helpful.

Gilhooly, K. J. (Ed.). (1989). *Human and machine problem solving.* New York: Plenum. This edited volume offers interesting contrasts between coverage of the research on human problem solving and the artificial intelligence approach.

Glover, J. A., Ronning, R. R., & Reynolds, C. R. (Eds.). (1989). *Handbook of creativity.* New York: Plenum. This book offers a good summary of the research on creativity, including issues such as measurement, cognitive models, and applications.

Levine, M. (1988). *Effective problem solving.* Englewood Cliffs, NJ: Prentice-Hall. Levine's how-to book covers the basics of problem solving described in this chapter and also includes more coverage of personality and social psychology, such as motivation and interpersonal problem solving.

ANSWERS TO DEMONSTRATIONS

Demonstration 10.5   In the hospital room problem, Ms. Anderson has mononucleosis, and she is in Room 104.

Demonstration 10.6   In the Hobbits-and-Orcs problem (with R representing the right bank and L representing the left bank), here are the steps in the solution:

1. Move 2 Orcs, R to L.
2. Move 1 Orc, L to R.
3. Move 2 Orcs, R to L.
4. Move 1 Orc, L to R.
5. Move 2 Hobbits, R to L.
6. Move 1 Orc, 1 Hobbit, L to R.
7. Move 2 Hobbits, R to L.
8. Move 1 Orc, L to R.
9. Move 2 Orcs, R to L.
10. Move 1 Orc, L to R.
11. Move 2 Orcs, R to L.

Demonstration 10.7   In the beginning, Mr. and Mrs. Renshaw both agree upon the number of plants to buy. Therefore, we know that 10, 4, and 5 must all go evenly into that number—whatever it is. Thus, the first thing to do is to find the smallest number that is evenly divisible by 10, 4, and 5; that number is 20. So we know that the original number of vegetable plants the Renshaws were thinking of buying could be any multiple of 20 (that is, 20, 40, 60, 80, and so on). But then they decide to buy 2 additional plants they had not originally planned to buy. Thus, the total number of plants they actually end up buying must be 2 more than the multiples of 20 listed earlier (that is, 22, 42, 62, 82, and so on). This means that 10, 4, and 5 will no longer go evenly into the total number of plants. However, the problem states that they eventually agree to buy 6 of each vegetable, so the total number of plants must be evenly divisible by 6. The smallest total number of plants that is evenly divisible by 6 is 42, so the answer is 6 (based on Novick, 1988, p. 513).

Demonstration 10.8   The numbers are in alphabetical order; your mental set probably suggested that the numbers were in some mathematical sequence, not a language-based sequence.

Demonstration 10.9(a)

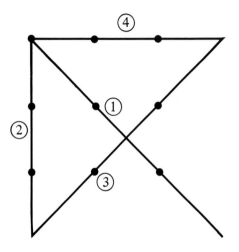

Incidentally, Adams (1979) lists a number of other, nontraditional solutions, such as cutting the puzzle apart into thirds, taping the dots together in a row, and drawing a single line through all nine dots.

Demonstration 10.9(b)

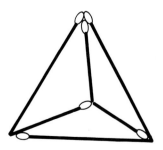

Demonstration 10.11   Answers to the remote associates items:

1. PRINCE
2. DOG
3. COLD
4. GLASSES
5. CLUB

6. BOAT
7. DEFENSE
8. BLACK
9. PIT
10. WRITER

C H A P T E R   1 1

LOGICAL REASONING AND DECISION MAKING

PREVIEW

This chapter considers how people perform two complex cognitive tasks, logical reasoning and decision making. The topics of problem solving (Chapter 10), logical reasoning, and decision making are all included within the topic of thinking.

Logical reasoning means transforming the given information in order to reach conclusions, and we will consider two kinds of reasoning tasks in this chapter—conditional reasoning and syllogisms. Conditional reasoning describes "if . . . , then . . . " relationships. People make several kinds of errors on conditional reasoning tasks; for example, they often fail to appreciate all possible interpretations of the premises. Syllogisms use quantitative words such as *all*, *some*, and *none*. Again, people make several kinds of errors; for example, they may rely too much on their background knowledge, rather than on the logical argument.

Decision making means assessing and choosing among several alternatives. This section of the chapter will emphasize the heuristics, or "rules of thumb," that we use in making decisions. Heuristics *usually* lead to the correct decision, but we sometimes apply them inappropriately. Psychologists study the inappropriate use of heuristics in order to discover how we normally use these heuristic guidelines. This chapter examines three heuristics we often use. The first is representativeness, in which we judge a sample to be likely because it looks similar to the population from which it is selected. For example, if you toss a coin six times, the outcome H T H H T T looks very likely. We pay so much attention to representativeness that we sometimes ignore important features such as sample size and base rates. A second heuristic, the availability heuristic, is used when we estimate frequency in terms of how easily we can think of examples of something. For instance, you estimate the number of psychology majors at your college to be large if you can easily think of people who are psychology majors. Unfortunately, availability is often influenced by two irrelevant factors—recency and familiarity—and so we may make decision errors when we use this heuristic. The third heuristic, the anchoring and adjustment heuristic, is used when we begin by guessing a first approximation (an anchor) and then make an adjustment, based on other information; the strategy is reasonable, except that our adjustments are typically too small. Another common phenomenon in decision making is the framing effect, in which the choice of wording and context influence the decision inappropriately. Finally, we'll discuss how people are often too confident about the accuracy of their decisions.

INTRODUCTION

Every day you use logical reasoning, although you might not spontaneously choose that label. For example, a friend tells you, "If I can find that newspaper ad for the apartment, I'll give you a call." The afternoon passes without a phone call, and you draw the logical conclusion, "My friend did not find the ad." Every day, you also make dozens of decisions. Should you see the new movie at the Riviera that your neighbor raved about or the horror film that is the season's box office favorite? Should you ask Professor Adams for the letter of recommendation, or should you try Professor Sanchez?

Problem solving (our topic in the previous chapter), logical reasoning, and decision making are interrelated, and we will note several similarities among these tasks. All three topics are included in the general category called *thinking*. **Thinking** is defined as going beyond the information given (Galotti, 1989). You begin with several bits of information, and you must manipulate that information to solve a problem, to reach a logical conclusion, or to make a decision. Most cognitive psychologists use the word *thinking* to refer to deliberate, conscious efforts to figure things out (Nickerson, 1986). In contrast, *thinking* does not usually include the automatic inferences we make in language understanding. When someone tells you that Paula drives to work, you infer that she owns a car, rather than a bus or a moving van. . . . But cognitive psychologists typically do not categorize that inference as *thinking*.

Our topics for this chapter—logical reasoning and decision making—are clearly related. **Reasoning** means transforming the given information in order to reach conclusions (Galotti, 1989). **Decision making** refers to assessing and choosing among several alternatives. In reasoning, the premises are either true or false, and the rules for drawing conclusions are specified. In decision making, on the other hand, the information is uncertain. Much of the information may be missing. Furthermore, no clear-cut rules tell us how to proceed from the information to the conclusions. In real life, the uncertainty of decision making is more common than the certainty of reasoning.

LOGICAL REASONING

In this section, we will consider two logical reasoning tasks, conditional reasoning and syllogisms. Although the specific operations differ for these tasks, some of the same factors influence performance. Furthermore, people make similar kinds of errors on these two tasks, such as failing to consider all possible interpretations of the statements. Finally, both tasks are challenging. The majority of college students typically have difficulty using the strategies of logical reasoning consistently (Nunmedal, 1987).

Conditional Reasoning

If the moon is shining, I can see without a flashlight.
I cannot see without a flashlight.
Therefore, the moon is not shining.

This example illustrates conditional reasoning. **Conditional reasoning** or **propositional reasoning** problems tell us about the relationship between conditions,

---

DEMONSTRATION 11.1

THE PROPOSITIONAL CALCULUS.

Decide which of the following conclusions are valid and which are invalid. The answers are at the end of the chapter.

1. Affirming the antecedent.

   If today is Tuesday, then I have by bowling class.
   Today is Tuesday.
   Therefore, I have my bowling class.

2. Affirming the consequent.

   If I have been at a buffet-style restaurant, then I have gained five pounds.
   I have gained five pounds.
   Therefore, I have been at a buffet-style restaurant.

3. Denying the antecedent.

   If I am a freshman, then I must register for next semester's classes today.
   I am not a freshman.
   Therefore, I must not register for next semester's classes today.

4. Denying the consequent.

   If the judge is fair, then Susan is the winner.
   Susan is not the winner.
   Therefore, the judge is not fair.

---

such as the relationship between the moon shining and needing a flashlight. The kind of conditional reasoning we consider in this section involves "if . . . , then . . . " relationships. Conditional reasoning situations occur frequently in daily life, yet they are surprisingly difficult to solve correctly. Formal principles for dealing with conditional reasoning have been devised, but people frequently contradict these principles.

The Propositional Calculus.
The propositional calculus* is a system for categorizing the kinds of reasoning used in analyzing propositions or statements. Four

---

* By tradition, the phrase *the propositional calculus* is used rather than *propositional calculus*.

basic kinds of conditional reasoning situations are illustrated in Demonstration 11.1. Let's first introduce some basic terminology. The word **antecedent** means the proposition that comes first; the antecedent is contained in the "if . . . " part of the sentence. The word **consequent** refers to the proposition that follows; it is the consequence. The consequent is contained in the "then . . . " part of the sentence. Sometimes we affirm part of the sentence, saying that it is true; sometimes we deny part of the sentence, saying that it is false.

Four conditional reasoning situations can occur:

1. **Affirming the antecedent** means that you say that the "if . . . " part of the sentence is true. This kind of reasoning leads to a valid, or correct, conclusion.
2. **Affirming the consequent** means that you say that the "then . . . " part of the sentence is true. This kind of reasoning leads to an incorrect conclusion. Notice in the second item that the conclusion, "Therefore I have been at a buffet-style restaurant," is incorrect because a person can gain five pounds in many other ways—eating dinner at the home of a friend who believes that everything tastes better with cream or butter added, staying home and consuming five pounds of chocolate fudge, or whatever.

   We can easily see why people are tempted to affirm the consequent: In real life we are often correct when we make this kind of reasoning error (Bell & Staines, 1981; Nickerson et al., 1985). For example, consider the propositions, "If a man is a football player, then he has a thick neck" and "John has a thick neck." It is a good bet that John is indeed a football player; however, in logical reasoning we cannot rely on statements such as "It is highly likely that . . . " As Theme 2 emphasizes, many cognitive errors can be traced to a strategy that usually works well.
3. **Denying the antecedent** means that you say that the "if . . . " part of the sentence is false. Denying the antecedent also leads to an incorrect conclusion. The conclusion of Item 3—"I must not register for next semester's classes today"—is false, because it is possible that the members of your own class, as well as freshmen, must register today.
4. **Denying the consequent** means that you say that the "then . . . " part of the sentence is false. This kind of reasoning leads to a correct conclusion.

The four kinds of reasoning are presented in a matrix in Table 11.1. Make certain that you understand these and can make up your own examples for each kind.

Try noticing how often you use the two correct kinds of reasoning. For example, a traffic sign might read, "Left turns permitted on weekends." This sign could be translated into the "if . . . , then . . . " form: "*If* it is a weekend, *then* left turns are permitted." You know that it is Saturday, a weekend day. By the method of affirming the antecedent, you can conclude that left turns are permitted. Similarly, a judge says, "If I find Tom Smith guilty, he is going to jail." You learn that Tom

| TABLE 11.1 | | |

THE PROPOSITIONAL CALCULUS: THE FOUR KINDS OF REASONING, WITH EXAMPLES FOR THE STATEMENT, "IF THIS IS AN APPLE, THEN THIS IS A FRUIT."

ACTION TAKEN	PORTION OF THE STATEMENT	
	ANTECEDENT	CONSEQUENT
Affirm	Affirming the Antecedent (valid) *This is an apple; therefore this is a fruit.*	Affirming the Consequent (invalid) *This is a fruit; therefore this is an apple.*
Deny	Denying the Antecedent (invalid) *This is not an apple; therefore this is not a fruit.*	Denying the Consequent (valid) *This is not a fruit; therefore this is not an apple.*

Smith did not go to jail, so you conclude by the method of denying the consequent that Tom was judged not guilty.

Also watch out for logical errors that you might be making. Think how the method of affirming the consequent might produce the wrong conclusion in the sentence, "If Mary likes me, then she will smile at me." The method of denying the antecedent also produces the wrong conclusion for the sentence, "If I get a D on this test, then I'll get a D in the course."

As you might guess, the four kinds of conditional reasoning tasks differ in their difficulty. Affirming the antecedent is easiest. As Rips (1981) notes, it is difficult to imagine what we could say to someone who says that the antecedent is true, yet the consequent is false. Taplin's (1971) research demonstrated that people were indeed most accurate in affirming the antecedent, next best in denying the consequent, and worst in denying the antecedent and in affirming the consequent. (Performance was equally poor for these last two kinds of reasoning). Notice, then, that people are best at the correct kinds of reasoning. They are worst at the incorrect kinds of reasoning, which they mistakenly believe to be correct.

Factors Affecting Conditional Reasoning.   Two factors that influence the error rate for conditional reasoning problems are the abstractness of the problem and whether the problem contains negative information.

You won't be surprised to learn that people are more accurate when the problem uses concrete examples, as in the case of the apples and fruit in Table 11.1. In contrast, they have difficulty when the material is abstract (Wason & Johnson-Laird, 1972). Even though this abstract reasoning problem is short, it is difficult:

> If an object is red, then it is rectangular.
> This object is not rectangular.
> Therefore, it is not red. (True or false?)

Other related research demonstrates that performance is better if the propositions are high in imagery (Clement & Falmagne, 1986).

Theme 3 of this book states that people can handle positive information better than negative information. A second factor that influences conditional reasoning is negation. Many studies have demonstrated that conditional reasoning is difficult if the item contains the negative word *not* in the premises (Evans, 1972; Galotti, 1989). Consider the following problem:

> If an object is not blue, then it is rectangular.
> This object is not rectangular.
> Therefore, it is blue. (True or false?)

People typically decide that no conclusion can be drawn in this problem; in fact, the conclusion is true.

You may recall from Chapter 8 that people have difficulty understanding double negatives. In the reasoning problem above, denying the consequent produces the conclusion, "It is not true that the object is not blue." You are likely to make a mistake in translating that sentence into the correct answer, "The object is blue."

Errors in Conditional Reasoning. People make errors when they draw conclusions on a conditional reasoning task, even when they have taken a course in logic (Cheng et al., 1986). Let's consider four areas in which errors are frequently made.

1. *Making only one model of the antecedent and consequent.* According to Johnson-Laird and Byrne (1991), people construct mental images to represent the premises; these mental images may not portray all the logical possibilities. As we saw in Chapter 10, people may not search the problem space as thoroughly as they should. Consider this reasoning problem:

> If she meets her friend, then she will go to a play.
> She did not meet her friend.

Byrne (1989) found that 46 percent of her college-student participants erroneously concluded, "She will not go to a play." Apparently, students constructed a single mental model in which the only way she could go to the play was by meeting her friend. In another condition, Byrne added an extra premise, "If she meets her brother, then she will go to a play." Now only 4 percent drew the wrong conclusion,

"She will not go to a play." Apparently, they could construct an additional mental model involving the brother; they now saw that she might go to the play, even without the friend.

2. *Making an illicit conversion.* Another interpretive error that people often make is an illicit conversion. An **illicit conversion** means that you inappropriately change part of the problem into another form. Wason and Johnson-Laird (1972) point out how this works when people use the method of denying the antecedent— an invalid method. The general form of this method is:

If *p*, then *q*.
p is not true.
Therefore, *q* is not true.

The problem is that people use illicit conversion when they see the first statement. They convert it—inappropriately—into:

If *q*, then *p*.

Then they attack that converted statement, using the method of denying the consequent, which is a valid method when used appropriately. They conclude, therefore, that *q* is not true.

In everyday reasoning situations, we can often use an illicit conversion without problems. Suppose that a friend is trying to guess what the dormitory will serve for breakfast, and she says, "If it's Tuesday, then we are having pancakes." This statement implies a one-to-one correspondence between days of the week and the breakfast dish. Thus, you can reasonably conclude that the two parts of the statement can be converted to yield the statement, "If we are having pancakes, then it is Tuesday." In a formal reasoning task—unlike in real life—we must consider that pancakes may be served more often than once a week.

3. *Trying to confirm a hypothesis, rather than trying to disprove it.* Try Demonstration 11.2 now, before reading further. This selection task has inspired more research than any other logical reasoning problem.

This task illustrates how people would much rather try to confirm a hypothesis than try to disprove it. Most people working on this classical selection task say that they would turn over the *E* and the 6 cards, or else just the *E* card; these strategies allow them to confirm their hypothesis. However, the correct strategy is to choose the 7 card, as well as the *E* card. Less than 10 percent of participants typically produce the correct solution (Gellatly, 1986b; Griggs & Cox, 1982). Furthermore, people with Ph.D. degrees are no more likely to answer the problem correctly than people with bachelor's degrees (Jackson & Griggs, 1988).

Let's see why *E* and 7 are the correct answers. First of all, you need to see what lies on the other side of the *E*. If it is an even number, the rule is correct. If it is an odd number, the rule is incorrect. However, you must also examine the other

---

DEMONSTRATION 11.2

AVOIDING DISPROVING HYPOTHESES.

Imagine that each of the squares below represents a card. Suppose that you know from previous experience that every card has a letter on one side and a number on the other side.

| E | J | 6 | 7 |

You are then given this rule about these four cards: "If a card has a vowel on one side, then it has an even number on the other side."

Your task is to decide which of these cards you would need to turn over in order to find out whether this rule is true or false. What is your answer? The answer is discussed in the text.

---

side of the 7, a choice that very few people select. The information about the other side of the 7 is very valuable—just as valuable as the information about the E. If the other side shows a consonant, the rule is still correct. However, if it shows a vowel, the rule is incorrect and must be rejected.

Let us examine that rule again, using the propositional calculus:

If a card has a vowel on its letter side, then it has an even number on its number side.

Recall that we have two correct conditional reasoning strategies: (1) To affirm the antecedent, we check out a vowel (in this case, the E) and (2) to deny the consequent, we must check out a number side that is *not* an even number (in this case, the 7). People are eager to affirm the antecedent, but they are reluctant to deny the consequent by searching for counterexamples. This would be an attempt to disprove a hypothesis, a strategy people systematically avoid.

You may wonder why we did not need to check on the J and the 6. If you look carefully, you will notice that the rule did not say anything about consonants, such as J. The other side of the J could have an odd number, an even number, or a giraffe, and we wouldn't care. The rule also doesn't specify what must appear on the other side of the even numbers, such as 6. Many people select the 6 to turn over because they perform an illicit conversion on the rule, so that it reads, "If a card has an even number on its number side, then it has a vowel on its letter side." Thus, they choose the 6 by mistake.

You may notice that this preference for confirming a hypothesis, rather than disproving it, corresponds to Theme 3 of this book. On the selection task, we see that when people are given a choice, they would rather seek out positive information than negative information. We would rather know what something *is* than what it *is not.*

In recent years, researchers have tested numerous versions of the classic selection task. Even a subtle change in the wording of the problem can change the results dramatically (Jackson & Griggs, 1990). As you may have guessed, performance is much better when the task is concrete and familiar (e.g., Cheng & Holyoak, 1985; Oakhill & Johnson-Laird, 1985; Pollard & Evans, 1987).

Let us consider a representative study. Griggs and Cox (1982) tested college students in Florida using a variation of the selection task. This task involved the drinking age, which was then 19. The problem was much more concrete and relevant to most college students. The participants in this study saw the following problem:

> On this task imagine that you are a police officer on duty. It is your job to ensure that people conform to certain rules. The cards in front of you have information about four people sitting at a table. On one side of a card is a person's age and on the other side of the card is what the person is drinking. Here is a rule: IF A PERSON IS DRINKING BEER, THEN THE PERSON MUST BE OVER 19 YEARS OF AGE. Select the card or cards that you definitely need to turn over to determine whether or not the people are violating the rule. (p. 415)

Four cards were presented, labeled DRINKING A BEER, DRINKING A COKE, 16 YEARS OF AGE, and 22 YEARS OF AGE, respectively.

Griggs and Cox found that 73 percent of the students who tried the drinking-age problem made the correct selection, in contrast to 0 percent who tried the standard, abstract form of the selection task. The difference in performance between concrete and abstract tasks is especially dramatic when the wording of the selection task implies some kind of social contract designed to prevent people from cheating (Cosmides, 1989; Gigerenzer & Hug, 1992). Cosmides even argues that evolution may have encouraged people to develop specialized skills in understanding important, adaptive problems. In particular, they may be especially competent in understanding the kinds of rules that are necessary for cooperative interactions in a society.

4. *Failing to transfer knowledge to a new task.* So far we have seen that people make errors in conditional reasoning because they create only one model of the premises, because they make illicit conversions, and because they avoid disproving hypotheses. Perhaps you could have predicted this fourth source of errors from what you learned in the chapter on problem solving. In that chapter we saw that people have trouble appreciating the similarity between a math problem they are currently working on and one they solved earlier. Similarly, people have trouble appreciating the similarity between two versions of the selection task illustrated in Demonstration 11.2 (Klaczynski et al., 1989). Furthermore, research has confirmed that students who study formal logic in philosophy classes have difficulty applying

their knowledge in new situations (Salmon, 1991). In general, then, the material on conditional reasoning does not provide much evidence for Theme 2 of this book; humans are not especially accurate when they solve "if . . . , then . . . " problems.

Syllogisms

Unfortunately, people are even less accurate when they work on logical tasks involving syllogisms. A **syllogism** (pronounced "*sill*-owe-jizz-um") consists of two premises, or statements that we must assume to be true, plus a conclusion. Syllogisms involve quantities, so they use the words *all, none, some,* or other similar terms. In conditional reasoning, the statements are often represented by the letters *p* and *q*. In syllogistic reasoning, the traditional symbols are A, B, and C. Thus, an example of a syllogism using these symbols is the following:

Some A are B.
Some B are C.
Therefore, some A are C.

Does that conclusion seem correct to you? At first glance, it might, and you can probably think of some concrete examples for which it would be true. However, there are some other examples for which it would not be true. For example, think about this syllogism:

Some women are Democrats.
Some Democrats are men.
Therefore, some women are men.

Sometimes the conclusion to a syllogism is either true or false. However, sometimes we cannot draw a conclusion from the syllogism—it may be true for some relationships and false for others. In these cases, such as in the A, B, and C example above, we conclude, "can't say." On the surface, it looks simple to decide whether your conclusion is "true," "false," or "can't say"—after all, how hard can *some* and *all* be? However, people have difficulty solving these reasoning problems.

It is important to stress that the correctness of the conclusion does *not* depend on the truth of the premises. I can make up some ridiculous premises, but the conclusion would be true as long as the basic form of the syllogism is true. For example, because the underlying logic is correct, the conclusion for this syllogism is true:

All elephants are fond of dry martinis.
All those who are fond of dry martinis are bankers.
Therefore, all elephants are bankers.

So, remember that you should ignore the content of syllogisms in deciding whether the conclusions are correct. We will discuss this issue again later in the chapter.

FIGURE 11.1

Euler's Circles, Showing Possible Interpretations of Four Different Relationships Between A and B.

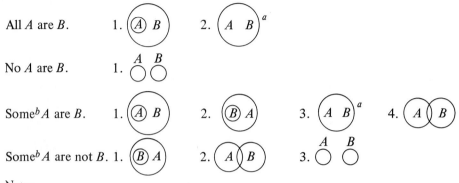

Notes:
[a]In the diagrams in which A and B are represented by a single circle, the sets A and B are identical.
[b]When logicians use the word *some*, it is different from the everyday usage, because *some* can also mean *all*. Thus, "Some A and B" can mean "All A and B."

One effective way to represent information in the premises of syllogisms is in terms of Euler's circles (pronounced, *Oi*-lurrs). **Euler's circles** show how two sets of items, called A and B, are related to each other. Figure 11.1 shows Euler's circles for four possible relationships, or **moods,** in a syllogism. Each of the three statements in a syllogism can be expressed in terms of each of these four kinds of moods: (1) All A are B, (2) no A are B, (3) some A are B, and (4) some A are not B.

Notice that the statement "No A are B" can be interpreted in only one way. However, the other moods are ambiguous, because each can be interpreted in at least two ways. For example, notice in Diagram 1 for "All A are B" that all parts of circle A are inside circle B, but some parts of circle B extend beyond the boundaries of circle A. Figure 11.1 also shows an alternative interpretation of "All A are B." Here, the two circles overlap completely. Incidentally, college students tend to prefer this second interpretation of the word *all* (Begg & Harris, 1982).

As you can see, the most ambiguous term is *some*. College students tend to interpret the word *some* as meaning "less than half" (Begg, 1987). This makes sense. When we hear, "Some students are honest," we automatically assume, "Some, *but not all*." After all, in normal communication, people are supposed to share with their listeners as much information as they know. If they mean to imply the kinds of set relationships shown for *some* in the first and third sets of circles, they should say *all* (Begg, 1987; Begg & Harris, 1982). Consistent with Theme 2, errors in our cognitive processes are generally "smart" errors, not random ones.

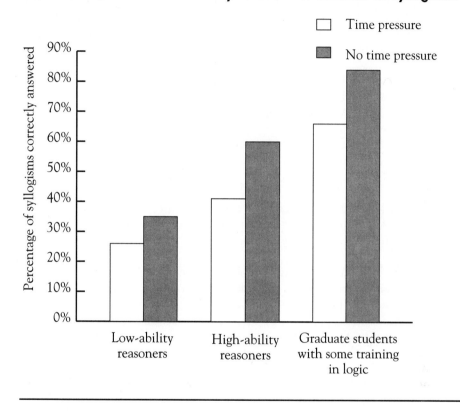

FIGURE 11.2

Effects of Time Pressure and Ability Level on Performance on Syllogisms.

□ Time pressure

▨ No time pressure

Percentage of syllogisms correctly answered

Low-ability reasoners

High-ability reasoners

Graduate students with some training in logic

Let us begin our examination of this difficult reasoning task by considering the factors affecting syllogisms and some common errors people make on this task. Then we'll discuss a theoretical explanation of how people solve syllogisms.

Factors Affecting Syllogisms. Several variables can influence performance on syllogisms. These include linguistic factors and time pressure.

The linguistic form of sentences is critical in determining the difficulty of syllogisms. As we saw with conditional reasoning tasks, problems are more difficult to solve when they include negative words such as *not*. Similarly, syllogisms are more difficult if they include negatives (Lippman, 1972). Furthermore, syllogisms are easier to solve if they use the active voice (Lippman, 1972). You may recall that Chapter 8 pointed out that people understand language better if it is in the active rather than the passive voice.

DEMONSTRATION 11.3

EXAMPLES OF SYLLOGISMS (BASED ON MARKOVITZ & NANTEL, 1989).

In each of these four syllogisms, decide whether or not the conclusions follow logically from the premises. Limit yourself only to the information contained in these premises. (The answers appear at the end of the chapter.)

1. Premise 1: All things that have a motor need oil.
   Premise 2: All automobiles need oil.
   Conclusion: Automobiles have motors.

2. Premise 1: All flowers have petals.
   Premise 2: Lapidars have petals.
   Conclusion: Lapidars are flowers.

3. Premise 1: All eastern countries are communist.
   Premise 2: Canada is not an eastern country.
   Conclusion: Canada is not communist.

4. Premise 1: All unemployed people are poor.
   Premise 2: Hudon is not unemployed.
   Conclusion: Hudon is not poor.

Time pressure also has a clear effect on accuracy in solving syllogisms. Galotti and her coauthors (1986) tested undergraduates who had scored either in the bottom third or the top third on a pretest of syllogistic reasoning ability, as well as graduate students who had previously studied logic. The students were first allowed only 20 seconds to solve each syllogism. With this little time, they could give only their first impression of the correct answer. Immediately afterward, they received the same problem and were allowed as much time as they wanted. Figure 11.2 shows the results. As you can see, results showed that expertise influenced reasoning ability, no matter how much time they had to solve the problem. Furthermore, students in each of the groups improved when they had more time on the problems. Syllogisms are challenging, and even high-ability students make errors when time is limited.

Errors in Syllogistic Reasoning. People make two common errors in solving syllogisms. They make illicit conversions, and they are influenced by belief bias.

We discussed illicit conversion in connection with conditional reasoning. People also perform illicit conversions for syllogisms. Specifically, they assume that the premise "All *A* are *B*" can also be interpreted as "All *B* are *A*." Notice that this assumption is correct for only one of the two interpretations of the word *all* in Figure 11.1. Research shows that about 30 percent of introductory psychology students consistently perform illicit conversions on syllogisms that use the word *all* (Newstead, 1989; Newstead & Griggs, 1983). As you can imagine, illicit conversion of premises is a common source of errors on syllogisms.

Before you read further, be sure you tried the syllogisms in Demonstration 11.3. This demonstration examines the **belief-bias effect** in syllogistic reasoning, which occurs when people make judgments based on prior beliefs, rather than on the rules of logic. Naturally, not everyone makes this kind of error. However, in a typical study, undergraduate students correctly accepted fewer than half of the conclusions in syllogisms where the conclusions were indeed valid, but unbelievable (Evans et al., 1983). People are often reluctant to say that a conclusion is valid if that conclusion contradicts common sense.

Similarly, Markovitz and Nantel (1989) gave French-Canadian college students a series of syllogisms; the English translations for some of them appeared in Demonstration 11.3. As you can see, some items described real objects, and the logical conclusion contradicted the students' prior beliefs. Other items substituted nonsense words in the syllogisms; therefore, no belief bias could influence students' conclusions.

The results showed that people were significantly more likely to believe the conclusions were correct when these conclusions were consistent with their prior beliefs. In contrast, when the syllogism used a nonsense word, they were more likely to detect the flaw in the logic. Now check your own answers. The first and second syllogisms have the same format. However, if you resemble the students in Markovitz and Nantel's study, the conclusion, "Automobiles have motors," seems entirely appropriate. In contrast, you may have caught the flaw in the structurally similar second syllogism; you are more likely to be critical in judging statements about nonsense words. Similarly, the third and the fourth syllogisms have the same format; were you more suspicious about the fourth one? (Incidentally, if these items are still puzzling, try drawing Euler's circles to represent the possible interpretations of each premise.)

How can we explain belief bias? According to Evans (1989), belief bias is an example of a heuristic that says, "You don't have to examine a syllogism's logic carefully when the conclusions are obviously believable." In other words, people "short-circuit" their usual critical approach when the conclusions are consistent with their prior beliefs. Theme 5 emphasizes that cognition involves both top-down and bottom-up processes, but top-down processes are sometimes overactive.

Some interesting research in social psychology illustrates an application of the belief-bias effect. Lord and his coauthors (1979) asked people who either supported or opposed capital punishment to read summaries of two studies on the topic. Then they rated how well the study had been conducted and whether it supported the conclusion. Half of the summaries presented results supporting capital punishment; the other half opposed capital punishment. Lord and his colleagues found that both supporters and opponents of capital punishment rated the studies as higher in quality if they conformed to their own prior beliefs. In other words, people tend to accept information uncritically if they agree with it.

The Analogical Theory of Syllogisms.

Johnson-Laird and his coauthors have developed a theory to explain how people solve syllogisms (Johnson-Laird & Bara, 1984; Johnson-Laird & Byrne, 1991; Johnson-Laird & Steedman, 1978). They restricted their investigations to concrete sentences, and they asked participants to supply a conclusion, rather than to judge the plausibility of a conclusion. For example, people might be asked to supply a conclusion for these two premises:

All of the artists are beekeepers.
Some of the beekeepers are clever.

(Conclusion?)

Johnson-Laird and his colleagues argue that people represent the premises of a syllogism in terms of **mental models,** or internal pictures of a problem. This emphasis on mental representations was inspired by one participant who described his solution strategy: "I thought of all the little . . . artists in the room and imagined that they all had beekeeper's hats on" (Johnson-Laird & Steedman, 1978, p. 77).

Johnson-Laird's notation system represents the first premise, "All of the artists are beekeepers," in this fashion:

```
    artist        artist
      ↓             ↓
 beekeeper    beekeeper    (beekeeper)    (beekeeper)
```

In this representation, an arrow represents the relationship between two items and can be translated "is a." Thus, each of the first two artists is a beekeeper. The parentheses around the other two beekeepers indicate that some beekeepers may not be artists. Johnson-Laird's theory is called an **analogical theory** because of the way people presumably represent the premises with mental analogies.

The theory argues that people then combine representations. For example, the previous syllogism could be represented:

```
All of the artists
are beekeepers                    artist       artist
                                    ↓            ↓
Some of the beekeepers    beekeeper    beekeeper    (beekeeper)    (beekeeper)
are clever                    ↓
                           clever      (clever)      (clever)
```

In the next stage, people draw their conclusion. If at least one positive path can be created, they conclude, "Some artists are clever." If there is at least one negative path, they conclude, "Some artists are not clever." If there are *only* negative paths, they conclude, "No artists are clever."

Notice how the strategy could lead to an error; some artists may be beekeepers, but not clever. (Try Euler's circles if you are not convinced.) In one study, 12 out of 20 people erroneously concluded, "Some artists are clever."

During the final stage, Johnson-Laird proposes that people test their initial representation by searching for counterexamples. For instance, can the established path between *artist* and *clever* be broken and still remain consistent with the original premises? In fact, you may realize that the only arrow between *beekeeper* and *clever* might be in the third column, not the first. People who search for counterexamples in this fashion would therefore reject the conclusion that some artists are clever.

In Chapter 10, we saw that problem-solvers often fail to search the entire problem space. In logical reasoning tasks, people also frequently conduct inadequate searches. Furthermore, we don't always have time to search for counterexamples. With time constraints, we are likely to conclude, "No valid conclusion can be drawn" (Johnson-Laird & Bara, 1984).

Some psychologists are skeptical about Johnson-Laird's analogical theory (e.g., Wetherick, 1989, 1991). However, many believe that this approach is the most broad ranging and promising theory that is currently available (e.g., Eysenck & Keane, 1990; Gilhooly, 1988). One strong feature of the model is that it explains how we are often tempted to draw the wrong conclusion for a syllogism. However, it also accounts for people who take a more critical approach and realize that the initial conclusion is not correct. For example, turn back to Figure 11.2, which examines time pressure and expertise. When reasoners have more time, they can leisurely examine the syllogisms and detect errors in their conclusions.

SECTION SUMMARY: LOGICAL REASONING

1. Conditional reasoning involves "if . . . , then . . . " relationships; performance is most accurate for the two valid categories, for concrete problems, and for affirmative (rather than negative) statements.
2. Sources of error in conditional reasoning include making only one model of the premises, making illicit conversions, trying to confirm a hypothesis rather than disprove it (for example, on a selection task), and failing to transfer knowledge to a new task.
3. Syllogisms involve quantitative statements using words such as *all*, *some*, and *none*; the words *all* and *some* are often misinterpreted.
4. Performance on syllogisms is most accurate with active, affirmative sentences and when there is no time pressure.
5. Two common errors in syllogistic reasoning are illicit conversion and the belief-bias effect.

6. Johnson-Laird's analogical theory proposes that people form mental models and try to find connections between the premises. After drawing conclusions, they may check for counterexamples.

DECISION MAKING

As we noted at the beginning of the chapter, reasoning uses established rules to draw clear-cut conclusions. In contrast, decision making involves uncertainty. Critical information is missing, and other information may be unreliable. Should you apply to graduate school or get a job after college? Should you take social psychology in the morning or the afternoon? On a more trivial level, should you bring your umbrella this afternoon? No list of rules, such as the propositional calculus, can help you assess the relative merits of graduate school or employment—given all the sources of potential uncertainty.

Psychologists have approached the study of decision making in several different ways. The different approaches are described in recent books about decision making (e.g., Dawes, 1988; Hogarth, 1990; Rachlin, 1989; Yates, 1990). Several approaches emphasize how people weigh the various costs and benefits of various outcomes. In this chapter, however, we will emphasize the approach that focuses on decision-making heuristics. As you'll recall from previous chapters, **heuristics** are rules of thumb or strategies that are likely to produce a correct solution. As a consequence, decision making is not perfectly accurate because people often fail to appreciate the limitations of these heuristics (Abelson & Levi, 1985). In the words of one theorist, humans are "sometimes systematically irrational" (Baron, 1991, p. 487).

Throughout this section, you will often see the names of two researchers, Daniel Kahneman and Amos Tversky. These two individuals proposed that a small number of heuristics guide human decision making. They emphasize that the strategies that normally guide us toward the correct decision may sometimes lead us astray—consistent with Theme 2 of this book. We need to stress, however, that these heuristics normally lead us to the correct decisions in our everyday lives.

Throughout this part of the chapter, we will discuss many studies that point out errors in decision making. These errors should not, however, lead you to conclude that humans are limited, foolish creatures (Crandall, 1984). Instead, keep in mind a caution expressed by Nisbett and Ross (1980). They argue that people's decision-making strategies are well adapted to handle a wide range of problems. However, these same strategies become a liability when they are applied beyond that range. Nisbett and Ross point out that psychologists interested in decision making emphasize errors that people make, and this emphasis on what can go wrong is parallel to the interest of researchers in perception in illusions:

Perception researchers have shown that in spite of, and largely because of, people's exquisite perceptual capacities, they are subject to certain perceptual illusions. No serious scientist, however, is led by such demonstrations to conclude that the perceptual system under study is inherently faulty. Similarly, we conclude from our own research that we are observing not an inherently faulty cognitive apparatus but rather, one that manifests certain explicable flaws. Indeed, in human inference as in perception, we suspect that many of people's failings will prove to be closely related to, or even an unavoidable cost of, their greatest strengths. (p. 14)

Once again, a heuristic that usually leads to correct conclusions can produce errors if it is used inappropriately. Let us explore three classic decision-making heuristics—representativeness, availability, and anchoring and adjustment. Then we will consider two general issues in decision making: (1) how wording and context influence decisions and (2) overconfidence in decision making.

The Representativeness Heuristic

Representativeness is probably the most important of the decision-making heuristics (Nisbett et al., 1983). Let us look at an example before we consider a formal definition. Suppose that you have a regular penny with one head (H) and one tail (T), and you toss it six times. Which outcome seems most likely?

```
H H H H H H
H H H T T T
T H H T H T
```

If you are like most people, you would guess that T H H T H T would be the most likely outcome of those three possibilities. After all, you know that if a coin is tossed six times, it is likely to come up tails three times and heads three times. It would be much less likely to come up heads all six times in your sample. Furthermore, you know that coin tossing should produce heads and tails in random order, and the order T H H T H T looks much more random than H H H T T T.

A sample looks **representative** if it is similar in important characteristics to the population from which it was selected. The specific definition of representativeness depends on how that sample was selected from the population (Pitz & Sachs, 1984). For example, if a sample was selected by a random process, then that sample must look random for people to judge it to be representative. Thus, T H H T H T is a sample that would be judged representative because it has an equal number of heads and tails, just like the population of all possible coin tosses. Furthermore, T H H T H T would be judged representative because the order of the T's and H's looks random rather than orderly.

Kahneman and Tversky (1972) pointed out that when people make decisions about the relative frequency of different samples, such as coin tosses, they often seem to be unaware of the true probabilities. For example, the *specific* sequence H H H H H H is just as likely to occur as the *specific* sequence T H H T H T. Each of these two sequences occurs 1/64 of the time. However, instead of using true probabilities, people use representativeness as a basis for decisions, believing that T H H T H T is more likely. Thus, we often use the **representativeness heuristic,** judging a sample to be likely on the basis of similarity and random-looking appearance. Here is another way of viewing representativeness, related to a topic discussed in Chapter 7. A sample looks representative if it resembles a prototype (Pitz & Sachs, 1984). The sample T H H T H T looks like a prototypical sample of coin tosses, whereas the sample H H H H H H does not.

Notice that the representativeness heuristic often leads to the correct choice in everyday decisions. For example, suppose that someone asked you which of the following choices would be more likely, if you were to select five people in the United States and measure their IQs: (1) 100, 100, 100, 100, 100, or (2) 140, 140, 140, 140, 140. You would note that both samples look too homogeneous. However, you would appropriately select the first option because it is similar in important characteristics to the population from which it was selected; namely, both the sample and the population have a mean of 100. Furthermore, the population has more IQs of 100 than IQs of 140. In summary, representativeness is generally a useful heuristic that leads us to the correct decision. When we overuse it, however, we can make incorrect decisions.

Let us consider some examples of how the representativeness heuristic emphasizes random-looking outcomes. Then we will see how people tend to ignore both sample size and base rate, as long as the sample looks representative. Finally, we will consider an interesting consequence of the representativeness heuristic, called the conjunction fallacy.

Random-Looking Outcomes and the Representativeness Heuristic.

According to the representativeness heuristic, we believe that random-looking outcomes are more likely than orderly looking outcomes—as long as the outcome is produced by a random process. Has a cashier ever added up your bill, and the sum looked *too* orderly, say $22.22? You might even be tempted to check the arithmetic, because addition is a process that should yield a random-looking outcome. You would be less likely to check the bill if it were $21.97, because that very random-looking outcome is a more representative kind of answer.

Kahneman and Tversky (1972) discuss how the representativeness heuristic operated during World War II. London was intensively bombed during this war. A few sections of the city were hit several times, whereas other sections were not hit at all. People therefore generally believed that a systematic plan must have guided the bombing; they did not believe that a random plan could have produced such an apparently orderly bombing pattern. However, a statistical analysis demonstrated that the pattern was in fact consistent with random bombing. People find it difficult to believe that a random process can produce occasional orderly patterns.

As an example of the representativeness heuristic, Kahneman and Tversky (1972) conducted several experiments that emphasize the importance of representativeness. In one study, for example, they asked people to make judgments about

TABLE 11.2

TWO DISTRIBUTIONS OF 20 MARBLES.

DISTRIBUTION 1		DISTRIBUTION 2	
Beth	4	Beth	4
Sally	4	Sally	4
Jerome	4	Jerome	3
Darlene	4	Darlene	4
Pedro	4	Pedro	5

families with six children. People judged the sequence G B B G B G to be more likely than the sequence B B B G G G. People base their decisions on representativeness, rather than on true probability.

Kahneman and Tversky also asked people to imagine that five children were playing a game involving the random distribution of 20 marbles. They were asked to guess which of two possible distributions would be more likely to occur; the distributions were similar to those in Table 11.2. Actually, the uniformity in Distribution 1 is statistically more likely than the nonuniformity in Distribution 2. (Distributions *similar* to Distribution 2 are likely, but that *exact* distribution is unlikely.) However, Distribution 2 looks more representative. This distribution is basically equal, with just enough deviation from equality to look random. People therefore judge Distribution 2 to be more likely. Now try Demonstration 11.4 before you read further.

DEMONSTRATION 11.4

SAMPLE SIZE AND REPRESENTATIVENESS.

A nearby town is served by two hospitals. About 45 babies are born each day in the larger hospital. About 15 babies are born each day in the smaller hospital. Approximately 50 percent of all babies are boys, as you know. However, the exact percentage of babies who are boys will vary from day to day. Some days it may be higher than 50 percent, some days it may be lower. For a period of one year, both the larger hospital and the smaller hospital recorded the number of days on which more than 60 percent of the babies born were boys. Which hospital do you think recorded more such days?

___ The larger hospital
___ The smaller hospital
___ About the same (say, within 5 percent of each other)

Sample Size and Representativeness. When we make a decision, representativeness is such a compelling heuristic that we often ignore other important information, such as sample size. How did you respond to Demonstration 11.4? Kahneman and Tversky (1972) asked college students this question, and most of them responded "about the same." Apparently it seems equally likely for a hospital to report having at least 60 percent baby boys born on a given day, whether the hospital is large or small. Thus sample size was ignored by the college students surveyed.

In reality, however, sample size is an important characteristic that should be considered whenever you make decisions. A large sample is statistically more likely than a small sample to reflect the true proportions in a population. For example, if about 50 percent of all babies are boys in a population, then a large sample is likely to have close to 50 percent boy babies. For instance, it is unlikely that 40 of the 45 babies in the large hospital—about 90 percent—would be boys. It is much more likely for about 90 percent of the babies in the small hospital to be boys; 13 boys out of 15 babies would not be an unusual outcome. However, people are usually unaware of the relationship between sample size and deviance from a population proportion. Representativeness guides their decisions, and deviations from representativeness—such as more than 60 percent boy babies—seem equally likely whether the sample is large or small.

Tversky and Kahneman (1971) point out that we should believe in the **law of large numbers,** which states that large samples will be representative of the population from which they are selected. The law of large numbers is a correct law. However, too often we also believe in an incorrect principle, which could be called "the law of small numbers"; this principle states that small samples will be representative of the population from which they are selected. The law of small numbers is not correct, but we often believe it anyway.

We often incorrectly apply the law of small numbers, not only in relatively abstract statistics problems, but also in social situations. For example, we may draw unwarranted conclusions about a group of people on the basis of a small number of group members (Quattrone & Jones, 1980; Read, 1983). Stereotypes are often formed by too much trust in the law of small numbers. One effective way of combating inappropriate stereotypes is to become acquainted with a large number of people from the target group, for example, through exchange programs with people in other countries.

In some cases, however, people appropriately favor the law of large numbers over the law of small numbers. For example, research by Well and his colleagues (1990) shows that college students know that the mean (average) for a large sample is likely to be close to the mean for the entire population. They also know that the mean for a small sample can be quite discrepant from the population mean. However, students fail to understand the implications of this information. Specifically, they do not realize that if the mean for a small sample is more variable, you are more likely to find a deviant mean (for example, more than 60 percent boys in a sample of babies).

People are also more likely to use the law of large numbers for problems in areas in which they have extensive experience. For example, people with experience in team sports appropriately use the law of large numbers (rather than the law of small numbers) for a decision about probable outcomes in a football game. Similarly, people with experience in acting are more likely to use the law of large numbers for a decision involving theater performances, in contrast to people with no experience in acting (Kunda & Nisbett, 1986). Also, there are tremendous individual differences in ability in answering sample-size problems (Pollard & Evans, 1983); some people find the task difficult, whereas others realize that large sample sizes are less likely to contain deviant distributions.

Fortunately, people can be trained to appreciate the law of large numbers. Fong and his colleagues (1986) included four conditions in their study:

1. a control group given no training;
2. a group given abstract training in the law of large numbers;
3. a group given examples about the law of large numbers; and
4. a group given both abstract training and examples.

The results showed that the control group answered 43 percent of the questions correctly, in contrast to 56 percent for the abstract-training group and 55 percent for the examples group. The group given both kinds of training performed best, with 64 percent of the questions correct. Thus, training can help people to some extent, though many people still fail to appreciate the law of large numbers.

In summary, representativeness is such a strong heuristic that people often

---

DEMONSTRATION 11.5

BASE RATES AND REPRESENTATIVENESS (FROM KAHNEMAN AND TVERSKY, 1973, P. 241).

Imagine that some psychologists have administered personality tests to 30 engineers and 70 lawyers, all people who are successful in their fields. Brief descriptions were written for each of the 30 engineers and the 70 lawyers. A sample description follows. Judge that description by indicating the probability that the person described is an engineer. Use a scale from 0 to 100.

Jack is a 45-year-old man. He is married and has four children. He is generally conservative, careful, and ambitious. He shows no interest in political and social issues and spends most of his free time on his many hobbies which include home carpentry, sailing, and mathematical puzzles.

The probability that the man is one of the 30 engineers in the sample of 100 is _____ percent.

ignore other characteristics of the sample that should be important, such as sample size. People will pay attention to the law of large numbers when judging the mean, when they have had experience in a problem area, and when they have received formal training.

Base Rate and Representativeness.

Representativeness is so compelling that people also ignore the **base rate,** or how often the item occurs in the population. Try Demonstration 11.5 before we proceed. Using problems like the one in this demonstration, Kahneman and Tversky (1973) showed that people rely on representativeness when they are asked to judge category membership. They ignore the relative proportions of the categories in the population (that is, the base rates), and they focus instead on the extent to which a description is representative of members of each category.

In one study, people were presented with a personality sketch of an imaginary person named Steve. Steve was described in the following words:

> Steve is very shy and withdrawn, invariably helpful, but with little interest in people, or in the world of reality. A meek and tidy soul, he has a need for order and structure, and a passion for detail. (Tversky & Kahneman, 1974, p. 1124)

After reading the passage, people were asked to judge Steve's occupation. A list of possibilities—such as farmer, salesperson, airline pilot, librarian, and physician—was supplied. If people pay attention to base rates, they should select a profession that has a high base rate in the population, such as a salesperson. However, people used the representativeness heuristic, and they tended to guess that Steve was a librarian. The description of Steve was highly similar to (that is, representative of) the stereotype of a librarian.

You might argue, however, that the experiment with Steve was unfair. After all, Tversky and Kahneman did not make the base rates of the various professions at all prominent in the problem. People may not have considered the fact that salespeople are more common than librarians. Well, the base rate was made very clear in Demonstration 11.5; you were told that the base rate was 30 engineers and 70 lawyers in the population. Did you make use of this base rate and guess that Jack was highly likely to be a lawyer? Most people ignored this base-rate information and judged on the basis of representativeness. In fact, this description is highly representative of our stereotype for engineers, and so people guess a high percentage for the answer to the question.

Kahneman and Tversky (1973) point out how their studies are related to Bayes' rule. **Bayes' rule** (also called Bayes' theorem) states that judgments should be influenced by two factors, base rate and the likelihood ratio. The **likelihood ratio** is the ratio of the probability that the description came from population A, divided by the probability that the description came from population B. For example, in the engineer-versus-lawyer decision, let us say that engineers represent population A and lawyers represent population B. Now the description in Demonstration 11.5

DEMONSTRATION 11.6

THE CONJUNCTION FALLACY.

Read the following paragraph:

> Linda is 31 years old, single, outspoken, and very bright. She majored in philosophy. As a student, she was deeply concerned with issues of discrimination and social justice, and also participated in antinuclear demonstrations.

Now rank the following options in terms of their likelihood in describing Linda. Give a ranking of 1 to the most likely option and a ranking of 8 to the least likely option:

_____ Linda is a teacher at an elementary school.
_____ Linda works in a bookstore and takes Yoga classes.
_____ Linda is active in the feminist movement.
_____ Linda is a psychiatric social worker.
_____ Linda is a member of the League of Women Voters.
_____ Linda is a bank teller.
_____ Linda is an insurance salesperson.
_____ Linda is a bank teller and is active in the feminist movement.

---

is probably much more representative of a typical engineer than of a typical lawyer. Thus, the likelihood ratio is very high, because the probability that the passage describes an engineer is greater than the probability that the passage describes a lawyer. We seem to base our decision on this likelihood ratio, and we tend to ignore base rates. However, Bayes' rule says that we must also pay attention to base rates. Because people often ignore base rates, they are not obeying Bayes' rule.

We should emphasize, however, that people vary widely in the way they tackle problems. In their summary of the research, Pollard and Evans (1983b) conclude that many people tend to ignore base rates, but a sizable minority do pay attention to them. They also conclude, unfortunately, that few people can apply the base-rate information properly. On the brighter side, other research shows that people who have been encouraged to use base rates in prior problems are likely to use them on future problems (Ginossar & Trope, 1987). Furthermore, after a training session on probability concepts such as base rates, students become more competent at solving problems that involve the representativeness heuristic (Gebotys & Claxton-Oldfield, 1989).

The Conjunction Fallacy and Representativeness. Try Demonstration 11.6 before you read further. Now inspect your answers. Which did you rank more likely, that Linda is a bank teller, or that Linda is a bank teller and is active in the feminist movement? Demonstration 11.6 represents one of the types of questions that Tversky and Kahneman (1983) tested in their study on the conjunction fallacy. Let us examine their experiment and then discuss the nature of the conjunction fallacy.

Tversky and Kahneman presented the "Linda" problem and another similar problem to three groups of people. One was a statistically naive group of undergraduates. The second group consisted of first-year graduate students who had taken one or more courses in statistics; this group had intermediate knowledge about the principles of probability. The third group consisted of doctoral students in a decision science program of a business school who had taken several advanced courses in probability and statistics; they were labeled the sophisticated group. In each case, the participants were asked to rank all eight statements according to their probability, with the rank of 1 assigned to the most likely statement.

Figure 11.3 shows the average rank for each of the two critical statements: (1) "Linda is a bank teller" and (2) "Linda is a bank teller and is active in the feminist movement" for each of the three groups. Notice that the people in all three groups thought that the second statement would be more likely than the first.

Think for a moment why this conclusion is statistically impossible. The **conjunction rule** states that the probability of a conjunction of two events cannot be larger than the probability of its constituent events. In the Linda problem, the conjunction of the two events—bank teller and feminist—cannot occur more often than either event by itself, for example, being a bank teller. (Contemplate some other examples of the conjunction rule; for example, the number of psychology majors who were born in the state of Iowa cannot be greater than the number of psychology majors.)

Tversky and Kahneman (1983) discovered, however, that most people commit the **conjunction fallacy:** They judge the probability of the conjunction to be greater than the probability of a constituent event. The conjunction fallacy can be traced to the representativeness heuristic. People judged the conjunction of "bank teller" and "feminist" to be more likely than the simple event "bank teller," because "feminist" is a characteristic that is very representative of (that is, similar to) someone who is single, outspoken, bright, a philosophy major, concerned about social justice, and an antinuclear activist. A person with these characteristics doesn't seem very likely to become a bank teller, but she seems highly likely to be a feminist. By adding to "bank teller" the extra detail of "feminist," we have made the description seem more plausible—even though that description is statistically less likely.

Psychologists have been particularly intrigued with the conjunction fallacy, because it demonstrates that people can ignore one of the most basic principles of probability theory. As Birnbaum and his colleagues (1990) write, "Many scholars have found it disturbing to think that humans might have been rational enough to invent probability theory but not rational enough to use it in their daily thought" (p. 477). The results on the conjunction fallacy have been replicated many times, with generally consistent findings (e.g., Birnbaum et al., 1990; Shafir et al., 1990; and Wolford et al., 1990).

FIGURE 11.3

The Influence of Type of Statement and Level of Statistical Sophistication on Likelihood Ratings. (Note: Low numbers on the ranking indicate that people think the event is more likely.)

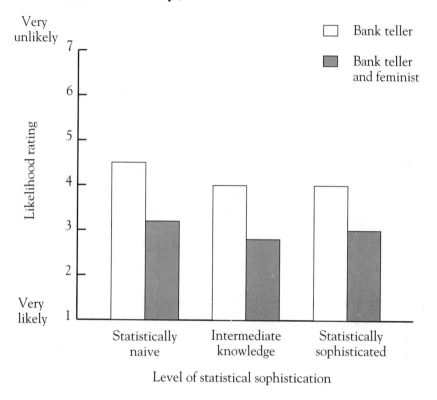

Some skeptics have wondered whether the conjunction fallacy can be traced to a simple verbal misunderstanding. For example, perhaps when people read, "Linda is a bank teller," they interpret that to mean that Linda is a bank teller who is *not* active in the feminist movement. (You'll recall that we discussed how people reading the word "some" in a syllogism problem in logical reasoning often understand it to mean "some, but not all"—a simple verbal misunderstanding.) However, we do not yet have much evidence for this explanation; the real villain is probably the overuse of the representativeness heuristic (Agnoli & Krantz, 1989). Once again, however, when people are taught alternative strategies, they can learn to use the representativeness heuristic more appropriately (Agnoli & Krantz, 1989).

AVAILABILITY AND LETTER ESTIMATES.

Some experts studied the frequency of appearance of various letters in the English language. They selected a typical passage in English and recorded the relative frequency with which various letters of the alphabet appeared in the first and the third positions in words. For example, in the word *language*, *L* appears in the first position and *N* appears in the third position. In this study, words with less than three letters were not examined. Consider the letter *K*. Do you think that the letter *K* is more likely to appear in the first position or the third position? Now estimate the ratio for the number of times it appeared in the first position in comparison to the number of times it appeared in the third position. For example, if you guess 2:1, this means that it appeared in the first position twice as often as in the third position; if you guess 1:2, this means that it appeared in the third position twice as often as in the first position.

Before we discuss a second decision-making heuristic, let's briefly review the representativeness heuristic. We use the representativeness heuristic when we make decisions based on whether a sample looks similar in important characteristics to the population it comes from. The representativeness heuristic is so appealing that we tend to ignore other important characteristics that *should* be considered—such as sample size and base rate—and we also fail to acknowledge that the probability of two events occurring together (for example, bank teller and feminist) needs to be smaller than the probability of just one of those events (for example, bank teller). In sum, the representativeness heuristic is basically helpful in our daily lives, but sometimes we tend to use it inappropriately.

◇ In Depth: **The Availability Heuristic**

A second important heuristic that people use in making decisions is availability. Because much recent research has been conducted on this heuristic, we will examine it in depth. You use the **availability heuristic** whenever you estimate frequency or probability in terms of how easy it is to think of examples of something (Tversky & Kahneman, 1973). In other words, people judge frequency by assessing whether relevant examples can be easily retrieved from memory or whether this memory retrieval requires great effort. This heuristic is generally helpful in everyday life. For example, suppose that someone asked you whether there were more psychology majors or more Spanish majors at your college. You have probably not memorized the enrollment statistics, so you would be likely to answer the question in terms of the relative availability of examples of psychology majors and Spanish majors. It is easy to retrieve names of psychology majors ("Karl, Lucia, Peter, . . . ") because your memory has stored the names of dozens of people you know in psychology. However, you have more trouble retrieving the names of Spanish majors. Because examples of psychology majors were relatively easy to retrieve, you conclude that there are more psychology majors at your college. Now try Demonstration 11.7 before you read further.

Recall that a heuristic is a rule of thumb that is generally accurate. The availability heuristic *is* generally accurate—probably more psychology majors than Spanish majors attend your college. Thus the availability heuristic is useful in judgment, insofar as availability is correlated with true, objective frequency—and it usually is. However, the availability heuristic can lead to errors. As we will see in this section, other factors influence memory retrieval but are *not* correlated with objective frequency. These factors distort availability and therefore decrease the accuracy of our judgments. We will see that recency and familiarity—both factors that influence memory—can potentially influence availability.

The availability heuristic makes sense, even though it can lead to errors. We know from our everyday experience that things we frequently see are easier to recall than things we seldom see. For instance, you have seen the names Kahneman and Tversky frequently in this chapter, and so you can remember the names easily. In contrast, the names Abelson and Levi were mentioned only once, and these names would probably be more difficult to remember. We know that greater frequency produces better memory, and so we turn the rule around when we are asked to judge frequency. We assume that if we have better memory for an item, then that item must have greater frequency. (If your memory about logical reasoning is strong, you will recognize this error as an illicit conversion.) The problem arises, as mentioned previously, because better memory (and hence availability) can be produced by factors other than frequency.

Let's make certain that you know how availability differs from representativeness. When we use the representativeness heuristic, we are given a specific example (such as T H T T H H or Linda the philosophy major). We then make judgments about whether the specific example is similar to the general category it is supposed to represent (such as coin-tosses or feminist bank tellers). In contrast, when we use the availability heuristic, we are given a general category and we must supply the specific examples (such as examples of psychology majors). Then we make judgments on the basis of the ease with which these specific examples come to mind. So here is a way to remember the two: If the problem begins with a specific example, you are dealing with the representativeness heuristic; if the problem begins with a general category, you are dealing with the availability heuristic.

A classic study on the availability heuristic asked people to consider two general categories, words with *k* in the first position and words with *k* in the third position; this task was illustrated in Demonstration 11.7. Tversky and Kahneman (1973) found that most people guess that about twice as many words with *k* appear in the first position, rather than in the third position. However, in reality, about twice as many *k*'s appear in the third position as in the first position.

Why do we overestimate the frequency of first-position *k*'s? Well, consider how you approached the question in Demonstration 11.7. You probably thought it was easy to recall examples of words beginning with *k* (kitty, koala, kitchen, kind, and so on). In contrast, it was difficult to search for words in terms of their third letter. If we make judgments on the basis of how easily examples come to mind, the first-position task wins hands-down. Consequently, we erroneously judge first-letter *k*'s to be more common.

We'll begin our exploration of availability by considering two factors that influence availability—recency and familiarity. Then we will examine a consequence of availability, called illusory correlations. Finally, we will see how availability operates when people try to imagine an event in the future.

Recency and Availability. Memory for items generally declines with the passage of time, and thus more recently experienced items are recalled better. As a result, more recent items are more available, and we judge them to be more likely than they really are. For example, if you had been asked, following the incident at the World Trade Center, to estimate the frequency of terrorist bombings in early 1993, your estimate would probably have been high. Recency also influences judgments about the probability of natural hazards. People rush to purchase earthquake insurance immediately after an earthquake. However, the purchase rate drops steadily thereafter, as the earthquake fades into history (Slovic et al., 1982).

An article in the *New England Journal of Medicine* points out how physicians can be influenced by the recency effect. The article describes a physician who was reluctant to recommend a particular medical procedure because a serious neurological disorder had developed in a patient of his who had recently undergone this procedure. The authors of the article comment upon the physician's decision making:

> The physician's conclusion is probably correct, though [we would] question his rationale. Recalling a patient who suffered a complication is an example of the availability heuristic, a bias that makes noteworthy outcomes seem more likely. (Pauker & Kopelman, 1992, p. 41)

Researchers in decision making should be delighted that their findings are being discussed in a prestigious medical journal. This kind of information can help physicians become more unbiased decision makers!

Familiarity and Availability. The familiarity of the examples can also produce a distortion in frequency estimation. For instance, people who are acquainted with many examples of divorce often provide higher estimates of divorce rates than do people who have rarely encountered divorce (Kozielecki, 1981). Furthermore—turning again to a medical example—physicians tend to have distorted ideas about the dangers of various diseases that are frequently discussed in medical journals. One study demonstrated a strong correlation between the number of journal articles about each disease and physicians' estimates about whether that disease was likely to be fatal (Christensen-Szalanski et al., 1983). This correlation held true, regardless of what the article actually said about the disease. Schwartz and Griffin (1986) point out a potential real-life problem that may occur: If journal coverage leads a doctor to believe that a disease is more dangerous than it really is, he or she may order screening tests that are actually unnecessary.

Journalists and broadcast newspeople overexpose us to some events and under-expose us to others (Slovic et al., 1982). For example, violent events such as tornadoes, fires, drownings, murders, and accidents are reported much more often than less dramatic causes of death, even though these less dramatic deaths actually occur more often in real life. Newspapers tend not to report deaths due to diabetes or emphysema, even though these diseases are responsible for 16 times as many deaths, in comparison with accidents. However, newspapers carry three times as many articles about accidents. One hundred times as many people die from diseases as are murdered, yet the newspapers carry three times as many articles about murders.

The problem is that media coverage makes some causes of death more available than others. As a consequence, people's estimates are influenced. In fact, the correlation between judged frequency of death and the number of deaths reported in newspapers is about +.70, a strong positive correlation. The press covered terrorist violence extensively in the mid-1980s, so people would not have guessed that in 1985, they were more likely to drown in their own bathtub than to die of a terrorist attack ("Please Go Away," 1986). Would you guess from the press coverage that more than twice as many U.S. residents are killed by falling than by dying in a fire ("Rating Threats," 1989)?

The media also misrepresent the frequency of other events. When television features fictional programs about violence and other antisocial behavior, viewers are guided by the availability heuristic. That is, they are likely to exaggerate the prevalence of antisocial behavior in our society (Berkowitz, 1984).

Did you know that the media can even influence your estimates of a country's population? Try asking a friend to estimate the populations of Indonesia, Nigeria, and Bangladesh. Each of these countries has a population of over 100 million people. However, Brown and Siegler (1992) found that undergraduate students who were tested in 1989 gave median population estimates of 19.5 million, 16.5 million, and 14.0 million, respectively. In 1989, these countries were not in the news. Because they were relatively unfamiliar, students gave low estimates. In contrast, El Salvador was frequently in the news during that era because of U.S. intervention in Latin America. The students estimated the population of El Salvador as 12 million, though its actual population was only 5 million. In summary, we underestimate the number of people in the countries that are seldom mentioned in the news, and we overestimate the number of people in frequently mentioned countries. The media create our cognitive realities.

The media can also influence viewers' ideas about the prevalence of different points of view. Nisbett and Ross (1980) note that protesters in the huge antiwar marches of the Vietnam era resented the media's distortion of antiwar and pro-war sympathizers. The media would often devote almost as much time to several

---

DEMONSTRATION 11.8

FAMILIARITY AND AVAILABILITY.

Read this list of names to several friends. After you have finished the entire list, ask your friends to estimate whether there were more men or women listed. Do not allow them to answer "about the same." (In reality, 14 women's names and 15 men's names are listed.)

Louisa May Alcott   Maxine Hong Kingston
John Dickson Carr   Virginia Woolf
Alice Walker   Robert Lovett
Thomas Hughes   Judy Blume
Laura Ingalls Wilder   George Nathan
Jack Lindsay   Allan Nevins
Edward George Lytton   Jane Austen
Margaret Mitchell   Henry Crabb Robinson
Michael Drayton   Joseph Lincoln
Edith Wharton   Emily Bronte
Henry Vaughan   Arthur Hutchinson
Judith Krantz   James Hunt
Agatha Christie   Alice Walker
Richard Watson Gilder   Brian Hooker
                                      Harriet Beecher Stowe

---

dozen counterprotesters as they devoted to the 100,000 protesters. The protesters were understandably concerned that the media made both protesters and counterprotesters equally available to television viewers. Viewers might therefore reach inaccurate conclusions about the sizes of the two groups. Notice whether you can spot the same tendency in current news broadcasts.

Try Demonstration 11.8, a modification of a study by Tversky and Kahneman (1973). See if your friends respond according to the familiarity of the examples, rather than true frequency. Tversky and Kahneman presented people with lists of 39 names. A typical list might contain 19 names of famous women and 20 names of less famous men. After hearing the list, they were asked to judge whether the list contained more men's names or more women's names. About 80 percent of the participants erroneously guessed that the group with the most famous, familiar names was the more frequent, even though it was objectively less frequent.

Illusory Correlation and Availability. So far, we have seen that availability—or the ease with which examples come to mind—is generally a useful heuristic. However, it can become "contaminated" by factors such as recency and frequency, leading to inappropriate decisions about an event's frequency. Now we turn to a third topic, to see how the availability heuristic can be responsible for an error called an *illusory correlation*. As you know, a correlation is a statistical relationship between two variables. *Illusory* is derived from the word *illusion*; it means deceptive or unreal. Therefore, an **illusory correlation** occurs when people believe that a statistical relationship exists between two variables, with no real evidence for this relationship. In particular, numerous studies show that people often believe that two kinds of events tend to occur together, when an honest tabulation would show that these two kinds of events occur together at just a chance level (Crocker, 1981; Trolier & Hamilton, 1986).

Consider this example of an illusory correlation. Research has shown that a person who is physically attractive is also perceived to be blessed with other desirable characteristics (Berscheid & Walster, 1974). For example, we believe that attractive people are also intelligent, witty, and imaginative. Indeed, attractiveness and these other good characteristics may actually be related. However, we probably distort the relationship, so that it appears stronger than it really is (Hirschberg, 1977).

Think of other examples of illusory correlations that people often proclaim. These illusory correlations may either have no basis in fact or much less basis than is commonly believed. For example, consider the following illusory correlations: females are unskilled at math, blondes are not very bright, gay people have psychological problems, and so forth.

An early investigation of illusory correlation was performed by Chapman and Chapman (1967, 1969), who approached the problem from a clinical psychology viewpoint. They were concerned that clinicians consistently reported associations between responses on projective tests and certain clinical symptoms. However, many studies have demonstrated that there is no true relationship between the responses and the symptom. How could intelligent people, well educated in scientific methods, maintain these illusory correlations? For example, one projective test is called the Draw-a-Person test. The test assumes that people project their emotions and motivations onto the figure they draw. Careful studies have demonstrated that the responses on this test are really unrelated to clinical symptoms. Nevertheless, many clinical psychologists believe that the Draw-a-Person test is useful. For example, they claim that paranoid or suspicious patients typically exaggerate the eyes, whereas dependent patients (who like to be cared for and fed) typically exaggerate the mouth.

Chapman and Chapman (1967) asked patients in a state hospital to take the Draw-a-Person test. These drawings were then paired *completely at random* with six symptoms, such as suspiciousness and dependence. College students then examined these drawings, paired together with the symptoms of the people who had presumably drawn them. Afterwards, they were asked to report what features of the drawings were most often paired with each symptom. Remember, now, that the stimuli had been arranged so that there was indeed no systematic relationship between the drawings and the symptoms. Nonetheless, the college students reported the same kind of associations that clinical psychologists report. College students who have had no experience in a clinical setting reported, for example, that drawings with exaggerated eyes had been done by the paranoid people, whereas drawings with exaggerated mouths had been done by dependent people. Chapman and Chapman (1969) also extended their findings to reports of homosexuality on the Rorschach test.

Notice, then, that the participants reported a correlation that did not really exist. How did this illusory correlation arise? Tversky and Kahneman (1974) point out that availability provides a reasonable explanation for illusory correlation. When people judge the frequency with which exaggerated eyes and paranoid symptoms occur together, they may make judgments in terms of the associative bond between these two events. In everyday life, we associate suspiciousness with the eyes more than with any other part of the body; this association is therefore particularly strong. Thus, our judgment about how often events occur together is heavily influenced by our previous ideas rather than by the actual events.

Theorists have proposed a variety of alternate explanations for illusory correlations, including unevenly distributed attention and characteristics of the memory trace (e.g., Slovic et al., 1974; Smith, 1991). However, let's explore the availability explanation in more detail.

When we try to determine whether two variables are related to each other, we really ought to consider four kinds of information. For example, suppose that we want to determine whether people who are gay are likely to have psychological problems. Incidentally, many people seem to believe in this illusory correlation, even though research shows no consistent relationship between sexual preference and psychological problems (e.g., Kurdek, 1987; Mannion, 1981). To do the research properly, we need to pay attention to the frequency of four possible combinations: gay people who have psychological problems, gay people who do not have psychological problems, straight people who have psychological problems, and straight people who do not have psychological problems. Imagine, for example, that researchers gathered the data in Table 11.3. Their decision should be based on a comparison of two ratios:

$$\frac{\text{gay people with psychological problems}}{\text{total number of gay people}} \quad \text{versus} \quad \frac{\text{straight people with psychological problems}}{\text{total number of straight people}}$$

Using the data from Table 11.3, for example, we would find that 3 out of the 12 gay people (or 25 percent) had psychological problems, and 5 out of the 20 straight people (also 25 percent) had psychological problems. We should therefore conclude that there is no relationship between sexual preference and psychological problems.

TABLE 11.3

A MATRIX SHOWING HYPOTHETICAL INFORMATION ABOUT SEXUAL PREFERENCE AND PSYCHOLOGICAL PROBLEMS.

	NUMBER IN EACH CATEGORY	
	GAY PEOPLE	STRAIGHT PEOPLE
People with Psychological Problems	3	5
People without Psychological Problems	9	15
Totals	12	20

Unfortunately, people often pay attention to only one cell in the matrix; this cell has exaggerated availability. Many people are likely to notice only gay people who have psychological problems, ignoring the important information in the other three cells. People with a bias against gay people might be especially likely to pay attention to this cell, and they continue to look for information that confirms their hypothesis that gay people have problems. You'll recall from the section on reasoning that people would rather try to confirm a hypothesis than try to disprove it, consistent with Theme 3 of this book.

By now, you may be thoroughly disgusted with the apparent inadequacy of humans' abilities to make competent decisions. However, in some cases, it may be helpful to be eager to detect correlations. For example, it is biologically adaptive to overdetect the correlations between particular food and illnesses (McArthur, 1980). We are more likely to survive if we remove a particular food dye from the market once we suspect a relationship between this dye and cancer.

Another error that is related to illusory correlations is called the halo effect. When the **halo effect** operates, we judge an individual to be high on many traits because we believe that he or she is high on one trait (Berger, 1984). For example, I am sometimes tempted to fall victim to the halo effect when filling out recommendations on my students' applications to graduate school. If a student has received a high grade on examinations in my cognitive psychology class and has also written a strong library-research paper, I give this student high ratings on characteristics related to this kind of performance, such as academic ability and organizational skills. However, I'm also tempted to provide high ratings on other traits, such as "creativity" and "works well with others"—even if I have no evidence for these skills. As Cooper's (1981) review of the literature on the halo effect points out, if we have even minimal reasons to believe that traits are related to each other, we are likely to make judgments as if the two traits are indeed correlated.

Causal Scenarios: The Power of Imagining.

So far, we have discussed decisions you can make by thinking of examples and judging the relative frequency of those examples. The correct answer to these decisions could be obtained by counting an unbiased list of the examples. For instance, the problem about first-letter versus third-letter *k*'s could be answered by counting letters in a passage of text.

In real life, however, we often judge probabilities in situations that cannot be evaluated by simply counting the list of examples. For example, what is the probability that Bill and Jane will get divorced? What is the probability that the operation on Jim's leg will be a success? Each marriage and each leg is unique, so we cannot provide an answer by counting examples of other people's marriages and legs.

Tversky and Kahneman (1973) argue that we still use the availability heuristic to judge the likelihood of various outcomes in situations like these. These two theorists believe that we make judgments by trying to construct causal scenarios. A **causal scenario** is a story in which one event causes another, leading from the original situation to the outcome. We then make a judgment about the likelihood of that outcome on the basis of the ease with which the causal scenario came to mind; if we can imagine it readily, the event seems likely. Thus, causal scenarios are similar to the availability heuristic, in which judgments are based on the ease with which examples come to mind.

For example, suppose that you want to judge the likelihood of your becoming a clinical psychologist. You might construct a causal scenario in which you do extremely well in your coursework, receive a high score on the Graduate Record Exam, receive strong letters of recommendation from your professors, graduate at the top of your class, get accepted into the graduate school of your choice, do well in graduate school, complete your dissertation in good time, receive your Ph.D., complete your internship, and set up your practice. If you have no difficulty imagining each of the events in this scenario, then you may judge the entire scenario as being likely. On the other hand, constructing a causal scenario for your becoming the president of the United States may be more difficult, and so you would judge the scenario as being unlikely.

Let us consider in more detail this concept that if a causal scenario comes readily to mind, people judge the outcome to be likely. A study by Gregory and his colleagues (1982) provides another illustration of this principle and also shows that the availability of the scenario can affect behavior. In one of a series of studies, these authors examined how imagining a causal scenario about using a cable television service actually influenced later attitudes and subscriptions to the service. A door-to-door canvasser in an Arizona city provided one group of residents with information about cable television. For example, the information described the advantages of cable TV in terms of spending time at home and avoiding the hassles of going out. Another group of residents was encouraged to develop personal scenarios. Here is an excerpt from the material in the imagination condition:

> Take a moment and imagine how CATV will provide you with a broader entertainment and informational service. When you use it properly, you will be able to plan in advance which of the events offered you wish to enjoy. Take a moment and think of how, instead of spending money on the babysitter and gas, and then having to put up with the hassles of "going out," you will be able to spend your time at home, with our family, alone, or with your friends. (p. 95)

The canvasser then asked a number of questions about the residents' attitudes toward cable television: The residents provided ratings ranging between 1 (for a negative attitude) and 7 (for a positive attitude). Figure 11.4 shows their responses on three of these items. As you can see, people were much more positive about cable television if they had constructed their own scenarios about how cable television could change their lives. Most convincing of all, Gregory and his coauthors (1982) contacted the local cable television service three months later to determine how many residents had actually subscribed to the service. The records showed that 20 percent of people in the information condition had done so, in contrast to 47 percent in the imagination condition! Clearly, causal scenarios have implications for consumer behavior.

Causal scenarios also have implications for personality psychology. Consider the research by Daniel Cervone (1989), who examined whether the power of imagination could extend to people's **self-efficacy,** which is the feeling individuals have that they are competent and effective. Cervone specifically examined how envisioning future activities could influence people's feelings of self-efficacy for solving problems that involve maze-like graphs. Prior to the task, undergraduate students were asked to think about factors that could influence their performance on the task. Some were instructed to imagine positive factors (for example, "What do you think are some personal characteristics, if any, that may make it easy for you to find solutions to the graphs?"). Others were instructed to imagine negative factors (for example, "What do you think are some personal characteristics, if any, that may make it difficult for you to find solutions to the graphs?"). Still others received no imagination instructions.

Cervone assessed the influence of these imagination instructions on two dependent variables. One variable was people's self-efficacy, measured in terms of the number of graph problems they expected to solve in comparison to performance on a different task (anagrams). As you can see from Figure 11.5a, people who were instructed to think of factors that would make the task difficult did indeed have lower levels of self-efficacy than those who either imagined factors that would make the task easy or who had no imagination instructions.

Cervone's second dependent variable involved task persistence; how many trials would an individual persist on the graph problems before switching to a different task, the anagrams? As you can see from Figure 11.5b, task persistence mirrored

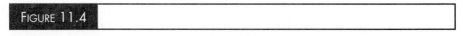

FIGURE 11.4

Attitudes Toward Cable Television on Several Questions, as a Function of Condition (Information Versus Imagination).

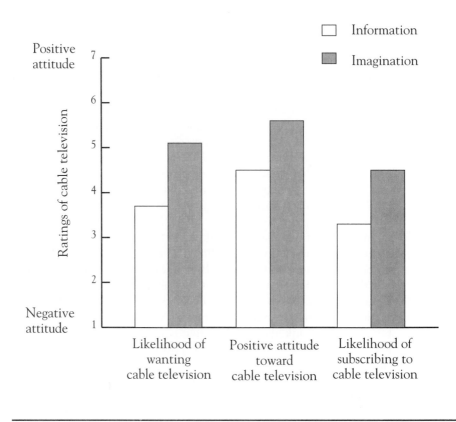

self-efficacy measures. Specifically, those people who had thought of factors that would make the task difficult gave up and switched to the anagrams much sooner than people in the other two groups.

The implications of Cervone's study are clear: If you want to boost your confidence and your persistence on a task, avoid thinking about the factors that could make you fail! Cervone also points out how therapists can encourage clients to take advantage of the availability heuristic; clients should be urged to imagine themselves coping successfully with an activity. Perhaps more important, they should be instructed to *avoid* imagining unsuccessful outcomes.

FIGURE 11.5

The Effect of Imaging Factors That Would Make a Task Easy or Difficult (or No Imagination Instructions) on Two Dependent Variables (a) Relative Level of Self-Efficacy and (b) Task Persistence (Based on Cervone, 1989).

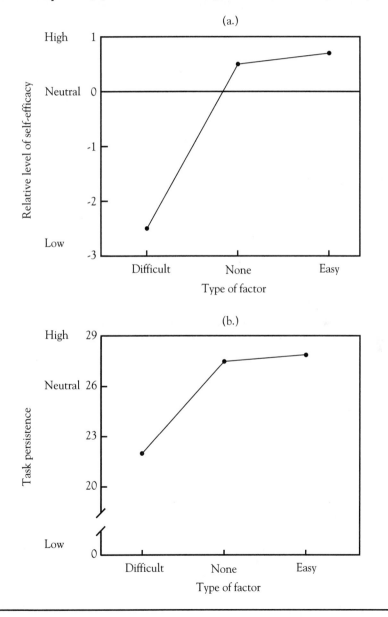

Let's consider one final component of causal scenarios. Kahneman and Tversky (1982) developed another aspect of causal scenarios, which they call the simulation heuristic. According to the **simulation heuristic,** we judge the probability of a particular goal in terms of the ease with which a mental simulation reaches that goal. In particular, Kahneman and Tversky examined the process people use in judging an event that nearly occurred. They asked people to read the following example:

> Mr. Crane and Mr. Tees were scheduled to leave the airport on different flights, at the same time. They traveled from town in the same limousine, were caught in a traffic jam, and arrived at the airport 30 minutes after the scheduled departure time of their flights.
> Mr. Crane is told that his flight left on time. Mr. Tees is told that his flight was delayed, and just left five minutes ago. Who is more upset? (p. 203)

It will not surprise you that 96 percent of a sample of students answered that Mr. Tees would be more upset. Why should this be? Both men had the same outcome. Kahneman and Tversky (1982) argue that people envision both Mr. Crane and Mr. Tees engaging in a simulation exercise, in order to test how close they came to reaching the flight in time. It is easier for us to see how Mr. Tees could construct a simulation in which he didn't stop to buy a newspaper, or in which he walked faster to the limousine stand, or in which the limousine didn't get caught in a traffic jam. It is difficult to see how Mr. Crane could construct a scenario saving 30 minutes. Once again, the ease with which examples or events come to mind is an important determinant in decision making.

Let us review what we've discussed about the availability heuristic, which is the heuristic of estimating frequency or probability in terms of how easily we can think of examples of something. Although this heuristic is generally accurate in our daily lives, availability can be contaminated by two factors that are not related to objective frequency—recency and familiarity. Furthermore, availability helps create illusory correlations, another error in decision making. Finally, we often judge likelihood in terms of the plausibility of causal scenarios, which are related to the availability heuristic; these causal scenarios can influence such behavior as subscribing to a cable-TV service, self-efficacy, and task persistence.

The Anchoring and Adjustment Heuristic

The third major heuristic, called anchoring and adjustment, has received less attention than the representativeness and availability heuristics. However, this cognitive strategy has many potential applications, for instance, in making estimates. In the **anchoring and adjustment heuristic,** we begin by guessing a first approximation—an **anchor**—and then we make adjustments to that number on the basis of additional information (Slovic et al., 1974; Tversky & Kahneman, 1982). This heuristic often leads to a reasonable answer, just as the representativeness and availability heuristics often lead to reasonable answers. However, people typically rely too heavily on the anchor, and their adjustments are too small. Notice, incidentally, that the anchoring and adjustment heuristic depends upon the availability heuristic, because highly available information is likely to serve as an anchor.

Jonathan Baron (1988) makes an interesting point about the anchoring and adjustment heuristic. This heuristic illustrates once more that we humans tend to endorse our current hypotheses or beliefs. Just as we saw with the selection task in conditional reasoning (Demonstration 11.2) and in illusory correlation, we feel comfortable about the status quo, and we often fail to consider other information as carefully as we should.

Let's begin by considering some examples of the anchoring and adjustment heuristic. Then we will see how this heuristic can be applied to estimating confidence intervals. Finally, we'll examine several applications to areas beyond cognitive psychology.

Examples of the Anchoring and Adjustment Heuristic. In one study, Tversky and Kahneman (1974) asked people to estimate various quantities. For example, a typical question might ask participants to estimate the percentage of African countries in the United Nations. Before requesting the reply, the experimenters spun a wheel while the participants looked on. At random, the wheel selected a number between 0 and 100. The participants were asked to indicate whether the answer to the question was higher or lower than the selected number,

---

DEMONSTRATION 11.9

THE ANCHORING AND ADJUSTMENT HEURISTIC.

Copy the two multiplication problems listed below on separate pieces of paper. Show each problem to at least five friends. In each case, ask the friend to estimate the answer within a 5-second period.

A. $8 \times 7 \times 6 \times 5 \times 4 \times 3 \times 2 \times 1$

B. $1 \times 2 \times 3 \times 4 \times 5 \times 6 \times 7 \times 8$

Now tally the answers separately for the two problems, listing the answers from smallest to largest. Calculate the median for each problem. (If you have an odd number of participants, the median is the answer in the middle of the distribution—with half larger and half smaller. If you have an even number of participants, the median is the average of the two answers in the middle of the distribution.)

and to reply to the question by moving upward or downward from that selected number.

Tversky and Kahneman (1974) found that the arbitrarily selected number acted as an anchor for the estimates. For example, if the wheel had stopped on 10, people estimated 25 as the percentage of African countries in the United Nations. If the wheel had stopped on 65, people estimated 45. In other words, a number that had no real relationship to the question acted as an anchor for the response. People made adjustments from this number, based on information related to the question. However, these adjustments were often far too conservative.

Tversky and Kahneman (1974) found that the anchoring effect was not reduced when people received money for more accurate guesses. Anchoring is such a trusted heuristic that we fail to abandon it even when we are promised modest wealth. Furthermore, an anchoring bias is also found among gamblers, whether in a Las Vegas casino (Lichtenstein & Slovic, 1973) or in a college research lab (Carlson, 1990).

Try Demonstration 11.9 for another example of the anchoring and adjustment heuristic. When high-school students were asked to estimate these mathematical products—and were allowed only 5 seconds to do so—they provided widely different answers as a function of the order of the numbers. When starting with a large number—8—the median estimate was 2,250 (that is, half of the students estimated higher than 2,250, and half estimated lower). In contrast, when starting with a small number—1—the median estimate was only 512 (Tversky & Kahneman, 1982). Interestingly, both groups seem to have anchored too heavily on the single-digit numbers in the question, because both median estimates are gross underestimates: The correct answer is 40,320. Notice whether the people you tested were influenced by the anchoring and adjustment heuristic.

We have discussed the three major heuristics separately, but in reality they often work together. For example, we discussed the halo effect in connection with the availability heuristic, in terms of how readily related characteristics come to mind. However, the halo effect is also related to anchoring and adjustment (Huber et al., 1987a). If I want to estimate whether a student is creative, I use that student's academic ability to provide an anchor, and then I make adjustments based on other information. Usually, however, those adjustments will not be as large as they should be.

Estimating Confidence Intervals. We use anchoring and adjustment when we estimate a single number. We also use this heuristic when we estimate **confidence intervals,** or ranges within which we expect a number to fall a certain percentage of the time. (For example, you might guess that the 98 percent confidence interval for the population of a particular town is 2,000–7,000, meaning that you think that there is a 98 percent chance that the population is between 2,000 and 7,000.)

Try Demonstration 11.10 to see how accurate your estimates are for various kinds of almanac information. The answers can be found at the end of this section.

DEMONSTRATION 11.10

ANCHORING AND ADJUSTMENT.

For each of the following questions, answer in terms of a range, rather than a single number. Specifically, you should supply a 98 percent confidence interval, which is the range within which you expect the correct answer to fall. For example, if you answer a question by supplying a 98 percent confidence interval that is 4,000 to 7,000, this means that you think there is only a 2 percent chance that the real answer is either less than 4,000 or more than 7,000. All questions are based on information in *The Information Please Almanac*. (The answers can be found at the end of the chapter.)

1. For the entire country of Canada, what is the population density (in terms of number of people per square mile)?
2. How many miles is it between Miami, Florida, and Los Angeles, California?
3. In what year did the first U.S. college establish coeducation?
4. In what year did the philosopher Plato die?
5. What is the size of Brazil, in square miles?
6. In 1988, how many U.S. residents lived below the poverty level?
7. What percent of adult Americans could not locate Central America on a map?
8. What is the literacy rate in Guatemala?
9. What is the average daily highest temperature for Toronto for the month of July?
10. How many people reported that they did not vote in the 1988 U.S. presidential election?

Slovic et al. (1974) point out how a typical decision maker might respond to a question asking for an estimate of the number of foreign cars imported into the United States in 1968:

> I think there were about 180 million people in the U.S. in 1968; there is about one car for every three people; thus there would have been about 60 million cars; the lifetime of a car is about 10 years, this suggests that there should be about 6 million new cars in a year but since the population and the number of cars is increasing let's make that 9 million for 1968; foreign cars make up about 10 percent of the U.S. market, thus there were probably about 900,000 foreign imports; to set my 98 percent confidence band, I'll add and subtract a few hundred thousand cars from my estimate of 900,000. (p. 195)

Check to see how many of your confidence interval estimates included the correct answer. If a large number of people were to answer a large number of questions, we would expect their confidence intervals to include the correct answer about 98 percent of the time, assuming that their estimation techniques are correct. However, studies have demonstrated that the confidence intervals actually include the correct answer only about 60 percent of the time (Fischhoff, 1982a; Slovic et al., 1974; Tversky & Kahneman, 1974). In other words, the confidence intervals that we estimate are too narrow.

Tversky and Kahneman (1974) point out how anchoring and adjustment are relevant when we make confidence-interval estimates. We arrive at a best estimate and use this figure as an anchor. We make adjustments upward and downward from this anchor to construct the confidence interval estimate. However, our adjustments are much too small. Look back over the quotation on the foreign car estimates and notice the number of times when a large estimation error could have occurred. Errors could have occurred in estimating the U.S. population, the ratio of cars to people, the lifetime of each car, and the percentage of cars that are foreign. Given the enormous potential for large errors, an adjustment of just a few hundred thousand is much too small. Again, we establish our anchor and we do not wander far from it in the adjustment process.

Think about applications of the anchoring and adjustment heuristic. Suppose that you are trying to guess how much you will make in tips in your summer job. You will probably make a first guess and then make adjustments in this figure. However, your final answer will depend too heavily on that first guess (which may not have been carefully chosen), and the adjustments will not adequately reflect all the additional factors that you consider after you made your first guess.

Nisbett and Ross (1980) summarize the anchoring and adjustment problem: " . . . once subjects have made a first pass at a problem, the initial judgment may prove remarkably resistant to further information, alternative modes of reasoning, and even logical or evidential challenges" (p. 41). Thus, we are amazingly "conservative." We are loyal to the original estimate, and we shut our eyes to new evidence. Consistent with a pattern we saw in Chapter 10, we often fail to conduct an adequate search of the problem space.

Applications of the Anchoring and Adjustment Heuristic.

You will recall that Daniel Cervone found that students' self-efficacy judgments could be influenced by the availability heuristic. Cervone and his coauthor Philip Peake (1986) found that these same kinds of self-efficacy judgments could be influenced by anchoring and adjustment. Specifically, college students were given an arbitrary anchor value that represented either high or low performance on graph problems. They were instructed to guess how well they would perform, relative to that anchor. Students who had received a high anchor value supplied much higher self-efficacy judgments than did students who had received a low anchor value. Furthermore, those with a high anchor value also persisted longer on a difficult task. Clearly, these findings have implications for motivating students in the school system and also for therapists who want to help their clients lead more productive lives.

Most of the applications of the anchoring and adjustment heuristic have been developed in connection with financial issues. For example, Smith and Kida (1991) examined whether the anchoring and adjustment heuristic is a problem for auditors, who are accountants responsible for checking financial records. In general, well-trained professionals were not heavily influenced by this heuristic. Reassuringly, experts are more accurate in adjusting their original results to reflect new information.

The anchoring and adjustment heuristic is also used when people make real-estate decisions. Northcraft and Neale (1987) asked undergraduate business school students as well as real-estate agents to make estimates about the value of a particular house. These estimates included the appraised value, an appropriate advertised selling price, a reasonable price to pay for the house, and the lowest acceptable offer. In each case, the participant was supplied with a 10-page packet of information about the house, including a listing price for the house. Each participant also toured the house. Some participants were given a listing price of $65,900, and some were given a listing price of $83,900.

Both the students and the real-estate agents tended to make judgments that were heavily influenced by the anchors that they had been given. For the students, for example, the lowest offer was about $63,000 when they had been given the less expensive anchor, in contrast to about $70,000 for the more expensive anchor. For the real-estate agents, the corresponding figures were $65,000 and $73,000. The results were replicated with a more expensive house and a different group of participants. In short, people use the anchoring and adjustment heuristic in the real world, as well as in the laboratory.

Let's review the last of the three decision-making heuristics. When we use the anchoring and adjustment heuristic, we begin by guessing a first approximation or anchor. Then we make adjustments to that anchor. This heuristic is generally a good one, but we typically fail to make large enough adjustments. The anchoring and adjustment heuristic accounts for our errors when we estimate confidence intervals; we usually supply ranges that are far too narrow, given the degree of uncertainty they should reflect. Finally, the anchoring and adjustment heuristic can be applied to judgments about self-efficacy and financial issues.

The Framing Effect

In 1983, Daniel Kahneman and Amos Tversky received the Distinguished Scientific Contributions Award from the American Psychological Association. In their honorary talk, they chose the topic of the framing effect (Kahneman & Tversky, 1984). The **framing effect** demonstrates that the way in which a question is worded (framed) and the background context of the choice itself can influence the outcome of the decision. In a sense, the frame makes one perspective more available than others. Let's consider the original research on the wording of the question, as well as the replications of this research. Then we will turn to the effects of background context.

Kahneman and Tversky's Research on the Wording of a Question.

The concept of the framing effect arose as part of Kahneman and Tversky's (1979)

DEMONSTRATION 11.11

THE FRAMING EFFECT AND THE WORDING OF A QUESTION (BASED ON TVERSKY & KAHNEMAN, 1981).

Try the following two problems:

Problem 1
Imagine that the United States is preparing for the outbreak of an unusual Asian disease, which is expected to kill 600 people. Two alternative programs to combat the disease have been proposed. Assume that the exact scientific estimate of the consequences of the programs are as follows:
   If Program A is adopted, 200 people will be saved.
   If Program B is adopted, there is a one-third probability that 600 people will be saved, and two-thirds probability that no people will be saved.
   Which program would you favor?

Problem 2
Now imagine the same situation, with these two alternatives:
   If Program C is adopted, 400 people will die.
   If Program D is adopted, there is a one-third probability that nobody will die, and two-thirds probability that 600 people will die.

theories about the way people construct internal representations of a decision problem. You'll recall that in Chapter 10 we discussed the internal representation of a problem as an important first step in problem solving. We also saw in that chapter that people often fail to realize that two problems share a deep-structure similarity. That is, people are distracted by the surface-structure differences. We will see that these statements also apply when people make decisions about uncertain events.

Try Problem 1 in Demonstration 11.11 before you read further. When Tversky and Kahneman (1981) presented this problem to 152 students in Canada and the United States, 72 percent chose Program A; only 28 percent chose Program B. Notice that the participants in this study were "risk averse"; that is, they preferred the certainty of saving 200 lives, rather than the risky prospect of a one-in-three possibility of saving 600 lives. Notice, however, that the benefits of the two programs are statistically equal.

Now inspect your answer to Problem 2. When 155 different students were given this problem, only 22 percent favored Program C, but 78 percent favored Program D. Here the participants were "risk-taking"; they preferred the two-in-three chance that 600 would die, rather than the guaranteed death of 400 people. Again, however, the benefits of the two programs are statistically equal. Furthermore, notice that Problem 1 and Problem 2 have identical deep structure. The only difference is that the outcomes are described in Problem 1 in terms of the lives saved, but in Problem 2 in terms of the lives lost.

The way that the question is framed—lives saved or lives lost—has an important effect on people's decisions. This framing changes people from focusing on the possible gains (lives saved) to focusing on the possible losses (lives lost). The change in focus is important because people tend to be risk-avoiding when dealing with possible gains, but risk-seeking when dealing with possible losses. In the case of Problem 1, we tend to prefer having 200 lives saved for sure; we avoid the option where there is a risk involved that no lives will be saved. In the case of Problem 2, we tend to prefer the risk that nobody will die (even though there is a good chance that 600 will die) rather than choose the option where 400 face certain death.

Kahneman and Tversky (1984) note that the influence of framing on decision making is both pervasive and robust. That is, the framing effect is as common among statistically sophisticated people as among naive people, and the magnitude of the effect is large. Furthermore, the framing effect is not eliminated when the experimenters point out to participants that their answers are contradictory. Even after participants reread the problems, they still are risk averse in the "lives saved" version and risk seeking in the "lives lost" version.

The framing effect is just as persistent as the famous Müller-Lyer illusion shown in Figure 11.6. You *know* that those lines are supposed to be the same length, just as you *know* that Problems 1 and 2 in Demonstration 11.11 are statistically identical. In both cases, however, the frame—either geometric or verbal—influences interpretations. (We will not pursue this analogy between visual illusions and framing, though, because the underlying mechanisms are different.)

FIGURE 11.6

The Müller-Lyer Illusion: Another Example in Which Context Influences Interpretation.

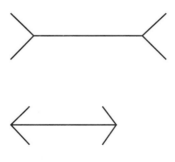

Replications of the Framing Effect for the Wording of a Question.

On the day I began writing this section on the framing effect, I needed to buy some smoked sausage at the grocery store. I was pleased to find a new "Lite" sausage, labeled "80% fat-free." Waiting in line, I realized I had fallen victim to the framing effect; would I have been so pleased to find this sausage if it had been labeled "20% fat"? Interestingly, Johnson (1987) confirmed that people are much more positive about ground beef that is labeled "80% lean," rather than "20% fat."

Numerous studies have replicated the framing effect; the way a question is worded has an important effect on people's decisions, and the framing effect is considered to be both robust and pervasive (Levin et al., 1988). For example, several studies have examined medical decisions. The framing effect holds true for decisions about receiving vaccinations (Slovic et al., 1982), treating lung cancer (McNeil et al., 1982), and genetic counseling (McNeil et al., 1988); physicians, as well as patients, may be influenced by this effect. The framing effect has also been demonstrated for gambling choices (Elliott & Archibald, 1989), for people buying refrigerators (Neale & Northcraft, 1986), for people making real-estate decisions (Northcraft & Neale, 1987), and for decisions about using automobile seat belts (Slovic et al., 1988).

Let us consider two studies in more detail. Huber and her colleagues (1987b) examined the effect of framing on personnel selection decisions. Imagine that you are an executive who needs to hire three new employees for a job; should you approach the task by rejecting the applicants who are less qualified, or by accepting the applicants who are more qualified? The participants in the study by Huber and her coauthors were students in courses on organizational behavior, and they were

---

DEMONSTRATION 11.12

THE FRAMING EFFECT AND BACKGROUND INFORMATION (BASED ON TVERSKY & KAHNEMAN, 1981).

Try the following two problems:

Problem 1
Imagine that you have decided to see a play and paid the admission price of $10 per ticket. As you enter the theater, you discover that you have lost the ticket. The seat was not marked, and the ticket cannot be recovered.

   Would you pay $10 for another ticket for the play?

Problem 2
Imagine that you have decided to see a play where admission is $10 per ticket. As you enter the theater, you discover that you have lost a $10 bill.

   Would you still pay $10 for a ticket for the play?

asked to read the resumes from 20 applicants for a position as a computer technician's assistant. They were informed that it would cost the company $300 to interview each job applicant. When people were instructed to accept the applicants who were high on the selection criteria, they chose to interview an average of 6 applicants. In contrast, when they were instructed to reject the applicants who were low on the selection criteria, they chose to interview an average of 10 applicants.

As you can see, this study demonstrates once more that the wording of a question determines whether people show risk-aversion or risk-seeking behavior. *Accepting* the candidates for interviews implies gains, so people demonstrate risk aversion; that is, they do not choose to interview risky candidates. *Rejecting* the candidates for interviews implies losses, so people demonstrate risk seeking; that is, they decide that they do want to interview those borderline candidates.

Incidentally, the way to remember this general effect—which may initially seem backwards—is that when people think the situation is good, they want to maintain the status quo, so they avoid risks. However, when they think the situation is bad, they want things to change, so they seek risks. In summary, a positive frame makes people avoid risks; a negative frame makes them seek risks (Schooler, 1992).

Let's consider one final example of how a question's wording influences decisions. Levin and his colleagues (1988) asked college students to estimate the incidence of cheating at their university. Before making these estimates, half of them were informed about a national survey reporting that 65 percent of students had cheated during their college career; the other half read a version reporting that 35 percent of students had never cheated. Those who saw the "cheated" version rated their university's incidence of cheating as being significantly higher than did those who saw the "never cheated" version.

As Huber and her colleagues (1987b) concluded in connection with the general framing effect, decision making often depends on whether the choice is presented as, "Is the pitcher half *empty?*" or, "Is the pitcher half *full?*" This area of research confirms Theme 4 of this textbook; the cognitive processes are indeed interrelated. In this case, language has a profound effect on decision making.

Background Information and the Framing Effect. Try Demonstration 11.12 before you read further. Notice that the amount of money involved is $10 in both cases, yet the decision frame differs for these two situations. As Kahneman and Tversky (1984) point out, we organize our mental expense accounts according to topics. We view going to the theater as a transaction in which the cost of the ticket is exchanged for the experience of seeing a play. Buying another ticket increases the cost of seeing that play to a level that many people find unacceptable. When Kahneman and Tversky asked people what they would do, only 46 percent said that they would pay $10 for another ticket (Problem 1). In contrast, in Problem 2, we don't tally the lost $10 bill in the same account; the loss is viewed as being generally irrelevant to the ticket. In Kahneman and Tversky's study, 88 percent of the participants said that they would purchase the ticket. Notice that the framing effect in these two problems refers to the background information for the problem, rather than the wording of the problem, as in previous examples.

Let's review how the framing effect operates. The wording of the question can influence decisions, so that people avoid risks when the wording implies gains, and they seek risks when the wording implies losses. In addition, background information can also influence decisions; we do not make choices in a vacuum (Payne et al., 1992). Both components of the framing effect illustrate that humans do not make decisions based solely on statistical information. Instead, context has an important impact on the choices we make.

Overconfidence in Decisions

So far, we have seen that decisions can be influenced by three decision-making heuristics. Furthermore, the framing effect demonstrates that wording and background information influence decision making inappropriately. Given these sources of error, people should not be very confident in their decision-making skills. Unfortunately, however, they are overconfident. **Overconfidence** means that people's confidence judgments are higher than the relative frequencies of the correct answers (Gigerenzer et al., 1991).

We have already seen two examples of overconfidence in decision making. In the section on illusory correlations, we emphasized that people are confident that two variables are related, when in fact the relationship is either weak or nonexistent. In the discussion of anchoring and adjustment, we saw that people are so confident in their estimation abilities that they supply very narrow confidence intervals for their estimates.

Robyn Dawes (1988, pp. 204–205) provides a vivid, everyday example of human overconfidence, as seen in this letter to "Dear Abby":

> DEAR ABBY: While standing in a check out line in a high-grade grocery store, I saw a woman directly in front of me frantically rummaging around in her purse, looking embarrassed. It seems her groceries had already been checked, and she was a dollar short. I felt sorry for her, so I handed her a dollar. She was very grateful, and she insisted on writing my name and address on a loose piece of paper. She stuck it in her purse and said, "I promise I'll mail you a dollar tomorrow." Well, that was three weeks ago, and I still haven't heard from her! Abby, I think I'm a fairly good judge of character, and I just didn't peg her as the kind that would beat me out of a dollar. The small amount of money isn't important, but what it did to my faith in people is. I'd like your opinion.
>
> SHY ONE BUCK

Dawes points out that this incident caused Shy One Buck to lose her faith in humanity. Ironically, her confidence in her ability to make decisions about people remained strong. Indeed, she appears to be overconfident; how could she possibly judge honesty from a single brief interaction?

Dawes discusses how people prefer to trust their own judgment over statistical predictions when making decisions. This overconfidence applies to a wide variety of different kinds of judgments, including decisions about how long people with a fatal disease will live, which firms will go bankrupt, which psychiatric inpatients have serious disorders, and which students will do well in graduate school. People consistently have more confidence in their own decisions than in predictions that are based on statistically combined objective measurements.

Other studies on the topic of overconfidence demonstrate that amateur bridge players are overconfident, though expert players are not (Keren, 1987). Furthermore, physicians are overconfident in judging that patients with coughs have pneumonia (Schwartz & Griffin, 1986). Even our political leaders make mistakes and are overconfident about their decisions. Peterson (1985) points out how decision makers focus on the similarity between a small number of variables in the present situation and a small number of variables in a previous situation. This rather casual similarity is welded into a justification for some political policy. For example, an emerging new government in Nicaragua in the late 1970s and early 1980s was seen as being similar to the government in Cuba. From scanty evidence, political leaders convince themselves that they—and we as citizens—should be very confident about their decisions.

Overconfidence is not simply a theoretical issue; it has real consequences for people's lives. For example, an article in the *APA Monitor* described how a panel of decision-making theorists analyzed the Vincennes incident (Bales, 1988). In July 1988, the USS Vincennes was in the Persian Gulf. Its radar system detected an airplane taking off from an Iranian airport, flying directly toward the ship. Captain Will Rogers had to decide whether the unknown aircraft was attacking his ship or whether it was simply a civilian airplane. Captain Rogers decided to launch two missiles at the aircraft. As both Rogers and the rest of the world soon learned, the plane was only a civilian airline, and all 290 passengers aboard the plane died when the plane was shot down. The psychologists pointed out that the captain had been overconfident about his original judgment, failing to verify the characteristics of the plane and whether it was ascending or descending.

We should remember, incidentally, that overconfidence is a characteristic of other cognitive tasks, as well as decision making. For example, you may recall from Chapter 8 that people were overconfident about how well they understood material they had read, even after answering many questions incorrectly. In connection with overconfidence in decision making, let's examine why people are overconfident. Then we will consider a specific kind of overconfidence, called the hindsight bias.

Reasons for Overconfidence. Our overconfidence in the correctness of our decisions arises from errors at many different stages in the decision-making process:

1. People are often unaware that their knowledge is based on very tenuous and uncertain assumptions (Slovic, 1982; Slovic et al., 1982).
2. Examples confirming our hypotheses are readily available, and we resist searching for counterexamples (Dawes, 1988; Koriat et al., 1980). You'll recall from the discussion of logical reasoning that people persist in confirming their current hypothesis, rather than looking for negative evidence.
3. People have difficulty *recalling* the other possible hypotheses (Gettys et al., 1986); decision making depends on memory (Theme 4). If you cannot recall the competing hypotheses, you are sure to be overly confident about the hypothesis you have endorsed.
4. A self-fulfilling effect operates (Einhorn & Hogarth, 1978, 1981). For example, admissions officers who judge that a candidate is particularly well qualified for admission to a program may feel that their judgment is supported when their candidate does well. However, the candidate's success may be due primarily to the positive effects of the program itself. Even the people who had been rejected might have been successful if they had been allowed to participate in the program.
5. When people are informed that most people are overconfident about the accuracy of their decisions, they fail to take this information into account when providing confidence judgments (Gigerenzer et al., 1991). In other words, they remain overconfident. Keep these findings in mind, and try to reduce your own overconfidence when you make important decisions.

The Hindsight Bias. Not only do we exaggerate our decision-making abilities, we also overestimate the accuracy of our hindsight. Specifically, people often show a hindsight bias, or a "knew-it-all-along" effect. The **hindsight bias** means that people overestimate the accuracy with which they could have predicted past events, given some information about the outcome. Furthermore, people deny that the information about the outcome actually influenced their judgment (Hawkins & Hastie, 1990). Consider this example: You have just been told that a couple, Chris and Pat, have broken up. You reply, "I'm not surprised. I could have predicted they wouldn't stay together." In reality, if you had been questioned yesterday, you might have judged that their relationship was strong. Today, armed with this new knowledge, you are overconfident that yesterday you would have known that Chris and Pat would break up.

Fischhoff (1975) provides a good example of a hindsight bias. In 1974, a prisoner named Cletus Bowles, who had been previously convicted of murder and bank robbery, was allowed to leave the penitentiary on a 4-hour social pass. He promptly fled and later allegedly murdered two people. The public demanded the resignation of the prison warden who had issued the pass. In retrospect, perhaps we could have predicted the escape. However, the prison warden may well have made a good decision, given the information he had at the time. Bowles had in fact been a model prisoner before he left the penitentiary. Unfortunately, however, good decisions can have bad outcomes. Notice why a hindsight bias is operating here. As you were reading about Cletus Bowles, weren't you tempted to conclude that the prison warden had been a fool? You in fact probably overestimated the extent to which he should have been able to predict that Bowles would harm someone.

Experimental evidence for the hindsight bias comes from several studies (e.g., Christensen-Szalanski & Willham, 1991; Fischhoff, 1977; Hawkins & Hastie, 1990; Slovic & Fischhoff, 1977). Demonstration 11.13 is based on a study by Slovic and Fischhoff (1977) called, "On the Psychology of Experimental Surprises." Perhaps you have had this experience. You are reading about an experiment in a textbook, and then you think to yourself that the results were not at all surprising. In fact, you "knew it all along." In reality, the hindsight bias may have led you to overestimate your confidence.

Slovic and Fischhoff (1977) asked people to make judgments about either a foresight version (such as Version A) or a hindsight version (such as Version B). The people in the foresight version were not told which outcome occurred, whereas the people in the hindsight condition were told the results. The results showed that people assigned much higher probabilities to the stated outcome if they were in the hindsight condition. For instance, combining three of the examples, the average probability of the initial outcome always being replicated was .38 for those who read the foresight version and .55 for those who read the hindsight version. (Think about your hindsight on this hindsight study. Did you "know it all along" that hindsight is better than foresight?)

The hindsight bias also operates when professionals make decisions. For example, consider a study in which five groups of physicians were given a case history and were asked for their medical opinions (Arkes et al., 1981). One group—the foresight group—was instructed to assign a probability estimate to each of four possible diagnoses. The four hindsight groups were also instructed to assign probability estimates, but each was told that a different one of the four possible diagnoses (for instance, hepatitis) was correct. When the hindsight groups had been told that one of the less likely diagnoses was correct, they assigned far greater probability estimates to these presumably correct diagnoses than did the foresight group. For example, only 16 percent of the foresight group guessed hepatitis for one particular case history. For members of the hepatitis hindsight group, however, hepatitis seemed like the most likely diagnosis; 38 percent guessed that hepatitis was indeed the diagnosis.

Here is an important practical application for this study on medical hindsight. Suppose that a patient who has been diagnosed by one physician as having a particular illness seeks a second opinion from another physician. The hindsight bias results in second opinions that tend to support the first opinion. Knowledge of the previous diagnosis contaminates the second physician's decision making.

A recent review of the literature on the hindsight bias has confirmed that this bias operates in nonlaboratory settings. In addition to medical decision making,

---

DEMONSTRATION 11.13

THE HINDSIGHT BIAS.

Find two friends who can spare a few minutes for an experiment. They should be tested separately, one friend hearing version A and one friend hearing version B. In each case, announce that you will read a paragraph and then ask a question.

Version A (foresight)

A goose egg was placed in a soundproof, heated box from time of laying to time of cracking. Approximately two days before it cracked, the experimenter began intermittently to play sounds of ducks quacking into the box. On the day after birth, the gosling was placed on a smooth floor equidistant from a duck and a goose, each of which was in a wire cage. The gosling was observed for two minutes. The possible outcomes were (a) the gosling approached the caged duck or (b) the gosling approached the caged goose (Slovic & Fischhoff, 1977, p. 546). If the gosling does approach the caged duck, what is the probability that in a replication of this experiment with ten additional goslings,

    a. all will approach the duck? _____ %
    b. some will approach the duck? _____ %
    c. none will approach the duck? _____ %

Note that these must sum to 100 percent.

Version B (hindsight)

Read the same story as in version A up to the Slovic and Fischhoff reference. Then read this ending:
    The initial gosling that was tested in this experiment approached the caged duck. Suppose that a replication of the experiment was performed with ten additional goslings. What is the probability that in this replication,

    a. all will approach the duck? _____ %
    b. some will approach the duck? _____ %
    c. none will approach the duck? _____ %

Note that these must sum to 100 percent.

    After you have tested your two subjects (or better still, five on each version), compare the percentages. Were people in the hindsight condition more likely to guess that all of the goslings would approach the duck?

Hawkins and Hastie (1990) point out that the hindsight bias also operates when people are making legal decisions and when people are asked to predict the outcomes of political elections. (For example, the hindsight bias clearly operated in the 1992 U.S. presidential elections.)

In another review of the literature, Christensen-Szalanski and Willham (1991) located 122 studies on the hindsight bias, and they conducted a meta-analysis on these studies. As discussed earlier in the book, the **meta-analysis technique** provides a statistical method for synthesizing numerous studies on a single topic. The meta-analysis on the hindsight studies showed that the overall magnitude of the effect was small, although it was especially likely to operate when people made judgments about almanac-type information and when people were working on an unfamiliar task.

Hawkins and Hastie (1990) discuss a variety of possible explanations for these results. For example, people may reconstruct their prior judgment by rejudging the outcome; in other words, people use cognitive strategies to make judgments consistent. Another cognitive explanation is that people might use anchoring and adjustment; they have been told that a particular outcome actually happened, that is, it was 100 percent certain. Therefore, they use this 100 percent value as an anchor, and they do not adjust their certainty downward as much as they should. An additional explanation is motivational, rather than cognitive; perhaps people simply want to look good in the eyes of the experimenter or other people who may be evaluating them. Did that result surprise me? Of course not; I knew it all along!

This chapter seems to provide little evidence for Theme 2. Especially compared to some of our astonishing memory and language capabilities, we humans are not especially accurate in logical reasoning or decision making. Part of this impression is created by psychologists' emphasis on studies about decision errors. In addition, some of our mistakes can be traced to the kinds of sensible errors and heuristics that usually prove useful. However, the reality is that humans also find some cognitive tasks more challenging than others.

SECTION SUMMARY: DECISION MAKING

1. Decision-making heuristics are typically useful in our daily lives; many errors in decision making occur because we use heuristics beyond the range for which they are intended.
2. The most common heuristic is representativeness. For example, people consider a sample to be likely if it matches important characteristics of the population from which it was selected.
3. People are so impressed by representativeness that they tend to pay too little attention to sample size and base rates; the representativeness heuristic also produces the conjunction fallacy.

4. We use the availability heuristic when we estimate frequency in terms of how easily we can remember examples of something; this heuristic can lead to errors when recency and familiarity influence availability.
5. An illusory correlation occurs when we believe that two variables are more strongly correlated than they really are; this error can be traced to the heightened availability of selected information.
6. To figure out the likelihood of a particular outcome, we often construct causal scenarios that lead from the original situation to the outcome; we use the availability of this causal scenario to judge likelihood.
7. When we use the anchoring and adjustment heuristic, we establish an anchor and make adjustments based on other information; the problem is that these adjustments are usually too small.
8. We also use the anchoring and adjustment heuristic when we estimate confidence intervals. We arrive at a single best estimate, and then we make very narrow adjustments upwards and downwards to establish a confidence interval.
9. The way in which a question is framed or worded can influence our decisions; when the wording implies gains, we tend to avoid risks; when the wording implies losses, we tend to seek out risks; background information can also influence our decisions inappropriately.
10. People are frequently overconfident about their decisions; this overconfidence also produces a hindsight bias.

CHAPTER REVIEW QUESTIONS

1. Describe the basic differences between logical reasoning and decision making, providing at least one example from your daily life that illustrates each cognitive process. Why do they both qualify as thinking?
2. Give an example of conditional reasoning and an example of a syllogism. How can the propositional calculus and Euler's circles be used to represent the logical outcomes of these two kinds of reasoning?
3. The discussion of conditional reasoning pointed out that people try to confirm a hypothesis; they seldom try to disprove it. How is this tendency related to the anchoring and adjustment heuristic?
4. Many reasoning errors seem to arise from failure to *understand* (for example, the meaning of specific terms, the possible interpretations of premises, or the fact that illicit conversions are not appropriate). Point out how many errors people make in reasoning can be traced to lack of understanding and other language factors. How is this related to the information on the framing effect in decision making?
5. Many of the errors people make in reasoning can be traced to overreliance on previous knowledge or overactive top-down processes. Discuss this point and relate it to the anchoring and adjustment heuristic.

6. Decide which heuristic each of the following everyday errors represents: (a) you decide that you are more likely to live in Massachusetts than in New Mexico, because you can more easily envision a sequence of events that brings you to Massachusetts; (b) someone asks you whether cardinals or robins are more common, and you respond on the basis of the number of birds of each kind that you have seen this winter; (c) one of your classes has 30 students, including two people named Scott and three named Jennifer, which seems too coincidental to be due to chance alone; and (d) you estimate the number of bottles of soda you will need for the Fourth of July picnic based on the Christmas party consumption, taking into account the fact that the weather will be warmer in July.

7. Imagine that your congressional district is in the midst of a hotly contested election; about 50 percent of the voters seem to favor each candidate. A poll of 200 voters says that Candidate A has 60 percent of the vote, whereas a different poll of 800 voters says that Candidate A has 55 percent of the votes. Why wouldn't these results surprise you, and what part of the chapter is this topic related to?

8. In the case of the representativeness heuristic, people fail to take into account two important factors that should be emphasized. In the case of the availability heuristic, people take into account two important factors that should be ignored. Discuss these statements, with reference to the information in the chapter, giving examples of each of these four kinds of errors.

9. Describe the variety of ways in which people tend to be overconfident in their decision making. Think of relevant examples from your own experience.

10. Imagine that you have been hired by your local high school district to create a course in critical thinking. Review the chapter and make 15 to 20 suggestions (each only a sentence long) on what material should be included in such a program.

NEW TERMS

thinking
reasoning
decision making
conditional reasoning
propositional reasoning
the propositional calculus
antecedent
consequent
affirm the antecedent

affirm the consequent
deny the antecedent
deny the consequent
illicit conversion
syllogism
Euler's circles
moods (in reasoning)
belief-bias effect
mental models

analogical theory	halo effect
heuristics	causal scenario
representative	self-efficacy
representativeness heuristic	simulation heuristic
law of large numbers	anchoring and adjustment heuristic
base rate	anchor
Bayes' rule	confidence intervals
likelihood ratio	framing effect
conjunction rule	overconfidence
conjunction fallacy	hindsight bias
availability heuristic	meta-analysis technique
illusory correlation	

RECOMMENDED READINGS

Dawes, R. M. (1988). *Rational choice in an uncertain world*. San Diego: Harcourt Brace Jovanovich. Dawes is a prominent researcher in the area of decision making, and his mid-level textbook provides a clear and interesting overview of the field; the text covers many topics other than decision-making heuristics.

Hawkins, S. A., & Hastie, R. (1990). Hindsight: Biased judgments of past events after the outcomes are known. *Psychological Bulletin, 107,* 311–327. This article provides a superb review of the topic and gives examples of both laboratory research and real-life decision making.

Johnson-Laird, P. N., & Byrne, R. M. J. (1991). *Deduction*. Hove, Great Britain: Erlbaum. This volume reviews the theory and research on conditional reasoning and syllogisms; it would be most appropriate for advanced undergraduates.

Payne, J. W., Bettman, J. R., & Johnson, E. J. (1992). Behavioral decision research: A constructive processing perspective. *Annual Review of Psychology, 43,* 87–131. This piece provides a guide to the most current research in the field, with some coverage of heuristics and the framing effect but additional coverage of other approaches.

Voss, J. F., Perkins, D. N., & Segal, J. W. (Eds.). (1990). *Informal reasoning and education*. Hillsdale, NJ: Erlbaum. Informal reasoning is a topic that includes both logical reasoning and decision making; it primarily applies to our everyday thinking processes. This book includes 23 chapters on topics such as informal reasoning in the judicial system, informal reasoning in inner-city children, and several chapters examining implications for education.

ANSWERS TO DEMONSTRATIONS

Demonstration 11.1

1. valid
2. invalid

3. invalid
4. valid

Demonstration 11.3   None of the conclusions follows logically from the premises.
Demonstration 11.10

1. 7 people per square mile
2. 2,757 miles
3. the year was 1833 (at Oberlin College)
4. 347 B.C.
5. 3,286,470 square miles
6. 63,743,000 people
7. 45%
8. 51 percent
9. 79°F or 26°C
10. 75,875,000 people.

C H A P T E R   1 2

COGNITIVE DEVELOPMENT

PREVIEW

This chapter examines how cognition develops in three areas: memory, metacognition, and language. Some skills improve as children mature to adulthood, and then they decline as adults reach old age. However, other skills show less change than might be expected.

According to recent research, even young infants have developed memories; for example, under the right conditions, 3-month-olds can remember an event that occurred 5 weeks earlier. Children's recognition memory is surprisingly accurate, but their short-term and long-term recall memory is considerably less accurate than in adults. Young children also fail to use memory strategies spontaneously when they want to remember something. Elderly adults are somewhat similar to young adults in sensory memory and some kinds of short-term and long-term memory tasks; however other kinds of memory (for example, long-term memory for prose) may decline.

Studies on metacognition reveal that children change in their metamemory and metacomprehension as they grow older. For example, older children are more accurate than young children in estimating their memory span. In general, however, young adults and elderly adults are comparable in their metamemory.

With respect to language development, young infants are remarkably competent in perceiving speech. As children mature, their skills increase dramatically in understanding word meaning, grammatical relationships, and the social aspects of language.

INTRODUCTION

The following conversation between two 4-year-old children was overheard in a playroom situation:

GIRL: (on toy telephone) David!
BOY: (not picking up second phone) I'm not home.
GIRL: When you'll be back?
BOY: I'm not here already.
GIRL: But when you'll be back?
BOY: Don't you know if I'm gone already, I went before so I can't talk to you! (Miller, 1981)

This dialogue captures the considerable language skills of young children, while illustrating some ways in which they differ from adults. As another 4-year-old boy remarked to his mother one morning, "You know, I thought I'd be a grown-up by now. . . . It sure is taking a long time!" (Rogoff, 1990, p. 3). He is absolutely correct, as we will see in this chapter. Four-year-olds have mastered some aspects of memory and language, but they still need to develop skills in memory performance, memory strategies, metacognition, syntax, and pragmatics.

This chapter will examine not only the cognitive development of young children, but also the cognitive skills of elderly people. As the chapter emphasizes, some cognitive skills decline during the aging process, but many other capabilities remain stable.

When we study the cognitive abilities of the very young and the very old, the research problems are even more complex than when we study young adults. How can young infants convey what they know, given their minimal language and motor skills? As Mandler (1990) remarked, researchers "have tended to confuse infants' motor incompetence with conceptual incompetence" (p. 240). Research with the elderly presents a different set of methodological problems. Many studies have compared the performance of young, healthy college students with the performance of elderly people whose health, self-confidence, and education are relatively poor. Although these factors cannot account for all of the cognitive differences associated with age, some of the results can be attributed to these confounding variables (Hulicka, 1982; Rebok, 1987; Salthouse, 1991; Salthouse & Kausler, 1985).

This chapter focuses on cognitive development in three areas: memory, metacognition, and language. Our examination of these topics will reveal that infants and young children are not helpless and that elderly people are quite competent.

THE DEVELOPMENT OF MEMORY

Many parts of this textbook have examined memory. Chapters 3, 4, and 5 focused specifically on memory, and the remaining chapters noted the contribution of memory to other cognitive processes. Now we will examine how memory develops from infancy and childhood through old age.

Memory in Infancy

Think about an infant you know, a baby under one year of age. Would you expect this baby to recognize his or her mother, to remember the location of hidden objects, or to imitate simple actions? Naturally, we cannot expect sophisticated memory feats from a young infant; after all, the synaptic connections in the portions of the cortex most relevant to memory will not reach the adult level until about 7 years of age (Siegler, 1989). Furthermore, we will underestimate infants' memory capacities unless we can create a task that depends upon a response the infant has already mastered (Kail, 1990). Fortunately, researchers have devised a number of methods to test infants' ability to remember people and objects. The research shows that infants have greater memory capabilities than you might expect. Indeed Theme 2, which emphasizes cognitive competence, can even be applied to infants.

Recognizing Mother. In our North American culture, infants generally spend more time with their mother than with any other person. Therefore, if they have substantial memory capacities at a young age, they should be able to demonstrate that they can recognize their mother's face. Research on visual recognition indicates that they seem to be able to distinguish their mothers from strangers somewhere between 1 and 3 months of age (Barrera & Maurer, 1981; Bushnell, 1982; Ruff, 1982). Even 2-*day*-olds have skills in this area. Bushnell and Sai (1987) separated these newborns from their mothers for a period of at least 5 minutes. Then the infants saw their mother standing next to a female stranger whose hair color and complexion were similar. These tiny infants looked reliably longer at their mothers, thereby indicating that they had already developed some ability to remember what she looked like.

Infants' ability to recognize their mothers' voices is equally remarkable. DeCasper and Fifer (1980) found that 3-day-old babies sucked on pacifiers at different rates to produce either the voices of their mothers or the voice of a female stranger. Impressively, these tiny babies produced their mothers' voices more often than the stranger's. It seems likely that they become accustomed to her voice while still in the uterus. DeCasper and Spence (1986) demonstrated that newborns prefer a particular Dr. Seuss passage that their mothers read aloud each day during the last three months of pregnancy, rather than a similar passage that had never been read.

Infants can even smell the difference between their mothers and strangers. In typical research on smell recognition, infants demonstrate their memory by turning their heads to a breastpad worn by their mothers, rather than a breastpad worn by a stranger. It is not clear exactly when smell recognition is acquired; estimates vary between 6 days and 6 weeks of age (Cernoch & Porter, 1985; Macfarlane, 1977; Russell, 1976).

Habituation Studies. In research using the **habituation procedure,** a stimulus is presented many times until the baby stops responding to it; then a new stimulus is introduced, and the experimenters notice whether the baby responds to the new stimulus. If the baby stops responding to the first stimulus but responds to the new one, the experimenters conclude that he or she demonstrates recognition memory. Much of this research tested 3-month-olds. As Small (1990) concludes, extensive research shows that infants at this age have immediate recognition memory for many types of visual patterns.

A classic study by Friedman (1972), using black-and-white checkerboards, demonstrated memory in infants who were only 1 to 4 days old. For example, Friedman might initially show an infant a checkerboard containing only 4 squares. During the first presentation, a typical infant might look at this design for most of the 60-second presentation period. After several additional presentations, however, he or she might look at the design for only 45 seconds, representing a significant decline. By looking less, infants demonstrate that they recognize the design from previous presentations.

How do we know that the decline in looking cannot be traced to simple fatigue? To address this issue, Friedman then showed infants a new design. For example, a

FIGURE 12.1

The Conjugate Reinforcement Situation.

baby who had previously seen the 4-square design would now be shown a 144-square design. A typical infant increased his or her looking time from 45 seconds to 55 seconds, demonstrating **dishabituation,** or recovery from habituation. Infants not only recognize a design from previous presentations, but they also demonstrate that a different design is unfamiliar.

The Conjugate Reinforcement Technique. The most extensive program of research on infant memory has been conducted by Carolyn Rovee-Collier and her associates, using the conjugate reinforcement technique. In the **conjugate reinforcement technique,** a mobile is placed above an infant's crib; a ribbon runs between the infant's ankle and the mobile, so that the infant's kicks produce motion in the mobile (see Figure 12.1). According to Rovee-Collier (1987), 6- to 16-week-old infants seem to like to play the game. After several minutes, they begin to kick rapidly and pump up the mobile; then they lie quietly and watch the parts of the mobile move. As the movement dies down, they typically shriek and then kick vigorously, thereby pumping it up again. In operant conditioning terms, the *response* is a foot kick, and the *reinforcement* is the movement of the mobile.

Let us examine how the conjugate reinforcement technique can be used to assess infant memory. All the training and testing take place in the infant's home crib, so that measurements are not distorted by the infant's reactions to new surroundings. For a 3-minute period at the beginning of the first session, the experimenter takes a baseline measure. During this time, the ribbon is attached to an "empty" mobile stand. The infants can view the mobile, attached to its own stand, but kicking does not activate the mobile. Thus, the baseline measure assesses kicking prior to learning.

Next, the experimenter moves one end of the ribbon from the empty mobile stand to the stand from which the mobile is hung. The babies are allowed 9 minutes to discover that their kicks can activate the mobile and to enjoy playing with it; this is the acquisition phase. Then the ribbon is unhooked and returned to the empty stand for 3 minutes in order to measure what they remember; this is the immediate retention test. The infants typically receive two training sessions spaced 24 hours apart.

Memory is then measured after 1 to 35 days have elapsed. The mobile is once again hung over the infant's crib, with the ribbon hooked to the empty stand. If the infant recognizes the mobile and recalls how to move it, then he or she will produce the foot-kick response. If this kicking rate equals the kicking rate during the immediate retention test, the retention ratio is 1.00. A retention ratio lower than 1.00 therefore indicates forgetting. Notice, then, that Rovee-Collier has devised a clever way to "ask" infants if they remember how to activate the mobile, as well as a clever, objective method of measuring memory. As you can see from Figure 12.2, 3-month-olds remember the stimulus quite well for the first eight days, but they show little recall 14 days after the original training. Notice that the retention ratio has fallen to 0.3.

The conjugate reinforcement technique has also been used to examine **memory reactivation,** a process in which memory improves by priming an inactive memory. Rovee-Collier and her colleagues study reactivation by presenting a reminder, a brief exposure to the moving mobile. Typically, this reminder is presented when the infant has almost completely forgotten how to activate the mobile, perhaps 13 days after the end of training when testing 3-month-olds.

Intriguingly, if the infants are tested only 15 minutes after the reminder, the infants show no signs of memory reactivation (Fagen & Rovee-Collier, 1983). However, 1 to 3 days after the reminder, infants show strong reactivation effects; they typically show a kicking rate roughly equal to their rate during the immediate retention test.

We adults occasionally show a similar reactivation effect. For example, I recently received a letter from a student who had been in my Peace Studies course 8 years earlier. She asked whether I could write a letter of recommendation for her, and she described several characteristics to help jog my memory, mentioning a survey

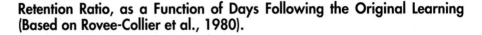

Retention Ratio, as a Function of Days Following the Original Learning (Based on Rovee-Collier et al., 1980).

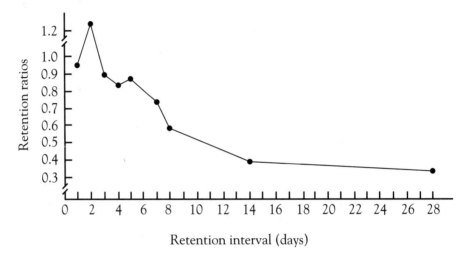

she had conducted. Nothing "clicked" until a day later when I suddenly remembered the details of her survey—and then her face and her excellent class performance came instantly to mind. Apparently infants often show this kind of memory reactivation, which is delayed by at least a day after the reminder. In fact, Rovee-Collier (1987) reports that about half of the 3-month-old infants in her study demonstrated recall 5 weeks after the original learning, when given a reminder on the previous day.

We saw in Chapter 5 that context is sometimes important in adult memory; contextual effects are even stronger for infants. For example, Rovee-Collier and her colleagues (1985) used the conjugate reinforcement technique to test 3-month-old infants whose cribs were lined with a crib bumper that had a distinctive, colorful pattern. (If you are not an expert in crib decor, look back at the patterned crib lining in Figure 12.2.) The infants' recall was excellent when they were tested after a 7-day delay. However, another group of infants was tested with the same mobile and the same delay—but a different crib bumper. This second group of infants showed no retention whatsoever! Without the proper environmental context, infants' memories decline sharply.

Remembering the Location of Objects. Infants can also remember the location of a hidden object. Baillargeon and Graber (1988) presented 7- and 8-month old infants with a distinctive-looking object, a white Styrofoam cup decorated with stars and dots, located on one of two placemats. After 3 seconds of viewing, identical screens were placed in front of the two placemats so that the object was no longer visible. Then a human hand emerged, wearing a long silver glove and a jingle-bell bracelet. The hand "tiptoed" back and forth for 15 seconds, then reached behind one of the two screens, and came out holding the white cup. Half of the time the cup came from behind the screen where it was supposed to be located, thereby representing a possible event. In the remaining instances, the cup came from behind the other screen, representing an impossible event.

Baillargeon and Graber found that 8-month-old infants looked significantly longer at the cup in the impossible-event condition, indicating that they were puzzled by its unexpected location. However, the 7-month-olds looked at the cup for an equal amount of time in both conditions, thus indicating they do not seem to remember the original location of an object after being hidden for a 15-second period. Thus, memory for location seems to emerge between 7 and 8 months of age.

Imitation. Most parents can remember examples of their infant imitating an action he or she had previously seen. But how can we encourage imitation so that it can be studied objectively? In a series of studies, 9- to 14-month-old infants watched an adult performing a number of actions with unusual objects, for example, moving a handle or pressing a button to produce a beeping noise. One day later, the objects were placed in front of the infant; the majority of the infants successfully imitated the adult's actions. However, when the delay was increased to one week, only the 14-month-olds repeated the actions (Meltzoff, 1988a, 1988b).

In summary, infants demonstrate memory on a number of tasks. Newborns can recognize the sight, sound, and smell of their mothers, and they can also recognize checkerboard designs. Three-month-olds can remember how to activate a mobile after a delay of more than a week; and with a reminder, they can recall the trick up to 5 weeks later. Eight-month-olds can recall the location of hidden objects, and 14-month-olds can remember how to imitate actions after a week-long delay.

Memory in Children

We have seen that researchers need to be extremely inventive when they study infant memory. Assessing children's memory is far easier, because children can respond verbally. However, the task is still far from simple, because children may have difficulty understanding task instructions, and they may be unable to identify certain stimuli (for example, letters of the alphabet). Let's consider three components of children's memory: (a) sensory and short-term memory, (b) long-term memory, and (c) memory strategies.

Sensory and Short-Term Memory. In general, studies of sensory memory show that children and adults have similar kinds of sensory memory (Engle et al., 1981; Hoving et al., 1978). Furthermore, both the capacity and the decay rates of iconic (visual) and echoic (auditory) memory are similar for adults and for 5-year-old children (Kail & Siegel, 1977). If we are looking for major differences between children and adults, we will have to look beyond sensory memory.

Short-term memory is often measured in terms of memory span. Tests of memory span usually measure the number of items that can be correctly recalled in order immediately after presentation. These tests have established that memory span improves as children grow older (Dempster, 1985; Harris, 1978). For example, the average 2-year-old may have a memory span of only two items, in contrast to about seven items for 12-year-olds and adults (Dempster, 1981).

We also know that young children are more likely than older children and adults to store material in a visual form in short-term memory. Specifically, Hitch and his colleagues (1988) found that 5-year-olds had difficulty recalling a series of drawings of visually similar objects, compared to a series of dissimilar drawings. However, 10-year-olds experienced no additional difficulty with visually similar objects. Apparently, older children engage in verbal rehearsal to keep items in short-term memory, so visual appearance is not relevant.

As Cairns and Valsiner (1984) conclude, all things being equal, older children and adults perform considerably better than young children. However, the interesting results appear when all things are *not* equal. We have discussed the issue of expertise throughout earlier chapters of this book. What happens when we compare children who are experts in a certain area with adults who are novices? Chi (1981) asked 10-year-old chess experts and adult chess novices to perform a standard digit span task. As expected, the adults performed much better; they recalled an average of two digits more than the children. However, Chi also asked these two groups of participants to memorize chess pieces and their positions on a chessboard. On this task the children excelled, recalling an average of three items more than the adults! It is unclear whether these results can be explained by the fact that the children have more knowledge about the subject matter of chess, or whether they were more motivated because the area was personally meaningful to them (Cairns & Valsiner, 1984).

Long-Term Memory. The literature on long-term memory has been summarized by Kail (1990) and Small (1990). In general, young children have excellent recognition memory but poor recall memory. In a study by Brown and Scott (1971), for example, 4-year-olds were accurate 75 percent of the time in their recognition of pictures that had been shown one week earlier.

Furthermore, some studies show that children have good recognition memory, even after a long delay. For example, Peters (1987) tested children between the ages of 3 and 8 for their facial recognition accuracy. Specifically, could they recognize the faces of their dentists and their dental hygienists? Each child visited the

DEMONSTRATION 12.1

AGE DIFFERENCES IN RECALL AND RECOGNITION.

In this experiment you will need to test a college-age person and a preschool child. You should reassure the child's parents that you are simply testing memory as part of a class project.

You will be examining both recall and recognition in this demonstration. First, assemble 20 common objects, such as a pen, pencil, piece of paper, leaf, stick, rock, book, key, apple, and so on. Place the objects in a box or cover them with a cloth.

You will use the same testing procedure for both people, although the preschool child will require more extensive explanation. Remove 10 objects in all, 1 at a time. Show each object for about 5 seconds and then conceal it again. After all 10 objects have been shown, ask each person to recall as many of the objects as possible. Do not provide feedback about the correctness of the responses. After recall is complete, test for recognition. Remove one object at a time, randomly presenting the old objects mixed in sequence with new objects. In each case, ask whether the object is old or new.

Count the number of correct recalls and the number of correct recognitions for each person. You should find that they both show a similar high level of performance on the *recognition* measures. However, the older person will *recall* far more than the younger person.

dentist's office for a routine check-up or to have a cavity filled; in each case, the children saw these two individuals for about 15 minutes. One group of children was given a recognition test 1 to 2 days later; the other group was tested between 3 and 4 weeks later. Both groups showed similar recognition accuracy. Furthermore, the age of the children did not affect the accuracy of their recognition of either the dentist or the hygienist.

In general, recall measures are more likely than recognition measures to reveal major differences between children's and adults' memory. For example, Myers and Perlmutter (1978) performed studies similar to those in Demonstration 12.1 using 2- and 4-year-old children. To test recognition, they showed children 18 objects. Then they presented 36 items, including the 18 previous objects and 18 new objects. As you can see in Figure 12.3, children were highly accurate on this recognition task; the 4-year-olds had almost perfect performance, and even the 2-year-olds recognized 80 percent of the items.

Myers and Perlmutter then tested recall in a different group of children. These children saw nine objects. After the experimenter had presented each item and named it, the children were told that they could keep all the objects that they correctly recalled. Despite the tempting incentive, recall was poor, as shown in Figure 12.3. Notice that the 2-year-olds recalled only 22 percent of the items. Myers and Perlmutter discuss many reasons for children's superior performance on recognition tests in contrast to recall tests. For example, recall—but not recognition—

FIGURE 12.3

Recognition and Recall for 2- and 4-year-olds.

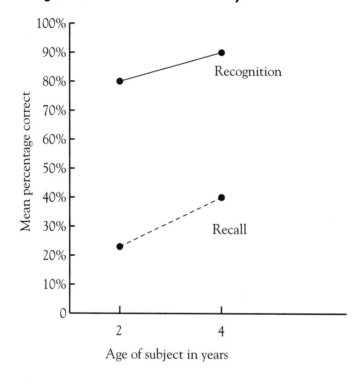

may require more active rehearsal strategies and more thorough searches of memory.

You may recall that Chapter 5 discussed **reality monitoring,** which is the process of trying to decide which memories are real and which are simply imagined. In general, children have more difficulty than adults in distinguishing between reality and fantasy (Ratner & Foley, in press). For example, I know an extremely bright child who had participated in an imaginary trip to the moon one day at school. Later that day, she claimed that she really *had* visited the moon.

Research has demonstrated age-related changes in reality monitoring. For example, in research by Foley and her colleagues (1987) and Harris and Foley (1992), children and adults either drew objects or imagined themselves drawing objects. Young children had more difficulty than older children in remembering which activities they had actually done and which they had imagined doing; older children also had more difficulty than adults. Similarly, in another study, 4-year-olds worked together with adults in making collages (Foley et al., 1993). The 4-year-olds made many errors in deciding which pieces they had placed on the collage and which had been placed there by adults. The children frequently claimed, "I did it," when the experimenter had actually contributed the pieces.

The information on children's relative accuracy in recognition memory and their relative inaccuracy in reality monitoring has important implications for children's eyewitness testimony. Should we trust children when they were the only witnesses to a robbery? Should we believe children who say they were sexually abused? Unfortunately, researchers disagree about the trustworthiness of children's memories (Ceci et al., 1987; DeAngelis, 1989; Doris, 1991). However, they generally agree that younger children are more suggestible than older children; younger children are more likely to incorporate false post-event information into their testimonies.

In contrast to the disagreement about the reliability of children's memories, researchers tend to agree that children use scripts in their memories. As you'll recall from Chapter 7, a **script** is a simple, well-structured sequence of events (Small, 1990). For example, children as young as 3 years of age can supply script-like answers to general questions such as "Can you tell me what happens when you have lunch at the day-care center?" (Nelson, 1986). Children respond by listing the critical actions in the appropriate time sequence, relying on generic information rather than specific episodes. In fact, children are more attentive to the typical, script-type aspects of events than to the distinctive aspects that make each event unique (Farrar & Goodman, 1990; Fivush & Hamond, 1990).

Memory Strategies. So far, our examination of children's memory has demonstrated that children differ most from adults in their recall memory. In contrast, children are most similar to adults in their sensory memory and their recognition memory. When adults want to remember something in recall memory, they are likely to make use of memory strategies. A possible explanation for children's relatively poor performance in recall is that they are not able to use memory strategies effectively.

Memory strategies are deliberate, goal-oriented behaviors we use to improve our memories (Kail, 1990). Young children may try to use some memory strategies, but the strategies may be faulty and the children may not use the strategies effectively (Wellman, 1988). In contrast, older children use more helpful strategies, and they use these strategies more consistently (e.g., Cairns & Valsiner, 1984; Kail, 1990; Small, 1990). Let's survey four major kinds of memory strategies: rehearsal, organization, imagery, and retrieval.

1. *Rehearsal,* or merely repeating items over and over, is not a particularly effective strategy. Some researchers are skeptical about whether mere rehearsal really

aids long-term memory. Nonetheless, it is useful in maintaining items in short-term memory. In a classic study on children's rehearsal patterns, Flavell and his colleagues (1966) asked 5-, 7-, and 10-year-olds to watch as the experimenter pointed to several objects in sequence. The children were told that they themselves would later have to point to the same objects in the same order. During the delay prior to recall, a trained lip-reader carefully noted any spontaneous lip movements that would indicate rehearsal. The results showed that the 7- and 10-year-olds were much more likely than the younger children to rehearse the items during the delay period.

As children grow older, they are more likely to rehearse. They are also likely to change with respect to the kind of material they select for rehearsal. Young children typically rehearse a single word, usually the one just presented. In contrast, older children and adults rehearse several words together (Kail, 1990). Furthermore, older children and adults rehearse at a faster rate (Hulme & Tordoff, 1989). As we saw in Chapter 4, short-term memory capacity is related to the number of items that can be rehearsed in a short period of time. Part of the reason that adults have larger short-term memory capacities may be that they can rehearse more quickly than children.

Another important point is that younger children benefit from rehearsal strategies, but they do not always use these strategies spontaneously (e.g., Baker-Ward et al., 1984; Flavell, 1985; Liben, 1982). As we will see in the section on metacognition, young children often fail to realize that they could enhance their memory performance by using strategies.

2. *Organizational strategies*, such as categorizing and grouping, are frequently used by adults, as we saw in Chapter 5. However, young children do not spontaneously group similar items together to aid memorization. Try Demonstration 12.2 and see if it illustrates children's reluctance to adopt organizational strategies.

This demonstration is based on a study by Moely and her colleagues (1969), in which children studied pictures from four categories: animals, clothing, furniture, and vehicles. During the 2-minute study period, they were told that they could rearrange the pictures in any order they wished. Younger children rarely moved the pictures next to other similar pictures, but older children frequently organized the pictures into categories. Other groups of children were specifically urged to organize the pictures. This training procedure encouraged even the younger children to adopt an organizational strategy, and this strategy increased their recall. Thus, children often have the ability to organize, though they are not aware that organization will enhance recall.

Children can use spatial organization, as well as semantic organization. Bjorklund and Zeman (1982) discovered that grade-school children frequently remembered the names of their classmates in terms of where they sat in the classroom. The children often seemed to discover these organizational strategies by chance. They began their list of classmates in random order, but frequently listed together

ORGANIZATIONAL STRATEGIES IN CHILDREN.

Make a photocopy of the pictures on this page and use scissors to cut them apart (or, alternatively, cut pictures out of magazines that belong to four different categories). In this experiment you will test a child between the ages of 4 and 8; ideally, it would be interesting to test children of several different ages. Arrange these pictures in random order in a circle facing the child. Instruct him or her to study the pictures so that they can be remembered later. Mention that the pictures can be rearranged in any order. After a two-minute study period, remove the pictures and ask the child to list as many items as possible. Notice two things in this demonstration: (1) Does the child rearrange the items at all during the study period? (2) Does the child show clustering during recall, with similar items appearing together?

two names of children who sat next to each other. This event often triggered an insight: "Aha! I can remember the names of kids by where they sit!"

In discussing rehearsal, we saw that children begin to use that strategy spontaneously when they are about 7 years of age. In contrast, children do not begin to use organizational strategies spontaneously until they are 9 or 10 (Kail, 1990). More complex strategies, such as organization, require more sophisticated cognitive abilities. A child who has the ability to organize objects in terms of semantic categories needs to pay attention to semantic features of items (for example, meaning, rather than shape) and needs to possess established categories for related objects (for example, vehicles).

3. *Imagery*, the topic discussed in Chapter 6, is an extremely useful device for improving memory in adults. Although imagery is also useful for older children, some evidence suggests that it may not be as useful for younger children (e.g., Reese, 1977). However, Kosslyn (1976) found that children as young as 6 spontaneously used mental images in various tasks. Furthermore, Yuille and Catchpole (1977) found that first-graders' memories improved after they had been trained to form interactive images. Specifically, these authors displayed pairs of objects, one at a time, and asked children to imagine the two objects playing together. After 5 minutes of this kind of training, one group of children learned 20 pairs of objects. Other children received no special training prior to learning the 20 pairs. Recall was measured both immediately and after a 1-week delay. In both immediate and delayed recall, training aided recall substantially. Thus, just 5 minutes of training can lead to a long-lasting improvement in learning. Fry and Lupart (1986) suggest that educators should offer more instruction on how to learn. In particular, young children can benefit from training designed to improve their memory.

4. In addition to strategies requiring rehearsal, organization, and imagery, adults also use *retrieval strategies*. When a cue is available that might help adults retrieve a memory, they use it spontaneously. In contrast, children who have been given a retrieval cue do not search their memories exhaustively (Ackerman, 1988).

We saw that young children do not seem to be aware that organizational strategies can enhance recall. Similarly, young children do not appreciate that retrieval cues can be helpful. In a representative experiment, Kobasigawa (1974) showed children pictures of items together with a retrieval cue (for example, a bear, a lion, and a monkey together with the retrieval cue of a picture of a zoo). One group of children then tried to recall the names without using the cue cards; their recall was quite low. Another group of children was handed the cue cards (for example, the zoo picture) and was instructed to supply the items that had been associated with each card. Children of all ages were uniformly accurate in this condition.

The most interesting results from Kobasigawa's study came from a third group, who were given the cue cards, face down, and were told to use them if they thought the cards would be helpful. The youngest children in that group (6-year-olds) seldom used the cue cards. In contrast, the oldest children (11-year-olds) made good use of the cue cards, and their recall was about twice that of the youngest children. In short, all children benefited when they were required to use retrieval cues. However, only the older children spontaneously used them.

In short, preschool children are unlikely to use memory strategies in a careful, consistent fashion. In fact, as we have suggested here and will further discuss in the section on metamemory, young children are not likely to appreciate that they need to use memory strategies. However, as children develop, they learn how to use four memory strategies—rehearsal, organization, imagery, and retrieval. Furthermore, they become aware that if they want to remember something, they would be wise to use these memory strategies, rather than merely trusting that they will remember important material.

◇ In Depth: **Memory in Elderly People**

Irele Hulicka (1982) provides an illustration of the way people judge cognitive errors made by elderly people. A 78-year-old woman served a meal to her guests, and the meal was excellent except that she had used Clorox instead of vinegar in the salad dressing. Her concerned relatives attributed the error to impaired memory and general intellectual decline, and they discussed placing her in a nursing home. As it turned out, someone else had placed the Clorox in the cupboard where the vinegar was kept. Understandably, she had reached for the wrong bottle, which was similar in size, shape, and color to the vinegar bottle.

Some time later, the same people were guests in another home. A young woman in search of hair spray reached into a bathroom cabinet and found a can of the right size and shape. She proceeded to drench her hair with Lysol. In this case, however, no one suggested that the younger woman be institutionalized; they merely teased her about her absentmindedness. Apparently, people are so convinced that elderly people have cognitive deficits that an incident considered humorous in a younger person provides proof of incompetence in an older person.

During the last decade, research on memory in the elderly has blossomed, and a wide variety of review articles and books have been published (e.g., Light, 1991; Light & Burke, 1988; Salthouse, 1989; Salthouse, 1991). The picture that emerges suggests complex developmental trends in various components of memory. As Lachman (1991) summarizes the data:

> Although there are indeed memory changes with aging, there is no evidence that these are widespread, pervasive, or irreversible. Rather, there is evidence of large individual differences in the nature and extent of memory problems. (p. 171)

Let us consider the research on sensory memory, short-term memory, and long-term memory; then we will examine potential explanations for some of the memory changes during aging.

Sensory Memory. In general, researchers have not discovered major developmental changes in sensory memory, that fragile storage system that records information for less than two seconds. Some studies, however, have reported moderate decline in iconic (or visual sensory) memory. For example, Walsh and Thompson (1978) found that iconic memory lasted an average of 289 milliseconds for a group of younger people whose average age was 21. It lasted an average of 248 milliseconds for a group of older people whose average age was 67. However, these differences may be attributed to the attention patterns in people of different ages (Rebok, 1987). Walsh and Thompson used the Sperling technique, which we described in Chapter 3. Elderly people tend to concentrate their attention on the top row of letters. In contrast, younger people can distribute their attention more flexibly throughout the visual display, thereby increasing their scores on Sperling-type tests. Other measures of assessing iconic memory have not found major differences in the iconic memory of young and elderly adults (e.g., Kline & Orme-Rogers, 1978; Kline & Schieber, 1981).

Echoic memory, or auditory sensory memory, is often measured with a dichotic memory task. Because divided-attention tasks are difficult for older people, any differences in measures of echoic memory may be traceable to attention problems, rather than echoic memory itself (Erber, 1982). In general, however, both researchers and theorists have concluded that the echoic memory of young and elderly adults do not differ substantially (Craik, 1977; Crowder, 1980). In summary, if we want to discover major ways in which the memories of 80-year-olds differ from the memories of 20-year-olds, we will have to look beyond sensory memory. Let us turn our attention to short-term and then long-term memory.

Short-Term Memory. How well do elderly people do on tasks requiring short-term memory, when material must be retained in memory for less than a minute? Some reviews of the research conclude that elderly people do not differ substantially from younger people (e.g., Bayles et al., 1987; Rebok, 1987; Rybash et al., 1986; West, 1985). However, other reviews suggest that age-related differences are clear-cut (e.g., Kausler, 1982; Cohen, 1988).

How can we resolve these discrepancies? If you have taken several previous psychology courses, you'll probably agree that your professors and your textbooks frequently use the phrase, "It all depends. . . . " In the case of short-term memory, whether we find age similarities or age differences all depends upon factors such as the nature of the task. In general, we find age similarities when the short-term memory task is relatively straightforward; we find age differences when the task is complicated and requires manipulation of information.

For example, Craik (1990) reports that younger and older adults showed no differences on a standard digit-span test, where people were instructed to recall a list of numbers in order. However, age differences were substantial for a task in which people were given short lists of unrelated words, with the instructions to report the words in correct alphabetical order. With lists that were five items long, for example, the average young participant reported 3.2 correct items, whereas the average elderly participant reported 1.7 correct items.

Perhaps one reason that elderly people perform reasonably well on a digit-span test is that it resembles everyday memory tasks, for example, remembering a phone number long enough to write it down. In contrast, consider a less familiar, more difficult task, remembering spatial locations. Salthouse and his coauthors (1988) presented a 5 × 5 matrix in which 7 of the 25 cells were highlighted as targets. Then the stimulus matrix was removed and the participants were instructed to indicate on a blank matrix which cells had been the targets in the previous display. The results showed that 20-year-olds identified an average of 4.3 items, 45-year-olds averaged 3.9 items, and 65-year-olds averaged 3.5 items. Thus, the age differences were not huge, but the decline was consistent. Similarly, when people were instructed to remember a list of English words that had been presented in random order, 17- to 19-year-olds recalled an average of 9.1 words, in contrast to 5.4 words for 60- to 78-year-olds (Rebok & Balcerak, 1989).

Let us consider a study by Elizabeth Stine and her coauthors (1989) in more detail, because it provides a good illustration of how age differences in short-term memory are more likely with more difficult tasks. This group of researchers was interested in examining people's recall for spoken English. They tested a group of young adults, aged 18 to 22 years, and a group of elderly adults, aged 65 to 73 years, who were similar in educational level and verbal ability. Stine and her colleagues used three kinds of material. All consisted of eight-word strings. However, some were normal sentences (e.g., "The rich soil was filled with sharp rocks"). Some had correct syntactic structure but were not meaningful because they contained some violation of semantic constraints (e.g., "The rich rocks were filled with sharp soil"). The third group of sentences were simply strings of eight words in random order with neither correct syntactic structure nor semantic content (e.g., "filled soil the sharp rich with were rocks").

This study also varied the rate at which the words were spoken. Normal English is spoken at the rate of between 100 and 200 words per minute. Stine and her colleagues used speech rates that varied from 275 words per minute (somewhat faster than normal) to 425 words per minute (much faster than normal).

As you can see from Figure 12.4a, the young and the elderly participants recalled a similar number of items when the words formed normal sentences; even at the fastest speed, the younger people recalled only slightly more material. When the word strings obeyed syntactic rules—but not semantic rules—the performance of the two groups diverged more substantially, especially at the faster speeds (Figure 12.4b). Furthermore, when the words were in entirely random order, obeying neither syntactic nor semantic rules, the two groups diverged sharply (Figure 12.4c). Notice that at the fastest speech rate, the younger participants recalled more than twice as many words as the older participants. In summary, in the situation most like everyday English, older adults have no problems. However, when the task is made more challenging and less familiar, with words spoken at a rapid-fire rate in random order, elderly people will be at a disadvantage.

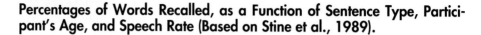

FIGURE 12.4

Percentages of Words Recalled, as a Function of Sentence Type, Participant's Age, and Speech Rate (Based on Stine et al., 1989).

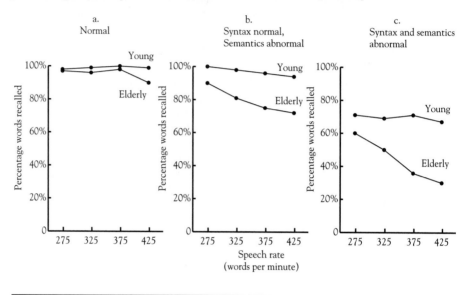

Long-Term Memory. Do elderly people differ from younger adults in their long-term memory? Once again, the answer is, "It all depends. . . ." In general, the age differences are smallest on tasks that involve recognition memory and on tasks that can be performed relatively automatically. However, age differences emerge on more challenging tasks.

A number of research papers and reviews of the literature argue that long-term recognition memory declines either slowly or not at all as people grow older (Craik et al., 1987; Craik & McDowd, 1987; Lavigne & Finley, 1990; Perlmutter, 1979). However, elderly people may have a significantly higher false-alarm rate; they may say that an item is old, when in fact they have never seen it before (Trahan et al., 1986).

Chapter 5 discussed the difference between explicit and implicit memory measures. As you may recall, an **explicit memory measure** requires the participant to remember information in an active fashion (for example, recall or recognition). In contrast, an **implicit memory measure** requires the participant to perform a task. In general, age differences are relatively small on implicit memory tasks. For example, Leah Light and Asha Singh (1987) tested implicit memory by presenting word fragments, such as P__P__R. Older adults and younger adults were equally likely to supply the word PAPER if they had previously been exposed to that word.

Similarly, elderly people show no deficit on two other implicit memory tasks, supplying examples of various categories (Light & Albertson, 1989) and filling in a missing word in a sentence (Lovelace & Coon, 1991). As Light and her coauthors conclude, elderly people and young people perform similarly when the memory task involves automatic activation processes. However, they are likely to perform differently when the task involves conscious efforts to recall details (Light et al., 1986).

Let us now turn to performance on long-term recall tasks, where age differences are likely to be more substantial. For example, consider the research on recall for prose, or lengthy passages of standard English. Fortunately, Elizabeth Zelinski and Michael Gilewski (1988) have conducted a meta-analysis on this extensive research. As you may recall, the **meta-analytic technique** is a statistical method for synthesizing numerous studies on a single topic. This meta-analysis of 36 studies showed that younger adults recalled significantly more material than older adults. However, the effect of age differences was much more prominent when the verbal material told a story than when it was an essay. Furthermore, differences in age were more prominent in people who were low in verbal ability. When the individuals in both groups had high verbal ability, the recall for the elderly people and the younger people were more similar.

Notice how the research on long-term memory obeys the "It all depends . . . " principle. Elderly people are similar to younger people in recognition memory and in implicit-memory performance. Even when we examine an area in which age differences are more prominent, such as prose recall, we cannot draw a simple conclusion, because highly verbal people are less likely to show a deficit and because essays are less likely to cause recall problems. In other words, memory deficits are far from universal among elderly people; age-related differences are found only among some people on specified tasks.

On some kinds of recall tasks, elderly people may be even more accurate than younger people. For instance, Rodgers and Herzog (1987) were interested in the accuracy of older people in supplying information on survey questionnaires. These authors asked a large sample of people to supply the kind of information that could be verified in publicly accessible records. For example, the questions included whether they had voted in the 1980 presidential election, the make and year of any cars they owned, and so forth. On these questions, people over the age of 60 were more accurate than people younger than 60. It is not clear what properties of this task encouraged this impressively strong recall from the elderly participants.

Explanations for Age Differences in Memory.   As you probably suspected, when we need to account for a complex pattern of results, the explanations will not be simple. Furthermore, I need to emphasize that we are seeking explanations for memory changes that accompany the normal aging process; disease-related memory deficits involve different mechanisms (e.g., Elias et al., 1991). To account for normal memory changes, we probably need to rely on several mechanisms, because no single explanation is sufficient. Let us consider some possible explanations, using the framework proposed by Leah Light (1991):

1. Memory strategies and metamemory could differ for elderly and young adults. Research suggests, for example, that elderly people are less likely to use organizational strategies when they need to memorize a long list of items (Smith, 1980). Some research also suggests that elderly people are less likely to use visual imagery spontaneously when they are learning material (Hulicka & Grossman, 1967; Weinstein et al., 1979). Elderly people are also less likely to benefit from instructions that urge the use of visual images (Smith, 1980). However, numerous studies summarized by Light (1991) and Salthouse (1991) conclude that elderly and young adults report using similar memory strategies. Furthermore, as Light (1991) concludes, and as we will see in the second section of this chapter, age differences in metamemory do not seem to be consistent enough to explain the differences in memory performance.

2. The semantic deficit hypothesis suggests that the elderly have impaired memory because their language processing skills are deficient. For example, they might encode material at a shallower level of processing. However, Light's (1991) review concludes, "Our literature review offers no support for the claim that deficits in semantic processing underlie memory problems in old age" (p. 346).

3. Another hypothesis suggests that elderly people have problems in deliberate recollection. As we saw earlier, elderly people experience the greatest problems with memory tasks that require the most effortful, deliberate processing. Recall suffers the most as we grow older; recognition suffers less, and implicit memory suffers the least. Light (1991) agrees that the data suggest a reasonably consistent pattern, but we cannot yet identify any mechanisms to explain why some performance is spared and some is impaired.

4. The hypothesis that has been most extensively researched in the past decade is that elderly people experience a reduction in their processing resources. For example, perhaps older adults have a more limited attention capacity than younger adults. Young adults can pay selective attention because inhibitory processes eliminate competing stimuli; if these inhibitory processes stop working so efficiently, working memory may be flooded by irrelevant information (e.g., Hartman & Hasher, 1991; Hasher & Zacks, 1988). However, Light (1991) concludes that the evidence for this explanation is mixed. A second "reduced processing resources" explanation is that the capacity of working memory (short-term memory) may be reduced in elderly people. Light concludes that this explanation can account for some of the age-related differences in memory, but not all. A final "reduced processing resources" explanation is that elderly people experience **cognitive slowing,** or a slower

rate of responding on cognitive tasks (e.g., Hale et al., 1991; Lima et al., 1991; Myerson et al., 1990; Salthouse, 1991). However, Light argues that the cognitive slowing hypothesis does not predict how elderly people perform on tasks requiring large memory loads.

Reviewing all four proposed mechanisms, Light (1991) argues that "These hypotheses, taken individually or collectively, do not provide an adequate account for the observed patterns of spared and impaired function in old age" (pp. 365–366). In fact, she titles her review article, "Memory and Aging: Four Hypotheses in Search of Data." Perhaps a refined version of one of the current hypotheses may be developed, or additional hypotheses may be proposed. However, at present we have a complex set of findings about memory in the elderly, but no satisfying explanation for these results.

SECTION SUMMARY: THE DEVELOPMENT OF MEMORY

1. Psychologists interested in the development of cognition encounter methodological problems in their research, particularly with studies on infants and elderly people.
2. Research demonstrates that newborns can recognize their mothers and also geometric designs; 3-month-olds can remember how to activate a mobile following a one-week delay; 8-month-olds can recall the location of hidden objects; and 14-month-olds can remember how to imitate actions after a one-week delay.
3. Compared to adults, children have similar sensory memory but reduced short-term memory; children have reasonably strong recognition memory, but poor recall memory. In addition, children have poor reality monitoring; however, like adults, their memory is based on scripts.
4. As they grow older, children make increasing use of memory strategies such as rehearsal, organization, imagery, and retrieval. Young children typically do not use memory strategies spontaneously, but they can be trained to use them effectively.
5. As adults grow older, sensory memory does not decline substantially; short-term memory remains intact for some tasks, but it is limited when the task is complicated and requires manipulation of information.
6. With respect to long-term memory, age differences are smallest for recognition memory tasks and for tasks that can be performed relatively automatically (for example implicit memory tasks); age differences in prose recall is substantial, especially for story recall and for people with low verbal ability.
7. Several potential explanations have been proposed to explain how age affects memory: memory strategies and metamemory, the semantic deficit hypothesis, the deliberate-recollection hypothesis, and the hypothesis about reduced

processing resources. Unfortunately, none of the current forms of these four hypotheses is strongly supported by the data.

THE DEVELOPMENT OF METACOGNITION

As we discussed in Chapter 7, **metacognition** is knowledge and awareness about cognitive processes—or our thoughts about thinking. Two important kinds of metacognition are metamemory (for example, realizing that you need to use a strategy to remember someone's name) and metacomprehension (for example, trying to decide whether you understood that definition of *metacognition*). In this section of the chapter, we will look at metacognition in children and in elderly people.

Metacognition in Children

Research on metacognition in children has been thriving for more than two decades. In fact, the first major research in metacognition focused on children rather than on college students (Flavell, 1971). Flavell argued that young children have extremely limited metacognition; they seldom monitor their memory, language, problem solving, or decision making (Flavell, 1979). Let us examine several components of children's metamemory, as well as the topic of metacomprehension.

Metamemory: How Memory Works. One aspect of metamemory is your knowledge about how memory works. Demonstration 12.3 includes some questions about this component of metamemory. Research shows that children as young as 6 years of age know that familiar items are easier to remember than unfamiliar ones (Kreutzer et al., 1975). Even younger children, 3 and 4 years of age, know that a small set of pictures can be remembered better than a large set (Yussen & Bird, 1979). These young children also know that personal variables, such as mood and fatigue, can affect how easily you learn new material (Hayes et al., 1987).

However, even 5-year-olds have rather unsophisticated ideas about how their memories work. For example, they are not yet aware that words are easier to remember when they are part of a narrative, rather than a list; they also do not realize that the gist of a passage is easier to remember than verbatim recall (Brown, 1975; Kreutzer et al., 1975). In other research, Beal (1985) told children about a boy who draws a picture to help him remember to take his lunch to school. Only 65 percent of the 5- and 6-year-olds in the study understood that the boy needed to find the picture *before* he left for school, rather than afterwards. In contrast, all 8-year-olds understood this point.

Metamemory: Realizing the Necessity of Effort. Another important component of metamemory is the awareness that if you really want to remember something, you must make an effort (Flavell & Wellman, 1977). Even young children

---

DEMONSTRATION 12.3

METAMEMORY IN ADULTS AND CHILDREN.

Ask a child the following questions. (Ideally, try to question several children of different ages). Compare the accuracy and/or the completeness of the answers with your own responses. Note that some questions should be adapted to a level appropriate for your subject.

1. A child will be going to a party tomorrow, and she wants to remember to bring her skates. What kinds of things can she do to help her remember them?
2. Suppose that I were to read you a list of words. How many words do you think you could recall in the correct order? (Then read the following list and count the number of words correctly recalled. Use only part of the list for the child.)

   cat   rug   chair   leaf   sky   book   apple   pencil   house   teacher

3. Two children want to learn the names of some rocks. One child learned the names last month but forgot them. The other child never learned the names. Who will have an easier time in learning the names?
4. Suppose that you memorize somebody's address. Will you remember it better after 2 minutes have passed or after 2 days have passed?
5. Suppose that you are memorizing two kinds of words. One kind of word is abstract (refers to things you cannot see or touch, such as *idea* or *religion*) and the other kind is concrete (refers to things that you can see and touch, such as *notebook* or *zebra*). Which kind of word will you learn better?
6. Two children want to remember some lists of words. One child has a list of 10 words, and the other has a list of 5 words. Which child will be more likely to remember all the words on the list correctly?
7. Two children are reading the same paragraph. The teacher tells one child to remember all the sentences in the paragraph and repeat them word for word. The teacher tells the other child to remember the main ideas of the paragraph. Which child will have an easier job?

---

have some appreciation for this fact. For example, in one study, an experimenter took 4-year-olds on brief walks through hallways (Acredolo et al., 1975). Some children were told beforehand that they would be asked to recall where the experimenter dropped her keys. Other children did not receive these instructions. In all cases, the experimenter dropped her keys and then picked them up. Children recalled the location much more accurately when they had been instructed beforehand to remember. With a simple task, then, children can make an effort to remember, and they can remember accurately.

However, young children do not seem to realize that effort and strategies are required to learn a list of items. When preschoolers and kindergartners are given a list of items to learn, with instruction to notify the experimenter when the list has been memorized, they spend most of the study time in unproductive activities. Also, they do not understand when something has been committed to memory. They typically report to the experimenter that they have satisfactorily memorized a list, yet testing reveals that they recall little (Gross, 1985).

Even older children have naive ideas about the effort required in memorization. I recall an example of this very vividly. A sixth-grade neighbor was visiting and doing her homework, which involved memorizing some information about the U.S. Constitution. My husband asked her how she was doing and whether it would be helpful if he quizzed her. She replied that she knew the material well, but he could quiz her if he wanted. Her recall turned out to be minimal for both factual and conceptual information. She had assumed that by allowing her eyes to wander over the text several times, the material had magically worked its way into memory. Of course, magical thinking is not limited to children. If your high-school courses were relatively easy for you, perhaps you reached college before you realized that effortful processing is essential in order to retain difficult material.

Metamemory: Accuracy of Predictions. In general, older children and adults are much more accurate than younger children in predicting their memory performance. For example, Yussen and Levy (1975) studied preschool children (mean age of 4.6 years), third-graders (mean age of 8.9), and college students (mean age of 20.2). Each person was first asked to estimate the number of picture names that he or she would be able to recall in correct order. Notice that this question measures metamemory because it asks people to think about their memory abilities. Next, Yussen and Levy measured everyone's true memory span on this task. They first presented a single picture and asked for recall, then two pictures, and then three. Testing continued with increasingly longer lists until people made errors in recall.

Figure 12.5 shows both memory estimates and actual memory spans for the three age groups. Notice that the preschoolers are wildly optimistic in their memory estimates. Unfortunately, this optimism may lull them into a false sense of security; they may not believe they need to spend any effort or use any strategies to memorize material (Kail, 1990). However, as people grow older, their estimates become more modest while their actual memory spans increase. Consequently, college students are quite realistic in their estimates about short-term memory.

Metamemory: The Relationship Between Metamemory and Memory Performance. Let us summarize several observations related to memory in young children: (1) their metamemory is faulty—they do not realize that they need to put effort into memorizing, and they do not realize how little they can remember;

FIGURE 12.5	

Estimated Versus Actual Memory Span, as a Function of Age.

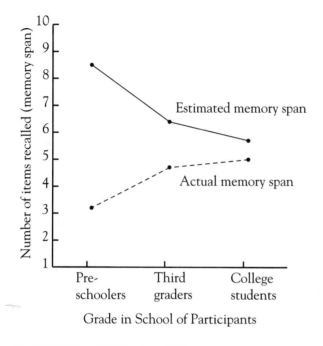

Estimated memory span

Actual memory span

Number of items recalled (memory span)

Pre-
schoolers

Third
graders

College
students

Grade in School of Participants

(2) they do not spontaneously use helpful memory strategies; and (3) relative to older children, their memory performance is poor.

Does a causal relationship link these three observations? Perhaps the three are related in this fashion:

Metamemory → Strategy Use → Memory Performance

Maybe a faulty metamemory means that children are not aware that they must use strategies to commit material to memory. If they do not use strategies, memory performance will suffer. Developmental psychologists are reasonably certain that strategy use is related to memory performance, as discussed in the previous section of this chapter. However, they disagree about whether the two ends in that chain of events—that is, metamemory and memory performance—are strongly related.

In a representative study, Cavanaugh and Borkowski (1980) interviewed children between the ages of kindergarten and fifth grade about metamemory. The children were questioned individually about the way they learned and remembered information, and their answers were scored for their level of memory awareness. As expected, older children were much more aware of their memory than younger children. Two weeks later, memory performance was tested for 30 pictures of objects. The correlations between metamemory scores and measures of memory performance were significant when the data were combined for all participants. However, when the researchers computed the correlations separately for each grade level, most of the correlations were not significant. In a later review of the literature, Cavanaugh and Perlmutter (1982) concluded that children's metamemory was only moderately correlated with their memory performance.

Other research is more optimistic. For example, Swanson (1987) demonstrated that children's metamemory scores were better than measures of language ability (for example, verbal IQ) in predicting how well the children performed on a variety of recall tests. Furthermore, Weed and her colleagues (1990) asked children whether they believed that they could control their academic success; could they do things to raise their grades in school? Children who scored high on this measure—which is a component of metamemory—also tended to perform better on a memory test. Furthermore, a review of the literature by Wellman (1985) and research by Andreassen and Waters (1989) conclude that metamemory and performance are fairly strongly linked.

Why do the research and the reviews on this topic reach such different conclusions about the correlation between metamemory and memory performance? Schneider (1984) points out that the correlations are much stronger when metamemory is assessed in terms of children's monitoring their own knowledge. For example, Wellman's (1985) review emphasized studies that assessed memory-monitoring skills. In a typical study, children might be asked to report when they were ready to be tested for recall; these measures of metamemory are indeed closely linked to memory performance. Schneider (1984) also pointed out that correlations between metamemory and performance are lower when metamemory is assessed in terms of children's knowledge about memory strategies (Cavanaugh & Borkowski, 1980; Cavanaugh & Perlmutter, 1982).

Schneider's conclusions make sense, especially because metamemory has many separate components, and they would not all be equally good predictors of memory performance. Nine-year-old Suzy may *know* that organization helps memory; if she doesn't use that strategy, however, that knowledge will not help her. In contrast, if she is very skilled in knowing when she is ready to be tested, she will probably perform well on a memory test.

In summary, we can probably conclude that metamemory—particularly memory monitoring—is related fairly strongly to memory performance. Consequently the proposed causal sequence (Metamemory → Strategy Use → Memory Performance) probably accounts for a substantial portion of the improvement in memory performance as children grow older.

Metacomprehension. Metacomprehension involves assessing whether you understand what you are reading or what is being said to you; it also involves your knowledge and thoughts about comprehension. Even young children know that reading comprehension is important. For example, both first-graders and sixth-graders believe that people who are good readers also perform better on other academic tasks (Yussen & Kane, 1983). However, young children often have inadequate ideas about reading and reading comprehension. For example, when a second-grader was asked how he viewed reading, he replied that reading was "stand up, sit down." When asked to explain, he replied that the teacher had him stand up to read, but when he made a mistake, he would sit down (Johns, 1986).

An important component of metacomprehension is your awareness of whether or not you understand what you are reading. You have probably had the sensation of reading a passage in a book, and suddenly becoming aware that you have not understood what you have been reading. You search back through the passage, trying to locate the point where the material first became unclear. As we grow older, we become increasingly skilled in identifying problems with comprehension.

Even young children can reveal that they do not understand a spoken message—though they may not be able to verbalize this confusion. For example, Flavell and his colleagues (1981) found that young children sometimes failed to identify a garbled message as being flawed. However, they revealed their difficulty in understanding by giving nonverbal messages: They looked puzzled, made funny expressions with their faces, and produced other body language that indicated, "I don't understand this message." This study is particularly interesting because it reveals that children know more about metacomprehension than they reveal verbally.

Good and poor students differ in their ability to assess their metacomprehension. Bransford and his colleagues (1982) constructed two passages about robots that were designed to wash windows. One passage described the functions of the robot and its properties, and it also explained how the properties helped the robot perform its functions. (For example, the suction-cup feet helped the robot climb the windows.) The second passage was similar, except that the explanations were omitted. Good and poor fifth-grade students were instructed to assess the difficulty of the passage after reading it. The good students were more likely to report that the version that omitted the explanations was more difficult and confusing than the one that contained the explanations. In contrast, the poor students were also more likely to feel they were ready for a test after only one rereading of the passage without the explanations. They didn't understand that they didn't understand!

In the discussion of metamemory, we noted that metamemory measures are not always correlated with memory performance. Is metacomprehension correlated with comprehension scores? Research by Cross and Paris (1988) revealed that the two factors were not closely related in their sample of third-graders, but they were related in their sample of fifth-graders. Apparently, by fifth grade, children can use their understanding about reading strategies to enhance their reading performance.

Metacognition in Elderly People

Research on metacognition in the elderly is limited almost exclusively to the topic of metamemory (Salthouse, 1991). Any of you who are concerned that all the interesting or worthwhile topics in psychology have already been examined should consider the possible research areas that are still unexplored. We know little about elderly people's thoughts about their attention patterns, comprehension, problem solving, and other cognitive processes. Our discussion of metacognition in the elderly is therefore limited to the area of metamemory.

In a way, we have already given away the punch line about age comparisons in metamemory. Earlier in the chapter, we discussed possible explanations for age differences in some areas in memory. One explanation we rejected stated that young and elderly adults might differ substantially in their metamemory. The evidence simply does not support major age differences in metamemory. Let us consider the findings in more detail:

1. Older and younger adults share similar beliefs about the properties of memory tasks (Light, 1991; Salthouse, 1991). Both groups have the same fundamental knowledge about how memory works, which strategies are most effective, and what kinds of material can be remembered most readily.

2. Older and younger adults have similar ability to monitor their memory performance. For example, the two groups are similar in their ability to predict, on an item-by-item basis, which items they can recall at a later time (Lovelace & Marsh, 1985). The similarity in accuracy rates holds true for three different memory tasks—free recall, paired-associate, and sentence memory (Rabinowitz et al., 1982).

3. On some measures of memory self-efficacy, the elderly receive lower scores than young adults. We discussed the general concept of self-efficacy in Chapter 11; **memory self-efficacy** is the feeling individuals have that their memories are competent and effective. Reviews of the research show that elderly people often score lower (e.g., Light, 1991; Lovelace, 1990). However, these lower measures may simply reflect—with accuracy—the fact that elderly people indeed have greater difficulty with some memory tasks. In other words, older and younger adults may be similar in the *accuracy* of their memory self-efficacy judgments.

4. The research on memory self-confidence is not consistent. In some research, older adults are more likely than younger adults to overestimate their memory performance. For example, Lovelace and Marsh (1985) asked people to study 60 pairs of unrelated English words, and the participants then rated their likelihood of recalling each item later. From these ratings, Lovelace and Marsh counted the number of items that people indicated they had more than a 50 percent chance of recalling correctly. These estimates were compared with the number of pairs each person actually recalled correctly. The younger adults (whose average age was 19) were quite accurate in their estimates, which were only 1.5 items higher than their actual recall. However,

the elderly people (whose average age was 67) were much less accurate. In fact, they estimated that they would recall 14.0 items more than they actually did recall.

Other research has also demonstrated overconfidence in the memory predictions of the elderly (e.g., Bruce et al., 1982; Herrmann, 1990; and Salthouse, 1991). However, some studies on estimation of memory performance show that the elderly are *underconfident*, not overconfident (e.g., Hertzog et al., 1990; Salthouse, 1991). The results probably depend upon the sample of elderly people that is being tested; active, healthy adults may be more likely to show overconfidence.

5. Elderly people are likely to report that memory failures have increased over the years. Lovelace and Twohig (1990) asked people whose average age was 68 to report whether they had noticed a change in their memory for certain items. The results showed that 42 percent reported that they were now more likely to have problems recalling the word they wanted during a conversation. In addition, 40 percent said that they were more likely to forget what they had intended to do (for example, why they went into a particular room). They also reported an increased incidence of forgetting the point of a conversation they had begun and an increased problem with remembering whether or not they had done a routine task. However, Lovelace and Twohig also found that in this sample of healthy, articulate adults, not a single participant reported that memory failures seriously hampered his or her daily activities. Their memory difficulties had increased in some areas, but they were still managing quite well.

In summary, our examination of metamemory in the elderly has revealed many age similarities in memory knowledge, memory monitoring, memory self-efficacy, memory self-confidence, and reported memory problems. As Salthouse (1991) concludes in his review of age comparisons in metamemory, "Results from the available studies do not appear to provide much support for the hypothesis of age differences in metacognitive functioning" (p. 211). Thus, young children's metamemory may be inferior compared to young adults' metamemory, but elderly adults experience no overwhelming metamemory impairment.

SECTION SUMMARY: THE DEVELOPMENT OF METACOGNITION

1. Young children have some awareness of the way memory works, but their knowledge increases as they mature.
2. Young children are not aware that they must use strategies to learn a list of items.
3. Older children and adults are much more accurate than younger children in

predicting their memory performance; young children are far too overconfident.

4. When metamemory is measured in terms of children's monitoring their own knowledge, metamemory is correlated with memory performance.

5. Young children may reveal that they do not understand a message by giving nonverbal signals; good and poor students differ in the accuracy of their metacomprehension.

6. Older and younger adults have similar knowledge about their memory and similar ability to monitor their memory.

7. The elderly score lower on measures of memory self-efficacy; however, age is not consistently related to overconfidence in predicting one's memory performance.

8. The elderly report an increase in the frequency of some memory problems, but they do not believe that these memory problems greatly impair their daily functioning.

THE DEVELOPMENT OF LANGUAGE

"Mama!" (8 months old)

"Wash hair." (1 year, 4 months old)

"Don't tickle my tummy, Mommy!" (1 year, 11 months old)

"My Grandma gave me this dolly, Cara. My Grandma is my Mommy's Mommy. I have another Grandma, too. She's my Daddy's Mommy. And Aunt Elli is my Daddy's sister." (2 years, 9 months old)

These selections from the early language of my daughter Sally are typical of the remarkable accomplishment involved in language acquisition. Individual children differ in the rate at which they master language (e.g., Bates et al., 1988). Still, within a period of two to three years, all normal children progress from one-word utterances to complex descriptions.

Language acquisition is often said to be the most spectacular of human accomplishments, and children's linguistic skills clearly exemplify Theme 2. For instance, Carey (1978) estimated that 6-year-old children have some mastery of about 14,000 words. To acquire this many words, children must learn about nine new words each day from the time they start speaking until their sixth birthday. If you are not impressed by a 14,000-word vocabulary, consider how much effort high school students must make to acquire 1,000 words in a foreign language—and those spectacular language learners are only waist high! Furthermore, children can combine these words into phrases that have never been heard before, such as "My dolly dreamed about toys" (2 years, 2 months).

With only a few exceptions (e.g., Light & Burke, 1988), researchers have typically ignored language skills in the elderly. Our discussion of language development will therefore be limited to infancy and childhood.

Language in Infancy

Let us begin by considering infants' early perception of speech sounds. Then we will look at their language production, including both verbal language and nonverbal gestures, as well as the characteristics of the language that parents use with infants.

Speech Perception in Infancy.

To acquire language, infants must distinguish between **phonemes,** or the smallest sound units in a language. However, the ability to make distinctions is only half of the struggle; infants must also be able to group together the sounds that are phonetically equivalent. Thus, language acquisition requires the ability to recognize that the sounds *b* and *p* are different from each other, whereas the sound *b* spoken by the deepest bass voice, in the middle of a word, is the same as the sound *b* spoken by the highest soprano voice, at the end of a word.

If you have recently seen a baby who is less than 6 months old, you might have been tempted to conclude that the baby's mastery of language was roughly equivalent to that of a tennis shoe. Until the early 1970s, psychologists were not much more optimistic. However, research has demonstrated that an infant's speech perception is surprisingly advanced. They can perceive almost all the speech contrasts used in language, either at birth or within the first few weeks of life (Bates et al., in press). Infants can also recognize similarities, an important early stage in the understanding of language. Infants' abilities are highly conducive to language learning (Kuhl, 1987; Miller & Eimas, 1983).

Peter Eimas and his coauthors (1971) were among the first to discover infants' capacity for speech perception. They used a method called **nonnutritive sucking,** in which babies suck on nipples to produce a particular sound. No liquid is delivered through the nipple, but the infant is required to suck at least two times each second to maintain the sound. Typically, babies begin each session by sucking frequently to maintain the sound. However, they then show habituation. Remember that habituation occurs when a stimulus is presented frequently, and the response rate decreases. Presumably, the sound is now too boring, and it is not worth the hard work of frequent sucking.

How can the nonnutritive sucking technique be used to provide insight into speech perception? Eimas and his colleagues shifted the speech sound after the 1- to 4-month-old infants had habituated to the first sound. For example, an infant who had shown habituation to *bah* was suddenly presented with a highly similar sound, *pah*. These infants show dishabituation. That is, when *pah* was presented, they suddenly started sucking vigorously once more. The infants showed more modest dishabituation to other sounds that were more similar to each other than *bah* and *pah*. However, infants showed no dishabituation when they continued to hear the *bah* sound; their response rate continued to decrease. Thus, the nonnutritive sucking technique revealed that infants respond at different rates to different sounds, and so they can perceive the difference between them.

Other research has demonstrated that 2-month-old infants can distinguish between the syllables *bad* and *bag* and that 6-month-old infants can distinguish between the similar nonsense words *kokodu* and *kokoba* (Eimas & Tartter, 1979; Goodsitt et al., 1984). In some cases, young infants are even better than older infants and adults in making phonemic distinctions. For example, English-speaking infants can make distinctions between phonemic contrasts that are important in Hindi, a language spoken in India. In Hindi, the *t* sound is sometimes made by placing the tongue against the back of the teeth and sometimes by placing the tongue farther back along the roof of the mouth. English does not distinguish between these two *t* sounds. Werker and Tees (1984) demonstrated that English-speaking infants can distinguish between these phonemes with about 95 percent accuracy when they are 6 to 8 months old. Accuracy drops to about 70 percent at 8 to 10 months of age, and to about 20 percent at 10 to 12 months of age. Thus, some kinds of phonemic distinctions are present in infancy but are later lost (Kuhl, 1987; Matlin & Foley, 1992).

Patricia Kuhl and her coworkers (1992) have tested infants in the United States and Sweden to determine when linguistic experience alters the perception of phonemes. They tested 6-month-old infants in both countries for their perception of two speech sounds. One vowel, the *ee* sound in American English, is a prototype vowel in American English, but it is not found in Swedish. A second vowel that is somewhat similar to *ee* but pronounced with a rounded mouth (we'll call it *y*) is a prototype in Swedish, but it is not found in American English.

As you can imagine, the methodology in this study was crucially important. Borrowing from operant conditioning methods, Kuhl and her colleagues trained the infants to turn their heads whenever they heard the vowel change from the prototype vowel to a computerized version that was slightly different from the prototype. The infants' head-turning responses were rewarded by activating a toy bear that pounded a miniature drum. This drumming bear was so enchanting that infants paid close attention to the prototype vowel, trying to detect any change in the sound.

The researchers analyzed the data to see if they could detect a phenomenon called the magnet effect. Adult speakers of a given language often demonstrate the **magnet effect**; they perceive nonprototypic sounds to be similar to their nearest prototype. Thus, a prototype acts like a magnet, drawing other speech sounds closer to it, much like a magnet attracts iron filings. If infants demonstrate the magnet effect, they will *not* turn their heads when the speech sound changes from the prototype to a variant. By not turning their head, infants are indicating that they regard the new, nonprototypic speech sound to be similar to the prototype.

FIGURE 12.6

Infants' Responses to Sounds That Were Similar to Prototypes in American English and in Swedish (Based on Kuhl et al., 1992).

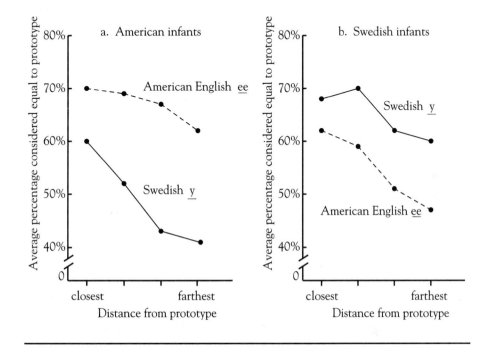

Figure 12.6 shows the results. Let's look first at the results for American infants. Figure 12.6(a) shows that they considered close to 70 percent of those nonprototypic speech sounds to be similar to the American English prototype *ee*; the magnet effect operated to draw even the more distant sounds in closer to the *ee* sound. However, their pattern was different for the Swedish sound, *y*. They were able to detect the difference between the prototype for the *y* sound and other sounds that were different—especially those that were far-removed from the *y* sound; only 40 percent of these were considered equal to the prototype *y*. In other words, infants turned their heads more often when the Swedish sound changed, and they were less likely to show the magnet effect.

As you can see, the pattern is neatly reversed for the Swedish infants. As Figure 12.6(b) shows, the Swedish infants demonstrated the magnet effect toward the prototypical *y* sound, but they were more likely to notice when the sound changed from the American English sound *ee* to its variants.

We need to emphasize the significance of this study. Basically, it illustrates that infants can learn about sounds by merely being exposed to language. These tiny infants are only 6 months old, and they have not yet uttered a single meaningful word in their native language. However, they already identify the prototypical sounds in their language, and they have already learned not to notice slight variations from those prototypes.

We have examined in some detail infants' appreciation of the auditory components of language. In addition, infants have a remarkable understanding of some social aspects of language. For example, Walker-Andrews (1986) played recordings of either a happy voice or an angry voice to 7-month-old infants. Meanwhile, the infants saw a pair of films—of one happy speaker and one angry speaker—projected side by side. The mouth region of the faces were covered so that the infants could not rely on lip movements to match the voice with the film. The results showed that infants who heard a happy voice tended to watch the happy face, whereas infants who heard an angry voice tended to watch the angry face. Thus even young infants appreciate that facial expression must correspond with vocal intonation.

The word *infant* originally meant "not speaking." Infants' speech *production* is certainly limited. However, their speech *perception* is impressively sophisticated, even when they are only a few months old.

Language Production in Infancy.

The early vocalizations of infants pass through a series of stages. By about 2 months of age, infants begin to make **cooing** noises, sounds that involve vowels such as *oo*. By about 6 to 8 months they have developed a kind of **babbling** that uses both consonants and vowels, repeating sounds in a series such as *dadada* (Bates et al., in press). Interestingly, deaf infants who have been exposed to sign language also begin at about this time to "babble" with their hands, producing systematic but meaningless actions that are not found in hearing children (Petitto & Marentette, 1991).

Researchers do not know what function babbling serves (Carroll, 1986; Locke, 1983). Does it provide the opportunity to imitate? Is babbling distinctly different from speech, or are the two linked? Although many aspects of babbling are unclear, we do know that babies realize that their vocal activity conveys information to others (Locke, 1983). Clearly, language development occurs in a social and communicative context (Cairns & Valsiner, 1984).

The first attempts at intentional communication occur at about 9 months of age. **Intentional communication** involves the expectation that an adult will help in reaching a desired goal (Bates, 1979). For example, an 8-month-old who wants a ball will reach out toward the ball and fuss. However, a 9-month-old who uses intentional communication will alternate eye contact between the ball and the parent, while fussing. The young infants apparently see some relationship among the goal, the adult, and the communication signal.

These advances in intentional communication may be linked to biological developments in the brain. Bates and her colleagues (in press) report that brain-imaging research has detected increased metabolic activity in the frontal lobe of the cortex in 8- to 10-month-old infants. The frontal lobe is associated with many "executive functions" that monitor behavior in adults. Links between other regions of the brain and the frontal lobe may be necessary before infants can master relatively sophisticated tasks like intentional communication, imitation, and retrieving hidden objects.

Infants typically begin to point between 8 and 14 months of age (Lempert & Kinsbourne, 1985). Pointing is thought to be particularly important because it calls another person's attention to an object or an event. Preverbal infants may point simply to attract the parent's attention, but an older infant often points and names simultaneously.

Another important social component of early language is turn-taking. Parents treat their babies as active conversational partners, each alternating politely and waiting for a response from the other (Carroll, 1986; Owens, 1992). Here is a sample conversation between a mother and her 3-month-old daughter, Ann:

ANN: (smiles)
MOM: Oh, what a nice little smile! Yes, isn't that nice? There.
ANN: (burps)
MOM: What a nice wind as well! Yes, that's better, isn't it? Yes.
ANN: (vocalizes)
MOM: Yes! There's a nice noise. (Snow, 1977)

Parents' Language to Infants. Language acquisition is facilitated by infants' impressive auditory skills, their memory capacity, and their receptivity to language. However, they also get a little help from their friends, most notably their parents. Adults who raise children tend to make language acquisition somewhat simpler by adjusting their language when speaking with them. The term **motherese** is used to refer to the language spoken to children; motherese language involves simple vocabulary, well-formed sentences, many repetitions, a focus on the here and now, high voice pitch, and slow rate of speech (Rice, 1989). Demonstration 12.4 illustrates motherese (De Hart, 1989).

You probably caught the gender-bias in the term *motherese*. Many fathers probably speak "motherese" to their infants and children. However, fathers who are secondary caregivers seem to be less "tuned in" to their offspring's communication needs, and their speech to infants tends to be more like their speech to adults. Also, when fathers do not understand something spoken by their children, they usually respond with a nonspecific question, such as "What?" In contrast, mothers make more specific requests for clarification, such as "Where should I put the Raggedy Andy?" (Sroufe et al., 1992; Tomasello et al., 1990). Obviously, it would be interesting to study the language patterns of fathers who are primary caregivers,

---

DEMONSTRATION 12.4

SPEAKING MOTHERESE.

Locate a doll that resembles an infant as closely as possible in features and size. Select a friend who has had experience with infants, and ask him or her to imagine that the doll is a niece or nephew who just arrived with parents for a first visit. Encourage your friend to interact with the baby as he or she normally would. Observe your friend's language for qualities such as pitch, variation in pitch, vocabulary, sentence length, repetition, and intonation. Also observe nonverbal communication. What qualities are different from the language used with adults?

---

as well as mothers who are secondary caregivers. When confounding variables are eliminated, gender differences are often minimal (Matlin, 1993b).

Research on a variety of language communities throughout the world shows major similarities in the language adults use with infants and children (Fernald, 1985). The rhythm of the speech helps young language learners break the stream of conversation into its major syntactic units (e.g., Gleason & Ratner, 1993b; Hirsh-Pasek et al., 1987). As Gleason and Ratner write:

> Parents say things like "See the birdie? Look at the birdie! What a pretty birdie!" These features probably make it easier for the infant to decode the language than if they heard, "Has it come to your attention that one of our better looking feathered friends is perched upon the windowsill?" (p. 311)

Language in Children

Sometime around their first birthday, most infants speak their first word. Let's look at the characteristics of these initial words, as well as the words spoken by older children. Then we will consider children's grammar, specifically morphology and syntax. Finally, we will examine how children master pragmatics, or the social rules of language.

Words. A child's first word usually refers to people or familiar objects (Bates et al., 1988). Why should these initial words refer to things, rather than actions, when research shows that children can learn the two categories equally readily (Oviatt, 1980)? One reason may be that the loudest word in an adult sentence is likely to be the name of an object (Messer, 1981). Furthermore, adults believe that infants are most interested in things, so we constantly name objects. For example, when children point to falling snow, we respond by naming the object—"Brr, snow"—rather than the action (Bridges, 1986).

In a large-scale study involving samples from three cities, parents estimated that their children produced an average of 12 words at 12 months of age, 179 words at

20 months, and 380 words at 28 months. However, we need to emphasize the tremendous range in vocabulary size for normal children. For example, the production vocabulary for 12-month-olds ranged between 0 and 52 words (Fenson et al., 1991). The sudden increase in vocabulary size between 12 and 28 months may be linked to rapid increases in synaptic connections in the cortex (Bates et al., in press).

Children's first words typically represent the basic level of categorization (Hoff-Ginsberg & Shatz, 1982; Mervis & Crisafi, 1982). In Chapter 7, we discussed how adults prefer to use the basic level of categorization (for example, *dog*), rather than the superordinate (for example, *animal*) or the subordinate (for example, *poodle*). Children also prefer the basic level, which makes sense, because this is the level of labels that parents usually supply to their children (Hoff-Ginsberg & Shatz, 1982).

How do children learn the meaning of a new term they have just heard? Chapter 8 emphasized that adults are guided by word context, and context is also critically important for young children. In a relevant study, Heibeck and Markman (1987) showed preschoolers pairs of objects and asked the children to select one of them. The request specifically used one familiar term and one unfamiliar term, such as "Bring me the chartreuse one. Not the blue one, the chartreuse one." Other requests used familiar and unfamiliar terms for shape and texture, as well as color. The children understood the requests, bringing the appropriate object with the unfamiliar label. When tested several minutes later, even 2-year-olds remembered the unfamiliar terms. The process of using context to make a reasonable guess about a word's meaning is called **fast mapping.**

Furthermore, children make a **taxonomic assumption;** they assume a label can apply to other objects of the same category. For example, Markman (1990) showed children a puppet, who spoke to them and made certain requests. For instance, the puppet might say, "I'm going to show you a *dax,* then I want you to think carefully and find another one." The children were shown a picture of a cow, and they were encouraged to select one of two pictures, a pig or a pail of milk. The children selected the pig 65 percent of the time. They made the taxonomic assumption that *dax* referred to all members of the taxonomic category *animal* or *farm animal*—rather than focusing on the specific properties of cows (for example, milk-givers).

Naturally, young children may apply a newly learned label to a category that is either too broad or too narrow. An **overextension** is the use of a word to refer to other objects in addition to the appropriate object. Clark (1975) describes the overextensions a child used for a unique word, *gumene.* Initially, *gumene* was applied to a coat button, but it was later used to refer to a collar stud, a door handle, a light switch, and other small round items. My daughter Beth used the word *baish* to refer initially to her blanket, and then the term was later applied to a diaper, a diaper pin, and a vitamin pill. Often, an object's shape is important in determining overextensions, but sometimes (as in the case of the vitamin pill) overextensions defy adult explanation. Incidentally, they frequently occur for properly pronounced English words as well as children's own invented words. You've

DEMONSTRATION 12.5

THE RELATIVE IMPORTANCE OF CHARACTERISTIC AND DEFINING FEATURES (FROM KEIL & BATTERMAN, 1984, p. 227).

Locate two or more children between the ages of 5 and 10. Read these four stories to each of them individually. Try to decide whether the child bases word meaning more on characteristic features or defining features.

1. These two girls look alike, dress alike, do well in the same subjects in school, like the same vegetables, and live in the same house. One of them, however, is 2 years older than the other one. Could these be twin sisters?
2. There are two girls who were born at the same time on the same day in the same room from the same mommy, but one of them lives in California and the other one lives in New York. Could these be twin sisters?
3. There is this place that sticks out of the land like a finger. Coconut trees and palm trees grow there, and the girls sometimes wear flowers in their hair because it's so warm all the time. There is water on all sides except one. Could that be an island?
4. On this piece of land, there are apartment buildings, snow, and no green things growing. This piece of land is surrounded by water on all sides. Could that be an island?

probably heard of children who call every adult male—including the mailman—"Daddy."

Research by Thomson and Chapman (1977) demonstrated that children around the age of 2 often showed overextensions for words such as *dog* and *ball*. For example, one child produced the name *dog* for nine species of dog and one toy dog—as he should—but also for two bears, a wolf, a fox, a doe, a rhinoceros, a hippopotamus, and a fish—all overextensions.

Children may also show an **underextension,** using a word in a narrower sense than adults do (Pinker, 1984b; Rogers, 1985). For example, they may apply the name *doggie* only to the family pet. Older children may refuse to believe that the word *animal* could apply to a praying mantis (Anglin, 1977).

Try Demonstration 12.5 to illustrate another important aspect of children's word usage. Specifically, the characteristics of children's word meaning change as they mature, particularly with respect to defining and characteristic features (Keil, 1989). As discussed in Chapter 7, **defining features** are the features that are essential to the meaning of the item, whereas **characteristic features** are those that are merely descriptive, but not essential. As you can see from Demonstration 12.5, for example, the defining features of twins are that they were born on the same day and have the same mother. The characteristic features are that they look alike, act alike, and live together.

Keil and Batterman (1984) read brief stories like those in Demonstration 12.5 to children who ranged in age from preschool to fourth grade. Each child was then asked if the thing or person described could be an *x* (twin, island, and so on). For each concept they investigated, one story had the correct defining features but lacked important characteristic features; the other story had important characteristic features but lacked the correct defining features. Children's responses changed very significantly as they grew older. Preschoolers and kindergartners relied heavily on characteristic features, as revealed in the following dialog with the experimenter about whether your mother's brother, who was 2 years old, could be your uncle:

EXPERIMENTER: Could he be an uncle?

CHILD: No . . . because he's little and 2 years old.

EXPERIMENTER: How old does an uncle have to be?

CHILD: About 24 or 25.

EXPERIMENTER: If he's 2 years old can he be an uncle?

CHILD: No . . . he can be a cousin. (p. 229)

Children in the second grade seemed to be in transition. For instance, they tended to know that sisters of different ages could not be twins. However, they usually insisted that people needed to live in the same house to be twins. By fourth grade, defining features predominated. These older children realized that characteristic features were nice to have, but not essential. As Nelson (1985) stresses, language development is basically a problem in the acquisition of culture. In American culture, uncles must meet kinship criteria, rather than age criteria.

Morphology.

Morphology. Children initially use the simple form of a word in every context, for example, "girl run," rather than "girl runs." However, they soon begin to master how to add on **morphemes** (basic units of meaning, which include endings such as *-s* and *-ed,* as well as simple words such as *run*). **Morphology** is the study of these basic units of meaning.

English-speaking children acquire morphemes in a fairly regular order between the ages of 1½ and 3½. For example, the first morpheme to develop is *-ing* (for example, *running*), plurals develop next, using the morpheme *-s* (for example, *girls*), and the regular past tense develops still later (for example, *kicked*) (Brown, 1973: Kuczaj, 1977).

After children begin learning the regular plurals and past tenses—like *girls* and *kicked*—they start to create their own regular forms, such as *mouses* and *runned.* This tendency to add the most customary morphemes to create new forms of irregular words is called **overregularization.** (Keep in mind, then, that *overgeneralization* refers to the tendency to broaden a word's meaning inappropriately, whereas *overregularization* refers to the tendency to add regular morphemes inappropriately.)

You'll recall our discussion of parallel distributed processing, in previous chapters; this approach argues that cognitive processes can be understood in terms of networks that link together neuron-like units. Two supporters of connectionism argue that this theory can explain how children acquire the past tenses of verbs (Rumelhart & McClelland, 1986b, 1987). The details of this model are beyond the scope of this chapter, but basically these theorists propose that the child's language system keeps a tally of the morpheme patterns. The system notes that *-ed* is the statistically most likely pattern, and so this ending is extended to new verbs, forming inappropriate past tenses, such as *runned, growed, goed,* and *eated.* Rumelart and McClelland believe that a child does not need to consult an internal set of rules to make these overregularizations; instead, patterns of excitation within neural networks can account for the phenomenon.

Other researchers have criticized the connectionist approach, on both theoretical and empirical grounds (e.g., Lachter & Bever, 1988; Pinker & Prince, 1988). At this point, we cannot yet anticipate whose argument will be supported by further research.

Syntax. At about 18 to 20 months of age, the average child begins to combine two words (Bates, 1991). An important issue that arises at this point is **syntax,** or the organizational rules for determining word order, sentence organization, and relationships between words (Owens, 1992). As children struggle with syntax, their rate of combining words is initially slow. However, it increases rapidly after the age of 2 (Anisfeld, 1984). Another factor that probably contributes to this rapid increase in word combinations is the growing capacity of short-term memory (Bates et al., 1988).

Children's two-word utterances express many different kinds of relationships, such as possessor-possessed ("Daddy pants"), action-object ("Eat cookie"), and action-place ("Sit chair"). Furthermore, a two-word phrase can have different meanings in different contexts; "Daddy car" may signify that Daddy is driving a car, or it may refer to Daddy's car, rather than Mommy's car (deVilliers & deVilliers, 1982).

Children learning all languages—not just English—use telegraphic speech (deVilliers & deVilliers, 1978; Slobin, 1979). **Telegraphic speech** is speech that includes content words, such as nouns and verbs, but omits the extra words that only serve a grammatical function, such as prepositions and articles. The name *telegraphic speech* is appropriate because when adults need to conserve words (for example, when sending a telegram or placing an advertisement in a newspaper), they also omit the extra words. Thus, "I lost a lady's wristwatch with a gold band at the concert at Kilbourne Hall on Saturday, June 20," becomes: "Lost: Lady's wristwatch, gold band at concert Kilbourne Hall June 20." Similarly, a child who wants to convey, "The puppy is sitting on my blanket," will say "Puppy blanket."

After children have reached the two-word stage, they begin to fill in the missing words and word endings and to master the complexities of word order. "Baby cry" becomes "The baby is crying," for example.

It is important to stress that language learning is an active process, consistent with Theme 1 of this book. As Rogers (1985) emphasizes, children learn language by actively constructing their own speech. Their speech includes phrases that adults would never say, such as "Allgone sticky," "Bye-bye hot," and "More page." Children's speech is far richer than a simple imitation of adult language.

Another example of the active nature of children's language is **crib speech,** or monologs that children produce when they are alone in their cribs. Kuczaj (1983) studied crib speech in 1- and 2-year-old children and found that they often practiced their linguistic skills when they were alone. One frequent pattern in their practice involved building longer phrases, as in the sequence, "Block. Yellow block. Look at all the yellow blocks." Substitutions were common, too: "What color blanket? What color map? What color glass?"

As children grow increasingly skilled in producing sophisticated language, they also grow increasingly skilled in understanding it. Consider, for example, how a child comes to understand the sentence "Pat hit Chris." How does the child know who is the actor in that sentence and who is the recipient of the action? In English, the word order of the sentence is the most important cue, and so it is tempting to assume that word order is similarly helpful in all languages. However, as Weist (1985) notes, young children learning Turkish or Polish use the endings of words, rather than word order information, to decode the meaning of sentences. Children seem to be clever strategists, who can use whatever syntax cues are available in their language.

Pragmatics. As we discussed in Chapter 9, the term **pragmatics** refers to the social rules of language. Children must learn what should be said (and what should *not* be said) in certain circumstances. They must learn how two speakers coordinate conversation, and they must learn how to behave as listeners, as well as speakers.

Every family has its stories about children's wildly inappropriate remarks to elderly relatives, friendly neighbors, and complete strangers. A 2-year-old I knew once told a woman that her husband looked like a monkey. The child's description was stunningly accurate, yet both the child's mother and the woman reacted more strongly to the fact that the child had broken a pragmatic rule than to the fact that she had produced a grammatically perfect and factually accurate sentence.

As Garvey (1984) notes, conversations could not operate without a system to reduce friction and minimize potential conflicts and embarrassments. An important component of children's developing language involves mastering the markers of courtesy such as *please, excuse me,* and *may I.* Garvey's observation of nursery-school children showed that 3- and 4-year-olds frequently requested permission using socially appropriate phrases such as "Can I _____" and "May I _____." These requests typically occurred in situations in which the addressee was either physically blocking something the speaker wanted to reach or had some claim on something the speaker wanted to use. Teachers, parents, and other caregivers encourage this kind of courtesy, for example by telling a child, "Ask Judy nicely if you can play with the bear" (Garvey, 1984; Snow et al., 1990).

Pragmatic rules also regulate certain rituals in our culture. Gleason and Weintraub (1976) examined the use of pragmatic rules in Halloween trick-or-treat routines, certainly a novel topic for a language study. Think about the pragmatic rules that would govern behavior on Halloween if you were a 10-year-old child. When the door opens, you say "Trick or treat." Greetings that would be perfectly appropriate on other nights, such as "Hi" or "Good evening," would clearly break an unspoken pragmatic rule. After the adult puts candy in your bag, you say "Thank you." As you leave, you say "Goodbye." Gleason and Weintraub mounted tape recorders near the doors of two suburban Boston homes and recorded each trick-or-treat conversation.

The youngest children, 2- and 3-year-olds, typically said nothing at all during the entire sequence. The 4- and 5-year-olds typically said only "Trick or treat." Somewhat older children added a "Thank you," but only the children over 10 produced the whole routine of "Trick or treat, thank you, goodbye." Gleason and Weintraub found that adults accompanying the children often explicitly coached the children in the three segments of the routine. Try checking with your parents to see if they, too, specifically trained you in the pragmatic rules of Halloween.

Children must also learn how to coordinate conversations. We discussed earlier that mothers and infants develop turn-taking in their social interactions. Sophisticated turn-taking requires each speaker to anticipate when the conversational partner will complete his or her remark—clearly a requirement that demands an impressive knowledge of the language structure (McTear, 1985). Young children have longer gaps in turn-taking than adults do, perhaps because they are not as skilled in anticipating the completion of a remark. Two-year-olds have conversational gaps that average about 1.5 seconds, in contrast to gaps of about 0.8 seconds in adults (McTear, 1985).

Children also learn how to adapt their language to the listener. Psychologists used to believe that children's language ignored the level of understanding of the listener, but we now acknowledge that they make appropriate adjustments. For example, Shatz and Gelman (1973) found that 4-year-olds modified their speech substantially when the listener was a 2-year-old rather than a peer or an adult. Specifically, the 4-year-olds described a toy to their 2-year-old listeners using short, simple utterances. However, when describing the toy to another 4-year-old or an adult, their utterances were much longer and more complex. Thus children understand some of the social aspects of language, such as the need to modify speech for younger listeners.

The next time you observe two adults conversing, notice how the listener responds to the speaker by smiling, gazing, and other gestures of interest. Miller, Lechner, and Rugs (1985) recorded these kinds of listener responses in young children who were discussing with an adult such topics as toys, a popular film, and siblings. All of these listener responses were much more abundant in the older children. For example, 8 percent of 3-year-olds said "uh-hum" at some point while the adult was speaking, in contrast to 50 percent of 5-year-olds. Furthermore, head nods increased from 67 percent to 100 percent.

Infants and children seem to be specially prepared to notice and interact socially (Wellman & Gelman, 1992). As Marilyn Shatz commented in an interview several years ago:

> Children are very impatient to be members of the family, genuine members. They learn very early that speech is the way to realize and maintain contact with other family members and, at the same time, to be taken seriously. A 2-year-old already has the goal of being a person in the family instead of a baby, of being someone to interact linguistically with instead of an object of discussion. (Roşu & Natanson, 1987, p. 5)

This enthusiasm about learning language encourages children to master the words, morphemes, syntax, and pragmatics of speech.

Throughout this chapter, we have seen examples of the early competence of infants and children. For instance, young infants are remarkably skilled at remembering faces and distinguishing speech sounds. These early skills foreshadow the remarkable cognitive skills that adults exhibit (Theme 2). Furthermore, children's active, inquiring interactions with the people, objects, and concepts in their world (Theme 1) help them develop memory, metamemory, and language. Finally, the research on the cognitive skills of elderly people reveal some deficits. However, their cognitive abilities usually remain both accurate and active throughout the lifespan.

SECTION SUMMARY: THE DEVELOPMENT OF LANGUAGE

1. Studies with infants reveal remarkable speech perception abilities; they can perceive differences between similar phonemes, show the magnet effect for prototypical phonemes in their language environment, and appreciate that a person's voice tone must correspond to the facial expression.
2. Language production in infancy includes cooing and babbling; other early skills are intentional communication, pointing, and turn-taking. The language that parents use with infants encourages their verbal development.
3. Young children rapidly acquire new words from context, but their word usage shows both overextensions and underextensions. As they mature, they begin to emphasize the defining features of words, rather than the characteristic features.
4. During language acquisition, children show overregularization, adding regular morphemes to words that have irregular plurals and past tenses.
5. Children's early word combinations are telegraphic; children make active efforts to master language.
6. Although young children frequently break pragmatic rules, they realize the importance of courtesy terms at an early age. As children mature, they

develop turn-taking, and they adapt their language to the listener. They also learn how listeners are supposed to respond to speakers.

CHAPTER REVIEW QUESTIONS

1. Up until the early 1970s, psychologists were pessimistic about the cognitive skills of infants and children. In 1979, Gelman said, "The time has come for us to turn our attention to what young children can do as well as what they cannot do" (p. 904). If you wanted to impress someone with infants' and children's cognitive abilities, what would you mention about their memory, metacognition, and language abilities?
2. Part of the difficulty with infant research is designing experiments that reveal the infant's true abilities. Describe how experimental procedures have been developed to uncover infants' skills in memory and language.
3. Compare children, young adults, and elderly people with respect to sensory memory, short-term memory, long-term recognition memory, and long-term recall memory. (In some cases, a conclusive answer may not be possible.)
4. What is one proposed explanation for children's memory performance, which involves memory strategies and metamemory? Discuss the evidence for this explanation, including information on the correlation between metamemory and memory performance.
5. In general, what kinds of memory tasks are especially difficult for elderly people? What explanations have been proposed for memory deficits in the elderly? Can metamemory account for these problems?
6. Given what you know about children's metamemory and strategy use, what could a third-grade teacher do to encourage students' memory skills?
7. Imagine that a friend of yours has an 11-month-old child who is just beginning to talk. Summarize what parents can expect to find in their children's language development before the child's fifth birthday.
8. Branthwaite and Rogers (1985) note that being a child is like being a spy, trying to break a code to discover the way in which the world works. Apply this idea to the development of word meaning, morphology, word order, and pragmatic rules.
9. Describe some of the pragmatic rules of language that are important in our culture, noting how the mastery of these rules changes with development. What other topics do you think would be worth investigating in connection with pragmatic rules?
10. Considering the information in this chapter, are infants as different from young adults as you had originally thought? Do the findings on elderly people surprise you, or do they match your original impressions?

NEW TERMS

habituation procedure
dishabituation
conjugate reinforcement technique
memory reactivation
reality monitoring
script
explicit memory measure
implicit memory measure
meta-analytic technique
cognitive slowing
metacognition
metacomprehension
memory self-efficacy
phonemes
nonnutritive sucking
magnet effect
cooing

babbling
intentional communication
motherese
fast mapping
taxonomic assumption
overextension
underextension
defining features
characteristic features
morphemes
morphology
overregularization
syntax
telegraphic speech
crib speech
pragmatics

RECOMMENDED READINGS

Kail, R. (1990). *The development of memory in children* (3rd ed.). New York: Freeman. This interesting book emphasizes the development of memory, memory strategies, and metamemory in children, but it also includes a chapter on infants' memory.

Light, L. L. (1991). Memory and aging: Four hypotheses in search of data. *Annual Review of Psychology, 42,* 333–376. Light's comprehensive review article is clearly written and honest, not bending the empirical research to fit any favored explanation.

Owens, R. E., Jr. (1992). *Language development: An introduction* (3rd ed.). New York: Merrill. Owens' textbook offers a very readable, comprehensive overview of language development, including coverage of topics such as neurolinguistics, pragmatics, adult language development, bilingualism, and language disorders.

Salthouse, T. A. (1991). *Theoretical perspectives on cognitive aging.* Hillsdale, NJ: Erlbaum. In addition to memory, Salthouse also examines reasoning and spatial abilities in the elderly.

Small, M. Y. (1990). *Cognitive development.* Fort Worth, TX: Harcourt Brace Jovanovich. Small's textbook covers cognitive development in infancy and childhood, covering reasoning, problem solving, and social cognition, in addition to the three topics covered in this chapter.

ONE LAST TASK

To review this book as comprehensively as possible, try this final task. On separate sheets of paper, list each of the five themes of this book. Then skim through each chapter, noting on the appropriate sheet each time a theme is mentioned. You can check the completeness of the lists by consulting the entries "Themes 1, 2, 3, 4, and 5" in the subject index. After completing the lists, try to synthesize the material within each of the five themes.

REFERENCES

Abelson, R. P. (1981). Psychological status of the script concept. *American Psychologist, 36*, 715–729.

Abelson, R. P., & Levi, A. (1985). Decision-making and decision theory. In G. Lindzey & E. Aronson (Eds.), *Handbook of social psychology* (3rd ed., Vol. 1, pp. 231–309). New York: Random House.

Ackerman, B. P. (1988). Search set access problems in retrieving episodic information from memory in children and adults. *Journal of Experimental Child Psychology, 45*, 234–261.

Acredolo, L. P., Pick, H. L., & Olsen, M. G. (1975). Environmental differentiation and familiarity as determinants of children's memory for spatial location. *Developmental Psychology, 11*, 495–501.

Adams, J. L. (1979). *Conceptual blockbusting* (2nd ed.). New York: Norton.

Adams, J. L. (1986). *The care and feeding of ideas: A guide to encouraging creativity.* Reading, MA: Addison-Wesley.

Adelson, E. H. (1978). Iconic storage: The role of rods. *Science, 201*, 544–546.

Adeyemo, S. A. (1990). Thinking imagery and problem-solving. *Psychological Studies, 35*, 179–190.

Adler, T. (1991, July). Memory researcher wins Troland award. *APA Monitor*, pp. 12–13.

Agnoli, F., & Krantz, D. H. (1989). Suppressing natural heuristics by formal instruction: The case of the conjunction fallacy. *Cognitive Psychology, 21*, 515–550.

Alba, J. W., & Hasher, L. (1983). Is memory schematic? *Psychological Bulletin, 93*, 203–231.

Allbritton, D. W., & Gerrig, R. J. (1991). Participatory responses in text understanding. *Journal of Memory and Language, 30*, 603–626.

Allport, A. (1989). Visual attention. In M. Posner (Ed.), *Foundations of cognitive science* (pp. 631–682). Cambridge, MA: MIT Press.

Amabile, T. M. (1982). Social psychology of creativity: A consensual assessment technique. *Journal of Personality and Social Psychology, 43*, 997–1013.

Amabile, T. M. (1983). *The social psychology of creativity.* New York: Springer-Verlag.

Amabile, T. M. (1990). Within you, without you: The social psychology of creativity, and beyond. In M. A. Runco & R. S. Albert (Eds.), *Theories of creativity* (pp. 61–91). Newbury Park, NY: Sage.

American Psychological Association. (1983). *Publication manual of the American Psychological Association* (3rd ed.). Washington, DC: Author.

Anderson, J. R. (1976). *Language, memory, and thought.* Hillsdale, NJ: Erlbaum.

Anderson, J. R. (1983a). *The architecture of cognition.* Cambridge, MA: Harvard University Press.

Anderson, J. R. (1983b). Retrieval of information from long-term memory. *Science, 220*, 25–30.

Anderson, J. R. (1985). *Cognitive psychology and its implications* (2nd ed.). New York: W. H. Freeman.

Anderson, J. R. (1987). Skill acquisition: Compilation of weak-method problem solutions. *Psychological Review, 94*, 192–210.

Anderson, J. R. (1990). *The adaptive character of thought.* Hillsdale, NJ: Erlbaum.

Anderson, J. R. (1991). Is human cognition adaptive? *Behavioral and Brain Sciences, 14*, 471–517.

Anderson, J. R., & Reder, L. (1979). An elaborative processing explanation of depth of processing. In L. S. Cermak & F. I. M. Craik (Eds.), *Levels of processing in human memory.* Hillsdale, NJ: Erlbaum.

Anderson, R. E. (1984). Did I do it or did I only imagine doing it? *Journal of Experimental Psychology: General, 113*, 594–613.

Andreassen, C., & Waters, H. S. (1989). Organization during study: Relationships between metamemory, strategy use, and performance. *Journal of Educational Psychology, 81*, 190–195.

Andrews, F. M. (1975). Social and psychological factors which influence the creative process. In I. A. Taylor & J. W. Getzels (Eds.), *Perspectives in creativity*. Chicago: Aldine.

Anglin, J. M. (1977). *Word, object, and conceptual development*. New York: Norton.

Anisfeld, M. (1984). *Language development from birth to three*. Hillsdale, NJ: Erlbaum.

Anisfeld, M., & Klenbort, I. (1973). On the functions of structural paraphrase: The view from the passive voice. *Psychological Bulletin, 79,* 117–126.

Arkes, H. R., Wortmann, R. L., Saville, P. D., & Harkness, A. R. (1981). Hindsight bias among physicians weighing the likelihood of diagnoses. *Journal of Applied Psychology, 66,* 252–254.

Atkinson, R. C., & Shiffrin, R. M. (1968). Human memory: A proposed system and its control processes. In K. W. Spence & J. T. Spence (Eds.), *The psychology of learning and motivation: Advances in research and theory* (Vol. 2). New York: Academic Press.

Baddeley, A. D. (1984). The fractionation of human memory. *Psychological Medicine, 14,* 259–264.

Baddeley, A. D. (1986). *Working memory*. Oxford, England: Clarendon Press.

Baddeley, A. D. (1988). Cognitive psychology and human memory. *Trends in Neurosciences, 11,* 176–181.

Baddeley, A. D. (1989). The uses of working memory. In P. R. Solomon, G. R. Goethals, C. M. Kelley, & B. R. Stephens (Eds.), *Memory: Interdisciplinary approaches* (pp. 107–123). New York: Springer-Verlag.

Baddeley, A. D. (1990). *Human memory: Theory and practice*. Boston: Allyn and Bacon.

Baddeley, A. D. (1992). Working memory. *Science, 255,* 556–559.

Baddeley, A. D., & Hitch, G. J. (1974). Working memory. In G. Bower (Ed.), *Recent advances in learning and memory* (Vol. 8, pp. 47–90). New York: Academic Press.

Baddeley, A. D., & Hitch, G. (1993). The recency effect: Implicit learning with explicit retrieval? *Memory and Cognition, 21,* 146–155.

Baddeley, A. D., Thomson, N., & Buchanan, M. (1975). Word length and the structure of short-term memory. *Journal of Verbal Learning and Verbal Behavior, 14,* 575–589.

Bahrick, H. P. (1984). Semantic memory content in permastore: Fifty years of memory for Spanish learned in school. *Journal of Experimental Psychology: General, 113,* 1–35.

Bahrick, H. P., & Hall, L. K. (1991). Lifetime maintenance of high school mathematics content. *Journal of Experimental Psychology: General, 120,* 20–33.

Bahrick, H. P., & Phelps, E. (1987). Retention of Spanish vocabulary over 8 years. *Journal of Experimental Psychology: Learning, Memory, and Cognition, 13,* 344–349.

Baillargeon, R., & Graber, M. (1988). Evidence of location memory in 8-month-old infants in a nonsearch AB task. *Developmental Psychology, 24,* 502–511.

Baker, L. (1989). Metacognition, comprehension monitoring, and the adult reader. *Educational Psychology Review, 1,* 3–38.

Baker-Ward, L., Ornstein, P. A., & Holden, D. J. (1984). The expression of memorization in early childhood. *Journal of Experimental Child Psychology, 37,* 555–575.

Bales, J. (1988, December). Vincennes: Findings could have helped avert tragedy, scientists tell Hill panel. *APA Monitor*, pp. 10–11.

Balota, D. A., Pollatsek, A., & Rayner, K. (1985). The interaction of contextual constraints and parafoveal visual information in reading. *Cognitive Psychology, 17,* 364–390.

Banaji, M. R., & Crowder, R. G. (1989). The bankruptcy of everyday memory. *American Psychologist, 44,* 1185–1193.

Banks, W. P., & Barber, G. (1977). Color information in iconic memory. *Psychological Review, 84,* 536–546.

Banks, W. P., & Kracijek, D. (1991). Perception. *Annual Review of Psychology, 42,* 305–331.

Barber, P. (1988). *Applied cognitive psychology*. London: Methuen.

Barclay, C. R. (1986). Schematization of autobiographical memory. In D. C. Rubin (Ed.), *Autobiographical memory* (pp. 82–99). New York: Cambridge University Press.

Barclay, C. R., & Wellman, H. M. (1986). Accuracies and inaccuracies in autobiographical memories. *Journal of Memory and Language, 25,* 93–103.

Baron, J. (1988). *Thinking and deciding.* New York: Cambridge University Press.

Baron, J. (1991). Some thinking is irrational. *Behavioral and Brain Sciences, 14,* 486–487.

Baron, J., & Strawson, C. (1976). Use of orthographic and word-specific knowledge in reading words aloud. *Journal of Experimental Psychology: Human Perception and Performance, 2,* 386–393.

Barrera, M., & Maurer, D. (1981). Recognition of mother's photographed face by the three-month-old infant. *Child Development, 52,* 714–716.

Barsalou, L. W. (1985). Ideals, central tendency, and frequency of instantiation as determinants of graded structure in categories. *Journal of Experimental Psychology: Learning, Memory, and Cognition, 11,* 629–654.

Barsalou, L. W. (1987). The instability of graded structure: Implications for the nature of concepts. In U. Neisser (Ed.), *Concepts and conceptual development: Ecological and intellectual factors in categorization.* New York: Cambridge University Press.

Barsalou, L. W. (1989). Intra-concept similarity and its implications for inter-concept similarity. In S. Vosniadou & A. Ortony (Eds.), *Similarity and analogical reasoning* (pp. 76–121). New York: Cambridge University Press.

Barsalou, L. W. (1990). On the indistinguishability of exemplar memory and abstraction in category representation. In T. K. Srull & R. S. Wyer (Eds.), *Advances in social cognition* (Vol. 3, pp. 61–88). Hillsdale, NJ: Erlbaum.

Barsalou, L. W. (1992). *Cognitive psychology: An overview for cognitive scientists.* Hillsdale, NJ: Erlbaum.

Barsalou, L. W., & Sewell, D. R. (1985). Contrasting the representation of scripts and categories. *Journal of Memory and Language, 24,* 646–665.

Bartlett, F. C. (1932). *Remembering: An experimental and social study.* Cambridge, England: Cambridge University Press.

Bates, E. (1979). *The emergence of symbols: Cognition and communication in infancy.* New York: Academic Press.

Bates, E. (1991). *Normal and abnormal language development.* Paper presented at the Venice Conference on Developmental Neuropsychology, San Servolo, Italy.

Bates, E., Bretherton, I., & Snyder, L. (1988). *From first words to grammar: Individual differences and dissociable mechanisms.* New York: Cambridge University Press.

Bates, E., & Elman, J. (in press). Connectionism and the study of change. In M. Johnson (Ed.), *Brain development and cognition: A reader.* Oxford: Blackwell Publishers.

Bates, E., Thal, D., & Janowsky, J. S. (in press). Early language development and its neural correlates. In I. Rapin & S. Segalowitz (Eds.), *Handbook of neuropsychology* (Vol. 6). Amsterdam: Elsevier.

Bayles, K. A., Kaszniak, A. W., & Tomoeda, C. K. (1987). *Communication and cognition in normal aging and dementia.* Boston: Little-Brown.

Beal, C. R. (1985). Development of knowledge about the use of cues to aid prospective retrieval. *Child Development, 56,* 631–642.

Beattie, G. (1983). *Talk: An analysis of speech and nonverbal behaviour in conversation.* Milton Keynes, England: Open University Press.

Bechtel, W., & Abrahamsen, A. (1991). *Connectionism and the mind: An introduction to parallel processing in networks.* Cambridge, MA: Basil Blackwell.

Begg, I. (1982). Imagery, organization, and discriminative processes. *Canadian Journal of Psychology, 36,* 273–290.

Begg, I. (1987). Some. *Canadian Journal of Psychology, 41,* 62–73.

Begg, I., & Harris, G. (1982). On the interpretation of syllogisms. *Journal of Verbal Learning and Verbal Behavior, 21,* 595–620.

Begg, I., & White, P. (1985). Encoding specificity in interpersonal communication. *Canadian Journal of Psychology, 39,* 70–87.

Bell, P. B., & Staines, P. J. (1981). *Reasoning and argument in psychology.* London: Routledge and Kegan Paul.

Bellezza, F. S. (1984). The self as a mnemonic device: The role of internal cues. *Journal of Personality and Social Psychology, 47*, 506–516.

Bellezza, F. S. (1986). Mental cues and verbal reports in learning. In G. H. Bower (Ed.), *The psychology of learning and motivation* (Vol. 20, pp. 237–273). New York: Academic Press.

Bellezza, F. S. (1987). Mnemonic devices and memory schemes. In M. McDaniel & M. Pressley (Eds.), *Imagery and related mnemonic processes* (pp. 34–55). New York: Springer-Verlag.

Bellezza, F. S., & Buck, D. K. (1988). Expert knowledge as mnemonic cues. *Applied Cognitive Psychology, 2*, 147–162.

Bereiter, C., & Bird, M. (1985). Use of thinking aloud in identification and teaching of reading comprehension strategies. *Cognition and Instruction, 2*, 131–156.

Berger, D. E., Pezdek, K., & Banks, W. P. (Eds.). (1987). *Applications of cognitive psychology: Problem solving, education, and computing.* Hillsdale, NJ: Erlbaum.

Berger, L. (1984). Halo effect. In R. J. Corsini (Ed.), *Encyclopedia of psychology* (Vol. 2, p. 90). New York: Wiley.

Berkowitz, L. (1984). Some effects of thoughts on anti- and prosocial influences of media events: A cognitive-neoassociation analysis. *Psychological Bulletin, 95*, 410–427.

Berscheid, E., & Walster, E. (1974). Physical attractiveness. In L. Berkowitz (Ed.), *Advances in experimental social psychology* (pp. 158–215). New York: Academic Press.

Besner, D., Davies, J., & Daniels, S. (1981). Reading for meaning: The effects of concurrent articulation. *Quarterly Journal of Experimental Psychology, 33A*, 415–437.

Bettman, J. R. (1986). Consumer psychology. *Annual Review of Psychology, 37*, 257–289.

Bialystok, E. (1987). Words as things. Development of word concept by bilingual children. *Studies in Second Language Acquisition, 9*, 133–140.

Bialystok, E. (1988). Levels of bilingualism and levels of linguistic awareness. *Developmental Psychology, 24*, 560–567.

Biederman, I. (1987). Recognition-by-components: A theory of human image understanding. *Psychological Review, 94*, 115–147.

Biederman, I. (1990). Higher-level vision. In E. N. Osherson, S. M. Kosslyn, & J. M. Hollerbach (Eds.), *An invitation to cognitive science* (Vol. 2, pp. 41–72). Cambridge, MA: MIT Press.

Birnbaum, M. H., Anderson, C. J., & Hynan, L. G. (1990). Theories of bias in probability judgment. In J. P. Caverni, J. M. Fabre, & M. Gonzalez (Eds.), *Cognitive biases* (pp. 477–478). Amsterdam: Elsevier.

Bjork, E. L., & Bjork, R. A. (1988). On the adaptive aspects of retrieval failure in autobiographical memory. In M. M. Gruneberg, P. E. Morris, & R. N. Sykes (Eds.), *Practical aspects of memory* (Vol. II). London: Wiley.

Bjork, R. A., & Richardson-Klavehn, A. (1987). On the puzzling relationship between environmental context and human memory. In C. Izawa (Ed.), *Current issues in cognitive processes* (pp. 313–344). Hillsdale, NJ: Erlbaum.

Bjorklund, D. F., & Zeman, B. R. (1982). Children's organization and metamemory awareness in the recall of familiar information. *Child Development, 53*, 799–810.

Black, J. B. (1984). The architecture of the mind [Review of *The architecture of cognition*]. *Contemporary Psychology, 29*, 853–854.

Blanchard, H. E. (1987). The effects of pronoun processing on information utilization during fixations in reading. *Bulletin of the Psychonomic Society, 25*, 171–174.

Blanchard, H. E., & Iran-Nejad, A. (1987). Comprehension processes and eye movement patterns in the reading of surprise-ending stories. *Discourse Processes, 10*, 127–138.

Blaney, P. H. (1986). Affect and memory: A review. *Psychological Bulletin, 99*, 229–246.

Bloom, C. P. (1988). The roles of schemata in memory for text. *Discourse Processes, 11*, 305–318.

Bloom, L. C., & Mudd, S. A. (1991). Depth of processing approach to face recognition: A test of two theories. *Journal of Experimental Psychology: Learning, Memory, and Cognition, 17*, 556–565.

Bock, J. K. (1986). Syntactic persistence in language production. *Cognitive Psychology, 18,* 355–387.

Bock, J. K. (1987). Co-ordinating words and syntax in speech plans. In A. W. Ellis (Ed.), *Progress in the psychology of language* (Vol. 3, pp. 337–390). London: Erlbaum.

Bond, M. H., & Lai, T. (1986). Embarrassment and code-switching into a second language. *Journal of Social Psychology, 126,* 179–186.

Bothwell, R. K., Brigham, J. C., & Malpass, R. S. (1989). Cross-racial identification. *Personality and Social Psychology Bulletin, 15,* 19–25.

Bower, G. H. (1970). Analysis of a mnemonic device. *American Scientist, 58,* 496–510.

Bower, G. H. (1976). Experiments on story understanding and recall. *Quarterly Journal of Experimental Psychology, 28,* 511–534.

Bower, G. H. (1987). Commentary on mood and memory. *Behavior Research Therapy, 25,* 443–455.

Bower, G. H. (1989). Mental models in text understanding. In A. F. Bennett & K. M. McConkey (Eds.), *Cognition in individual and social contexts* (pp. 129–144). Amsterdam, Holland: Elsevier Science.

Bower, G. H., & Clark, M. C. (1969). Narrative stories as mediators for serial learning. *Psychonomic Science, 14,* 181–182.

Bower, G. H., Clark, M. C., Lesgold, A. M., & Winzenz, D. (1969). Hierarchical retrieval schemes in recall of categorized word lists. *Journal of Verbal Learning and Verbal Behavior, 8,* 323–343.

Bower, G. H., & Gilligan, S. G. (1979). Remembering information related to one's self. *Journal of Research in Personality, 13,* 420–432.

Bower, G. H., & Mayer, J. D. (1985). Failure to replicate mood-dependent retrieval. *Bulletin of the Psychonomic Society, 23,* 39–42.

Bower, G. H., & Mayer, J. D. (1989). In search of mood-dependent retrieval. *Journal of Social Behavior and Personality, 4,* 121–156.

Bower, G. H., & Morrow, D. G. (1990). Mental models in narrative comprehension. *Science, 247,* 44–48.

Bower, G. H., & Springston, F. (1970). Pauses as recoding points in letter series. *Journal of Experimental Psychology, 83,* 421–430.

Bower, G. H., & Winzenz, D. (1970). Comparison of associative learning strategies. *Psychonomic Science, 20,* 119–120.

Bowers, K. S. (1984). On being unconsciously influenced and informed. In K. S. Bowers & D. Meichenbaum (Eds.), *The unconscious reconsidered* (pp. 227–272). New York: Wiley.

Bowers, K. S., & Meichenbaum, D. (1984). *The unconscious reconsidered.* New York: Wiley.

Bradshaw, J. L., & Nettleton, N. C. (1974). Articulatory inference and the MOWN-DOWN heterophone effect. *Journal of Experimental Psychology, 102,* 88–94.

Brandimonte, M. A., Hitch, G. J., & Bishop, D. V. M. (1992). Influence of short-term memory codes on visual image processing: Evidence from image transformation tasks. *Journal of Experimental Psychology: Learning, Memory, and Cognition, 18,* 157–165.

Bransford, J. D., Barclay, J. R., & Franks, J. J. (1972). Sentence memory: A constructive versus interpretive approach. *Cognitive Psychology, 3,* 193–209.

Bransford, J. D., & Franks, J. J. (1971). Abstraction of linguistic ideas. *Cognitive Psychology, 2,* 331–350.

Bransford, J. D., Franks, J. J., Morris, C. D., & Stein, B. S. (1979). Some general constraints on learning and memory research. In L. S. Cermak & F. I. M. Craik (Eds.), *Levels of processing in human memory* (pp. 331–354). Hillsdale, NJ: Erlbaum.

Bransford, J. D., & Johnson, M. K. (1972). Contextual prerequisites for understanding: Some investigations of comprehension and recall. *Journal of Verbal Learning and Verbal Behavior, 11,* 717–726.

Bransford, J. D., Sherwood, R. D., & Sturdevant, T. (1987). Teaching thinking and problem solving. In J. B. Baron & R. J. Sternberg (Eds.), *Teaching thinking skills* (pp. 162–181). New York: Freeman.

Bransford, J. D., & Stein, B. S. (1984). *The IDEAL problem solver.* New York: Freeman.

Bransford, J. D., Stein, B. S., Vye, N. J., Franks, J. J., Aubel, P. M., Meznynsky, K. J., & Perfetto, G. A. (1982). Differences in approaches to learning: An overview. *Journal of Experimental Psychology: General, 111,* 390–398.

Branthwaite, A., & Rogers, D. (1985). Introduction. In A. Branthwaite & D. Rogers (Eds.), *Children growing up* (pp. 1–2). Milton Keynes, England: Open University Press.

Brewer, W. F., & Treyens, J. C. (1981). Role of schemata in memory for places. *Cognitive Psychology, 13,* 207–230.

Bridges, A. (1986). Actions and things: What adults talk about to one-year-olds. In S. A. Kuczaj & M. D. Barrett (Eds.), *The development of word meaning* (pp. 225–255). New York: Springer-Verlag.

Brigham, T. C., & Malpass, R. S. (1985). The role of experience and context in the recognition of faces of own- and other-race. *Journal of Social Issues, 41,* 139–155.

Broadbent, D. E. (1958). *Perception and communication.* New York: Pergamon.

Brooks, L. R. (1968). Spatial and verbal components of the act of recall. *Canadian Journal of Psychology, 22,* 349–368.

Brown, A. L. (1975). The development of memory: Knowing, knowing about knowing, and knowing how to know. In H. W. Reese (Ed.), *Advances in child development and behavior* (Vol. 10). New York: Academic Press.

Brown, A. L., & Scott, M. S. (1971). Recognition memory for pictures in preschool children. *Journal of Experimental Child Psychology, 11,* 401–412.

Brown, A. S. (1991). A review of the tip-of-the-tongue experience. *Psychological Bulletin, 109,* 204–223.

Brown, J. A. (1958). Some tests of the decay theory of immediate memory. *Quarterly Journal of Experimental Psychology, 10,* 12–21.

Brown, N. R. (1990). Organization of public events in long-term memory. *Journal of Experimental Psychology: General, 119,* 297–314.

Brown, N. R., & Siegler, R. S. (1992). The role of availability in the estimation of national populations. *Memory & Cognition, 20,* 406–412.

Brown, P., Keenan, J. M., & Potte, G. R. (1986). The self-reference effect with imagery encoding. *Journal of Personality and Social Psychology, 51,* 897–906.

Brown, P., & Levinson, S. C. (1987). *Politeness: Some universals of language usage.* Cambridge, England: Cambridge University Press.

Brown, R. (1973). *A first language: The early stages.* Cambridge, MA: Harvard University Press.

Brown, R. (1986). *Social psychology* (2nd ed.). New York: The Free Press.

Brown, R. (1990). Foreword. In M. G. Johnson & T. B. Henley (Eds.), *Reflections on the Principles of Psychology: William James after a century* (pp. xv–xvii). Hillsdale, NJ: Erlbaum.

Brown, R., & Kulik, J. (1977). Flashbulb memories. *Cognition, 5,* 73–99.

Brown, R., & McNeill, D. (1966). The "tip of the tongue" phenomenon. *Journal of Verbal Learning and Verbal Behavior, 5,* 325–377.

Brown, R. T. (1989). Creativity: What are we to measure? In J. A. Glover, R. R. Ronning, & C. R. Reynolds (Eds.), *Handbook of creativity* (pp. 3–32). New York: Plenum.

Brown, S. I., & Walter, M. I. (1990). *The art of problem posing* (2nd ed.). Hillsdale, NJ: Erlbaum.

Bruce, P. R., Coyne, A. C., & Botwinick, J. (1982). Adult age differences in metamemory. *Journal of Gerontology, 37,* 354–357.

Bruce, V. (1988). Perceiving. In G. Claxton (Ed.), *Growth points in cognition* (pp. 32–65). New York: Routledge.

Bruck, M., Cavanagh, P., & Ceci, S. J. (1991). Fortysomething: Recognizing faces at one's 25th reunion. *Memory & Cognition, 19,* 221–228.

Bryant, D. J., Tversky, B., & Franklin, N. (1992). Internal and external spatial frameworks for representing described scenes. *Journal of Memory and Language, 31,* 74–98.

Bushnell, I. W. R. (1982). Discrimination of faces by young infants. *Journal of Experimental Psychology, 33,* 298–308.

Bushnell, I. W. R., & Sai, F. (1987). *Neonatal recognition of the mother's face.* University of Glasgow Report, 87/1.

Byrne, R. M. J. (1989). Suppressing valid inferences with conditionals. *Cognition, 31,* 61–83.

Cairns, R. B., & Valsiner, J. (1984). Child psychology. *Annual Review of Psychology, 35,* 553–577.

Caramazza, A., Yenni-Komshian, G., Zurif, E., & Carbone, E. (1973). The acquisition of a new phonological contrast: The case of stop consonants in French-English bilinguals. *Journal of the Acoustical Society of America, 54,* 421–428.

Carey, S. (1978). The child as word learner. In M. Halle, J. Bresnan, & G. A. Miller (Eds.), *Linguistic theory and psychological reality.* Cambridge, MA: MIT Press.

Carlson, B. W. (1990). Anchoring and adjustment in judgments under risk. *Journal of Experimental Psychology: Learning, Memory, and Cognition, 16,* 665–676.

Carlson, L., Zimmer, J. W., & Glover, J. A. (1981). First-letter mnemonics: DAM (Don't Aid Memory). *Journal of General Psychology, 104,* 287–292.

Carlson, R. A., Sullivan, M. A., & Schneider, W. (1989). *Journal of Experimental Psychology: Learning, Memory, and Cognition, 15,* 517–526.

Carroll, D. W. (1986). *Psychology of language.* Monterey, CA: Brooks/Cole.

Cassell, J., & McNeill, D. (1991). Gesture and the poetics of prose. *Poetics today, 12,* 375–403.

Cattell, J. M. (1886). The time it takes to see and name objects. *Mind, 11,* 63–65.

Cavanaugh, J. C., & Borkowski, J. G. (1980). Searching for metamemory-memory connections: A developmental study. *Developmental Psychology, 16,* 441–453.

Cavanaugh, J. C., & Perlmutter, M. (1982). Metamemory: A critical examination. *Child Development, 53,* 11–28.

Cave, K. R., & Kosslyn, S. M. (1989). Varieties of size-specific visual selection. *Journal of Experimental Psychology: General, 118,* 148–164.

Ceci, S. J., & Bronfenbrenner, U. (1991). On the demise of everyday memory: "The rumors of my death are much exaggerated" (Mark Twain). *American Psychologist, 46,* 27–31.

Ceci, S. J., & Liker, J. (1986a). Academic and nonacademic intelligence: An experimental separation. In R. J. Sternberg & R. K. Wagner (Eds.), *Practical intelligence: Nature and origins of competence in the everyday world* (pp. 119–142). New York: Cambridge University Press.

Ceci, S. J., & Liker, J. K. (1986b). A day at the races: A study of IQ, expertise, and cognitive complexity. *Journal of Experimental Psychology: General, 115,* 255–266.

Ceci, S. J., & Liker, J. K. (1988). Stalking the IQ-expertise relation: When the critics go fishing. *Journal of Experimental Psychology: General, 117,* 96–100.

Ceci, S. J., Toglia, M. P., & Ross, D. F. (Eds.). (1987). *Children's eyewitness memory.* New York: Springer-Verlag.

Cernoch, J. M., & Porter, R. H. (1985). Recognition of maternal axillary odors by infants. *Child Development, 56,* 1593–1598.

Cervone, D. (1989). Effects of envisioning future activities on self-efficacy judgments and motivation: An availability heuristic interpretation. *Cognitive Therapy and Research, 13,* 247–261.

Cervone, D., & Peake, P. K. (1986). Anchoring, efficacy, and action: The influence of judgmental heuristics on self-efficacy judgments and behavior. *Journal of Personality and Social Psychology, 50,* 492–501.

Chafe, W., & Danielewicz, J. (1987). Properties of spoken and written language. In R. Horowitz & S. J. Samuels (Eds.), *Comprehending oral and written language* (pp. 83–113). San Diego: Academic Press.

Chambers, D., & Reisberg, D. (1985). Can mental images be ambiguous? *Journal of Experimental Psychology: Human Perception and Performance, 11,* 317–328.

Chang, T. M. (1986). Semantic memory: Facts and models. *Psychological Bulletin, 99,* 199–220.

Chapman, L. J., & Chapman, J. P. (1967). Genesis of popular but erroneous psychodiagnostic observations. *Journal of Abnormal Psychology, 72,* 193–204.

Chapman, L. J., & Chapman, J. P. (1969). Illusory correlations as an obstacle to the use of valid psychodiagnostic signs. *Journal of Abnormal Psychology, 74,* 271–280.

Chastain, G. (1981). Phonological and orthographic factors in the word-superiority effect. *Memory & Cognition, 9,* 389–397.

Chastain, G. (1986). Word-to-letter inhibition: Word-inferiority and other interference effects. *Memory & Cognition, 14,* 361–368.

Cheng, P. W. (1985). Restructuring versus automaticity: Alternative accounts of skill acquisition. *Psychological Review, 92,* 414–423.

Cheng, P. W., & Holyoak, K. J. (1985). Pragmatic reasoning schemas. *Cognitive Psychology, 17,* 391–416.

Cheng, P. W., Holyoak, K. J., Nisbett, R. E., & Oliver, L. M. (1986). Pragmatic versus syntactic approaches to training deductive reasoning. *Cognitive Psychology, 18,* 293–328.

Cherry, C. (1953). Some experiments on the recognition of speech with one and with two ears. *Journal of the Acoustical Society of America, 25,* 975–979.

Chi, M. T. H. (1981). Knowledge development and memory performance. In M. Friedman, J. P. Das, & N. O'Connor (Eds.), *Intelligence and learning* (pp. 221–230). New York: Plenum.

Chi, M. T. H., Glaser, R., & Farr, M. J. (Eds.). (1988). *The nature of expertise.* Hillsdale, NJ: Erlbaum.

Chi, M. T. H., Glaser, R., & Rees, E. (1982). Expertise in problem solving. In R. Sternberg (Ed.), *Advances in the psychology of human intelligence* (Vol. 1, pp. 7–75). Hillsdale, NJ: Erlbaum.

Chomsky, N. (1957). *Syntactic structures.* The Hague: Mouton Publishers.

Chomsky, N. (1965). *Aspects of the theory of syntax.* Cambridge, MA: MIT Press.

Chomsky, N. (1973). Conditions on transformations. In S. R. Anderson & P. Rosenbaum (Eds.), *A festschrift for Morris Halle.* New York: Holt, Rinehart and Winston.

Chomsky, N. (1981). *Lectures on government and binding.* Dordrecht, Netherlands: Foris.

Christensen-Szalanski, J. J. J., Beck, D. E., Christensen-Szalanski, C. M., & Koepsell, T. D. (1983). The effect of journal coverage on physicians' perception of risk. *Journal of Applied Psychology, 68,* 278–284.

Christensen-Szalanski, J. J. J., & Willham, C. F. (1991). The hindsight bias: A meta-analysis. *Organizational Behavior and Human Decision Processes, 48,* 147–168.

Christianson, S. A. (1989). Flashbulb memories: Special, but not so special. *Memory & Cognition, 17,* 435–443.

Churchland, P. M., & Churchland, P. S. (1990, January). Could a machine think? *Scientific American,* pp. 32–37.

Clark, E. V. (1975). Knowledge, context, and strategy in the acquisition of meaning. In D. P. Dato (Ed.), *Georgetown University Round Table on Languages and Linguistics 1975.* Washington, DC: Georgetown University Press.

Clark, H. H. (1985). Language use and language users. In G. Lindzey & E. Aronson (Eds.), *Handbook of social psychology* (2nd ed., Vol. 2, pp. 179–231). New York: Random House.

Clark, H. H., & Chase, W. G. (1972). On the process of comparing sentences against pictures. *Cognitive Psychology, 3,* 472–517.

Clark, H. H., & Clark, E. V. (1977). *Psychology and language: An introduction to psycholinguistics.* New York: Harcourt Brace Jovanovich.

Clark, H. H., & Wilkes-Gibbs, D. (1986). Referring as a collaborative process. *Cognition, 22,* 1–39.

Clement, C. A., & Falmagne, R. J. (1986). Logical reasoning, world knowledge, and mental imagery: Interconnections in cognitive processes. *Memory & Cognition, 14,* 299–307.

Clement, J. (1991). Nonformal reasoning in experts and in science students: The use of analogies, extreme cases, and physical intuition. In J. Voss, D. Perkins, & J. Siegel (Eds.), *Informal reasoning and education.* Hillsdale, NJ: Erlbaum.

Cohen, G. (1983). *The psychology of cognition* (2nd ed.). London: Academic Press.

Cohen, G. (1988). Age differences in memory for texts: Production deficiency or processing limitations? In L. L. Light & D. M. Burke (Eds.), *Language, memory, and aging* (pp. 171–190). New York: Cambridge University Press.

Cohen, G. (1989). *Memory in the real world.* London: Erlbaum.

Cohen, G., Eysenck, M. W., & LeVoi, M. E. (1986). *Memory: A cognitive approach.* Milton Keynes, England: Open University Press.

Cohen, J. D., Dunbar, K., & McClelland, J. L. (1990). On the control of automatic processes:

A parallel distributed processing account of the Stroop effect. *Psychological Review, 97,* 332–361.

Cole, R. A. (1973). Listening for mispronunciations: A measure of what we hear during speech. *Perception & Psychophysics, 14,* 153–156.

Cole, R. A., & Jakimik, J. (1980). A model of speech perception. In R. A. Cole (Ed.), *Perception and production of fluent speech* (pp. 133–163). Hillsdale, NJ: Erlbaum.

Cole, R. A., & Scott, B. (1974). Toward a theory of speech perception. *Psychological Review, 81,* 348–374.

Collins, A. M., & Loftus, E. F. (1975). A spreading-activation theory of semantic memory. *Psychological Review, 82,* 407–428.

Collins, A. M., & Quillian, M. R. (1969). Retrieval time from semantic memory. *Journal of Verbal Learning and Verbal Behavior, 8,* 240–248.

Coltheart, M. (1980). Iconic memory and visual persistence. *Perception & Psychophysics, 27,* 183–228.

Coltheart, M., Patterson, K. E., & Marshall, J. C. (1980). *Deep dyslexia.* London: Routledge and Kegan Paul.

Conrad, R. (1964). Acoustic confusions in immediate memory. *British Journal of Psychology, 55,* 75–84.

Conway, M. A. (1991). In defense of everyday memory. *American Psychologist, 46,* 19–26.

Cooper, L. A., & Shepard, R. N. (1973). Chronometric studies of the rotation of mental images. In W. G. Chase (Ed.), *Visual information processing.* New York: Academic Press.

Cooper, L. A., & Shepard, R. N. (1984). Turning something over in the mind. *Scientific American, 251*(6), 106–114.

Cooper, W. E., Tye-Murray, N., & Eady, S. J. (1985). Acoustical cues to the reconstruction of missing words in speech perception. *Perception & Psychophysics, 38,* 30–40.

Cooper, W. H. (1981). Ubiquitous halo. *Psychological Bulletin, 90,* 218–244.

Corballis, M. C. (1986). Memory scanning: Can subjects scan two sets at once? *Psychological Review, 93,* 113–114.

Corbetta, M., Meizin, F. M., Shulman, G. L., & Petersen, S. E. (1991). Shifting attention in space, direction versus visual hemifield: Psychophysics and PET. *Journal of Blood Flow and Metabolism, 11,* 909.

Coren, S., Ward, L. M., & Enns, S. (1994). *Sensation & perception* (4th ed.). Fort Worth, TX: Harcourt Brace.

Corteen, R. S., & Wood, B. (1972). Autonomic responses to shock-associated words in an unattended channel. *Journal of Experimental Psychology, 94,* 308–313.

Cosmides, L. (1989). The logic of social exchange: Has natural selection shaped how humans reason? Studies with the Wason selection task. *Cognition, 31,* 187–276.

Cowan, N. (1984). On short and long auditory stores. *Psychological Bulletin, 96,* 341–370.

Cowan, N. (1988). Evolving conceptions of memory storage, selective attention, and their mutual constraints within the human information-processing system. *Psychological Bulletin, 104,* 163–191.

Craik, F. I. M. (1977). Age differences in human memory. In J. E. Birren & K. W. Schaie (Eds.), *Handbook of the psychology of aging.* New York: Van Nostrand Reinhold.

Craik, F. I. M. (1979). Levels of processing: Overview and closing comments. In L. S. Cermak & F. I. M. Craik (Eds.), *Levels of processing in human memory* (pp. 447–461). Hillsdale, NJ: Erlbaum.

Craik, F. I. M. (1990). Changes in memory with normal aging: A functional view. In R. J. Wurtman (Ed.), *Advances in Neurology: Vol. 51. Alzheimer's Disease* (pp. 201–205). New York: Raven Press.

Craik, F. I. M. (1991). Will cognitivism bury experimental psychology? *Canadian Psychology/ Psychologie canadienne, 32,* 440–444.

Craik, F. I. M., Byrd, M., & Swanson, J. M. (1987). Patterns of memory loss in three elderly samples. *Psychology and Aging, 2,* 79–86.

Craik, F. I. M., & Lockhart, R. S. (1972). Levels of processing: A framework for memory research. *Journal of Verbal Learning and Verbal Behavior, 11,* 671–684.

Craik, F. I. M., & Lockhart, R. S. (1986). CHARM is not enough: Comments on Eich's model of cued recall. *Psychological Review, 93,* 360–364.

Craik, F. I. M., & McDowd, J. M. (1987). Age differences in recall and recognition. *Journal of Experimental Psychology: Learning, Memory, and Cognition, 13,* 474–479.

Craik, F. I. M., & Tulving, E. (1975). Depth of processing and the retention of words in episodic memory. *Journal of Experimental Psychology: General, 104,* 268–294.

Crandall, C. S. (1984). The overcitation of examples of poor performance: Fad, fashion, or fun? *American Psychologist, 39,* 1499.

Crocker, J. (1981). Judgment of covariation by social perceivers. *Psychological Bulletin, 90,* 272–292.

Cross, D. R., & Paris, S. G. (1988). Developmental and instructional analyses of children's metacognition and reading comprehension. *Journal of Educational Psychology, 80,* 131–142.

Crovitz, H. F. (1990). Association, cognition, and neural networks. In M. G. Johnson & T. B. Henley (Eds.), *Reflections on the Principles of Psychology: William James after a century* (pp. 167–182). Hillsdale, NJ: Erlbaum.

Crowder, R. G. (1980). Echoic memory and the study of aging memory systems. In L. W. Poon, J. L. Fozard, L. S. Cermak, D. Arenberg, & L. W. Thompson (Eds.), *New directions in memory and aging: Proceedings of the George A. Talland Memorial Conference* (pp. 181–204). Hillsdale, NJ: Erlbaum.

Crowder, R. G. (1982a). Decay of auditory memory in vowel discrimination. *Journal of Experimental Psychology: Learning, Memory, and Cognition, 8,* 153–162.

Crowder, R. G. (1982b). The demise of short-term memory. *Acta Psychologica, 50,* 291–323.

Crowder, R. G., & Wagner, R. K. (1992). *The psychology of reading* (2nd ed.). New York: Oxford University Press.

Cutler, B. L., Penrod, S. D., & Martens, T. K. (1987). The reliability of eyewitness identification: The role of system and estimator variables. *Law and Human Behavior, 11,* 233–258.

Daneman, M., & Green, I. (1986). Individual differences in comprehending and producing words in context. *Journal of Memory and Language, 25,* 1–18.

Danks, J. H., & End, L. J. (1987). Processing strategies for reading and listening. In R. Horowitz & S. J. Samuels (Eds.), *Comprehending oral and written language* (pp. 271–294). San Diego: Academic Press.

Darke, S. (1988). Anxiety and working memory capacity. *Cognition and Emotion, 2,* 145–154.

Darwin, C. J. (1976). The perception of speech. In E. C. Carterette & M. P. Friedman (Eds.), *Handbook of Perception* (Vol. 7, pp. 175–226). New York: Academic Press.

Darwin, C. J., Turvey, M. T., & Crowder, R. G. (1972). An auditory analogue of the Sperling partial report procedure: Evidence for brief auditory storage. *Cognitive Psychology, 3,* 255–267.

Davies, G., & Jenkins, F. (1985). Witnesses can be misled by police composite pictures: How and when. In F. L. Denmark (Ed.), *Social/ecological psychology and the psychology of women* (pp. 103–115). Amsterdam: Elsevier Science Publishers.

Davies, G. M. (1988). Faces and places: Laboratory research on context and face recognition. In G. M. Davies & D. M. Thomson (Eds.), *Memory in context: Context in memory* (pp. 35–53). Chichester, England: John Wiley & Sons.

Davies, G. M., & Thomson, D. M. (Eds.). (1988). *Memory in context: Context in memory.* Chichester, England: John Wiley & Sons.

Dawes, R. M. (1988). *Rational choice in an uncertain world.* San Diego: Harcourt Brace Jovanovich.

Dawson, M. E., & Schell, A. M. (1982). Electrodermal responses to attended and nonattended significant stimuli during dichotic listening. *Journal of Experimental Psychology: Human Perception and Performance, 8,* 315–324.

DeAngelis, T. (1989, September). Controversy marks child witness meeting. *APA Monitor,* pp. 1, 8–9.

DeCasper, A. J., & Fifer, W. P. (1980). Of human bonding: Newborns prefer their mothers' voices. *Science, 208,* 1174–1176.

DeCasper, A. J., & Spence, M. J. (1986). Prenatal maternal speech influences newborns' perception of speech sounds. *Infant Behavior and Development, 9,* 133–150.

Deese, J. (1984). *Thought into speech: The psychology of language*. Englewood Cliffs, NJ: Prentice-Hall.

de Groot, A. (1986). Perception and memory versus thought: Some old ideas and recent findings. In B. Kleinmuntz (Ed.), *Problem solving*. New York: Wiley.

De Jong, G. (1982). Skimming stories in real time: An experiment in integrated understanding. In W. Lehnert & M. H. Ringle (Eds.), *Natural language processing*. Hillsdale, NJ: Erlbaum.

De Jong, T., & Ferguson-Hessler, M. G. M. (1986). Cognitive structures of good and poor novice problem solvers in physics. *Journal of Educational Psychology, 78*, 279–288.

Dell, G. S. (1985). Putting production back in psycholinguistics [Review of *Language production: Vol. 2. Development, writing, and other language processes*]. *Contemporary Psychology, 30*, 129–130.

Dell, G. S. (1986). A spreading-activation theory of retrieval in sentence production. *Psychological Review, 93*, 283–321.

Dember, W. N. (1990). William James on sensation and perception. *Psychological Science, 1*, 163–166.

Dempster, F. N. (1981). Memory span: Sources of individual and developmental differences. *Psychological Bulletin, 89*, 63–100.

Dempster, F. N. (1985). Short-term memory development in childhood and adolescence. In C. J. Brainerd & M. Pressley (Eds.), *Basic processes in memory development* (pp. 209–248). New York: Springer-Verlag.

Dennett, D. C. (1991). *Consciousness explained*. Boston: Little, Brown and Company.

Desrochers, A., & Begg, I. (1987). A theoretical account of encoding and retrieval processes in the use of imagery-based mnemonic techniques: The special case of the keyword method. In M. A. McDaniel & M. Pressley (Eds.), *Imagery and related mnemonic processes* (pp. 56–77). New York: Springer-Verlag.

Deutsch, J. A., & Deutsch, D. (1963). Attention: Some theoretical considerations. *Psychological Review, 70*, 80–90.

deVilliers, J. G., & deVilliers, P. A. (1978). *Language acquisition*. Cambridge, MA: Harvard University Press.

deVilliers, J. G., & deVilliers, P. A. (1982). Language development. In R. Vasta (Ed.), *Strategies and techniques of child study* (pp. 117–159). New York: Academic Press.

Devolder, P. A., & Pressley, M. (1989). Metamemory across the adult lifespan. *Canadian Psychology, 30*, 578–587.

Diaz, R. M. (1985). Bilingual cognitive development: Addressing three gaps in current research. *Child Development, 56*, 1376–1388.

Di Lollo, V. (1977). Temporal characteristics of iconic memory. *Nature, 267*, 241–243.

Di Lollo, V. (1980). Temporal integration in visual memory. *Journal of Experimental Psychology: General, 109*, 75–97.

Di Lollo, V., & Dixon, P. (1988). Two forms of persistence in visual information processing. *Journal of Experimental Psychology: Human Perception and Performance, 14*, 671–681.

Di Lollo, V., & Hogben, J. H. (1987). Suppression of visible persistence as a function of spatial separation between inducing stimuli. *Perception & Psychophysics, 41*, 345–354.

Doctor, E. A., & Coltheart, M. (1980). Children's use of phonological encoding when reading for meaning. *Memory & Cognition, 8*, 195–209.

Dodd, B., & Campbell, R. (1986). *Hearing by eye: The psychology of lip reading*. London: Erlbaum.

Donley, R. D., & Ashcraft, M. H. (1992). The methodology of testing naive beliefs in the physics classroom. *Memory & Cognition*, 381–391.

Dooling, D. J., & Christiaansen, R. E. (1977). Levels of encoding and retention of prose. In G. H. Bower (Ed.), *The psychology of learning and motivation: Advances in research and theory* (Vol. 11). New York: Academic Press.

Doris, J. (Ed.). (1991). *The suggestibility of children's recollections: Implications for eyewitness testimony*. Washington, DC: American Psychological Association.

Du Boulay, B. (1989). Nonadversary problem solving by machine. In K. J. Gilhooly (Ed.), *Human and machine problem solving* (pp. 13–37). New York: Plenum.

Duncan, E. M., & Bourg, T. (1983). An examination of the effects of encoding and decision processes on the rate of mental rotation. *Journal of Mental Imagery, 7*, 33–56.

Duncker, K. (1945). On problem solving. *Psychological Monographs, 58* (Whole No. 270).

D'Ydewalle, G., Delhaye, P., & Goessens, L. (1985). Structural, semantic, and self-reference processing of pictorial advertisements. *Human Learning, 4*, 29–38.

Ebbinghaus, H. (1913). *Memory: A contribution to experimental psychology*. New York: Columbia Teacher's College. (Original work published 1885)

Eimas, P. D., Siqueland, E. R., Jusczyk, P., & Vigorito, J. (1971). Speech perception in infants. *Science, 171*, 303–306.

Eimas, P. D., & Tartter, V. C. (1979). On the development of speech perception: Mechanisms and analogies. In H. W. Reese & L. P. Lipsitt (Eds.), *Advances in child development and behavior* (pp. 155–194). New York: Academic Press.

Einhorn, H. J., & Hogarth, R. M. (1978). Confidence in judgment: Persistence of the illusion of validity. *Psychological Review, 85*, 395–416.

Einhorn, H. J., & Hogarth, R. M. (1981). Behavioral decision theory: Processes of judgment and choice. *Annual Review of Psychology, 32*, 53–88.

Einstein, G. O., & McDaniel, M. A. (1987). Distinctiveness and the mnemonic benefits of bizarre imagery. In M. A. McDaniel & M. Pressley (Eds.), *Imagery and related mnemonic processes* (pp. 78–102). New York: Springer-Verlag.

Einstein, G. O., McDaniel, M. A., & Lackey, S. (1989). *Journal of Experimental Psychology: Learning, Memory, and Cognition, 15*, 137–146.

Elias, J. W., Elias, M. F., & Elias, P. K. (1991). Normal aging and disease as contributors to the study of cognitive processing in aging. In J. D. Sinnott & J. C. Cavanaugh (Eds.), *Bridging paradigms: Positive development in adulthood and cognitive aging* (pp. 27–41). New York: Praeger.

Elliott, C. S., & Archibald, R. B. (1989). Subjective framing and attitudes toward risk. *Journal of Economic Psychology, 10*, 321–328.

Ellis, A., & Beattie, G. (1986). *The psychology of language and communication*. New York: Guilford.

Ellis, H. D. (1984). Practical aspects of face memory. In G. L. Wells & E. F. Loftus (Eds.), *Eyewitness testimony: Psychological perspectives* (pp. 12–37). Cambridge: Cambridge University Press.

Engle, R. W., Fidler, D. S., & Reynolds, L. H. (1981). Does echoic memory develop? *Journal of Experimental Child Psychology, 32*, 459–473.

Enns, J. T., & Rensink, R. A. (1991). Preattentive recovery of three-dimensional orientation from line drawings. *Psychological Review, 98*, 335–351.

Erber, J. T. (1982). Memory and age. In T. M. Field, A. Huston, H. C. Quay, L. Troll, & G. E. Finley (Eds.), *Review of human development* (pp. 569–585). New York: Wiley.

Ericsson, K. A. (1985). Memory skill. *Canadian Journal of Psychology, 39*, 188–231.

Ericsson, K. A. (1988). Analysis of memory performance in terms of memory skill. In R. J. Sternberg (Ed.), *Advances in the psychology of human intelligence*, (Vol. 4, pp. 137–179). Hillsdale, NJ: Erlbaum.

Ericsson, K. A., & Polson, P. G. (1988). An experimental analysis of the mechanisms of a memory skill. *Journal of Experimental Psychology: Learning, Memory, and Cognition, 14*, 305–316.

Ericsson, K. A., & Simon, H. A. (1980). Verbal reports as data. *Psychological Review, 87*, 215–251.

Ericsson, K. A., & Simon, H. A. (1984). *Protocol analysis*. Cambridge, MA: MIT Press.

Ericsson, K. A., & Smith, J. (1991a). Prospects and limits of the empirical study of expertise: An introduction. In K. A. Ericsson & J. Smith (Eds.), *Toward a general theory of expertise: Prospects and limits* (pp. 1–38). New York: Cambridge University Press.

Ericsson, K. A., & Smith, J. (Eds.). (1991b). *Toward a general theory of expertise: Prospects and limits*. New York: Cambridge University Press.

Ervin-Tripp, S. (1976). Is Sybil there? The structure of some American English directives. *Language in Society, 5*, 25–66.

Ervin-Tripp, S. (1993). Conversational discourse. In J. B. Berko-Gleason & N. B. Ratner (Eds.), *Psycholinguistics*. Fort Worth, TX: Harcourt Brace Jovanovich.

Estes, W. K. (1978). Perceptual processing in letter recognition and reading. In E. C. Carterette & M. P. Friedman (Eds.), *Handbook of perception* (Vol. 9, pp. 163–220). New York: Academic Press.

Estes, W. K. (1988). Human learning and memory. In R. C. Atkinson, R. J. Herrnstein, G. Lindzey, & R. D. Luce (Eds.), *Stevens' handbook of experimental psychology* (Vol. 2, pp. 351–415). New York: Wiley.

Estes, W. K. (1991). Cognitive architectures from the standpoint of an experimental psychologist. *Annual Review of Psychology, 42,* 1–28.

Evans, J. St B. T. (1972). Reasoning with negatives. *British Journal of Psychology, 63,* 213–219.

Evans, J. St B. T. (1983). Introduction. In J. St B. T. Evans (Ed.), *Thinking and reasoning: Psychological approaches* (pp. 1–15). London: Routledge & Kegan Paul.

Evans, J. St B. T. (1989). *Bias in human reasoning: Causes and consequences.* Hove, United Kingdom: Erlbaum.

Evans, J. St B. T., Barston, J. L., & Pollard, P. (1983). On the conflict between logic and belief in syllogistic reasoning. *Memory & Cognition, 11,* 295–306.

Evans, R. B. (1990). William James and his *Principles.* In M. G. Johnson & T. B. Henley (Eds.), *Reflections on The Principles of Psychology: William James after a century* (pp. 11–31). Hillsdale, NJ: Erlbaum.

Eysenck, M. W. (1982). *Attention and arousal.* Berlin: Springer-Verlag.

Eysenck, M. W. (1984). *A handbook of cognitive psychology.* London: Erlbaum.

Eysenck, M. W. (1990a). Creativity. In M. W. Eysenck (Ed.), *The Blackwell dictionary of cognitive psychology* (pp. 86–87). Oxford, England: Basil Blackwell.

Eysenck, M. W. (1990b). Introduction. In M. W. Eysenck (Ed.), *Cognitive psychology: An international review* (pp. 1–7). Chichester, England: John Wiley & Sons.

Eysenck, M. W., & Keane, M. T. (1990). *Cognitive psychology: A student's handbook.* London: Lawrence Erlbaum.

Fagen, J. W., & Rovee-Collier, C. (1983). Memory retrieval: A time-locked process in infancy. *Science, 222,* 1349–1351.

Faigley, L., & Miller, T. P. (1982). What we learn from writing on the job. *College English, 44,* 557–559.

Farah, M. J. (1988). Is visual imagery really visual? Overlooked evidence from neuropsychology. *Psychological Review, 95,* 307–317.

Farah, M. J., Peronnet, F., Gonon, M. A., & Giard, M. H. (1988). Electrophysiological evidence for a shared representational medium for visual images and percepts. *Journal of Experimental Psychology: General, 117,* 248–257.

Farah, M. J., & Smith, A. F. (1983). Perceptual interference and facilitation with auditory imagery. *Perception & Psychophysics, 33,* 475–478.

Farrar, M. J., & Goodman, G. S. (1990). Developmental differences in the relation between scripts and episodic memory: Do they exist? In R. Fivush & J. A. Hudson (Eds.), *Knowing and remembering in young children* (pp. 30–64). New York: Cambridge University Press.

Farthing, G. W. (1992). *The psychology of consciousness.* Englewood Cliffs, NJ: Prentice Hall.

Fenson, L., Dale, P., Reznick, S., Thal, D., Bates, E., Hartung, J., Pethick, S., & Reilly, J. (1991). *The MacArthur Communicative Development Inventories: Technical Manual.* San Diego: San Diego State University.

Ferber, R. (1991). Slip of the tongue or slip of the ear? On the perception and transcription of naturalistic slips of the tongue. *Journal of Psycholinguistic Research, 20,* 105–122.

Ferguson-Hessler, M. G. M., & DeJong, T. (1987). On the quality of knowledge in the field of electricity and magnetism. *American Journal of Physics, 55,* 492–497.

Fernald, A. (1985). Four-month-old infants prefer to listen to motherese. *Infant Behavior and Development, 8,* 181–195.

Finke, R. A. (1989). *Principles of mental imagery.* Cambridge, MA: MIT Press.

Finke, R. A., & Kosslyn, S. M. (1980). Mental imagery acuity in the peripheral visual field. *Journal of Experimental Psychology: Human Perception and Performance, 6,* 126–139.

Finke, R. A., Pinker, S., & Farah, M. J. (1989). Reinterpreting visual patterns in mental imagery. *Cognitive Science, 13*, 51–78.

Finke, R. A., & Schmidt, M. J. (1978). The quantitative measure of pattern representation in images using orientation-specific color aftereffects. *Perception & Psychophysics, 23*, 515–520.

Finke, R. A., & Shepard, R. N. (1986). Visual functions of mental imagery. In K. R. Boff, L. Kaufman, & J. Thomas (Eds.), *Handbook of perception and human performance* (Vol. 2, pp. 37-1–37-55). New York: Wiley.

Fischhoff, B. (1975). The silly certainty of hindsight. *Psychology Today, 8*, 71–72, 76.

Fischhoff, B. (1977). Perceived informativeness of facts. *Journal of Experimental Psychology: Human Perception and Performance, 3*, 349–358.

Fischhoff, B. (1982). Debiasing. In D. Kahneman, P. Slovic, & A. Tversky (Eds.), *Judgment under uncertainty: Heuristics and biases* (pp. 422–444). New York: Cambridge University Press.

Fisher, D. L. (1984). Central capacity limits in consistent mapping, visual search tasks: Four channels or more? *Cognitive Psychology, 16*, 449–484.

Fiske, S. T., & Taylor, S. E. (1991). *Social cognition* (2nd ed.). New York: McGraw-Hill.

Fivush, R., & Hamond, N. R. (1990). Autobiographical memory across the preschool years: Toward reconceptualizing childhood amnesia. In R. Fivush & J. A. Hudson (Eds.), *Knowing and remembering in young children* (pp. 223–248). New York: Cambridge University Press.

Flagg, P. W., Potts, G. R., & Reynolds, A. G. (1975). Instructions and response strategies in recognition memory for sentences. *Journal of Experimental Psychology: Human Learning and Memory, 1*, 592–598.

Flavell, J. H. (1971). First discussant's comments. What is memory development the development of? *Human Development, 14*, 272–278.

Flavell, J. H. (1979). Metacognition and cognitive monitoring. *American Psychologist, 34*, 906–911.

Flavell, J. H. (1985). *Cognitive development* (2nd ed.). Englewood Cliffs, NJ: Prentice-Hall.

Flavell, J. H., Beach, D. R., & Chinsky, J. M. (1966). Spontaneous verbal rehearsal in a memory task as a function of age. *Child Development, 37*, 283–299.

Flavell, J. H., Speers, J. R., Green, F. L., & August, D. L. (1981). The development of comprehension monitoring and knowledge about communication. *Monographs of the Society for Research in Child Development, 46* (5, Serial No. 192).

Flavell, J. H., & Wellman, H. M. (1977). Metamemory. In R. V. Kail, Jr., & J. W. Hagen (Eds.), *Perspectives on the development of memory and cognition* (pp. 3–34). Hillsdale, NJ: Erlbaum.

Fletcher, C. R. (1981). Short-term memory processes in text comprehension. *Journal of Verbal Learning and Verbal Behavior, 20*, 564–574.

Flores d'Arcais, G. B. (1988). Language perception. In F. J. Newmeyer (Ed.), *Linguistics: The Cambridge survey* (Vol. 3, pp. 97–123). Cambridge, England: Cambridge University Press.

Flower, L. S., & Hayes, J. R. (1980). The dynamics of composing: Making plans and juggling constraints. In L. W. Gregg & E. R. Steinberg (Eds.), *Cognitive processes in writing* (pp. 31–50). Hillsdale, NJ: Erlbaum.

Fodor, J. A., & Pylyshyn, Z. W. (1988). Connectionism and cognitive architecture: A critical analysis. *Cognition, 28*, 3–71.

Foley, M. A., Aman, C., & Gutch, D. (1987). Discriminating between action memories: Children's use of kinesthetic cues and visible consequences. *Journal of Experimental Child Psychology, 44*, 335–347.

Foley, M. A., Ratner, H. H., & Passalacqua, C. (1993). *Appropriating the actions of another: Implications for children's memory and learning.* Unpublished manuscript, Skidmore College.

Fong, G. T., Krantz, D. H., & Nisbett, R. E. (1986). The effects of statistical training on thinking about everyday problems. *Cognitive Psychology, 18*, 253–292.

Forster, K. (1981). Priming and the effects of sentence and lexical contexts on naming time: Evidence for autonomous lexical processing. *Quarterly Journal of Experimental Psychology, 33A*, 465–495.

Foss, D. J. (1970). Some effects of ambiguity upon sentence comprehension. *Journal of Verbal Learning and Verbal Behavior, 9,* 699–706.

Foss, D. J. (1988). Experimental pssycholinguistics. *Annual Review of Psychology, 39,* 301–348.

Foss, D. J., & Speer, S. R. (1991). Global and local context effects in sentence processing. In R. R. Hoffman & D. S. Palermo (Eds.), *Cognition and the symbolic processes: Applied and ecological perspectives* (pp. 115–139). Hillsdale, NJ: Erlbaum.

Foti, R. J., & Lord, R. G. (1987). Prototypes and scripts: The effects of alternative methods of processing information on rating accuracy. *Organizational Behavior and Human Decision Processes, 39,* 318–340.

Franklin, N., & Tversky, B. (1990). Searching imagined environments. *Journal of Experimental Psychology: General, 119,* 63–76.

Franklin, N., Tversky, B., & Coon, V. (1992). Switching points of view in spatial mental models. *Memory & Cognition, 20,* 507–518.

Franks, J. J., & Bransford, J. D. (1971). Abstraction of visual patterns. *Journal of Experimental Psychology, 90,* 65–74.

Frick, R. W. (1988). Issues of representation and limited capacity in the auditory short-term store. *British Journal of Psychology, 79,* 213–240.

Frick, R. W. (1990). The visual suffix effect in tests of the visual short-term store. *Bulletin of the Psychonomic Society, 28,* 101–104.

Friedman, S. (1972). Habituation and recovery of visual response in the alert human newborn. *Journal of Experimental Child Psychology, 13,* 339–349.

Fromkin, V. A. (1993). Speech production. In J. B. Berko-Gleason & N. B. Ratner (Eds.), *Psycholinguistics.* Fort Worth, TX: Harcourt Brace Jovanovich.

Fry, P. S., & Lupart, J. L. (1986). *Cognitive processes in children's learning.* Springfield, IL: Charles C. Thomas.

Galotti, K. M. (1989). Approaches to studying formal and everyday reasoning. *Psychological Bulletin, 105,* 331–351.

Galotti, K. M., Baron, J., & Sabini, J. P. (1986). Individual differences in syllogistic reasoning: Deduction rules or mental models? *Journal of Experimental Psychology: General, 115,* 16–25.

Ganellen, R. J., & Carver, C. S. (1985). Why does self-reference promote incidental encoding? *Journal of Experimental Social Psychology, 21,* 284–300.

Gardner, H. (1985). *The mind's new science: A history of the cognitive revolution.* New York: Basic Books.

Gardner, H. (1988, August). *Scientific psychology: Should we bury it or praise it?* Paper presented at the annual meeting of the American Psychological Association, Atlanta, GA.

Gardner, R. C., & Lambert, W. E. (1959). Motivational variables in second-language acquisition. *Canadian Journal of Psychology, 13,* 266–272.

Gärling, T., Böök, A., & Lindberg, E. (1985). Adults' memory representations of the spatial properties of their everyday physical environment. In R. Cohen (Ed.), *The development of spatial cognition* (pp. 141–184). Hillsdale, NJ: Erlbaum.

Garman, M. (1990). *Psycholinguistics.* Cambridge, England: Cambridge University Press.

Garner, R. (1987). *Metacognition and reading comprehension.* Norwood, NJ: Ablex.

Garner, W. R. (1979). Letter discrimination and identification. In A. D. Pick (Ed.), *Perception and its development: A tribute to Eleanor J. Gibson* (pp. 111–144). Hillsdale, NJ: Erlbaum.

Garrett, M. F. (1984). The organization of processing structures for language production: Applications to aphasic speech. In D. Caplan, A. R. Lecours, & A. Smith (Eds.), *Biological perspectives on language.* Cambridge, MA: MIT Press.

Garvey, C. (1984). *Children's talk.* Cambridge, MA: Harvard University Press.

Gebotys, R. J., & Claxton-Oldfield, S. P. (1989). Errors in the quantification of uncertainty: A product of heuristics or minimal probability knowledge base? *Applied Cognitive Psychology, 3,* 237–250.

Geiselman, R. E., & Glenny, J. (1977). Effects of imagining speakers' voices on the retention of words presented visually. *Memory & Cognition, 5,* 499–504.

Gellatly, A. (1986a). Solving problems. In A. Gellatly (Ed.), *The skilful mind: An introduction to cognitive psychology* (pp. 171–182). Milton Keynes, England: Open University Press.

Gellatly, A. (1986b). Skill at reasoning. In A. Gellatly (Ed.), *The skilful mind: An introduction to cognitive psychology* (pp. 159–170). Milton Keynes, England: Open University Press.

Gelman, R. (1979). Preschool thought. *American Psychologist, 34,* 900–905.

Genesee, F., Tucker, R., & Lambert, W. E. (1975). Communication skills of bilingual children. *Child Development, 46,* 1010–1014.

Gerrig, R. J., & Littman, M. L. (1990). Disambiguation by community membership. *Memory & Cognition, 18,* 331–338.

Gettys, C. F., Mehle, T., & Fisher, S. (1986). Plausibility assessments in hypothesis generation. *Organizational Behavior and Human Decision Processes, 37,* 14–33.

Gibbs, R. W. (1986). What makes some indirect speech acts conventional? *Journal of Memory and Language, 25,* 181–196.

Gibson, E. J. (1969). *Principles of perceptual learning and development.* New York: Prentice-Hall.

Gigerenzer, G., Hoffrage, U., & Kleinbölting, H. (1991). Probabilistic mental models: A Brunswikian theory of confidence. *Psychological Review, 98,* 506–528.

Gigerenzer, G., & Hug, K. (1992). Domain-specific reasoning: Social contracts, cheating, and perspective change. *Cognition, 43,* 127–171.

Gilhooly, K. J. (1982). *Thinking: Directed, undirected, and creative.* London: Academic Press.

Gilhooly, K. J. (1988). *Thinking: Directed, undirected, and creative* (2nd ed.). London: Academic Press.

Gilhooly, K. J. (Ed.). (1989). *Human and machine problem solving.* New York: Plenum.

Ginossar, Z., & Trope, Y. (1987). Problem solving in judgment under uncertainty. *Journal of Personality and Social Psychology, 52,* 464–474.

Glanzer, M. (1982). Short-term memory. In C. R. Puff (Ed.), *Handbook of research methods in human memory and cognition* (pp. 63–98). New York: Academic Press.

Glaser, R., & Chi, M. T. H. (1988). Overview. In M. T. H. Chi, R. Glaser, & M. J. Farr (Eds.), *The nature of expertise* (pp. xv–xxxvi). Hillsdale, NJ: Erlbaum.

Gleason, J. B., & Ratner, N. B. (Eds.). (1993a). *Psycholinguistics.* Fort Worth, TX: Harcourt Brace Jovanovich.

Gleason, J. B., & Ratner, N. B. (1993b). Language development in children. In J. B. Gleason & N. B. Ratner (Eds.), *Psycholinguistics.* Fort Worth, TX: Harcourt Brace Jovanovich.

Gleason, J. B., & Weintraub, S. (1976). The acquisition of routines in child language. *Language in Society, 5,* 129–136.

Glenberg, A. M., Sanocki, T., Epstein, W., & Morris, C. (1987). Enhancing calibration of comprehension. *Journal of Experimental Psychology: General,* 119–136.

Glover, J. A., Ronning, R. R., & Reynolds, C. R. (Eds.). (1989). *Handbook of creativity.* New York: Plenum.

Glucksberg, S. (1989). Metaphors in conversation: How are they understood? Why are they used? *Metaphor and Symbolic Activity, 4,* 125–143.

Glucksberg, S., Kreuz, R. J., & Rho, S. H. (1986). Context can constrain lexical access: Implications for models of language comprehension. *Journal of Experimental Psychology: Learning, Memory, and Cognition, 12,* 323–335.

Goldenberg, G., Podreka, I., Steiner, M., Suess, E., Deecke, L., & Willmes, K. (1988). Pattern of regional cerebral blood flow related to visual and motor imagery: Results of emission computerized tomography. In M. Denis, J. Engelkamp, & J. T. E. Richardson (Eds.), *Cognitive and neuropsychological approaches to mental imagery,* (pp. 363–373). Dordrecht, The Netherlands: Martinus Nijhoff Publishers.

Goldstein, A. G., Chance, J. E., & Schneller, G. R. (1989). Frequency of eyewitness identification in criminal cases: A survey of prosecutors. *Bulletin of the Psychonomic Society, 27,* 71–74.

Goldstein, E. B. (1989). *Sensation and perception* (3rd ed.) Belmont, CA: Wadsworth.

Goodglass, H., & Butters, N. (1988). Psychobiology of cognitive processes. In R. C. Atkinson, R. J. Herrnstein, G. Lindzey, & R. D. Luce (Eds.), *Stevens' handbook of experimental psychology* (Vol. 2, pp. 863–952). New York: Wiley.

Goodsitt, J. V., Morse, P. A., VerHoeve, J. N., & Cowan, N. (1984). Infant speech recognition in multisyllabic contexts. *Child Development, 55,* 903–910.

Goodwin, C. (1981). *Conversational organization.* New York: Academic Press.

Gordon, W. J. J. (1961). *Synectics: The development of creative capacity.* New York: Harper & Row.

Gowin, D. B. (1981). *Educating.* Ithaca, NY: Cornell University Press.

Graf, P., & Schacter, D. (1985). Implicit and explicit memory for new associations in normal and amnesic subjects. *Journal of Experimental Psychology: Learning, Memory, and Cognition, 11,* 501–518.

Green, B. F., McCloskey, M., & Caramazza, A. (1985). The relation of knowledge to problem solving, with examples from kinematics. In S. F. Chipman, J. W. Segal, & R. Glaser (Eds.), *Thinking and learning skills* (Vol. 2, pp. 127–139). Hillsdale, NJ: Erlbaum.

Green, G. M. (1989). *Pragmatics and natural language understanding.* Hillsdale, NJ: Erlbaum.

Greene, J. (1986). *Language understanding: A cognitive approach.* Milton Keynes, England: Open University Press.

Greene, R. L. (1986a). Sources of recency effects in free recall. *Psychological Bulletin, 99,* 221–228.

Greene, R. L. (1986b). A common basis for recency effects in immediate and delayed recall. *Journal of Experimental Psychology: Learning, Memory, and Cognition, 12,* 413–418.

Greene, R. L., & Samuel, A. G. (1986). Recency and suffix effects in serial recall of musical stimuli. *Journal of Experimental Psychology: Learning, Memory, and Cognition, 12,* 517–524.

Greeno, J. G. (1974). Hobbits and Orcs: Acquisition of a sequential concept. *Cognitive Psychology, 6,* 270–292.

Greeno, J. G. (1977). Process of understanding in problem solving. In N. J. Castellan, Jr., D. B. Pisoni, & G. R. Potts (Eds.), *Cognitive theory* (Vol. 2, pp. 43–84). Hillsdale, NJ: Erlbaum.

Greeno, J. G., & Simon, H. A. (1988). Problem solving and reasoning. In R. C. Atkinson, R. J. Herrnstein, G. Lindzey, & R. D. Luce (Eds.), *Stevens' handbook of experimental psychology*

(2nd ed., Vol. 2, pp. 589–672). New York: Wiley.

Greenwald, A. G., & Banaji, M. R. (1989). The self as a memory system: Powerful, but ordinary. *Journal of Personality and Social Psychology, 57,* 41–54.

Gregory, W. L., Cialdini, R. B., & Carpenter, K. M. (1982). Self-relevant scenarios as mediators of likelihood estimates and compliance: Does imagining make it so? *Journal of Personality and Social Psychology, 43,* 89–99.

Griggs, R. A., & Cox, J. R. (1982). The elusive thematic-materials effect in Wason's selection task. *British Journal of Psychology, 73,* 407–420.

Groninger, L. D. (1971). Mnemonic imagery and forgetting. *Psychonomic Science, 23,* 161–163.

Gross, T. F. (1985). *Cognitive development.* Monterey, CA: Brooks/Cole.

Gruneberg, M. M. (1978). The feeling of knowing, memory blocks and memory aids. In M. M. Gruneberg & P. Morris (Eds.), *Aspects of memory* (pp. 186–214). London: Methuen.

Guilford, J. P. (1967). *The nature of human intelligence.* New York: McGraw-Hill.

Haber, R. N. (1983a). The impending demise of the icon: A critique of the concept of iconic storage in visual information processing. *The Behavioral and Brain Sciences, 6,* 1–11.

Haber, R. N. (1983b). The icon is really dead. *Behavioral and Brain Sciences, 6,* 43–55.

Haber, R. N. (1985). An icon can have no worth in the real world: Comments on Loftus, Johnson, and Shimamura's "How much is an icon worth?" *Journal of Experimental Psychology: Human Perception and Performance, 11,* 374–378.

Haberlandt, K., Berian, C., & Sandson, J. (1980). The episode schema in story processing. *Journal of Verbal Learning and Verbal Behavior, 19,* 635–650.

Haberlandt, K., & Bingham, G. (1984). The effect of input direction on the processing of script statements. *Journal of Verbal Learning and Verbal Behavior, 23,* 162–177.

Haensly, P. A., & Reynolds, C. R. (1989). Creativity and intelligence. In J. A. Glover, R. R. Ronning, & C. R. Reynolds (Eds.), *Handbook of creativity* (pp. 135–145). New York: Plenum.

Hakuta, K. (1986). *Mirror of language: The debate on bilingualism.* New York: Basic Books.

Hale, S., Lima, S. D., & Myerson, J. (1991). General cognitive slowing in the nonlexical domain: An experimental validation. *Psychology and Aging, 6,* 512–521.

Halpern, D. F. (1987). Analogies as a critical thinking skill. In D. E. Berger, K. Pezdek, & W. P. Banks (Eds.), *Applications of cognitive psychology: Problem solving, education, and computing* (pp. 75–86). Hillsdale, NJ: Erlbaum.

Halpern, D. F. (1989). *Thought and knowledge: An introduction to critical thinking* (2nd ed.). Hillsdale, NJ: Erlbaum.

Halpern, D. F., Hansen, C., & Riefer, D. (1990). Analogies as an aid to understanding and memory. *Journal of Educational Psychology, 82,* 298–305.

Halpin, J. A., Puff, C. R., Mason, H. F., & Marston, S. P. (1984). Self-reference and incidental recall by children. *Bulletin of the Psychonomic Society, 22,* 87–89.

Handel, S. (1989). *Listening: An introduction to the perception of auditory events.* Cambridge, MA: MIT Press.

Hardiman, P. T., Dufresne, R., & Mestre, J. P. (1989). The relation between problem categorization and problem solving among experts and novices. *Memory & Cognition, 17,* 627–638.

Hardyck, C. D., & Petrinovitch, L. R. (1970). Subvocal speech and comprehension level as a function of the difficulty level of reading material. *Journal of Verbal Learning and Verbal Behavior, 9,* 647–652.

Harley, B. (1986). *Age in second language acquisition.* San Diego, CA: College–Hill Press.

Harris, G., Begg, I., & Upfold, D. (1980). On the role of the speaker's expectations in interpersonal communication. *Journal of Verbal Learning and Verbal Behavior, 19,* 597–607.

Harris, J. E. (1984). Remembering to do things: A forgotten topic. In J. E. Harris & P. E. Morris (Eds.), *Everyday memory, actions and absentmindedness* (pp. 71–92). London: Academic Press.

Harris, J. F., & Foley, M. A. (1992). *Developmental comparisons of memories for real and imagined events.* Unpublished manuscript.

Harris, P. L. (1978). Developmental aspects of memory. A review. In M. M. Gruneberg, P. E. Morris, & R. N. Sykes (Eds.), *Practical aspects of memory* (pp. 369–377). London: Academic Press.

Harris, R. J., Lee, D. J., Hensley, D. L., & Schoen, L. M. (1988). The effect of cultural script knowledge on memory for stories over time. *Discourse Processes, 11,* 413–431.

Harris, R. J., Sardarpoor-Bascom, F., & Meyer, T. (1989). The role of cultural knowledge in distorting recall for stories. *Bulletin of the Psychonomic Society, 27,* 9–10.

Harris, R. J., Trusty, M. L., Bechtold, J. I., & Wasinger, L. (1989). Memory for implied versus directly stated advertising claims. *Psychology & Marketing, 6,* 87–96.

Hartman, M., & Hasher, L. (1991). Aging and suppression: Memory for previously relevant information. *Psychology and Aging, 6,* 587–594.

Hasher, L., & Zacks, R. T. (1988). Working memory, comprehension, and aging: A review and a new view. *The Psychology of Learning and Motivation, 22,* 193–225.

Haviland, S. E., & Clark, H. H. (1974). What's new? Acquiring new information as a process in comprehension. *Journal of Verbal Learning and Verbal Behavior, 13,* 512–521.

Hawkins, H. L., & Presson, J. C. (1986). Auditory information processing. In K. R. Boff, L. Kaufman, & J. P. Thomas (Eds.), *Handbook of perception and human performance* (Vol. II, pp. 26-1-26-44). New York: Wiley.

Hawkins, S. A., & Hastie, R. (1990). Hindsight: Biased judgments of past events after the outcomes are known. *Psychological Bulletin, 107,* 311–327.

Hayes, D. S., Scott, L. C., Chemelski, B. E., & Johnson, J. (1987). Physical and emotional states as memory-relevant factors: Cognitive monitoring by young children. *Merrill-Palmer Quarterly, 33,* 473–487.

Hayes, J. R. (1978). *Cognitive psychology: Thinking and creating.* Homewood, IL: Dorsey Press.

Hayes, J. R. (1989a). Writing research: The analysis of a very complex task. In D. Klahr & K. Kotovsky (Eds.), *Complex information processing: The impact of Herbert A. Simon* (pp. 209–234). Hillsdale, NJ: Erlbaum.

Hayes, J. R. (1989b). *The complete problem solver* (2nd ed.). Hillsdale, NJ: Erlbaum.

Hayes, J. R. (1989c). Cognitive processes in creativity. In J. A. Glover, R. R. Ronning, & C. R. Reynolds (Eds.), *Handbook of creativity* (pp. 135–145). New York: Plenum.

Hayes, J. R., & Flower, L. S. (1986). Writing research and the writer. *American Psychologist, 41*, 1106–1113.

Hayes, J. R., Flower, L. S., Schriver, K. A., Stratman, J., & Carey, L. (1987). Cognitive processes in revision. In S. Rosenberg (Ed.), *Advances in psycholinguistics: Vol. 2. Reading, writing, and languages processing.* Cambridge, England: Cambridge University Press.

Hearnshaw, L. S. (1987). *The shaping of modern psychology.* London: Routledge & Kegan Paul.

Hearst, E. (1979). One hundred years: Themes and perspectives. In E. Hearst (Ed.), *The first century of experimental psychology* (pp. 1–38). Hillsdale, NJ: Erlbaum.

Hearst, E. (1991). Psychology and nothing. *American Scientist, 79*, 432–443.

Heibeck, T. H., & Markman, E. M. (1987). Word learning in children: An examination of fast mapping. *Child Development, 58*, 1021–1034.

Hennessey, B. A., & Amabile, T. M. (1984, April). *The effect of reward and task label on children's verbal creativity.* Paper presented at the annual meeting of the Eastern Psychological Association, Baltimore, MD.

Hennessey, B. A., & Amabile, T. M. (1988). The conditions of creativity. In R. J. Sternberg (Ed.), *The nature of creativity: Contemporary psychological perspectives* (pp. 11–38). New York: Cambridge University Press.

Herrmann, D. J. (1990). Self-perceptions of memory performance. In W. K. Schaie, J. Rodin, & C. Schooler (Eds.), *Self-directedness and efficacy: Causes and effects throughout the life course* (pp. 199–211). Hillsdale, NJ: Erlbaum.

Herrmann, D. J. (1991). *Super memory.* Emmaus, PA: Rodale Press.

Herrmann, D. J., & Petro, S. J. (1990). Commercial memory aids. *Applied Cognitive Psychology, 4*, 439–450.

Herrmann, D. J., Rea, A., & Andrzejewski, S. (1987, August). *The need for a new approach to memory training.* Paper presented at the Second Practical Aspects of Memory Conference, Cardiff, Wales.

Herrmann, D. J., & Searleman, A. (1990). The new multimodal approach to memory improvement. *The Psychology of Learning and Motivation, 26*, 175–205.

Hershey, D. A., Walsh, D. A., Read, S. J., & Chulef, A. S. (1990). The effects of expertise on financial problem solving: Evidence for goal-directed, problem-solving scripts. *Organizational Behavior and Human Decision Processes, 46*, 77–101.

Hertzog, C., Dixon, R. A., & Hultsch, D. F. (1990). Relationships between metamemory, memory predictions, and memory task performance in adults. *Psychology and Aging, 5*, 215–227.

Hill, J. W., & Bliss, J. C. (1968). Modeling a tactile sensory register. *Perception & Psychophysics, 4*, 91–101.

Hill, R. D., Evankovich, K. D., Sheikh, J. I., & Yesavage, J. A. (1987). Imagery mnemonic training in a patient with primary degenerative dementia. *Psychology and Aging, 2*, 204–205.

Hinsley, D., Hayes, J. R., & Simon, H. A. (1977). From words to equations: Meaning and representation in algebra word-problems. In P. Carpenter & M. Just (Eds.), *Cognitive processes in comprehension* (pp. 89–108). Hillsdale, NJ: Erlbaum.

Hintzman, D. L. (1978). *The psychology of learning and memory.* San Francisco: Freeman.

Hintzman, D. L. (1986). "Schema abstraction" in a multiple-trace memory model. *Psychological Review, 93*, 411–428.

Hirschberg, N. W. (1977). Predicting performance in graduate school. Human judgment and decision processes in applied settings. In M. F. Kaplan & S. Schwartz (Eds.), *Human judgment and decision processes in applied settings* (pp. 95–124). New York: Academic Press.

Hirsh-Pasek, K., Kemler Nelson, D., Jusczyk, P., Cassidy, K., Druss, B., & Kennedy, L. (1987). Clauses are perceptual units for young infants. *Cognition, 26*, 269–286.

Hirst, W. (1984). Factual memory? *The Behavioral and Brain Sciences, 7*, 241–242.

Hirst, W. (1986). The psychology of attention. In J. E. LeDoux & W. Hirst (Eds.), *Mind and brain* (pp. 105–141). Cambridge, England: Cambridge University Press.

Hirst, W. (1988). Improving memory. In M. S. Gazzaniga (Ed.), *Perspectives in memory research* (pp. 219–244). Cambridge, MA: Bradford.

Hirst, W. (1989). On consciousness, recall, recognition, and the architecture of memory. In S. Lewandowsky, J. C. Dunn, & K. Kirsner (Eds.), *Implicit memory: Theoretical issues* (pp. 33–46). Hillsdale, NJ: Erlbaum.

Hirst, W., Spelke, E., Reaves, C. C., Caharack, G., & Neisser, U. (1980). Dividing attention without alternation or automaticity. *Journal of Experimental Psychology: General, 109,* 98–117.

Hirtle, S. C., & Jonides, J. (1985). Evidence of hierarchies in cognitive maps. *Memory & Cognition, 13,* 208–217.

Hirtle, S. C., & Mascolo, M. F. (1986). Effect of semantic clustering on the memory of spatial locations. *Journal of Experimental Psychology: Learning, Memory, and Cognition, 12,* 182–189.

Hitch, G. J., Halliday, S., Schaafstal, A. M., & Schraagen, M. C. (1988). Visual working memory in young children. *Memory & Cognition, 16,* 120–132.

Hoff-Ginsberg, E., & Shatz, M. (1982). Linguistic input and the child's acquisition of language. *Psychological Bulletin, 92,* 3–26.

Hoffman, J. E. (1986). The psychology of perception. In J. E. LeDoux & W. Hirst (Eds.), *Mind and brain: Dialogues in cognitive neuroscience* (pp. 7–32). New York: Cambridge University Press.

Hogarth, R. M. (Ed.). (1990). *Insights in decision making.* Chicago: University of Chicago Press.

Holland, J. H., Holyoak, K. J., Nisbett, R. E., & Thagard, P. R. (1987). *Induction: Processes of inference, learning, and discovery.* Cambridge, MA: MIT Press.

Holmes, V. M. (1984). Parsing strategies and discourse context. *Journal of Psycholinguistic Research, 13,* 237–257.

Holmes, V. M., Kennedy, A., & Murray, W. S. (1987). Syntactic structure and the garden path. *Quarterly Journal of Experimental Psychology, 39A,* 277–293.

Holyoak, K. J., & Koh, K. (1987). Surface and structural similarity in analogical transfer. *Memory & Cognition, 15,* 332–340.

Hornby, P. A. (1974). Surface structure and presupposition. *Journal of Verbal Learning and Verbal Behavior, 13,* 530–538.

Horowitz, L. M., Wright, J. C., Lowenstein, E., & Parad, H. W. (1981). The prototype as a construct in abnormal psychology: 1. A method for deriving prototypes. *Journal of Abnormal Psychology, 90,* 568–574.

Horton, D. L., & Mills, C. B. (1984). Human learning and memory. *Annual Review of Psychology, 35,* 361–394.

Hoving, K. L., Spencer, T., Robb, K., & Schulte, D. (1978). Developmental changes in visual information processing. In P. A. Ornstein (Ed.), *Memory development in children* (pp. 21–68). Hillsdale, NJ: Erlbaum.

Hubel, D. H. (1982). Explorations of the primary visual cotex, 1955–1978. *Nature, 299,* 515–524.

Hubel, D. H., & Wiesel, T. N. (1965). Receptive fields of single neurons in two nonstriate visual areas (18 and 19) of the cat. *Journal of Neurophysiology, 28,* 229–289.

Hubel, D. H., & Wiesel, T. N. (1979). Brain mechanisms and vision. *Scientific American, 241*(3), 150–162.

Huber, V. L., Neale, M. A., & Northcraft, G. B. (1987a). Judgment by heuristics: Effects of ratee and rater characteristics and performance standards on performance-related judgments. *Organizational Behavior and Human Decision Processes, 40,* 149–169.

Huber, V. L., Neale, M. A., & Northcraft, G. B. (1987b). Decision bias and personnel selection strategies. *Organizational Behavior and Human Decision Processes, 40,* 136–147.

Huey, E. B. (1968). *The psychology and pedagogy of reading.* Cambridge, MA: MIT Press. (Original work published 1908)

Hulicka, I. M. (1982). Memory functioning in late adulthood. In F. I. M. Craik & S. Trehub (Eds.), *Aging and cognitive processes* (pp. 331–351). New York: Plenum.

Hulicka, I. M., & Grossman, J. L. (1967). Age-group comparison for the use of mediators in paired-associate learning. *Journal of Gerontology, 22,* 46–57.

Hulme, C., & Tordoff, V. (1989). Working memory development: The effects of speech rate, word length, and acoustic similarity on serial recall. *Journal of Experimental Child Psychology, 47*, 72–87.

Humphreys, M. S., Bain, J. D., & Pike, R. (1989). Different ways to cue a coherent memory system: A theory for episodic, semantic, and procedural tasks. *Psychological Review, 96*, 208–233.

Hunt, E. (1989). Cognitive science: Definition, status, and questions. *Annual Review of Psychology, 40*, 603–629.

Hunt, E., & Lansman, M. (1986). Unified model of attention and problem solving. *Psychological Review, 93*, 446–461.

Hunt, R. R., & Elliott, J. M. (1980). The role of nonsemantic information in memory: Orthographic distinctiveness effects on retention. *Journal of Experimental Psychology: General, 109*, 49–74.

Hurford, J. R. (1991). The evolution of the critical period for language acquisition. *Cognition, 40*, 159–201.

The 1991 Information Please Almanac (1991). Boston: Houghton Mifflin.

Intons-Peterson, M. J. (1983). Imagery paradigms: How vulnerable are they to experimenters' expectations? *Journal of Experimental Psychology: Learning, Memory, and Cognition, 10*, 699–715.

Intons-Peterson, M. J. (1993). External memory aids and their relation to memory. In C. Izawa (Ed.), *Cognitive psychology applied*. Hillsdale, NJ: Erlbaum.

Intons-Peterson, M. J., & Fournier, J. (1986). External and internal memory aids: When and how often do we use them? *Journal of Experimental Psychology: General, 115*, 267–280.

Intons-Peterson, M. J., & McDaniel, M. A. (1991). Symmetries and asymmetries between imagery and perception. In C. Cornoldi & M. A. McDaniel (Eds.), *Imagery and cognition* (pp. 47–76). New York: Springer-Verlag.

Intons-Peterson, M. J., & Newsome, G. L., III. (1992). External memory aids: Effects and effectiveness. In D. Herrmann, H. Weingartner, A. Searleman, & C. McEvoy (Eds.), *Memory improvement: Implications for memory theory* (pp. 101–121). New York: Springer Verlag.

Intons-Peterson, M. J., Russell, W., & Dressel, S. (1992). The role of pitch in auditory imagery. *Journal of Experimental Psychology: Human Perception and Performance, 18*, 233–240.

Intons-Peterson, M. J., & Smyth, M. M. (1987). The anatomy of repertory memory. *Journal of Experimental Psychology: Learning, Memory, and Cognition, 13*, 490–500.

Irwin, D. E., Zacks, J. L., & Brown, J. S. (1990). Visual memory and the perception of a stable visual environment. *Perception & Psychophysics, 47*, 35–46.

Irwin, D. E., & Yeomans, J. M. (1986). Sensory registration and informational persistence. *Journal of Experimental Psychology: Human Perception and Performance, 12*, 343–360.

Jackson, S. L., & Griggs, R. A. (1988). Education and the selection task. *Bulletin of the Psychonomic Society, 26*, 327–330.

Jackson, S. L., & Griggs, R. A. (1990). The elusive pragmatic reasoning schemas effect. *The Quarterly Journal of Experimental Psychology, 42A*, 353–373.

Jacoby, L. L. (1983). Remembering the data: Analyzing interactive processes in reading. *Journal of Verbal Learning and Verbal Behavior, 22*, 485–508.

James, W. (1890). *The principles of psychology*. New York: Henry Holt.

Jarvella, R. J. (1971). Syntactic processing of connected speech. *Journal of Verbal Learning and Verbal Behavior, 10*, 409–416.

Jenkins, F., & Davies, G. (1985). Contamination of facial memory through exposure to misleading composite pictures. *Journal of Applied Psychology, 70*, 164–176.

Jenkins, J. J. (1974). Remember that old theory of memory? Well, forget it. *American Psychologist, 29*, 785–795.

Jespersen, O. (1922). *Language*. London: George Allen and Unwin.

Johns, J. L. (1986). Students' perceptions of reading: Thirty years of inquiry. In D. B. Yaden, Jr., & S. Templeton (Eds.), *Metalinguistic awareness and beginning literacy: Conceptualizing what it means to read and write* (pp. 31–40). Portsmouth, NH: Heinemann.

Johnson, J. S., & Newport, E. L. (1989). Critical effects in second language learning: The influence of maturational state on the acquisition of English as a second language. *Cognitive Psychology, 21*, 60–99.

Johnson, M. K. (1988). Reality monitoring: An experimental phenomenological approach. *Journal of Experimental Psychology: General, 117*, 390–394.

Johnson, M. K., & Hasher, L. (1987). Human learning and memory. *Annual Review of Psychology, 38*, 631–668.

Johnson, M. K., & Raye, C. L. (1981). Reality monitoring. *Psychological Review, 88*, 67–85.

Johnson, N. F. (1991). Holistic models of word recognition. In R. R. Hoffman & D. S. Palermo (Eds.), *Cognition and the symbolic processes: Applied and ecological perspectives* (pp. 79–94). Hillsdale, NJ: Erlbaum.

Johnson, R. D. (1987). Making judgments when information is missing: Inferences, biases, and framing effects. *Acta Psychologica, 66*, 69–72.

Johnson-Laird, P. N. (1974). Experimental psycholinguistics. *Annual Review of Psychology, 25*, 135–160.

Johnson-Laird, P. N. (1988). *The computer and the mind: An introduction to cognitive science.* Cambridge, MA: Harvard University Press.

Johnson-Laird, P. N., & Bara, B. G. (1984). Syllogistic inference. *Cognition, 16*, 1–61.

Johnson-Laird, P. N., & Byrne, R. M. J. (1991). *Deduction.* Hove, Great Britain: Erlbaum.

Johnson-Laird, P. N., Herrmann, D. J., & Chaffin, R. (1984). Only connections: A critique of semantic networks. *Psychological Bulletin, 96*, 292–315.

Johnson-Laird, P. N., & Steedman, M. (1978). The psychology of syllogisms. *Cognitive Psychology, 10*, 64–99.

Johnston, W. A., & Dark, V. J. (1986). Selective attention. *Annual Review of Psychology, 37*, 43–75.

Jolicoeur, P. (1985). The time to name disoriented natural objects. *Memory & Cognition, 13*, 289–303.

Jolicoeur, P., & Kosslyn, S. M. (1985a). Demand characteristics in image scanning experiments. *Journal of Mental Imagery, 9*, 41–50.

Jolicoeur, P., & Kosslyn, S. M. (1985b). Is time to scan visual images due to demand characteristics? *Memory & Cognition, 13*, 320–332.

Jolicoeur, P., & Landau, M. J. (1984). Effects of orientation on the identification of simple visual patterns. *Canadian Journal of Psychology, 38*, 80–93.

Jolicoeur, P., Snow, D., & Murray, J. (1987). The time to identify disoriented letters: Effects of practice and font. *Canadian Journal of Psychology, 41*, 303–316.

Jonides, J., Naveh-Benjamin, M., & Palmer, J. (1985). Assessing automaticity. *Acta Psychologica, 60*, 157–171.

Jordan, K., & Huntsman, L. A. (1990). Image rotation of misoriented letter strings: Effects of orientation cuing and repetition. *Perception & Psychophysics, 48*, 363–374.

Jusczyk, P. W. (1986). Speech perception. In K. R. Boff, L. Kaufman, & J. P. Thomas (Eds.), *Handbook of perception and human performance* (pp. 27-1–27-57). Hillsdale, NJ: Erlbaum.

Just, M. A., & Carpenter, P. A. (1984). Reading skills and skilled reading in the comprehension of text. In H. Mandl, N. L. Stein, & T. Trabasso (Eds.), *Learning and comprehension of text* (pp. 307–329). Hillsdale, NJ: Erlbaum.

Just, M. A., & Carpenter, P. A. (1985). Cognitive coordinate systems: Accounts of mental rotation and individual differences in spatial ability. *Psychological Review, 92*, 137–172.

Just, M. A., & Carpenter, P. A. (1987). *The psychology of reading and language comprehension.* Newton, MA: Allyn and Bacon.

Just, M. A., & Carpenter, P. A. (1992). A capacity theory of comprehension: Individual differences in working memory. *Psychological Review, 99*, 122–149.

Kahneman, D., & Tversky, A. (1972). Subjective probability: A judgment of representativeness. *Cognitive Psychology, 3*, 430–454.

Kahneman, D., & Tversky, A. (1973). On the psychology of prediction. *Psychological Review, 80*, 237–251.

Kahneman, D., & Tversky, A. (1979). Prospect theory: An analysis of decision under risk. *Econometrica, 47*, 263–291.

Kahneman, D., & Tversky, A. (1982). The simulation heuristic. In D. Kahneman, P. Slovic, & A. Tversky (Eds.), *Judgment under uncertainty: Heuristics and biases* (pp. 201–208). New York: Cambridge University Press.

Kahneman, D., & Tversky, A. (1984). Choices, values, and frames. *American Psychologist, 39*, 341–350.

Kahney, H. (1986). *Problem solving: A cognitive approach*. Milton Keynes, England: Open University Press.

Kail, R. V., Jr. (1990). *The development of memory in children* (3rd ed.). New York: Freeman.

Kail, R. V., Jr., & Siegel, A. W. (1977). The development of mnemonic encoding in children. From perception to abstraction. In R. V. Kail, Jr., & J. W. Hagen (Eds.), *Perspectives on the development of memory and cognition* (pp. 61–88). Hillsdale, NJ: Erlbaum.

Kardash, C. A. M., Royer, J. M., & Greene, B. A. (1988). Effects of schemata on both encoding and retrieval of information from prose. *Journal of Educational Psychology, 80*, 324–329.

Kasper, L. F., & Glass, A. L. (1988). An extension of the keyword method facilitates the acquisition of simple Spanish sentences. *Applied Cognitive Psychology, 2*, 137–146.

Katz, A. N. (1981). Knowing about the sensory properties of objects. *Quarterly Journal of Experimental Psychology, 33A*, 39–49.

Katz, A. N. (1987). Self-reference in the encoding of creative-relevant traits. *Journal of Personality, 55*, 97–120.

Kaufman, N. J., Randlett, A. L., & Price, J. (1985). Awareness of the use of comprehension strategies in good and poor college readers. *Reading Psychology, 6*, 1–11.

Kaufmann, G. (1985). A theory of symbolic representation in problem solving. *Journal of Mental Imagery, 9*, 51–70.

Kausler, D. H. (1982). *Experimental psychology and human aging*. New York: Wiley.

Keane, M. T. (1988). *Analogical problem solving*. Chichester, England: Ellis Horwood.

Keil, F. C. (1989). *Concepts, kinds, and cognitive development*. Cambridge, MA: MIT Press.

Keil, F. C. (1991). On being more than the sum of the parts: The conceptual coherence of cognitive science. *Psychological Science, 2*, 283, 287–293.

Keil, F. C., & Batterman, N. (1984). A characteristic-to-defining shift in the development of word meaning. *Journal of Verbal Learning and Verbal Behavior, 23*, 221–236.

Kellogg, R. T. (1987). Effects of topic knowledge on the allocation of processing time and cognitive effort to writing processes. *Memory & Cognition, 15*, 256–266.

Kellogg, R. T. (1988). Attentional overload and writing performance: Effects of rough draft and outline strategies. *Journal of Experimental Psychology: Learning, Memory, and Cognition, 14*, 355–365.

Kellogg, R. T. (1989). Idea processors: Computer aids for planning and composing text. In B. K. Britton & S. M. Glynn (Eds.), *Computer writing environments: Theory, research, and design* (pp. 57–92). Hillsdale, NJ: Erlbaum.

Kellogg, R. T. (1990). Effectiveness of prewriting strategies as a function of task demands. *American Journal of Psychology, 103*, 327–342.

Kendler, H. H. (1987). *Historical foundations of modern psychology*. Pacific Grove, CA: Brooks/Cole.

Kent, D. (1990, January). A conversation with Lynn Cooper. *APS Observer, 3*, 11–13.

Keren, G. (1984). On the importance of identifying the correct "problem space." *Cognition, 16*, 121–128.

Keren, G. (1987). Facing uncertainty in the game of bridge: A calibration study. *Organizational Behavior and Human Decision Processes, 39*, 98–114.

Kiewra, K. A. (1985). Investigation notetaking and review: A depth of processing alternative. *Educational Psychologist, 20*, 23–32.

Kihlstrom, J. F. (1987). The cognitive unconscious. *Science, 237*, 1445–1452.

Kimball, J. P. (1973). Seven principles of surface structure parsing in natural language. *Cognition, 2*, 15–47.

King, J., & Just, M. A. (1991). Individual differences in syntactic processing: The role of working memory. *Journal of Memory and Language, 30*, 580–602.

Kintsch, W. (1984). Approaches to the study of the psychology of language. In T. G. Bever, J. M. Carroll, & L. A. Miller (Eds.), *Talking minds: The study of language in cognitive science* (pp. 111–145). Cambridge, MA: MIT Press.

Kintsch, W. (1988). The role of knowledge in discourse comprehension: A construction-integration model. *Psychological Review, 95*, 163–182.

Kintsch, W., & Buschke, H. (1969). Homophones and synonyms in short-term memory. *Journal of Experimental Psychology, 80*, 403–407.

Kintsch, W., & Greeno, J. G. (1985). Understanding and solving word arithmetic problems. *Psychological Review, 92*, 109–129.

Kintsch, W., & Van Dijk, T. A. (1978). Toward a model of text comprehension and production. *Psychological Review, 85*, 363–394.

Klaczynski, P. A., Gelfand, H., & Reese, H. W. (1989). Transfer of conditional reasoning: Effects of explanations and initial problem types. *Memory & Cognition, 17*, 208–220.

Klatzky, R. L. (1980). *Human memory: Structures and processes* (2nd ed.). San Francisco: Freeman.

Klein, S. B., & Kihlstrom, J. F. (1986). Elaboration, organization, and the self-reference effect in memory. *Journal of Experimental Psychology: General, 115*, 26–38.

Kline, D. W., & Orme-Rogers, C. (1978). Examination of stimulus persistence as the basis for superior visual identification performance among older adults. *Journal of Gerontology, 33*, 76–81.

Kline, D. W., & Schieber, F. (1981). What are the age differences in visual sensory memory? *Journal of Gerontology, 36*, 86–89.

Kobasigawa, A. (1974). Utilization of retrieval cues by children in recall. *Child Development, 45*, 127–134.

Koestler, A. (1964). *The act of creation.* London: Hutchinson.

Koriat, A., Ben-Zur, H., & Nussbaum, A. (1990). Encoding information for future action: Memory for to-be-performed tasks versus memory for to-be-recalled tasks. *Memory & Cognition, 18*, 568–578.

Koriat, A., Lichtenstein, S., & Fischhoff, B. (1980). Reasons for confidence. *Journal of Experimental Psychology: Human Learning and Memory, 6*, 107–118.

Koriat, A., & Melkman, R. (1987). Depth of processing and memory organization. *Psychological Research, 49*, 183–188.

Kosslyn, S. M. (1975). Information representation in visual images. *Cognitive Psychology, 7*, 341–370.

Kosslyn, S. M. (1976). Using imagery to retrieve semantic information: A developmental study. *Child Development, 47*, 433–444.

Kosslyn, S. M. (1981). The medium and the message in mental imagery: A theory. *Psychological Review, 88*, 46–65.

Kosslyn, S. M. (1983). *Ghosts in the mind's machine: Creating and using images in the brain.* New York: Norton.

Kosslyn, S. M. (1987). Seeing and imagining in the cerebral hemispheres: A computational approach. *Psychological Review, 94*, 148–175.

Kosslyn, S. M. (1988). Aspects of a cognitive neuroscience of mental imagery. *Science, 240*, 1621–1626.

Kosslyn, S. M. (1990). Mental imagery. In D. N. Osherson, S. M. Kosslyn, & J. M. Hollerback (Eds.), *Visual cognition and action: An invitation to cognitive science* (Vol. 2, pp. 73–97). Cambridge, MA: MIT Press.

Kosslyn, S. M., Ball, T. M., & Reiser, B. J. (1978). Visual images preserve metric spatial information: Evidence from studies of image scanning. *Journal of Experimental Psychology: Human Perception & Performance, 4*, 47–60.

Kosslyn, S. M., & Koenig, O. (1992). *Wet mind: The new cognitive neuroscience.* New York: The Free Press.

Kosslyn, S. M., Seger, C., Pani, J. R., & Hillger, L. A. (1990). When is imagery used in everyday life? A diary study. *Journal of Mental Imagery, 14*, 131–152.

Kotovsky, K., Hayes, J. R., & Simon, H. A. (1985). Why are some problems hard? Evidence from Tower of Hanoi. *Cognitive Psychology, 17*, 248–294.

Kotovsky, K., & Kushmerick, N. (1991). Processing constraints and problem difficulty: A model. *Proceedings of the 13th Annual Meeting of the Cognitive Science Society*. Hillsdale, NJ: Erlbaum.

Kotovsky, K., & Simon, H. A. (1990). What makes some problems really hard: Explorations in the problem space of difficulty. *Cognitive Psychology, 22*, 143–183.

Kounios, J., Osman, A. M., & Meyer, D. E. (1987). Structure and process in semantic memory: New evidence based on speed-accuracy decomposition. *Journal of Experimental Psychology: General, 116*, 3–25.

Kozielecki, J. (1981). *Psychological decision theory*. Warsaw, Poland: Polish Scientific Publishers.

Kreutzer, M. A., Leonard, C., & Flavell, J. H. (1975). An interview study of children's knowledge about memory. *Monographs of the Society for Research in Child Development, 40*(1, Serial No. 159).

Krueger, L. E. (1992). The word-superiority effect and phonological recoding. *Memory & Cognition, 20*, 685–694.

Kuczaj, S. A., II. (1977). The acquisition of regular and irregular past tense forms. *Journal of Verbal Learning and Verbal Behavior, 16*, 589–600.

Kuczaj, S. A. (1983). *Crib speech and language play*. New York: Springer-Verlag.

Kuhl, P. K. (1987). Perception of speech and sound in early infancy. In P. Salapatek & L. Cohen (Eds.), *Handbook of infant perception* (Vol. 2, pp. 275–382). Orlando, FL: Academic Press.

Kuhl, P. K. (1989). On babies, birds, modules, and mechanisms: A comparative approach to the acquisition of vocal communication. In R. J. Dooling & S. H. Hulse (Eds.), *The comparative psychology of audition: Perceiving complex sounds* (pp. 379–419). Hillsdale, NJ: Erlbaum.

Kuhl, P. K., Williams, K. A., Lacerda, F., Stevens, K. N., & Lindblom, B. (1992). Linguistic experience alters phonetic perception in infants by 6 months of age. *Science, 255*, 606–608.

Kunda, Z., & Nisbett, R. E. (1986). The psychometrics of everyday life. *Cognitive Psychology, 18*, 195–224.

Kurdek, L. A. (1987). Sex role self schema and psychological adjustment in coupled homosexual and heterosexual men and women. *Sex Roles, 17*, 549–562.

LaBerge, D. L. (1990). Attention. *Psychological Science, 1*, 156–162.

Lachman, M. E. (1991). Perceived control over memory aging: Developmental and intervention perspectives. *Journal of Social Issues, 47*, 159–175.

Lachter, J., & Bever, T. G. (1988). The relation between linguistic structure and associative theories of language learning—A constructive critique of some connectionist learning models. *Cognition, 28*, 195–247.

Lambert, W. E. (1987). The effects of bilingual and bicultural experiences on children's attitudes and social perspectives. In P. Homel, M. Palij, & D. Aaronson (Eds.), *Childhood bilingualism: Aspects of linguistic, cognitive, and social development* (pp. 197–228). Hillsdale, NJ: Erlbaum.

Lambert, W. E. (1990). Persistent issues in bilingualism. In B. Harley, P. Allen, J. Cummins, & M. Swain (Eds.), *The development of second language proficiency* (pp. 201–218). Cambridge, England: Cambridge University Press.

Lambert, W. E. (1992). Challenging established views on social issues. *American Psychologist, 47*, 533–542.

Lambert, W. E., Genesee, F., Holobow, N., & Chartrand, L. (1991). *Bilingual education for majority English-speaking children*. Montreal, Quebec, Canada: McGill University, Psychology Department.

Langer, E. J. (1989). *Mindlessness/mindfulness*. Reading, MA: Addison-Wesley.

Larkin, J. H. (1983). The role of problem representation in physics. In D. Gentner & A. L. Stevens (Eds.), *Mental models* (pp. 75–98). Hillsdale, NJ: Erlbaum.

Larkin, J. H. (1985). Understanding, problem representations, and skill in physics. In S. F. Chipman, J. W. Segal, & R. Glaser (Eds.), *Thinking and learning skills* (Vol. 2, pp. 141–159). Hillsdale, NJ: Erlbaum.

Larkin, J. H., & Simon, H. A. (1987). Why a diagram is (sometimes) worth ten thousand words. *Cognitive Science, 11*, 65–99.

Lau, R. R., & Sears, D. O. (Eds.). (1986). *Political cognition*. Hillsdale, NJ: Erlbaum.

Lave, J. (1988). *Cognition in practice*. New York: Cambridge University Press.

Lavigne, V. D., & Finley, G. E. (1990). Memory in middle-aged adults. *Educational Gerontology, 16*, 447–461.

Leal, L. (1987). Investigation of the relation between metamemory and university students' examination performance. *Journal of Educational Psychology, 79*, 35–40.

LeDoux, J. E., & Hirst, W. (1986). Cognitive neuroscience: An overview. In J. E. LeDoux & W. Hirst (Eds.), *Mind and brain: Dialogues in cognitive neuroscience*. Cambridge, MA: Cambridge University Press.

Lehnert, W. G. (1984). The architecture of the mind [Review of *The architecture of cognition*]. *Contemporary Psychology, 29*, 854–856.

Lempert, H., & Kinsbourne, M. (1985). Possible origin of speech in selective orienting. *Psychological Bulletin, 97*, 62–73.

Lenneberg, E. H. (1967). *Biological foundations of language*. New York: Wiley.

Lesgold, A. (1988). Problem solving. In R. J. Sternberg & E. E. Smith (Eds.), *The psychology of human thought* (pp. 188–213). Cambridge, England: Cambridge University Press.

Levelt, W. J. M. (1989). *Speaking: From intention to articulation*. Cambridge, MA: MIT Press.

Levin, I. P., Schnittjer, S. K., & Thee, S. L. (1988). Information framing effects in social and personal decisions. *Journal of Experimental Social Psychology, 24*, 520–529.

Levine, M. A. (1988). *Effective problem solving*. Englewood Cliffs, NJ: Prentice-Hall.

Lewandowsky, S., Dunn, J. C., & Kirsner, K. (Eds.). (1989). *Implicit memory: Theoretical issues*. Hillsdale, NJ: Lawrence Erlbaum.

Liben, L. S. (1982). The developmental study of children's memory. In T. M. Field, A. Huston, H. C. Quay, L. Troll, & G. E. Finley (Eds.), *Review of human development* (pp. 269–289). New York: Wiley.

Liberman, A. M. (1992). The relation of speech to reading and writing. In R. Frost & L. Katz (Eds.), *Orthography, phonology, morphology, and meaning*. Amsterdam, Holland: North-Holland.

Liberman, A. M., & Mattingly, I. G. (1989). A specialization for speech perception. *Science, 243*, 489–494.

Lichtenstein, S., & Slovic, P. (1973). Response-induced reversals of preference in gambling: An extended replication in Las Vegas. *Journal of Experimental Psychology, 101*, 16–20.

Light, L. L. (1991). Memory and aging: Four hypotheses in search of data. *Annual Review of Psychology, 42*, 333–376.

Light, L. L., & Albertson, S. A. (1989). Direct and indirect tests of memory for category exemplars in young and older adults. *Psychology and Aging, 4*, 487–492.

Light, L. L., & Burke, D. (Eds.). (1988). *Language, memory, and aging*. New York: Cambridge University Press.

Light, L. L., & Singh, A. (1987). Implicit and explicit memory in young and older adults. *Journal of Experimental Psychology: Learning, Memory, and Cognition, 13*, 531–541.

Light, L. L., Singh, A., & Capps, J. L. (1986). Dissociation of memory and awareness in young and older adults. *Journal of Clinical and Experimental Neuropsychology, 8*, 62–74.

Lima, S. D., Hale, S., & Myerson, J. (1991). How general is general slowing? Evidence from the lexical domain. *Psychology and Aging, 6*, 416–425.

Linde, C., & Labov, W. (1975). Spatial networks as a site for the study of language and thought. *Language, 51*, 924–939.

Lindsley, J. R. (1975). Producing simple utterances: How far ahead do we plan? *Cognitive Psychology, 7*, 1–19.

Lippman, M. F. (1972). The influence of grammatical transform in a syllogistic reasoning task. *Journal of Verbal Learning and Verbal Behavior, 11*, 424–430.

List, J. A. (1986). Age and schematic differences in the reliability of eyewitness testimony. *Developmental Psychology, 22*, 50–57.

Locke, J. L. (1983). *Phonological acquisition and change*. New York: Academic Press.

Lockhart, R. S. (1989). The role of theory in understanding implicit memory. In S. Lewandowsky, J. C. Dunn, & K. Kirsner (Eds.), *Implicit memory: Theoretical issues* (pp. 3–13). Hillsdale, NJ: Erlbaum.

Loftus, E. F. (1979). *Eyewitness testimony*. Cambridge, MA: Harvard University Press.

Loftus, E. F., Donders, K., Hoffman, H. G., & Schooler, J. W. (1989). Creating new memories that are quickly accessed and confidently held. *Memory & Cognition, 17*, 607–616.

Loftus, E. F., & Hoffman, H. G. (1989). Misinformation and memory: The creation of new memories. *Journal of Experimental Psychology: General, 118*, 100–104.

Loftus, E. F., & Ketcham, K. (1991). *Witness for the defense*. New York: St. Martin's Press.

Loftus, E. F., Miller, D. G., & Burns, H. J. (1978). Semantic integration of verbal information into visual memory. *Journal of Experimental Psychology: Human Learning and Memory, 4*, 19–31.

Loftus, G. R. (1983). The continuing persistence of the icon. *The Behavioral and Brain Sciences, 6*, 28.

Loftus, G. R. (1985). On worthwhile icons: Reply to Di Lollo and Haber. *Journal of Experimental Psychology: Human Perception and Performance, 11*, 384–388.

Loftus, G. R., Duncan, J., & Gehrig, P. (1992). On the time course of perceptual information that results from a brief visual presentation. *Journal of Experimental Psychology: Human Perception and Performance, 18*, 530–549.

Loftus, G. R., Johnson, C. A., & Shimamura, A. P. (1985). How much is an icon worth? *Journal of Experimental Psychology: Human Perception and Performance, 11*, 1–13.

Long, G. M. (1980). Iconic memory: A review and critique of the study of short-term visual storage. *Psychological Bulletin, 88*, 785–820.

Long, G. M., & Beaton, R. J. (1982). The case for peripheral persistence: Effects of target and background luminance on a partial-report task. *Journal of Experimental Psychology: Human Perception and Performance, 8*, 383–391.

Lord, C. G., Ross, L., & Lepper, M. R. (1979). Biased assimilation and attitude polarization: The effects of prior theories on subsequently considered evidence. *Journal of Personality and Social Psychology, 37*, 2098–2109.

Lovelace, E. A. (1984). Metamemory: Monitoring future recallability during study. *Journal of Experimental Psychology: Learning, Memory, and Cognition, 10*, 756–766.

Lovelace, E. A. (1990). Aging and metacognitions concerning memory function. In E. A. Lovelace (Ed.), *Aging and cognition: Mental processes, self awareness and interventions* (pp. 157–188). Amsterdam: Elsevier.

Lovelace, E. A., & Coon, V. E. (1991). Aging and word finding: Reverse vocabulary and Cloze tests. *Bulletin of the Psychonomic Society, 29*, 33–35.

Lovelace, E. A., & Marsh, G. R. (1985). Prediction and evaluation of memory performance by young and old adults. *Journal of Gerontology, 40*, 192–197.

Lovelace, E. A., & Twohig, P. T. (1990). Healthy older adults' perceptions of their memory functioning and use of mnemonics. *Bulletin of the Psychonomic Society, 28*, 115–118.

Luce, P. A., & Pisoni, D. B. (1987). Speech perception: New directions in research, theory, and applications. In H. Winitz (Ed.), *Human communication and its disorders, A review 1987* (pp. 1–87). Norwood, NJ: Ablex.

Luchins, A. S. (1942). Mechanization in problem solving. *Psychological Monographs, 54* (Whole No. 248).

Lupker, S. J. (1990). Information processing: A reminder of past glories [Review of *Experimental psychology: An information processing approach*]. *Contemporary Psychology, 35*, 1140–1142.

MacDonald, M. C., Just, M. A., & Carpenter, C. M. (1992). Working memory constraints on the processing of syntactic ambiguity. *Cognitive Psychology, 24*, 56–98.

Macfarlane, A. (1977). *The psychology of childbirth*. Cambridge, MA: Harvard University Press.

Mackay, H., & Osgood, C. E. (1959). Hesitation phenomena in spontaneous English speech. *Word, 15*, 19–44.

MacLeod, C. M. (1991). Half a century of research on the Stroop effect: An integrative review. *Psychological Bulletin, 109*, 163–203.

MacLeod, C. M., & Bassili, J. N. (1989). Are implicit and explicit tests differentially sensitive to item-specific vs. relational information? In S. Lewandowsky, J. C. Dunn, & K. Kirsner (Eds.), *Implicit memory: Theoretical issues* (pp. 159–172). Hillsdale, NJ: Erlbaum.

Mägiste, E. (1986). Selected issues in second and third language learning. In J. Vaid (Ed.), *Language processing in bilinguals: Psycholinguistic and neuropsychological perspectives*. Hillsdale, NJ: Erlbaum.

Maier, N. R. F. (1931). Reasoning in humans: II. The solution of a problem and its appearance in consciousness. *Journal of Comparative Psychology, 12*, 181–194.

Maki, R. H., & Berry, S. L. (1984). Metacomprehension of text material. *Journal of Experimental Psychology: Learning, Memory, and Cognition, 10*, 663–679.

Malt, B. C. (1990). Features and beliefs in the mental representation of categories. *Journal of Memory and Language, 29*, 289–315.

Malt, B. C., & Smith, E. E. (1984). Correlated properties in natural categories. *Journal of Verbal Learning and Verbal Behavior, 23*, 250–269.

Mandler, G. (1985). *Cognitive psychology: An essay in cognitive science*. Hillsdale, NJ: Erlbaum.

Mandler, J. M. (1984). *Stories, scripts, and scenes: Aspects of schema theory*. Hillsdale, NJ: Erlbaum.

Mandler, J. M. (1990). A new perspective on cognitive development in infancy. *American Scientist, 78*, 236–243.

Mandler, J. M., & Johnson, N. S. (1977). Remembrance of things parsed: Story structure and recall. *Cognitive Psychology, 9*, 111–151.

Mannion, K. (1981). psychology and the lesbian: A critical review of the research. In S. Cox (Ed.), *Female Psychology* (pp. 256–274). New York: St. Martin's.

Mansfield, T. S., & Busse, T. V. (1981). *The psychology of creativity and discovery*. Chicago: Nelson-Hall.

Mäntysalo, S., & Näätänen, R. (1987). The duration of a neuronal trace of an auditory stimulus as indicated by event-related potentials. *Biological Psychology, 24*, 183–195.

Markman, E. M. (1990). Constraints children place on word meanings. *Cognitive Science, 14*, 57–77.

Markovits, H., & Nantel, G. (1989). The belief-bias effect in the production and evaluation of logical conclusions. *Memory & Cognition, 17*, 11–17.

Marr, D. (1982). *Vision*. San Francisco: Freeman.

Marr, D., & Nishihara, H. K. (1978). Representation and recognition of the spatial organization of three-dimensional shapes. *Proceedings of the Royal Society of London B, 200*, 269–294.

Marshall, J. C. (1977). Minds, machines and metaphors. *Social Studies of Science, 7*, 475–488.

Martin, E. (1970). Toward an analysis of subjective phrase structure. *Psychological Bulletin, 74*, 153–166.

Martin, R. C. (1993). Short-term memory and sentence processing: Evidence from neuropsychology. *Memory and Cognition, 21*, 176–183.

Martindale, C. (1991). *Cognitive psychology: A neural-network approach*. Pacific Grove, CA: Brooks/Cole.

Mason, M. (1978). From print to sound in mature readers as a function of reader ability and two forms of orthographic regularity. *Memory & Cognition, 6*, 568–581.

Massaro, D. W. (1987). *Speech perception by ear and eye: A paradigm for psychological inquiry*. Hillsdale, NJ: Erlbaum.

Massaro, D. W. (1989). Multiple book review of *Speech perception by ear and eye: A paradigm for psychological inquiry*. *Behavioral and Brain Sciences, 12*, 741–794.

Massaro, D. W., & Cohen, M. M. (1990). Perception of synthesized audible and visible speech. *Psychological Science, 1*, 55–63.

Matlin, M. W. (1979). *Human experimental psychology*. Monterey, CA: Brooks/Cole.

Matlin, M. W. (1993a). "But I thought I was going to ace that test!": Metacognition and the college student. Paper presented at the meeting of the Southeastern Psychological Association, Atlanta, GA.

Matlin, M. W. (1993b). *The Psychology of Women* (2nd ed.). Fort Worth, TX: Harcourt Brace Jovanovich.

Matlin, M. W., & Foley, H. J. (1992). *Sensation and perception* (3rd ed.). Boston: Allyn & Bacon.

Matlin, M. W., & Stang, D. J. (1978). *The Pollyanna Principle: Selectivity in language, memory, and thought.* Cambridge, MA: Schenkman.

Matlin, M. W., Stang, D. J., Gawron, V. J., Freedman, A., & Derby, P. L. (1979). Evaluative meaning as a determinant of spew position. *Journal of General Psychology, 100,* 3–11.

Mattingly, I. G., & Liberman, A. M. (1988). Specialized perceiving systems for speech and other biologically significant sounds. In G. M. Edelman, W. E. Gall, & W. M. Cowan (Eds.), *Auditory function* (pp. 775–793). New York: Wiley.

Mayer, J. D. (1986). How mood influences cognition. In N. E. Sharkey (Ed.), *Advances in cognitive science* (pp. 290–314). Chichester, West Sussex, England: Ellis Horwood.

Mayer, J. D., & Bower, G. H. (1986). Learning and memory for personality prototypes. *Journal of Personality and Social Psychology, 51,* 473–492.

Mayer, R. E. (1982). The psychology of mathematical problem solving. In F. K. Lester & J. Garofalo (Eds.), *Mathematical problem solving: Issues in research* (pp. 1–13). Philadelphia, PA: The Franklin Institute.

Mayer, R. E. (1983). *Thinking, problem solving, cognition.* New York: Freeman.

Mayer, R. E. (1985). Implications of cognitive psychology for instruction in mathematical problem solving. In E. A. Silver (Ed.), *Teaching and learning mathematical problem solving* (pp. 123–138). Hillsdale, NJ: Erlbaum.

Mayer, R. E. (1989). Human nonadversary problem solving. In K. J. Gilhooly (Ed.), *Human and machine problem solving* (pp. 39–81). New York: Plenum.

McArthur, D. J. (1982). Computer vision and perceptual psychology. *Psychological Bulletin, 92,* 283–309.

McArthur, L. Z. (1980). Illusory causation and illusory correlation: Two epistemological accounts. *Personality and Social Psychology Bulletin, 6,* 507–519.

McClelland, J. L. (1981). Retrieving general and specific knowledge from stored knowledge of specifics. *Proceedings of the Third Annual Conference of the Cognitive Science Society,* (pp. 170–172) Hillsdale, NJ: Erlbaum..

McClelland, J. L. (1988). Connectionist models and psychological evidence. *Journal of Memory and Language, 27,* 107–123.

McClelland, J. L., & Rumelhart, D. E. (1981). An interactive activation model of context effects in letter perception: Part 1: An account of basic findings. *Psychological Review, 88,* 375–407.

McClelland, J. L., Rumelhart, D. E., & Hinton, G. E. (1986). The appeal of parallel distributed processing. In D. E. Rumelhart, J. L. McClelland, and the PDP Research Group (Eds.), *Parallel distributed processing* (Vol. 1, pp. 3–44). Cambridge, MA: MIT Press.

McClelland, J. L., Rumelhart, D. E., & the PDP Research Group. (1986). *Parallel distributed processing* (Vol. 2). Cambridge, MA: MIT Press.

McCloskey, M., & Cohen, N. J. (1989). Catastrophic interference in connectionist networks: The sequential learning problem. *The Psychology of Learning and Motivation, 24,* 109–165.

McCloskey, M., Wible, C. G., & Cohen, N. J. (1988). Is there a special flashbulb-memory mechanism? *Journal of Experimental Psychology: General, 11,* 171–181.

McConkie, G. W. (1983). Eye movements and perception during reading. In K. Rayner (Ed.), *Eye movements in reading: Perceptual and language processes* (pp. 65–96). New York: Academic Press.

McConkie, G. W., & Zóla, D. (1984). Eye movement control during reading: The effect of word units. In W. Prinz & A. F. Sanders (Eds.), *Cognition and motor processes* (pp. 63–74). Berlin: Springer-Verlag.

McDaniel, M. A., & Pressley, M. (Eds.). (1987). *Imagery and related mnemonic processes.* New York: Springer-Verlag.

McDaniel, M. A., Pressley, M., & Dunay, P. K. (1987). Long-term retention of vocabulary after keyword and context learning. *Journal of Educational Psychology, 79,* 87–89.

McKeachie, W. J., Pintrich, P. R., & Lin, Y. (1985). Teaching learning strategies. *Educational Psychology, 20*, 153–160.

McKelvie, S. J. (1984). Relationship between set and functional fixedness: A replication. *Perceptual and Motor Skills, 58*, 996–998.

McKoon, G., & Ratcliff, R. (1986). Automatic activation of episodic information in a semantic memory task. *Journal of Experimental Psychology: Learning, Memory, and Cognition, 12*, 108–115.

McKoon, G., & Ratcliff, R. (1992a). Spreading activation versus compound cue accounts of priming: Mediated priming revisited. *Journal of Experimental Psychology: Learning, Memory, and Cognition, 18*, 1155–1172.

McKoon, G., & Ratcliff, R. (1992b). Inference during reading. *Psychological Review, 99*, 440–466.

McKoon, G., Ratcliff, R., & Dell, G. S. (1986). A critical evaluation of the semantic-episodic distinction. *Journal of Experimental Psychology: Learning, Memory, and Cognition, 12*, 295–306.

McKoon, G., Ratcliff, R., & Seifert, C. (1989). Making the connection: Generalized knowledge structures in story understanding. *Journal of Memory and Language, 28*, 711–734.

McLaughlin, M. L. (1984). *How talk is organized.* Beverly Hills: Sage.

McNamara, T. P. (1986). Mental representations of spatial relations. *Cognitive Psychology, 18*, 87–121.

McNamara, T. P., Hardy, J. K., & Hirtle, S. C. (1989). Subjective hierarchies in spatial memory. *Journal of Experimental Psychology: Learning, Memory, and Cognition, 15*, 211–217.

McNamara, T. P., Ratcliff, R., & McKoon, G. (1984). The mental representation of knowledge acquired from maps. *Journal of Experimental Psychology: Learning, Memory, and Cognition, 10*, 723–732.

McNaughton, B. L., & Morris, R. G. M. (1987). Hippocampal synaptic enhancement and information storage within a distributed memory system. *Trends in Neurosciences, 10*, 408–415.

McNeil, B. J., Pauker, S. G., Sox, H. C., & Tversky, A. (1982). On the elicitation of preferences for alternative therapies. *New England Journal of Medicine, 306*, 1259–1262.

McNeil, B. J., Pauker, S. G., & Tversky, A. (1988). On the framing of medical decisions. In D. E. Bell, H. Raiffa, & A. Tversky (Eds.), *Decision making: Descriptive, normative, and prescriptive interactions* (pp. 562–568). New York: Cambridge University Press.

McNeill, D. (1985). So you think gestures are nonverbal? *Psychological Review, 92*, 350–371.

McTear, M. F. (1985). *Children's conversations.* Oxford, England: Basil Blackwell.

McTear, M. F. (1988). *Understanding cognitive science.* Chichester, England: Ellis Horwood.

Meacham, J. A. (1982). A note on remembering to execute planned actions. *Journal of Applied Developmental Psychology, 3*, 121–133.

Meacham, J. A., & Singer, J. (1977). Incentive in prospective remembering. *Journal of Psychology, 97*, 191–197.

Medin, D. L. (1989). Concepts and conceptual structure. *American Psychologist, 44*, 1469–1481.

Medin, D. L., & Schaffer, M. M. (1978). A context theory of classification learning. *Psychological Review, 85*, 207–238.

Medin, D. L., Wattenmaker, W. D., & Hampson, S. E. (1987). Family resemblances, conceptual cohesiveness, and category construction. *Cognitive Psychology, 19*, 242–279.

Mednick, S. A., & Mednick, M. T. (1967). *Examiner's manual, Remote Associates Test.* Boston, MA: Houghton Mifflin.

Mehler, J. (1963). Some effects of grammatical transformation on the recall of English sentences. *Journal of Verbal Learning and Verbal Behavior, 2*, 346–351.

Melton, A. W. (1963). Implications of short-term memory for a general theory of memory. *Journal of Verbal Learning and Verbal Behavior, 2*, 1–21.

Meltzoff, A. N. (1988a). Infant imitation after a 1-week delay: Long-term memory for novel acts and multiple stimuli. *Developmental Psychology, 24*, 470–476.

Meltzoff, A. N. (1988b). Infant imitation and memory: Nine-months-olds in immediate and deferred tests. *Child Development, 59,* 217–225.

Merck, Sharp & Dome. (1980). *Medical mnemonics handbook.* West Point, PA: Author.

Mervis, C. B., Catlin, J., & Rosch, E. (1976). Relationships among goodness-of-example, category norms, and word frequency. *Bulletin of the Psychonomic Society, 7,* 283–284.

Mervis, C. B., & Crisafi, M. A. (1982). Order of acquisition of subordinate, basic, and superordinate categories. *Child Development, 53,* 258–266.

Messer, D. (1981). Non-linguistic information which could assist the young child's interpretation of adults' speech. In W. P. Robinson (Ed.), *Communication in development.* London: Academic Press.

Metcalfe, J. (1986). Premonitions of insight predict impending error. *Journal of Experimental Psychology: Learning, Memory, and Cognition, 12,* 623–634.

Metcalfe, J., & Wiebe, D. (1987). Intuition in insight and noninsight problem solving. *Memory & Cognition, 15,* 238–246.

Meyer, B. J. F., Brandt, D. M., & Bluth, C. J. (1980). Use of top level structure in text: Key for reading comprehension of ninth grade students. *Reading Research Quarterly, 16,* 72–103.

Miller, G. A. (1956). The magical number seven, plus or minus two: Some limits on our capacity for processing information. *Psychological Review, 63,* 81–97.

Miller, G. A. (1962). *Psychology: The science of mental life.* New York: Harper & Row.

Miller, G. A. (1979). *A very personal history.* Address to Cognitive Science Workshop. Massachusetts Institute of Technology, Cambridge, MA.

Miller, G. A. (1981). *Language and speech.* San Francisco: Freeman.

Miller, G. A. (1985). Trends and debates in cognitive psychology. In A. M. Aitkenhead & J. M. Slack (Eds.), *Issues in cognitive modeling* (pp. 3–11). London: Erlbaum.

Miller, J. L. (1990). Speech perception. In D. N. Osherson & H. Lasnik (Eds.), *Language: An invitation to cognitive science* (pp. 69–93). Cambridge, MA: MIT Press.

Miller, J. L., & Eimas, P. D. (1983). Studies on the categorization of speech by infants. *Cognition, 13,* 135–166.

Miller, J. R., & Kintsch, W. (1980). Readability and recall of short prose passages. A theoretical analysis. *Journal of Experimental Psychology: Human Learning and Memory, 6,* 335–354.

Miller, L. C., Lechner, R. E., & Rugs, D. (1985). Development of conversational responsiveness: Preschoolers' use of responsive listener cues and relevant comments. *Developmental Psychology, 21,* 473–480.

Mills, C. J. (1983). Sex-typing and self-schemata effects on memory and response latency. *Journal of Personality and Social Psychology, 45,* 163–172.

Milner, B. (1966). Amnesia following operation on the temporal lobes. In C. W. M. Whitty & O. L. Zangwill (Eds.), *Amnesia following operation on the temporal lobes* (pp. 109–133). London: Butterworth.

Mitchell, D. B. (1991). Implicit memory, explicit theories [Review of *Implicit memory: Theoretical issues*]. *Contemporary Psychology, 36,* 1060–1061.

Moar, I., & Bower, G. H. (1983). Inconsistency in spatial knowledge. *Memory & Cognition, 11,* 107–113.

Moely, B. E., Olson, F. A., Halwes, T. G., & Flavell, J. H. (1969). Production deficiency in young children's clustered recall. *Developmental Psychology, 1,* 26–34.

Moody, D. B., Stebbins, W. C., & May, B. J. (1990). Auditory perception of communication signals by Japanese monkeys. In W. C. Stebbins & M. A. Berkley (Eds.), *Comparative perception: Complex signals* (pp. 311–343). New York: Wiley.

Moray, N. (1959). Attention in dichotic listening: Affective cues and the influence of instructions. *Quarterly Journal of Experimental Psychology, 11,* 56–60.

Morris, M. W., & Murphy, G. L. (1990). Converging operations on a basic level in event taxonomies. *Memory & Cognition, 18,* 407–418.

Morris, N. (1987). Exploring the visuo-spatial scratch pad. *The Quarterly Journal of Experimental Psychology, 39A*, 409–430.

Morris, N., & Jones, D. M. (1990). Memory updating in working memory: The role of the central executive. *British Journal of Psychology, 81*, 111–121.

Morris, P. E. (1978). Sense and nonsense in traditional mnemonics. In M. M. Gruneberg, P. E. Morris, & R. N. Sykes (Eds.), *Practical aspects of memory* (pp. 155–163). London: Academic Press.

Morris, P. E. (1988). Memory research: Past mistakes and future prospects. In G. Claxton (Ed.), *Growth points in cognition* (pp. 91–110). London: Routledge.

Moscovitch, M., & Craik, F. I. M. (1976). Depth of processing, retrieval cues, and uniqueness of encoding as factors in recall. *Journal of Verbal Learning and Verbal Behavior, 15*, 447–458.

Mountcastle, V. B. (1979). An organizing principle for cerebral function: The unit module and the distributed system. In F. O. Schmitt (Ed.), *The neurosciences: Fourth study program*. Cambridge, MA: MIT Press.

Moyer, R. S. (1973). Comparing objects in memory: Evidence suggesting an internal psychophysics. *Perception & Psychophysics, 13*, 180–184.

Moyer, R. S., & Dumais, S. T. (1978). Mental comparisons. In G. H. Bower (Ed.), *The psychology of learning and motivation* (Vol. 12, pp. 117–156). New York: Academic Press.

Mumford, M. D., & Gustafson, S. B. (1988). Creativity syndrome: Integration, application, and innovation. *Psychological Bulletin, 103*, 27–43.

Murphy, G. L., & Smith, E. E. (1982). Basic level superiority in picture categorization. *Journal of Verbal Learning and Verbal Behavior, 21*, 1–20.

Myers, N. A., & Perlmutter, M. (1978). Memory in the years from two to five. In P. A. Ornstein (Ed.), *Memory development in children* (pp. 191–218). Hillsdale, NJ: Erlbaum.

Myerson, J., Hale, S., Wagstaff, D., Poon, L. W., & Smith, G. A. (1990). The information-loss model: A mathematical theory of age-related cognitive slowing. *Psychological Review, 97*, 475–487.

Näätänen, R. (1982). Processing negativity: An evoked potential reflection of selective attention. *Psychological Bulletin, 92*, 605–640.

Näätänen, R. (1985). Selective attention and stimulus processing: Reflections in event-related potentials, magnetoencephalogram, and regional cerebral blood flow. In M. I. Posner & O. S. Marin (Eds.), *Attention and performance XI* (pp. 355–373). Hillsdale, NJ: Erlbaum.

Näätänen, R. (1986). Neurophysiological basis of the echoic memory as suggested by event-related potentials and magnetoencephalogram. In F. Klix & H. Hagendorf (Eds.), *Human memory and cognitive capabilities* (pp. 615–628). Amsterdam: Elsevier.

Naveh-Benjamin, M., & Ayres, T. J. (1986). Digit span, reading rate, and linguistic relativity. *Quarterly Journal of Experimental Psychology, 38*, 739–751.

Neale, M. A., & Northcraft, G. B. (1986). Experts, amateurs, and refrigerators: Comparing expert and amateur negotiators in a novel task. *Organizational Behavior and Human Decision Processes, 38*, 305–317.

Neisser, U. (1963). The multiplicity of thought. *British Journal of Psychology, 54*, 1–14.

Neisser, U. (1967). *Cognitive psychology*. New York: Appleton.

Neisser, U. (1987). From direct perception to conceptual structure. In U. Neisser (Ed.), *Concepts and conceptual development* (pp. 11–24). New York: Cambridge University Press.

Neisser, U. (1988). What is ordinary memory the memory of? In U. Neisser & E. Winograd (Eds.), *Remembering reconsidered: Ecological and traditional approaches to the study of memory* (pp. 356–373). New York: Cambridge University Press.

Neisser, U. (1989). Domains of memory. In P. R. Solomon, G. R. Goethals, C. M. Kelley, & B. R. Stephens (Ed.), *Memory: Interdisciplinary approaches* (pp. 67–83). New York: Springer-Verlag.

Neisser, U., & Becklen, R. (1975). Selective looking: Attending to visually significant events. *Cognitive Psychology, 7*, 480–494.

Nelson, K. (1985). *Making sense: The acquisition of shared meaning.* Orlando, FL: Academic Press.

Nelson, K. (1986). *Event knowledge: Structure and function in development.* Hillsdale, NJ: Erlbaum.

Nelson, T. O. (1977). Repetition and depth of processing. *Journal of Verbal Learning and Verbal Behavior, 16,* 151–171.

Nelson, T. O. (Ed.). (1992). *Metacognition: Core readings.* Boston, MA: Allyn & Bacon.

Nelson, T. O., & Leonesio, R. J. (1988). Allocation of self-paced study time and the "labor-in-vain effect." *Journal of Experimental Psychology: Learning, Memory, and Cognition, 14,* 676–686.

Newell, A., & Simon, H. A. (1972). *Human problem solving.* Englewood Cliffs, NJ: Prentice-Hall.

Newport, E. L. (1990). Maturational constraints on language learning. *Cognitive Science, 14,* 11–28.

Newport, E. L., and Supalla, T. (1993). *Critical period effects in the acquisition of a primary language.* Unpublished manuscript, University of Rochester.

Newstead, S. E. (1989). Interpretational errors in syllogistic reasoning. *Journal of Memory and Language, 28,* 78–91.

Newstead, S. E., & Griggs, R. (1983). Drawing inferences from quantified statements: A study of the square of opposition. *Journal of Verbal Learning and Verbal Behavior, 22,* 535–546.

Nickerson, R. S. (1986). Reasoning. In R. F. Dillon & R. J. Sternberg (Eds.), *Cognition and instruction* (pp. 343–373). Orlando, FL: Academic Press.

Nickerson, R. S. (1990). William James on reasoning. *Psychological Science, 1,* 167–171.

Nickerson, R. S., Perkins, D. N., & Smith, E. E. (1985). *The teaching of thinking.* Hillsdale, NJ: Erlbaum.

Nisbett, R. E., Krantz, D. H., Jepson, C., & Kunda, Z. (1983). The use of statistical heuristics in everyday inductive reasoning. *Psychological Review, 90,* 339–363.

Nisbett, R. E., & Ross, L. (1980). *Human inference: Strategies and shortcomings of social judgment.* Englewood Cliffs, NJ: Prentice-Hall.

Nisbett, R. E., & Wilson, T. D. (1977). Telling more than we can know. Verbal reports on mental processes. *Psychological Review, 84,* 231–259.

Nist, S. L., & Mealey, D. L. (1991). Teacher-directed comprehension strategies. In R. F. Flippo & D. C. Caverly (Eds.), *Teaching reading and study strategies at the college level* (pp. 42–85). Newark, Delaware: International Reading Association.

Norman, D. A. (1982). *Learning and memory.* San Francisco: W. H. Freeman.

Northcraft, G. B., & Neale, M. A. (1987). Experts, amateurs, and real estate: An anchoring-and-adjustment perspective on property pricing decisions. *Organizational Behavior and Human Decision Processes, 39,* 84–97.

Novick, L. R. (1988). Analogical transfer, problem similarity, and expertise. *Journal of Experimental Psychology: Learning, Memory, and Cognition, 14,* 510–520.

Novick, L. R., & Coté, N. (1992). The nature of expertise in anagram solution. *Proceedings of the Fourteenth Annual Conference of the Cognitive Science Society* (pp. 450–455). Hillsdale, NJ: Erlbaum.

Novick, L. R., & Holyoak, K. J. (1991). Mathematical problem solving by analogy. *Journal of Experimental Psychology: Learning, Memory, and Cognition, 17,* 398–415.

Nunmedal, S. G. (1987). Developing reasoning skills in college students. In D. E. Berger, K. Pezdek, & W. P. Banks (Eds.), *Applications of cognitive psychology: Problem solving, education, and computing* (pp. 87–97). Hillsdale, NJ: Erlbaum.

Oakhill, J. V., & Johnson-Laird, P. N. (1985). Rationality, memory, and the search for counterexamples. *Cognition, 20,* 79–94.

O'Regan, K. (1979). Saccade size control in reading: Evidence for the linguistic control hypothesis. *Perception & Psychophysics, 25,* 501–509.

O'Regan, K. (1980). The control of saccade size and fixation duration in reading: The limits of linguistic control. *Perception & Psychophysics, 28,* 112–117.

Ormrod, J. E., Ormrod, R. K., Wagner, E. D., & McCallin, R. C. (1988). Reconceptualizing map learning. *American Journal of Psychology, 101,* 425–433.

Osborn, A. (1957). *Applied imagination*. New York: Charles Scribner's Sons.

Osgood, C. E. (1953). *Method and theory in experimental psychology*. New York: Oxford University Press.

Osherson, E. N., Kosslyn, S. M., & Hollerbach, J. M. (Eds.). (1990). *An invitation to cognitive science*. Cambridge, MA: MIT Press.

Oviatt, S. (1980). The emerging ability to comprehend language: An experimental approach. *Child Development, 51*, 97–106.

Overheard. (1992, July 13). *Newsweek*, p. 15.

Owens, R. E., Jr. (1992). *Language development: An introduction* (3rd ed.). New York: Merrill.

Paivio, A. (1978a). On exploring visual knowledge. In B. S. Randhawa and W. E. Coffman (Eds.), *Visual learning, thinking and communication* (pp. 113–132). New York: Academic Press.

Paivio, A. (1978b). Comparisons of mental clocks. *Journal of Experimental Psychology: Human Perception and Performance, 4*, 61–71.

Palmer, C. F., Jones, R. K., Hennessy, B. L., Unze, M. G., & Pick, A. D. (1989). How is a trumpet known? The "basic object level" concept and the perception of musical instruments. *American Journal of Psychology, 102*, 17–37.

Palmer, S. E. (1975a). Visual perception and world knowledge: Notes on a model of sensory-cognitive interaction. In D. A. Norman & D. E. Rumelhart (Eds.), *Explorations in cognition* (pp. 279–307). San Francisco: Freeman.

Palmer, S. E. (1975b). The effects of contextual scenes on the identification of objects. *Memory & Cognition, 3*, 519–526.

Palmer, S. E. (1987). PDP: A new paradigm for cognitive theory [Review of *Parallel distributed processing: Explorations in the microstructure of cognition*]. *Contemporary Psychology, 32*, 925–928.

Palmere, M., Benton, S. L., Glover, J. A., & Ronning, R. (1983). Elaboration and recall of main ideas in prose. *Journal of Educational Psychology, 75*, 898–907.

Parkin, A. J. (1984). Levels of processing, context, and facilitation of pronunciation. *Acta Psychologica, 55*, 19–29.

Pauker, S. G., & Kopelman, R. I. (1992). Clinical problem solving. *The New England Journal of Medicine, 326*, 40–43.

Payne, J. W., Bettman, J. R., & Johnson, E. J. (1992). Behavioral decision research: A constructive processing perspective. *Annual Review of Psychology, 43*, 87–131.

Peal, E., & Lambert, W. E. (1962). The relation of bilingualism to intelligence. *Psychological Monographs, 546*.

Perfetti, C. A., & Bell, L. (1991). Phonemic activation during the first 40 ms. of word identification: Evidence from backward masking and priming. *Journal of Memory and Language, 30*, 473–486.

Perlmutter, M. (1979). Age differences in adults' free recall, cued recall, and recognition. *Journal of Gerontology, 34*, 533–539.

Peters, D. P. (1987). The impact of naturally occurring stress on children's memory. In S. J. Ceci, M. P. Toglia, & D. F. Ross (Eds.), *Children's eyewitness memory* (pp. 122–141). New York: Springer-Verlag.

Petersen, S. E., Fox, P. T., Posner, M. I., Mintun, M., & Raichle, M. E. (1988). Positron emission tomographic studies of the cortical anatomy of single-word processing. *Nature, 331*, 585–589.

Peterson, L. R., & Peterson, M. (1959). Short-term retention of individual verbal items. *Journal of Experimental Psychology, 58*, 193–198.

Peterson, M. A., Kihlstrom, J. F., Rose, P. M., & Glisky, M. L. (1992). Mental images can be ambiguous: Reconstruals and reference-frame reversals. *Memory & Cognition, 20*, 107–123.

Peterson, S. A. (1985). Neurophysiology, cognition, and political thinking. *Political Psychology, 6*, 495–518.

Petitto, L., & Marentette, P. F. (1991). Babbling in the manual mode: Evidence for the ontogeny of language. *Science, 251*, 1493–1499.

Pillemer, D. B., Goldsmith, L. R., Panter, A. T., & White, S. H. (1988). Very long-term memories of the first year in college. *Journal of Experimental Psychology: Learning, Memory, and Cognition, 14*, 709–715.

Pillemer, D. B., Koff, E., Rhinehart, E. D., & Rierdan, J. (1987). Flashbulb memories of menarche and adult menstrual distress. *Journal of Adolescence, 10,* 187–199.

Pinker, S. (1984a). Visual cognition: An introduction. *Cognition, 18,* 1–63.

Pinker, S. (1984b). *Language learnability and language development.* Cambridge, MA: Harvard University Press.

Pinker, S. (1985). Visual cognition: An introduction. In S. Pinker (Ed.), *Visual cognition* (pp. 1–63). Cambridge, MA: MIT Press.

Pinker, S., & Mehler, J. (Eds.). (1988). *Connections and symbols.* Cambridge, MA: MIT Press.

Pinker, S., & Prince, A. (1988). On language and connectionism: Analysis of a parallel distributed processing model of language acquisition. *Cognition, 28,* 73–193.

Pitz, G. F., & Sachs, N. J. (1984). Judgment and decision: Theory and application. *Annual Review of Psychology, 35,* 139–163.

"Please Go Away." (1986, May 19). *The New Republic,* pp. 7–8.

Pollard, P., & Evans, J. St B. T. (1983). The role of "representativeness" in statistical inference: A critical appraisal. In J. St B. T. Evans (Ed.), *Thinking and reasoning: Psychological approaches* (pp. 107–134). London: Routledge & Kegan Paul.

Pollard, P., & Evans, J. St B. T. (1987). Content and context effects in reasoning. *American Journal of Psychology, 100,* 41–60.

Pollatsek, A., & Rayner, K. (1989). Reading. In M. I. Posner (Ed.), *Foundations of cognitive science* (pp. 401–436). Cambridge, MA: MIT Press.

Poon, L. W. (1980). A systems approach for the assessment and treatment of memory problems. In J. M. Ferguson & C. B. Taylor (Eds.), *The comprehensive handbook of behavior medicine* (Vol. 1, pp. 191–212). New York: Spectrum.

Poplack, S. (1980). "Sometimes I'll start a sentence in English *y termino en español.*" *Linguistics, 18,* 561–618.

Posner, M. I. (1986). Overview. In K. R. Boff, L. Kaufman, & J. P. Thomas (Eds.), *Handbook of perception and human performance* (pp. v-3–v-10). New York: Wiley.

Posner, M. I. (Ed.). (1989). *Foundations of cognitive science.* Cambridge, MA: MIT Press.

Posner, M. I. (1991). *Interaction of arousal and selection in the posterior attention network.* Unpublished paper, University of Oregon.

Posner, M. I., Goldsmith, R., & Welton, K. E., Jr. (1967). Perceived distance and the classification of distorted patterns. *Journal of Experimental Psychology, 73,* 28–38.

Posner, M. I., Grossenbacher, P. G., & Compton, P. E. (1991). *Visual attention.* Unpublished paper, University of Oregon.

Posner, M. I., & Keele, S. W. (1967). Decay of visual information from a single letter. *Science, 158,* 137–139.

Posner, M. I., & McLeod, P. (1982). Information processing models—in search of elementary operations. *Annual Review of Psychology, 33,* 477–514.

Posner, M. I., & Petersen, S. E. (1990). The attention system of the human brain. *Annual Review of Neuroscience, 13,* 25–42.

Posner, M. I., Petersen, S. E., Fox, P. T., & Raichle, M. E. (1988). Localization of cognitive operations in the human brain. *Science, 240,* 1627–1631.

Posner, M. I., & Rothbart, M. K. (1991). Attentional mechanisms and conscious experience. In D. Milner & M. Rugg (Eds.), *The neurospychology of consciousness.* Orlando, FL: Academic Press.

Postman, L. (1975). Verbal learning and memory. *Annual Review of Psychology, 26,* 291–335.

Pressley, M., & Ghatala, E. S. (1988). Delusions about performance on multiple-choice comprehension tests. *Reading Research Quarterly, 23,* 454–464.

Pressley, M., Levin, J. R., & Ghatala, E. S. (1984). Memory strategy monitoring in adults and children. *Journal of Verbal Learning and Verbal Behavior, 23,* 270–288.

Pressley, M., Levin, J. R., & Ghatala, E. S. (1988). Strategy-comparison opportunities promote long-term strategy use. *Contemporary Educational Psychology, 13,* 157–168.

Prideaux, G. D. (1985). *Psycholinguistics.* New York: Guilford Press.

Pryor, J. B., & Merluzzi, T. V. (1985). The role of expertise in processing social interaction scripts. *Journal of Experimental Social Psychology, 21*, 362–379.

Pylyshyn, Z. W. (1978). Imagery and artificial intelligence. In C. W. Savage (Ed.), Minnesota studies in the philosophy of science: Vol. 9. *Perception and cognition issues in the foundations of psychology* (pp. 19–56). Minneapolis: University of Minnesota Press.

Pylyshyn, Z. W. (1984). *Computation and cognition.* Cambridge, MA: MIT Press.

Quattrone, G. A., & Jones, E. E. (1980). The perception of variability within in-groups and out-groups: Implications for the law of small numbers. *Journal of Personality and Social Psychology, 38*, 141–152.

Quinlan, P. T., & Humphreys, G. W. (1987). Visual search for targets defined by combinations of color, shape, and size: An examination of the task constraints on feature and conjunction searches. *Perception & Psychophysics, 41*, 455–472.

Rabinowitz, J. C., Ackerman, B. P., Craik, F. I. M., & Hinchley, J. L. (1982). Aging and metamemory: The roles of relatedness and imagery. *Journal of Gerontology, 37*, 688–695.

Rachlin, H. (1989). *Judgment, decision, and choice.* New York: Freeman.

Ransdell, S. E., & Fischler, I. (1987). Memory in a monolingual mode: When are bilinguals at a disadvantage? *Journal of Memory and Language, 26*, 392–405.

Ratcliff, R. (1990). Connectionist models of recognition memory: Constraints imposed by learning and forgetting functions. *Psychological Review, 97*, 285–308.

Ratcliff, R., & McKoon, G. (1978). Priming in item recognition: Evidence for the propositional structure of sentences. *Journal of Verbal Learning and Verbal Behavior, 17*, 403–417.

Ratcliff, R., & McKoon, G. (1988). A retrieval theory of priming in memory. *Psychological Review, 95*, 385–408.

Rating Threats. (1989, March 27). *Time Magazine,* p. 27.

Ratner, H. H., & Foley, M. A. (in press). A unifying framework for the development of children's memory for activity. *Advances in Child Development and Behavior.*

Ratner, N. B., & Gleason, J. B. (1993). An introduction to psycholinguistics: What do language users know? In J. B. Gleason & N. B. Ratner (Eds.), *Psycholinguistics.* Fort Worth, TX: Harcourt Brace Jovanovich.

Rayner, K., & Pollatsek, A. (1989). *The psychology of reading.* Englewood Cliffs, NJ: Prentice Hall.

Read, S. J. (1983). Once is enough: Causal reasoning from a single instance. *Journal of Personality and Social Psychology, 45*, 323–334.

Read, S. J., & Cesa, I. L. (1991). This reminds me of the time when . . . : Expectation failures in reminding and explanation. *Journal of Experimental Social Psychology, 27*, 1–25.

Reason, J. (1984). Absent-mindedness and cognitive control. In J. E. Harris & P. E. Morris (Eds.), *Everyday memory, actions and absent-mindedness* (pp. 113–132). London: Academic Press.

Reason, J., & Mycielska, K. (1982). *Absent-minded? The psychology of mental lapses and everyday errors.* Englewood Cliffs, NJ: Prentice-Hall.

Rebok, G. W. (1987). *Life-span cognitive development.* New York: Holt, Rinehart and Winston.

Rebok, G. W., & Balcerak, L. J. (1989). Memory self-efficacy and performance differences in young and old adults: The effects of mnemonic training. *Developmental Psychology, 25*, 714–721.

Reed, S. K. (1972). Pattern recognition and categorization. *Cognitive Psychology, 3*, 383–407.

Reed, S. K. (1974). Structural descriptions and the limitations of visual images. *Memory & Cognition, 2*, 329–336.

Reed, S. K. (1977). Facilitation of problem solving. In N. J. Castellan, Jr., D. B. Pisoni, & G. R. Potts (Eds.), *Cognitive theory* (Vol. 2, pp. 3–20). Hillsdale, NJ: Erlbaum.

Reed, S. K., Dempster, A., & Ettinger, M. (1985). Usefulness of analogous solutions for solving algebra word problems. *Journal of Experimental Psychology: Learning, Memory, and Cognition, 11*, 106–125.

Reeder, G. D., McCormick, C. B., & Esselman, E. D. (1987). Self-referent processing and recall of prose. *Journal of Educational Psychology, 79,* 243–248.

Reese, H. W. (1977). Imagery and associative memory. In R. V. Kail & J. W. Hagen (Eds.), *Perspectives on the development of memory and cognition* (pp. 113–176). Hillsdale, NJ: Erlbaum.

Reicher, G. M. (1969). Perceptual recognition as a function of meaningfulness of stimuli material. *Journal of Experimental Psychology, 81,* 275–280.

Reisberg, D. (Ed.). (1992). *Auditory imagery.* Hillsdale, NJ: Erlbaum.

Reisberg, D., Culver, L. C., Heuer, F., & Fischman, D. (1986). *Journal of Mental Imagery, 10,* 51–74.

Reitman, W. R. (1964). Heuristic decision procedures, open constraints, and the structure of ill-defined problems. In M. W. Shelley & G. L. Bryan (Eds.), *Human judgments and optimality.* New York: Wiley.

Reynolds, A. G. (1991a). The cognitive consequences of bilingualism. In A. G. Reynolds (Ed.), *Bilingualism, multiculturalism, and second language learning: The McGill Conference in Honour of Wallace E. Lambert* (pp. 145–182). Hillsdale, NJ: Erlbaum.

Reynolds, A. G. (Ed.). (1991b). *Bilingualism, multiculturism, and second language learning: The McGill Conference in Honour of Wallace E. Lambert.* Hillsdale, NJ: Erlbaum.

Rhodes, G., Brennan, S., & Carey, S. (1987). Identification and ratings of caricatures: Implications for mental representations of faces. *Cognitive Psychology, 19,* 473–497.

Ribbiting Evidence. (1987, August 10). *Time Magazine,* p. 31.

Rice, M. L. (1989). Children's language acquisition. *American Psychologist, 44,* 149–156.

Richardson-Klavehn, A., & Bjork, R. A. (1988). Measures of memory. *Annual Review of Psychology, 39,* 475–543.

Richman, H. B., & Simon, H. A. (1989). Context effects in letter perception: Comparison of two theories. *Psychological Review, 96,* 417–432.

Rips, L. J. (1981). Cognitive processes in propositional reasoning. *Psychological Review, 90,* 38–71.

Robinson, D. L., & Petersen, S. E. (1986). The neurobiology of attention. In J. E. LeDoux & W. Hirst (Eds.), *Mind and brain: Dialogues in cognitive neuroscience* (pp. 142–171). Cambridge: Cambridge University Press.

Rodgers, W. L., & Herzog, A. R. (1987). Interviewing older adults: The accuracy of factual information. *Journal of Gerontology, 42,* 387–394.

Roediger, H. L., III. (1980). Levels of processing: Criticism and development [Review of *Levels of processing in human memory*]. *Contemporary Psychology, 25,* 20–21.

Roediger, H. L., III. (1990). Implicit memory: Retention without remembering. *American Psychologist, 45,* 1043–1056.

Roediger, H. L., III. (1991). *Remembering, knowing, and reconstructing the past.* Paper presented at the Annual Convention of the American Psychological Association, San Francisco, CA.

Roediger, H. L., III, & Craik, F. I. M. (Eds.). (1989). *Varieties of memory and consciousness: Essays in honour of Endel Tulving.* Hillsdale, NJ: Erlbaum.

Roediger, H. L., Srinivas, K., & Weldon, M. S. (1989). Dissociations between implicit measures of retention. In S. Lewandowsky, J. C. Dunn, & K. Kirsner (Eds.), *Implicit memory: Theoretical issues* (pp. 67–84). Hillsdale, NJ: Erlbaum.

Roediger, H. L., III, Weldon, M. S., & Challis, B. H. (1989). Explaining dissociations between implicit and explicit measures of retention: A processing account. In H. L. Roediger, III, & F. I. M. Craik (Eds.), *Varieties of memory and consciousness* (pp. 3–41). Hillsdale, NJ: Erlbaum.

Rogers, D. (1985). Language development. In A. Branthwaite & D. Rogers (Eds.), *Children growing up* (pp. 82–93). Milton Keynes, England: Open University Press.

Rogers, T. B. (1983). Emotion, imagery, and verbal codes: A closer look at an increasingly complex interaction. In J. Yuille (Ed.), *Imagery,* memory, and cognition (pp. 285–305). Hillsdale, NJ: Erlbaum.

Rogers, T. B., Kuiper, N. A., & Kirker, W. S. (1977). Self-reference and the encoding of personal information. Journal of Personality and Social Psychology, 35, 677–688.

Rogoff, B. (1984). Introduction: Thinking and learning in social context. In B. Rogoff & J. Lave (Eds.), Everyday cognition: Its development in social context (pp. 1–8). Cambridge, MA: Harvard University Press.

Rogoff, B. (1990). Apprenticeship in thinking: Cognitive development in social context. New York: Oxford.

Romaine, S. (1989). Bilingualism. Oxford, England: Basil Blackwell.

Rosch, E. H. (1973). Natural categories. Cognitive Psychology, 4, 328–350.

Rosch, E. H. (1975a). Cognitive reference points. Cognitive Psychology, 7, 532–547.

Rosch, E. H. (1975b). The nature of mental codes for color categories. Journal of Experimental Psychology: Human Perception and Performance, 1, 303–322.

Rosch, E. H. (1977). Human categorization. In N. Warren (Ed.), Advances in cross-cultural psychology (Vol. 1). London: Academic Press.

Rosch, E. H. (1988). Coherences and categorization: A historical view. In F. S. Hessel (Ed.), The development of language and language researchers: Essays in honor of Roger Brown (pp. 373–392). Hillsdale, NJ: Erlbaum.

Rosch, E. H., & Mervis, C. B. (1975). Family resemblances: Studies in the internal structure of categories. Cognitive Psychology, 7, 573–605.

Rosch, E. H., Mervis, C. B., Gray, W. D., Johnson, D. M., & Boyes-Braem, P. (1976). Basic objects in natural categories. Cognitive Psychology, 8, 382–439.

Roşu, D., & Natanson, K. (1987, December). Out of the mouths of babes. Michigan Today, p. 5.

Rovee-Collier, C. K. (1987, April). Infant memory. Paper presented at the annual meeting of the Eastern Psychological Association, Crystal City, Virginia.

Rovee-Collier, C. K., Griesler, P. C., & Earley, L. A. (1985). Contextual determinants of retrieval in three-month-old infants. Learning and Motivation, 16, 139–157.

Rovee-Collier, C. K., Sullivan, M. W., Enright, M., Lucas, D., & Fagen, J. W. (1980). Reactivation of infant memory. Science, 208, 1159–1161.

Rubin, D. C., & Baddeley, A. D. (1989). Telescoping is not time compression: A model of the dating of autobiographical events. Memory & Cognition, 17, 653–661.

Rubin, D. C., & Kozin, M. (1984). Vivid memories. Cognition, 16, 81–95.

Rueckl, J. G., & Oden, G. C. (1986). The integration of contextual and featural information during word identification. Journal of Memory and Language, 25, 445–460.

Ruff, H. A. (1982). The development of object perception in infancy. In T. M. Field, A. Huston, H. C. Quay, L. Troll, & G. E. Finley (Eds.), Review of human development (pp. 93–106). New York: Wiley.

Rumelhart, D. E., & McClelland, J. L. (1982). An interactive activation model of context effects in letter perception: Part 2. The contextual enhancement effect and some tests and extensions of the model. Psychological Review, 89, 60–94.

Rumelhart, D. E., McClelland, J. L., & the PDP Research Group. (1986a). Parallel distributed processing (Vol. 1). Cambridge, MA: MIT Press.

Rumelhart, D. E., & McClelland, J. L. (1986b). On learning the past tenses of English verbs. In J. L. McClelland & D. E. Rumelhart (Eds.), Parallel distributed processing: Explorations in the microstructure of cognition (Vol. 2, pp. 216–271). Cambridge, MA: MIT Press.

Rumelhart, D. E., & McClelland, J. L. (1987). Learning the past tenses of English verbs: Implicit rules or parallel distributed processing? In B. MacWhinney (Ed.), Mechanisms of language acquisition (pp. 195–248). Hillsdale, NJ: Erlbaum.

Rumelhart, D. E., & Norman, D. A. (1988). Representation in memory. In R. C. Atkinson, R. J. Herrnstein, G. Lindzey, & R. D. Luce (Eds.), Stevens' handbook of experimental psychology (2nd ed., Vol. 2, pp. 511–587). New York: Wiley.

Russell, J. A. (1990). In defense of a prototype approach to emotion concepts. *Journal of Personality and Social Psychology, 60,* 37–47.

Russell, J. A., & Ward, L. M. (1982). Environmental psychology. *Annual Review of Psychology, 33,* 651–688.

Russell, M. J. (1976). Human olfactory communication. *Nature, 260,* 520–522.

Ryan, C. (1983). Reassessing the automaticity-control distinction: Item recognition as a paradigm case. *Psychological Review, 90,* 171–178.

Rybash, J. M., Hoyer, W. J., & Roodin, P. A. (1986). *Adult cognition and aging.* New York: Pergamon.

Sachs, J. (1967). Recognition memory for syntactic and semantic aspects of a connected discourse. *Perception & Psychophysics, 2,* 437–442.

Safire, W. (1979, May 27). "I led the pigeons to the flag." *The New York Times Magazine,* pp. 9–10.

Sakitt, B. (1976). Iconic memory. *Psychological Review, 83,* 257–276.

Sakitt, B., & Long, G. M. (1979). Spare the rod and spoil the icon. *Journal of Experimental Psychology: Human Perception and Performance, 5,* 19–30.

Salasoo, A., & Pisoni, D. B. (1985). Interaction of knowledge sources in spoken word identification. *Journal of Memory and Language, 24,* 210–231.

Salmon, M. H. (1991). Informal reasoning and informal logic. In J. F. Voss, D. N. Perkins, & J. W. Segal (Eds.), *Informal reasoning and education* (pp. 153–168). Hillsdale, NJ: Erlbaum.

Salthouse, T. A. (1988). Effects of aging on verbal abilities: Examination of the psychometric literature. In L. L. Light & D. M. Burke (Eds.), *Language, memory, and aging* (pp. 17–35). New York: Cambridge University Press.

Salthouse, T. A. (1989). Age-related changes in basic cognitive processes. In M. Storandt & G. R. VandenBos (Eds.), *The adult years: Continuity and change* (pp. 5–40). Washington, DC: American Psychological Association.

Salthouse, T. A. (1991). *Theoretical perspectives on cognitive aging.* Hillsdale, NJ: Erlbaum.

Salthouse, T. A., & Kausler, D. H. (1985). Memory methodology in maturity. In C. J. Brainerd

& M. Pressley (Eds.), *Basic processes in memory development* (pp. 279–311). New York: Springer-Verlag.

Salthouse, T. A., Kausler, D. H., & Saults, J. S. (1988). Investigation of student status, background variables, and the feasibility of standard tasks in cognitive aging research. *Psychology and Aging, 3,* 29–37.

Sams, H., Paavilainen, P., Alho, K., & Näätänen, N. (1985). Auditory frequency discrimination and event-related potentials. *Electroencephalography and Clinical Neurophysiology, 62,* 437–448.

Samuel, A. G. (1981). Phonemic restoration: Insights from a new methodology. *Journal of Experimental Psychology: General, 110,* 474–494.

Samuel, A. G. (1987). Lexical uniqueness effects on phonemic restoration. *Journal of Memory and Language, 26,* 36–56.

Samuel, A. G., & Ressler, W. H. (1986). Attention within auditory word perception: Insights from the phonemic restoration illusion. *Journal of Experimental Psychology: Human Perception and Performance, 12,* 70–79.

Sanford, A. J. (1985). *Cognition and cognitive psychology.* New York: Basic Books.

Schacter, D. L. (1990a). Memory. In M. I. Posner (Ed.), *Foundations of cognitive science* (pp. 683–725). Cambridge, MA: MIT Press.

Schacter, D. L. (1990b). Perceptual representation systems and implicit memory: Toward a resolution of the multiple memory systems debate. *Annals of the New York Academy of Sciences, 608,* 543–571.

Schacter, D. L., Bowers, J., & Booker, J. (1989). Intention, awareness, and implicit memory: The retrieval intentionality criterion. In S. Lewandowsky, J. C. Dunn, & K. Kirsner (Eds.), *Implicit memory: Theoretical issues* (pp. 47–65). Hillsdale, NJ: Erlbaum.

Schacter, D. L., Cooper, L. A., Delaney, S. M., Peterson, M. A., & Tharan, M. (1991). Implicit memory for possible and impossible objects: Constraints on the construction of structural descriptions. *Journal of Experimental Psychology: Learning, Memory, and Cognition, 17,* 3–19.

Schank, R. C. (1982). *Dynamic memory*. New York: Cambridge University Press.

Schank, R. C., & Abelson, R. P. (1977). *Scripts, plans, goals, and understanding*. Hillsdale, NJ: Erlbaum.

Schank, R. C., & the Yale AI Project. (1975). *SAM—A story understander*. (Research Report No. 43). New Haven, CT: Yale University, Committee on Computer Science.

Schneider, W. (1984). Developmental trends in the metamemory-memory behavior relationship: An integrative review. In D. L. Forrest-Pressley & T. G. Waller (Eds.), *Cognition, metacognition, and communication*. New York: Academic Press.

Schneider, W. (1987). Connectionism: Is it a paradigm shift for psychology? *Behavior Research Methods, Instruments, & Computers, 19*, 73–83.

Schneider, W. (1993). Variety of working memory as seen in biology and in connectionist/control architectures. *Memory and Cognition, 21*, in press.

Schneider, W., & Shiffrin, R. M. (1977). Controlled and automatic information processing: I. Detection, search, and attention. *Psychological Review, 84*, 1–66.

Schneider, W., & Shiffrin, R. M. (1985). Categorization (restructuring) and automatization: Two separable factors. *Psychological Review, 92*, 424–428.

Schoenfeld, A. H. (1982). Some thoughts on problem-solving research and mathematics education. In F. K. Lester & J. Garofalo (Eds.), *Mathematical problem solving: Issues in research* (pp. 27–37). Philadelphia, PA: The Franklin Institute.

Schooler, J. W., Gerhard, D., & Loftus, E. F. (1986). Qualities of the unreal. *Journal of Experimental Psychology: Learning, Memory, and Cognition, 12*, 171–181.

Schwartz, N. H., & Kulhavy, R. W. (1988). Encoding tactics in the retention of maps. *Contemporary Educational Psychology, 13*, 72–85.

Schwartz, S., & Griffin, T. (1986). *Medical thinking: The psychology of medical judgment and decision making*. New York: Springer-Verlag.

Schwartz, S. H. (1971). Modes of representation and problem solving: Well evolved is half solved. *Journal of Experimental Psychology, 91*, 347–350.

Schweickert, R. (1987). Short-term memory; long-term goals [Review of *Working memory*]. *Contemporary Psychology, 32*, 940–942.

Schweickert, R., & Boruff, B. (1986). Short-term memory capacity: Magic number or magic spell? *Journal of Experimental Psychology: Learning, Memory, and Cognition, 12*, 419–425.

Scott, S. (1973). *The relation of divergent thinking to bilingualism: Cause or effect?* Unpublished manuscript. Department of Psychology, McGill University.

Searle, J. R. (1990a). Minds, brains, and programs. In J. L. Garfield (Ed.), *Foundations of cognitive science: The essential readings* (pp. 189–208). New York: Paragon.

Searle, J. R. (1990b, January). Is the brain's mind a computer program? *Scientific American*, pp. 26–31.

Segal, S. J. (1971). Processing of the stimulus in imagery and perception. In S. J. Segal (Ed.), *Imagery: Current cognitive approaches*. New York: Academic Press.

Segal, S. J., & Fusella, V. (1970). Influence of imaged pictures and sounds on detection of visual and auditory signals. *Journal of Experimental Psychology, 83*, 458–464.

Segal, S. J., & Gordon, P. (1969). The Perkey effect revisited: Paradoxical threshold or signal detection error. *Perceptual and Motor Skills, 28*, 791–797.

Seidenberg, M. S., & McClelland, J. L. (1989). A distributed, developmental model of word recognition and naming. *Psychological Review, 96*, 523–568.

Seifert, C. M. (1990). Content-based inferences in text. *The Psychology of Learning and Motivation, 25*, 103–122.

Seifert, C. M., McKoon, G., Abelson, R. P., & Ratcliff, R. (1986). Memory connections between thematically similar episodes. *Journal of Experimental Psychology: Learning, Memory, and Cognition, 12*, 220–231.

Seifert, C. M., Robertson, S. P., & Black, J. B. (1985). Types of inferences generated during reading. *Journal of Memory and Language, 24*, 405–422.

Shafir, E. B., Smith, E. E., & Osherson, D. N. (1990). Typicality and reasoning fallacies. *Memory & Cognition, 18,* 229–239.

Shallice, T., & Warrington, E. K. (1970). Independent functioning of verbal memory stores: A neuropsychological study. *Quarterly Journal of Experimental Psychology, 22,* 261–273.

Shapiro, P. N., & Penrod, S. D. (1986). Meta-analysis of facial identification studies. *Psychological Bulletin, 100,* 139–156.

Sharkey, N. E. (1986). A model of knowledge-based expectations in text comprehension. In J. A. Galambos, J. B. Black, & R. P. Abelson (Eds.), *Knowledge structures* (pp. 49–70). Hillsdale, NJ: Erlbaum.

Sharkey, N. E., & Mitchell, D. C. (1985). Word recognition in a functional context: The use of scripts in reading. *Journal of Memory and Language, 24,* 253–270.

Sharkey, N. E., & Sharkey, A. J. C. (1987a). KAN: A knowledge access network model. In R. G. Reilly (Ed.), *Communication failure in dialogue and discourse* (pp. 287–307). Amsterdam: Elsevier.

Sharkey, N. E., & Sharkey, A. J. C. (1987b). What is the point of integration? The loci of knowledge-based facilitation in sentence processing. *Journal of Memory and Language, 26,* 255–276.

Shatz, M., & Gelman, R. (1973). The development of communication skills: Modifications in the speech of young children as a function of listener. *Monographs of the Society for Research in Child Development, 38* (2, Serial No. 152).

Shaughnessy, J. J., & Mand, J. L. (1982). How permanent are memories for real life events? *American Journal of Psychology, 95,* 51–65.

Shepard, R. N. (1978). Externalization of mental images and the act of creation. In B. S. Randhawa & W. E. Coffman (Eds.), *Visual learning, thinking, and communication* (pp. 133–190). New York: Academic Press.

Shepard, R. N., & Chipman, S. (1970). Second-order isomorphism of internal representation: Shapes of states. *Cognitive Psychology, 1,* 1–17.

Shepard, R. N., & Cooper, L. A. (Eds.). (1982). *Mental images and their transformations.* Cambridge, MA: MIT Press.

Shepard, R. N., & Metzler, J. (1971). Mental rotation of three-dimensional objects. *Science, 171,* 701–703.

Shepherd, J. W., Ellis, H. D., & Davies, G. M. (1982). *Identification evidence.* Aberdeen, Great Britain: Aberdeen University Press.

Sherman, M. A. (1976). Adjectival negation and the comprehension of multiply negated sentences. *Journal of Verbal Learning and Verbal Behavior, 15,* 143–157.

Sherry, D. F., & Schacter, D. L. (1987). The evolution of multiple memory systems. *Psychological Review, 94,* 439–454.

Shiffrin, R. M., & Schneider, W. (1977). Controlled and automatic human information processing: II. Perceptual learning, automatic attending, and a general theory. *Psychological Review, 84,* 127–190.

Shiffrin, R. M., & Schneider, W. (1984). Automatic and controlled processing revisited. *Psychological Review, 91,* 269–276.

Shoben, E. J. (1984). Semantic and episodic memory. In R. S. Wyer, Jr., & T. K. Srull (Eds.), *Handbook of social cognition* (Vol. 2, pp. 213–231). Hillsdale, NJ: Erlbaum.

Shoben, E. J. (1988). The representation of knowledge. In M. McTear (Ed.), *Understanding cognitive science* (pp. 102–119). New York: Wiley.

Shoben, E. J., Wescourt, K. T., & Smith, E. E. (1978). Sentence verification, sentence recognition, and the semantic/episodic distinction. *Journal of Experimental Psychology: Human Learning and Memory, 4,* 304–317.

Siegler, R. S. (1989). Mechanisms of cognitive development. *Annual Review of Psychology, 40,* 353–379.

Simon, H. A. (1973). The structure of ill-structured problems. *Artificial Intelligence, 4,* 181–201.

Simon, H. A. (1974). How big is a chunk? *Science, 183,* 482–488.

Simon, H. A. (1981). Cognitive science: The newest science of the artificial. In D. A. Norman (Ed.), *Perspectives on cognitive science* (pp. 13–25). Hillsdale, NJ: Erlbaum.

Simon, H. A. (1990). Invariants of human behavior. *Annual Review of Psychology, 41,* 1–19.

Simon, H. A. (1992a). What is an "explanation" of behavior *Psychological Science, 3,* 150–160.

Simon, H. A. (1992b). *Why the mind needs an eye: The uses of mental imagery.* Paper presented at the Convention of the American Psychological Association, Washington, DC.

Simon, H. A., & Hayes, J. R. (1976). The understanding process: Problem isomorphs. *Cognitive Psychology, 8,* 165–190.

Simpson, G. B. (1984). Lexical ambiguity and its role in models of word recognition. *Psychological Bulletin, 96,* 316–340.

Simpson, G. B., & Burgess, C. (1985). Activation and selection processes in the recognition of ambiguous words. *Journal of Experimental Psychology: Human Perception and Performance, 11,* 28–39.

Singer, M. (1990). *Psychology of language: An introduction to sentence and discourse processes.* Hillsdale, NJ: Erlbaum.

Sinnott, J. D. (1989). Background: About this book and the field of everyday problem solving. In J. D. Sinnott (Ed.), *Everyday problem solving: Theory and applications* (pp. 1–6). Westport, CT: Praeger.

Slobin, D. I. (1966). Grammatical transformations and sentence comprehension in childhood and adulthood. *Journal of Verbal Learning and Verbal Behavior, 5,* 219–227.

Slobin, D. I. (1979). *Psycholinguistics* (2nd ed.). Glenview, IL: Scott, Foresman.

Slovic, P. (1982). Toward understanding and improving decisions. In W. C. Howell & E. A. Fleishman (Eds.), *Human performance and productivity* (pp. 157–183). Hillsdale, NJ: Erlbaum.

Slovic, P., & Fischhoff, B. (1977). On the psychology of experimental surprises. *Journal of Experimental Psychology: Human Perception and Performance, 3,* 544–551.

Slovic, P., Fischhoff, B., & Lichtenstein, S. (1982). Facts versus fears: Understanding perceived risk. In D. Kahneman, P. Slovic, & A. Tversky (Eds.), *Judgment under uncertainty: Heuristics and biases* (pp. 463–489). New York: Cambridge University Press.

Slovic, P., Fischhoff, B., & Lichtenstein, S. (1988). Response mode, framing, and information-processing effects in risk assessment. In D. E. Bell, H. Raiffa, & A. Tversky (Eds.), *Decision making: Descriptive, normative, and prescriptive interactions* (pp. 152–166). Cambridge: Cambridge University Press.

Slovic, P., Kunreuther, H., & White, G. F. (1974). Decision processes, rationality and adjustment to natural hazards. In G. F. White (Ed.), *Natural hazards, local, national and global.* New York: Oxford University Press.

Small, M. Y. (1990). *Cognitive development.* San Diego, CA: Harcourt Brace Jovanovich.

Smith, A. D. (1980). Age differences in encoding, storage, and retrieval. In L. W. Poon, J. L. Fozard, L. S. Cermak, D. Arenberg, & L. W. Thompson (Eds.), *New directions in memory and aging* (pp. 23–46). Hillsdale, NJ: Erlbaum.

Smith, E. E. (1978). Theories of semantic memory. In W. K. Estes (Ed.), *Handbook of learning and cognitive processes* (Vol. 6). Hillsdale, NJ: Erlbaum.

Smith, E. E. (1989). Concepts and induction. In M. I. Posner (Ed.), *Foundations of cognitive science* (pp. 501–526). Cambridge, MA: MIT Press.

Smith, E. E., Shoben, E. J., & Rips, L. J. (1974). Structure and process in semantic memory: A featural model for semantic decisions. *Psychological Review, 81,* 214–241.

Smith, E. R. (1991). Illusory correlation in a simulated exemplar-based memory. *Journal of Experimental Social Psychology, 27,* 107–123.

Smith, J. F., & Kida, T. (1991). Heuristics and biases: Expertise and task realism in auditing. *Psychological Bulletin, 109,* 472–489.

Smith, S. M. (1988). Environmental context-dependent memory. In G. M. Davies & D. M. Thomson (Eds.), *Memory in context: Context in memory* (pp. 13–34). Chichester, England: Wiley.

Smith, S. M., Glenberg, A., & Bjork, R. A. (1978). Environmental context and human memory. *Memory & Cognition, 6,* 342–353.

Smyth, M. M., Morris, P. E., Levy, P., & Ellis, A. W. (1987). *Cognition in action.* Hillsdale, NJ: Erlbaum.

Snodgrass, J. G. (1987). How many memory systems are there really?: Some evidence from the picture fragment completion task. In C. Izawa

(Ed.), *Current issues in cognitive processes* (pp. 135–173). Hillsdale, NJ: Erlbaum.

Snow, C. E. (1977). The development of conversation between mothers and babies. *Journal of Child Language, 4,* 1–22.

Snow, C. E. (1993). Bilingualism and second language acquisition. In J. B. Berko-Gleason & N. B. Ratner (Eds.), *Psycholinguistics.* Fort Worth, TX: Harcourt Brace Jovanovich.

Snow, C. E., Perlmann, R. Y., & Gleason, J. Berko. (1990). Developmental perspectives on politeness: Sources of children's knowledge. *Journal of Pragmatics, 14,* 289–305.

Snowman, J. (1987). Explorations in mnemonic training. In M. A. McDaniel & M. Pressley (Eds.), *Imagery and related mnemonic processes* (pp. 377–391). New York: Springer-Verlag.

Spelke, E., Hirst, W., & Neisser, U. (1976). Skills of divided attention. *Cognition, 4,* 215–230.

Sperling, G. (1960). The information available in brief visual presentations. *Psychological Monographs, 74,* 1–29.

Spilich, G. J., Vesonder, G. T., Chiesi, H. L., & Voss, J. F. (1979). Text processing of domain-related information for individuals with high and low domain knowledge. *Journal of Verbal Learning and Verbal Behavior, 18,* 275–290.

Spoehr, K. T., & Lehmkuhle, S. W. (1982). *Visual information processing.* San Francisco: Freeman.

Sporer, S. L. (1991). Deep—deeper—deepest? Encoding strategies and the recognition of human faces. *Journal of Experimental Psychology: Learning, Memory, and Cognition, 17,* 323–333.

Squire, L. R. (1987). *Memory and brain.* New York: Oxford University Press.

Sroufe, L. A., Cooper, R. G., & DeHart, G. B. (1992). *Child development: Its nature and course* (2nd ed.). New York: McGraw-Hill.

Standing, L. (1973). Learning 10,000 pictures. *Quarterly Journal of Experimental Psychology, 25,* 207–222.

Stanovich, K. E., & West, R. F. (1981). The effect of sentence processing on ongoing word recognition: Tests of a two-process theory. *Journal of Experimental Psychology: Human Perception and Performance, 7,* 658–672.

Stanovich, K. E., & West, R. F. (1983). On priming by a sentence context. *Journal of Experimental Psychology: General, 112,* 1–36.

Stemberger, J. P. (1991). Speaking of language, . . . [Review of *Speaking: From intention to articulation*]. *Contemporary Psychology, 36,* 119–120.

Sternberg, R. J. (1990). Wisdom and its relations to intelligence and creativity. In R. J. Sternberg (Ed.), *Wisdom: Its nature, origins, and development* (pp. 142–159). New York: Cambridge University Press.

Sternberg, R. J., & Powell, J. S. (1983). Comprehending verbal comprehension. *American Psychologist, 38,* 878–893.

Stevens, A., & Coupe, P. (1978). Distortions in judged spatial relations. *Cognitive Psychology, 10,* 422–437.

Stillings, N. A., Feinstein, M. H., Garfield, J. L., Rissland, E. L., Rosenbaum, D. A., Weisler, S. E., & Baker-Ward, L. (1987). *Cognitive science: An introduction.* Cambridge, MA: MIT Press.

Stine, E. L., Wingfield, A., & Poon, L. W. (1989). Speech comprehension and memory through adulthood: The roles of time and strategy. In L. W. Poon, D. C. Rubin, & B. A. Wilson (Eds.), *Everyday cognition in adulthood and later life* (pp. 195–221). New York: Cambridge University Press.

Stroop, J. R. (1935). Studies of interference in serial verbal reactions. *Journal of Experimental Psychology, 18,* 643–662.

Suzuki-Slakter, N. S. (1988). Elaboration and metamemory during adolescence. *Contemporary Educational Psychology, 13,* 206–220.

Svartik, J. (1966). *On voice in the English verb.* The Hague: Mouton.

Swanson, H. L. (1987). The influence of verbal ability and metamemory on future recall. *British Journal of Educational Psychology, 57,* 179–190.

Sweller, J., & Levine, M. (1982). Effects of goal specificity on means-end analysis and learning. *Journal of Experimental Psychology: Learning, Memory, and Cognition, 8,* 463–474.

Tahka, S., Wood, M., & Loewenthal, K. (1981). Age changes in the ability to replicate foreign pronunciation and intonation. *Language and Speech, 24,* 363–372.

Tanaka, J. W., & Taylor, M. (1991). Object categories and expertise: Is the basic level in the eye of the beholder? *Cognitive Psychology, 23*, 457–482.

Taplin, J. E. (1971). Reasoning with conditional sentences. *Journal of Verbal Learning and Verbal Behavior, 10*, 219–225.

Tartter, V. C. (1986). *Language processes.* New York: Holt, Rinehart and Winston.

Taylor, H. A., & Tversky, B. (1992). Spatial mental models derived from survey and route descriptions. *Journal of Memory and Language, 31*, 261–292.

Taylor, I., & Taylor, M. M. (1983). *The psychology of reading.* New York: Academic Press.

Taylor, I., & Taylor, M. M. (1990). *Psycholinguistics: Learning and using language.* Englewood Cliffs, NJ: Prentice Hall.

Thomas, J. C. (1974). An analysis of behavior in the Hobbits-Orcs program. *Cognitive Psychology, 6*, 257–269.

Thomas, J. C. (1989). Problem solving by human-machine interaction. In K. J. Gilhooly (Ed.), *Human and machine problem solving* (pp. 317–362). New York: Plenum.

Thompson, C. P., Skowronski, J. J., & Lee, D. J. (1988). Reconstructing the date of a personal event. In M. M. Gruneberg, P. E. Morris, & R. N. Sykes (Eds.), *Practical aspects of memory: Current research and issues* (Vol. 1, pp. 241–246). New York: Wiley.

Thomson, J. R., & Chapman, R. S. (1977). Who is "Daddy" revisited: The status of two-year-olds' overextended words in use and comprehension. *Journal of Child Language, 4*, 359–375.

Thorndyke, P. W. (1976). The role of inferences in discourse comprehension. *Journal of Verbal Learning and Verbal Behavior, 15*, 437–446.

Thorndyke, P. W. (1981). Distance estimation from cognitive maps. *Cognitive Psychology, 13*, 526–550.

Thorndyke, P. W. (1984). Applications of schema theory in cognitive research. In J. R. Anderson & S. M. Kosslyn (Eds.), *Tutorials in learning and memory* (pp. 167–192). San Francisco: W. H. Freeman.

Thorndyke, P. W., & Goldin, S. E. (1983). Spatial learning and reasoning skill. In H. L. Pick, Jr., & L. P. Acredolo (Eds.), *Spatial orientation* (pp. 195–217). New York: Plenum.

Timberlake, W. (1984). An ecological approach to learning. *Learning and motivation, 15*, 321–333.

Tomasello, M., Conti-Ramsden, G., & Ewert, B. (1990). Young children's conversations with the mothers and fathers: Differences in breakdown and repair. *Journal of Child Language, 17*, 115–130.

Townsend, D. J., Carrithers, C., & Bever, T. G. (1987). Listening and reading processes in college- and middle school-age readers. In R. Horowitz & S. J. Samuels (Eds.), *Comprehending oral and written language* (pp. 217–242). San Diego: Academic Press.

Trahan, D. E., Larrabee, G. J., & Levin, H. S. (1986). Age-related differences in recognition memory for pictures. *Experimental Aging Research, 12*, 147–150.

Treisman, A. M. (1960). Contextual cues in selective listening. *Quarterly Journal of Experimental Psychology, 12*, 242–248.

Treisman, A. M. (1964). Monitoring and storage of irrelevant messages and selective attention. *Journal of Verbal Learning and Verbal Behavior, 3*, 449–459.

Treisman, A. M. (1986, November). Features and objects in visual processing. *Scientific American, 255*(5), 114B–125.

Treisman, A. M. (1988). Features and objects: The fourteenth Bartlett Memorial Lecture. *Quarterly Journal of Experimental Psychology, 40A*, 201–237.

Treisman, A. M. (1990). Visual coding of features and objects: Some evidence from behavioral studies. In National Research Council (Ed.), *Advances in the modularity of vision: Selections from a symposium on frontiers of visual science* (pp. 39–61). Washington, DC: National Academy Press.

Treisman, A. (1991). Search, similarity, and integration of features between and within dimensions. *Journal of Experimental Psychology: Human Perception and Performance, 17*, 652–676.

Treisman, A. M., & Gelade, G. (1980). A feature-integration theory of attention. *Cognitive Psychology, 12,* 97–136.

Treisman, A. M., & Gormican, S. (1988). Feature analysis in early vision: Evidence from search asymmetries. *Psychological Review, 95,* 15–48.

Treisman, A. M., & Schmidt, H. (1982). Illusory conjunction in the perception of objects. *Cognitive Psychology, 14,* 107–141.

Treisman, A. M., & Souther, J. (1985). Search asymmetry: A diagnostic for preattentive processing of separable features. *Journal of Experimental Psychology: General, 114,* 285–310.

Treisman, A. M., & Souther, J. (1986). Illusory words: The roles of attention and of top-down constraints in conjoining letters to form words. *Journal of Experimental Psychology: Human Perception and Performance, 12,* 3–17.

Treisman, A. M., Vieira, A., & Hayes, A. (1992). Automaticity and preattentive processing. *American Journal of Psychology, 105,* 341–362.

Trolier, T. K., & Hamilton, D. L. (1986). Variables influencing judgments of correlational relations. *Journal of Personality and Social Psychology, 50,* 879–888.

Tulving, E. (1966). Subjective organization and effects of repetition in multi-trial free-recall learning. *Journal of Verbal Learning and Verbal Behavior, 5,* 193–197.

Tulving, E. (1972). Episodic and semantic memory. In E. Tulving & W. Donaldson (Eds.), *Organization of memory.* New York: Academic Press.

Tulving, E. (1983). *Elements of episodic memory.* New York: Oxford University Press.

Tulving, E. (1984). Precis, *Elements of episodic memory. The Behavioral and Brain Sciences, 7,* 223–268.

Tulving, E. (1985). How many memory systems are there? *American Psychologist, 40,* 385–398.

Tulving, E. (1986). What kind of a hypothesis is the distinction between episodic and semantic memory? *Journal of Experimental Psychology: Learning, Memory, and Cognition, 12,* 307–311.

Tulving, E. (1987). Multiple memory systems and consciousness. *Human Neurobiology, 6,* 67–80.

Tulving, E. (1989, July/August). Remembering and knowing the past. *American Scientist, 77,* 361–367.

Tulving, E. (1991). Memory research is not a zero-sum game. *American Psychologist, 46,* 41–42.

Tulving, E., & Schacter, D. L. (1990). Priming and human memory systems. *Science, 247,* 301–306.

Tversky, A., & Kahneman, D. (1971). Belief in the law of small numbers. *Psychological Bulletin, 76,* 105–110.

Tversky, A., & Kahneman, D. (1973). Availability: A heuristic for judging frequency and probability. *Cognitive Psychology, 5,* 207–232.

Tversky, A., & Kahneman, D. (1974). Judgments under uncertainty: Heuristics and biases. *Science, 185,* 1124–1131.

Tversky, A., & Kahneman, D. (1981). The framing of decisions and the psychology of choice. *Science, 211,* 453–458.

Tversky, A., & Kahneman, D. (1982). Judgment under uncertainty: Heuristics and biases. In D. Kahneman, P. Slovic, & A. Tversky (Eds.), *Judgment under uncertainty: Heuristics and biases* (pp. 3–20). New York: Cambridge University Press.

Tversky, A., & Kahneman, D. (1983). Extensional versus intuitive reasoning: The conjunction fallacy in probability judgment. *Psychological Review, 90,* 293–315.

Tversky, B. (1981). Distortions in memory for maps. *Cognitive Psychology, 13,* 407–433.

Tversky, B. (1991a). Distortions in memory for visual displays. In S. R. Ellis, M. Kaiser, & A. Grunewald (Eds.), *Spatial instruments and spatial displays* (pp. 61–75). Hillsdale, NJ: Erlbaum.

Tversky, B. (1991b). Spatial mental models. *The Psychology of Learning and Motivation, 27,* 109–145.

Tversky, B., & Hemenway, K. (1984). Objects, parts, and categories. *Journal of Experimental Psychology: General, 113,* 169–193.

Tversky, B., & Schiano, D. J. (1989). Perceptual and conceptual factors in distortions in memory for graphs and maps. *Journal of Experimental Psychology: General, 118,* 387–398.

Ucros, C. G. (1989). Mood state-dependent memory: A meta-analysis. *Cognition and Emotion*, *3*, 139–167.

Underwood, B. J., Boruch, R. F., & Malmi, R. A. (1978). Composition of episodic memory. *Journal of Experimental Psychology: General*, *107*, 393–419.

Underwood, N. R., & McConkie, G. W. (1985). Perceptual span for letter distinctions during reading. *Reading Research Quarterly*, *20*, 153–162.

Valian, V. (1985). Saying what we mean, more or less [Review of *Speech and situation: A psychological conception of situated speaking*]. *Contemporary Psychology*, *30*, 140–141.

van der Heijden, A. H. C. (1981). *Short-term visual information forgetting*. London: Routledge & Kegan Paul.

VanLehn, K. (1989). Problem solving and cognitive skill acquisition. In M. I. Posner (Ed.), *Foundations of cognitive science* (pp. 527–579). Cambridge, MA: MIT Press.

Van Oostendorp, H. (1991). Inferences and integrations made by readers of script-based texts. *Journal of Research in Reading*, *14*, 3–20.

Van Orden, G. C. (1987). A rows is a rose: Spelling, sound and reading. *Memory and Cognition*, *15*, 181–198.

Van Orden, G. C., Pennington, B. F., & Stone, G. O. (1990). Word identification in reading and the promise of subsymbolic psycholinguistics. *Psychological Review*, *97*, 488–522.

Vosniadou, S., & Ortony, A. (Eds.). (1989). *Similarity and analogical reasoning*. New York: Cambridge University Press.

Voss, J. F., Greene, T. R., Post, T. A., & Penner, B. C. (1983). Problem solving skill in social sciences. In G. Power (Ed.), *The psychology of learning and motivation: Advances in research and theory* (Vol. 17). New York: Academic Press.

Voss, J. F., Perkins, D. N., & Segal, J. W. (Eds.). (1990). *Informal reasoning and education*. Hillsdale, NJ: Erlbaum.

Voss, J. F., & Post, T. A. (1988). On the solving of ill-structured problems. In M. T. H. Chi, R. Glaser, & M. J. Farr (Eds.), *The nature of expertise* (pp. 261–285). Hillsdale, NJ: Erlbaum.

Wagner, R. K., & Torgesen, J. K. (1987). The nature of phonological processing and its causal role in the acquisition of reading skills. *Psychological Bulletin*, *101*, 192–212.

Waldrop, M. M. (1987). The workings of working memory. *Science*, *237*, 1564–1567.

Walker-Andrews, A. S. (1986). Intermodal perception of expressive behaviors: Relation of eye and voice? *Developmental Psychology*, *22*, 373–377.

Wallace, B. (1984). Apparent equivalence between perception and imagery in the production of various visual illusions. *Memory & Cognition*, *12*, 156–162.

Wallace, B., & Fisher, L. E. (1983). *Consciousness and behavior*. Boston, MA: Allyn and Bacon.

Walsh, D. A., & Thompson, L. W. (1978). Age differences in visual sensory memory. *Journal of Gerontology*, *33*, 383–387.

Ward, T. B., & Scott, J. (1987). Analytic and holistic modes of learning family-resemblance concepts. *Memory & Cognition*, *15*, 42–54.

Wardlaw, K. A., & Kroll, N. E. A. (1976). Autonomic responses to shock-associated words in a non-attended message: A failure to replicate. *Journal of Experimental Psychology: Human Perception and Performance*, *2*, 357–360.

Warren, R. M. (1970). Perceptual restoration of missing speech sounds. *Science*, *167*, 392–393.

Warren, R. M. (1984). Perceptual restoration of obliterated sounds. *Psychological Bulletin*, *96*, 371–383.

Warren, R. M., & Warren, R. P. (1970, December). Auditory illusions and confusions. *Scientific American*, *223*(6), 30–36.

Warrington, E. K., & Weiskrantz, L. (1970). Amnesic syndrome: Consolidation or retrieval? *Nature*, *228*, 629–630.

Wason, P. C., & Johnson-Laird, P. N. (1972). *Psychology of reasoning: Structure and content*. Cambridge, MA: Harvard University Press.

Wasow, T. (1989). Grammatical theory. In M. I. Posner (Ed.), *Foundations of cognitive science* (pp. 161–205). Cambridge, MA: MIT Press.

Watson, J. B. (1924). *Behaviorism*. Chicago, IL: University of Chicago Press.

Weatherford, D. L. (1985). Representing and manipulating spatial information from different environments: Models to neighborhoods. In R. Cohen (Ed.), *The development of spatial cognition* (pp. 41–70). Hillsdale, NJ: Erlbaum.

Weed, K., Ryan, E. B., & Day, J. (1990). Metamemory and attributions as mediators of strategy use and recall. *Journal of Educational Psychology, 82,* 849–855.

Wegner, D. M. (1992). You can't always think what you want: Problems in the suppression of unwanted thoughts. *Advances in Experimental Social Psychology, 25,* 193–225.

Wegner, D. M., Schneider, D. J., Carter, S. R., III., & White, T. L. (1987). Paradoxical effects of thought suppression. *Journal of Personality and Social Psychology, 53,* 5–13.

Weinstein, C. E., Duffy, M., Underwood, V. L., & MacDonald, J. E. (1979). *Whose learning strategies deficit . . . the elderly's or the researcher's?* Paper presented at the annual meeting of American Psychological Association, New York.

Weisberg, R. W. (1986). *Creativity: Genius and other myths.* New York: Freeman.

Weisstein, N. (1973). Beyond the yellow Volkswagen detector and the grandmother cell: A general strategy for the exploration of operations in human pattern recognition. In R. L. Solso (Ed.), *Contemporary issues in cognitive psychology* (pp. 17–51). Washington, DC: Wilston/Wiley.

Weist, R. M. (1985). Cross-linguistic perspective on cognitive development. In T. M. Schlechter & M. P. Toglia (Eds.), *New directions in cognitive science* (pp. 191–216). Norwood, NJ: Ablex.

Weldon, M. S., & Roediger, H. L., III. (1987). Altering retrieval demands reverses the picture superiority effect. *Memory & Cognition, 15,* 269–280.

Well, A. D., Pollatsek, A., & Boyce, S. J. (1990). Understanding the effects of sample size on the variability of the mean. *Organizational Behavior and Human Decision Processes, 47,* 289–312.

Wellman, H. M. (1985). A child's theory of mind: The development of conceptions of cognition. In S. R. Yussen (Ed.), *The growth of reflection in children* (pp. 169–203). New York: Academic Press.

Wellman, H. M. (1988). The early development of memory strategies. In F. W. Weinert & M. Perlmutter (Eds.), *Memory development: Universal changes and individual differences* (pp. 3–29). Hillsdale, NJ: Erlbaum.

Wellman, H. M., & Gelman, S. A. (1992). Cognitive development: Foundational theories of core domains. *Annual Review of Psychology, 43,* 337–375.

Wells, G. L., & Hrciw, B. (1984). Memory for faces: Encoding and retrieval operations. *Memory & Cognition, 12,* 338–344.

Werker, J. F., & Tees, R. C. (1984). Cross-language speech perception: Evidence for perceptual reorganization during the first year of life. *Infant Behavior and Development, 7,* 49–63.

West, R. (1985). *Memory fitness over 40.* Gainesville, FL: Tried.

Wetherick, N. E. (1989). Psychology and syllogistic reasoning. *Philosophical Psychology, 2,* 111–124.

Wetherick, N. E. (1991). What goes on in the mind when we solve syllogisms? In R. H. Logie & M. Denis (Eds.), *Mental images in human cognition* (pp. 255–267). Amsterdam: Elsevier.

Wheeler, D. (1970). Processes in word recognition. *Cognitive Psychology, 1,* 59–85.

Wickelgren, W. A. (1965). Acoustic similarity and intrusion errors in short-term memory. *Journal of Experimental Psychology, 70,* 102–108.

Wickelgren, W. A. (1973). The long and the short of memory. *Psychological Bulletin, 80,* 425–438.

Wickens, D. D., Dalezman, R. E., & Eggemeier, F. T. (1976). Multiple encoding of word attributes in memory. *Memory & Cognition, 4,* 307–310.

Wilkinson, I. A. G. (1992). Basic research in beginning reading: Something old, something new [Review of *Learning to read: Basic research and its implications*]. *Contemporary Psychology, 37,* 564–566.

Wilson, B. A. (1984). Memory therapy in practice. In B. A. Wilson & N. Moffat (Eds.), *Clinical management of memory problems* (pp. 89–111). Rockville, MD: Aspen.

Wilson, B. A. (1987). *Rehabilitation of memory.* New York: Guilford.

Wittgenstein, L. (1953). *Philosophical investigations*. New York: Macmillan.

Wittrock, M. C. (1974). Learning as a generative process. *Educational Psychologist, 11,* 87–95.

Wolff, A. S., Mitchell, D. H., & Frey, P. W. (1984). Perceptual skill in the game of Othello. *Journal of Psychology, 118,* 7–16.

Wolford, G., Taylor, H. A., & Beck, J. R. (1990). The conjunction fallacy? *Memory & Cognition, 18,* 47–53.

Woltz, D. J. (1988). An investigation of the role of working memory in procedural skill acquisition. *Journal of Experimental Psychology: General, 117,* 319–331.

Wurtz, R. H., Goldberg, M. E., & Robinson, D. L. (1982, June). Brain mechanisms of visual attention. *Scientific American, 246,* 124–136.

Wyer, R. S., & Srull, T. K. (1986). Human cognition in its social context. *Psychological Review, 93,* 322–359.

Yaniv, I., & Meyer, D. E. (1987). Activation and metacognition of inaccessible stored information: Potential bases for incubation effects in problem solving. *Journal of Experimental Psychology: Learning, Memory, and Cognition, 13,* 187–205.

Yates, J. F. (1990). *Judgment and decision making*. Englewood Cliffs, NJ: Prentice Hall.

Yuille, A. L., & Ullman, S. (1990). Computational theories of low-level vision. In D. N. Osherson, S. M. Kosslyn, & J. M. Hollerbach (Eds.), *An invitation to cognitive science* (Vol. 2, pp. 5–39). Cambridge, MA: MIT Press.

Yuille, J. C. (1983). The crisis in theories of mental imagery. In J. C. Yuille (Ed.), *Imagery, memory and cognition* (pp. 263–284). Hillsdale, NJ: Erlbaum.

Yuille, J. C. (1985). A laboratory-based experimental methodology is inappropriate for the study of mental imagery. *Journal of Mental Imagery, 9,* 137–150.

Yuille, J. C., & Catchpole, M. J. (1977). Imagery and children's associative learning. In A. M. Lesgold, J. W. Pellegrino, S. D. Fokkema, & R. Glaser (Eds.), *Cognitive psychology and instruction*. New York: Plenum.

Yussen, S. R., & Bird, J. E. (1979). The development of metacognitive awareness in memory, communication, and attention. *Journal of Experimental Child Psychology, 19,* 502–508.

Yussen, S. R., & Kane, P. T. (1983). Children's ideas about intellectual ability. In R. Leahy (Ed.), *Conceptions of inequality*. New York: Academic Press.

Yussen, S. R., & Levy, V. M. (1975). Developmental changes in predicting one's own span of short-term memory. *Journal of Experimental Child Psychology, 19,* 502–508.

Zebrowitz, L. A. (1990). *Social perception*. Pacific Grove, CA: Brooks/Cole.

Zelinski, E. M., & Gilewski, M. J. (1988). Memory for prose and aging: A meta-analysis. In M. L. Howe & C. J. Brainerd (Eds.), *Cognitive development in adulthood: Progress in cognitive development research* (pp. 133–158). New York: Springer-Verlag.

NAME INDEX

Key terms are printed in bold
type.